P9-CPW-120

The Essential Guide to User Interface Design

Second Edition

An Introduction to GUI Design
Principles and Techniques

Wilbert O. Galitz

Wiley Computer Publishing

John Wiley & Sons, Inc.

NEW YORK · CHICHESTER · WEINHEIM · BRISBANE · SINGAPORE · TORONTO

*To my wife and business partner, Sharon,
for many years of love and support in our
home and office.*

*To our grandchildren, Mitchell, Barry, Deirdra,
and Spencer Galitz, Lauren and Scott Roepel,
and Shane Watters. May one or more of them
pick up the writing torch.*

Publisher: Robert Ipsen
Executive Editor: Robert Elliott
Assistant Editor: Emilie Herman
Associate Managing Editor: John Atkins
Text Design & Composition: Publishers' Design and Production Services, Inc.

Designations used by companies to distinguish their products are often claimed as trademarks. In all instances where John Wiley & Sons, Inc., is aware of a claim, the product names appear in initial capital or ALL CAPITAL LETTERS. Readers, however, should contact the appropriate companies for more complete information regarding trademarks and registration.

This book is printed on acid-free paper. ∞

Published by John Wiley & Sons, Inc.

Published simultaneously in Canada.

Wiley also publishes its books in a variety of electronic formats. Some content that appears in print may not be available in electronic books.

This publication is designed to provide accurate and authoritative information in regard to the subject matter covered. It is sold with the understanding that the publisher is not engaged in professional services. If professional advice or other expert assistance is required, the services of a competent professional person should be sought.

Library of Congress Cataloging-in-Publication Data:

ISBN: 0-471-084646

Printed in the United States of America.
10 9 8 7 6 5 4 3 2 1

Contents

Preface

This second edition of the *Essential Guide to User Interface Design* is about designing clear, easy-to-understand-and-use interfaces and screens for graphical and Web systems. It is the seventh in a long series of books by the author addressing screen and interface design. Over the past two decades these books have evolved and expanded as interface technology has changed and research knowledge has expanded.

The first book in the series, called *The Handbook of Screen Format Design,* was published in 1981. It presented a series of screen design guidelines for the text-based technology of that era. Through the 1980s and early 1990s the book's content was regularly updated to reflect current technology and published under different, but similar, titles. In 1994, graphical user interface, or GUI, systems having assumed interface dominance, the newest version of the book, which focused exclusively on graphical system interface design, was released. It was titled *It's Time To Clean Your Windows.* The follow-on and updated version of *It's Time To Clean Your Windows* was the first edition of this book, *The Essential Guide to User Interface Design.* The impetus for this newest edition of *The Essential Guide to User Interface Design* has been the impact of the World Wide Web on interface and screen design. This new edition incorporates an extensive compilation of Web interface design guidelines, and updates significant general interface findings over the past several years.

Is Good Design Important?

Is good design important? It certainly is! Ask the users whose productivity improved 25–40 percent as a result of well-designed screens, or the company that saved $20,000 in operational costs simply by redesigning one window. (These studies are described in Chapter 1.)

What comprises good design? To be truly effective, good screen design requires an understanding of many things. Included are the characteristics of people: how we see, understand, and think. It also includes how information must be visually presented to enhance human acceptance and comprehension, and how eye and hand movements must flow to minimize the potential for fatigue and injury. Good design must also consider the capabilities and limitations of the hardware and software of the human-computer interface.

What does this book do? This book addresses interface and screen design from the user's perspective, spelling out hundreds of principles of good design in a clear and concise manner. It blends the results of screen design research, knowledge concerning people, knowledge about the hardware and software capabilities of the interface, and my practical experience, which now spans 40 years in display-based systems.

Looking ahead, an example of what this book will accomplish for you is illustrated in Figures P.1 through P.4. Figure P.1 is an actual existing interface screen. It looks bad but you do not realize how really horrible it is until you look at Figure P.2, a redesigned version. The same goes for Figure P.3, an original screen, and Figure P.4, a redesigned version. This book will present the rules for the redesigned screens, and the rationale and reasoning that explains why they are much friendlier. We'll fully analyze these screens later in this text. Sprinkled throughout the pages will also be many other examples of good and bad design.

How This Book Is Organized

This book is composed of two parts. Part 1, provides an introduction to the human-computer interface. Chapter One examines what an interface is, its importance, and its history. Chapter Two reviews the two dominant user interfaces today, the graphical user interface (GUI) and the World Wide Web (WWW or Web). GUI interfaces are looked at in terms of their components, characteristics, and advantages over the older text-based systems. Web interfaces are compared to both GUI interfaces and conventional printed documents. The differing characteristics of three distinct Web environments, the Internet,

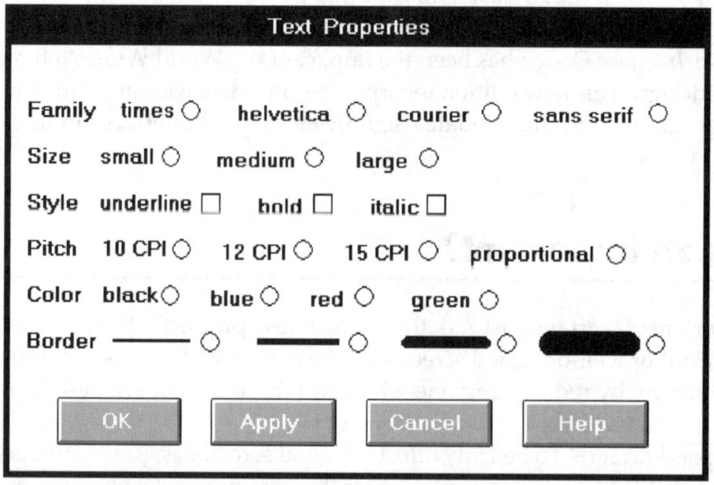

Figure P.1 An existing screen.

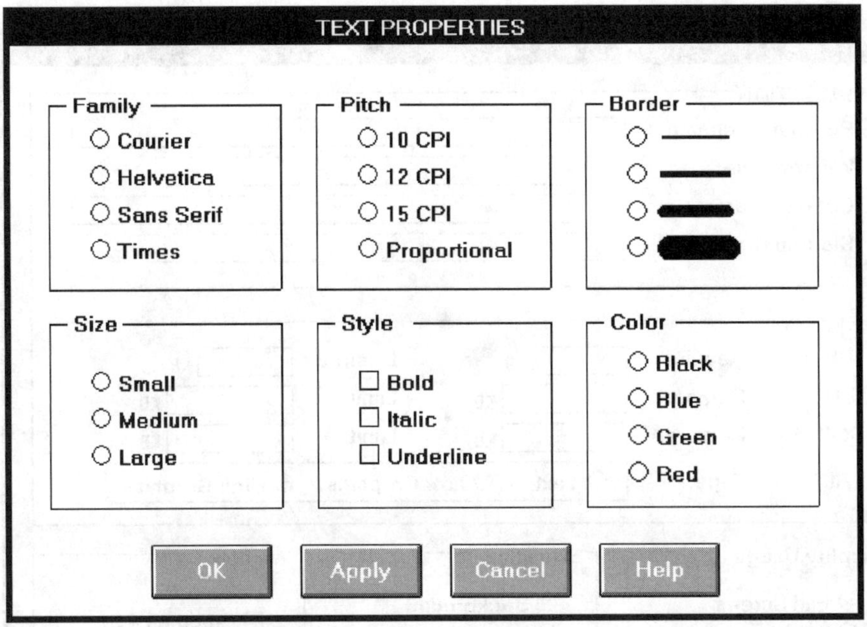

TEXT PROPERTIES

Family
- ○ Courier
- ○ Helvetica
- ○ Sans Serif
- ○ Times

Pitch
- ○ 10 CPI
- ○ 12 CPI
- ○ 15 CPI
- ○ Proportional

Border
- ○ ────
- ○ ━━━━
- ○ ━━━━
- ○ ━━━━

Size
- ○ Small
- ○ Medium
- ○ Large

Style
- ☐ Bold
- ☐ Italic
- ☐ Underline

Color
- ○ Black
- ○ Blue
- ○ Green
- ○ Red

[OK] [Apply] [Cancel] [Help]

Figure P.2 A redesigned screen.

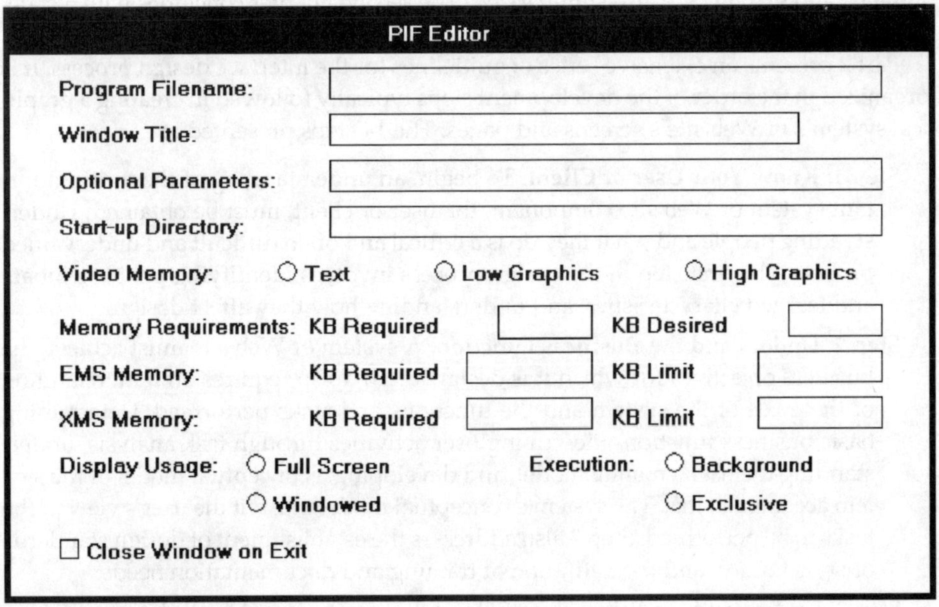

PIF Editor

Program Filename: [   ]

Window Title: [   ]

Optional Parameters: [   ]

Start-up Directory: [   ]

Video Memory: ○ Text ○ Low Graphics ○ High Graphics

Memory Requirements: KB Required [   ] KB Desired [   ]

EMS Memory: KB Required [   ] KB Limit [   ]

XMS Memory: KB Required [   ] KB Limit [   ]

Display Usage: ○ Full Screen   Execution: ○ Background
                ○ Windowed   ○ Exclusive

☐ Close Window on Exit

Figure P.3 An existing screen.

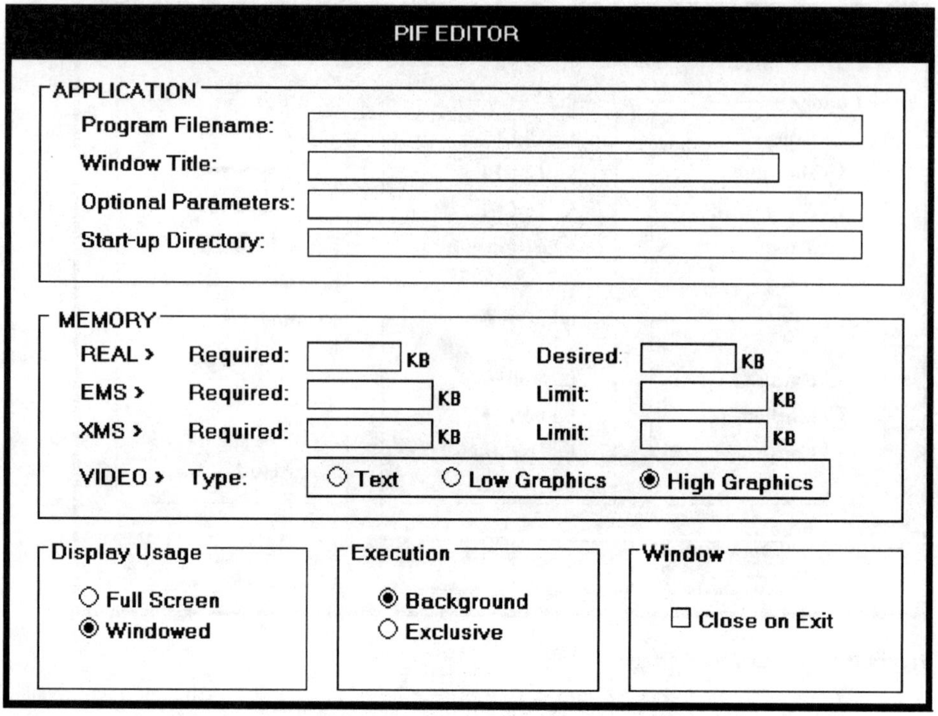

Figure P.4 A redesigned screen.

intranet, and extranet are also summarized. The second chapter concludes with a statement of the basic underlying principles for interface design.

Part 2 presents an extensive series of guidelines for the interface design process. It is organized in the order of the development steps typically followed in creating a graphical system's or Web site's screens and pages. The 14 steps presented are:

Step 1: Know Your User or Client. To begin, an understanding of the most important system or Web site component, the user or client, must be obtained. Understanding people and what they do is a critical and often difficult and undervalued process. The first step in the design process involves identifying people's innate and learned characteristics, and understanding how they affect design.

Step 2: Understand the Business Function. A system or Web site must achieve the business objectives for which it is designed. To do so requires an understanding of the goals of the system and the functions and tasks performed. Determining basic business functions, describing user activities through task analysis, understanding the user's mental model, and developing a conceptual model of the system accomplish this. The system's conceptual model must fit the user's view of the tasks to be performed. Step 2 also addresses the establishment of design standards or style guides, and the definition of training and documentation needs.

Step 3: Understand the Principles of Good Screen Design. A well-designed screen must reflect the needs and capabilities of its users, be developed within the physical constraints imposed by the hardware on which it is displayed, and effectively utilize the capabilities of its controlling software. Step 3 involves understanding the capabilities of, and limitations imposed by, people, hardware, and software in designing screens and Web pages. It presents an enormous number of general design principles for organizing and presenting information to people.

Step 4: Develop System Menus and Navigation Schemes. Graphical systems and Web sites are heavily menu-oriented. Menus are used to designate commands, properties that apply to an object, documents, and windows. To accomplish these goals, a variety of menu styles are available to choose from. Step 4 involves understanding how menus are used, and selecting the proper kinds for specific tasks. The principles of menu design are described, and the purpose and proper usage of various menu types are detailed. In this step Web site navigation schemes are also discussed.

Step 5: Select the Proper Kinds of Windows. Graphical screen design will consist of a series of windows. Step 5 involves understanding how windows are used and selecting the proper kinds for the tasks. The elements of windows are described, and the purpose and proper usage of various types of windows are detailed.

Step 6: Select the Proper Device-Based Controls. In addition to the keyboard, a system or Web site might offer the user a mouse, trackball, joystick, graphic tablet, touch screen, light pen, or some other similar device. Step 6 consists of identifying the characteristics and capabilities of these various control mechanisms and providing the proper ones for users and their tasks.

Step 7: Choose the Proper Screen-Based Controls. The designer is presented an array of screen-based controls to choose from. Selecting the right one for the user and the task is often difficult. But, as with device-based controls, making the right choice is critical to system success. A proper fit between user and control will lead to fast, accurate performance. A poor fit will result in lower productivity, more errors, and often user dissatisfaction. Step 7 consists of identifying the characteristics and capabilities of these various screen-based controls and guidelines for providing the proper ones for users and their tasks.

Step 8: Write Clear Text and Messages. Creating text and messages in a form the user wants and understands is absolutely necessary for system acceptance and success. Rules for writing text and messages for systems and Web sites are presented.

Step 9: Provide Effective Feedback and Guidance and Assistance. Effective feedback and guidance and assistance are also necessary elements of good design. This step presents the guidelines for presenting to the user feedback concerning the system and its processing status. It also describes the system response times necessary to meet user needs. Step 9 also describes the kinds of guidance and assistance that should be included in a system, and presents important design guidelines for the various kinds.

Step 10: Provide Effective Internationalization and Accessibility. People from different cultures, and people who speak different languages may use graphical systems and Web sites. Guidelines for accommodating different cultures and languages in a design are presented. People with disabilities may also be users. Design considerations for these kinds of users are also described.

Step 11: Create Meaningful Graphics, Icons, and Images. Graphics, including icons and images, are an integral part of design. Design guidelines for various types of graphics are presented. Icons are also described, including a discussion of what kinds of icons exist, what influences their usability, and how they should be designed so they are meaningful and recognizable.

Step 12: Choose the Proper Colors. Color, if used properly, can emphasize the logical organization of a screen, facilitate the discrimination of screen components, accentuate differences, and make displays more interesting. If used improperly, color can be distracting and cause visual fatigue, impairing a system's usability. Step 12 involves understanding color and how to use it effectively on textual and statistical graphics screens, and in Web sites.

Step 13: Organize and Layout Windows and Pages. After determining all the components of a screen or page, the screen or page must be organized and its elements presented clearly and meaningfully. Proper presentation and organization will encourage the quick and accurate comprehension of information and the fastest possible execution of user tasks. Step 13 addresses the rules for laying out all screen elements and controls in the most effective manner possible.

Step 14: Test, Test, and Retest. A host of factors must be considered in design and numerous trade-offs will have been made. Indeed, the design of some parts of the system may be based on skimpy data and simply reflect the most educated guess possible. Also, the implications for some design decisions may not be fully appreciated until the results can be seen. Waiting until after a system has been implemented to uncover any deficiencies and make any design changes can be aggravating, costly, and time-consuming. To minimize these kinds of problems, interfaces and screens must be continually tested and refined as development proceeds. Step 14 reviews the kinds of tests that can be performed, and discusses creating, evaluating, and modifying prototypes in an iterative manner. It also reviews final system testing and ongoing evaluations of working systems.

Because Part 2 is organized into what appear to be nonoverlapping linear tasks, this does not mean to imply, however, that the actual design process will fall into such neat categories—one step finishing and only then the next step starting. In reality, some steps will run concurrently or overlap, and design iterations will cause occasional movements backward as well as forward. If any of these steps are omitted, or carelessly performed, a product's foundation will be flawed. A flawed foundation is difficult to correct afterwards.

The readers of the previous edition of this book will note that the order in which the steps are presented has been slightly modified and the number of design steps has increased from 12 to 14. The most notable reordering change is the repositioning of the step "Organize and Layout Windows and Pages" to near the end of the development process. This was done to accommodate the much greater importance of graphical components in Web site design. The increase in the number of steps resulted from material previously covered in one step being separated into three steps. "Write Clear Text and Messages," "Provide Effective Feedback and Guidance and Assistance," and "Provide Effective Internationalization and Accessibility" are now addressed separately in order to emphasize the importance of each of these activities.

This book is both a reference book and a textbook. A set of related bulleted listings of guidelines, many with illustrative examples, are first presented in checklist form. Each checklist is then followed by more detailed explanatory text providing necessary rationale and any research upon which they are based. The reader can use the narrative to gain an understanding of the reasoning behind the guidelines and use the bulleted listings as a checklist for design.

Scattered throughout the book are many illustrations of design, both good and bad. These illustrations have been made as generic as possible, without intending to reflect any one graphical product or system. In view of the ever-changing interface landscape, this seems the most practical approach. The screen examples, however, were created using Microsoft's Visual Basic, so an illustrative bias will exist in this direction.

Research citations have been confined to those in the last decade or so. Older citations have been included, however, when they are extremely relevant to a guideline or a guideline's discussion. Finally, also sprinkled throughout the book are a collection of design myths to be discounted and maximums to be adhered to.

Who Should Read This Book

This book, while essentially an introduction to interface design, will be useful for any GUI system or Web page developer. For the developer with limited experience, a reading of its entire contents is appropriate. For the more experienced developer a perusal of its extensive contents will undoubtedly identify topics of further interest. The experienced developer will also find a review of the bulleted guidelines useful in identifying topics to be read more thoroughly. All readers will also find the bulleted checklists a handy reference guide in their development efforts.

From Here

Thank you for your interest in interface and screen design. The reader with any thoughts or comments is invited to contact me.

Bill Galitz
Wilbert O. Galitz, Inc.
P.O. Box 1477
Surprise, Arizona 85378
(623) 214-2944
wogalitz@earthlink.net

Acknowledgments

My gratitude to Bob Elliott of John Wiley & Sons, Inc. for guiding this book through two editions. I would also like to thank Emilie Herman for editorial guidance and support throughout the writing process and John Atkins for managing the production process.

My gratitude is also extended to the multitude of user interface researchers and designers without whose work this book would not have been possible.

I would also like to acknowledge and thank for their contributions several people who have been instrumental in the shaping of my long career. They are: Ralph Notto, Gaithersburg, Maryland, who many, many, years ago, gave me my first job in the not-then-widely-practiced field of business systems user interface design; Jack Endicott, Chicago, Illinois, who provided me with the opportunity to write my first book; Ed Kerr and Larry Grodman, Wellesley, Massachusetts, who made it feasible for me to establish my own company; and Bob Bailey, Salt Lake City, Utah, and Michael Patkin, Adelaide, SA, Australia, colleagues who have provided me with many useful insights over the years. Thanks also to Rob and Trish Barnett, Canberra, ACT, Australia, who provided important logistical support when it was sorely needed.

Finally, I would like to thank the many organizations and individuals who have used my services over the past couple of decades. Without your support, this book, and others, would not have been possible.

About the Author

Wilbert (Bill) O. Galitz is an internationally respected consultant, author, and instructor with a long and illustrious career in Human Factors and user-interface design. For many years he has consulted, lectured, written about, and conducted seminars and workshops on these topics worldwide. Now the author of ten books, his first book, *Human Factors in Office Automation*, published in 1980, was critically acclaimed internationally. This book was the first to address the entire range of human factors issues involved in business information systems. As a result, he was awarded the Administrative Management Society's Olsten Award. Other books have included *User-Interface Screen Design* and *It's Time to Clean Your Windows*. He has long been recognized as a world authority on the topic of screen design.

Bill's career now spans more than 40 years in information systems and he has been witness to the amazing transformation of technology over this time span. Before forming his own consulting company in 1981, he worked for CNA Insurance and the Insurance Company of North America (now CIGNA) where he designed the user-interfaces and developed screen design standards for a variety of business information systems. His work experience also includes an appointment at South Africa's National Institute for Personnel Research, and a number of years with UNIVAC (now UNISYS), and the System Develop Corporation. At UNIVAC he performed the human engineering of the company's first commercial display terminal, and completed a pioneering study on the operational aspects of large-scale computer systems.

A native of Chicago, Bill possesses a B.A. in Psychology from Lake Forest College in Illinois and an M.S. in Industrial Psychology from Iowa State University. He currently resides in Surprise, Arizona.

Part One

The User Interface—
An Introduction
and Overview

The user interface is the most important part of any computer system. Why? It *is* the system to most users. It can be seen, it can be heard, and it can be touched. The piles of software code are invisible, hidden behind phosphor, keyboards, and the mouse. The goals of interface design are simple, to make working with a computer easy, productive, and enjoyable.

This first part of this book, Part 1, provides an introduction to the human-computer interface. Chapter One examines what an interface is, its importance, and its history. Chapter 2 reviews the two dominant user interfaces, the graphical user interface (GUI) and the World Wide Web (WWW or Web). GUI interfaces are looked at in terms of their components, characteristics, and advantages over the older text-based systems. Web interfaces are compared to both GUI interfaces and conventional printed documents. The differing characteristics of three distinct Web environments, the Internet, intranet, and extranet are also summarized. The second chapter concludes with a statement of the basic underlying principles for interface design.

Part 2 of this book presents and examines an extensive collection of interface design guidelines. It is composed of 14 steps, beginning with "Know Your User or Client" and concluding with guidelines for usability testing. A complete overview of Part 2 will be found in the Part 2 Introduction.

The Importance of the User Interface

In these times of metaphors, mice, widgets/controls, links, applets, and usability, the user interface is being scrutinized, studied, written about, and talked about like never before. This welcome attention, along with the proliferation of usability laboratories and product testing, has significantly raised the usability of products we are presenting to our users today. People's voices have finally been heard above the din. Their combined voices, frustrated, fed up with complicated procedures and incomprehensible screens, have finally become overwhelming. "We're no longer going to peacefully accept products that mess up our lives and put everything we work on at risk," they are saying. They're also saying "That's just the way it is" is no longer tolerable as an answer to a problem. Examples of good design, when they have occurred, have been presented as vivid proof that good design is possible.

We developers have listened. Greatly improved technology in the late twentieth century eliminated a host of barriers to good interface design and unleashed a variety of new display and interaction techniques wrapped into a package called the graphical user interface, or, as it is commonly called, GUI or "gooey." Almost every graphical platform now provides a style guide to assist in product design. Software to aid the GUI design process proliferates. Hard on the heels of GUIs has come the amazingly fast intrusion of the World Wide Web into the everyday lives of people. Web site design has greatly expanded the range of users and introduced additional interface techniques such as multimedia. (To be fair, in some aspects it has dragged interface design backwards as well, but more about that later.)

It is said that the amount of programming code devoted to the user interface now exceeds 50 percent. Looking backwards, we have made great strides in interface design. Looking around today, however, too many instances of poor design still abound. Looking ahead, it seems that much still remains to be done.

Defining the User Interface

User interface design is a subset of a field of study called *human-computer interaction* (HCI). Human-computer interaction is the study, planning, and design of how people and computers work together so that a person's needs are satisfied in the most effective way. HCI designers must consider a variety of factors: what people want and expect, what physical limitations and abilities people possess, how their perceptual and information processing systems work, and what people find enjoyable and attractive. Technical characteristics and limitations of the computer hardware and software must also be considered.

The *user interface* is the part of a computer and its software that people can see, hear, touch, talk to, or otherwise understand or direct. The user interface has essentially two components: input and output. *Input* is how a person communicates his or her needs or desires to the computer. Some common input components are the keyboard, mouse, trackball, one's finger (for touch-sensitive screens), and one's voice (for spoken instructions). *Output* is how the computer conveys the results of its computations and requirements to the user. Today, the most common computer output mechanism is the display screen, followed by mechanisms that take advantage of a person's auditory capabilities: voice and sound. The use of the human senses of smell and touch output in interface design still remain largely unexplored.

Proper interface design will provide a mix of well-designed input and output mechanisms that satisfy the user's needs, capabilities, and limitations in the most effective way possible. The best interface is one that it not noticed, one that permits the user to focus on the information and task at hand, not the mechanisms used to present the information and perform the task.

The Importance of Good Design

With today's technology and tools, and our motivation to create really effective and usable interfaces and screens, why do we continue to produce systems that are inefficient and confusing or, at worst, just plain unusable? Is it because:

1. We don't care?
2. We don't possess common sense?
3. We don't have the time?
4. We still don't know what really makes good design?

I take the view that the root causes are Number 4, with a good deal of Number 3 thrown in. We *do* care. But we never seem to have time to find out what makes good design, nor to properly apply it. After all, many of us have other things to do in addition to designing interfaces and screens. So we take our best shot given the workload and time constraints imposed upon us. The result, too often, is woefully inadequate.

I discounted the "we don't possess common sense" alternative years ago. If, as I have heard thousands of times, interface and screen design were really a matter of common sense, we developers would have been producing *almost identical* screens for similar applications and functions for many years. When was the last time you saw two designers create almost identical screen solutions, based on the same requirements, without the aid of design guidelines or standards (or with them as well)?

A well-designed interface and screen is terribly important to our users. It is their window to view the capabilities of the system. To many, *it is* the system, being one of the few visible components of the product we developers create. It is also the vehicle through which many critical tasks are presented. These tasks often have a direct impact on an organization's relations with its customers, and its profitability.

A screen's layout and appearance affect a person in a variety of ways. If they are confusing and inefficient, people will have greater difficulty in doing their jobs and will make more mistakes. Poor design may even chase some people away from a system permanently. It can also lead to aggravation, frustration, and increased stress. I've heard of one user who relieved his frustrations with his computer with a couple of well-aimed bullets from a gun. I recently heard of another who, in a moment of extreme exasperation and anger, dropped his PC out of his upper-floor office window.

The Benefits of Good Design

Imagine the productivity benefits we could gain through proper design. Based on an actual system requiring processing of 4.8 million screens per year and illustrated in Table 1.1, an analysis established that if poor clarity forced screen users to spend one extra second per screen, almost one additional person-year would be required to process all screens. Twenty extra seconds in screen usage time adds an additional 14 person-years.

The benefits of a well-designed screen have also been under experimental scrutiny for many years. One researcher, for example, attempted to improve screen clarity and readability by making screens less crowded. Separate items, which had been combined on the same display line to conserve space, were placed on separate lines instead. The result: screen users were about 20 percent more productive with the less-crowded version. Other researchers reformatted a series of screens following many of the same concepts to be described in this book. The result: screen users of the modified screens completed transactions in 25 percent less time and with 25 percent fewer errors than those who used the original screens.

Another researcher has reported that reformatting inquiry screens following good design principles reduced decision-making time by about 40 percent, resulting in a sav-

Table 1.1   Impact of Inefficient Screen Design on Processing Time

ADDITIONAL SECONDS REQUIRED PER SCREEN IN SECONDS	ADDITIONAL PERSON-YEARS REQUIRED TO PROCESS 4.8 MILLION SCREENS PER YEAR
1	.7
5	3.6
10	7.1
20	14.2

ings of 79 person-years in the affected system. In a second study comparing 500 screens, it was found that the time to extract information from displays of airline or lodging information was 128 percent faster for the best format than for the worst.

Other studies have also shown that the proper formatting of information on screens does have a significant positive effect on performance. Cope and Uliano (1995) found that *one* graphical window redesigned to be more effective would save a company about $20,000 during its first year of use.

In recent years, the productivity benefits of well-designed Web pages have also been scrutinized. Baca and Cassidy (1999) redesigned an organization's home page because users were complaining they were unable to find information they needed. These designers established a usability objective specifying that after redesign users should be able to locate the desired information 80 percent of the time. After one redesign, 73 percent of the searches were completed with an average completion time of 113 seconds. Additional redesigns eventually improved the success rate to 84 percent, and reduced the average completion time to 57 seconds. The improvement in search success rate between the first redesign and final redesign was 15 percent; the improvement in search time was about 50 percent. (This study also points out the value of iterative testing and redesign.)

Fath and Henneman (1999) evaluated four Web sites commonly used for online shopping. Participants performed shopping tasks at each site. In three of the Web sites only about one-half of the shopping tasks could be completed, in the fourth 84 percent were successful. (In the former, one-third of the shopping tasks could not be completed at all.) The more successful, and more usable, site task completion rate was about 65 percent higher than that of the less successful sites. We can only speculate how this might translate into dollars.

Other benefits also accrue from good design (Karat, 1997). Training costs are lowered because training time is reduced, support line costs are lowered because fewer assist calls are necessary, and employee satisfaction is increased because aggravation and frustration are reduced. Another benefit is, ultimately, that an organization's customers benefit because of the improved service they receive.

Identifying and resolving problems during the design and development process also has significant economic benefits. Pressman (1992) has shown that for every dollar spent fixing a problem during product design, $10 would be spent if the problem was fixed during development, and $100 would be spent fixing it after the product's release. A general rule of thumb: every dollar invested in usability returns $10 to $100 (IBM, 2001).

How many screens are used each day in our technological world? How many screens are used each day in your organization? Thousands? Millions? Imagine the possible savings. Proper screen design might also, of course, lower the costs of replacing "broken" PCs.

A Brief History of the Human-Computer Interface

The need for people to communicate with each other has existed since we first walked upon this planet. The lowest and most common level of communication modes we share are movements and gestures. Movements and gestures are language-independent, that is, they permit people who do not speak the same language to deal with one another.

The next higher level, in terms of universality and complexity, is spoken language. Most people can speak one language, some two or more. A spoken language is a very efficient mode of communication if both parties to the communication understand it.

At the third and highest level of complexity is written language. While most people speak, not all can write. But for those who can, writing is still nowhere near as efficient a means of communication as speaking.

In modern times, we have the typewriter, another step upward in communication complexity. Significantly fewer people type than write. (While a practiced typist can find typing faster and more efficient than handwriting, the unskilled may not find this the case.) Spoken language, however, is still more efficient than typing, regardless of typing skill level.

Through its first few decades, a computer's ability to deal with human communication was inversely related to what was easy for people to do. The computer demanded rigid, typed input through a keyboard; people responded slowly using this device and with varying degrees of skill. The human-computer dialog reflected the computer's preferences, consisting of one style or a combination of styles using keyboards, commonly referred to as Command Language, Question and Answer, Menu Selection, Function Key Selection, and Form Fill-In. For more details on the screens associated with these dialogs see Galitz (1992).

Throughout the computer's history, designers have been developing, with varying degrees of success, other human-computer interaction methods that utilize more general, widespread, and easier-to-learn capabilities: voice and handwriting. Systems that recognize human speech and handwriting now exist, although they still lack the universality and richness of typed input.

Introduction of the Graphical User Interface

Finally, in the 1970s, another dialog alternative surfaced. Research at Xerox's Palo Alto Research Center provided an alternative to the typewriter, an interface using a form of human gesturing, the most basic of all human communication methods. The Xerox systems, Altus and STAR, introduced the mouse and pointing and selecting as the primary human-computer communication method. The user simply pointed at the screen, using the mouse as an intermediary. These systems also introduced the graphical user interface as we know it today. Ivan Sutherland at the Massachusetts Institute of Technology (MIT) is given credit for first introducing graphics with his Sketchpad program in 1963. Lines, circles, and points could be drawn on a screen using a light pen. Xerox worked on developing handheld pointing devices in the 1960s and patented a mouse with wheels in 1970. In 1974, Xerox patented today's ball mouse, after a researcher was suddenly inspired to turn a track ball upside down.

Xerox was never able to market the STAR successfully, but Apple quickly picked up the concept and the Macintosh, released in 1984, was the first successful mass-market system. A new concept was born, revolutionizing the human-computer interface. A chronological history of GUIs is found in Table 1.2.

Table 1.2   Chronological History of Graphical User Interfaces

1973	Pioneered at the Xerox Palo Alto Research Center. —First to pull together all the elements of the modern GUI.
1981	First commercial marketing as the Xerox STAR. —Widely introduced pointing, selection, and mouse.
1983	Apple introduces the Lisa. — Features pull-down menus and menu bars.
1984	Apple introduces the Macintosh. — Macintosh is the first successful mass-marketed system.
1985	Microsoft Windows 1.0 released. Commodore introduces the Amiga 1000.

1987	X Window System becomes widely available.
	IBM's System Application Architecture released.
	    — Including Common User Access (CUA).
	IBM's Presentation Manager released.
	    — Intended as graphics operating system replacement for DOS.
	Apple introduces the Macintosh II.
	    — The first color Macintosh.

1988	NeXT's NeXTStep released. — First to simulate three-dimensional screen.
1989	UNIX-based GUIs released. — Open Look by AT&T and Sun Microsystems. — Innovative appearance to avoid legal challenges. — Motif, for the Open Software Foundation by DEC and Hewlett-Packard. — Appearance and behavior based on Presentation Manager. Microsoft Windows 3.0 released.
1992	OS/2 Workplace Shell released. Microsoft Windows 3.1 released.
1993	Microsoft Windows NT released.
1995	Microsoft Windows 95 released.
1996	IBM releases OS/2 Warp 4. Microsoft introduces NT 4.0.
1997	Apple releases the Mac OS 8.
1998	Microsoft introduces Windows 98.
1999	Apple releases Mac OS X Server. — A UNIX-based OS.
2000	Microsoft Windows 2000 released. Microsoft Windows ME released
2001	Microsoft Windows XP released

The Blossoming of the World Wide Web

The seeds of the Internet were planted in the early 1960s. J. C. R. Licklider of MIT proposed a global network of computers in 1962 and moved to the Defense Advanced Projects Research Agency (DARPA) to lead the development work. In 1969 the Internet, then known as ARPANET, was brought online, connecting the computers at four major universities. Over the next few years, additional universities and research institutions were added to the network. One major goal of the Internet was to provide a communications network that would still function if some of the sites were destroyed by a nuclear attack.

Then, in 1974, Bolt, Beranek and Newman released Telenet, the first commercial version of ARPANET, and the public was exposed to how computers could be used in daily life. The early Internet was not user-friendly, being used by computer experts, engineers, scientists, and librarians. The Internet continued to develop, mature, and expand throughout the 1970s. Through the late 1970s and into the 1980s, the common language of all Internet computers, TCP/IP, was created. The Internet, as it is known today, came in to existence, and in 1982 the term Internet was coined. During the mid-1980s the increasing availability of PCs and super-minicomputers allowed many companies to also attach to the Internet. In 1990 ARPANET was decommissioned, leaving only the vast network of networks called the Internet. In 1991, Gopher, the first really friendly interface, was developed at the University of Minnesota. While designed to ease campus communications, it was freely distributed on the Internet.

In 1989 another significant event took place when Tim Berners-Lee and others at the European Laboratory for Particle Physics (CERN) proposed a new protocol for distributing information. This protocol was based upon hypertext, a system of embedding links in text to go to other text. The language created in conjunction with the protocol was the Hypertext Markup Language (HTML). In 1991, it was released on the Internet. HTML presented a limited set of objects and interaction styles and in many ways was a step backwards for interface design, especially when compared to the growth of interactive computing over the previous four decades. It was never, however, intended to be as flexible as the GUI interface, and users were expected to be more technical, more interested in function than form.

The hypertext concept was first presented in 1945 by Vannear Bush, and the term itself was coined in 1965. The first hypertext system released to the user community was the University of Vermont's PROMIS in 1976. Apple's HyperCard helped bring the idea to a wider audience in 1988. Berners-Lee's work is credited with hatching the World Wide Web in 1991.

In 1992, Delphi was the first to provide commercial online Internet access to subscribers. The first popular graphics-based hypertext browser was Mosaic, created by the National Center for Supercomputing Applications (NCSA) at the University of Illinois in 1993. Mosaic was one of the ingredients contributing to the initial overwhelming success of the Web, and it provided the basis for browsers to follow, including Netscape and Microsoft's Internet Explorer. (NCSA halted development of Mosaic in 1997.)

The Netscape Navigator browser, first released in 1994, was the product of some of those who left the University of Illinois' NCSA project to work for a newly founded company called Mosaic Communications. (Mosaic was later renamed Netscape Communications.) The potential for Web browsing software such as Mosaic had become obvious, and a need was waiting to be fulfilled. Netscape Navigator was the most successful browser until Microsoft declared war and entered the market with its Internet Explorer, also based upon Mosaic, in 1995. That year also saw the coming online of AOL, CompuServe, Prodigy, Yahoo, and Lycos. The Internet's shift to a commercial entity was now complete. The National Science Foundation (NSF) which had been sponsoring the Internet, also ended its the support that year. In 1994, The World Wide Web Consortium (W3C) was formed to promote and develop standards for the Web. Today, the Web is the nation's superhighway.

A chronological history of the Internet is found in Table 1.3. This table, and the above discussion, is based upon Howe (2001) and PBS's "Life on the Internet" timeline. The reader seeking more detailed historical information is referred to these Web documents.

Table 1.3   Chronological History of the Internet

1945	Hypertext concept presented by Vannear Bush.
1960	J. C. R. Licklider of MIT proposes a global network of computers.
1962	Design and development begins on network called ARPANET
1969	ARPANET is brought online. — Connects computers at four major universities. — Additional universities and research institutions soon added to the network.
1973	ARPANET goes international.
1974	Bolt, Beranek and Newman releases Telenet. — The first commercial version of ARPANET.
1976	University of Vermont's PROMIS released. — The first hypertext system released to the user community.
1982	The term Internet is coined.
1983	TCP/IP architecture now universally adopted.
1988	Apple's HyperCard released. —Presents the hypertext idea to a wider audience. —The first Internet worm unleashed.
1989	Tim Berners-Lee and others at the European Laboratory for Particle Physics (CERN) propose a new protocol for distributing information. Based upon hypertext
1990	HTML created. — In conjunction with Berners-Lees protocol. ARPANET is decommissioned
1991	HTML code released on the Internet by Tim Berners-Lee. Berners-Lee's work is credited with hatching the World Wide Web. Gopher developed at the University of Minnesota. — First really friendly interface.

Table 1.3   (*Continued*)

1992	Delphi released. – First to provide commercial online Internet access to subscribers. Mosaic created by the National Center for Supercomputing Applications (NCSA) at the University of Illinois. – The first popular graphic-based hypertext browser.
1994	Netscape Navigator Version 1.0 released. World Wide Web Consortium founded. – To promote and develop Web standards.
1995	Microsoft Internet Explorer Versions 1.0 and 2.0 released. AOL, CompuServe, Prodigy, Yahoo, and Lycos come online. National Science Foundation ends Internet support. HTML 2.0 approved as proposed Web standard. Netscape Navigator Versions 2.0 and 3.0 released. Microsoft Internet Explorer Version 3.0 released. Opera Version 2.1 released. – Browser for computers with small resources. – Written from scratch (not based upon Mosaic). – Version 2.1 the first widely available. HTML 3.2 draft released. NCSA halts development of Mosaic. Netscape Navigator Version 4.0 released. Microsoft Internet Explorer Version 4.0 released. Opera Version 3.0 released. HTML 4.0 certified as proposed standard. Microsoft Internet Explorer Version 5.0 released. XHTML 1.0 first working draft released.

A Brief History of Screen Design

While developers have been designing screens since a cathode ray tube display was first attached to a computer, more widespread interest in the application of good design principles to screens did not begin to emerge until the early 1970s, when IBM introduced its 3270 cathode ray tube text-based terminal. The 3270 was used in myriad ways in the office, and company-specific guidelines for good screen design occasionally began to surface (e.g., Galitz and DiMatteo, 1974). Typically, however, design at this time period had little to guide it, being driven by hardware and telephone line transmission issues. A 1970s screen often resembled the one pictured in Figure 1.1. It usually consisted of many fields (more than are illustrated here) with very cryptic and often unintelligible captions. It was visually cluttered, and often possessed a command field that challenged the user to remember what had to be keyed into it. Ambiguous messages often required referral to a manual to interpret. Effectively using this kind of screen required a great deal of practice and patience. Most early screens were monochromatic, typically presenting green text on black backgrounds.

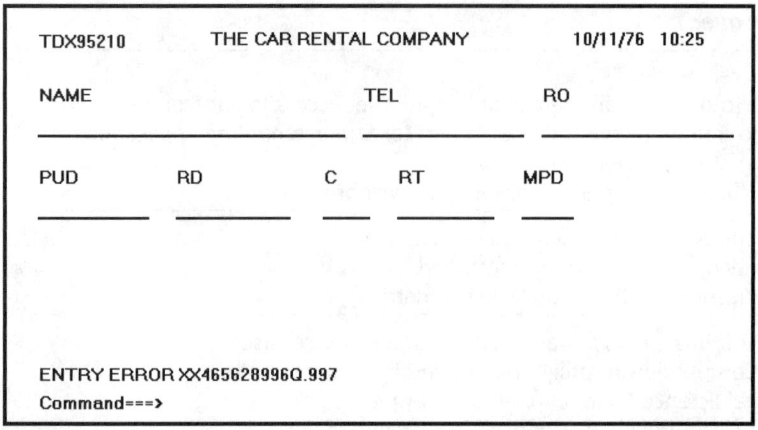

```
TDX95210            THE CAR RENTAL COMPANY              10/11/76  10:25

NAME                            TEL            RO
_____       _____     _____

PUD         RD          C       RT        MPD
_____     _____     ___     _____   _____




ENTRY ERROR XX465628996Q.997
Command===>
```

Figure 1.1 A 1970s screen.

At the turn of the decade guidelines for text-based screen design were finally made widely available (Galitz, 1980, 1981) and many screens began to take on a much less cluttered look through concepts such as grouping and alignment of elements, as illustrated in Figure 1.2. User memory was supported by providing clear and meaningful field captions and by listing commands on the screen, and enabling them to be applied through function keys. Messages also became clearer. These screens were not entirely clutter-free, however. Instructions and reminders to the user had to be inscribed on the screen in the form of prompts or completion aids such as the codes PR and SC. Not all 1980s screens looked like this, however. In the 1980s, 1970s-type screens were still being designed, and many still reside in systems today.

The advent of graphics yielded another milestone in the evolution of screen design, as illustrated in Figure 1.3. While some basic design principles did not change, groupings and alignment, for example, borders were made available to visually enhance

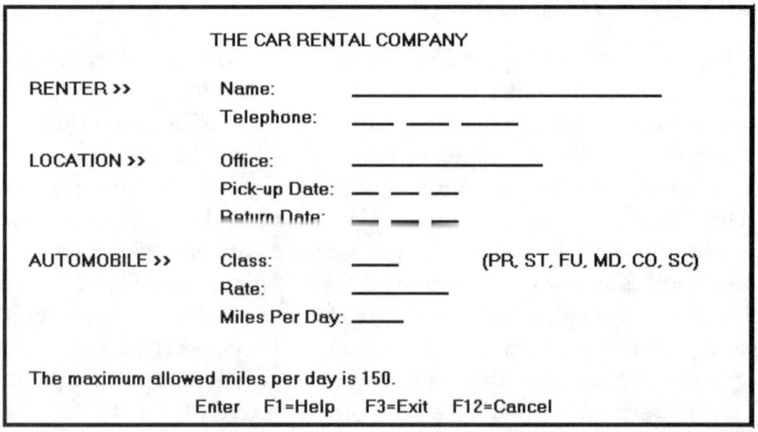

```
                 THE CAR RENTAL COMPANY

RENTER >>        Name:        _____
                 Telephone:   ____ ____ _____

LOCATION >>      Office:      _____
                 Pick-up Date:  ___ ___ ___
                 Return Date:   ___ ___ ___

AUTOMOBILE >>    Class:       _____        (PR, ST, FU, MD, CO, SC)
                 Rate:        _____
                 Miles Per Day: _____

The maximum allowed miles per day is 150.
            Enter   F1=Help   F3=Exit   F12=Cancel
```

Figure 1.2 A 1980s screen.

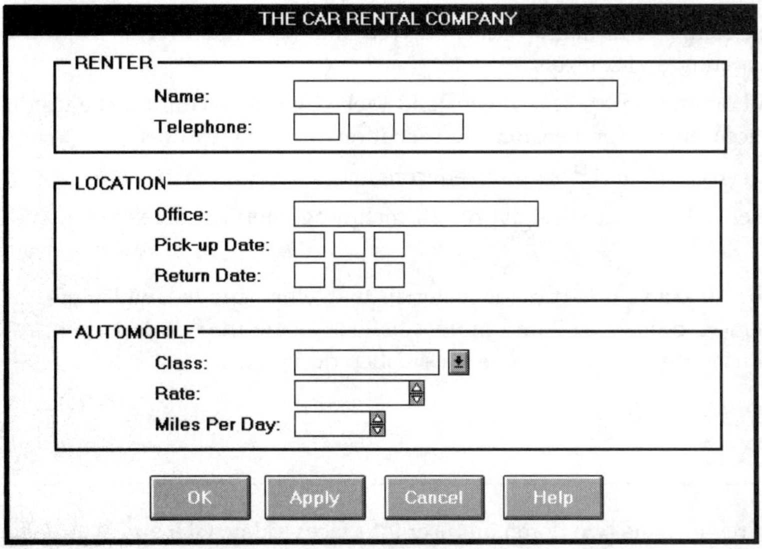

Figure 1.3   A 1990s and beyond screen.

groupings, and buttons and menus for implementing commands replaced function keys. Multiple properties of elements were also provided, including many different font sizes and styles, line thicknesses, and colors. The entry field was supplemented by a multitude of other kinds of controls, including list boxes, drop-down combination boxes, spin boxes, and so forth. These new controls were much more effective in supporting a person's memory, now simply allowing for selection from a list instead of requiring a remembered key entry. Completion aids disappeared from screens, replaced by one of the new listing controls. Screens could also be simplified, the much more powerful computers being able to quickly present a new screen.

In the 1990s, our knowledge concerning what makes effective screen design continued to expand. Coupled with ever-improving technology, the result was even greater improvements in the user-computer screen interface as the new century dawned.

The Purpose of This Book

This book's first objective is to present the important practical guidelines for good interface and screen design. It is intended as a ready reference source for all graphical and Web systems. The guidelines reflect a mix of human behavior, science, and art, and are organized within the context of the GUI design process. The specific objectives are to enable the reader to do the following:

- Understand the many considerations that must be applied to the interface and screen design process.
- Understand the rationale and rules for an effective interface design methodology.

- Identify the components of graphical and Web interfaces and screens, including windows, menus, and controls.

- Design and organize graphical screens and Web pages to encourage the fastest and most accurate comprehension and execution of screen features.

- Choose screen colors and design screen icons.

- Perform the User Interface design process, including interface development and testing.

The book's other objective is to provide materials that, when applied, will allow our users to become more productive—and more satisfied—using the interfaces we produce. A satisfied user also means, of course, a satisfied designer.

What's Next?

The next chapter reviews the two dominant user interfaces today, GUI and Web. GUI interfaces are looked at in terms of their components, characteristics, and advantages over the older text-based systems. Web interfaces are compared to both GUI interfaces and conventional printed documents. The differing characteristics of three distinct Web environments, the Internet, intranet, and extranet are also summarized. The next chapter concludes with a statement of the basic underlying principles for interface design.

CHAPTER 2

Characteristics of Graphical and Web User Interfaces

The graphical user interface differed significantly from its text-based forefather. The Web interface differs from a GUI interface in significant ways also, not all differences, however, can be considered interface advancements. In this chapter, the characteristics of a GUI interface will be reviewed, including the concept it introduced: direct manipulation. Then, Web characteristics will be reviewed, including the differences between GUI and Web interface design, and the differences between printed page and Web design.

The Graphical User Interface

In brief, a graphical user interface can be defined as follows. A *user interface,* as recently described, is a collection of techniques and mechanisms to interact with something. In a *graphical* interface, the primary interaction mechanism is a pointing device of some kind. This device is the electronic equivalent to the human hand. What the user interacts with is a collection of elements referred to as *objects*. They can be seen, heard, touched, or otherwise perceived. Objects are always visible to the user and are used to perform tasks. They are interacted with as entities independent of all other objects. People perform operations, called *actions*, on objects. The operations include accessing and modifying objects by pointing, selecting, and manipulating. All objects have standard resulting behaviors.

The Popularity of Graphics

Graphics revolutionized design and the user interface. A graphical screen bore scant resemblance to its earlier text-based colleagues. Whereas the older text-based screen possessed a one-dimensional, text-oriented, form-like quality, graphic screens assumed a three-dimensional look. Information floated in windows, small rectangular boxes seemed to rise above the background plane. Windows could also float above other windows. Controls appeared to rise above the screen and move when activated. Lines appeared to be etched into the screen. Information could appear, and disappear, as needed, and in some cases text could be replaced by graphical images called icons. These icons could represent objects or actions.

Screen navigation and commands are executed through menu bars and pull-downs. Menus "pop up" on the screen. In the screen body, selection fields such as radio buttons, check boxes, list boxes, and palettes coexisted with the reliable old text entry field. More sophisticated text entry fields with attached or drop-down menus of alternatives also became available. Screen objects and actions were selected through use of pointing mechanisms, such as the mouse or joystick, instead of the traditional keyboard.

Increased computer power and the vast improvement in the display enable the user's actions to be reacted to quickly, dynamically, and meaningfully. This new interface is characterized as representing one's "desktop" with scattered notes, papers, and objects such as files, trays, and trashcans arrayed around the screen. It is sometimes referred to as the WIMP interface: windows, icons, menus, and pointers.

Graphic presentation of information utilizes a person's information-processing capabilities much more effectively than other presentation methods. Properly used, it reduces the requirement for perceptual and mental information recoding and reorganization, and also reduces the memory loads. It permits faster information transfer between computers and people by permitting more visual comparisons of amounts, trends, or relationships; more compact representation of information; and simplification of the perception of structure. Graphics also can add appeal or charm to the interface and permit greater customization to create a unique corporate or organization style.

The Concept of Direct Manipulation

The term used to describe this style of interaction for graphical systems was first used by Shneiderman (1982). He called them "direct manipulation" systems, suggesting that they possess the following characteristics:

The system is portrayed as an extension of the real world. It is assumed that a person is already familiar with the objects and actions in his or her environment of interest. The system simply replicates them and portrays them on a different medium, the screen. A person has the power to access and modify these objects, among which are windows. A person is allowed to work in a familiar environment and in a familiar way, focusing on the data, not the application and tools. The physical organization of the system, which most often is unfamiliar, is hidden from view and is not a distraction.

Continuous visibility of objects and actions. Like one's desktop, objects are continuously visible. Reminders of actions to be performed are also obvious, labeled buttons replacing complex syntax and command names. Cursor action and motion occurs in physically obvious and intuitively natural ways. Nelson (1980) described this concept as "virtual reality," a representation of reality that can be manipulated. Hatfield (1981) is credited with calling it "WYSIWYG" (what you see is what you get). Rutkowski (1982) described it as "transparency," where one's intellect is applied to the task, not the tool. Hutchins, Hollan, and Norman (1986) considered it direct involvement with the world of objects rather than communicating with an intermediary.

One problem in direct manipulation, however, is that there is no direct analogy on the desk for all necessary windowing operations. A piece of paper on one's desk maintains a constant size, never shrinking or growing. Windows can do both. Solving this problem required embedding a control panel, a familiar concept to most people, in a window's border. This control panel is manipulated, not the window itself.

Actions are rapid and incremental with visible display of results. Since tactile feedback is not yet possible (as would occur with one's hand when one touches something), the results of actions are immediately displayed visually on the screen in their new and current form. Auditory feedback may also be provided. The impact of a previous action is quickly seen, and the evolution of tasks is continuous and effortless.

Incremental actions are easily reversible. Finally, actions, if discovered to be incorrect or not desired, can be easily undone.

Earlier Direct Manipulation Systems

Using the above definition, the concept of direct manipulation actually preceded the first graphical system. The earliest full-screen text editors possessed similar characteristics. Screens of text resembling a piece of paper on one's desk could be created (extension of real world) and then reviewed in their entirety (continuous visibility). Editing or restructuring could be easily accomplished (through rapid incremental actions) and the results immediately seen. Actions could be reversed when necessary. It took the advent of graphical systems to crystallize the direct manipulation concept, however.

Indirect Manipulation

In practice, direct manipulation of *all* screen objects and actions may not be feasible because of the following:

- The operation may be difficult to conceptualize in the graphical system.
- The graphics capability of the system may be limited.
- The amount of space available for placing manipulation controls in the window border may be limited.

- It may be difficult for people to learn and remember all the necessary operations and actions.

When this occurs, *indirect manipulation* is provided. Indirect manipulation substitutes words and text, such as pull-down or pop-up menus, for symbols, and substitutes typing for pointing. Most window systems are a combination of both direct and indirect manipulation. A menu may be accessed by pointing at a menu icon and then selecting it (direct manipulation). The menu itself, however, is a textual list of operations (indirect manipulation). When an operation is selected from the list, by pointing or typing, the system executes it as a command.

Which style of interaction—direct manipulation, indirect manipulation, or a combination of both—is best, under what conditions and for whom, remains a question whose answer still eludes us.

Graphical Systems: Advantages and Disadvantages

Graphical systems burst upon the office with great promise. The simplified interface they presented was thought to reduce the memory requirements imposed on the user, make more effective use of one's information-processing capabilities, and dramatically reduce system learning requirements. Experience indicates that for many people they have done all these things.

Advantages

The success of graphical systems has been attributed to a host of factors. The following have been commonly referenced in literature and endorsed by their advocates as advantages of these systems.

Symbols recognized faster than text. Research has found that symbols can be recognized faster and more accurately than text, and that the graphical attributes of icons, such as shape and color, are very useful for quickly classifying objects, elements, or text by some common property. An example of a good classification scheme that speeds up recognition are the icons developed for indicating the kind of message being presented to the user of the system. The text of an informational message is preceded by an "i" in a circle, a warning message by an exclamation point, and a critical message by another unique symbol. These icons allow speedy recognition of the type of message being presented.

Faster learning. Research has also found that a graphical, pictorial representation aids learning, and symbols can also be easily learned.

Faster use and problem solving. Visual or spatial representation of information has been found to be easier to retain and manipulate and leads to faster and more successful problem solving. Symbols have also been found to be effective in conveying simple instructions.

Easier remembering. Because of greater simplicity, it is easier for casual users to retain operational concepts.

More natural. Graphic representations of objects are thought to be more natural and closer to innate human capabilities. In human beings, actions and visual skills emerged before languages. It has also been suggested that symbolic displays are more natural and advantageous because the human mind has a powerful image memory.

Exploits visual/spatial cues. Spatial relationships are usually found to be understood more quickly than verbal representations. Visually thinking is believed to be better than logical thinking.

Fosters more concrete thinking. Displayed objects are directly in the high-level task domain, or directly usable in their presented form. There is no need mentally to decompose tasks into multiple commands with complex syntactic form. The need for abstract thinking is therefore minimized.

Provides context. Displayed objects are visible, providing a picture of the current context.

Fewer errors. More concrete thinking affords fewer opportunities for errors. Reversibility of actions reduces error rates because it is always possible to undo the last step. Error messages are less frequently needed.

Increased feeling of control. The user initiates actions and feels in control. This increases user confidence and hastens system mastery.

Immediate feedback. The results of actions furthering user goals can be seen immediately. Learning is quickened. If the response is not in the desired direction, the direction can be changed quickly.

Predictable system responses. Predictable system responses also speed learning.

Easily reversible actions. The user has more control. This ability to reverse unwanted actions also increases user confidence and hastens system mastery.

Less anxiety concerning use. Hesitant or new users feel less anxiety when using the system because it is so easily comprehended, is easy to control, and has predictable responses and reversible actions.

More attractive. Direct-manipulation systems are more entertaining, cleverer, and more appealing. This is especially important for the cautious or skeptical user.

May consume less space. Icons may take up less space than the equivalent in words. More information can often be packed in a given area of the screen. This, however, is not always the case.

Replaces national languages. Language-based systems are seldom universally applicable. Language translations frequently cause problems in a text-based system. Icons possess much more universality than text and are much more easily comprehended worldwide.

Easily augmented with text displays. Where graphical design limitations exist, direct-manipulation systems can easily be augmented with text displays. The reverse is not true.

Low typing requirements. Pointing and selection controls, such as the mouse or trackball, eliminate the need for typing skills.

Smooth transition from command language system. Moving from a command language to a direct-manipulation system has been found to be easy. The reverse is not true.

Disadvantages

The body of positive research, hypotheses, and comment concerning graphical systems is being challenged by some studies, findings, and opinions that indicate that graphical representation and interaction may not necessarily always be better. Indeed, in some cases, it may be poorer than pure textual or alphanumeric displays. Trying to force all system components into a graphical format may be doing a disservice to the user. Some also feel that, as graphical systems are becoming increasingly sophisticated and continue to expand, interfaces have become increasingly more complex, sometimes arcane, and even bizarre. Among the disadvantages put forth are these:

Greater design complexity. The elements and techniques available to the graphical screen designer far outnumber those that were at the disposal of the text-based screen designer. Controls and basic alternatives must be chosen from a pile of choices numbering in excess of 50. (Conversely, alternatives available to the text-based screen designer numbered about 15.) This design potential may not necessarily result in better design, unless the choices are thoughtfully selected and consistently and simply applied. Proper window types must also be chosen and colors selected from a seemingly unending rainbow of alternatives. With graphics, the skill of the designer is increasingly challenged. Poor design can undermine acceptance.

Learning still necessary. The first time one encounters many graphical systems, what to do is not immediately obvious. The meanings of many words and icons may not be known. It is not often possible to guess their meanings, especially the more arbitrary symbols. How to use a pointing device may also have to be learned. A severe learning and remembering requirement is imposed on many users, and it takes a while to get up to speed. A text-based system could easily be structured to incorporate a set of clear instructions: (1) Do this, (2) now do this, and so on.

System providers estimate that becoming accustomed to a graphical interface should require about eight hours of training. Other experts say the learning time is closer to 20 or 30 hours.

Lack of experimentally-derived design guidelines. The graphical interface is still burdened today by a lack of widely available experimentally-derived design guidelines. Early on, more developer interest existed in solving technical rather than usability issues, so few studies to aid in making design decisions were performed. Today, studies being performed in usability laboratories are rarely published. This occurs because of a number of factors. First, builders of platforms and packages will not publish their study results because they want to maintain a competitive advantage. If a better way is found to do something, or present something, why tell the competition? Let them make the same mistake, or find the answer themselves.

Second, the studies are often specific to a particular function or task. They may not be generally applicable. Third, it takes time and effort to publish something. The developer in today's office seldom has the time. Finally, it is also difficult to develop studies evaluating design alternatives because of increased GUI complexity. Too many variables that must be controlled make meaningful cause-and-effect relationships very difficult to uncover.

Consequently, there is too little understanding of how most design aspects relate to productivity and satisfaction.

Inconsistencies in technique and terminology. Many differences in technique, terminology, and look and feel exist among various graphical system providers, and even among successive versions of the same system. These inconsistencies occur because of copyright and legal implications, product differentiation considerations, and our expanding knowledge about the interface. The result is that learning, and relearning, for both designers and users is much more difficult than it should be.

Working domain is the present. While direct-manipulation systems provide context, they also require the user to work in the "present." Hulteen (1988), in a parody of "WYSIWYG," suggests "What you see is all you get." Walker (1989) argued that language takes you out of the here and now and the visually present. Language, she continues, makes it easier to find things.

Not always familiar. Symbolic representations may not be as familiar as words or numbers. We have been exposed to words and numbers for a long time. Research has found that numeric symbols elicit faster responses than graphic symbols in a visual search task. One developer had to modify a new system during testing by replacing iconic representations with a textual outline format. The users, lawyers, were unfamiliar with icons and demanded a more familiar format.

Human comprehension limitations. Human limitations may also exist in terms of one's ability to deal with the increased complexity of the graphical interface. The variety of visual displays can still challenge all but the most sophisticated users. The number of different icons that can be introduced is also restricted because of limitations in human comprehension. Studies continually find that the number of different symbols a person can differentiate and deal with is much more limited than text. Some researchers note that claims for the easy understanding of pictograms are exaggerated, and that recognizing icons requires much perceptual learning, abstracting ability, and intelligence.

The motor skills required may also challenge all but the most sophisticated users. Correctly double-clicking a mouse, for example, is difficult for some people.

Window manipulation requirements. Window handling and manipulation times are still excessive and repetitive. This wastes time and interrupts the decision-making needed to perform tasks and jobs.

Production limitations. The number of symbols that can be clearly produced using today's technology is still limited. A body of recognizable symbols must be produced that are equally legible and equally recognizable using differing technologies. This is extremely difficult today.

Few tested icons exist. Icons, like typefaces, must appear in different sizes, weights, and styles. As with text, an entire font of clearly recognizable symbols must be developed. It is not simply a question of developing an icon and simply enlarging or reducing it. Changing an icon's size can differentially affect symbol line widths, open areas, and so forth, dramatically affecting its recognizability. Typeface design is literally the product of 300 years of experimentation and study. Icons must be researched, designed, tested, and then introduced into the marketplace. The consequences of poor or improper design will be confusion and lower productivity for users.

Inefficient for touch typists. For an experienced touch typist, the keyboard is a very fast and powerful device. Moving a mouse or some other pointing mechanism may be slower.

Inefficient for expert users. Inefficiencies develop when there are more objects and actions than can fit on the screen. Concatenation for a command language is impossible.

Not always the preferred style of interaction. Not all users prefer a pure iconic interface. A study comparing commands illustrated by icons, icons with text, or text-only, found that users preferred alternatives with textual captions.

Not always fastest style of interaction. Another study has found that graphic instructions on an automated bank teller machine were inferior to textual instructions.

Increased chances of clutter and confusion. A graphical system does not guarantee elimination of clutter on a screen. Instead, the chance for clutter is increased, thereby increasing the possibility of confusion. How much screen clutter one can deal with is open to speculation. The possibility that clutter may exist is evidenced by the fact that many people, when working with a window, expand it to fill the entire display screen. This may be done to reduce visual screen clutter. Mori and Hayashi (1993) found that visible windows, not the focus of attention, degraded performance in the window being worked on.

The futz and fiddle factor. With the proliferation of computer games, computer usage can be wasteful of time. Stromoski (1993) estimates that five hours a week in the office are spent playing and tinkering. Experts have said that the most used program in Microsoft Windows is Solitaire! Tinkering includes activities such as creating garish documents reflecting almost every object property (font size, style, color, and so on.) available.

Futzing and fiddling does have some benefits, however. It is a tool for learning how to use a mouse, for example, and it is a vehicle for exploring the system and becoming familiar with its capabilities. It is of value when done in moderation.

May consume more screen space. Not all applications will consume less screen space. A listing of names and telephone numbers in a textual format will be more efficient to scan than a card file.

Hardware limitations. Good design also requires hardware of adequate power, processing speed, screen resolution, and graphic capability. Insufficiencies in these areas can prevent a graphic system's full potential from being realized.

Some Studies and a Conclusion

The many benefits of one interaction style versus another are anecdotal. This has often made the debate between advocates of graphical and other styles of interaction more emotional than scientific. This is certainly true for many of the arguments. Over the past couple of decades a variety of studies have been performed comparing graphical systems with other interaction styles. In some usability studies graphical systems were found superior, in other studies other interaction techniques were found superior, and in some cases no differences were found. Perhaps the best conclusion was drawn by Whiteside, Jones, Levy, and Wixon (1985) who compared the usability characteristics of seven systems, including the direct-manipulation, menu, and command language styles of interaction. They found that user performance did not depend on the type of system. There were large differences in learnability and usability among all. How well the system was *designed* was the best indicator of success, not the style of interaction.

Research and experience have shown that different interface styles also have different strengths and weaknesses. Some concepts and tasks are very hard to convey symbolically and do not seem to be suited for a pure graphical presentation. Other concepts and tasks, however, may be well suited to such an approach. Which tasks are best suited for which styles still needs continuing study. Finally, all users may not like all aspects of a graphical system. The design should reflect this. In summary, the following is clear:

- The design of an interface, and not its interaction style, is the best determinant of ease of use.
- User preferences must be considered in choosing an interaction style.
- In the overwhelming majority of cases, words are more meaningful to users than icons.
- The content of a graphic screen is critical to its usefulness. The wrong presentation or a cluttered presentation may actually lead to greater confusion, not less.
- The success of a graphical system depends on the skills of its designers in following established principles of usability.

Characteristics of the Graphical User Interface

A graphical system possesses a set of defining concepts. Included are sophisticated visual presentation, pick-and-click interaction, a restricted set of interface options, visualization, object orientation, extensive use of a person's recognition memory, and concurrent performance of functions.

Sophisticated Visual Presentation

Visual presentation is the visual aspect of the interface. It is what people see on the screen. The sophistication of a graphical system permits displaying lines, including drawings and icons. It also permits the displaying of a variety of character fonts, including different sizes and styles. The display of 16 million or more colors is possible on some screens. Graphics also permit animation and the presentation of photographs and motion video.

The meaningful interface elements visually presented to the user in a graphical system include windows (primary, secondary, or dialog boxes), menus (menu bar, pull-down, pop-up, cascading), icons to represent objects such as programs or files, assorted screen-based controls (text boxes, list boxes, combination boxes, settings, scroll bars, and buttons), and a mouse pointer and cursor. The objective is to reflect visually on the screen the real world of the user as realistically, meaningfully, simply, and clearly as possible.

Pick-and-Click Interaction

Elements of a graphical screen upon which some action is to be performed must first be identified. The motor activity required of a person to identify this element for a proposed action is commonly referred to as *pick*, the signal to perform an action as *click*. The primary mechanism for performing this pick-and-click is most often the mouse and its buttons. The user moves the mouse pointer to the relevant element (pick) and the action is signaled (click). Pointing allows rapid selection and feedback. The eye, hand, and mind seem to work smoothly and efficiently together.

The secondary mechanism for performing these selection actions is the keyboard. Most systems permit pick-and-click to be performed using the keyboard as well.

Restricted Set of Interface Options

The array of alternatives available to the user is what is presented on the screen or what may be retrieved through what is presented on the screen, nothing less, nothing more. This concept fostered the acronym WYSIWYG.

Visualization

Visualization is a cognitive process that allows people to understand information that is difficult to perceive, because it is either too voluminous or too abstract. It involves changing an entity's representation to reveal gradually the structure and/or function of the underlying system or process. Presenting specialized graphic portrayals facilitates visualization. The best visualization method for an activity depends on what people are trying to learn from the data. The goal is not necessarily to reproduce a realistic graphical image, but to produce one that conveys the most relevant information. Effective visualizations can facilitate mental insights, increase productivity, and foster faster and more accurate use of data.

Object Orientation

A graphical system consists of objects and actions. *Objects* are what people see on the screen. They are manipulated as a single unit. A well-designed system keeps users focused on objects, not on how to carry out actions. Objects can be composed of *subobjects*.

For example, an object may be a document. The document's subobjects may be a paragraph, sentence, word, and letter.

IBM's System Application Architecture Common User Access Advanced Interface Design Reference (SAA CUA) (IBM, 1991) breaks objects into three meaningful classes: data, container, and device. *Data objects* present information. This information, either text or graphics, normally appears in the body of the screen. It is, essentially, the screen-based controls for information collection or presentation organized on the screen.

Container objects are objects to hold other objects. They are used to group two or more related objects for easy access and retrieval. There are three kinds of container objects: the workplace, folders, and workareas. The *workplace* is the desktop, the storage area for all objects. *Folders* are general-purpose containers for long-term storage of objects. *Workareas* are temporary storage folders used for storing multiple objects currently being worked on.

Device objects represent physical objects in the real world, such as printers or trash baskets. These objects may contain others for acting upon. A file, for example, may be placed in a printer for printing of its contents.

Microsoft Windows specifies the characteristics of objects depending upon the relationships that exist between them. Objects can exist within the context of other objects, and one object may affect the way another object appears or behaves. These relationships are called collections, constraints, composites, and containers.

A *collection* is the simplest relationship—the objects sharing a common aspect. A collection might be the result of a query or a multiple selection of objects. Operations can be applied to a collection of objects.

A *constraint* is a stronger object relationship. Changing an object in a set affects some other object in the set. A document being organized into pages is an example of a constraint.

A *composite* exists when the relationship between objects becomes so significant that the aggregation itself can be identified as an object. Examples include a range of cells organized into a spreadsheet, or a collection of words organized into a paragraph.

A *container* is an object in which other objects exist. Examples include text in a document or documents in a folder. A container often influences the behavior of its content. It may add or suppress certain properties or operations of objects placed within it, control access to its content, or control access to kinds of objects it will accept.

These relationships help define an object's *type*. Similar traits and behaviors exist in objects of the same object type.

Another important object characteristic is *persistence*. Persistence is the maintenance of a state once it is established. An object's state (for example, window size, cursor location, scroll position, and so on) should always be automatically preserved when the user changes it.

Properties or Attributes of Objects

Objects also have properties or attributes. Properties are the unique characteristics of an object. Properties help to describe an object and can be changed by users. Examples of properties are text styles (such as normal or italics), font sizes (such as 10 or 12 points), or window background colors (such as black or blue).

Actions

In addition to objects are actions. People take actions on objects. They manipulate objects in specific ways (commands) or modify the properties of objects (property or attribute specification).

Commands are actions that manipulate objects. They may be performed in a variety of ways, including by direct manipulation or through a command button. They are executed immediately when selected. Once executed, they cease to be relevant. Examples of commands are opening a document, printing a document, closing a window, and quitting an application.

Property/attribute specification actions establish or modify the attributes or properties of objects. When selected, they remain in effect until deselected. Examples include selecting cascaded windows to be displayed, a particular font style, or a particular color.

The following is a typical *property/attribute specification sequence:*

1. The user selects an object—for example, several words of text.
2. The user then selects an action to apply to that object, such as the action BOLD.
3. The selected words are made bold and will remain bold until selected and changed again.

A series of actions may be performed on a selected object. Performing a series of actions on an object also permits and encourages system learning through exploration.

Application versus Object or Data Orientation

Earlier graphical systems were usually application-oriented, a continuation of the philosophy that enveloped text-based systems. When a text-based system was developed, it was called an application. As graphical systems evolved, developers usually thought in terms of applications as well. When a real picture of the user began to emerge, it finally became evident that people thought in terms of tasks, not applications. They choose objects and then act upon them.

An application-oriented approach takes an action:object approach, like this:

Action> 1. An application is opened (for example, word processing).

Object> 2. A file or other object selected (for example, a memo).

An object-oriented object:action approach does this:

Object> 1. An object is chosen (a memo).

Action> 2. An application is selected (word processing).

The object-action approach permits people to more easily focus on their task and minimizes the visibility of the operating system and separate applications. Many experienced users may have difficulty in switching from one approach to another since an old interaction behavior must be unlearned and a new one learned. New users should not experience these problems, since it more accurately reflects a person's thinking. In any one interface, it is critical that a consistent orientation be maintained, either an object:action or an action:object approach.

Views

Views are ways of looking at an object's information. IBM's SAA CUA describes four kinds of views: composed, contents, settings, and help.

Composed views present information and the objects contained within an object. They are typically associated with data objects and are specific to tasks and products being worked with. *Contents* views list the components of objects. *Settings* views permit seeing and changing object properties. *Help* views provide all the help functions.

Use of Recognition Memory

Continuous visibility of objects and actions encourages use of a person's more powerful recognition memory. The "out of sight, out of mind" problem is eliminated.

Concurrent Performance of Functions

Graphic systems may do two or more things at one time. Multiple programs may run simultaneously. When a system is not busy on a primary task, it may process background tasks (cooperative multitasking). When applications are running as truly separate tasks, the system may divide the processing power into time slices and allocate portions to each application (preemptive multitasking). Data may also be transferred between programs. It may be temporarily stored on a "clipboard" for later transfer or be automatically swapped between programs.

The Web User Interface

The expansion of the World Wide Web since the early 1990s has been truly amazing. Once simply a communication medium for scientists and researchers, its many and pervasive tentacles have spread deeply into businesses, organizations, and homes around the world. Unlike earlier text-based and GUI systems that were developed and nurtured in an organization's Data Processing and Information Systems groups, the Web's roots were sown in a market-driven society thirsting for convenience and information.

Web interface design is essentially the design of navigation and the presentation of information. It is about content, not data. Proper interface design is largely a matter of properly balancing the structure and relationships of menus, content, and other linked documents or graphics. The design goal is to build a hierarchy of menus and pages that feels natural, is well structured, is easy to use, and is truthful. The Web is a navigation environment where people move between pages of information, not an application environment. It is also a graphically rich environment.

Web interface design is difficult for a number of reasons. First, its underlying design language, HTML, was never intended for creating screens to be used by the general population. Its scope of users was expected to be technical. HTML was limited in objects and interaction styles and did not provide a means for presenting information in the most effective way for people. Next, browser navigation retreated to the pre-GUI era. This era was characterized by a "command" field whose contents had to be learned, and a navigational organization and structure that lay hidden beneath a mostly dark and blank screen. GUIs eliminated the absolute necessity for a command field, providing menus related to the task and the current contextual situation. Browser navigation is mostly confined to a "Back" and "Forward" concept, but "back-to-where" and "forward-to-where" is often unremembered or unknown. Ill-timed use of the Back button can destroy many minutes worth of work. Remaining navigation was willed to Web pages themselves, where the situation only worsened. Numerous links were provided to destinations unknown, invisible navigation buttons lay unrecognizable on the screen, and linked jumps two paragraphs down the page were indistinguishable from those that went to the Ukraine. Also, form completion and submission was essentially a form of batch processing. Forms were completed, transmitted, and then edited instead of the editing being interactive, occurring as the entry process was accomplished. Web interface design is now struggling to recover from these giant steps backward.

Web interface design is also more difficult because the main issues concern information architecture and task flow, neither of which is easy to standardize. It is more difficult because of the availability of the various types of multimedia, and the desire of many designers to use something simply because it is available. It is more difficult because users are ill defined, and the user's tools so variable in nature.

Today, then, the Web interface is a victim of its poor foundation. It is also a victim of its explosive and haphazard growth. Looking forward, interface design tools will mature, research-based design guidelines will become increasingly available (and will be applied), and knowledge of users and their needs will expand. Then, the ultimate goal of a Web that feels natural, is well structured, and is easy to use will reach fruition.

The Popularity of the Web

While the introduction of the graphical user interface revolutionized the user interface, the Web has revolutionized computing. It allows millions of people scattered across the globe to communicate, access information, publish, and be heard. It allows people to control much of the display and the rendering of Web pages. Aspects such as typography and colors can be changed, graphics turned off, and decisions made whether or not to transmit certain data over nonsecure channels or whether to accept or refuse cookies. Nowhere in the history of computing has the user been given so much control.

Web usage has reflected this popularity. The number of Internet hosts has risen dramatically. In 1984, hosts online exceeded 1,000; in 1987, 10,000; in 1989, 100,000, in 1990, 300,000; in 1992 hosts exceeded one million. Commercialization of the Internet saw even greater expansion of the growth rate. In 1993, Internet traffic was expanding at a 341,634 percent annual growth rate. In 1996, there were nearly 10 million hosts online and 40 million connected people (PBS Timeline).

User control has had some decided disadvantages for some Web site owners as well. Users have become much more discerning about good design. Slow download times, confusing navigation, confusing page organization, disturbing animation, or other undesirable site features often results in user abandonment of the site for others with a more agreeable interface. People are quick to vote with their mouse, and these warnings should not go unheeded.

Characteristics of a Web Interface

A Web interface possesses a number of characteristics, some similar to a GUI interface, and, as has already been shown, some different. In the following paragraphs many of these specific commonalities and differences will be examined. Also, the differing characteristics of printed page design and Web page design will be compared.

GUI versus Web Page Design

GUI and Web interface design do have similarities. Both are software designs, they are used by people, they are interactive, they are heavily visual experiences presented through screens, and they are composed of many similar components. Significant differences do exist, however. The following paragraphs highlight the other most significant differences. Table 2.1 provides a summary listing. Parts of this discussion are based upon Berry (2000) and Nielsen (1997a).

Devices. In *GUI* design, the characteristics of interface devices such as monitors and modems are well defined, and design variations tend to be restricted. Monitor display capabilities, such as installed fonts and screen size, are established and easily considered in the design process. In *Web* design, no assumptions about the user's interface devices can be made. User devices may range from handheld mechanisms to high-end workstations. (In GUI design, the difference in screen area between a laptop and a high-end workstation is a factor of six, in Web page design this difference may be as high as 100.) Connection speed bandwidths may also vary by a factor of 1,000. Consequently, WYSIWYG no longer exists in page design. In GUI design, the layout of a screen will look exactly as specified, Web page look will be greatly influenced by both the hardware and software. With the Web, the designer has to relinquish full control and share responsibility for the interface with users and their hardware and software.

User focus. *GUI* systems are about well-defined applications and data, about transactions and processes. Thorough attention must usually be addressed to tasks in need of completion. The *Web* is about information and navigation, an environment where people move back and forth in an unstructured way among many pages of information. Web use is most often characterized browsing and visual scanning of information to find what information is needed.

Data/information. *GUI* data is typically created and used by known and trusted sources, people in the user's organization or reputable and reliable companies and organizations. The properties of the system's data are generally known, and the information is typically organized in an understandable and meaningful fashion. A notion of shared data exists, as does a notion of data privacy. The *Web* is full of unknown content typically placed there by others unknown to the user. Typical users don't put information on the Web (except for publishing their own pages). The reliability and truthfulness of found information cannot always be ascertained and trusted. Web content is usually highly variable in organization, and the privacy of the information is often suspect.

User tasks. *GUI* system users install, configure, personalize, start, use, and upgrade programs. They open, use, and close data files. Fairly long times are spent within

Table 2.1 GUI versus Web Design

	GUI	WEB
Devices	User hardware variations limited. User hardware characteristics well defined. Screens appear exactly as specified.	User hardware variations enormous. Screen appearance influenced by hardware being used.
User Focus	Data and applications.	Information and navigation.
Data/ Information	Typically created and used by known and trusted sources. Properties generally known. Typically placed into system by users or known people and organizations. Typically organized in a meaningful fashion. A notion of private and shared data exists.	Full of unknown content. Source not always trusted. Often not placed onto the Web by users or known people and organizations. Highly variable organization. Privacy often suspect.
User Tasks	Install, configure, personalize, start, use, and upgrade programs. Open, use, and close data files. Fairly long times spent within an application. Familiarity with applications often achieved.	Link to a site, browse or read pages, fill out forms, register for services, participate in transactions, download and save things. Movement between pages and sites very rapid. Familiarity with many sites not established.
User's Conceptual Space	Controlled and constrained by program.	Infinite and generally unorganized.
Presentation Elements	Windows, menus, controls, data, toolbars, messages, and so on. Many transient, dynamically appearing and disappearing. Presented as specified by designer. Generally standardized by toolkits and style guides.	Two components, browser and page. Within page, any combination of text, images, audio, video, and animation. May not be presented as specified by the designer—dependent on browser, monitor, and user specifications. Little standardization.

Navigation	Through menus, lists, trees, dialogs, and wizards. Not a strong and visible concept. Constrained by design. Generally standardized by toolkits and style guides.	Through links, bookmarks, and typed URLs. Significant and highly visible concept. Few constraints, frequently causing a lost "sense of place." Few standards. Typically part of page design, fostering a lack of consistency.
Context	Enables maintenance of a better sense of context. Restricted navigation paths. Multiple viewable windows.	Poorer maintenance of a sense of context. Single-page entities. Unlimited navigation paths. Contextual clues become limited or are difficult to find.
Interaction	Interactions such as clicking menu choices, pressing buttons, selecting list choices, and cut/copy/paste occur within context of active program.	Basic interaction is a single click. This can cause extreme changes in context, which may not be noticed.
Response Time	Nearly instantaneous.	Quite variable, depending on transmission speeds, page content, and so on. Long times can upset the user.
Visual Style	Typically prescribed and constrained by toolkit. Visual creativity allowed but difficult. Little significant personalization.	Fosters a more artistic, individual, and unrestricted presentation style. Complicated by differing browser and display capabilities, and bandwidth limitations. Limited personalization available.
System Capability	Unlimited capability proportional to sophistication of hardware and software.	Limited by constraints imposed by the hardware, browser, software, client support, and user willingness to allow features because of response time, security, and privacy concerns.
Task Efficiency	Targeted to a specific audience with specific tasks. Only limited by the amount of programming undertaken to support it.	Limited by browser and network capabilities. Actual user audience usually not well understood. Often intended for anyone and everyone.

(continues)

Table 2.1 *(Continued)*

	GUI	WEB
Consistency	Major objective exists within and across applications. Aided by platform toolkit and design guidelines. Universal consistency in GUI products generally created through toolkits and design guidelines.	Sites tend to establish their own identity. Frequently standards set within a site. Frequent ignoring of GUI guidelines for identical components, especially controls.
User Assistance	Integral part of most systems and applications. Accessed through standard mechanisms. Documentation, both online and offline, usually provided. Personal support desk also usually provided.	No similar help systems. The little available help is built into the page. Customer service support, if provided, oriented to product or service offered.
Integration	Seamless integration of all applications into the platform environment a major objective. Toolkits and components are key elements in accomplishing this objective.	Apparent for some basic functions within most Web sites (navigation, printing, and so on.) Sites tend to achieve individual distinction rather than integration.
Security	Tightly controlled, proportional to degree of willingness to invest resources and effort. Not an issue for most home PC users.	Renowned for security exposures. Browser-provided security options typically not understood by average users. When employed, may have function-limiting side effects.
Reliability	Tightly controlled in business systems, proportional to degree of willingness to invest resources and effort.	Susceptible to disruptions caused by user, telephone line and cable providers, Internet service providers, hosting servers, and remotely accessed sites.

an individual application, and people become familiar with many of its features and its design. *Web* users do things like linking to sites, browsing or reading pages, filling out forms, registering for services, participating in transactions, and downloading and saving things. Movement between pages and sites is often a very rapid activity, with people not gaining familiarity with many sites. The typical Web user has no notion of programs and tends to be much less aware of computer mechanics. Most GUI and Web users to not want to spend the effort required to set up or install anything.

User's conceptual space. In a *GUI* environment the user's conceptual space is controlled by the program and application. A user's access to data is constrained, and space is made available where their data can be stored and managed. A *Web* user's space is infinite and generally unorganized. Little opportunity for meaningful organization of personal information exists.

Presentation elements. The main presentation elements for *GUIs* are various kinds of windows, menus, controls, toolbars, messages, and data. Many elements are transient, dynamically appearing and disappearing based upon the current context of the interaction. They are also generally standardized as a result of the toolkits and style guides used. Elements are presented on screens exactly as specified by the designer. *Web* systems possess two components: the browser and page. Many browsers are substantially GUI applications with traditional GUI presentation elements. Within a page itself, however, any combination of text, images, audio, video, and animation may exist. Complex, cluttered, and visually distracting pages are easy to generate and often exist. This occurs because many designers have focused on implementing that which is new, pretty, or attention getting, with little thought given to usability. The availability of interface style guides and guidelines to aid the design process is not known (or they are ignored). Common toolkits and industry conventions, however, are now being proposed and will be slowly adopted. Also contributing to page design problems is the fact that a page may not be presented exactly as specified by the designer. The exact look of a page is dependent on browser and monitor used. Extreme variations in screen sizes for presenting pages can and do exist. Finally, the user can change the look of a page by modifying its properties.

Navigation. *GUI* users navigate through structured menus, lists, trees, dialogs, and wizards. Paths are constrained by design (grayed out menu choices, for example), and the navigation mechanisms standardized by toolkits and style guides. Navigation is a weakly established concept, a supplement to more important task functions and actions. Some aspects of a GUI do provide a strong sense of navigation, the ellipsis on "to another window" intent indicators such as "Open...," command buttons such as "OK" and "Cancel" that direct the user's focus to another window, and wizards. Others aspects of GUI design do not provide a strong sense of navigation—button pressing, for example, that does not result in something visible happening (for example, pressing an Apply button).

Web users control their own navigation through links, bookmarks, and typed URLs. Navigation is a significant and highly visible concept with few constraints. The immense size of the Web, and the user's ability to easily wander just about anywhere, frequently causes a lost "sense of place," or "Where am I right now?"

feeling. Web navigation has few standards beyond the browser's Back button and underlined links. Typically most navigation is part of page design that fosters a lack of consistency, and often confuses users. Establishing a continual sense of place for the user is a critical aspect of Web page design.

Context. *GUI* systems enable the user to maintain a better sense of context. Paths are restricted, and multiple overlapping windows may be presented and be visible, enabling users to remember how what they are doing fits into the overall task picture. *Web* pages are single entities with almost unlimited navigation paths. They do not bring up separate dialog boxes to ask questions, provide or request supplemental information, or present messages. Contextual clues become limited or are hard to find.

Interaction. *GUI* interactions consist of such activities as clicking menu choices, pressing buttons, selecting choices from list, keying data, and cutting, copying, or pasting within context established by an open window and an active program. The basic *Web* interaction is a single click. This click can cause extreme changes in context such as moving to another site or changing the displayed information within a site. The user may not notice subtle changes when they occur. Additionally, the browser provides parallel mechanisms like the Back button that may function differently depending on context. The distinction between an action and a navigation link is not always obvious.

Response time. Compared to the Web, response times with a *GUI* system are fairly stable, if not nearly instantaneous. *Web* response times can be quite variable, and often aggravatingly slow. Line transmission speeds, system loads, and page content can have a dramatic impact. Long response times can upset and frustrate users.

Visual style. In *GUI* systems, the visual style is typically prescribed and constrained by toolkit. (Exceptions are entertainment and multimedia applications.) Visual creativity in screen design is allowed but it is difficult to do. While some user options and style choices do exist, little opportunity exists for screen personalization. In *Web* page design, a more artistic, individual, and unrestricted presentation style is allowed and encouraged. Much design freedom exists, but differing browser and display capabilities, multiple screen sizes, and bandwidth limitations, often complicate and restrict this freedom. Limited personalization of the system is available, at a browser or site level, for users.

System capability. *GUI* system capabilities are only limited in proportion to the capability of the hardware in terms of speed, memory, and configuration, and the sophistication of the software. The *Web* is more constrained, being limited by constraints imposed by the hardware, browser, and software. It is also limited by the willingness of the page owner to provide certain functions and elements, and the willingness of the user to allow features because of response time, security, and privacy issues and concerns.

Task efficiency. *GUI* systems are targeted to a specific audience performing specific tasks. Generally, the efficiency of performing a task is only limited by the amount of programming undertaken to support it. Browser and network capabilities limit *Web* task efficiency. The actual user audience is usually not well understood, since many Web sites are intended for anyone and everyone.

Consistency. Consistency in *GUI* system design is a major objective in most development efforts. While they are far from perfect, an attempt is made to be consistent both within applications and across applications. Many organizations possess interface and screen design standards and toolkits to aid in the standardization process. Toolkits and guidelines also allow a certain degree of universal consistency in GUI products. In *Web* page design, the heavy emphasis on graphics, a lack of design standards, and the desire of Web sites to establish their own identities results in very little consistency across sites. Web sites often establish standards within a site, but in too many instances developers ignore guidelines existing for GUI components used in Web pages. These problems are especially found in the presentation of screen controls on pages.

User assistance. User assistance is an integral part of most *GUI* systems applications. This assistance is accessed through standard mechanisms such as the F1 key and Help menus. Message and status areas are also provided on the screen. Documentation, both online and offline, is normally provided, as is a support desk to answer user questions and provide guidance and assistance. *Web* pages do not yet provide similar help systems. What little help that is available is built into the page. Customer service support, if provided, is generally oriented to the product or service offered. GUI browsers may provide GUI-type assistance, so the user sees two different assistance approaches. Deficiencies in Web page help then become more obvious.

Integration. A primary goal of most *GUI* applications is the seamless integration of all pieces. Common functions are supported across applications and import/export capabilities exist. Again, toolkits and their components are key elements in accomplishing this objective. In *Web* design, some integration is apparent within a site for basic functions such as navigation and printing. But because sites strive for individual distinction, interoperability between sites is almost nonexistent.

Security. In a *GUI* environment, security and data access can be tightly controlled, in proportion to the degree of willingness of an organization to invest resources and effort. For home applications, security is not an issue for most PC users. The *Web* is renowned for security exposures. This is a major inhibitor of Web use for both businesses and consumers. Browser-provided security options have typically not been well understood by average Web users. When employed, these security options often have function-limiting side effects. (Disabled cookies, for example.) Attempts to create a more trustworthy appearance are being made through the use of security levels and passwords to assure users that the Web is a secure environment.

Reliability. Like security, reliability in *GUI* systems is established and controlled in proportion to the degree of willingness of an organization to invest resources and effort. The computer being used influences reliability as does, if applicable, the local area network. Both are in the control of the using organization. *Web* reliability is susceptible to disruptions from many directions. Telephone line and cable providers, Internet service providers, hosting servers, and remotely accessed sites all can contribute to the problem. Accessed applications and user mistakes may also cause reliability problems. A lack of reliability can be a great inhibitor of Web use.

In conclusion, from a design implication perspective, GUI and Web differences can be extensive. Today, these differences must be considered in any Web page design, although many GUI interface design techniques and guidelines are applicable in page design. Tomorrow, many of these GUI-Web differences will diminish or disappear as the discrepancies are addressed by technology.

In developing a Web system, always evaluate each GUI guideline for direct applicability in any development effort. Also, do not simply transport a GUI application or design "en toto" to the Web without evaluating it in terms of the implications described above. Some applications or designs may require significant changes, others a simple "fine-tuning." One so far unmentioned aspect that both GUI and Web systems *do* have in common, is "know your user." Involving them throughout the redesign process will ensure the best transition to the Web. (More about knowing your users follows in Step 1 "Know Your User or Client.")

Printed Pages versus Web Pages

While Internet history spans but a few years, that of the printed page measures more than five and one-half centuries. Research and experience with printed pages through these centuries has created a fundamental and accepted set of guidelines for editorial style, element presentation, and text organization. Many of the basic guidelines, clear, comprehensive, and consistent, can and are being applied to Web page design. Web page design, however, is different in many aspects from the design of books, documents, newspapers, and other similar materials. These differences require a rethinking, researching, and reformulating of a number of these guidelines for use in Web page design. Many of these differences have already been identified. Others will surface as Web experience grows and research is conducted. In the following paragraphs, the major differences between print and Web page design are briefly described. Implications for Web page design are also summarized.

Page size. Printed pages are generally larger than their Web counterparts. They are also fixed in size, not variable like Web pages. A printed page can be designed as one entity, the designer being assured that the completed final product will possess an integrated and complete look. Web pages, while usually designed as a complete entity, are presented in pieces, pieces whose dimensions differ depending on the user's technology (browser, monitor, and so on). The visual impact of the printed page is maintained in hard-copy form, while on the Web all that usually exists are snapshots of page areas. The visual impact of a Web page is substantially degraded, and the user may never see some parts of the page because their existence is not known or require scrolling to bring into view. The design implications: the top of a Web page is its most important element, and signals to the user must always be provided that parts of a page lie below the surface.

Page rendering. Printed pages are immensely superior to Web pages in rendering. Printed pages are presented as complete entities, and their entire contents are available for reading or review immediately upon appearance. Web pages elements are often rendered slowly, depending upon things like line transmission speeds and page content. Dozens of seconds may be consumed waiting for a page to completely appear. Impatient users may not wait, moving on to somewhere else. Design implications: Provide page content that downloads fast, and give people elements to read immediately so the sense of passing time is diminished. (The ultimate goal: a bandwidth fast enough to download a Web page as fast as one can turn a paper page.)

Page layout. With the printed page, layout is precise with much attention given to it. With Web pages layout is more of an approximation, being negatively influenced by deficiencies in design toolkits and the characteristics of the user's browser and hardware, particularly screen sizes. Design implication: Understand the restrictions and design for the most common user tools.

Page resolution. Today, the resolution of displayed print characters still exceeds that of screen characters, and screen reading is still slower than reading from a document. Design implication: Provide an easy way to print long Web documents. (The ultimate goal: a screen resolution sharp enough to render type crisply enough so that screen reading speed reaches that of newspaper reading.)

User focus. Printed pages present people with entire sets of information. Estimations of effort needed to deal with the document are fairly easily made, size and the nature of the material being strong contributors. Some printed pages may be read sequentially (a novel) and others (a newspaper) partially and somewhat sequentially (the sports section first, perhaps?). Others forms of printed material may simply be skimmed (a sales brochure), but this skimming is usually systematic in some way. Web pages present people with individual snapshots of information, often with few clues as to structure and sequence, and rarely with a few cues as to length and depth. People also have a sense that the body of Web information potentially available is almost unlimited, and that information paths can lead everywhere and anywhere. With few content size cues available and a huge information base, a common resulting behavior of Web users is to skim the information presented, looking for what is most relevant to their task or need. This is done for personal efficiency and so as not to tax one's patience. Design implications: Create easy to scan pages and limit the word count of textual content. Also, provide overviews of information organization schemes, clear descriptions of where links lead, and estimations of sizes of linked pages and materials.

Page navigation. Navigating printed materials is as simple as page turning. It is a motor skilled learned early in life and never thought of as navigation or a design element. Substantial interaction between pages is rare, since the process is essentially sequential. Navigating the Web requires innumerable decisions concerning which of many possible links should be followed. It requires asking oneself questions such as these: What is at the end of this link? Where is it? Will it address my need or solve my problem? Design implications are similar to the above—provide overviews of information organization schemes and clear descriptions of where links lead.

Sense of place. With paper documents you derive a sense of where you are through a mixture of graphic and editorial organization, and size cues supplied by the design of the document. The document is an object with physical characteristics. Paging through printed material is an orderly process, sequential and understandable. Electronic documents provide none of these physical cues. All that is visible is a small collection of text, graphics, and links hinting that much else lies *somewhere* underneath. Moving through the Web links can cause radical shifts in location and context. Paging using the browser's Back button steps one back through links visited and may involve passing through different documents. Fixed locations that provide cues to support one's memory concerning the location of things are nonexistent. All these factors cause a person to easily lose a sense of place and lead to confusion. Design implication: Build cues into Web pages to aid the user in maintaining a sense of place.

Interactivity. Printed page design involves letting the eyes traverse static information, selectively looking at information and using spatial combinations to make page elements enhance and explain each other. Web design involves letting the hands move the information (scrolling, pointing, expanding, clicking, and so on) in conjunction with the eyes. Information relationships, static or dynamic, are expressed chronologically as part of the interaction and user movements. Doing is more memorable and makes a stronger impact than simply seeing. No print precedents exist for this style of interaction. A better understanding of this process (as well as better hardware and software) is needed to enhance interactivity.

Page independence. Because moving between Web pages is so easy, and almost any page in a site can be accessed from anywhere else, pages must be made freestanding. Every page is independent, and its topic and contents must be explained without assumptions about any previous page seen by the user. Printed pages, being sequential, fairly standardized in organization, and providing a clear sense of place, are not considered independent. Specific types of content (table of contents, author, index, and so on) are easily found in well-established document locations. Design implication: Provide informative headers and footers on each Web page.

In conclusion, many of the basic print guidelines can be applied to Web page design. As shown above, however, printed material design differs from Web page design in many aspects. New guidelines must continue to be developed, implemented, and modified as necessary as technology advances and our understanding of Web interaction increases. For the moment, apply existing guidelines where relevant, and new guidelines as necessary. Part 2 of this book describes many of these guidelines. What must be avoided are things that made sense in the print world, but do not meets today's needs in Web interface design.

The Merging of Graphical Business Systems and the Web

Another strength of the Web lies in its ability to link databases and processing occurring on a variety of machines within a company or organization. Within a closed system, queries against databases can be made, internal communication performed, and information useful for employees can be made available. Current systems can also be implemented with more traditional GUI interfaces. The graphical business system and the Web will merge into a common entity. These Web systems are called intranets.

Characteristics of an Intranet versus the Internet

An intranet has many of the same characteristics as the Internet. They differ, however, in some important ways. The following discussion is partly based upon Nielsen (1997b).

Users. The users of intranets, being organization employees, know a lot about the organization, its structure, its products, its jargon, and its culture. Internet sites are used by customers and others who know much less about the organization, and often care less about it. The intranet user's characteristics and needs can be much more specifically defined then can those of the general Internet user.

Tasks. An intranet is used for an organization's everyday activities, including complex transactions, queries, and communications. The Internet is mainly used to find information, with a supplementary use being simple transactions.

Type of information. An intranet will contain detailed information needed for organizational functioning. Information will often be added or modified. The Internet will usually present more stable information: marketing and customer or client information, reports, and so forth.

Amount of information. Typically, an intranet site will be much larger than an organization's Internet site. Massive amounts of information and processes seem to be needed to make an organization function. It has been estimated that an intranet site can be ten to one hundred times larger than its corresponding public site.

Hardware and software. Since intranets exist in a controlled environment, the kinds of computers, monitors, browsers, and other software can be restricted or standardized. The need for cross-platform compatibility is minimized or eliminated, permitting more predictable design. Upgraded communications also permit intranets to run from a hundred to a thousand times faster than typical Internet access can. This allows the use of rich graphics and multimedia, screen elements that contribute to very slow download times for most Internet users.

Design philosophy. Implementation on the intranet of current text-based and GUI applications will present a user model similar to those that have existed in other domains. This will cause a swing back to more traditional GUI designs—designs that will also incorporate the visual appeal of the Web, but eliminate many of its useless, promotional, and distracting features. The resulting GUI hybrids will be richer and much more effective.

Some specific intranet design guidelines will be found in Part 2 of this book.

Extranets

An extranet is a special set of intranet Web pages that can be accessed from outside an organization or company. Typical examples include those for letting customers check on an order's status or letting suppliers view requests for proposals. An extranet is a blend of the public Internet and the intranet, and its design should reflect this. Some specific extranet design guidelines will also be found in Part 2.

Principles of User Interface Design

An interface must really be just an extension of a person. This means that the system and its software must reflect a person's capabilities and respond to his or her specific needs. It should be useful, accomplishing some business objectives faster and more efficiently than the previously used method or tool did. It must also be easy to learn, for people want to do, not learn to do. Finally, the system must be easy and fun to use, evoking a sense of pleasure and accomplishment not tedium and frustration.

The interface itself should serve as both a connector and a separator: a connector in that it ties the user to the power of the computer, and a separator in that it minimizes the possibility of the participants damaging one another. While the damage the user inflicts on the computer tends to be physical (a frustrated pounding of the keyboard), the damage caused by the computer is more psychological (a threat to one's self-esteem).

Throughout the history of the human-computer interface, various researchers and writers have attempted to define a set of general principles of interface design. What follows is a compilation of these principles. They reflect not only what we know today, but also what we think we know today. Many are based on research, others on the collective thinking of behaviorists working with user interfaces. These principles will continue to evolve, expand, and be refined as our experience with GUIs and the Web increases. We will begin with the first set of published principles, those for the Xerox STAR.

Principles for the Xerox STAR

The design of the Xerox STAR was guided by a set of principles that evolved over its lengthy development process (Smith, Harslem, Irby, Kimball, and Verplank, 1982; Verplank, 1988). These principles established the foundation for graphical interfaces.

The illusion of manipulable objects. Displayed objects that are selectable and manipulable must be created. A design challenge is to invent a set of displayable objects that are represented meaningfully and appropriately for the intended application. It must be clear that these objects can be selected, and how to select them must be self-evident. When they are selected should also be obvious, because it should be clear that the selected object will be the focus of the next action. Verplank calls this "graphics with handles on it." Standalone icons easily fulfilled this requirement. The handles for windows were placed in the borders (window-specific commands, pop-up menus, scroll bars, and so on).

Visual order and viewer focus. Attention must be drawn, at the proper time, to the important and relevant elements of the display. Effective visual contrast between various components of the screen is used to achieve this goal (STAR was monochromatic so color was not used). Animation is also used to draw attention, as is sound. Feedback must also be provided to the user. Since the pointer is usually the focus of viewer attention, it is a useful mechanism for providing this feedback (by changing shapes).

Revealed structure. The distance between one's intention and the effect must be minimized. Most often, the distance between intention and effect is lengthened as system power increases. The relationship between intention and effect must be tightened and made as apparent as possible to the user. The underlying structure is often revealed during the selection process.

Consistency. Consistency aids learning. Consistency is provided in such areas as element location, grammar, font shapes, styles, and sizes, selection indicators, and contrast and emphasis techniques.

Appropriate effect or emotional impact. The interface must provide the appropriate emotional effect for the product and its market. Is it a corporate, professional, and secure business system? Should it reflect the fantasy, wizardry, and bad puns of computer games?

A match with the medium. The interface must also reflect the capabilities of the device on which it will be displayed. Quality of screen images will be greatly affected by a device's resolution and color-generation capabilities.

General Principles

The design goals in creating a user interface are described below. They are fundamental to the design and implementation of all effective interfaces, including GUI and Web ones. These principles are general characteristics of the interface, and they apply to all aspects. Specific guidelines on how to implement many of these goals will be presented in Part 2. The compilation is presented alphabetically, and the ordering is not intended to imply degree of importance. They are derived from the various principles described in Galitz (1992), IBM (1991, 2001), Mayhew (1992), Microsoft (1992, 1995, 2001), Open Software Foundation (1993), and Verplank (1988).

Aesthetically Pleasing

- Provide visual appeal by following these presentation and graphic design principles:
  — Provide meaningful contrast between screen elements.
  — Create groupings.
  — Align screen elements and groups.
  — Provide three-dimensional representation.
  — Use color and graphics effectively and simply.

A design aesthetic, or visually pleasing composition, is attractive to the eye. It draws attention subliminally, conveying a message clearly and quickly. Visual appeal makes a computer system accessible and inviting. A lack of visually pleasing composition is disorienting, obscures the intent and meaning, and slows down and confuses the user. Visual appeal is terribly important today because most human-computer communication occurs in the visual realm.

Visual appeal is provided by following the presentation and graphic design principles to be discussed, including providing meaningful contrast between screen elements, creating spatial groupings, aligning screen elements, providing three-dimensional representation, and using color and graphics effectively. Good design combines power, functionality, and simplicity with a pleasing appearance.

Clarity

- The interface should be visually, conceptually, and linguistically clear, including:
  — Visual elements
  — Functions
  — Metaphors
  — Words and text

The interface must be clear in visual appearance, concept, and wording. Visual elements should be understandable, relating to the user's real-world concepts and functions. Metaphors, or analogies, should be realistic and simple. Interface words and text should be simple, unambiguous, and free of computer jargon.

Compatibility

- Provide compatibility with the following:
  — The user
  — The task and job
  — The product
- Adopt the user's perspective.

User compatibility. Design must be appropriate and compatible with the needs of the user or client. Effective design starts with understanding the user's needs and adopting the user's point of view. One very common error among designers is to assume that users are all alike. A glance around the office should quickly put this assumption to rest. Another common error is to assume that all users think, feel, and behave exactly like the developer. Studies have proven otherwise. Users have quite different needs, aspirations, and attitudes than developers. A system reflecting only the knowledge and attitudes of its designers cannot be successful.

"Know the user" is *the* fundamental principle in interface design. User compatibility can only happen if understanding truly occurs.

Task and job compatibility. The organization of a system should match the tasks a person must do to perform the job. The structure and flow of functions should permit easy transition between tasks. The user must never be forced to navigate between applications or many screens to complete routine daily tasks.

Product compatibility. The intended user of a new system is often the user of other systems or earlier versions of the new system. Habits, expectations, and a level of knowledge have been established and will be brought to bear when learning the new system. If these habits, expectations, and knowledge cannot be applied to the new system, confusion results and learning requirements are greatly increased. While compatibility across products must always be considered in relation to improving interfaces, making new systems compatible with existing systems will take advantage of what users already know and reduce the necessity for new learning.

Comprehensibility

- A system should be easily learned and understood. A user should know the following:
  — What to look at
  — What to do
  — When to do it
  — Where to do it
  — Why to do it
  — How to do it
- The flow of actions, responses, visual presentations, and information should be in a sensible order that is easy to recollect and place in context.

A system should be understandable, flowing in a comprehensible and meaningful order. Strong clues to the operation of objects should be presented. The steps to complete a task should be obvious. Reading and digesting long explanations should never be necessary.

Configurability

- Permit easy personalization, configuration, and reconfiguration of settings.
  — Enhances a sense of control.
  — Encourages an active role in understanding.

Easy personalization and customization through configuration and reconfiguration of a system enhances a sense of control, encourages an active role in understanding, and allows for personal preferences and differences in experience levels. It also leads to higher user satisfaction.

Some people will prefer to personalize a system to better meet their preferences. Other people will not, accepting what is given. Still others will experiment with reconfiguration and then give up, running out of patience or time. For these latter groups of users a good default configuration must be provided.

Consistency

- A system should look, act, and operate the same throughout. Similar components should:
  — Have a similar look.
  — Have similar uses.
  — Operate similarly.
- The same action should always yield the same result.
- The function of elements should not change.
- The position of standard elements should not change.

Design consistency is the common thread that runs throughout these guidelines. It is the cardinal rule of all design activities. Consistency is important because it can reduce requirements for human learning by allowing skills learned in one situation to be transferred to another like it. While any new system must impose some learning requirements on its users, it should avoid encumbering productive learning with nonproductive, unnecessary activity. Consistency also aids learning of the system's mental model.

In addition to increased learning requirements, *inconsistency* in design has a number of other prerequisites and by-products, including:

- More specialization by system users.
- Greater demand for higher skills.
- More preparation time and less production time.
- More frequent changes in procedures.
- More error-tolerant systems (because errors are more likely).
- More kinds of documentation.
- More time to find information in documents.
- More unlearning and learning when systems are changed.
- More demands on supervisors and managers.
- More things to do wrong.

Inconsistencies in design are caused by differences in people. Several designers might each design the same system differently. Inconsistencies also occur when those performing design activities are pressured by time constraints. All too often the solutions in those cases are exceptions that the user must learn to handle. People, however, perceive a system as a single entity. To them, it should look, act, and feel similar throughout. Excess learning requirements become a barrier to users achieving and maintaining high performance and can ultimately influence user acceptance of the system.

Can consistency make a big difference? One study found that user thinking time nearly doubled when the position of screen elements, such as titles and field captions, was varied on a series of menu screens.

Design consistency is achieved by developing and applying design standards or guidelines. In the late 1980s the computer industry and many using organizations finally awakened to the need for them, and a flurry of graphical user interface guideline documents were developed and published. These guidelines specify the appearance and behavior of the GUI user interface. They describe the windows, menus, and various controls available, including what they look like and how they work. They also provide some guidance on when to use the various components.

Examples of industry-produced guidelines include Apple's *Macintosh Human Interface Guidelines* (1992b), Digital Equipment Corporation's *XUI Style Guide* (1988), IBM's *System Application Architecture Common User Access* (1987, 1989a, 1989b, 1991, 1992), Sun Microsystem's *OPEN LOOK Graphical User Interface Application Style Guidelines*

(1990), Open Software Foundation's *OSF/MOTIF Style Guide* (1993), and Microsoft's *The Windows Interface* (1992) and *The Windows Interface Guidelines for Software Design* (1995).

The Web has burst upon the scene with few standards and guidelines to direct design. Many GUI and printed material principles are applicable but they have been applied in a haphazard manner. New research-based guidelines are desperately needed.

Organizations working on traditional interface guidelines or standards include the International Standards Organization (ISO), the American National Standards Institute (ANSI), and the Human Factors and Ergonomics Society (Billingsley, 1996). The development of Web design guidelines has been one focus of the World Wide Web Consortium (2001).

Control

- The user must control the interaction.
  - — Actions should result from explicit user requests.
  - — Actions should be performed quickly.
  - — Actions should be capable of interruption or termination.
  - — The user should never be interrupted for errors.
- The context maintained must be from the perspective of the user.
- The means to achieve goals should be flexible and compatible with the user's skills, experiences, habits, and preferences.
- Avoid modes since they constrain the actions available to the user.
- Permit the user to customize aspects of the interface, while always providing a proper set of defaults.

Control is feeling in charge, feeling that the system is responding to your actions. Feeling that a machine is controlling you is demoralizing and frustrating. The interface should present a tool-like appearance. Control is achieved when a person, working at his or her own pace, is able to determine what to do, how to do it, and then is easily able to get it done. Simple, predictable, consistent, flexible, customizable, and passive interfaces provide control. Lack of control is signaled by unavailable systems, long delays in system responses, surprising system actions, tedious and long procedures that cannot be circumvented, difficulties in obtaining necessary information, and the inability to achieve the desired results. The feeling of control has been found to be an excellent mitigator of the work stress associated with many automated systems

In general, avoid modes since they restrict the actions available to the user at any given time. If modes must be used, they should be visually obvious (for example, a changed mouse pointer shape). Existing modes must also be easy to learn and easy to remove.

Directness

- Provide direct ways to accomplish tasks.
  - Available alternatives should be visible.
  - The effect of actions on objects should be visible.

Tasks should be performed directly. Available alternatives should be visible, reducing the user's mental workload. Directness is also best provided by the object-action sequence of direct-manipulation systems. Tasks are performed by directly selecting an object, then selecting an action to be performed, and then seeing the action being performed.

Efficiency

- Minimize eye and hand movements, and other control actions.
  - Transitions between various system controls should flow easily and freely.
  - Navigation paths should be as short as possible.
  - Eye movement through a screen should be obvious and sequential.
- Anticipate the user's wants and needs whenever possible.

Eye and hand movements must not be wasted. One's attention must be captured by relevant elements of the screen when needed. Sequential eye movements between screen elements should be predictable, obvious, and short. Web pages must be easily scannable. All navigation paths should be as short as possible. Manual transitions between various system controls should also be as short as possible. Avoid frequent transitions between input devices such as the keyboard and mouse.

Always try to anticipate the user's wants and needs. At each step in a process, present to the user all the information and tools needed to complete the process. Do not require user to search for and gather necessary information and tools.

Familiarity

- Employ familiar concepts and use a language that is familiar to the user.
- Keep the interface natural, mimicking the user's behavior patterns.
- Use real-world metaphors.

Build on the user's existing knowledge. Build into the interface concepts, terminology, workflows, and spatial arrangements already familiar to the user. Operations should mimic one's behavior patterns; dialogs should mimic one's thought processes and vocabulary. Familiar concepts enable people to get started and become productive quickly.

Flexibility

- A system must be sensitive to the differing needs of its users, enabling a level and type of performance based upon:
  — Each user's knowledge and skills.
  — Each user's experience.
  — Each user's personal preference.
  — Each user's habits.
  — The conditions at that moment.

Flexibility is the system's ability to respond to individual differences in people. Permit people to choose the method of interaction that is most appropriate to their situation. People should be able to interact with a system in terms of their own particular needs, including knowledge, experience, and personal preference. Flexibility is accomplished by providing multiple ways to access application functions and perform tasks. It is also accomplished through permitting system customization. Another benefit of flexibility is that it contributes to increased user control. A flexible system is a versatile system.

Flexibility is not without dangers. Highly flexible systems can confuse inexperienced people, causing them to make more errors. For this reason, flexibility appears desirable only for experienced users. The novice user should not be exposed to system flexibility at the start, but only as experience is gained. The concept of "progressive disclosure," to be discussed in the simplicity guideline to follow, is also applicable here.

Another problem with flexibility is that it may not always be used, some people prefer to continue doing things in the way they first learned. A variety of factors may account for this, including an unwillingness to invest in additional learning, or, perhaps, new ways may not be obvious. The former problem may be addressed by making the new ways as easy and safe to learn as possible, the latter by including in training and reference materials not only information about how to do things, but when they are likely to be useful.

Forgiveness

- Tolerate and forgive common and unavoidable human errors.
- Prevent errors from occurring whenever possible.
- Protect against possible catastrophic errors.
- When an error does occur, provide constructive messages.

It is often said "to err is human." The corollary to that statement, at least in computer systems, might be "to forgive is good design." People will make mistakes; a system should tolerate those that are common and unavoidable. A forgiving system keeps people out of trouble.

People like to explore and learn by trial and error. A system oversensitive to erroneous inputs will discourage users from exploring and trying new things. Learning will be inhibited, and people will be overcautious, working slowly and carefully to avoid mistakes. Productivity will then suffer. A fear of making a mistake and not being able to recover from it has always been a primary contributor to fear of dealing with computers.

Prevent errors from occurring by anticipating where mistakes may occur and designing to prevent them. Permit people to review, change, and undo actions whenever necessary. Make it very difficult to perform actions that can have tragic results. When errors do occur, present clear instructions on how to correct them.

Predictability

- The user should be able to anticipate the natural progression of each task.
  — Provide distinct and recognizable screen elements.
  — Provide cues to the result of an action to be performed.
- All expectations should be fulfilled uniformly and completely.

Tasks, displays, and movement through a system should be anticipatable based on the user's previous knowledge or experience. All actions should lead to results the user expects. Screen elements should be distinct and recognizable. Current operations should provide clues as to what will come next. Anticipation, or predictability, reduces mistakes and enables tasks to be completed more quickly. All expectations possessed by the user should be fulfilled uniformly and completely. Predictability is greatly enhanced by design consistency.

Recovery

- A system should permit:
  — Commands or actions to be abolished or reversed.
  — Immediate return to a certain point if difficulties arise.
- Ensure that users never lose their work as a result of:
  — An error on their part.
  — Hardware, software, or communication problems.

A person should be able to retract an action by issuing an *undo* command. Knowing that an action can be reversed reduces much of the distress of new users, who often worry about doing something wrong. The return point could be the previous action, previous screen, a recent closure point, or the beginning of some predetermined period, such as back 10 screens or some number of minutes. Reversing or abolishing an action is analogous to using an eraser to eliminate a pencil mark on a piece of paper.

The goal is stability, or returning easily to the right track when a wrong track has been taken. Recovery should be obvious, automatic, and easy and natural to perform. In short, it should be hard to get into deep water or go too far astray. Easy recovery from an action greatly facilitates learning by trial and error and exploration. If an action is not reversible, and its consequences are critical, it should be made difficult to accomplish. Always ensure that users never lose their work as a result of their own errors or technical glitches.

Responsiveness

- The system must rapidly respond to the user's requests.
- Provide immediate acknowledgment for all user actions:
  — Visual.
  — Textual.
  — Auditory.

A user request must be responded to quickly. Knowledge of results, or feedback, is a necessary learning ingredient. It shapes human performance and instills confidence. All requests to the system must be acknowledged in some way. Feedback may be visual, the change in the shape of the mouse pointer, or textual, taking the form of a message. It may also be auditory, consisting of a unique sound or tone.

Never leave the screen blank for more than a moment, because the user may think the system has failed. If a request requires an unusually long processing time, or one that is longer than customary, provide an interim "in-progress" message. Also provide some unique form of communication if a user action results in a problem or possible problem.

Substantial or more informative feedback is most important for the casual or new system user. Expert users are often content to receive more modest feedback.

Simplicity

- Provide as simple an interface as possible.
- Five ways to provide simplicity:
  — Use progressive disclosure, hiding things until they are needed.
    • Present common and necessary functions first.
    • Prominently feature important functions.
    • Hide more sophisticated and less frequently used functions.
  — Provide defaults.
  — Minimize screen alignment points.
  — Make common actions simple at the expense of uncommon actions being made harder.
  — Provide uniformity and consistency.

Simplicity is the opposite of complexity. Complexity is a measure of the number of choices available at any point in the human-computer interaction. A great deal of functionality and power is usually associated with high complexity. Complexity most often overwhelms and confuses new and casual users of systems. Complex systems are often not fully used, or used ineffectively, because a person may follow known but more cumbersome methods instead of easier but undiscovered or unfamiliar methods.

A system lacking complexity may have a different set of faults. It may be tedious to use or not accomplish much. It is better, however, to provide less functionality that will get effectively used than to provide too much functionality, yielding an interface hopelessly complex and extremely difficult to use. Complexity, then, is a two-edged sword. To effectively solve problems, it must be present without being apparent. The goal, then, is to provide a complex system while masking the complexity through a simple interface. There are several ways to minimize this complexity.

Progressive disclosure. Introduce system components gradually so the full complexity of the system is not visible at first encounter. Teach fundamentals first. Then, slowly introduce advanced or more sophisticated functions. This is called the layered, or spiral, approach to learning. Such an approach was first described by Carroll and Carrithers (1984) who called it the "Training-Wheels System." They found that by disabling portions of the system that were not needed and could lead to errors and confusion, improved system learning efficiency was achieved.

Provide defaults. Providing defaults is another form of system layering. When a system is first presented, provide a set of defaults for all system-configurable items. The new user will not be burdened with these decisions and can concentrate on the fundamentals first. Defaults can later be changed, if desired, as experience increases.

Minimize screen alignment points. A larger number of alignment points of elements displayed on a screen are associated with greater screen visual complexity. Minimizing these alignment points minimizes visual complexity. This concept will be discussed more fully later.

Make common actions simple. Make common actions within a system easier to accomplish than uncommon actions. The benefit will be greater overall system efficiency.

Provide uniformity and consistency. Inconsistency is really a foolish form of complexity. It forces a person to learn that things that appear different are not different.

Transparency

■ Permit the user to focus on the task or job, without concern for the mechanics of the interface.
— Workings and reminders of workings inside the computer should be invisible to the user.

Never force the user to think about the technical details of the system. One's thoughts must be directed to the task, not the computer communication process. Reminders of the mechanics of the interface occur through the use of technical jargon, the heavy use of codes, and the presentation of computer concepts and representations.

Trade-Offs

- Final design will be based on a series of trade-offs balancing often-conflicting design principles.
- People's requirements always take precedence over technical requirements.

Design guidelines often cover a great deal of territory and often conflict with one another or with technical requirements. In such conflicts the designer must weigh the alternatives and reach a decision based on trade-offs concerning accuracy, time, cost, and ease of use. Making these trade-offs intelligently requires a thorough understanding of the user and all design considerations. The ultimate solution will be a blend of experimental data, good judgment, and the important user needs.

This leads to a second cardinal rule of graphical system development: *Human requirements always take precedence over technical requirements.* It may be easier for the designer to write a program or build a device that neglects user ease, but final system judgment will always come down to one simple fact: How well does the system meet the needs of the user?

What's Next?

Let's now move ahead to Part 2, the interface design process. Specific guidelines for good interface design will be presented within the context of GUI and Web characteristics and the general principles just described.

Part Two

The User Interface Design Process

Part 2 presents an extensive series of guidelines for the interface design process. It is organized in the order of the development steps typically followed in creating a graphical system's or Web site's screens and pages. In total, 14 steps are presented, beginning with "Know Your User or Client" and ending with a discussion of testing. Other topics addressed include considerations in screen design, navigation, screen-based controls, writing messages, and text, color, and graphics. This organization scheme enables all the interface design activities to be addressed easily, clearly, and sequentially.

Let us first look at several critical general aspects of the design the process. "Obstacles and Pitfalls in the Development Path" points out the realities of designing for people, and some reasons why design may not live up to expectations. "Designing for People: The Five Commandments" lists the guidelines that are the cornerstones of the entire design process. Then, the concept of *usability*, the primary objective on any development effort, is defined and discussed. Finally, the desired composition of the interface development *design team* is described.

Obstacles and Pitfalls in the Development Path

Developing a computer system is never easy. The path is littered with obstacles and traps, many of them human in nature. Gould (1988) has made these general observations about design:

- Nobody ever gets it right the first time.
- Development is chock-full of surprises.
- Good design requires living in a sea of changes.
- Making contracts to ignore change will never eliminate the need for change.
- Even if you have made the best system humanly possible, people will still make mistakes when using it.
- Designers need good tools.
- You must have behavioral design goals like performance design goals.

The first five conditions listed will occur naturally because people are people, both as users and as developers. These kinds of behavior must be understood and accepted in design. User mistakes, while they will always occur, can be reduced. Guidelines in the various design steps address this problem. Behavioral design goals are reviewed in Step 2 "Understand the Business Function."

Pitfalls in the design process exist because of a flawed design process, including a failure to address critical design issues, an improper focus of attention, or development team organization failures. Common pitfalls are:

- No early analysis and understanding of the user's needs and expectations.
- A focus on using design features or components that are "neat" or "glitzy."
- Little or no creation of design element prototypes.
- No usability testing.
- No common design team vision of user interface design goals.
- Poor communication between members of the development team.

"Know Your User or Client" is addressed in Step 1, prototypes and testing are addressed in Step 14 "Test, Test, and Retest." The development team is discussed shortly.

Designing for People: The Five Commandments

The complexity of a graphical or Web interface will always magnify any problems that do occur. While obstacles to design will always exist, pitfalls can be eliminated if the following design commandments remain foremost in the designer's mind.

Gain a complete understanding of users and their tasks. The users are the customers. Today, people expect a level of design sophistication from all interfaces, including Web sites. The product, system or Web site must be geared to people's needs, not those of the developers. A wide gap in technical abilities, goals, and attitudes often exists between users and developers. A failure to understand the differences will doom a product or system to failure.

Solicit early and ongoing user involvement. Involving the users in design from the beginning provides a direct conduit to the knowledge they possess about jobs, tasks, and needs. Involvement also allows the developer to confront a person's resistance to change, a common human trait. People dislike change for a variety of reasons, among them fear of the unknown and lack of identification with the system. Involvement in design removes the unknown and gives the user a stake in the system or identification with it. One caution, however: user involvement should be based on job or task knowledge, not status or position. The boss seldom knows what is really happening out in the office.

Perform rapid prototyping and testing. Prototyping and testing the product will quickly identify problems and allow you to develop solutions. The design process is complex and human behavior is still not well understood. While the design guidelines that follow go a long way toward achieving ease of use, all problems cannot possibly be predicted. Prototyping and testing must be continually performed during all stages of development to uncover all potential defects.

   If thorough testing is not performed before product release, the testing will occur in the user's office. Encountering a series of problems early in system use will create a negative first impression in the customer's mind, and this may harden quickly, creating attitudes that may be difficult to change.

   It is also much harder and more costly to fix a product after its release. In many instances, people may adapt to, or become dependent upon, a design, even if it is inefficient. This also makes future modifications much more difficult.

Modify and iterate the design as much as necessary. While design will proceed through a series of stages, problems detected in one stage may force the developer to revisit a previous stage. This is normal and should be expected. Establish user performance and acceptance criteria and continue testing and modifying until all design goals are met.

Integrate the design of *all* the system components. The software, the documentation, the help function, and training needs are all important elements of a graphical system or Web site and all should be developed concurrently. A system is being constructed, not simply software. Concurrent development of all pieces will point out possible problems earlier in the design process, allowing them to be more effectively addressed. Time will also exist for design trade-offs to be thought out more carefully.

Usability

Bennett (1979) was the first to use the term *usability* to describe the effectiveness of human performance. In the following years a more formal definition was proposed by Shackel (1981) and modified by Bennett (1984). Finally, Shackel (1991) simply defined usability as "the capability to be used by humans easily and effectively, where,

   easily   = to a specified level of subjective assessment,

   effectively = to a specified level of human performance."

Usability Assessment in the Design Process

Usability assessment should begin in the early stages of the product development cycle and should be continually applied throughout the process. The assessment should include the user's entire experience, and all the product's important components. Usability assessment methods are discussed more fully in Step 14 "Test, Test, and Retest."

Common Usability Problems

Mandel (1994) lists the 10 most common usability problems in graphical systems as reported by IBM usability specialists. They are:

1. Ambiguous menus and icons.
2. Languages that permit only single-direction movement through a system.
3. Input and direct manipulation limits.
4. Highlighting and selection limitations.
5. Unclear step sequences.
6. More steps to manage the interface than to perform tasks.
7. Complex linkage between and within applications.
8. Inadequate feedback and confirmation.
9. Lack of system anticipation and intelligence.
10. Inadequate error messages, help, tutorials, and documentation.

The Web, with its dynamic capabilities and explosive entrance into our lives, has unleashed what seems like more than its own share of usability problems. Many are similar to those outlined above. Web usability characteristics particularly wasteful of people's time, and often quite irritating, are:

Visual clutter. A lack of "white space," meaningless graphics, and unnecessary and wasteful decoration often turn pages into jungles of visual noise. Meaningful content lies hidden within the unending forest of vines and trees, forcing the user to waste countless minutes searching for what is relevant. Useless displayed elements are actually a form of visual noise.

Impaired information readability. Page readability is diminished by poor developer choices in typefaces, colors, and graphics. Use of innumerable typefaces and kaleidoscopic colors wrestle meaning from the screen. A person's attention is directed towards trying to understand why the differences exist, instead of being focused toward identifying and understanding the page's content. Backgrounds that are brightly colored or contain pictures or patterns greatly diminish the legibility of the overwritten text.

Incomprehensible components. Some design elements give the user no clue as to their function, leaving their purpose not at all obvious. Some icons and graphics, for example, are shrouded in mystery, containing no text to explain what they do. Some buttons don't look at all like command buttons, forcing the user to "minesweep" the screen with a mouse to locate the objects that can be used to do something. Command buttons or areas that give no visual indication that they are clickable often won't be clicked. Language is also often confusing, with the developer's terminology being used, not that of the user.

Annoying distractions. Elements constantly in motion, scrolling marquees or text, blinking text, or looping continually running animations compete with meaningful content for the user's eye's and attention—and destroy a page's readability. Automatically presented music or other sounds interrupt one's concentration, as do nonrequested pop-up widows, which must be removed, wasting more of the user's time. A person's senses are under constant attack, and the benefits afforded by one's peripheral vision are negated.

Confusing navigation. A site's structure often resembles a maze of twisting pages into which the user wanders and is quite soon lost. Poor, little, or no organization exists among pages. The size and depth of many Web sites can eventually lead to a "lost in space" feeling as perceived site structure evaporates as one navigates. Embarking on a side trip can lead to a radical change in context or a path with no signposts or landmarks. Navigation links lead to dead-ends from which there is no return, or boomerang you right back to the spot where you are standing without you being aware of it. Some navigation elements are invisible. (See mystery icons and minesweeping above.) Confusing navigation violates expectations and results in disturbing unexpected behavior.

> **MYTH**   **Usability is nothing but common sense.**

Inefficient navigation. A person must transverse content-free pages to find what is meaningful. One whole screen is used to point to another. Large graphics waste screen space and add to the page count. The path through the navigation maze is often long and tedious. Reams of useless data must be sifted through before a need can be fulfilled. Massive use of short pages with little content often creates the feeling that one is "link drunk."

Inefficient operations. Time is wasted doing many things. Page download times can be excessive. Pages that contain, for example, large graphics and maps, large chunky headings, or many colors, take longer to download than text. Excessive information fragmentation can require navigation of long chains of links to reach relevant material, also accelerating user disorientation.

Excessive or inefficient page scrolling. Long pages requiring scrolling frequently lead to the user's losing context as related information's spatial proximity increases and some information entirely disappears from view and, therefore, from memory. Out of sight is often out of mind. If navigation elements and important content are hidden below the page top, they may be missed entirely. To have to scroll to do something important or complete a task can be very annoying; especially if the scrolling is caused by what the user considers is an irrelevancy or noise.

Information overload. Poorly organized or large amounts of information taxes one's memory and can be overwhelming. Heavy mental loads can result from making decisions concerning which links to follow and which to abandon, given the large number of choices available. Or from trying to determine what information is important, and what is not. Or from trying to maintain one's place in a huge forest of information trees. One easily becomes buried in decisions and information. Requiring even minimal amounts of learning to use a Web site adds to the mental load.

Design inconsistency. Design inconsistency has not disappeared with the Web. It has been magnified. The business system user may visit a handful of systems in one day, the Web user may visit dozens, or many more. It is expected that site differences will and must exist because each Web site owner strives for its own identity. For the user's sake, however, some consistency must exist to permit a seamless flow between sites. Consistency is needed in, for example, navigation element location on a page and the look of navigation buttons (raised). The industry is diligently working on this topic and some "common practices" are already in place. The learning principle of rote memorization, however, is still being required *within* many sites. For example, the industry practice of using different standard link colors for unvisited sites (blue) and visited sites (purple) is often violated. This forces users to remember different color meanings in different places, and this also causes confusion between links and underlined text. Design guidelines for graphical user interfaces have been available for many years. Too often they are ignored (or the designer is unaware of them). Examples of inappropriate uses abound in design. The use of check boxes instead of radio buttons for mutually exclusive options, for example. Or the use of drop-down list boxes instead of combination boxes when the task mostly requires keyboard form fill-in. The Web is a form of the graphical user interface, and GUI guidelines should be followed.

Outdated information. One important value of a Web site is its "currentness." Outdated information destroys a site's credibility in the minds of many users, and therefore its usefulness. A useless site is not very usable.

Stale design caused by emulation of printed documents and past systems. The Web is a new medium with expanded user interaction and information display possibilities. While much of what we have learned in the print world and past information systems interface design can be ported to the Web, all of what we know should not be blindly moved from one to the other. Web sites should be rethought and redesigned using the most appropriate and robust design techniques available.

Some of these usability problems are a result of the Web's "growing pains." For other problems developers themselves can only be blamed, for they too often have created a product to please themselves and "look cool," not to please their users. Symptoms of this approach include overuse of bleeding edge technology, a focus on sparkle, and jumping to implement the latest Internet technique or buzzword. These problems, of course, did not start with the Web. They have existed since designers began building user interfaces.

Some Practical Measures of Usability

Usability, or the lack thereof, can often be sensed by a simple observation of, or talking to, people using an interface. While these measures lack scientific rigor, they do provide an indication that there may be usability problems.

Are people asking a lot of questions or often reaching for a manual? Many questions or frequent glances at manuals are signs that things are not as clear and intuitive as they should be. When in doubt, the first reaction of many people is to ask someone for assistance. When no one is around, then we look in a manual.

Are frequent exasperation responses heard? "Oh damn!" or similar reactions are usually used to express annoyance or frustration. Their frequency, and loudness, may foretell a strong rejection of a product. The absence of exasperation, however, may not represent acceptance. Some people are not as expressive in their language, or are better able to smother their feelings.

Are there many irrelevant actions being performed? Are people doing things the hard way? Are there incidental actions required for, but not directly related to, doing a job? These include excessive mouse clicks or keyboard strokes to accomplish something, or going through many operations to find the right page in a manual or the right window or page in the display.

Are there many things to ignore? Are there many elements on the screen that the user must disregard? Are there many "doesn't pertain to me" items? If so, remember, they still consume a portion of a person's visual or information-processing capacities, detracting from the capacities a person could devote to relevant things.

Do a number of people want to use the product? None of us goes out of our way to make our own lives more difficult. (Unfortunately, other people may, however.) We tend to gravitate to things easy to work with or do. If a lot of people want to use it, it probably has a higher usability score. Attitudes may be a very powerful factor in a system's or Web site's acceptance.

Some Objective Measures of Usability

Shackel (1991) presents the following more objective criteria for measuring usability. How *effective* is the interface? Can the required range of tasks be accomplished:

- At better than some required level of performance (for example, in terms of speed and errors)?
- By some required percentage of the specified target range of users?
- Within some required proportion of the range of usage environments?

How *learnable* is the interface? Can the interface be learned:

- Within some specified time from commissioning and start of user training?
- Based on some specified amount of training and user support?
- Within some specified relearning time each time for intermittent users?

How *flexible* is the interface? Is it flexible enough to:

- Allow some specified percentage variation in tasks and/or environments beyond those first specified?

What are the *attitudes* of the users? Are they:

- Within acceptable levels of human cost in terms of tiredness, discomfort, frustration, and personal effort?
- Such that satisfaction causes continued and enhanced usage of the system?

Human performance goals in system use, like any other design goal, should be stated in quantitative and measurable ways. Without performance goals you will never know if you have achieved them, or how successful the system really is. Clear and concrete goals also provide objectives for usability testing and ensure that a faulty or unsatisfactory product will not be released.

Values for the various criteria should be specified in absolute terms. An absolute goal might be "Task A must be performed by a first-time user in 12 minutes with no errors with 30 minutes of training and without referring to a manual." Goals may also be set in relative terms. For example, "Task B must be performed 50 percent faster than it was using the previous system."

The level of established goals will depend on the capabilities of the user, the capabilities of the system, and the objectives of the system. In addition to providing commitments to a certain level of quality, goals become the foundation for the system test plan.

The Design Team

Provide a balanced design team, including specialists in:

- Development
- Human factors
- Visual design
- Usability assessment
- Documentation
- Training

Effective design and development requires the application of very diverse talents. No one person possesses all the skills to perform all the necessary tasks; the best that can be hoped for is that one person may possess a couple of skills. A balanced design team with very different talents must be established. Needed are specialists in development to define requirements and write the software, human factors specialists to define behavioral requirements and apply behavioral considerations, and people with good visual design skills. Also needed are people skilled in testing and usability assessment, documentation specialists, and training specialists.

Also, select team members who can effectively work and communicate with one another. To optimize communication, locate the team members in close proximity to one another.

Know Your
User or Client

The journey into the world of interface design and the screen design process must begin with an understanding of the system user, the *most important* part of any computer system. It is the user whose needs a system is built to serve. Understanding people and what they do is a difficult and often undervalued process but very critical because of the gap in knowledge, skills, and attitudes existing between system users and developers that build them. To create a truly usable system, the designer must always do the following:

- Understand how people interact with computers.
- Understand the human characteristics important in design.
- Identify the user's level of knowledge and experience.
- Identify the characteristics of the user's needs, tasks, and jobs.
- Identify the user's psychological characteristics.
- Identify the user's physical characteristics.
- Employ recommended methods for gaining understanding of users.

Understanding How People Interact
with Computers

We will start by looking at some characteristics of computer systems, past and present, that have caused, and are causing, people problems. We will then look at the effect these problems have.

Why People Have Trouble with Computers

Although system design and its behavioral implications have come under intense scrutiny in the last decade or so, as we have seen, this has not always been the case. Historically, the design of business computer systems has been the responsibility of programmers, systems analysts, and system designers, many of whom possess extensive technical knowledge but little behavioral training. In recent years the blossoming of the Web, with its extensive graphical capabilities, has found graphic artists being added to design teams. Like those who have come before them, most graphical artists also possess extensive technical knowledge in their profession but little training in usability. Design decisions, therefore, have rested mostly on the designers' intuition concerning the user's capabilities and the designer's wealth of specialized knowledge. Consequently, poorly designed interfaces have often gone unrecognized.

The intuition of designers or of anyone else, no matter how good or bad they may be at what they do, is error-prone. It is much too shallow a foundation on which to base design decisions. Specialized knowledge lulls one into a false sense of security. It enables one to interpret and deal with complex or ambiguous situations on the basis of context cues not visible to users, as well as a knowledge of the computer system that users do not possess. The result is a system that appears perfectly useful to its designers but one that the user is unable or unwilling to face up to and master.

What makes a system difficult to use in the eyes of its user? Listed below are several contributing factors that apply to traditional business systems.

Use of jargon. Systems often speak in a strange language. Words that are completely alien to the office or home environment or used in different contexts, such as *file-spec*, *abend*, *segment*, and *boot*, proliferate. Learning to use a system often requires learning a new language.

Non-obvious design. Complex or novel design elements are not obvious or intuitive, but they must nevertheless be mastered. Operations may have prerequisite conditions that must be satisfied before they can be accomplished, or outcomes may not always be immediate, obvious, or visible. The overall framework of the system may be invisible, with the effect that results cannot always be related to the actions that accomplish them.

Fine distinctions. Different actions may accomplish the same thing, depending upon when they are performed, or different things may result from the same action. Often these distinctions are minute and difficult to keep track of. Critical distinctions are not made at the appropriate time, or distinctions having no real consequence are made instead, as illustrated by the user who insisted that problems were caused by pressing the Enter key "in the wrong way."

Disparity in problem-solving strategies. People learn best by doing. They have trouble following directions and do not always read instructions before taking an action. Human problem solving can best be characterized as "error-correcting" or "trial and error," whereby a tentative solution is formulated based on the available evidence and then tried. This tentative solution often has a low chance of success, but the action's results are used to modify one's next attempt and so increase the chance of success. Most early computer systems, however, have enforced an "error-preventing" strategy, which assumes that a person will not take an action until a high degree of confidence exists in its success. The result is that when people head down wrong one-way paths, they often get entangled in situations difficult, or impossible, to get out of. The last resort action? Turn off the computer and start again.

Design inconsistency. The same action may have different names: for example, "save" and "keep," "write" and "list." The same command may cause different things to happen. The same result may be described differently: for example, "not legal" and "not valid." Or the same information may be ordered differently on different screens. The result is that system learning becomes an exercise in rote memorization. Meaningful or conceptual learning becomes very difficult.

Responses to Poor Design

Unfortunately, people remember the one thing that went wrong, not the many that go right, so problems are ascribed an abnormal level of importance. Errors are a symptom of problems. The magnitude of errors in a computer-based system has been found to be as high as 46 percent for commands, tasks, or transactions. Errors, and other problems that befuddle one, lead to a variety of psychological and physical user responses.

Psychological

Typical psychological responses to poor design are:

Confusion. Detail overwhelms the perceived structure. Meaningful patterns are difficult to ascertain, and the conceptual model or underlying framework cannot be understood or established.

Annoyance. Roadblocks that prevent a task being completed, or a need from being satisfied, promptly and efficiently lead to annoyance. Inconsistencies in design, slow computer reaction times, difficulties in quickly finding information, outdated information, and visual screen distractions are a few of the many things that may annoy users.

Frustration. An overabundance of annoyances, an inability to easily convey one's intentions to the computer, or an inability to finish a task or satisfy a need can cause frustration. Frustration is heightened if an unexpected computer response cannot be undone or if what really took place cannot be determined. Inflexible and unforgiving systems are a major source of frustration.

Panic or stress. Unexpectedly long delays during times of severe or unusual pressure may introduce panic or stress. Some typical causes are unavailable systems or long response times when the user is operating under a deadline or dealing with an irate customer.

Boredom. Boredom results from improper computer pacing (slow response times or long download times) or overly simplistic jobs.

These psychological responses diminish user effectiveness because they are severe blocks to concentration. Thoughts irrelevant to the task at hand are forced to the user's attention, and necessary concentration is impossible. The result, in addition to higher error rates, is poor performance, anxiety, and dissatisfaction.

Physical

Psychological responses frequently lead to, or are accompanied by, the following physical reactions.

Abandonment of the system. The system is rejected and other information sources are relied upon. These sources must, of course, be available and the user must have the discretion to perform the rejection. In business systems this is a common reaction of managerial and professional personnel. With the Web, almost all users can exercise this option.

Partial use of the system. Only a portion of the system's capabilities are used, usually those operations that are easiest to perform or that provide the most benefits. Historically, this has been the most common user reaction to most computer systems. Many aspects of many systems often go unused.

Indirect use of the system. An intermediary is placed between the would-be user and the computer. Again, since this requires high status and discretion, it is another typical response of managers or others with authority.

Modification of the task. The task is changed to match the capabilities of the system. This is a prevalent reaction when the tools are rigid and the problem is unstructured, as in scientific problem solving.

Compensatory activity. Additional actions are performed to compensate for system inadequacies. A common example is the manual reformatting of information to match the structure required by the computer. This is a reaction common to workers whose discretion is limited, such as clerical personnel.

Misuse of the system. The rules are bent to shortcut operational difficulties. This requires significant knowledge of the system and may affect system integrity.

Direct programming. The system is reprogrammed by its user to meet specific needs. This is a typical response of the sophisticated worker.

These physical responses also greatly diminish user efficiency and effectiveness. They force the user to rely upon other information sources, to fail to use a system's complete capabilities, or to perform time-consuming "work-around" actions.

People and Their Tasks

The user in today's office is usually overworked, fatigued, and continually interrupted. The home user may also experience these same conditions, and often the pressures associated with children and family life as well. All computer users do tend to share the following: they tend not to read documentation, they do not understand well the problems the computer can aid in solving, and they know little about what information is available to meet their needs. Moreover, the users' technical skills have often been greatly overestimated by the system designer, who is usually isolated psychologically and physically from the users' situation. Unlike the users, the designer is capable of resolving most system problems and ambiguities through application of experience and technical knowledge. Often the designer cannot really believe that anyone is incapable of using the system created.

The user, while being subjected to the everyday pressures of the office and home, frequently does not care about how technically sophisticated a system or Web site is. The user may even be computer illiterate, and possibly even antagonistic. He or she wants to spend time using a computer, not learning to use it. His or her objective is simply to get some work done, a task performed, or a need satisfied. Today, many users have also learned to expect certain level of design sophistication. It is in this environment our system will be placed.

Important Human Characteristics in Design

We are complex organisms with a variety of attributes that have an important influence on interface and screen design. Of particular importance in design are perception, memory, visual acuity, foveal and peripheral vision, sensory storage, information processing, learning, skill, and individual differences.

Perception

Perception is our awareness and understanding of the elements and objects of our environment through the physical sensation of our various senses, including sight, sound, smell, and so forth. Perception is influenced, in part, by *experience*. We classify stimuli based on models stored in our memories and in this way achieve understanding. In essence, we tend to match objects or sensations perceived to things we already know. Comparing the accumulated knowledge of the child with that of an adult in interpreting the world is a vivid example of the role of experience in perception.

Other perceptual characteristics include the following:

Proximity. Our eyes and mind see objects as belonging together if they are near each other in space.

Similarity. Our eyes and mind see objects as belonging together if they share a common visual property, such as color, size, shape, brightness, or orientation.

Matching patterns. We respond similarly to the same shape in different sizes. The letters of the alphabet, for example, possess the same meaning, regardless of physical size.

Succinctness. We see an object as having some perfect or simple shape because perfection or simplicity is easier to remember.

Closure. Our perception is synthetic; it establishes meaningful wholes. If something does not quite close itself, such as a circle, square, triangle, or word, we see it as closed anyway.

Unity. Objects that form closed shapes are perceived as a group.

Continuity. Shortened lines may be automatically extended.

Balance. We desire stabilization or equilibrium in our viewing environment. Vertical, horizontal, and right angles are the most visually satisfying and easiest to look at.

Expectancies. Perception is also influenced by expectancies; sometimes we perceive not what is there but what we expect to be there. Missing a spelling mistake in proofreading something we write is often an example of a perceptual expectancy error; we see not how a word *is* spelled, but how we *expect* to see it spelled.

Context. Context, environment, and surroundings also influence individual perception. For example, two drawn lines of the same length may look the same length or different lengths, depending on the angle of adjacent lines or what other people have said about the size of the lines.

Signals versus noise. Our sensing mechanisms are bombarded by many stimuli, some of which are important and some of which are not. Important stimuli are called signals; those that are not important or unwanted are called noise. Signals are more quickly comprehended if they are easily distinguishable from noise in our sensory environment. Noise interferes with the perception of signals to the extent that they are similar to one another. Noise can even mask a critical signal. For example, imagine a hidden word puzzle where meaningful words are buried in a large block matrix of alphabetic characters. The signals, alphabetic characters constituting meaningful words, are masked by the matrix of meaningless letters.

The elements of a screen assume the quality of signal or noise, depending on the actions and thought processes of the user. Once a screen is first presented and has to be identified as being the correct one, the screen's title may be the signal, the other elements it contains simply being noise. When the screen is being used, the data it contains becomes the signal, and the title now reverts to noise. Other elements of the screen rise and fall in importance, assuming the roles of either signals or noise, depending on the user's needs of the moment. The goal in design is to allow screen elements to easily assume the quality of signal or noise, as the needs and tasks of the user change from moment to moment.

The goal in design, then, is to utilize our perceptual capabilities so a screen can be structured in the most meaningful and obvious way.

Memory

Memory is not the most stable of human attributes, as anyone who has forgotten why they walked into a room, or forgotten a very important birthday, can attest. Today, memory is viewed as consisting of two components, long-term and short-term (or working) memory. This has not always been the case. In the 1950s, most researchers believed there was only one memory system; the short-term component was not recognized or accepted. It was in this era that the classic memory study was published (Miller, 1956) indicating that memory limit is 7 ± 2 "chunks" of information. Shortly after this the concept of a short-term memory was identified and, in the 1970s, the view of short-term memory was broadened and called "working memory."

Short-term, or working, memory receives information from either the senses or long-term memory, but usually cannot receive both at once, the senses being processed separately. Within short-term memory a limited amount of information processing takes place. Information stored within it is variously thought to last from 10 to 30 seconds, with the lower number being the most reasonable speculation. Based upon research over the years, estimates of working memory storage capacity has gradually been lowered from Miller's 7 ± 2 items to a size of 3–4 items today.

Knowledge, experience, and familiarity govern the size and complexity of the information that can be remembered. To illustrate, most native English-speaking people would find remembering English words much easier than remembering an equal number of words in Russian. For a Russian-speaking person the opposite would be true. Short-term memory is easily overloaded. It is highly susceptible to the interference of such distracting tasks as thinking, reciting, or listening, which are constantly erasing and overwriting it. Remembering a telephone number long enough to complete the dialing operation taxes the memory of many people.

In performance, research indicates that a greater working memory is positively related to increased reading comprehension, drawing inferences from text, reasoning skill, and learning technical information (Baddeley, 1992). Research indicates, as well, that when performing complex tasks, working memory can be increased through applying two senses, vision and audition, rather than one (Williams, 1998). Research also indicates that performance can be degraded when a person must attend to multiple information sources, and then must integrate the information before understanding occurs.

Long-term memory contains the knowledge we possess. Information received in short-term memory is transferred to it and encoded within it, a process we call learning. It is a complex process requiring some effort on our part. The learning process is improved if the information being transferred from short-term memory has structure and is meaningful and familiar. Learning is also improved through repetition. Unlike short-term memory, with its distinct limitations, long-term memory capacity is thought to be unlimited. An important memory consideration, with significant implications for interface design, is the difference in ability to recognize or recall words. The human active vocabulary (words that can be recalled) typically ranges between 2,000 and 3,000 words. Passive vocabulary (words that can be recognized) typically numbers about 100,000. Our power of recognition, therefore, is much greater than our power of recall, and this phenomenon should be utilized in design. To do this, one should present, whenever possible, lists of alternatives to remind people of the choices they have.

MAXIM   **Minimize the need for a mighty memory.**

Other general ways to reduce user memory loads, reduce the need for mental integration, and expand working memory, thus enhancing system usability include:

- Presenting information in an organized, structured, familiar, and meaningful way.
- Placing all required information for task performance in close physical proximity.
- Giving the user control over the pace of information presentation.

Sensory Storage

Sensory storage is the buffer where the automatic processing of information collected from our senses takes place. It is an unconscious process, large, attentive to the environment, quick to detect changes, and constantly being replaced by newly gathered stimuli. In a sense, it acts like radar, constantly scanning the environment for things that are important to pass on to higher memory.

Though seemingly overwhelmed at times by noise, it can occasionally detect, proverbially, a tree through a forest. One good example is what is sometimes called the "cocktail party affect." Have you ever been at a party when, across the room, through the din of voices, someone mentions your name, and you hear it? In spite of the noise, your radar was functioning.

Repeated and excessive stimulation can fatigue the sensory storage mechanism, making it less attentive and unable to distinguish what is important (called *habituation*). Avoid unnecessarily stressing it. Design the interface so that all aspects and elements serve a definite purpose. Eliminating interface noise will ensure that important things will be less likely to be missed.

Visual Acuity

The capacity of the eye to resolve details is called *visual acuity*. It is the phenomenon that results in an object becoming more distinct as we turn our eyes toward it and rapidly losing distinctness as we turn our eyes away—that is, as the visual angle from the point of fixation increases. It has been shown that relative visual acuity is approximately halved at a distance of 2.5 degrees from the point of eye fixation (Bouma, 1970). Therefore, a five-degree diameter circle centered around an eye fixation character on a display has been recommended as the area near that character (Tullis, 1983) or the maximum length for a displayed word (Danchak, 1976).

If one assumes that the average viewing distance of a display screen is 19 inches (475 mm), the size of the area on the screen of optimum visual acuity is 1.67 inches (41.8 mm) in diameter. Assuming "average" character sizes and character and line spacings, the number of characters on a screen falling within this visual acuity circle is 88, with 15 characters being contained on the widest line, and seven rows being consumed, as illustrated in Figure 1.1.

The eye's sensitivity increases for those characters closest to the fixation point (the "0") and decreases for those characters at the extreme edges of the circle (a 50/50 chance exists for getting these characters correctly identified). This may be presumed to be a visual "chunk" of a screen and will have implications for screen grouping guidelines to be presented later. (Remember, it is the physical size of the circle, five degrees, that is critical, not the number of characters. A larger or smaller character size will decrease or increase the number of viewable characters.)

```
      3213123
     54321212345
    6543211123456
   765432101234567
    6543211123456
     54321212345
      3213123
```

Figure 1.1   Size of area of optimum visual acuity on a screen.

The eye is also never perfectly steady as it sees; it trembles slightly. This tremor improves the detection of edges of objects being looked at, thus improving acuity. This tremor, however, can sometimes create problems. Patterns of closely spaced lines or dots are seen to shimmer. This movement can be distracting and disturbing. Patterns for fill-in areas of screens (bars, circles, and so on.) must be carefully chosen to avoid this visual distraction.

Foveal and Peripheral Vision

Foveal vision is used to focus directly on something; *peripheral vision* senses anything in the area surrounding the location we are looking at, but what is there cannot be clearly resolved because of the limitations in visual acuity just described. Foveal and peripheral vision maintain, at the same time, a cooperative and a competitive relationship. Peripheral vision can aid a visual search, but can also be distracting.

In its cooperative nature, peripheral vision is thought to provide clues to where the eye should go next in the visual search of a screen. Patterns, shapes, and alignments peripherally visible can guide the eye in a systematic way through a screen.

In its competitive nature, peripheral vision can compete with foveal vision for attention. What is sensed in the periphery is passed on to our information-processing system along with what is actively being viewed foveally. It is, in a sense, visual noise. Mori and Hayashi (1993) experimentally evaluated the effect of windows in both a foveal and peripheral relationship and found that performance on a foveal window deteriorates when there are peripheral windows, and the performance degradation is even greater if the information in the peripheral is dynamic or moving. Care should be exercised in design to utilize peripheral vision in its positive nature, avoiding its negative aspects.

Information Processing

The information that our senses collect that is deemed important enough to do something about then has to be processed in some meaningful way. Recent thinking (Lind, Johnson, and Sandblad, 1992) is that there are two levels of information processing going on within us. One level, the highest level, is identified with consciousness and working memory. It is limited, slow, and sequential, and is used for reading and understanding. You are utilizing this higher level now reading this book.

In addition to this higher level, there exists a lower level of information processing, and the limit of its capacity is unknown. This lower level processes familiar information rapidly, in parallel with the higher level, and without conscious effort. We look rather than see, perceive rather than read. Repetition and learning results in a shift of control from the higher level to the lower level.

Both levels function simultaneously, the higher level performing reasoning and problem solving, the lower level perceiving the physical form of information sensed. You've probably experienced this difference in working with screens. When a screen is displayed, you usually will want to verify that it is the one you want. If you're new to a system, or if a screen is new to you, you rely on its concrete elements to make that determination, its title, the controls and information it contains, and so forth. You consciously look at the screen and its components using this higher-level processing.

As you become experienced and familiar with screens, however, a newly presented screen can be identified very quickly with just a momentary glance. Just its shape and structure adequately communicate to you that it is the correct screen for the context in which you are working. Your reasoning and problem solving continues unhindered; your lower-level information processing has assumed the screen identity task.

What assists this lower-level information processing? Visual distinctiveness of a screen is a strong contributor. If a screen is jammed with information and cluttered, it loses its uniqueness and can only be identified through the more time-consuming, and thought-interrupting, reading process.

Mental Models

As a result of our experiences and culture, we develop mental models of things and people we interact with. A mental model is simply an internal representation of a person's current understanding of something. Usually a person cannot describe this mental mode and most often is unaware it even exists. Mental models are gradually developed in order to understand something, explain things, make decisions, do something, or interact with another person. Mental models also enable a person to predict the actions necessary to do things if the action has been forgotten or has not yet been encountered.

When confronting a new computer system, people will bring their own expectations and preconceptions based upon mental models they have formed doing things in their daily life. If the system conforms to the mental models a person has developed, the model is reinforced and the system's use feels more "intuitive." If not, difficulties in learning to use the system will be encountered. This is why in design it is critical that a user's mental models be to identified and understood.

A person already familiar with one computer system will bring to another system a mental model containing specific visual and usage expectations. If the new system complies with already-established models, it will be much easier to learn and use. The key to forming a transferable mental model of a system is design consistency and design standards.

Movement Control

Once data has been perceived and an appropriate action decided upon, a response must be made; in many cases the response is a movement. In computer systems, movements include such activities as pressing keyboard keys, moving the screen pointer by pushing a mouse or rotating a trackball, or clicking a mouse button. Particularly important in screen design is Fitts' Law (1954). This law states that:

- The time to acquire a target is a function of the distance to and size of the target.

This simply means that the bigger the target is, or the closer the target is, the faster it will be reached. The implications in screen design are:

- Provide large objects for important functions.
- Take advantage of the "pinning" actions of the sides, top, bottom, and corners of the screen.

Big buttons are better than small buttons. They provide a larger target for the user to access with the screen pointer. Create toolbar icons that "bleed" into the edges of a display, rather than those leaving a one-pixel non-clickable edge along the display boundary. The edge of the screen will stop or "pin" the pointer's movement at a position over toolbar, permitting much faster movement to the toolbar. A one-pixel edge will require more careful positioning of the pointer over the toolbar.

Learning

Learning, as has been said, is the process of encoding in long-term memory information that is contained in short-term memory. It is a complex process requiring some effort on our part. Our ability to learn is important—it clearly differentiates people from machines. Given enough time people can improve their performance in almost any task. Too often, however, designers use our learning ability as an excuse to justify complex design. Because people can be taught to walk a tightrope is no excuse for incorporating tightropes in a design when walkways are feasible.

A design developed to minimize human learning time can greatly accelerate human performance. People prefer to stick with what they know, and they prefer to jump in and get started. Unproductive time spent learning is something frequently avoided.

Regarding the learning process, evidence derived from studies of people learning a computer system parallels that found in studies of learning in other areas. People prefer to be active, to explore, and to use a trial-and-error approach. There is also evidence that people are very sensitive to even minor changes in the user interface, and that such changes may lead to problems in transferring from one system to another. Moreover, just the "perception" of having to learn huge amounts of information is enough to keep some people from even using a system. Learning can be enhanced if it:

- Allows skills acquired in one situation to be used in another somewhat like it. Design consistency accomplishes this.
- Provides complete and prompt feedback.
- Is phased, that is, it requires a person to know only the information needed at that stage of the learning process.

Skill

The goal of human performance is to perform skillfully. To do so requires linking inputs and responses into a sequence of action. The essence of skill is performance of actions or movements in the correct time sequence with adequate precision. It is characterized by consistency and economy of effort. Economy of effort is achieved by establishing a work pace that represents optimum efficiency. It is accomplished by increasing mastery of the system through such things as progressive learning of shortcuts, increased speed, and easier access to information or data.

Skills are hierarchical in nature, and many basic skills may be integrated to form increasingly complex ones. Lower-order skills tend to become routine and may drop out of consciousness. System and screen design must permit development of increasingly skillful performance.

Individual Differences

In reality, there is no average user. A complicating but very advantageous human characteristic is that we all differ—in looks, feelings, motor abilities, intellectual abilities, learning abilities and speed, and so on. In a keyboard data entry task, for example, the best typists will probably be twice as fast as the poorest and make 10 times fewer errors. Individual differences complicate design because the design must permit people with widely varying characteristics to satisfactorily and comfortably learn the task or job, or use the Web site. In the past this has usually resulted in bringing designs down to the level of lowest abilities or selecting people with the minimum skills necessary to perform a job. But technology now offers the possibility of tailoring jobs to the specific needs of people with varying and changing learning or skill levels. Multiple versions of a system can easily be created. Design must provide for the needs of all potential users.

Human Considerations in Design

The human characteristics described above are general qualities we all possess. There are also a host of other human aspects in which people may vary greatly. These are also important and must be identified in the design process. The kinds of user/task characteristics that must be established are summarized in Table 1.1 and more fully described in the following paragraphs. A number of these considerations are derived from Mayhew (1992).

The User's Knowledge and Experience

The knowledge possessed by a person, and the experiences undergone, shape the design of the interface in many ways. The following kinds of knowledge and experiences should be identified.

Computer Literacy

Are the users highly technical such as programmers or experienced data entry clerks? Do they have moderate computer experience or none at all? Will they be familiar with computer concepts and terms, the keyboard and its keys, and a mouse or other input mechanisms? If familiar, how familiar?

System Experience

Are users already familiar with the interaction requirements of the new system, somewhat familiar, or not familiar at all? Have users worked with similar systems? If so, what kind? What are the similarities? The differences? The same questions can be asked for Web systems.

At one time or another, various schemes have been proposed to classify the different and sometimes changing characteristics of people as they become more experienced using a system. Words to describe the new, relatively new, or infrequent user

Table 1.1   Important User/Task Considerations

KNOWLEDGE/EXPERIENCE	
Computer Literacy	Highly technical or experienced, moderate computer experience, or none.
System Experience	High, moderate, or low knowledge of a particular system and its methods of interaction.
Application Experience	High, moderate, or low knowledge of similar systems.
Task Experience	Level of knowledge of job and job tasks.
Other Systems Use	Frequent or infrequent use of other systems in doing job.
Education	High school, college, or advanced degree.
Reading Level	Less than 5th grade, 5th–12th, more than 12th grade.
Typing Skill	Expert (135 WPM), skilled (90 WPM), good (55 WPM), average (40 WPM), or "hunt and peck" (10 WPM).
Native Language or Culture	English, another, or several.
JOB/TASK/NEED	
Type of System Use	Mandatory or discretionary use of the system.
Frequency of Use	Continual, frequent, occasional, or once-in-a-lifetime use of system.
Task or Need Importance	High, moderate, or low importance of the task being performed.
Task Structure	Repetitiveness or predictability of tasks being automated, high, moderate, or low.
Social Interactions	Verbal communication with another person required or not required.
Primary Training	Extensive or formal training, self-training through manuals, or no training.
Turnover Rate	High, moderate, or low turnover rate for jobholders.
Job Category	Executive, manager, professional, secretary, clerk.
Lifestyle	For Web e-commerce systems, includes hobbies, recreational pursuits, and economic status.
PSYCHOLOGICAL CHARACTERISTICS	
Attitude	Positive, neutral, or negative feeling toward job or system.
Motivation	Low, moderate, or high due to interest or fear.
Patience	Patience or impatience expected in accomplishing goal.
Expectations	Kinds and reasonableness.
Stress Level	High, some, or no stress generally resulting from task performance.
Cognitive Style	Verbal or spatial, analytic or intuitive, concrete or abstract.
PHYSICAL CHARACTERISTICS	
Age	Young, middle aged, or elderly.
Gender	Male or female.
Handedness	Left, right, or ambidextrous.
Disabilities	Blind, defective vision, deafness, motor handicap.

Derived from Mayhew, 1992.

have included *naive, casual, inexperienced,* or *novice.* At the other end of the experience continuum lie terms such as *experienced, full-time, frequent, power,* or *expert.* In between these extremes is a wide range of *intermediate* or *intermittent* users. The words describing these categories are less important than the behavioral characteristics they imply. Experience to date has uncovered some basic differences in the feelings of ease of use based upon proficiency level. What is easy for the new user is not always perceived as easy for the "old hand," and vice versa. For simplicity in this discussion, the term *novice* will be used for the new user, the term *intermediate* for those in between, and the term *expert,* for the most proficient.

In business systems, *novice* users have been found to:

- Depend on system features that assist recognition memory: menus, prompting information, and instructional and help screens.
- Need restricted vocabularies, simple tasks, small numbers of possibilities, and very informative feedback.
- View practice as an aid to moving up to expert status.

For years novice users have been told they are stupid and have been conditioned to accept the blame for their failure to understand and use a system or product. (Note the popularity of the manuals with "dummy" in the title.) These novice users have been forced to struggle through their "dumbness" to achieve mastery, because they had few other choices. If people cannot effectively use a system, then, who is to blame? It would seem the fault lies in the design of the system, for people cannot be redesigned.

Experts, on the other hand:

- Rely upon free recall.
- Expect rapid performance.
- Need less informative feedback.
- Seek efficiency by bypassing novice memory aids, reducing keystrokes, chunking and summarizing information, and introducing new vocabularies.

The needs of the intermediate user fall somewhere in between these extremes.

In Web systems, in addition to the above, novice users have been found to need overviews, buttons to select actions, and guided tours; intermediate users want an orderly structure, obvious landmarks, reversibility, and safety as they explore; and experts like smooth navigation paths, compact but in-depth information, fast page downloads, extensive services to satisfy their varied needs, and the ability to change or rearrange the interface.

In actuality, the user population of most systems is spread out along the continuum anchored by these two extremes. And, equally important, the behavior of any one user at different times may be closer to one extreme or the other. A person may be very proficient—an expert—in one aspect of a system and ignorant—a novice—in other aspects at the same time. Becoming an expert in use of the Web is particularly challenging. The faces of Web sites are continually changing, and individual sites are rarely used enough for expert competence to be established.

Microsoft has identified the problems that novice and intermediate users have in using their Windows systems. Novice users often have difficulties:

- Dragging and double-clicking using the mouse. Distinguishing between double-clicks and two separate clicks is particularly confusing
- In window management. That overlapping windows represent a three-dimensional space is not always realized. Hidden windows are assumed to be gone and no longer exist.
- In file management. The organization of files and folders nested more than two levels deep is difficult to understand. Structure is not as apparent as with physical files and folders.

Intermediate Windows users may understand the file hierarchy but often have difficulties with other aspects of file management such as moving or copying. These kinds of problems must be considered in design.

Exactly how experts and novices actually differ from one another in terms of knowledge, problem-solving behavior, and other human characteristics has been the subject of some research in recent years. Summarizing some of the findings, experts possess the following traits:

- They possess an integrated conceptual model of a system.
- They possess knowledge that is ordered more abstractly and more procedurally.
- They organize information more meaningfully, orienting it toward their task.
- They structure information into more categories.
- They are better at making inferences and relating new knowledge to their objectives and goals.
- They pay less attention to low-level details.
- They pay less attention to surface features of a system.

Novices exhibit these characteristics:

- They possess a fragmented conceptual model of a system.
- They organize information less meaningfully, orienting it toward surface features of the system.
- They structure information into fewer categories.
- They have difficulty in generating inferences and relating new knowledge to their objectives and goals.
- They pay more attention to low-level details.
- They pay more attention to surface features of the system.

A well-designed system, therefore, must support at the same time novice and expert behavior, as well as all levels of behavior in between. The challenge in design is to provide for the expert's needs without introducing complexity for those less experienced. In general, the following graphical system aspects are seen as desirable expert shortcuts:

- Mouse double-clicks.
- Pop-up menus.
- Tear-off or detachable menus.
- Command lines.

Microsoft Windows expert shortcuts are summarized in Table 1.2.

Table 1.2   Microsoft Windows Expert Aids

• The Windows Explorer	For easy file management and information browsing.
• Shortcuts	For quickly accessing all objects.
• Property Sheets	All objects carry context-sensitive properties that can be easily accessed and customized.
• Pop-up Menus (Right-Clicking)	Commands to perform common actions.
• Quick Viewers	To review a file without opening the application that created it.

Application Experience

Have users worked with a similar application (for example, word processing, airline reservation, and so on)? Are they familiar with the basic application terms? Or does little or no application experience exist?

Task Experience

Are users experienced with the task being automated? If it is an insurance claim system, do users have experience with paying claims? If it is a banking system, do users have experience in similar banking applications? Or do users possess little or no knowledge of the tasks the system will be performing?

Other System Use

Will the user be using other systems while using the new system? If so, they will bring certain habits and expectancies to the new system. The more compatibility between systems, the lower the learning requirements for the new system and the higher the productivity using all systems.

MYTH   **Developers have been working with users for a long time. They always know everything users want and need.**

Education

What is the general educational level of users? Do they generally have high school degrees, college degrees, or advanced degrees? Are the degrees in specialized areas related to new system use?

Reading Level

For textual portions of the interface, the vocabulary and grammatical structure must be at a level that is easily understood by the users. Reading level can often be inferred from one's education level.

Typing Skill

Is the user a competent typist or of the hunt-and-peck variety? Is he or she familiar with the standard keyboard layout or other newer layouts? A competent typist may prefer to interact with the system exclusively through the keyboard, whereas the unskilled typist may prefer the mouse.

Native Language and Culture

Do the users speak English, another language, or several other languages? Will the screens be in English or in another language? Other languages often impose different screen layout requirements. Are there cultural or ethnic differences between users? Will icons, metaphors, and any included humor or clichés be meaningful for all the user cultures?

In conclusion, most of these kinds of user knowledge and experience are independent of one another, so many different user profiles are possible. It is also useful to look ahead, assessing whether future users will possess the same qualities.

The User's Tasks and Needs

The user's tasks and needs are also important in design. The following should be determined:

Mandatory or Discretionary Use

Users of the earliest computer systems were *mandatory* or nondiscretionary. That is, they required the computer to perform a task that, for all practical purposes, could be performed no other way. Characteristics of mandatory use can be summarized as follows:

- The computer is used as part of employment.
- Time and effort in learning to use the computer are willingly invested.
- High motivation is often used to overcome low usability characteristics.
- The user may possess a technical background.
- The job may consist of a single task or function.

The mandatory user must learn to live comfortably with a computer, for there is really no other choice. Examples of mandatory use today include a flight reservations clerk booking seats, an insurance company employee entering data into the computer so a policy can be issued, and a programmer writing and debugging a program. The toll exacted by a poorly designed system in mandatory use is measured primarily by productivity, for example, errors and poor customer satisfaction.

In recent years, as technology and the Web has expanded into the office, the general business world, and the home, a second kind of user has been more widely exposed to the benefits, and problems, of technology. In the business office this other kind of user is much more self-directed than the mandatory user, not being told how to work but being evaluated on the results of his or her efforts. For him or her, it is not the means but the results that are most important. In short, this user has never been told how to work in the past and refuses to be told so now. This newer kind of user is the office executive, manager, or other professional, whose computer use is completely *discretionary.*

In the general business world and at home, discretionary users also include the people who are increasingly being asked to, or want to, interact with a computer in their everyday lives. Examples of this kind of interaction include library information systems, bank automated teller machines (ATMs), and the Internet. Common general characteristics of the discretionary user are as follows:

- Use of the computer or system is not absolutely necessary.
- Technical details are of no interest.
- Extra effort to use the system may not be invested.
- High motivation to use the system may not be exhibited.
- May be easily disenchanted.
- Voluntary use may have to be encouraged.
- Is from a heterogeneous culture.

For the business system discretionary user, the following may also be appropriate:

- Is a multifunction knowledge worker.
- The job can be performed without the system.
- May not have expected to use the system.
- Career path may not have prepared him or her for system use.

Quite simply, this discretionary user often judges a system on the basis of expected effort versus results to be gained. If the benefits are seen to exceed the effort, the system will be used. If the effort is expected to exceed the benefits, it will not be used. Just the *perception* of a great effort to achieve minimal results is often enough to completely discourage system use, leading to system rejection, a common discretionary reaction.

The discretionary user, or potential user, exhibits certain characteristics that vary. A study of users of ATMs identified five specific categories. Each group was about equal in size, encompassing about 20 percent of the general population. The groups, and their characteristics, are the following:

- People who understand technology and like it. They will use it under any and all circumstances.
- People who understand technology and like it, but will only use it if the benefits are clear.
- People who understand technology but do not like it. They will use it only if the benefits are overwhelming.
- People who do not understand anything technical. They might use it if it is very easy.
- People who will never use technology of any kind.

Again, clear and obvious benefits and ease of learning to use a system dominate these usage categories.

Frequency of Use

Is system use a continual, frequent, occasional, or once-in-a-lifetime experience? Frequency of use affects both learning and memory. People who spend a lot of time using a system are usually willing to spend more time learning how to use it in seeking efficiency of operation. They will also more easily remember how to do things. Occasional or infrequent users prefer ease of learning and remembering, often at the expense of operational efficiency.

Task or Need Importance

How important is the task or need for the user? People are usually willing to spend more time learning something if it makes the task being performed or need being fulfilled more efficient. For less important things, ease of learning and remembering are preferred, because extensive learning time and effort will not be tolerated.

Task Structure

How structured is the task being performed? Is it repetitive and predictable or not so? In general, the less structure, the more flexibility should exist in the interface. Highly structured tasks require highly structured interfaces.

Social Interactions

Will the user, in the normal course of task performance, be engaged in a conversation with another person, such as a customer, while using the system? If so, design should not interfere with the social interaction. Neither the user nor the person to whom the user is talking must be distracted in any way by computer interaction requirements. The design must accommodate the social interaction. User decision-making required by the interface should be minimized and clear eye-anchors built into the screen to facilitate eye-movements by the user between the screen and the other person.

Primary Training

Will the system training be extensive and formal, will it be self-training from manuals, or will training be impossible? With less training, the requirement for system ease of use increases.

Turnover Rate

In a business system, is the turnover rate for the job high, moderate, or low? Jobs with high turnover rates would not be good candidates for systems requiring a great deal of training and learning. With low turnover rates, a greater training expense can be justified. With jobs possessing high turnover rates, it is always useful to determine why. Perhaps the new system can restructure monotonous jobs, creating more challenge and thereby reducing the turnover rate.

Job Category

In a business system, is the user an executive, manager, professional, secretary, or clerk? While job titles have no direct bearing on design per se, they do enable one to predict some job characteristics when little else is known about the user. For example, executives and managers are most often discretionary users, while clerks are most often mandatory ones. Secretaries usually have typing skills, and both secretaries and clerks usually have higher turnover rates than executives and managers.

Lifestyle

For Web e-commerce systems, user information to be collected includes hobbies, recreational pursuits, economic status, and other similar more personal information.

The User's Psychological Characteristics

A person's psychological characteristics also affect one's performance of tasks requiring motor, cognitive, or perceptual skills.

Attitude and Motivation

Is the user's attitude toward the system positive, neutral, or negative? Is motivation high, moderate, or low? While all these feelings are not caused by, and cannot be controlled by, the designer, a positive attitude and motivation allows the user to concentrate on the productivity qualities of the system. Poor feelings, however, can be addressed by designing a system to provide more power, challenge, and interest for the user, with the goal of increasing user satisfaction.

Patience

Is the user patient or impatient? Recent studies of the behavior of Web users indicate they are becoming increasingly impatient. They are exhibiting less tolerance for Web use learning requirements, slow response times, and inefficiencies in navigation and locating desired content.

Stress Level

Will the user be subject to high levels of stress while using the system? Interacting with an angry boss, client, or customer, can greatly increase a person's stress level. High levels of stress can create confusion and cause one to forget things one normally would not. System navigation or screen content may have to be redesigned for extreme simplicity in situations that can become stressful.

Expectations

What are user's expectations about the system or Web site? Are they realistic? Is it important that the user's expectations be realized?

Cognitive Style

People differ in how they think about and solve problems. Some people are better at verbal thinking, working more effectively with words and equations. Others are better at spatial reasoning—manipulating symbols, pictures, and images. Some people are analytic thinkers, systematically analyzing the facets of a problem. Others are intuitive, relying on rules of thumb, hunches, and educated guesses. Some people are more concrete in their thinking, others more abstract. This is speculative, but the verbal, analytic, concrete thinker might prefer a textual style of interface. The spatial, intuitive, abstract thinker might feel more at home using a multimedia graphical interface.

The User's Physical Characteristics

The physical characteristics of people can also greatly affect their performance with a system.

Age

Are the users children, young adults, middle-aged, senior citizens, or very elderly? Age can have an affect on both computer and system usage. Older people may not have the manual dexterity to accurately operate many input devices. A double-click on a mouse, for example, is increasingly more difficult to perform as dexterity declines. With age, the eye's capability also deteriorates, affecting screen readability. Memory ability also diminishes. Recent research on the effects of age and system usability has found the following:

Young adults (aged 18–36), in comparison to older adults (aged 64–81) (Mead et al., 1997; Piolat et al., 1998):

- Use computers and ATMs more often.
- Read faster.
- Possess greater reading comprehension and working memory capacity.
- Possess faster choice reaction times.
- Possess higher perceptual speed scores.
- Complete a search task at a higher success rate.
- Use significantly less moves (clicks) to complete a search task.
- Are more likely to read a screen a line at a time.

Older adults, as compared to young adults:

- Are more educated.
- Possess higher vocabulary scores.
- Have more difficulty recalling previous moves and location of previously viewed information.
- Have more problems with tasks that require three or more moves (clicks).
- Are more likely to scroll a page at a time
- Respond better to full pages rather than long continuous scrolled pages.

Hearing

As people age, they require louder sounds to hear, a noticeable attribute in almost any everyday activity. Cohen (1994) found the following preferred levels for listening to speech at various age levels:

Age in Years	Sound Level in dB
25	57
45	65
65	74
85	85

Vision

Older adults read prose text in smaller type fonts more slowly than younger adults (Charness and Dijkstra, 1999). For older adults they recommend:

- 14-point type in 4-inch wide columns.
- 12-point type in 3-inch wide columns.

Ellis and Kurniawan (2000) recommend the following fonts for older users:

- San serif (Arial, Helvetica, and Verdana).
- Black type on a white background.

Ellis and Kurniawan (2000) and Czaja (1997) suggest Web links should be:

- Distinct and easy to see.
- Large (at least 180×22 pixels for a button).
- Surrounded by a large amount of white space.

Cognitive Processing

Brain processing also appears to slow with age. Working memory, attention capacity, and visual search appear to be degraded. Tasks where knowledge is important show the smallest age effect and tasks dependent upon speed show the largest effect (Sharit and Czaja, 1994).

Other age-related studies have compared people's performance with their time-of-day preferences (Intons-Peterson et al., 1998; Intons-Peterson et al., 1999). Older people were found to prefer to perform in the morning; younger people had no significant time of day preferences. In a memory test, younger users were able to perform well at all times in the day, older users, however, performed best during their preferred times.

The above research conclusions should be considered preliminary. They do illustrate, however, the kinds of differences age can play in making design decisions.

Gender

A user's sex may have an impact on both motor and cognitive performance. Women are not as strong as men, so moving heavy displays or controls may be more difficult. Women also have smaller hands than men, so controls designed for the hand size of one may not be used as effectively by the other. Significantly more men are color-blind than women, so women may perform better on tasks and screens using color-coding.

Handedness

A user's handedness, left or right, can affect ease of use of an input mechanism, depending on whether it has been optimized for one or the other hand. Research shows that for adults:

- 87 percent are right-handed.
- 13 percent are left-handed or can use both hands without a strong preference for either one.
- No gender or age differences exist.
- There is a strong cultural bias, in China and Japan only 1 percent of people are left-handed.

> **MAXIM**　**Ease of use promotes use.**

Disabilities

Blindness, defective vision, color-blindness, poor hearing, deafness, and motor handicaps can affect performance on a system not designed with these disabilities in mind. People with special needs must be considered in design. This is especially true for systems like the Web that permit unlimited user access.

Human Interaction Speeds

The speed at which people can perform using various communication methods has been studied by a number of researchers. The following, as summarized by Bailey (2000), have been found to be typical interaction speeds for various tasks. These speeds are also summarized in Table 1.3.

> **Reading.** The average adult, reading English prose in the United States, has a reading speed in the order of 250–300 words per minute. Proofreading text on paper has been found to occur at about 200 words per minute, on a computer monitor, about 180 words per minute (Ziefle, 1998).
>
> Nontraditional reading methods have also been explored in research laboratories. One technique that has dramatically increased reading speeds is called Rapid Serial Visual Presentation, or RSVP. In this technique single words are presented one at a time in the center of a screen. New words continually replace old words at a rate set by the reader. Bailey (1999a) tested this technique with a sample of people whose paper document reading speed was 342 words per minute. (With a speed range of 143 to 540 words per minute.) Single words were presented on a screen in sets at a speed sequentially varying ranging from 600 to 1,600 words per minute. After each set a comprehension test was administered.

Table 1.3   Average Human Interaction Speeds

Reading	
Prose text:	250–300 words per minute.
Proofreading text on paper:	200 words per minute.
Proofreading text on a monitor:	180 words per minute.
Listening:	150–160 words per minute.
Speaking to a computer:	105 words per minute.
After recognition corrections:	25 words per minute.
Keying	
Typewriter	
Fast typist:	150 words per minute and higher.
Average typist:	60–70 words per minute.
Computer	
Transcription:	33 words per minute.
Composition:	19 words per minute.
Two finger typists	
Memorized text:	37 words per minute.
Copying text:	27 words per minute.
Hand printing	
Memorized text:	31 words per minute.
Copying text:	22 words per minute.

For measured comprehension scores of 75 percent or higher, the average reading speed was 1,212 words per minute. This is about 3.5 times faster than reading in the traditional way. Bailey concludes that computer technology can help improve reading speeds, but nontraditional techniques must be used.

Listening. Words can be comfortably heard and understood at a rate of 150 to 160 words per minute. This is generally the recommended rate for audio books and video narration (Williams, 1998). Omoigui, et al, (1999) did find, however, that when normal speech is speeded up using compression, a speed of 210 words per minute results in no loss of comprehension.

Speaking. Dictating to a computer occurs at a rate of about 105 words per minute (Karat, et al., 1999; Lewis, 1999). Speech recognizer misrecognitions often occur, however, and when word correction times are factored in, the speed drops significantly, to an average of 25 words per minute. Karat, et al. (1999) also found that the speaking rate of new users was 14 words per minute during transcription and 8 words per minute during composition.

Keying. Fast typewriter typists can key at rates of 150 words per minute and higher. Average typing speed is considered to be about 60–70 words per minute. Computer keying has been found to be much slower, however. Speed for simple transcription found by Karat, et al. (1999) was only 33 words per minute and for composition only 19 words per minute. In this study, the fastest typists typed at only 40 words per minute, the slowest at 23 words per minute. Brown (1988) reports that two-finger typists can key memorized text at 37 words per minute and copied text at 27 words per minute. Something about the computer, its software, and the keyboard does seem to significantly degrade the keying process. (And two-finger typists are not really that bad off after all.)

Hand printing. People hand print memorized text at about 31 words per minute. Text is copied at about 22 words per minute (Brown, 1988).

Performance versus Preference

Occasionally, when asked, people may prefer an interface design feature that actually yields poorer performance than another feature. Numerous instances of performance/preference differences have been reported in the literature (Andre and Wickens, 1995). Examples include pointing with a mouse or cursor, alternative menu interaction techniques, use of color, two-dimensional versus three-dimensional displays, and prototype fidelity.

Preferences are influenced by a number of things, including familiarity, aesthetics, novelty, and perceived effort in feature use. Rarely are people aware of the many human mechanisms responsible for the speed and accuracy of human-computer interaction. Ideally, in design, always augment preferences with performance measures and try to achieve an optimized solution. Where optimization is impossible, however, implement the feature that provides the best performance, and, very importantly, explain to the user why this is being done. In these cases the user may *not* always be right.

Methods for Gaining an Understanding of Users

Gould (1988) suggests using the following kinds of techniques to gain an understanding of users, their tasks and needs, the organization where they work, and the environment where the system may be used.

- Visit user locations, particularly if they are unfamiliar to you, to gain an understanding of the user's work environment.
- Talk with users about their problems, difficulties, wishes, and what works well now. Establish direct contact; avoid relying on intermediaries.
- Observe users working or performing a task to see what they do, their difficulties, and their problems.
- Videotape users working or performing a task to illustrate and study problems and difficulties.
- Learn about the work organization where the system may be installed.
- Have users think aloud as they do something to uncover details that may not otherwise be solicited.
- Try the job yourself. It may expose difficulties that are not known, or expressed, by users.

- Prepare surveys and questionnaires to obtain a larger sample of user opinions.

- Establish testable behavioral target goals to give management a measure for what progress has been made and what is still required.

These techniques will be addressed in a more detailed basis in the next step, "Understand the Business Function."

In conclusion, this chapter has addressed *the* most important principle in interface and screen design. Simply stated, it is this: *Know your user, client, or customer.*

Understand the
Business Function

A thorough understanding of the user has been obtained, and the focus now shifts to the business function being addressed. Requirements must be determined and user activities being performed must be described through task analysis. From these, a conceptual model of the system will be formulated. Design standards must also be created (if not already available), usability goals established, and training and documentation needs determined.

A detailed discussion of all of these topics is beyond the scope of this book. The reader in need of more detail is referred to books exclusively addressing systems analysis, task analysis, usability, training, and documentation. The general steps to be performed are:

- Perform a business definition and requirements analysis.
- Determine basic business functions.
- Describe current activities through task analysis.
- Develop a conceptual model of the system.
- Establish design standards or style guides.
- Establish system usability design goals.
- Define training and documentation needs.

Business Definition and Requirements Analysis

The objective of this phase is to establish the need for a system. A requirement is an objective that must be met. A product description is developed and refined, based on input from users or marketing. There are many techniques for capturing information for determining requirements. Keil and Carmel (1995), Popowicz (1995), and Fuccella et al. (1999) described many of the methods summarized in Table 2.1 and discussed shortly. They have also provided insights into their advantages and disadvantages. The techniques listed are classified as direct and indirect. Direct methods consist of face-to-face meetings with, or actual viewing of, users to solicit requirements. Indirect methods impose an intermediary, someone or something, between the users and the developers.

Before beginning the analysis, the developer should be aware of the policies and work culture of the organization being studied. He or she should also be familiar with any current system or process the new system is intended to supplement or replace.

Table 2.1   Some Techniques for Determining Requirements

DIRECT METHODS

Individual Face-to-Face Interview
- A one-on-one visit with the user to obtain information. It may be structured or somewhat open-ended.

Telephone Interview or Survey
- A structured interview conducted via telephone.

Traditional Focus Group
- A small group of users and a moderator brought together to verbally discuss the requirements.

Facilitated Team Workshop
- A facilitated, structured workshop held with users to obtain requirements information. Similar to the Traditional Focus Group.

Observational Field Study
- Users are observed and monitored for an extended time to learn what they do.

Requirements Prototyping
- A demo, or very early prototype, is presented to users for comments concerning functionality.

User-Interface Prototyping
- A demo, or early prototype, is presented to users to uncover user-interface issues and problems.

Usability Laboratory Testing
- Users at work are observed, evaluated, and measured in a specially constructed laboratory.

Card Sorting for Web Sites
- A technique to establish groupings of information for Web sites.

INDIRECT METHODS

MIS Intermediary
- A company representative defines the user's goals and needs to designers and developers.

Paper Survey or Questionnaire
- A survey or questionnaire is administered to a sample of users using traditional mail methods to obtain their needs.

Electronic Survey or Questionnaire
- A survey or questionnaire is administered to a sample of users using e-mail or the Web to obtain their needs.

Electronic Focus Group
- A small group of users and a moderator discuss the requirements online using workstations.

Marketing and Sales
- Company representatives who regularly meet customers obtain suggestions or needs, current and potential.

Support Line
- Information collected by the unit that helps customers with day-to-day problems is analyzed (Customer Support, Technical Support, Help Desk, etc.).

E-Mail or Bulletin Board
- Problems, questions, and suggestions from users posted to a bulletin board or through e-mail are analyzed.

User Group
- Improvements are suggested by customer groups who convene periodically to discuss software usage.

Competitor Analyses
- A review of competitor's products or Web sites is used to gather ideas, uncover design requirements and identify tasks.

Trade Show
- Customers at a trade show are presented a mock-up or prototype and asked for comments.

Other Media Analysis
- An analysis of how other media, print or broadcast, present the process, information, or subject matter of interest.

System Testing
- New requirements and feedback are obtained from ongoing product testing

Direct Methods

The significant advantage of the direct methods is the opportunity they provide to hear the user's comments in person and firsthand. Person-to-person encounters permit multiple channels of communication (body language, voice inflections, and so on) and provide the opportunity to immediately follow up on vague or incomplete data. Here are some recommended direct methods for getting input from users.

Individual Face-to-Face Interview

A one-on-one visit is held with the user. It may be structured or more open-ended. The interview must have focus and topics to be covered must be carefully planned so data is collected in a common framework, and to ensure that all important aspects are thoroughly covered. A formal questionnaire should not be used, however. Useful topics to ask the user to describe in an interview include:

- The activities performed in completing a task or achieving a goal or objective.
- The methods used to perform an activity.
- What interactions exist with other people or systems.

It is also very useful to also uncover any:

- Potential measures of system usability
- Unmentioned exceptions to standard policies or procedures.
- Relevant knowledge the user must possess to perform the activity.

If designing a Web site, the following kinds of interview questions are appropriate for asking potential users:

- Present a site outline or proposal and then solicit comments on the thoroughness of content coverage, and suggestions for additional content.
- Ask users to describe situations in which the proposed Web site might be useful.
- Ask users to describe what is liked and disliked about the Web sites of potential competitors.
- Ask users to describe how particular Web site tasks should be accomplished.

Time must also be allowed for free conversation in interviews. Recording the session for playback to the entire design team provides all involved with some insights into user needs.

Advantages of a personal interview are that you can give the user your full attention, can easily include follow-up questions to gain additional information, will have more time to discuss topics in detail, and will derive a deeper understanding of your users, their experiences, attitudes, beliefs, and desires. Disadvantages of interviews are that they can be costly and time-consuming to conduct, and someone skilled in interviewing techniques should perform them.

The interviewer must establish a positive relationship with the user, ask questions in a neutral manner, be a good listener, and know when and how to probe for more information.

Telephone Interview or Survey

This interview is conducted using the telephone. It must have structure and be well planned. Arranging the interview in advance allows the user to prepare for it. Telephone interviews are less expensive and less invasive than personal interviews. They can be used much more frequently and are extremely effective for very specific information. Telephone interviews have some disadvantages. It is impossible to gather contextual information, such as a description of the working environment, replies may be easily influenced by the interviewer's comments, and body language cues are missing. Also, it may be difficult to contact the right person for the telephone interview.

MAXIM   **Know thy users, for they are not you.**

Traditional Focus Group

A small group of users (8 to 12) and a moderator are brought together to discuss the requirements. While the discussion is loosely structured, the range of topics must be determined beforehand. A typical session lasts about two hours. The purpose of a focus group is to probe user's experiences, attitudes, beliefs, and desires, and to obtain their reactions to ideas or prototypes. Focus groups are not usually useful for establishing how users really work or what kinds of usability problems they really have. Focus group discussion can be influenced by group dynamics, for good or bad. Recording of the session, either video or audio, will permit later detailed analysis of participants comments. Again, the recording can also be played for the entire design team, providing insights into user needs for all developers. Setting up focus group involves the following:

- Establish the objectives of the session.
- Select participants representing typical users, or potential users.
- Write a script for the moderator to follow.
- Find a skilled moderator to facilitate discussion, to ensure that the discussion remains focused on relevant topics, and to ensure that everyone participates.
- Allow the moderator flexibility in using the script.
- Take good notes, using the session recording for backup and clarification.

Facilitated Team Workshop

A facilitated team workshop is similar in structure and content to a traditional focus group but is slightly less formal. A common technique used in system requirements determination for many years, it is now being replaced (at least in name) by focus groups. Team workshops have had the potential to provide much useful information. Like focus groups, they do require a great deal of time to organize and run.

Observational Field Study

To see and learn what users actually do, they are watched and followed in their own environment, office, or home, in a range of contexts for a period of time. Observation provides good insight into tasks being performed, the working environment and conditions, the social environment, and working practices. It is more objective, natural, and realistic. Observation, however, can be time-consuming and expensive. Video recording of the observation sessions will permit detailed task analysis. Playing the recording for the entire design team again provides all involved with some insights into user tasks.

Requirements Prototyping

A demonstration model, or very early prototype, is presented to users for their comments concerning functionality. Prototypes are discussed more fully in Step 14, "Test, Test, and Retest."

User-Interface Prototyping

A demonstration model, or early prototype, is presented to users to uncover user-interface issues and problems. Again, prototypes are discussed more fully in Step 14.

Usability Laboratory Testing

A special laboratory is constructed and users brought in to perform actual newly designed tasks. They are observed and results measured, and evaluated to establish the usability of the product at that point in time. Usability tests uncover what people actually do, not what they think they do, a common problem with verbal descriptions. The same scenarios can be presented to multiple users, providing comparative data from several users. Problems uncovered may result in modification of the requirements. Usability labs can generate much useful information but are expensive to create and operate. Usability labs are also discussed in Step 14.

Card Sorting for Web Sites

This is a technique used to establish hierarchical groupings of information for Web sites. It is normally used only after gathering substantial site content information using other analysis techniques. Potential content topics are placed on individual index cards and users are asked to sort the cards into groupings that are meaningful to them. Card sorting assists in building the site's structure, map, and page content. Briefly, the process is as follows:

- From previous analyses, identify about 50 content topics and inscribe them on index cards. Limit topics to no more than 100.

- Provide blank index cards for names of additional topics the participant may want to add, and colored blank cards for groupings that the participant will be asked to create.
- Number the cards on the back.
- Arrange for a facility with large enough table for spreading out cards.
- Select participants representing a range of users. Use one or two people at a time and 5 to 12 in total.
- Explain the process to the participants, saying that you are trying to determine what categories of information will be useful, what groupings make sense, and what the groupings should be called.
- Ask the participants to sort the cards and talk out loud while doing so. Advise the participants that additional content cards may be named and added as they think necessary during the sorting process.
- Observe and take notes as the participants talk about what they are doing. Pay particular attention to the sorting rationale.
- Upon finishing the sorting, if a participant has too many groupings ask that they be arranged hierarchically.
- Ask participants to provide a name for each grouping on the colored blank cards, using words that the user would expect to see that would lead them to that particular grouping.
- Make a record of the groupings using the numbers on the back of each card.
- Reshuffle the cards for the next session.
- When finished, analyze the results looking for commonalities among the different sorting sessions.

The sorting can also be accomplished on the Web. The National Institute of Standards and Technology (NIST, 2001) has developed a card-sorting tool. The designer sets up the cards and names the categories. The user then sorts by dragging and dropping.

Indirect Methods

An indirect method of requirements determination is one that places an intermediary between the developer and the user. This intermediary may be electronic or another person. Using an intermediary can certainly provide useful information. Working through an intermediary, however, takes away the multichannel communication advantages of face-to-face user-developer contact. Some electronic intermediaries do provide some advantages, as will be described. Imposition of a human intermediary can also create these additional problems. First, there may be a filtering or distortion of the message, either intentional or unintentional. Next, the intermediary may not possess a complete, or current, understanding of user's needs, passing on an incomplete or incorrect message. Finally, the intermediary may be a mechanism that discourages direct user-developer contact for political reasons. Indirect methods include the following.

MIS Intermediary

A company representative who defines the user's goals and needs to designers and developers fulfills this intermediary role. This representative may come from the Information Services department itself, or he or she may be from the using department. While much useful information can be provided, all too often this person does not have the breadth of knowledge needed to satisfy all design requirements.

Paper Survey or Questionnaire

A paper questionnaire or survey is administered to a sample of users to obtain their needs. Questionnaires have the potential to be used for a large target audience located most anywhere, and are much cheaper than customer visits. They generally, however, have a low return rate, often generating responses only from those "very happy" or "very unhappy." They may take a long time to collect and may be difficult to analyze. Questionnaires are useful for determining a user's attitudes, experiences and desires, but not for determining actual tasks and behaviors. Questionnaires should be composed mostly of closed questions (yes/no, multiple choice, short answer, and so on). Open-ended questions require much more analysis. Questionnaires should be relatively short and created by someone experienced in their design.

Electronic Survey or Questionnaire

A questionnaire or survey is administered to a sample of users via e-mail or the Web. Characteristics, advantages, and disadvantages are similar to paper surveys and questionnaires. They are, however, significantly less expensive then mailed surveys. The speed of their return can also be much faster than those distributed in a paper format. In creating an electronic survey:

- Determine the survey objectives.
- Determine where you will find the people to complete the survey.
- Create a mix of multiple choice and open-ended questions requiring short answers addressing the survey objectives.
- Keep it short, about 10 items or less is preferable.
- Keep it simple, requiring no more than 5–10 minutes to complete.

Also consider a follow-up more detailed survey, or surveys, called *iterative surveys*. Ask people who complete and return the initial survey if they are willing to answer more detailed questions. If so, create and send the more detailed survey. Among other things, the detailed survey content can address questions the initial survey raises. A useful follow-up survey goal is to ask the participant to prioritize their needs and to rank expected user tasks according to their importance. A third follow-up survey can also be designed to gather additional information about the most important requirements and tasks. Iterative surveys, of course, take a longer time to complete. Don't forget to thank participants for their help and time.

Electronic Focus Group Similar

An electronic focus group is similar to a traditional focus group except that the discussion is accomplished electronically using specialized software on a workstation, e-mail, or a Web site. As with the direct methods, the opportunity to immediately follow up on vague or incomplete data exists. All comments, ideas, and suggestions are available in hard-copy form for easier analysis. Specialized software can provide ratings or rankings of items presented in lists, a task requiring much more effort in a traditional focus group.

Other advantages of electronic focus groups over traditional focus groups are that the discussion is less influenced by group dynamics; has a smaller chance of being dominated by one or a few participants; can be anonymous, leading to more honest comments and less caution in proposing new ideas; can generate more ideas in a shorter time since all participants can communicate at once; and can lead to longer sessions since the participant is in a more comfortable "home environment" and not confined to a conference room. Among the disadvantages are that the depth and richness of verbal discussions does not exist and the communication enhancement aspects of seeing participant's body language are missing.

Marketing and Sales

Company representatives who regularly meet customers obtain suggestions or needs, current and potential. This information is collected inexpensively, since the representative is going to visit the company anyway. Business representatives do have knowledge of the nature of customers, the business, and the needs that have to be met. Some dangers: the information may be collected from the wrong people, the representative may unintentionally bias questions, there may be many company "filters" between the representative's contact and the end user, and quantities may sometimes be exaggerated. ("Lots of people are complaining about . . ." may mean only one or two.) The developers should know the interests and bias of the representatives collecting the information.

Support Line

Information is collected by the unit that helps customers with day-to-day problems (Customer Support, Technical Support, Help Desk, and so on). This is fairly inexpensive and the target user audience is correct. The focus of this method is usually only on problems, however.

E-Mail, Bulletin Boards or Guest Book

Problems, questions, and suggestions by users posted to a bulletin board, a guest book, or through e-mail are gathered and evaluated. Again, the focus of this method is usually only on problems. The responsibility is on the user to generate the recommendations, but this population often includes unhappy users. This is a fairly inexpensive method.

User Group

Improvements suggested by customer groups who convene periodically to discuss system and software usage are evaluated. User groups have the potential to provide a lot of good information, if organized properly. They require careful planning, however.

Competitor Analysis

Reviews of competitor's products, or Web sites, can also be used to gather ideas, uncover design requirements, and identify tasks. The designers can perform this evaluation or, even better, users can be asked to perform the evaluation.

Trade Show

Customers at a trade show can be exposed to a mock-up or prototype and asked for comments. This method is dependent on the knowledge level of the customers and may provide only a superficial view of most prominent features.

Other Media Analysis

Analyze how other media, print or broadcast, present the process, information, or subject matter of interest. Findings can be used to gather ideas, uncover design requirements, and identify better ways to accomplish or show something.

System Testing

New requirements and feedback stemming from ongoing system testing can be accumulated, evaluated, and implemented as necessary.

Requirements Collection Guidelines

- Establish 4 to 6 different developer-user links.
- Provide most reliance on direct links.

Keil and Carmel (1995) evaluated the suitability and effectiveness of various requirements-gathering methods by collecting data on 28 projects in 17 different companies. Fourteen of the projects were rated as relatively successful, 14 as relatively unsuccessful. Each requirements collection method was defined as a developer-user *link*. Their findings and conclusions:

Establish 4 to 6 Different Developer-User Links

The more successful projects had utilized a greater number of developer-user links than the less successful projects. The mean number of links for the successful projects:

5.4; the less successful: 3.2. This difference was statistically significant. Few projects used more than 60 percent of all possible links. Keil and Carmel recommend, based upon their data, that, at minimum, four different developer-user links must be established in the requirements-gathering process. They also concluded that the law of diminishing returns begins to set in after six links.

Effectiveness ratings of the most commonly used links in their study were also obtained. (Not all the above-described techniques were considered in their study.) On a 1 to 5 scale (1 = ineffective, 5 = very effective) the following methods had the highest ratings:

Custom projects (software developed for internal use and usually not for sale):

Facilitated Teams	5.0
User-Interface Prototype	4.0
Requirements Prototype	3.6
Interviews	3.5

Package projects (software developed for external use and usually for sale):

Support Line	4.3
Interviews	3.8
User-Interface Prototype	3.3
User Group	3.3

Provide the Most Reliance on Direct Links

The problems associated with the less successful projects resulted, at least in part, from too much reliance on indirect links, or using intermediaries. Ten of the 14 less successful projects had used none, or only one, *direct* link. The methods with the highest effectiveness ratings listed above were mostly direct links.

Keil and Carmel caution that number of links is only a partial measure of user participation. How well the link is employed in practice is also very important.

Determining Basic Business Functions

A detailed description of what the product will do is prepared. Major system functions are listed and described, including critical system inputs and outputs. A flowchart of major functions is developed. The process the developer will use is summarized as follows:

- Gain a complete understanding of the user's mental model based upon:
  - The user's needs and the user's profile.
  - A user task analysis.
- Develop a conceptual model of the system based upon the user's mental model. This includes:
  - Defining objects.
  - Developing metaphors.

The user interface activities described in Steps 1 and 3 are usually performed concurrently with these steps.

Understanding the User's Mental Model

The next phase in interface design is to thoroughly describe the expected system user or users and their current tasks. The former will be derived from the kinds of information collected in Step 1 "Understand the User or Client," and the requirements analysis techniques described above. A goal of task analysis, and a goal of understanding the user, is to gain a picture of the user's mental model. A mental model is an internal representation of a person's current conceptualization and understanding of something. Mental models are gradually developed in order to understand, explain, and do something. Mental models enable a person to predict the actions necessary to do things if the actions have been forgotten or have not yet been encountered.

Performing a Task Analysis

User activities are precisely described in a task analysis. Task analysis involves breaking down the user's activities to the individual task level. The goal is to obtain an understanding of why and how people currently do the things that will be automated. Knowing why establishes the major work goals; knowing how provides details of actions performed to accomplish these goals. Task analysis also provides information concerning workflows, the interrelationships between people, objects, and actions, and the user's conceptual frameworks. The output of a task analysis is a complete description of all user tasks and interactions.

Work activities are studied and/or described by users using the techniques just reviewed; direct observation, interviews, questionnaires, or obtaining measurements of actual current system usage. Measurements, for example, may be obtained for the frequency with which tasks are performed or the number of errors that are made.

One result of a task analysis is a listing of the user's current tasks. This list should be well documented and maintained. Changes in task requirements can then be easily incorporated as design iteration occurs. Another result is a list of objects the users see as important to what they do. The objects can be sorted into the following categories:

- Concrete objects—things that can be touched.
- People who are the object of sentences—normally organization employees, customers, for example.
- Forms or journals—things that keep track of information.
- People who are the subject of sentences—normally the users of a system.
- Abstract objects—anything not included above.

Developing Conceptual Models

The output of the task analysis is the creation, by the designer, of a conceptual model for the user interface. A conceptual model is the general conceptual framework through which the system's functions are presented. Such a model describes how the interface will present objects, the relationships between objects, the properties of objects, and the actions that will be performed. A conceptual model is based on the user's mental model. Since the term mental model refers to a person's current level of knowledge about something, people will *always* have them. Since mental models are influenced by a person's experiences, and people have different experiences, no two user mental models are likely to be exactly the same. Each person looks at the interface from a slightly different perspective.

The goal of the designer is to facilitate for the user the development of useful *mental model of the system*. This is accomplished by presenting to the user a *meaningful conceptual model of the system*. When the user then encounters the system, his or her *existing mental model* will, hopefully, mesh well with the system's conceptual model. As a person works with a system, he or she then develops a *mental model of the system*. The system mental model the user derives is based upon system's behavior, including factors such as the system inputs, actions, outputs (including screens and messages), and its feedback and guidance characteristics, all of which are components of the conceptual model. Documentation and training also play a formative role. Mental models will be developed regardless of the particular design of a system, and then they will be modified with experience. What must be avoided in design is creating for the user a conceptual model that leads to the creation of a false mental model of the system, or that inhibits the user from creating a meaningful or efficient mental model.

Guidelines for Designing Conceptual Models

- Reflect the user's mental model, not the designer's.
- Draw physical analogies or present metaphors.
- Comply with expectancies, habits, routines, and stereotypes.
- Provide action-response compatibility.
- Make invisible parts and process of a system visible.
- Provide proper and correct feedback.
- Avoid anything unnecessary or irrelevant.
- Provide design consistency.
- Provide documentation and a help system that will reinforce the conceptual model.
- Promote the development of both novice and expert mental models.

Unfortunately, little research is available to assist the software designer in creating *conceptual models*. Development of a user's mental model can be aided, however, by following these general guidelines for conceptual model development.

Reflect the user's mental model, not the designer's. A user will have different expectations and levels of knowledge than the designer. So, the mental models of the user and designer will be different. The user is concerned with the task to be performed, the business objectives that must be fulfilled. The designer's model is focused on the design of the interface, the kinds of objects, the interaction methods, and the visual representations on the screen. Objects must be defined, along with their relationships, behaviors, and properties. Interaction methods must also be defined, such as input mechanisms, interaction techniques, and the contents of menus. Visual screen representations must also be created, including functionality and appearance.

Draw physical analogies or present metaphors. Replicate what is familiar and well known. Duplicate actions that are already well learned. The success of graphical systems can be attributed, in part, to their employing the desktop metaphor. A metaphor, to be effective, must be widely applicable within an interface. Metaphors that are only partially or occasionally applicable should not be used. In the event that a metaphor cannot be explicitly employed in a new interface, structure the new interface in terms of familiar aspects from the manual world.

Comply with expectancies, habits, routines, and stereotypes. Create a system that builds on knowledge, habits, routines, and expectancies that already exist. Use familiar associations, avoiding the new and unfamiliar. With color, for example, accepted meanings for red, yellow, and green are already well established. Use words and symbols in their customary ways. Replicate the language of the user, and create icons reflecting already known images.

Provide action-response compatibility. All system responses should be compatible with the actions that elicit them. Names of commands, for example, should reflect the actions that will occur. The organization of keys in documentation or help screens should reflect the ordering that actually exists on the keyboard.

Make invisible parts of the system visible. Systems are composed of parts and processes, many of which are invisible to the user. In creating a mental model, a person must make a hypothesis about what is invisible and how it relates to what is visible. New users of a system often make erroneous or incomplete assumptions about what is invisible and develop a faulty mental model. As more experience is gained, their mental models evolve to become more accurate and complete. Making invisible parts of a system visible will speed up the process of developing correct mental models.

An example of a process being made visible can be illustrated by moving a document between files. In a command language interface, the document must be moved through a series of typed commands. The file is moved invisibly, and the user assumes correctly, unless an error message is received. In a graphical direct-manipulation system, the entire process is visible, with the user literally picking up the file in one folder by clicking on it, and dragging it to another folder.

Provide Proper and Correct Feedback. Be generous in providing feedback. Keep a person informed of what is happening, and what has happened, at all times, including:

- *Provide a continuous indication of status.* Mental models are difficult to develop if things happen, or are completed, unknown to the user. During long processing sequences, for example, interim status messages such as loading, "opening . . ." or "searching . . ." reassure the user and enable him or her to understand internal processes and more accurately predict how long something will take. Such messages also permit the pinpointing of problems if they occur.

- *Provide visible results of actions.* For example, highlight selected objects, display new locations of moved objects, and show files that are closed.

- *Display actions in progress.* For example, show a window that is being changed in size actually changing, not simply the window in its changed form. This will strengthen cause-and-effect relationships in the mental model.

- *Present as much context information as possible.* To promote contextual understanding, present as much background or historical information as possible. For example, on a menu screen or in navigation, maintain a listing of the choices selected to get to the current point. On a query or search screen, show the query or search criteria when displaying the results.

- *Provide clear, constructive, and correct error messages.* Incomplete or misleading error messages may cause false assumptions that violate and weaken the user's mental model. Error messages should always be structured to reinforce the mental model. For example, error messages addressing an incomplete action should specify *exactly* what is missing, not simply advise a person that something is incomplete.

Avoid the unnecessary or irrelevant. Never display irrelevant information on the screen. People may try to interpret it and integrate it into their mental models, thereby creating a false one. Irrelevant information might be unneeded data fields, screen controls, system status codes, or error message numbers. If potentially misleading information cannot be avoided, point this out to the user.

Also, do not overuse display techniques, or use them in meaningless ways. Too much color, for example, may distract people and cause them to make erroneous assumptions as they try to interpret the colors. The result will be a faulty and unclear mental model.

Provide design consistency. Design consistency reduces the number of concepts to be learned. Inconsistency requires the mastery of multiple models. If an occasional inconsistency cannot be avoided, explain it to the user. For example, if an error is caused by a user action that is inconsistent with other similar actions, explain in the error message that this condition exists. This will prevent the user from falsely assuming that the model he or she has been operating under is incorrect.

Provide documentation and a help system that will reinforce the conceptual model. Consistencies and metaphors should be explicitly described in the user documentation. This will assist a person in learning the system. Do not rely on the people to uncover consistencies and metaphors themselves. The help system should offer advice aimed at improving mental models.

Promote the development of both novice and expert mental models. Novices and experts are likely to bring to bear different mental models when using a system. It will be easier for novices to form an initial system mental model if they are protected from the full complexity of a system. Employ levels of functionality that can be revealed through progressive disclosure.

Defining Objects

- Determine all objects that have to be manipulated to get work done. Describe:
  — The objects used in tasks.
  — Object behavior and characteristics that differentiate each kind of object.
  — The relationship of objects to each other and the people using them.
  — The actions performed.
  — The objects to which actions apply.
  — State information or attributes that each object in the task must preserve, display, or allow to be edited.
- Identify the objects and actions that appear most often in the workflow.
- Make the several most important objects very obvious and easy to manipulate.

All *objects* that have to be manipulated to get work done must be clearly described. Their behavioral characteristics must be established and the attributes that differentiate each kind of object must be identified. Relationships of objects to each other and the people using them must be determined. The actions people take on objects must also be described. State information or attributes that each object in the task must preserve, display, or allow to be edited must be defined.

The most important objects must be made very obvious and easy to manipulate. Weinschenk (1995) suggests that if the most important objects are not obvious in the workflow, go through the workflow document highlighting all nouns and verbs associated with nouns. Frequently appearing nouns are possible major objects. Frequently appearing verbs are actions pointing to possible major objects.

Developing Metaphors

- Choose the analogy that works best for each object and its actions.
- Use real-world metaphors.
- Use simple metaphors.
- Use common metaphors.
- Multiple metaphors may coexist.
- Use major metaphors, even if you can't exactly replicate them visually.
- Test the selected metaphors.

A *metaphor* is a concept where one's body of knowledge about one thing is used to understand something else. Metaphors act as building blocks of a system, aiding understanding of how a system works and is organized. Select a metaphor or analogy for the defined objects. Choose the analogy that works best for the objects and their actions.

Real-world metaphors are most often the best choice. Replicate what is familiar and well known. Duplicate actions that are already well learned. If a faster or better way exists to do something, however, use it. Use simple metaphors, as they are almost always the most powerful. Use common metaphors; uniqueness adds complexity. Multiple metaphors may coexist. Use major metaphors even if you can't exactly replicate them visually on the screen. Exactly mimicking the real world does not always aid understanding. It can lead a person to expect behavioral limitations that do not actually exist. A representation will be satisfactory. Finally, test the selected metaphors. Do they match one's expectations and experiences? Are they easily understood or quickly learned? Change them, if testing deems it necessary.

A common metaphor in a graphical system is the desktop and its components, items such as folders and a trash bin. The Web utilizes a library metaphor for the activities of browsing and searching. Browsing in a library occurs when you wander around book stacks looking for something interesting to read. When searching you devise an active plan to find some specific information. For example, first, check the topic in the card catalog. Next, ask the librarian, and so forth.

A word of caution in creating metaphors, however. Today's technology permits doing a lot of things, many not even thinkable in the old manual world (or even the old computer world). Do not constrain yourself from developing a more powerful interface because a current metaphor just happens to exist. If you do limit yourself, you may find yourself in the position of the farm tractor designers of the early last century. In developing a new tractor, the metaphor was the horse and plow. Reins controlled the horse, so reins were installed on the tractor for controlling it as well. Needless to say it was not successful. We do not want to read about you sometime later this century.

The User's New Mental Model

When the system is implemented, and a person interacts with the new system and its interface, an attempt will be made by the person to understand the system based upon the existing mental model brought to the interaction. If the designer has correctly reflected the user's mental model in design, the user's mental model is reinforced and a feeling that the interface is intuitive will likely develop. Continued interaction with the system may influence and modify the user's concept of the system, and his or her mental model may be modified as well. Refinement of this mental model, a normal process, is aided by well-defined distinctions between objects and being consistent across all aspects of the interface.

What happens, however, if the new system does not accurately reflect the user's existing mental model? The results include breakdowns in understanding, confusion, errors, loss of trust, and frustration. Another result is an inability to perform the task or job.

Historically, when system designers have known in advance there was a gap between their conceptual model and the mental model the user would bring to the new system, designers have tried to bridge this gap through extensive documentation and training. The problems with this approach are: people are unproductive while being trained, people rarely read the documentation and training materials, and, even if the training material is read, the material is presented out of context. This creates difficulties for the users in understanding the material's relevance to their needs and goals.

Design Standards or Style Guides

A design standard or style guide documents an agreed-upon way of doing something. In interface design it describes the appearance and behavior of the interface and provides some guidance on the proper use of system components. It also defines the interface standards, rules, guidelines, and conventions that must be followed in detailed design. It will be based on the characteristics of the system's hardware and software, the principles of good interface and screen design, the needs of system users, and any unique company or organization requirements that may exist.

Value of Standards and Guidelines

Developing and applying design standards or guidelines achieves design consistency. This is valuable to *users* because the standards and guidelines:

- Allow faster performance.
- Reduce errors.
- Reduce training time.
- Foster better system utilization.
- Improve satisfaction.
- Improve system acceptance.

They are valuable to system *developers* because they:

- Increase visibility of the human-computer interface.
- Simplify design.
- Provide more programming and design aids, reducing programming time.
- Reduce redundant effort.
- Reduce training time.
- Provide a benchmark for quality control testing.

Business System Interface Standards and Guidelines

While some businesses and organizations developed and implemented human-computer interface design standards as far back as the 1970s (for example, see Galitz and DiMatteo, 1974), it was not until the late 1980s the computer industry in general and other end-user organizations, fully awakened to their need. Then, a flurry of guideline documents began to appear. Some were for internal company or organization use only; others were published for general consumption by companies such as IBM (1987), Sun Microsystems (1990), Apple Computer (1992b), and Microsoft (1992). These guidelines have been updated over the last decade, and today many of these interface guidelines are published on the Web as well.

Concurrently government and trade organizations also began working on developing interface guidelines and standards. Organizations addressing these issues have included the International Standards Organization (ISO), the American National Standards Institute (ANSI), and the Human Factors and Ergonomics Society.

Unfortunately, past research on guideline utilization in business systems has hardly been encouraging. Standards conformance problems identified include difficulties in finding information being sought, difficulties in interpreting information, and numerous rules violations. Thovtrup and Nielsen (1991), for example, reported that designers were only able to achieve a 71 percent compliance with a two-page standard in a laboratory setting. In an evaluation of three real systems, they found that the mandatory rules of the company's screen design standard were violated 32 to 55 percent of the time.

Thovtrup and Nielsen, in analyzing why the rules in the screen design standard were broken, found a very positive designer attitude toward the standard, both in terms of its value and content. Rules were not adhered to, however, for the following reasons:

- An alternative design solution was better than that mandated by the standard.
- Available development tools did not allow compliance with the standard.
- Compliance with the standard was planned, but time was not yet available to implement it.
- The rule that was broken was not known or was overlooked.

Web Guidelines and Style Guides

Web interface design issues have also unleashed a plethora of Web-specific design guidelines and style guides, many of which are found on the Web itself. These guidelines can be seen on the sites of the various computer companies and interface consulting firms, in newsletters, and even on personal Web sites. While many of the traditional interface guidelines are applicable in a Web environment, the Web does impose a host of additional considerations.

The haste to publish Web design guidelines has been fueled by the explosive growth of the Web and a corresponding explosive growth in the number of developers creating sites for public access. In the brief existence of the Web, there has not been an opportunity for conventions and style guides to be properly developed and then accepted by the development community. This situation is made worse by the fact that many Web developers have had limited knowledge of traditional interface issues and concerns, and many are unfamiliar with the traditional interface design guidelines. Web guideline documents have attempted to fill this void.

Since a Web user can freely move among a seemingly endless supply of sites, no site will be seen in isolation. Commonality is of even greater importance than in business systems, where movement occurs between small numbers of applications. Today, many uniquely Web standards and guidelines are evolving by trial and error. Things are being tried to see what works best. De facto standards are being established when an overwhelming majority of big sites focus on one way to do something. An example is a menu bar that now frequently appears down the left side of the page. Standards and conventions will continue to evolve with experience and as the results of usability research become available. Worldwide standards are also being looked at by organizations such as the World Wide Web Consortium (2001).

Document Design

- Include checklists to present principles and guidelines.
- Provide a rationale for why the particular guidelines should be used.
- Provide a rationale describing the conditions under which various design alternatives are appropriate.
- Include concrete examples of correct design.
- Design the guideline document following recognized principles for good document design.
- Provide good access mechanisms such as a thorough index, a table of contents, glossaries, and checklists.

Checklists and rationale. Provide checklists for presenting key principles and guidelines. Checklists permit ease in scanning, ease in referring to key points, and make a document more readable by breaking up long sequences of text. Also provide a rationale for why the particular guidelines should be used. Understanding the reasoning will increase guideline acceptance. This is especially important if the guideline is a deviation from a previous design practice. Also, when two or more design alternatives exist, provide a rationale describing the conditions under which the alternatives are appropriate. It may not be easy for designers to infer when various alternatives are appropriate. You have probably noticed that this book uses a checklist format to present key guidelines and thoughts, and guideline rationale is described in the text.

Concrete examples. To be effective, a guideline must include many concrete examples of correct design. Learning by imitation is often a way we learn.

Document design and access. Always design the document, be it paper or electronic, by following recognized principles for good document design. This greatly enhances readability. Provide good access mechanisms such as a thorough index, a table of contents, glossaries, and checklists. An unattractive or hard to use document will not be inviting and consequently will not be used.

Design Support and Implementation

- Use all available reference sources in creating the guidelines.
- Use development and implementation tools that support the guidelines.
- Begin applying the guidelines immediately.

Available Reference Sources. Use all the available reference design sources in creating your guidelines. References include this text, other books on user interface design, project-specific guidelines, and the style guides for interface design and Web design created by companies such as Apple, IBM, Microsoft, and Sun. Other reference sources that meet your needs should also be utilized.

Tools. Use tools that support implementation of the guidelines you have established. Development tools make the design process much easier. If the design tools cannot support the guideline, it cannot be adhered to.

Applying the Guidelines. Two questions often asked are, "Is it too late to develop and implement standards?" and "What will be the impact on systems and screens now being used?" To address these questions, researchers reformatted several alphanumeric inquiry screens to improve their comprehensibility and readability. When these reformatted screens were presented to expert system users, decision-making time remained the same but errors were reduced. For novice system users, the reformatted screens brought large improvements in learning speed and accuracy. Therefore, it appears, that changes that enhance screens will benefit *both* novice and expert users already familiar with the current screens. It is never too late to begin to change.

System Training and Documentation Needs

Training and documentation are also an integral part of any development effort.

Training

System training will be based on user needs, system conceptual design, system learning goals, and system performance goals. Training may include such tools as formal or video training, manuals, online tutorials, reference manuals, quick reference guides, and online help. (Various types of training methods are more fully addressed in Step 9.) Training needs must be established and training components developed as the design process unfolds. This will ensure that the proper kinds of training are defined, properly integrated with the design, and developed correctly. This will also assure that the design is not imposing an unreasonable learning and training requirement on the user. Any potential problems can also be identified and addressed earlier in the design process, reducing later problems and modification costs.

MYTH   **That problems can be handled with documentation and training.**

Documentation

System documentation is a reference point, a form of communication, and a more concrete design—words that can be seen and understood. It will also be based on user needs, system conceptual design, and system performance goals. Creating documentation during the development progress will uncover issues and reveal omissions that might not otherwise be detected until later in the design process. As with training, any potential problems can be identified and addressed earlier in the design process, again reducing later problems and modification costs.

Understand the Principles of Good Screen Design

A well-designed screen:

- Reflects the capabilities, needs, and tasks of its users.
- Is developed within the physical constraints imposed by the hardware on which it is displayed.
- Effectively utilizes the capabilities of its controlling software.
- Achieves the business objectives of the system for which it is designed.

To accomplish these goals, the designer must first understand the principles of good screen design. What follows is an extensive compilation of general screen design guidelines for the user interface. It begins with a detailed series of guidelines dealing with user considerations, including the test for a good design, organizing screen elements, screen navigation and flow, visually pleasing composition, typography, and reading, browsing, and searching on the Web. The step concludes with considerations imposed by a system's hardware and software.

Human Considerations in Screen Design

Use of a screen, and a system, is affected by many factors. These include: how much information is presented on a screen, how a screen is organized, the language used on the screen, the distinctiveness of the screen's components, its aesthetics, and a screen's consistency with other screens. First, let's look at what aspects of poor screen design can be distracting to the user, what a user is looking for in good design, and the kinds of things screen users do interacting with a system or Web site. Then, we'll address the principles of good design.

How to Distract the Screen User

Barnett (1993) has compiled a list of factors that, when poorly designed, hinder the use of paper forms. These factors certainly apply to electronic forms and screens as well, and include:

- Unclear captions and badly worded questions. These cause hesitation, and rereading, in order to determine what is needed or must be provided. They may also be interpreted incorrectly, causing errors.
- Improper type and graphic emphasis. Important elements are hidden. Emphasis is drawn away from what is important to that which is not important.
- Misleading headings. These also create confusion and inhibit one's ability to see existing relationships.
- Information requests perceived to be irrelevant or unnecessary. The value of what one is doing is questioned, as is the value of the system.
- Information requests that require one to backtrack and rethink a previous answer, or look ahead to determine possible context. Inefficiency results, and mistakes increase.
- Cluttered, cramped layout. Poor layout creates a bad initial impact and leads to more errors. It may easily cause system rejection.
- Poor quality of presentation, legibility, appearance, and arrangement. Again, this degrades performance, slowing the user down and causing more errors.

Howlett (1995) based upon her experiences at Microsoft suggests the most common problems in visual interface design are:

- Visual inconsistency in screen detail presentation and with the operating system.
- Lack of restraint in the use of design features and elements.
- Overuse of three-dimensional presentations.
- Overuse of too many bright colors.
- Poorly designed icons.
- Bad typography
- Metaphors that are either overbearing or too cute, or too literal thereby restricting design options.

These kinds of problems, she concludes, lead to screens that can be chaotic, confusing, disorganized, distracting, or just plain ugly.

Web screens, as were recently described, also present to the user a variety of distractions. Summarized below, these distractions include:

- Numerous visual and auditory interruptions.
- Extensive visual clutter.

- Poor information readability.
- Incomprehensible screen components.
- Confusing and inefficient navigation.
- Inefficient operations and extensive waste of user time.
- Excessive or inefficient page scrolling.
- Information overload.
- Design inconsistency.
- Outdated information.
- Stale design caused by emulation of printed documents and past systems.

Poor design is not a new phenomenon. It has existed since people began interacting with media used for presenting and collecting information. Some of the distractions have been around a long time; others are fairly new, the byproduct of technological advances. Interface distractions cause a person to think about things they shouldn't have to think about, and divert one's attention from performing a task or satisfying a need. All distractions must be eliminated in design.

What Screen Users Want

What are people looking for in the design of screens? One organization asked a group of screen users and got the following responses:

- An orderly, clean, clutter-free appearance.
- An obvious indication of what is being shown and what should be done with it.
- Expected information located where it *should* be.
- A clear indication of what relates to what, including options, headings, captions, data, and so forth.
- Plain, simple English.
- A simple way of finding out what is in a system and how to get it out.
- A clear indication of when an action can make a permanent change in the data or system.

The desired direction is toward simplicity, clarity, and understandability—qualities lacking in many of today's screens.

What Screen Users Do

When interacting with a computer, a person:

1. **Identifies a task to be performed or need to be fulfilled.** The task may be very structured, including activities such as: enter this data from this form into the system, answer a specific question regarding the status of an order, or collect the necessary information from a customer to make a reservation. Alternatively, the task may have some structure but also include more free-form activities, including

answering questions such as: what is the best local rehabilitation program in which to enroll my client, or what are my customer's exact needs and then which of our products features are best suited for him or her. Finally, the need may be very general or even vague. Where should I take an exotic vacation near a beautiful beach? Where can I get the best price on a new PC?

2. **Decides how the task will be completed or the need fulfilled.** For a structured or semi-structured task a set of transaction screens will be available. The proper transaction is identified and the relevant screen series retrieved. To satisfy a general or vague need will require browsing or searching through screens that might possibly have relevance.

3. **Manipulates the computer's controls.** To perform the task or satisfy the need, the keyboard, mouse, and other similar devices are used to select choices from lists, choose commands to be performed, key data into text boxes, and so forth.

MAXIM **People will spend many, many, hours *staring* at your screens.**

4. **Gathers the necessary data.** Using structured and semi-structured transaction screens information is collected from its source: a form, a coworker, or a customer. This information is identified on the screen, or placed on the screen, through control manipulation. To satisfy a general or vague need may require following Web site links down many paths. Path activities may also require other kinds of control manipulation as well.

5. **Forms judgments resulting in decisions relevant to the task or need.** Structured transactions will require minimal decision-making. Has all the data been collected and is the data valid? Has the transaction been successfully accepted by the system? If not accepted, why not? Semi-structured transactions, in addition, may require decisions such as: Which set of screens, from all available, should I use to complete this process? How much information is needed to complete the sale of this particular product, make a reservation in this hotel, or complete the enrollment process for a specific program? To satisfy a general or vague need will require decisions like: Where should I look to get my answer? Which link should I follow? Is this all the information I need? How do I order it?

Interface Design Goals

To make an interface easy and pleasant to use, then, the goal in design is to:

- Reduce visual work.
- Reduce intellectual work.
- Reduce memory work.
- Reduce motor work.
- Minimize or eliminate any burdens or instructions imposed by technology.

The result will always be improved user productivity and increased satisfaction. Let's begin our review of the principles of good design by applying the following simple test to all screens.

The Test for a Good Design

■ Can all screen elements be identified by cues other than by reading the words that make them up?

A simple test for good screen design does exist. A screen that passes this test will have surmounted the first obstacle to effectiveness. The test is this: Can all screen elements (field captions, data, title, headings, text, types of controls, and so on) be identified without reading the words that identify or comprise them? That is, can a component of a screen be identified through cues independent of its content? If this is so, a person's attention can quickly be drawn to the part of the screen that is relevant at that moment. People look at a screen for a particular reason, perhaps to locate a piece of information such as a customer name, to identify the name of the screen, or to find an instructional or error message. The *signal* at that moment is that element of interest on the screen. The *noise* is everything else on the screen. Cues independent of context that differentiate the components of the screen will reduce visual search times and minimize confusion.

Try this test on the front page of your morning newspaper. Where is the headline? A story heading? The weather report? How did you find them? The headline was identified probably by its large and bold type size; story headings, again by a type size visually different than other page components; the weather report, probably by its location (bottom right? top left?). Imagine finding the headline on the front page of the newspaper if the same type size and style were used for all components and their positions changed from day to day. If this is true of a screen, screen scanning will be a lengthy and cumbersome process, and the screen will not be appealing to use.

Unfortunately, many of today's screens cannot pass this simple test and are unnecessarily difficult to use. Almost all the tools available to the creator of the newspaper's front page are now available to the screen designer. Technology has added some additional weapons. An effective solution can be achieved. It simply involves the thoughtful use of display techniques, consistent location of elements, the proper use of "white space" and groupings, and an understanding of what makes visually pleasing composition. The best interfaces make everything on the screen *obvious*.

Screen Meaning and Purpose

■ Each screen element . . .
  — Every control
  — All text
  — The screen organization
  — All emphasis
  — Each color
  — Every graphic
  — All screen animation
  — Each message
  — All forms of feedback

- Must . . .
  — Have meaning to screen users.
  — Serve a purpose in performing tasks.

All elements of a screen must have meaning to users and serve a purpose in performing tasks or fulfilling needs. If an element does not have meaning, do not include it on the screen because it is *noise*. Noise is distracting, competes for the screen user's attention, and contributes to information overload. That which is important will be more difficult to find.

Organizing Screen Elements Clearly and Meaningfully

Visual clarity is achieved when the display elements are organized and presented in meaningful and understandable ways. A clear and clean organization makes it easier to recognize screen's essential elements and to ignore its secondary information when appropriate. Clarity is influenced by a multitude of factors: consistency in design, a visually pleasing composition, a logical and sequential ordering, the presentation of the proper amount of information, groupings, and alignment of screen items. What must be avoided is visual clutter created by indistinct elements, random placement, and confusing patterns.

Consistency

- Provide real-world consistency. Reflect a person's experiences, expectations, work conventions, and cultural conventions.
- Provide internal consistency. Observe the same conventions and rules for all aspects of an interface screen, and all application or Web site screens, including:
  — Operational and navigational procedures.
  — Visual identity or theme.
  — Component.
    • Organization.
    • Presentation.
    • Usage.
    • Locations.
- Follow the same conventions and rules across all related interfaces.
- Deviate only when there is a clear benefit for the user.

Quite simply, consistency greatly aids learning. It establishes an expectation and permits a person to employ conceptual learning and transfer training. Inconsistency forces one to memorize, and remember, a variety of different ways to do something or interpret what is presented on the screen. Inconsistency makes it difficult for a coherent structure to emerge. It can also be distracting, causing a person to wonder why things are different. Inconsistency also creates a screen variation that makes it difficult to notice another variation that may be important for a person's task or need.

In Web site design consistency greatly enhances visual scanning, a common user activity. It also fosters a sense of place, reassuring a person that he or she is rooted in a certain location. This provides stability and reduces navigation confusion.

MYTH **Users can get used to anything!**

So, be consistent with the real world in which a person already exists. This world will already have been well learned and possess an established mental model. Generalization to the system interface will most easily occur. Provide internal consistency so that learning may be focused on the task or job, not on irrelevancies. As far as consistent location of screen elements, people do tend to have good memories for the locations of things. Take advantage of this phenomenon. The graphical system products and style guides have established consistent locations for most screen elements, as well as numerous other conventions. In Web site design location and presentation consistency is slowly evolving. Follow all current conventions and new conventions as they are established. Also be consistent across user interfaces for all the reasons already mentioned.

If an inconsistency will *benefit* the user, such as calling attention to something extremely critical, consider deviating from consistency. Be wary of too many deviations, though, as the impact of each inconsistency will be diminished screen usability.

Ordering of Screen Data and Content

- Divide information into units that are logical, meaningful, and sensible.
- Organize by the degree interrelationship between data or information.
- Provide an ordering of screen units of information and elements that is prioritized according to the user's expectations and needs.
- Possible ordering schemes include:
  — Conventional.
  — Sequence of use.
  — Frequency of use.
  — Function.
  — Importance.
  — General to specific.
- Form groups that cover all possibilities.
- Ensure that information that must be compared is visible at the same time.
- Ensure that only information relative to the users tasks or needs is presented on the screen.

An organizational scheme's goal is to keep to a minimum the number of information variables the user must retain in short term memory. A logical, meaningful, and sensible arrangement of screen data and content will lower this memory requirement. In ordering screens or pages, units of information and screen elements should be prioritized according to the user's needs and expectations. People develop expectations on how to accomplish certain tasks and find different types of information. A meaningful organization permits faster graphical system or Web site learning. In Web site design it is also easier to develop a clear navigation system if the site is meaningfully organized. Clear organization also makes it easier for Web users to find what they need, and to predict where a navigation link will take them.

The nature of the information should suggest ways to divide and organize information. A technique to aid in organizing Web sites is that of Card Sorting described in Step 2 "Understand the Business Function." Common information ordering schemes include the following:

Conventional. Through convention and custom, some ordering schemes have evolved for certain elements. Examples are by days of the week, by months of the year, by one's name and address, or along a timeline. These elements should always be ordered in the customary way.

Sequence of use. Sequence of use grouping involves arranging information items in the order in which they are commonly received or transmitted, or in natural groups. An address, for example, is normally given by street, city, state, and zip code. Another example of natural grouping is the league standings of football teams, appearing in order of best to worst records.

Frequency of use. Frequency of use is a design technique based on the principle that information items used most frequently should be grouped at the beginning, the second most frequently used items grouped next, and so forth.

Function or category. Information items are grouped according to their purpose or by some common parameter. All items pertaining to insurance coverage, for example, may be placed in one location. Transportation vehicles may be grouped within the categories of planes, trains, and automobiles. Such grouping also allows convenient group identification using headings for the user. Sub-categories with sub-headings may also be established.

Importance. Importance grouping is based on the information's importance to the user's task or need. Important items are placed first or in the most prominent position. Items may be organized from best to worst or largest to smallest.

General to specific. If some data is more general than others, the general elements should precede the specific elements. This will usually occur when there is a hierarchical relationship among data elements. This is a common Web site organization scheme.

Screen layout normally reflects a combination of these techniques. Information may be organized functionally but, within each function, individual items may be arranged by sequence or importance. Numerous permutations are possible. The ordering scheme established must encompass all the information.

Ensure that information that must be compared is always visible to the user at the same time. A common problem in design is forcing the user to remember things located on different screens, or within a screen but scrolled out of sight. The corollary is ensure that only information relative to the tasks or needs at hand is presented on a screen. Irrelevant information is noise.

Upper-Left Starting Point

■ Provide an obvious starting point in the screen's upper-left corner.

Eyeball fixation studies indicate that in looking at displays of information, usually one's eyes move first to the upper-left center of the display, and then quickly move through the display in a clockwise direction. Streveler and Wasserman (1984) found that visual targets located in the upper-left quadrant of a screen were found fastest and those located in the lower- right quadrant took longest to find.

Provide an obvious starting point in the upper-left corner of the screen. This is near the location where visual scanning begins and will permit a left-to-right, top-to-bottom reading of information or text as is common in Western cultures.

Screen Navigation and Flow

■ Provide an ordering of screen information and elements that:
— Is rhythmic, guiding a person's eye through the display.
— Encourages natural movement sequences.
— Minimizes pointer and eye movement distances.
■ Locate the most important and most frequently used elements or controls at the top left.
■ Maintain a top-to-bottom, left-to-right flow.
■ Assist in navigation through a screen by:
— Aligning elements.
— Grouping elements.
— Using of line borders.
■ Through focus and emphasis, sequentially, direct attention to items that are:
  1. Critical.
  2. Important.
  3. Secondary.
  4. Peripheral.
■ Tab through window in logical order of displayed information.
■ Locate command buttons at end of the tabbing order sequence.
■ When groups of related information must be broken and displayed on separate screens, provide breaks at logical or natural points in the information flow.

Screen navigation should be obvious and easy to accomplish. Navigation can be made obvious by grouping and aligning screen controls, and judiciously using line borders to guide the eye. Sequentially, direct a person's attention to elements in terms of their importance. Using the various display techniques, focus attention on the most important parts of a screen. Always tab through a screen in the logical order of the information displayed, and locate command buttons at the end of the tab order sequence. Guidelines for accomplishing all of these general objectives will be found in subsequent pages.

The direction of movement between screen items should be obvious, consistent, and rhythmic. The eye, or pointer, should not be forced or caused to wander long distances about the display seeking the next item. The eye can be guided through the screen with lines formed through use of white space and display elements. More complex movements may require the aid of display contrasts. Sequence of use can be made more obvious through the incorporation of borders around groupings of related information or screen controls. Borders provide visual cues concerning the arrangement of screen elements, because the eye will tend to stay within a border to complete a task. Aligning elements will also minimize screen scanning and navigation movements. In establishing eye movement through a screen, also consider that the eye tends to move sequentially, for example:

- From dark areas to light areas.
- From big objects to little objects.
- From unusual shapes to common shapes.
- From highly saturated colors to unsaturated colors.

These techniques can be used initially to focus a person's attention to one area of the screen and then direct it elsewhere.

For screens containing data, locate the most important or frequently used screen controls to the top left of the screen where initial attention is usually directed. This will also reduce the overall number of eye and manual control movements needed to work with a screen.

Then, maintain a top-to-bottom, left-to-right flow through the screen. This is contrary to the older text-based screen cursor movement direction that precedes left to right, then top to bottom. This top-to-bottom orientation is recommended for information *entry* for the following reasons:

- Eye movements between items will be shorter.
- Control movements between items will be shorter.
- Groupings are more obvious perceptually.
- When one's eye moves away from the screen and then back, it returns to about the same place it left, even if it is seeking the next item in a sequence (a visual anchor point remains).

Unfortunately, most product style guides recommend a left-to-right orientation. This orientation is based upon the presumption that since people read left-to-right, a screen must be organized in this way. Many screens, however, do not present text but listings of small pieces of information that must be scanned. All the research on human scanning finds a top-to-bottom presentation of information is best.

Why do we persist in this left-to-right orientation for nontextual screens? A common screen metaphor applied in today's systems is that of the paper form. We often see a paper form exactly replicated on a screen. Unfortunately, the left-to-right orientation of the typical form is poorly suited to the needs and characteristics of its user. Its complexity is generally higher than it should be, and its sequentiality is often not as obvious as it should be and certainly not at all efficient.

The left-to-right orientation of paper forms was not dictated by human needs but by mechanical considerations. The metaphor for earliest display screens five decades ago (although this term was not used then) was the typewriter. The left-to-right orientation of the typewriter was developed to permit one to type text on paper, a significant enhancement over handwriting as a medium of human communication. At some point early in the typewriter's life, however, its ability to be used to complete paper forms also became evident. So, we started designing forms to be completed by typewriter. They had to be filled out left-to-right because the design of the typewriter made any other completion method very difficult for a person to do.

Our earliest display screens reflected this left-to-right entry orientation and have done so for many years. Today, in our display-based world, the typewriter's mechanical limitations no longer exist. Let's shed the artificial constraints we have imposed upon ourselves and get rid of the left-to-right orientation for nontextual screens. A top-to-bottom orientation has many more advantages for the screen user.

Top-to-bottom orientation is also recommended for presenting displays of read-only information that must be scanned. This will be described shortly.

Visually Pleasing Composition

- Provide visually pleasing composition with the following qualities:
  — Balance.
  — Symmetry.
  — Regularity.
  — Predictability.
  — Sequentiality.
  — Economy.
  — Unity.
  — Proportion.
  — Simplicity.
  — Groupings.

Eyeball fixation studies also indicate that during the initial scanning of a display in a clockwise direction, people are influenced by the symmetrical balance and weight of the titles, graphics, and text of the display. The human perceptual mechanism seeks order and meaning, trying to impose structure when confronted with uncertainty. Whether a screen has meaningful and evident form or is cluttered and unclear is immediately discerned. A cluttered or unclear screen requires that some effort be expended in learning and understanding what is presented. The screen user who must deal with the display is forced to spend time to learn and understand. The user who has an option concerning whether the screen will or will not be used may reject it at this point if the perceived effort in understanding the screen is greater than the perceived gain in using it.

An entity's design composition communicates to a person nonverbally, but quite powerfully. It is an unconscious process that attracts, motivates, directs, or distracts. Meaningfulness and evident form are significantly enhanced by a display that is pleasing to one's eye. Visually pleasing composition draws attention subliminally, conveying a positive message clearly and quickly. A lack of visually pleasing composition is disorienting, obscures the intent and meaning, slows one down and confuses one.

The notion of what is artistic has evolved throughout history. Graphic design experts have, through perceptual research, derived a number of principles for what constitutes a visually pleasing appearance. These include: balance, symmetry, regularity, predictability, economy, unity, sequentiality, proportion, simplicity, and groupings. Keep in mind that this discussion of visually pleasing composition does not focus on the words on the screen, but on the perception of structure created by such qualities as spacing, shapes, intensities, and colors, and the relationship of screen elements to one another. It is as if the screen were viewed through "squinted eyes," causing the words themselves to become a blur.

Balance

- Create screen balance by providing an equal weight of screen elements, left and right, top and bottom.

Balance, illustrated in Figure 3.1, is stabilization or equilibrium, a midway center of suspension. The design elements have an equal weight, left to right, top to bottom. The opposite of balance is instability; the design elements seemingly ready to topple over.

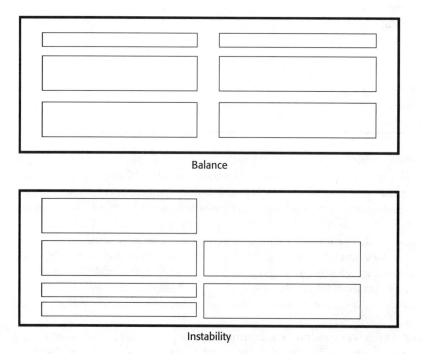

Balance

Instability

Figure 3.1   Balance (versus instability).

Our discomfort with instability, or imbalance, is reflected every time we straighten a picture hanging askew on the wall. Balance is most often informal or asymmetrical, with elements of different colors, sizes and shapes being positioned to strike the proper relationships.

Dark colors, unusual shapes, and larger objects are "heavier," whereas light colors, regular shapes, and small objects are "lighter." Balance on a screen is accomplished through centering the display itself, maintaining an equal weighting of components on each side of the horizontal and vertical axis, and centering titles and illustrations

In Web page design, vertical, or left-to-right balance is usually the most important concept. Web pages are often scrollable thereby shifting the horizontal, or top-to-bottom, balance point as the screen is scrolled. Horizontal balance is therefore more difficult to maintain.

Symmetry

- Create symmetry by replicating elements left and right of the screen centerline.

Symmetry, illustrated in Figure 3.2, is axial duplication: A unit on one side of the centerline is exactly replicated on the other side. This exact replication creates formal balance, but the difference is that balance can be achieved without symmetry. Symmetry's

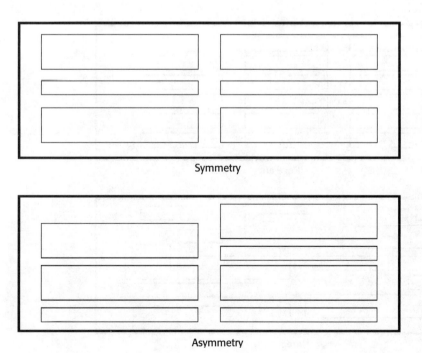

Symmetry

Asymmetry

Figure 3.2 Symmetry (versus asymmetry).

opposite is asymmetry. Our eye tends to perceive something as more compressed or compact when it is symmetric. Asymmetric arrays are perceived as larger.

Regularity

- Create regularity by establishing standard and consistently spaced horizontal and vertical alignment points.
- Also, use similar element sizes, shapes, colors, and spacing.

Regularity, illustrated in Figure 3.3, is a uniformity of elements based on some principle or plan. Regularity in screen design is achieved by establishing standard and consistently spaced column and row starting points for screen elements. It is also achieved by using elements similar in size, shape, color, and spacing. The opposite of regularity, irregularity, exists when no such plan or principle is apparent. A critical element on a screen will stand out better, however, if it is not regularized

Predictability

- Create predictability by being consistent and following conventional orders or arrangements.

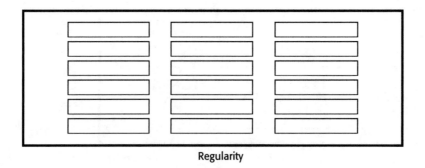

Regularity

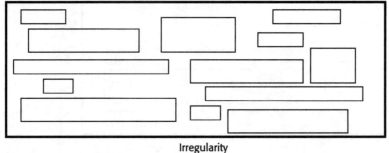

Irregularity

Figure 3.3 Regularity (versus irregularity).

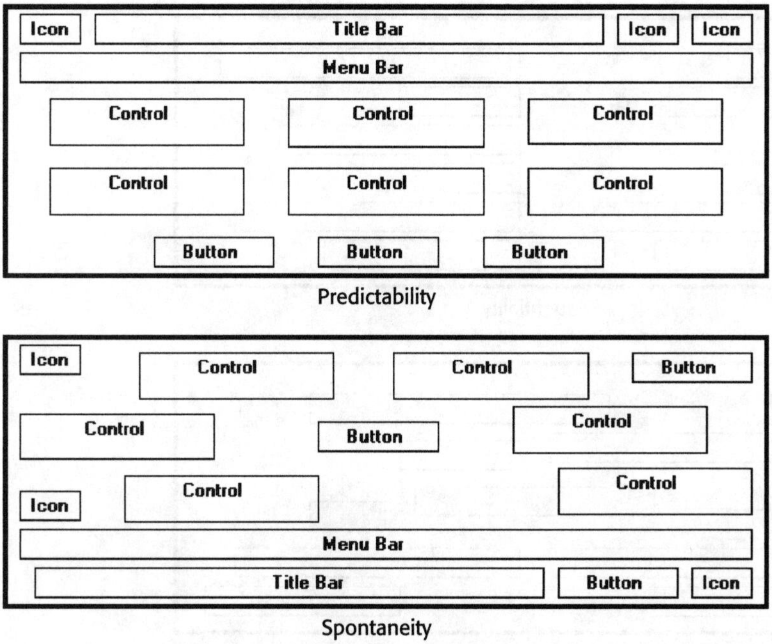

Figure 3.4   Predictability (versus spontaneity).

Predictability, illustrated in Figure 3.4, suggests a highly conventional order or plan. Viewing one screen enables one to predict how another will look. Viewing part of a screen enables one to predict how the rest of the screen will look. The opposite of predictability—spontaneity—suggests no plan and thus an inability to predict the structure of the remainder of a screen or the structure of other screens. In screen design predictability is also enhanced through design consistency.

Sequentiality

- Provide sequentiality by arranging elements to guide the eye through the screen in an obvious, logical, rhythmic, and efficient manner.
- The eye tends to be attracted to:
    — A brighter element before one less bright.
    — Isolated elements before elements in a group.
    — Graphics before text.
    — Color before black and white.
    — Highly saturated colors before those less saturated.
    — Dark areas before light areas.
    — A big element before a small one.
    — An unusual shape before a usual one.
    — Big objects before little objects.

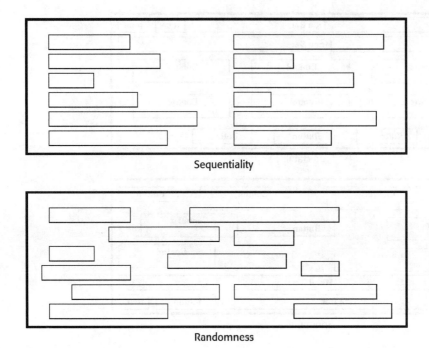

Sequentiality

Randomness

Figure 3.5   Sequentiality (versus randomness).

Sequentiality, illustrated in Figure 3.5, is a plan of presentation to guide the eye through the screen in a logical, rhythmic order, with the most important information significantly placed. Sequentiality can be achieved by alignment, spacing, and grouping as illustrated. The opposite of sequentiality is randomness, whereby an arrangement and flow cannot be detected.

The eye tends to move first to the elements listed above, and then from one to the other. For example, it moves from highly saturated colors to unsaturated colors, from dark to light areas, from big to little objects, and from unusual to usual shapes.

Economy

■ Provide economy by using as few styles, display techniques, and colors as possible.

Economy, illustrated in Figure 3.6, is the frugal and judicious use of display elements to get the message across as simply as possible. The opposite is intricacy, the use of many elements just because they exist. The effect of intricacy is ornamentation, which often detracts from clarity. Economy in screen design means mobilizing just enough display elements and techniques to communicate the desired message, and no more. Historically, the use of color in screens has often violated this principle, with screens sometimes taking on the appearance of Christmas trees.

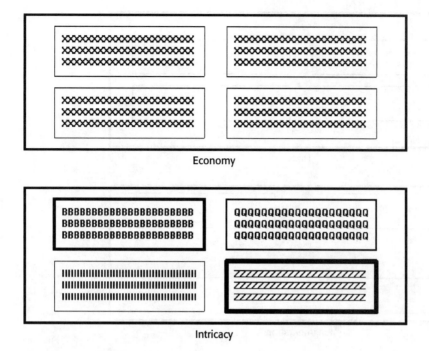

Figure 3.6 Economy (versus intricacy).

Unity

■ Create unity by:
— Using similar sizes, shapes, or colors for related information.
— Leaving less space between elements of a screen than the space left at the margins.

Unity, illustrated in Figure 3.7, is coherence, a totality of elements that is visually all one piece. With unity, the elements seem to belong together, to dovetail so completely that they are seen as one thing. The opposite of unity is fragmentation, each piece retaining its own character. In screen design similar sizes, shapes, and colors promote unity, as does *white space*—borders at the display boundary. Unity should exist between related screens, and Web site screens, as well.

Proportion

■ Create windows and groupings of data or text with aesthetically pleasing proportions.

Down through the ages, people and cultures have had preferred *proportional* relationships. What constitutes beauty in one culture is not necessarily considered the same

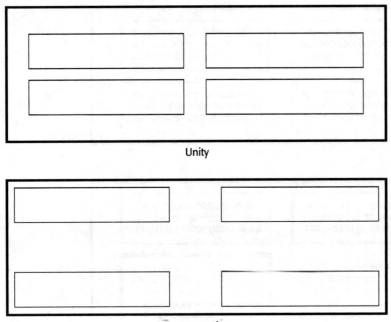

Unity

Fragmentation

Figure 3.7   Unity (versus fragmentation).

by another culture, but some proportional shapes have stood the test of time and are found in abundance today.

Marcus (1992) describes the following shapes, illustrated in Figure 3.8, as aesthetically pleasing.

Square (1:1). The simplest of proportions, it has an attention-getting quality and suggests stability and permanence. When rotated it becomes a dynamic diamond, expressing movement and tension.

Square root of two (1:1.414). A divisible rectangle yielding two pleasing proportional shapes. When divided equally in two along its length, the two smaller shapes that result are also both square roots of two rectangles. This property only occurs with this proportion and is often used in book design. An open book has the same outside proportion as the individual pages within it. The square root of two has been adopted as a standard paper size in many countries of the world (the United States excluded).

Golden rectangle (1:1.618). An old (fifth century B.C.) proportion is the golden rectangle. Early Greek architecture used this proportion, and a mathematical relationship exists between this number and growth patterns in plant and animal life. This "divine division of a line" results when a line is divided such that the smaller part is to the greater part as the greater part is to the whole. The golden rectangle also has another unique property. A square created from part of the rectangle leaves a remaining area with sides also in the golden rectangle proportion.

Square root of three (1:1.732). Used less frequently than the other proportions, its narrowness gives it a distinctive shape.

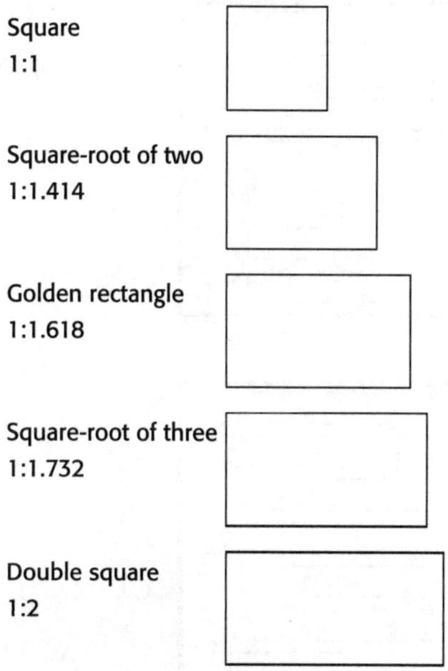

Square
1:1

Square-root of two
1:1.414

Golden rectangle
1:1.618

Square-root of three
1:1.732

Double square
1:2

Figure 3.8   Pleasing proportions.

> **Double square (1:2).** In Japan, the tatami mat used for floor covering usually comes in this proportion. Rectangles more elongated than this one have shapes whose distinctiveness is more difficult to sense.

While these pleasing shapes have passed the test of time, not everything we encounter conforms to these principles. The American letter paper size has a ratio of 1:1.29, a typical American television screen has a ratio of 1:1.33, and CRT screens typically have ratios in the range of about 1:1.33 to 1:1.50.

In screen design, aesthetically pleasing proportions should be considered for major components of the screen, including window sizes, Web page sizes, graphics, and groupings of data or text.

Simplicity (Complexity)

- Optimize the number of elements on a screen, within limits of clarity.
- Minimize the alignment points, especially horizontal or columnar.
  — Provide standard grids of horizontal and vertical lines to position elements.

Simplicity, illustrated in Figure 3.9, is directness and singleness of form, a combination of elements that results in ease of comprehending the meaning of a pattern. The opposite pole on the continuum is complexity. The scale created may also be considered a scale of complexity, with extreme complexity at one end and minimal complexity (simplicity) at the other. While the graphics designer usually considers this concept as *simplicity*, we will address it as *complexity* since it has been addressed by this term in the screen design literature, where an objective measure of it has been derived.

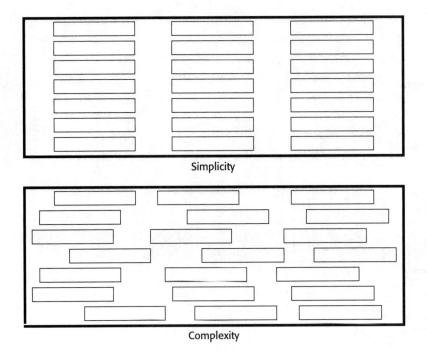

Figure 3.9 Simplicity (versus complexity).

This measure of complexity was derived by Tullis (1983) based on the work of Bonsiepe (1968), who proposed a method of measuring the complexity of typographically designed pages through the application of information theory (Shannon and Weaver, 1949). To illustrate, this measure involves the following steps:

1. Draw a rectangle around each element on a screen, including captions, controls, headings, data, title, and so on.

2. Count the number of elements and horizontal alignment points (the number of columns in which a field, inscribed by a rectangle, starts).

3. Count the number of elements and vertical alignment points (the number of rows in which an element, inscribed by a rectangle, starts).

This has been done for the text-based screens illustrated in Figures 3.10 and 3.11. These screens are examples from the earlier study by Tullis (1981) described in the introduction. They are an original read-only inquiry screen (Figure 3.10) from the screens whose mean search time was 8.3 seconds, and a redesigned screen (Figure 3.11) from the screens whose mean search time was 5.0 seconds.

A complexity calculation using information theory for each screen is as follows:

- Figure 3.10 (original):

   22 fields with 6 horizontal (column) alignment points = 41 bits.
   22 fields with 20 vertical (row) alignment points = 93 bits.
   Overall complexity = 134 bits.

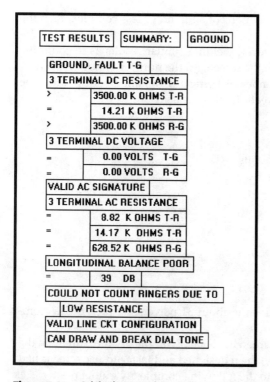

Figure 3.10 Original screen, from Tullis (1981), with title, captions, and data inscribed by rectangles.

- Figure 3.11 (redesigned):

  18 fields with 7 horizontal (column) alignment points = 43 bits.
  18 fields with 8 vertical (row) alignment points = 53 bits.
  Overall complexity = 96 bits.

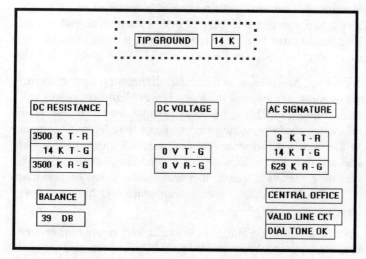

Figure 3.11 Redesigned screen, from Tullis (1981), with title, captions, and data inscribed by rectangles.

The redesigned screen is, thus, about 28 percent simpler, or less complex, than the original screen.

An easier method of calculation, however, yielding similar results, is to count the following: (1) the number of elements on the screen, (2) the number of horizontal (column) alignment points, and (3) the number of vertical (row) alignment points. The sums for the original and redesigned screens by this measure are:

- Figure 3.10 (original):

  22 elements.
  6 horizontal (column) alignment points.
  20 vertical (row) alignment points.
  48 = complexity.

- Figure 3.11 (redesigned):

  18 elements.
  7 horizontal (column) alignment points.
  8 vertical (row) alignment points.
  33 = complexity.

By this calculation the redesigned screen is about 31 percent simpler, or less complex, than the original screen.

By both calculations the redesigned screen has a *lower* complexity measure than the original screen. In the Tullis (1981) study, the redesigned and faster-to-use screens had lower complexity measures. This leads to the following complexity guidelines:

- Optimize the number of elements on a screen, within limits of clarity.
- Minimize the alignment points, especially horizontal or columnar.

Obviously, the way to minimize screen complexity is to reduce the number of controls displayed. Fewer controls will yield lower complexity measures. This is unrealistic, however, since ultimate simplicity means nothing is there, which obviously does not accomplish very much. Indeed, Vitz (1966) has found that people have subjective preferences for the right amount of information, and too little is as bad as too much. The practical answer, then, is to optimize the amount of information displayed, within limits of clarity. What is optimum must be considered in light of guidelines to follow, so a final judgment must be postponed.

Alignment. What can be done, however, is to minimize alignment points, most importantly horizontal or columnar alignment points. Fewer alignment points will have a strong positive influence on the complexity calculation. Tullis (1983) has also found, in a follow-up study of some other screens, that fewer alignment points were among the strongest influences creating positive viewer feelings of visually pleasing composition. Grose, Partush, Nadir, and Shtub (1998) also performed a study examining various screen factors and usability. They found that good alignment was related to shorter screen search times and higher viewer preferences for a screen.

Misalignments and uneven spacing, no matter how slight, can create bothersome unconscious disruptions to our perceptual systems. When things don't align, a sense of clutter and disorganization often results. In addition to reducing complexity, alignment helps create balance, regularity, sequentiality, and unity. Alignment also reduces variation on a screen. Common alignments are associated with a group identity of their own. Anything that breaks that alignment is quickly seen as an exception.

In laying out a screen, imagine a grid of horizontal and vertical lines beneath it. Use these grids to position elements and to achieve common alignment points.

Groupings

- Provide functional groupings of associated elements.
- Create spatial groupings as closely as possible to five degrees of visual angle (1.67 inches in diameter or about 6 to 7 lines of text, 12 to 14 characters in width).
- Evenly space controls within a grouping, allowing 1/8 to 1/4 inch between each.
- Visually reinforce groupings:
  — Provide adequate separation between groupings through liberal use of white space.
  — Provide line borders around groups.
- Provide meaningful titles for each grouping.

Grouping screen elements aids in establishing structure, meaningful relationships, and meaningful form. In addition to providing aesthetic appeal, past research has found that grouping aids in information recall and results in a faster screen search. The study by Grose, Parush, Nadir, and Shtub (1998) found that providing groupings of screen elements containing meaningful group titles was also related to shorter screen search times. In this study groupings also contributed to stronger viewer preferences for a screen.

The perceptual principles of proximity, closure, similarity, and matching patterns foster visual groupings. But the search for a more objective definition of what constitutes a group has gone on for years. Tullis, in his 1981 study, described an objective method for establishing groups based on the work of Zahn (1971) using the Gestalt psychologists' law of proximity. For the Tullis (1981) screens shown in Figures 3.12 and 3.13:

1. Compute the mean distance between each character and its nearest neighbor. Use a character distance of 1 between characters adjacent horizontally and 2 between characters adjacent vertically (between rows).
2. Multiply the mean distance derived by 2.
3. Connect with a line any character pair that is closer than the distance established in step 2.

This has been done for these inquiry screens and the results illustrated in Figures 3.12 and 3.13. Boxes have been included around the derived groupings.

- Figure 3.12 (original):
  Mean distance between characters = 1.05.
  Twice the mean distance = 2.10.
  A line is drawn between characters 1 or 2 apart, not 3 or more.
  Resulting number of groups = 3.

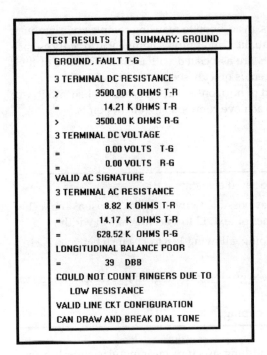

Figure 3.12 Original screen, from Tullis (1981), with grouping indicated by bold boxes.

■ Figure 3.13 (redesigned):
Mean distance between characters = 1.09.
Twice the mean distance = 2.18.
A line is drawn between characters 1 or 2 apart, not 3 or more.
Resulting number of groups = 13.

Tullis found that the redesigned screens had more groupings than the originals.

To use a simplified version of this formula, connect with a line all characters on the screen separated by no more than one space horizontally and no blank lines vertically. Groupings will become immediately obvious.

Tullis also calculated another grouping measure: the average size of each screen's group. The average size of the three groups in the original screen is 13.3 degrees in visual angle, whereas the 13 groups on the redesigned screen average 5.2 degrees visual angle. The redesigned screen group size, interestingly, closely matches the 5 degree visual acuity screen chunk described in Step 1 "Know Your User or Client." It seems that groups 5 degrees or less in size can be scanned with one eye fixation per group. Therefore, screens with these size groupings can be searched faster. Groupings larger than five degrees require more eye fixations per grouping, slowing down screen scanning time. So, in addition to complexity, the Tullis redesigned screens differ from the original screens by some grouping measures. The more effective redesigned screens have a *greater number* of *smaller size* groups.

Tullis, in his 1983 follow-up study, also found that groupings were the strongest determinant of a screen's visual search time. If the size of a group on a screen increased, or the number of groups increased, search time also increased. Number and size of

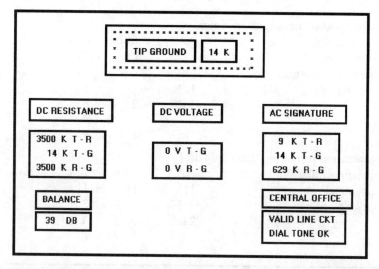

Figure 3.13   Redesigned screen, from Tullis (1981), with grouping indicated by bold boxes.

groups have an opposite relationship, however; if the number of groups increases, their size usually decreases. If the size increases, the number of groups usually decreases. What proves to be most effective is a middle-ground solution, a medium number of medium-sized groups. The grouping guidelines described above are based upon this and other research presented.

Functional, semantic groups are those that make sense to the user. Related information should be displayed together. A logical place to "break" a screen is between functional groups of information, but a massive grouping of information should be broken up into smaller groups. The most reasonable point is every five rows. A six- or seven-row grouping may be displayed without a break, if necessary, but do not exceed seven rows.

The 11- to 15-character width limitation must take into consideration the data to be displayed. Confining data to this width makes no sense if it thus suffers a reduction in comprehensibility. Legibility and comprehension are most important.

To give unity to a display, the space between groups should be less than that of the margins. The most common and obvious way to achieve spacing is through white or blank space, but there are other ways. Alternatives include: contrasting display features such as differing intensity levels, image reversals (white characters on a black background versus black characters on a white background), borders, and color. Spacing, however, appears to be stronger than color. Two studies (Haubner and Benz, 1983; Haubner and Neumann, 1986) found that adequate spacing, not color, is a more important determinant of ease of use for uncluttered, highly structured inquiry screens.

Perceptual Principles and Functional Grouping

- Use visual organization to create functional groupings.
  - Proximity: 000   000   000
  - Similarity: AAABBBCCC
  - Closure: []   []   []
  - Matching patterns: >>   < >

- Combine visual organization principles in logical ways.

— Proximity and similarity:	AAA	BBB	CCC
— Proximity and closure:	[ ]	[ ]	[ ]
— Matching patterns and closure:	( )	< >	{ }
— Proximity and ordering:	1234	1	5
	5678	2	6
		3	7
		4	8

- Avoid visual organization principles that conflict.

— Proximity opposing similarity:	AAA	ABB	BBC	CCC
— Proximity opposing closure:	] [	] [	] [	
— Proximity opposing ordering:	1357	1	2	
	2468	3	4	
		5	6	
		7	8	

Perceptual principles can be used to aid screen functional groupings.

Use visual organization to create functional grouping. The most common perceptual principle used in screen design to aid visual groupings has been the proximity principle. The incorporation of adequate spacing between groups of related elements enhances the "togetherness" of each grouping. Space should always be considered a design component of a screen. The objective should never be to get rid of it. The similarity principle can be used to call attention to various groupings by displaying them in a different intensity, font style, or color. The closure and matching patterns principles involve using lines, borders, and unique symbols to identify and relate common information.

Combine visual organization principles in logical ways. Visual organization principles can be combined to enhance groupings. Proximity, a very strong perceptual principle, can guide the eye through an array of information to be scanned in a particular direction. Scanning direction can also be made obvious through similarity (color, intensity, and so on) or matching patterns (lines or borders).

Avoid visual organization principles that conflict. Principles may not always be compatible, however. When the viewer encounters incompatibilities, confusion results. In the examples above, proximity destroys similarity, proximity overwhelms closure, and proximity overwhelms logical ordering.

Grouping Using White Space

- Provide adequate separation between groupings through liberal use of white space.
- For Web pages, carefully consider the trade-off between screen white space and the requirement for page scrolling.

Today, the term white space is a misnomer, a carry-over from the white paper of printed forms. It might more appropriately simply be called space, reflecting the variety of colors capable of being displayed by today's screens. Whatever we call it, space should be considered a screen element of equal importance to all others. It is not wasted space. It defines and separates screen elements, and gives a screen proportion and meaningful form, thus assisting in providing the distinctiveness that is so desired. Space is also used to direct attention to adjacent areas that do contain important information. Remember, if a screen is perceived as a homogeneous, cluttered mass, information will only be found through an exhaustive search of the entire screen.

In Web page design, the "provide white space" principle directly confronts another principle, "minimize the need for scrolling" (to be discussed shortly). Web pages are typically longer than the maximum visible area of the display on which they are presented. To see the entire page requires screen scrolling. An abundance of white space, therefore, creates a need for excessive scrolling. It also makes page scanning more difficult and moves information further apart spatially, making the determination of information relationships more difficult.

Web page guideline information addressing this problem is somewhat contradictory. Recommendations include "use white space sparingly" (Usability.gov), "minimize the use of white space in search tasks" (Bailey, 1999c), and users rating poorly sites with large amounts of white space and sparse text (Festa, 1998). On the other hand, a characteristic of the top 100 Web sites is "lots of white space" (Grok.com). The most practical recommendation at the moment is that for longer pages the use of white space should be reduced, but certainly not at the expense of page clarity. Each page must be evaluated in terms of its specific content, the relationships existing between the various pieces of content, and the page's scanning and visual search requirements. A trade-off that best meets all these needs must then be established and implemented.

Grouping Using Borders

- Incorporate line borders for:
  — Focusing attention on groupings or related information.
  — Guiding the eye through a screen.
- Do not exceed three line thicknesses or two line styles on a screen, however.
  — Use a standard hierarchy for line presentation.
- Create lines consistent in height and length.
- Leave sufficient padding space between the information and the surrounding borders.
- For adjacent groupings with borders, whenever possible, align the borders left, right, top, and bottom.
- Use rules and borders sparingly.
- In Web page design:
  — Be cautious in using horizontal lines as separators between page sections.
  — Reserve horizontal lines for situations in which the difference between adjacent areas must be emphasized.

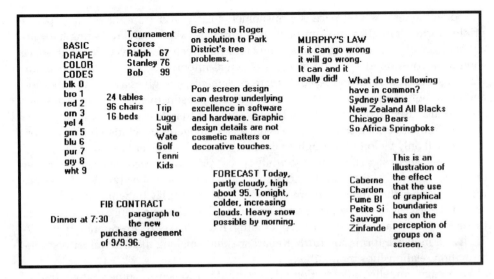

Figure 3.14 The effect of line or graphical borders. Groupings without borders.

Line borders. Line borders, or rules, can greatly enhance a screen. Research has found that information displayed with a border around it is easier to read, better in appearance, and preferable. Figures 3.14 and 3.15 illustrate identical screens with and without borders around groupings. While many groupings are obvious without borders, borders certainly reinforce their existence.

Lines or rules assist in focusing attention on related information. They also aid in separating groupings of information from one another. Draw borders around elements to be grouped. Microsoft Windows provides a control called the *Group*

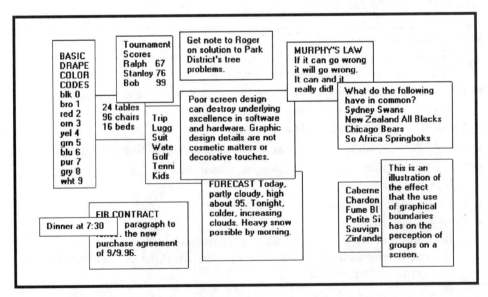

Figure 3.15 The effect of line or graphical borders. Groupings with borders.

Box to establish a frame around a group of related controls (see Step 7 "Choose the Proper Screen-Based Controls"). Rules also serve to guide the viewer's eye in the desired direction. Use vertical rulings to convey to the screen viewer that a screen should be scanned from top to bottom.

Line thickness variations. Too many variations in line thickness on a screen create clutter and are distracting. Use no more than three line weights at one time, or two different styles. Use a standard hierarchy for rules, the thickest to differentiate major components, the thinnest for minor separation. Consider a thin border for individual controls, a slightly thicker border for groupings, and the thickest borders for windows themselves.

Consistent line widths and heights. Similarly, variations in line widths and heights are distracting. Create horizontal lines of equal widths across the screen and vertical lines of equal height whenever possible. This will provide better balance.

Sufficient space padding. When placing information within borders leave "breathing room," sufficient space between the information and the borders themselves. Avoid looking like you are trying to stuff 6 pounds into a 5-pound sack.

Alignment. For adjacent groupings with borders, whenever possible, align the borders left, right, top, and bottom. The most important alignment points are left and top. Do not create right and bottom alignment by leaving excessive white space within the area encompassed by the border. This is not visually appealing.

Use lines and borders sparingly. Too many lines and borders on a screen also create clutter and can be distracting. Like any display technique, lines and borders must be used sparingly.

Web pages. In Web page design be cautious in using horizontal lines as separators between page sections. Users may assume they have reached the bottom of the page, missing what follows. Separator lines may also make the screen look more cluttered. In general, reserve horizontal lines for situations where the difference between adjacent areas must be emphasized.

Grouping Using Backgrounds

■ Consider incorporating a contrasting background for related information.
 — The background should not have the "emphasis" of the screen component that should be attended to. Consider about a 25 percent gray screening.
 — Reserve higher contrast or "emphasizing" techniques for screen components to which attention should be drawn.

Information can also be visually tied together through using a background that contrasts with the remainder of the screen. The background should just be a background, however; visual emphasis should be directed toward foreground material. A common failing of many screens is that the background is too highly emphasized. Consider about a 25 percent gray screening. Always reserve the higher contrast or emphasizing techniques for screen components in need of attention. Be very conservative in the variety of different backgrounds used. Background colors may also be used to relate or separate screen groupings. Color by itself is a poor separator of screen elements, however. A border is always needed to properly set off adjacent areas of different colors. Colors should also be used with caution since the user may have the ability to change them. This may result in undesirable effects. Finally, less variation is always better than more. An additional discussion on color screen backgrounds is found in Step 12 "Choose the Proper Colors."

MAXIM   **Working with a system should never be painful; instead it should be so painless you forget what you are doing!**

Visual Style in Web Page Design

- Maintain a consistent and unified visual style throughout the pages of an entire Web site.
- Base the visual style on:
  — The profile and goals of the Web site owner.
  — The profile, tastes, and expectations of the Web site user.

The style of a Web site, its visual characteristics, including color, typography, and graphics; the shape of its design elements; and the relationship of its components to one another, including their locations, should be maintained throughout the entire Web site. This will provide unity and harmony to the Web site and give it a consistent identity. Unity and consistency will also aid users in navigation, reinforcing for them that they are anchored in a specific place within the universe of information space. It will also enable the users to become comfortable and familiar with the Web site.

Visual style must reflect the needs and goals of the Web site owner and will vary depending upon the Web site's purpose; presenting facts, marketing, entertainment, and so forth. The tastes and expectations of the Web site's users are also critically important. It must be appealing to its expected viewers, motivating them to explore its entire contents. Sun Microsystems (1998) in a redesign of their Web site reported that a great visual appearance made users think more highly of their site. The visual design style must always be evaluated along with other components of the system. (See Step 14 "Test, Test, and Retest.")

Amount of Information

- Present the proper amount of information for the task.
  — Too little is inefficient.
  — Too much is confusing.
- Present all information necessary for performing an action or making a decision on one screen, whenever possible.
  — People should not have to remember things from one screen to the next.
- Restrict screen or window density levels to no more than about 30 percent.

Proper amount of information. Presenting too much information on a screen is confusing; there will be greater competition among a screen's components for a person's attention. Visual search times will be longer, and meaningful structure will be more difficult to perceive. Presenting too little information is inefficient and may tax a person's memory as information contained on multiple screens may have to be remembered.

Present all necessary information. In general; present all information necessary for performing an action or making a decision on one screen. If information located on different screens must be remembered, a person's memory will again be taxed. Developing a screen with all the necessary information requires careful analysis of the user's tasks.

Screen density. One objective measure of "how much" should go on a screen has been developed: "density." Density, by definition, is a calculation of the proportion of display character positions on the screen, or an area of the screen containing something. Density is clearly related to complexity, since both measure "how much is there." Complexity looks at elements, density at characters, so they should rise and fall together.

In general, studies show that increasing the density of a display increases the time and errors in finding information. There are two types of density to be calculated on a screen: overall and local.

Overall density is a measure of the percentage of character positions on the entire screen containing data. Danchak (1976) stated that density (loading, as he called it) should not exceed 25 percent. Reporting the results of a qualitative judgment of "good" screens, he found their density was on the order of 15 percent. Tullis, in his 1981 study, reported that the density of screens from an up and running successful system ranged from 0.9 to 27.9 percent, with a mean of 14.2 percent. Using this and other research data, he concluded that the common upper density limit appears to be about 25 percent.

Thacker (1987) compared screens with densities of 14 percent, 29 percent, and 43 percent. Response time increased significantly as screen density increased. He found, however, that the time increase between 14 percent and 29 percent was much smaller than the time increase between 29 percent and 43 percent. He also found increased error rates with greater density, the 43 percent density screens showing significantly more errors.

Local density is a measure of how "tightly packed" the screen is. A measure of local density, derived by Tullis, is the percentage of characters in the 88-character visual acuity circle described in Step 1, modified by the weighting factors illustrated below.

```
        012222210
      0123445443210
     023456777654320
    01235679+97653210
     023456777654320
      0123445443210
        012222210
```

```
TEST RESULTS   SUMMARY:   GROUND

GROUND, FAULT T-G
3 TERMINAL DC RESISTANCE
>          3500.00 K OHMS T-R
=            14.21 K OHMS T-R
>          3500.00 K OHMS R-G
3 TERMINAL DC VOLTAGE
=             0.00 VOLTS   T-G
=             0.00 VOLTS   R-G
VALID AC SIGNATURE
3 TERMINAL AC RESISTANCE
=             8.82  K OHMS T-R
=            14.17  K OHMS T-R
=           628.52 K OHMS R-G
LONGITUDINAL BALANCE POOR
=            39   DBB
COULD NOT COUNT RINGERS DUE TO
   LOW RESISTANCE
VALID LINE CKT CONFIGURATION
CAN DRAW AND BREAK DIAL TONE
```

Figure 3.16   Original screen, from Tullis (1981).

For every character on the screen, a local density is calculated using the above weighting factors, and then an average for all characters on the screen is established.

Figures 3.16 and 3.17 are the original and redesigned screens from the 1981 Tullis study. Density measures for these screens are:

- Figure 3.16 (original):

  Overall density = 17.9 percent.
  Local density = 58.0 percent.

- Figure 3.17 (redesigned):

  Overall density = 10.8 percent.
  Local density = 35.6 percent.

In both cases, the more effective redesigned screen had lower density measures. In his 1983 follow-up study, Tullis found a lower local density to be the most important characteristic, creating a positive "visually pleasing" feeling.

The research does suggest some density guidelines for screens. Maintain overall density levels no higher than about 30 percent. This upper overall density recommendation should be interpreted with extreme care. Density, by itself, does not affect whether or not what is displayed "makes sense." This is a completely different question. Density can always be reduced through substituting abbreviations for whole

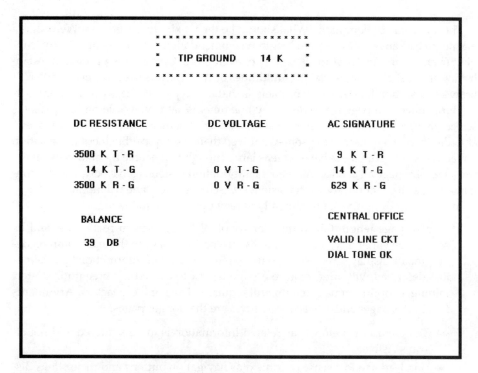

Figure 3.17 Redesigned screen, from Tullis (1981).

words. The cost of low density in this case may be illegibility and poorer comprehension. Indeed, poorly designed screens have been redesigned to achieve greater clarity and have actually ended up with higher density measures than the original versions. How it all "hangs together" can never be divorced from how much is there.

In conclusion, all this density research was performed using text-based screens. With many boxed or specialized controls found on graphical screens, such as list boxes or sliders, it is much more difficult to calculate density as has just been illustrated. Is it necessary to do so on graphical screens? Not really. The research was described to show the value of reducing density in screen design. From a practical standpoint, if the guidelines for alignment and groupings are adhered to, screen density will usually be reduced to an acceptable level.

Web Page Size

- Minimize page length.
  — Restrict to two or three screens of information.
- Place critical or important information at the very top so it is always viewable when the page is opened.
  — Locate it within the top 4 inches of page.

The answer to the question "What should be the maximum length of a Web page?" has no precise answer. Maximum length recommendations in the literature vary, running from "short" to "1–2" to "3" to "5" to even more. One serious problem in establishing an exact page size is that the multitudes of Web viewers use a variety of different browsers and monitors. Another problem is that font types and sizes can vary, impacting how much of a page is visible at any one time. What is viewable on one person's screen, then, may not be entirely visible on another. Another problem is that the viewable depth of a Web screen is somewhat less than the typical business information screen. Very few Web users have screens large enough that enable them to view an entire letter-size page all at once. A business information system, conversely, usually contains standardized applications, consistent size screens, and standard monitors.

In Web page design, what is generally agreed upon is the following:

Minimize page length Given the scarcity of Web page screen real estate, and its screen size variability, it is not practical to confine a page to the least common denominator display screen size. To fulfill the "Amount of Information" guidelines just described will often require a page length to exceed a "screenfull." Determining an optimum page length will require balancing these factors. Arguments for shorter pages and *against longer pages* are that longer pages:

- Tax the user's memory, as related information is more scattered and not always visible.
- Can lead to a lost sense of context as navigation buttons and major links disappear from view.
- Display more content and a broader range of navigation links making it more difficult for users to find and then decide upon what path to follow.
- Require excessive page scrolling, which may become cumbersome and inefficient.
- Are less conducive to the "chunking" information organization scheme commonly employed in Web sites.

Arguments *for longer pages* are that they:
- Resemble the familiar structure of paper documents.
- Require less "clicks" for navigating through a Web site.
- Are easier to download and print for later reading.
- Are easier to maintain because they possess fewer category navigation links to other pages.

Critical or important information at the very top. Critical or important information should be placed where it will be immediately visible when the page is displayed. In Web page design, this is referred to as "above the fold," a term borrowed from newspaper page layout. Above the fold is about the top 4 inches of a page. "Below the fold" will usually require scrolling to access and may not always be seen.

Deciding on Long versus Short Pages

- To find specific information quickly:
  — Create many links to short pages.

- To understand an entire concept without interruption:
  — Present the entire concept in one page with internal links to subtopics.
- To print all or most of the content to read offline:
  — Use one long page or prepare a version that uses one page.
- If page will be loading over slow modems and all pages are not needed:
  — Create a comprehensive contents page with links to many short pages.

Page size will also vary, depending upon the user's task and motivation, the page's purpose, and the Web page provider's objectives. If the user is interested and motivated, a longer page may be warranted, reducing the user's effort in reloading pages. If the user is being "sold" a product, advertising practices should be employed, including keeping pages short. If the page's purpose is strictly navigation, then one screen is most practical so that all navigation choices are visible. What must be determined in establishing page length, then, is the user's reading "rhythm" (Levine, 1995). Weinschenk (2001) provides the above page length recommendations based upon differing user needs.

Scrolling and Paging

- Scrolling:
  — Avoid scrolling to determine a page's contents.
  — Minimize vertical page scrolling.
  — When vertical scrolling is necessary to view an entire page:
    • Provide contextual cues within the page that it must be scrolled to view its entire contents.
    • Provide a unique and consistent "end of page" structure.
  — Avoid horizontal page scrolling.
- Paging:
  — Encourage viewing a page through "paging."
  — Create a second version of a Web site, one consisting of individual screens that are viewed through "paging."

In screen design over the past couple of decades the favored method of asking the user to move between screens of information has been through paging. A full screen of information is presented, the user does what is necessary to do to the screen, and then the entire screen is transmitted through a key action. If other user actions are then necessary to accomplish an objective, another full screen is presented and the process continues until an ending is reached. This method of interaction was practical and efficient for computer and monitor technology existing at that time, and it presented the user consistent and meaningful "chunks" of information to work on. Screen scrolling as an interaction method was also used over this time period but on a much more limited basis.

User performance using paging and scrolling has been the subject of occasional research efforts. One early study found that for novice users, paging through screens yielded better performance and was preferred. Dillon (1992), however, in a review of the research literature found no reliable differences using either method.

The scrolling technique used today in viewing screens was also established through research. There are two possible ways to control and view a scrolling screen, the telescope and the microscope approaches. In the *telescope* method, the model is that of a telescope, the window moves around the screen data much as a telescope scans the stars in the night sky. In the *microscope* approach, the screen data appears to move under a fixed viewing window, the way an object placed under a microscope is manually moved around to see it in its entirety. The research found that the telescope approach is more natural and causes fewer errors, and it was implemented. This is why, when scrolling today, clicking the up arrow on the scroll bar causes the data displayed on a screen to move downward. The data is not actually moving, the telescope through which the data is being viewed is moving upward.

Web technological requirements have tilted the scale toward scrolling as the favored method of page viewing. Early in it's popular life scrolling seemed to cause some difficulties for Web users, Nielsen (1996) reporting that only 10 percent of users went beyond what was visible on the screen by using scrolling. Apparently in 1996 paging was a well-ingrained habit. As user familiarity with the Web increased, so did scrolling familiarity, and in 1999 Nielsen (1999b) reported that most users were now used to scrolling, having gained the understanding that things were often hidden from view. In spite of its seeming acceptance, excessive page scrolling can be cumbersome and slow. It also can disrupt the user's perception of spatial location within a page, especially while the text is scrolling. To minimize these problems, do the following.

Avoid scrolling to determine page contents. A page's subject should be immediately recognizable. Elements crucial to identifying a page's contents must be viewable without requiring page scrolling. If not visible when the page is first displayed, these elements may never be seen. Place these content-identifying elements "above the fold," or in the top 4 inches of the page.

Minimize vertical scrolling. Some scrolling may be necessary to view the entire contents of a page. Minimize the requirement for vertical scrolling when defining, organizing, and laying out a page's components. For example, avoid large graphics and excessive amounts of white space. Place closest to the page's top the information most likely to be needed.

Provide contextual scrolling cues and a unique end-of-page structure. Lower parts of a page may be overlooked, especially if the visible portion appears to satisfy the user's needs and the user erroneously concludes that no more can be done. For pages exceeding one screen in length, provide contextual cues to the user that part of the page is hidden and that viewing the entire page will necessitate scrolling. Organize the information, for example, so that it is obvious there is more to follow. An incomplete alphabetical arrangement of information would be one such clue. Also, be cautious in placing screen-wide horizontal lines between groupings of content. This could convey to a causal user that the page's bottom has been reached. To identify the page bottom, provide a visually unique and consistent ending on all pages. A row of navigation links and other elements such as copyrights, e-mail address, and other contact information can signify "The End." Do not place these ending elements in other locations within the page or other pages. They will convey falsely to the user that the end has been reached.

Avoid horizontal scrolling. While some vertical scrolling is now acceptable in Web page design, horizontal scrolling must be avoided. A page too wide to be completely displayed within the confines of a screen will require continuous scrolling as reading is performed. This is extremely cumbersome and inefficient.

Encourage use of paging. Full-screen paging on the Web can be done by using the page-up and page-down keys or clicking on the scroll bar page-up or page-down icons. Text is then moved by the number of lines equaling screen size. This is almost always faster than scrolling a line at a time. Some recent studies have addressed the issue of Web page scrolling and paging.

Piolat, Roussey, and Thunin (1998) found, as in past studies, no significant differences between paging and scrolling in text reading. Paging users, however, were better at: building mental representations of the text, finding relevant information, and remembering the main ideas. Blinn and Biers (1999) found that, when searching Web sites with shorter pages, information was found faster using paging as opposed to scrolling. Mead, Spaulding, Sit, and Walker (1997) addressed the effects of an inexperienced user's age on paging and scrolling. Older users (64–81) were more likely to use a page at a time while reading; younger users (19–36) tended to scroll a line at a time. Older users also performed best when using short full pages of information rather than continuous long pages. Paging navigation, it seems, does have advantages for users. Encourage its use.

Paging version. Ensure the availability of full pages for reading and searching on the Web and, by creating a second version of a Web site, one consisting of individual screens that are viewed through "paging."

Distinctiveness

- Individual screen controls, and groups of controls, must be perceptually distinct.
  — Screen controls:
    - Should not touch a window border.
    - Should not touch each other.
  — Field and group borders:
    - Should not touch a window border.
    - Should not touch each other.
  — Buttons:
    - Should not touch a window border.
    - Should not touch each other.
- A button label should not touch the button border.
- Adjacent screen elements must be displayed in colors or shades of sufficient contrast with one another.

Elements of screen must be distinct, clearly distinguished from one another. Distinctiveness can be enhanced through separation and contrast.

All screen elements must be perceptually distinct. Distinctiveness is achieved by providing adequate separation between adjacent elements and screen boundaries and providing adequate separation between parts of an element. Screen controls, field and group borders, and buttons should not touch window borders or each other. Colors or shades used for adjacent screen elements must also contrast well with one another. Guidelines for color and shading are described in Step 12.

Focus and Emphasis

- Visually emphasize the:
  - Most prominent element.
  - Most important elements.
  - Central idea or focal point.
- To provide emphasis use techniques such as:
  - Higher brightness.
  - Reverse polarity or inverse video.
  - Larger and distinctive font.
  - Underlining.
  - Blinking.
  - Line rulings and surrounding boxes or frames.
  - Contrasting color.
  - Larger size.
  - Positioning.
  - Isolation.
  - Distinctive or unusual shape.
  - White space.
- De-emphasize less important elements.
- To ensure that emphasized screen elements stand out, avoid:
  - Emphasizing too many screen elements.
  - Using too many emphasis techniques.
  - Screen clutter.
- In Web page design:
  - Call attention to new or changed content.
  - Ensure that page text is not overwhelmed by page background.

Apply a visual emphasis technique to highlight the most important or prominent parts of a screen. An emphasized element should contrast with the rest of the screen, calling the user's eyes to it.

Brightness. A brighter element has a good attention-getting quality and no disturbing features. It may be used to indicate items in error, and increased brightness is the best vehicle for calling attention to data on inquiry screens. Do not use more than two brightness levels on a screen. If brightness has a fault, it is that displays with improperly set manual screen contrast controls can diminish its effectiveness, even causing it to disappear. This can be a major problem for displays placed in exceptionally bright viewing conditions.

Reverse polarity. Inverse video reverses an element's polarity. For example, on a screen with a specific level of dark text and a specific level of light background, certain elements can be emphasized by displaying them in the reverse: a text of the same lightness as that used on the regular screen on a background of the same darkness as is used on the regular screen.

For old text-based screens, reverse polarity meant displaying dark text on a light background, or reversing the standard light text on dark background. During the 1980s several studies comparing this reverse were performed and, in general, no differences in performance, eye-scanning behavior, or feelings of visual fatigue were uncovered. One study, however, did find reverse polarity more visually fatiguing, while another found green and orange phosphor reverse polarity screens easier to read but found no differences in white phosphor readability. These studies contributed to the popularity of orange phosphor screens at that time. In those days, it was generally found that people preferred dark background screens to white background screens because of the harshness and excessive brightness of backgrounds. There was one benefit to light background screens, however. Dark background screens can create a viewing problem, their mirror-like surfaces reflecting light from other outside sources back into the screen viewer's eyes. Light background screens absorb most of this light, instead of reflecting it back to the screen viewer.

For *elements* of screens—pieces of data, messages, and so on—reverse polarity has a very high attention-getting quality. It can be effectively used for items selected, items in error, information being acted upon, or information of current relevance.

Some cautions should be taken with reverse polarity. If reverse polarity is used to identify one kind of element, such as a text box or other boxed control, avoid what can best be described as the crossword puzzle effect—the haphazard arrangement of elements on the screen creating an image that somewhat resembles a typical crossword puzzle. An arrangement of elements might be created that tries to lead the eye in directions that the designer has not intended or causes elements to compete for the viewer's attention. The cause of this problem is using reverse polarity for too many purposes or by poor alignment and columnization of elements selected for this emphasis. Conservative use and alignment and columnization rules will minimize this effect.

If reverse polarity is used to highlight information such as messages or actions to be taken, allow an extra reversed character position on each side of the information. This will leave a margin around the information, improving legibility and giving it a more pleasing look. Last, reverse polarity can make text harder to read if the screen resolution and character sizes are not sufficient. A light screen background can actually bleed into its dark characters, reducing their legibility. This is a phenomenon called *iridescence.*

Fonts. Differences in fonts have a moderate attention-getting capability. Their varying sizes and shapes can be used to differentiate screen components. Larger, bolder letters can be used to designate higher-level screen pieces, such as different levels of headings, if the headings are used to search for something. Do not use larger fonts, however, for entry/modification (conversational) and display/read-only screens, because this will place too much emphasis in the headings themselves.

Emphasis should go to the screen data. If you are using multiple fonts, never use more than two styles or weights, and three sizes, on a screen.

Underlining. Underlining is a moderate attention-getting mechanism but it can reduce legibility, so it should be used conservatively and carefully. In graphical systems it is commonly used to designate keyboard equivalents or mnemonics. In Web pages it is used to designate navigation links.

Blinking. Blinking has a very high attention-getting capability, but it reduces text readability and is disturbing to most people. It often causes visual fatigue if used excessively. Therefore, it should be reserved for urgent situations and times when a quick response is necessary. A user should be able to turn off the blinking once his or her attention has been captured. The recommended blink rate is 2–5 Hz, with a minimum "on" time of 50 percent. An alternative to consider is creating an "on" cycle considerably longer than the "off," a wink rather than a blink.

Line rulings and surrounding boxes or frames. Use lines to emphasize and guide the user's eye through the screen. Use horizontal rulings as a substitute for spaces when breaking a screen into pieces. Use vertical rulings to convey to the screen viewer that a screen should be scanned from top to bottom. Use rules to surround radio button and check box controls, and other groupings of controls or important single controls. While many groupings are obvious without borders, borders certainly reinforce their existence. Use no more than three line thicknesses or two line styles on a screen.

Colors. Use color to emphasize and assist in the identification of screen components. Some colors appear brighter than others. Display no more than four colors at one time on a screen essentially alphanumeric in nature, six on a statistical graphics screen. Color considerations will be extensively reviewed in Step 12.

Other emphasis techniques. Other emphasis techniques include: displaying the element in a *larger size*, placing an element in a *position* where the eye first meets the screen, *isolating* the element from the remainder of the screen, presenting the element in a *distinctive or unusual shape*, and using *white space* to emphasize blocks of text. One's eyes will also be drawn to the start of any text following white space.

De-emphasize less important elements. To designate an element as not applicable or not active, dim it or gray it out.

Avoid too much emphasis. An emphasized element must, of course, attract the user's eye to it. The attraction capability of a mechanism is directly related to how well it stands out from its surroundings. Emphasis will loose it attracting value if too many different items on a screen are emphasized. A few hands raised for attention are much easier to deal with than many hands raised. Focus problems will also be created if too many emphasizing techniques are used within a screen. The user's attention will be drawn to the differences in techniques, and his or her information processing system will try to understand why the differences exist, instead focusing on the information itself. Minimization of clutter also assists a user in focusing on the most crucial part of a screen. In using emphasis, conservatism and simplicity is the key.

Web page emphasis. The dynamic nature of the Web and its available screen design tools raise some other emphasis considerations. New or changed Web page content should be emphasized to immediately call the user's attention to it when a page is presented. Inappropriate page backgrounds may degrade an emphasis technique's usability. Background graphics, pictures, patterns, or textures may reduce the technique's attention-getting quality, as well as reduce text legibility.

Conveying Depth of Levels or a Three-Dimensional Appearance

- Use perspective, highlighting, shading, and other techniques to achieve a three-dimensional appearance.
- Always assume that a light source is in the upper-left corner of the screen.
- Display command buttons above the screen plane.
- Display screen-based controls on, or etched or lowered below, the screen plane.
- Do not overdo things, and avoid:
  — Using perspective for noninteractive elements.
  — Providing too much detail.

The spatial composition of a screen can also be communicated by using perspective, highlighting, shading, and other techniques to achieve a three-dimensional appearance. In creating shadows, always assume that the light source is in the upper-left corner of the screen. To visually communicate function, consider displaying command buttons raised above the screen. Conversely, display screen-based controls on, or etched or lowered below, the screen plane. Consistently follow this concept on all screens. One caution, do not overdo things or the effect will be lost and visual clutter will emerge. Avoid using perspective for noninteractive elements, and do not provide too much detail.

Techniques used to achieve a three-dimensional appearance include overlapping, drop shadows, highlighting and lowlighting, growing and shrinking, and beveled edges (Marcus, 1992).

Overlapping. Fully display the window or screen element of current relevance and partially hide beneath it other screen windows or elements, as illustrated in Figure 3.18. The completeness or continuity of outline of the relevant element will make it appear nearer than those partially covered.

Drop shadows. To further aid in the perception of the placement of a pull-down above a screen, or a window above a screen or another window, locate a heavier

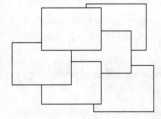

Figure 3.18   Overlapping screen elements.

line along the bottom and right edges of the pull-down or window. This creates the impression of a shadow caused by a light source in the upper-left corner of the screen, reinforcing the nearness of the important element. The light source should always appear to be upper left, the shadow lower right.

Highlighting and lowlighting. Highlighted or brighter screen elements appear to come forward, while lowlighted or less bright elements recede. Attention will be directed to the highlighted element.

Shrinking and growing. Important elements can be made to grow in size, while less important elements remain small or shrink. An icon, for example, should expand to a window when it is selected. The movement, as it expands, will focus attention upon it.

Beveled edges. A beveled edge (lines that are not at right angles to the screen element borders) will also give the impression of depth. With beveled edges, windows, buttons, and menu bar choices will appear to rise from the screen. To strengthen the three-dimensional aspect of the screen element, give it a drop shadow by shading the bottom and right sides with either a tone of gray or a darker shade of the basic screen color.

Texture change. Texture is the surface quality of an object. Varying the object's pattern of light and dark areas creates it. Increased density of an object implies a further distance. Increase the density of nonapplicable screen elements, and display currently relevant elements less densely. If textures are used as a code on screens, Shurtleff (1993) recommends using no more than six or seven. Also, a texture change should convey information that is not immediately apparent from name, shape, or other physical characteristic of an object. Finally, provide consistency; establish only one meaning for a texture.

Color change. Objects farther away appear hazy and less saturated. Increase haziness as screen element importance diminishes; display currently relevant elements more vividly.

Size change. Objects farther away appear smaller. Decrease the size of nonapplicable screen elements; display currently relevant elements as larger.

Clarity change. Objects not at the eye's focus distance appear fuzzy or blurred. Display nonapplicable elements as blurred, and currently relevant screen elements as clear.

Vertical location. The horizon appears higher, objects up close lower. Present currently applicable screen elements at the bottom of the screen, present nonapplicable elements at the screen's top.

Spacing change. Faraway objects appear more closely spaced, closer objects more widely spaced. Display nonapplicable elements as more closely spaced, currently applicable screen elements as more widely spaced.

Receding lines. Parallel lines converging and receding to a vanishing point imply depth.

Motion change. Objects moving at uniform speeds appear to be moving more slowly the farther away they are.

Presenting Information Simply and Meaningfully

- Provide legibility.
  — Information is noticeable and distinguishable.
- Provide readability.
  — Information is identifiable, interpretable, and attractive.
- Present information in usable form.
  — Translations, transpositions, and references to documentation should not be required to interpret and understand information.
- Utilize contrasting display features.
  — To attract and call attention to different screen elements.
- Create visual lines.
  — Implicit and explicit, to guide the eye.
- Be consistent.
  — In appearance and procedural usage.

Following are guidelines for presenting information on screens. The fundamental goals are clarity and simplicity in form, comprehensibility in organization, efficient information assimilation, and pleasantness in tone.

Legibility. Legibility is distinguishableness. Is the type of the proper kind and of adequate size and clarity for viewers of all ages? Is the contrast between text and its background adequate? In general, the legibility of screen text still does not match that of text presented on paper.

Readability. Is the information written at an understandable level for all users? Is it direct, simple, and easy to comprehend? Is visual interference minimized? When we read, we use the shape of a word as a strong aid in comprehension; often we do not read individual letters but recognize word shapes. Words are given more distinctive shapes by letter "ascenders" and "descenders." A lowercase letter's height is called its "x" height (the height of the letter x). Other letters are identical in height to the "x," such as the "e," "a," and "n" in the word "explain." Ascenders are letter strokes that rise above the x—the tops of the "l" and "i" in "explain," for example. Descenders are letter strokes that drop below the x—the bottom of the "p" in "explain." Research indicates that in the reading process the top half of a letter is the most important part of a word in comprehension. The top halves of letters are more distinctive than their bottom halves.

Usability. Screen information should be presented in a directly usable form. Reference to documentation or other extra steps for interpretation should never be required. In graphical system design, content consisting of words and text is much faster to comprehend and use than content in a graphical form.

Contrasting display features. Use contrasting display features to call attention to different screen components, items being operated upon, or urgent items. Usable features include such things as letter style, size, and color. Features chosen should provide perceptual cues to aid in screen component identification so that attention may be quickly and accurately focused. Perceptual cues clarify structure and relationships, and give hints to the reader. Good readers make great use of the typographic and semantic cues found in well-presented text.

Visual lines. The eye should be guided vertically or horizontally implicitly through the screen through the use of white space and content, typefaces, and control alignments. In situations where a large amount of information must be presented on one screen, eye movement direction may also be communicated to the viewer explicitly, through the drawing of actual vertical or horizontal rules. Purposeless, unfettered wandering of the eye should be discouraged.

Consistency. Methods chosen to present information must, of course, always be consistent in visual appearance and procedural usage.

Typography

In typography, by definition a typeface is the name of a type, such as Times New Roman, Arial, Verdana, or Helvetica. A font is a typeface of a particular size, such as Times Roman 16 point or Arial 12 point. In screen design, the terms have become somewhat interchangeable. In this discussion, the term font will be used to encompass both types and sizes.

In screen design, different fonts are used to organize information, establish importance, establish a reading order, and create a particular mood. A seemingly unending supply of typefaces, styles, and sizes are available for these purposes. Operating system and Web browser providers have also provided default fonts for various system components. Many screen users also have the ability to change fonts to suit their own liking, although many rarely do.

As these guidelines are presented, note the limits in the number of font variations recommended. Using too many techniques at one time only leads to screen clutter and the impression of confusion.

Font Types and Families

- Use simple, common, readable fonts.
    — Any sans serif such as Helvetica or Verdana.
    — Times Roman.
- Use no more than two families, compatible in terms of line thicknesses, capital letter height, and so on.
    — Assign a separate purpose to each family.
    — Allow one family to dominate.

Visually simple, common, readable fonts are needed for clarity on most screens, including business system applications and the text content of Web pages. Ornate, specialty, or "cool" fonts should be avoided because they are not familiar and may degrade on the screen, reducing legibility. Helvetica and Verdana, designed especially for use on screens, are sans serif typefaces, and they are considered more contemporary. Times Roman possesses very small serifs, and it is considered more conservative and traditional.

Generally, sans serif typefaces are recommended (serifs are the small cross strokes that appear on the arms of some letters) if the type is 10 or fewer points in size, if the display environment is less than ideal, or if the screen is of low resolution. The serifs can wash out under these conditions. Fonts with serifs, it is felt, provide better links between letters in a word, provide a horizontal guideline for the eye, and help in distinguishing one letter from another. Recent research (Boyarski, Neuwirth, Forlizzi, and Regli, 1998) compared reading speeds for the 10-point serif fonts Georgia and Times Roman with the 10-point sans serif font Verdana. Monitor resolution was 640 by 480 pixels. No significant differences in reading speed were found.

All typefaces are named, some after their designers (for example, Garamond), some after locations where they originated (Helvetica after Switzerland), and other for the publications for which they were designed (Times). Within each typeface are style variations: regular, italics, boldface, outlines, and shadows. These groupings are called *famili*es.

A family of styles is designed to complement one another, creating unity in design. An example of a family is that of Times illustrated in Figure 3.19.

Similar typefaces are grouped into what are called *races*. One kind of race is called *roman*, which contains the Times typeface illustrated here as well as the Bookman, Schoolbook, and Palatino typefaces. A second race is *sans serif*, where the typefaces Helvetica and Avant Garde reside. Another race is named Old English. An effective design can almost always be achieved by staying within one typeface race. If it is necessary to mix typeface families on a screen do the following:

- Never mix families within the same race. Typographic noise is created.
- Assign a separate purpose to each family. A sans serif typeface for the title and headings and a roman typeface for the body is a good combination. The opposite is also acceptable.
- Allow one family to dominate.

Times Roman

Times Italic

Times Bold

Times Bold Italic

Times Outline

Times Shadow

Figure 3.19   The Times family of type.

Professional designers rarely use anything but the traditional, simple typefaces. These fonts have been crafted through centuries of use. When in doubt, use the same font and its variants for all design needs. This better than a risky aesthetic decision.

Font Size

- Use no more than three sizes.
  - Consider "X" height.
- For graphical systems use:
  - 12 point for menus.
  - 10 point for windows.
- For Web pages use:
  - 12–14 points for body text.
  - 18–36 points for titles and headings.
- For line spacing use one to one and one-half times font size.

- Never change established type sizes to squeeze in more text.

Font sizes are described by points—the distance between the top of a letter's ascender and the bottom of its descender. One point equals 1/12 inch. Font sizes should be large enough to be legible on standard monitors. Also, a typeface displayed on a personal computer will look 2–3 points larger than the same typeface on a Macintosh.

Variations in type sizes should also be minimized, no more than three being the maximum to be displayed at one time on a screen. In selecting a typeface it is important to consider its *x-height*, or the height of its lowercase x and other similar letters. Two typefaces may share the same point size but one may *appear* significantly larger because its x-height is larger, as illustrated in Figure 3.20. Legibility can be affected by x-height.

Many systems use a 12-point type for menus and 10-point for windows. Dropping below eight points significantly degrades legibility. In Web page design larger type sizes are recommended, 12–14 points for body text and 18–36 points for titles and headings. Line spacing should be one to one and one-half times font size. For comparison purposes, recommended paper document type sizes and styles are as follows:

Chapter headings:	24-point bold
Section headings:	18-point bold
Subsection headings:	14-point bold
Paragraph headings:	12-point bold
Body text:	10-point
Annotations/footnotes:	8-point

Never change a selected type size for a screen component to squeeze something in. The differences in size will be noticeable and very disturbing.

abcdefghijklmnopqrstuvwxyz

abcdefghijklmnopqrstuvwxyz

abcdefghijklmnopqrstuvwxyz

Figure 3.20   Types with same point size and different x heights (from top to bottom, Gatsby, Times Roman, and Avant Garde).

Font Styles and Weight

- Use no more than:
  - — Two styles of the same family.
    - Standard and *italic*.
    - *Italic* is best presented in a serif font.
  - — Two weights.
    - Regular and **bold**.
    - **Bold** is best presented in a sans serif font.
- Use *italics* when you want to call attention.
- Use **bold** when you want to call attention or create a hierarchy.
- In Web pages, use an <u>underline</u> only to indicate a navigation link.

Styles. Italics may be used to emphasize something or attract attention on a screen. Because it may be hard to read on many monitors, it should be used sparingly. Boyarski, Neuwirth, Forlizzi, and Regli (1998) in their study did compare Verdana Standard with Verdana Italic, but found no differences in reading speed. (Technically, a sans serif type is slanted, not truly "italics".) For the Verdana font, larger use seems justified. Italic is best presented in a serif font. In general, though, restrict italics to words or short phrases; don't use it for large blocks of text. Never use more than two styles at one time. A standard font and its italics is a good combination. Because of degraded legibility, outline and shadow style variations should be used only with extreme caution on screens

Boldface. Use bold when you want to call attention to something. Typically, screens will be used again and again, and something bold often becomes too visually heavy. Use of too much bold is considered shouting, and nothing stands out. Like italics, use bold sparingly, restricting it to words or short phrases. Don't use it for large blocks of text. Bold's most effective use is for titles, headings, and key items. Restrict a font to two weights, regular and bold, although in Web page design, use of more weights is acceptable. Bold is best presented in a sans serif font. The differing stroke widths of serif fonts cause presentation problems over different font sizes.

Underline. In Web pages, an underline is used to designate a navigation link. It should only be used for this purpose. Its use in any other way will be confusing to the user.

Font Case

- Use mixed-case for:
  — Control captions.
  — Data.
  — Control choice descriptions.
  — Text.
  — Informational messages.
  — Instructional information.
  — Menu descriptions.
  — Button descriptions.
- Consider using upper case or capitalization for:
  — Title.
  — Section headings.
  — Subsection headings.
  — Caution and warning messages.
  — Words or phrases small in point size.
- Use all lower case with caution.

The screen designer often has the choice of whether to display screen components in mixed case or upper case. Upper case means all capital letters. Mixed case usually implies a predominance of lowercase letters with occasional capitalization as needed (initial letter of first word, acronyms, abbreviations, proper nouns, and so on).

The research on textual material is clear. One of the earliest studies, Tinker (1955), in a study of reading from hard-copy materials, found that mixed-case text is significantly faster to read than uppercase text. Subsequent studies also found large advantages in reading speed and reading comprehension for mixed-case text. The advantage of mixed-case over uppercase text is that it gives a word a more distinctive shape. Uppercase letters are all the same height; lowercase letters have different heights. These height differences aid comprehension.

The research on screen captions and menu choice descriptions, however, leans in another direction. Studies have found that captions and menu choice descriptions using uppercase characters are searched faster than those using mixed-case characters.

Why this difference? The materials giving better results for mixed-case text appear to be of a longer, textual nature. The caption materials appear to be single words or short phrases. It may be that the superiority of mixed-case text does not exhibit itself until text of an extended nature is read. Why short uppercase captions were actually superior to mixed-case ones is unknown. In light of this research, the following is recommended.

Mixed case. Always use mixed case for anything textual in nature, including text itself, messages, instructional information, figure and table descriptions, and so forth. Text, messages, and instructions reflect the years of research on readability. Also use mixed case for most other screen components, including control captions, data, control choice descriptions, and menu descriptions. These mixed-case recommendations also reflect what is becoming a de facto standard, found in various product style guides.

One choice in using mixed case is whether to use the *sentence style* or *headline style* of presentation. Sentence style is what you are reading now, the initial sentence letter is capitalized and the remainder of the sentence is lower case (except for acronyms, abbreviations, proper nouns, and so on). For anything more than one sentence in length, the sentence style must be followed in presenting textual information. For short phrases, such as control captions and headings, the more declarative headline style may be used.

Upper case. Unfortunately, most style guides, such as IBM's *SAA CUA* and Microsoft's *Windows Interface Guidelines,* recommend presenting *everything* on a screen in mixed case. That this is an extrapolation of the textual reading research to all written words can only be assumed.

Contrary to style guide recommendations, on screens capitalization can and should be judiciously used. Consider using uppercase text for the screen title and, most importantly, for all screen headings. Capitalization will set headings off from the many other screen components described above, which are displayed in mixed case. Headings on screens are a learning aid. They enable the user to become familiar with screen organization and relationships. With experience, the screen user finds headings less important. Capitalization will set them off from the remaining screen elements, making them easier to ignore when they are no longer needed. Screen design research does not discount using upper case.

On Web screens, the endless variety of display techniques (different fonts, font sizes, font weights, and so on) makes the use of capitalization for component differentiation much less necessary. On all screens, however, do consider using capitalization to call attention to important things, including caution and warning messages. Also, capitalization may be substituted for mixed case when a small font size is necessary within a screen component, and the small size degrades word legibility.

All lower case. In an attempt to be different, text or sentences in all lower case have begun to appear, that is, there is no initial capital letter on the first sentence word. Be cautious in using this approach; it does not conform to the mental model concerning sentence structure we have well ingrained within us. The visual beginning of a sentence anchor point has disappeared, it looks out of context, and it looks very casual. This style is rarely appropriate for a business application.

Defaults

- For graphical operating systems, use the standard system fonts.
- For Web pages design for the default browser fonts.
- Consider that the user may change the fonts.

A system's default fonts should be used to ensure usability and consistency. They must be known in the design process. Unfortunately, defaults may vary by operating system and browser.

Graphical systems. Use the standard system fonts. For example, with Microsoft Windows 98 and NT 4.0 the default is MS Sans Serif 8 point. For Windows 2000 it is Tahoma 8 point, although it must be set.

Web pages. Not all browsers provide the same typographic operations. If a page is designed using a font that the user does not have installed, the browser displays its default fonts. Many older browsers support only two fonts, Times Roman and Courier. Newer browsers support more fonts but they must be installed on the machine doing the browsing. Default fonts may include Times New Roman, Arial, Helvetica, and Verdana. It is best to stick with the fonts installed on the users' computers. Available options must be known before beginning the design process.

Consistency

- Establish a consistent hierarchy and convention for using typefaces, styles, and sizes.
  - Decide on a font for each different level of importance in the hierarchy.
  - Communicate hierarchy with changes in:
    - Size.
    - Weight.
    - Color.

To aid screen learning and improve screen scanning and readability, apply typeface size and style conventions in a consistent manner to all screen components. First, determine the hierarchy or levels of importance to be presented within an application or Web site, then, decide on a font for each level of the hierarchy. In a graphical business system, screen elements include the title, section headings, subsection headings, control captions, data, instructional information, and so forth. In Web site design important elements include the page heading, section headings, body text, icon captions, lists of navigation links, and so forth. Finally, communicate the hierarchy through variations is font size, weight, and color. Ensure that there is adequate visual contrast between elements composing the hierarchy. (Do not forget, however, that screen element location and its positional relationship to other screen elements also aid in the elements identification.)

Some cautionary reminders: Choose and combine font families with care, and too many font variations will only create visual clutter.

Other

- Always consider the visual capabilities of the user.
- Always verify that the design has succeeded using the selected fonts.

Age considerations. Unfortunately, as we all know, the eye's capability begins to diminish as we age. The eye begins it aging process in our early thirties. At 40 the process accelerates, and by age 50 most people need 50 percent more light to read by than they did when they were in their twenties. Failing to be able to read a menu in a dimly lit restaurant is often the first time we become aware of this problem. Smaller type sizes and text with insufficient background contrast may be more difficult for older people to use. Type sizes, styles backgrounds should always be chosen considering the ages of the screen users.

Font selection verification. Always check that the design has succeeded using the selected fonts. Ensure that the screens are legible and readable from all viewing distances and angles.

Paper versus Screen Reading

■ Provide a facility for printing out a hard copy of documents.

Printing technology has been evolving for several centuries. Factors such as type size and style, character and line spacing, and column and margin widths have been the focus of research for a good part of that time. The product of this research is highly readable and attractive printed material. Conversely, CRT-based characters are a relatively new innovation, with many technical limitations. The result is a displayed character that often lacks the high quality a paper medium can provide. This disparity in quality has resulted in performance differences when paper and screen reading of materials have been compared. Various researchers over the years have found screen reading speeds as much as 40 percent slower, and more error prone.

More recent research indicates that, as display resolution improves, the reading speed differences are being reduced, if not eliminated. Reading performance, using both hard-copy paper documents and monitors at different resolutions, was the subject of two studies by Ziefle (1998). In the first study she compared paper printed at 255 dots per inch (dpi) and monitors whose resolutions were 832×600 pixels (60 dpi) and 1664×1200 pixels (120 dpi). A 19-inch monitor showing black characters on a light background was used, and reading speeds and proofreading accuracy were compared. Ziefle found no difference in performance between the monitors with different resolutions. There was, however, a significant advantage for hard-copy over monitor usage. Reading from paper was faster, 200 words per minute to 180 wpm, and proofreading accuracy was higher. Reading from paper was also preferred by 80 percent of the users. The remaining 20 percent preferred the higher resolution screen (1664×1200).

Gujar, Harrison, and Fishkin (1998), however, compared text written on paper with text presented on screens and found no statistically significant differences in reading time and detected errors. Participants, though, rated reading from paper significantly better than reading from screens.

For extended reading, the hard-copy display of material still appears to have significant advantages, however, and will probably continue to for some time. People prefer reading from paper. Necessary screen-reading motor activities (scrolling, paging, and so on) are more cumbersome than the page-turning task of reading from a paper. Paper reading also offers much more convenience, the reader being much less constrained physically and environmentally. (Paper reading can be performed by the pool, in bed, or any place else where significant light exists.) Always provide a facility for printing hard copies of documents.

Screen Elements

Elements of a screen include control captions, the data or information displayed on the screen, headings and headlines, instructional information, and the screen's title. The following guidelines address these screen components.

Captions/Labels

- Identify controls with captions or labels.
- Fully spell them out in a language meaningful to the user.
- Display them in normal intensity.
- Use a mixed-case font.
- Capitalize the first letter of each significant word.
- End each caption with a colon (:).
- Choose distinct captions that can be easily distinguished from other captions.
  — Minimal differences (one letter or word) cause confusion.

Identify controls with captions. All screen controls should have captions or labels that identify the content of the control. The context in which information is found in the world at large provides cues to the information's meaning. A number on a telephone dial is readily identifiable as a telephone number; the number on a metal plate affixed to the back of an automobile is readily identified as a license number. The same information displayed on a screen, being out of context, may not be readily identifiable.

There are, however, some exceptions to this rule on read-only or inquiry screens. The structure of the data itself in some cases may be enough to identify its meaning. The most obvious example is name, street, city, state, and zip code. Date may be another possibility. Elimination of these common captions will serve further to clean up read-only screens. Before eliminating them, however, it should be determined that all screen users will be able to identify these fields all the time.

Structure and size. Captions on screens must clearly and concisely describe the information displayed. They are very important for inexperienced screen users. As one becomes more experienced, their importance diminishes. Therefore, captions should be fully spelled out in the natural language of the user. In general, abbreviations and contractions should not be used. To achieve the alignment recommendations to be discussed shortly, an occasional abbreviation or contraction may be necessary, but choose those that are common in the everyday language of the application or those that are meaningful and easily learned. Also, display captions in a moderate brightness or intensity. Visual emphasis will be directed to the screen data or information.

Significant word capitalization. With mixed-case field captions, capitalize the first letter of each significant word using the headline style previously described. A caption is not a sentence but the name for an area into which information will be keyed. This makes it a proper noun. In situations in which a caption is phrased as a question, it is a sentence, and then only its initial letter should be capitalized. Never begin a caption or sentence with a lowercase letter. A capital letter makes it easier for the eye to identify the start of each caption.

Unfortunately, IBM's SAA CUA and Microsoft's Windows style guides do not follow the headline style of using a capital letter for the initial letter of each significant word of the caption. They prefer and recommend the sentence style, capitalization of the initial letter of the first word only (except for acronyms, abbreviations, proper nouns, and so on).

Designate with a colon. A caption should be ended with a colon (:) to clearly identify it as such. The colon is unobtrusive, does not physically resemble a letter or number, and is grammatically meaningful, since it is used chiefly to direct attention to matter that follows. Unfortunately, many graphical systems do not follow this convention, and captions visually blend with other screen elements. The Windows style guide *does* recommend using a colon after captions.

Since the recommended entry area for an entry control will be a box, adequately distinguishing the caption from the entry field itself, the inclusion of a colon may seem redundant. However, read-only, display, and inquiry screens are most effective if the data displayed is not presented in a box, making a colon to distinguish caption from data absolutely necessary. Including a colon after all captions, therefore, will provide consistency across all screens.

Distinctiveness. Captions that are similar often repeat the same word or words over and over again. This directs a viewer's attention to the pattern created by the repetitive word, increases the potential for confusion, adds to density, and adds to screen clutter. A better solution is to incorporate the common words into headings, subheadings, or group identifiers, as illustrated in Figure 3.21.

Data Fields

- For entry or modifiable data fields, display data within:
  — A line box.
  — A reverse polarity box.
- For inquiry or display/read-only screens, display data on the normal screen background.
- Visually emphasize the data fields.

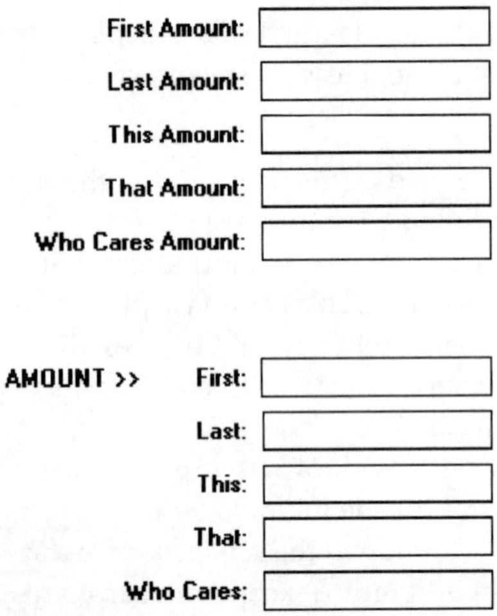

First Amount:	_____
Last Amount:	_____
This Amount:	_____
That Amount:	_____
Who Cares Amount:	_____

AMOUNT >>

First:	_____
Last:	_____
This:	_____
That:	_____
Who Cares:	_____

Figure 3.21 Providing better control caption discrimination. (The redundant word "amount" is incorporated into a heading.)

Two kinds of data fields are found on screens, those into which data may be entered or that contain data that may be modified, and those that only present data that cannot be changed. The design rules for each kind differ.

Entry/modifiable fields. An entry or modifiable field must possess the following qualities:

- Draw a person's attention to the fact that information must be keyed or selected in it.
- Not detract from the legibility of characters being keyed into it.
- Permit easy designation of the kind or structure of the entry required, such as incorporation of slashes (/) in a date field.
- Indicate the maximum size of the entry required.

    In an early study using text-based screens, it was found that people overwhelmingly preferred that something displayed on a screen indicate where data must be entered. In another study, it was found that the best alternatives for defining an entry field were a broken line underscore or a box. An underscore was traditionally used on text-based screens; the box is now recommended for, and should be used on, graphical screens.

Display/read-only screens. For inquiry or display/read-only screens, it is best for the data to be presented on the background of the screen. This permits easier scanning and information location; the reasoning will be discussed in the "Display/Read-Only" screen organization section following shortly.

Visual emphasis. Data or information is the most important part of any screen. It should be highlighted in some manner, either through higher intensity, boldness, or a brighter color. Headings and captions are most important for the new or casual user. As people become familiar with a system and screens, their attention is immediately drawn to the data when a screen is presented. An experienced user will often work with a screen just perusing the data, ignoring captions and headings. Highlight the data so it will attract the user's eyes. Other screen elements will be easier to ignore.

Control Captions/Data Fields

- Differentiate captions from data fields by using:
  — Contrasting features, such as different intensities, separating columns, boxes, and so forth.
  — Consistent physical relationships.

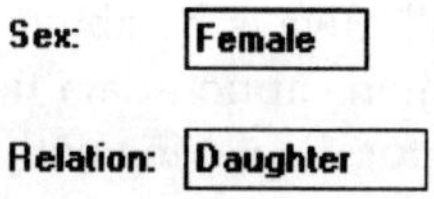

Figure 3.22

- For single data fields:
  — Place the caption to left of the data field.

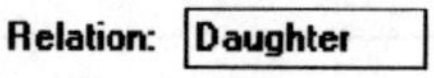

Figure 3.23   Relation: [Daughter]

  — Align the caption with the control's data.
  — Alternately, place the caption above the data field.
  —Align captions justified, upper left to the data field.

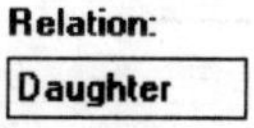

Figure 3.24

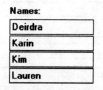

  — Maintain consistent positional relations within a screen, or within related screens, whenever possible.
- For multiple listings of columnar-oriented data, place the caption above the columnized data fields.

Figure 3.25

Names:
[Deirdra]
[Karin]
[Kim]
[Lauren]

Captions must be complete, clear, easy to identify, easy to scan, and distinguishable from other captions and data fields.

Differentiating captions from data. Captions and data should be visually distinguishable in some manner so that they do not have to be read in context to determine which is which. A common failing of many past screens is that the captions and data have the same appearance and blend into one another when the screen is filled. This makes differentiation difficult and increases caption and field data search time. Methods that can be used to accomplish differentiation, in addition to designating captions with a colon, are using contrasting display features and consistent positional relationships.

Single data fields. The recommended location for the caption is to the left of the data field and horizontally aligned with the field data. Alternately, the caption for a single data field may be positioned left-aligned above the data field. Maintain consistent positional relationships within a screen, and between multiple related screens whenever possible.

Columnar-oriented listings. For multiple listings of columnar data, place the caption above the data fields. Left/justify the caption above the data fields. Use horizontal caption formats for single fields and a columnar caption orientation for repeating fields to provide better discrimination between single and repeating fields. The single-field caption will always precede the data, and captions for repeating columnar fields will always be above the top data field. Figures 3.28 through 3.44 illustrate common caption-data field discrimination problems and the recommended solutions for displaying both entry/modifiable fields and display/read-only/inquiry fields.

Control Caption/Data Field Justification

■ 1. First Approach
   — Left-justify both captions and data fields.
   — Leave one space between the longest caption and the data field column.

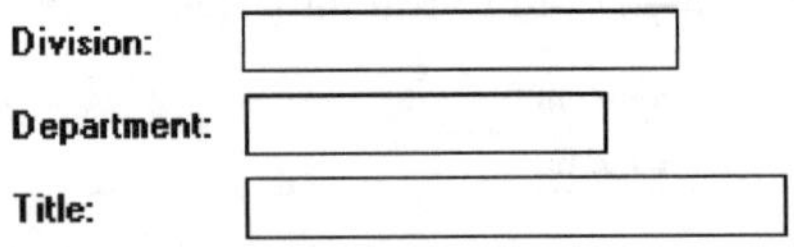

Division:

Department:

Figure 3.26   Title:

■ 2. Second Approach
   — Left-justify data fields and right-justify captions to data fields.
   — Leave one space between each.

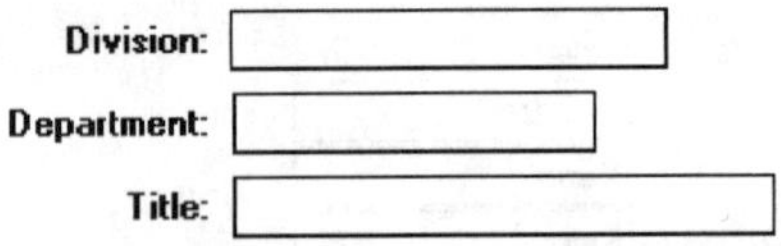

Division:

Department:

Figure 3.27   Title:

Figures 3.28 through 3.44 contain a series of screens in a variety of formats containing either entry/modification fields or display/read-only fields. The author's comments are found with each screen. What are your thoughts?

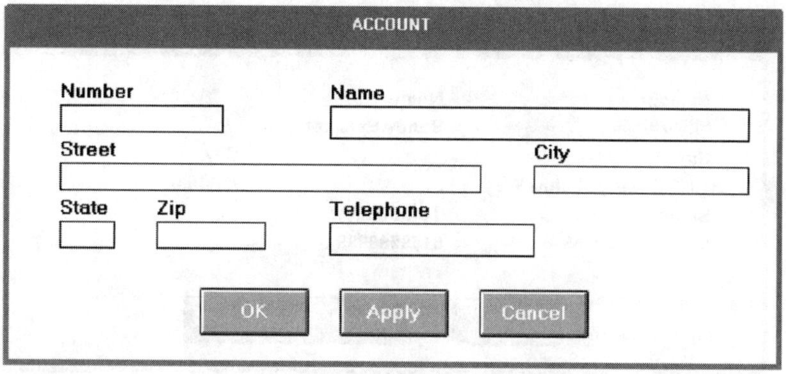

Figure 3.28   Entry screen with captions above single data fields. Captions distinct from data but with poor alignment and organization of fields. Left-to-right orientation and no groupings. Fair readability.

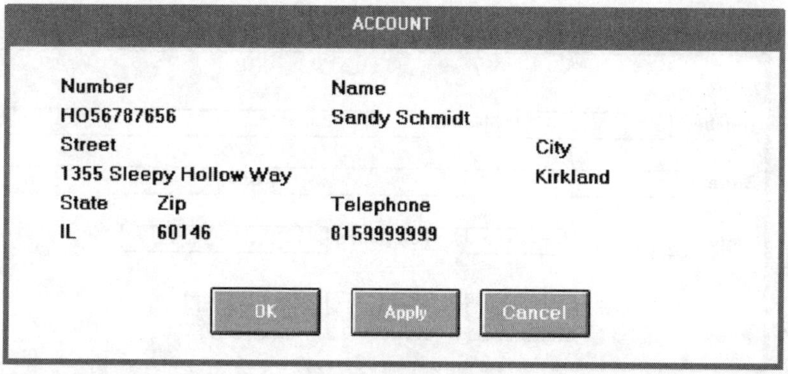

Figure 3.29   Display/read-only inquiry screen maintaining same structure as 3.22. Extremely poor differentiation of captions and data. Crowded look and extremely poor readability.

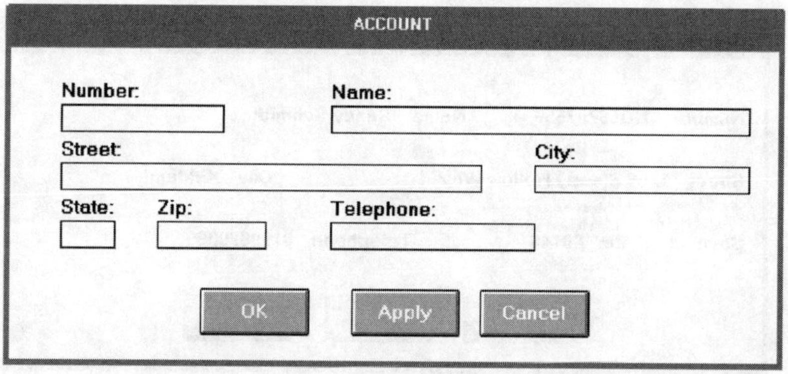

Figure 3.30   Entry screen in 3.28 with colons attached to captions. Captions somewhat more distinctive but still with poor alignment and organization of fields, left-to-right orientation and no groupings. Fair readability.

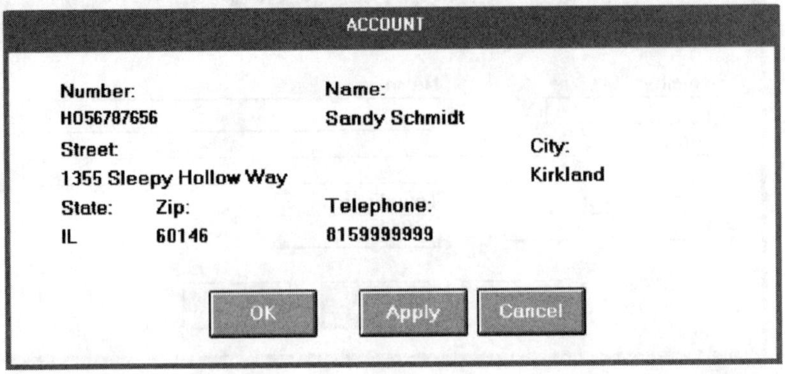

Figure 3.31 Display/read-only screen maintaining same structure as 3.30. Somewhat better differentiation of captions and data than 3.29 but still with a crowded look and poor readability.

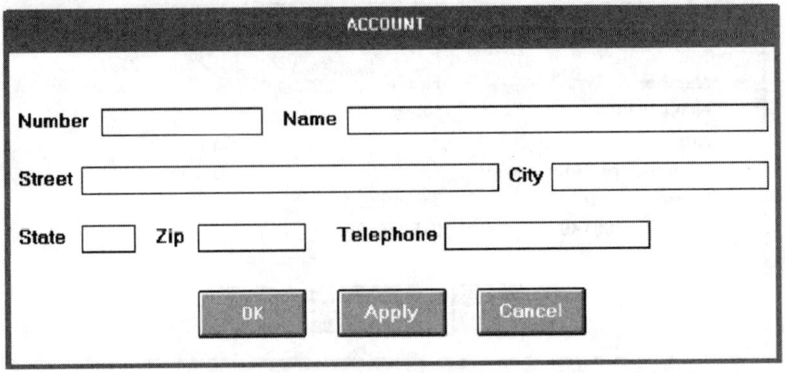

Figure 3.32 Entry/modification screen with captions to left of single data fields. Captions distinct from data but with poor alignment and organization of fields. Left-to-right orientation and no groupings. Fair readability.

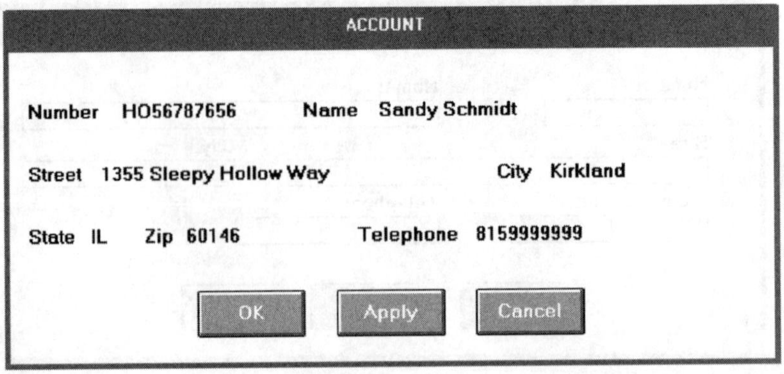

Figure 3.33 Display/read-only screen maintaining same structure as 3.32. Extremely poor differentiation of captions and data. Less crowded look than previous display/inquiry screens but still poor readability.

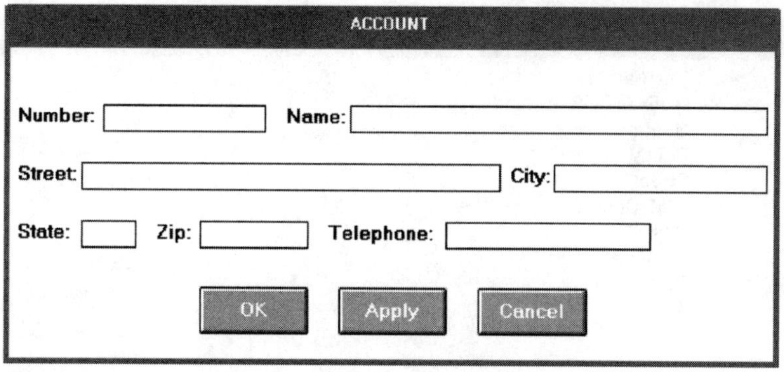

Figure 3.34   Entry/modification screen in 3.32 with colons attached to captions. Captions somewhat more distinctive but still poor alignment and organization of fields, left-to-right orientation and no groupings. Fair readability.

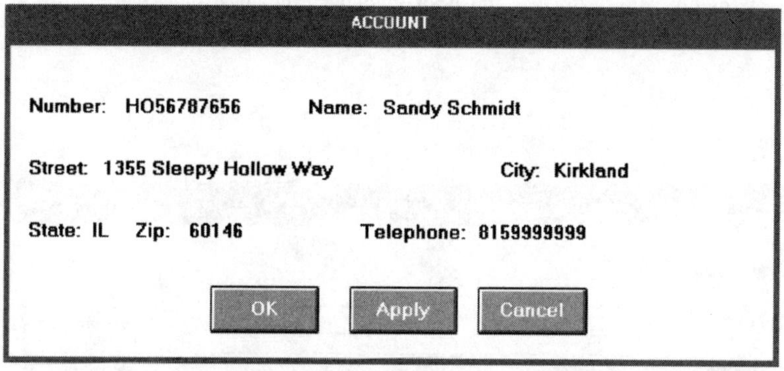

Figure 3.35   Display/read-only screen maintaining same structure as 3.34. Somewhat better differentiation of captions and data than 3.33 but still poor readability.

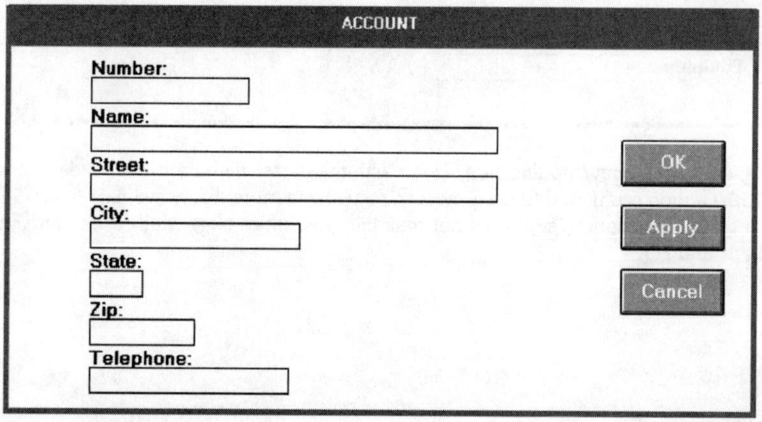

Figure 3.36   Entry/modification screen with much better alignment and readability than previous screens. Captions crowd data fields, however. Also, has no groupings and does not maintain post office suggested format for City, State, and Zip.

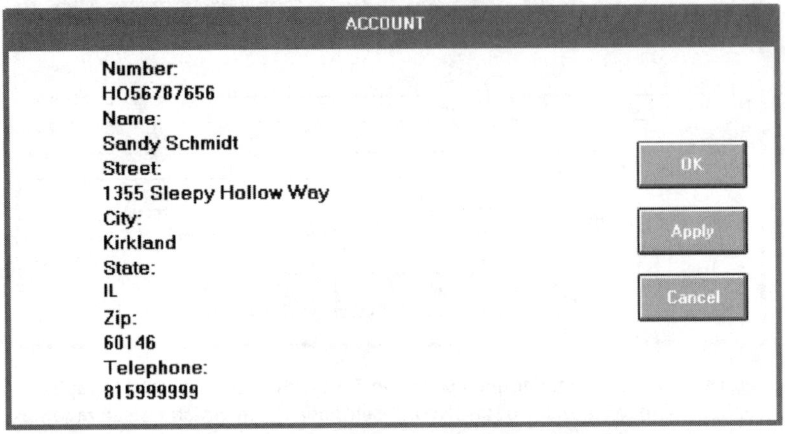

Figure 3.37 Display/read-only screen maintaining same aligned structure as 3.36. Captions not very distinctive and poor readability. Again, it looks very dense and crowded.

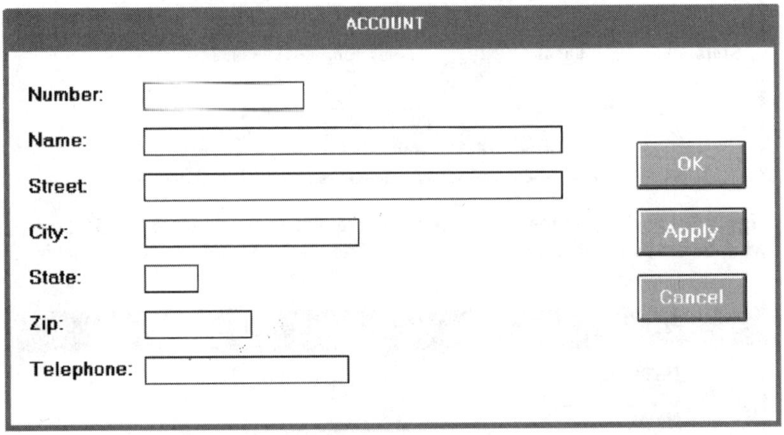

Figure 3.38 Entry/modification screen with the better alignment and readability of 3.36. Caption positioned to left, however, resulting in more distinctive data fields. Still no groupings, though, and does not maintain post office suggested format for City, State, and Zip.

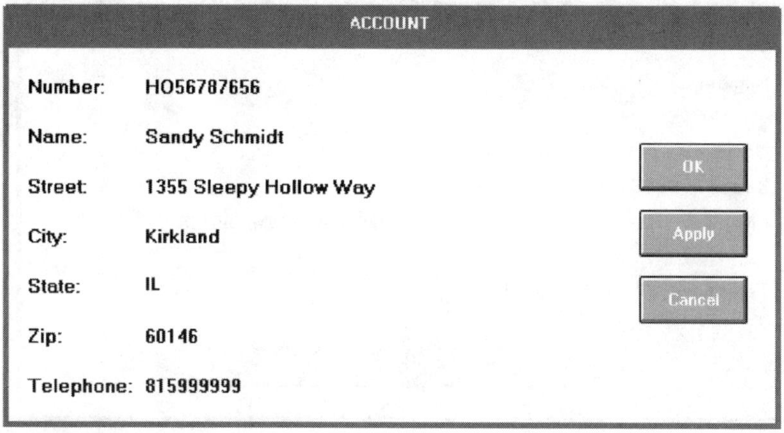

Figure 3.39 Display/read-only screen maintaining same alignment and positioning of captions of 3.38. Captions and data much more distinctive. Still no groupings though, and does not maintain post office suggested format for City, State, and Zip.

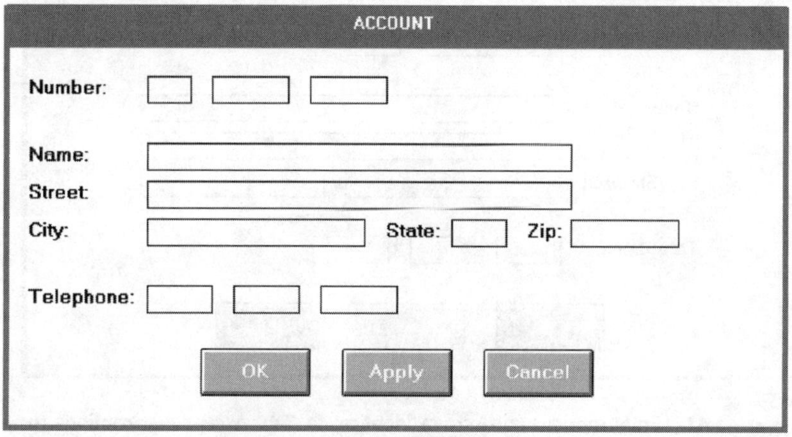

Figure 3.40 Entry/modification screen providing alignment, groupings, and the suggested and familiar post office address format. Data fields also segmented to enhance readability (Number and Telephone).

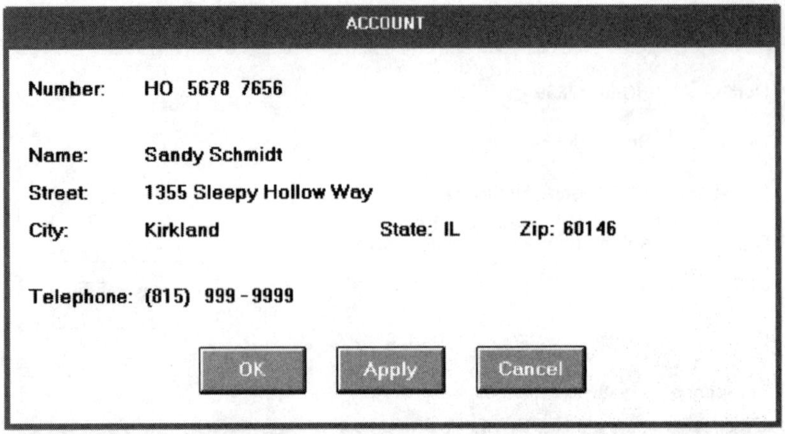

Figure 3.41 Display/read-only screen maintaining same item alignment and positioning, and data field segmentation as 3.40. Some data distinctiveness is lost and minor crowding occurs, however, because of the location of the captions for State and Zip between data fields.

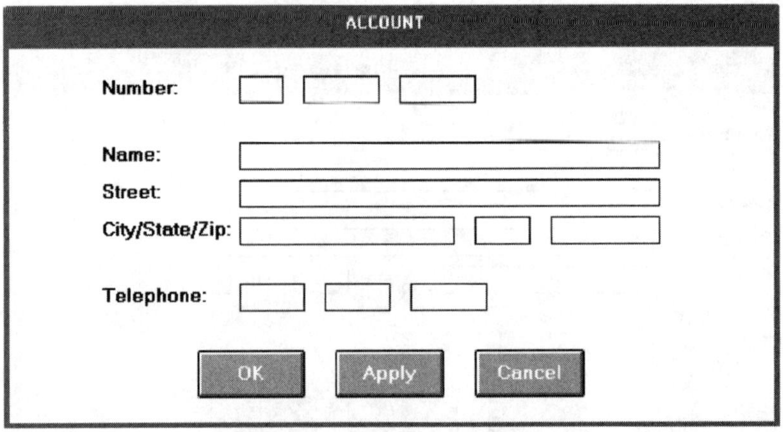

Figure 3.42 Entry/modification screen identical to 3.40 except that captions for State and Zip are stacked with City, enhancing distinctiveness and readability of the data fields. The screen also achieves a more compact and balanced look. The recommended style for this kind of entry screen.

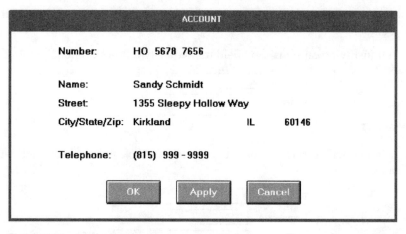

Figure 3.43 Display/read-only screen maintaining same alignment, item positioning, and data segmentation as 3.42. Good readability but the lengthy caption City/State/Zip does impinge upon the distinctiveness for the data.

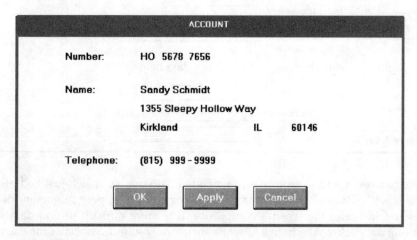

Figure 3.44 Display/read-only screen identical to 3.43 except that the captions Street and City/State/Zip have been eliminated to improve data field distinctiveness. The content of the data should make the identity of these fields obvious. The recommended style for this kind of display/read-only screen.

Justification of single captions and data fields can be accomplished in several ways. These include:

A. Left-justifying captions; data field immediately follows caption.

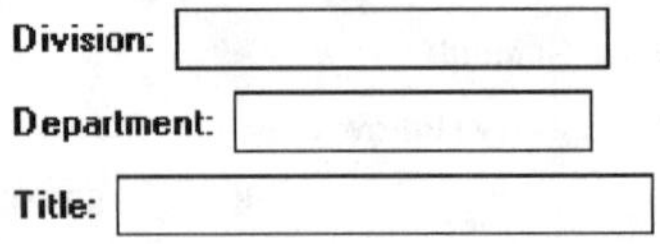

Division:

Department:

Figure 3.45   Title:

B. Left-justifying captions; left-justifying data fields; colon (:) associated with captions.

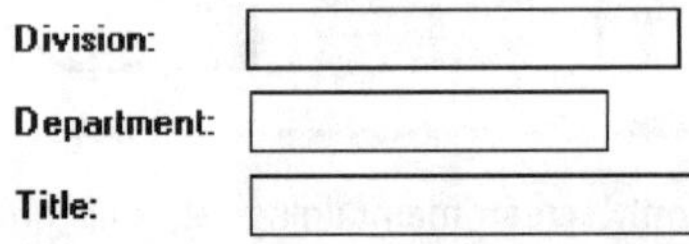

Division:

Department:

Figure 3.46   Title:

C. Left-justifying captions; left-justifying data fields; colon (:) associated with data field.

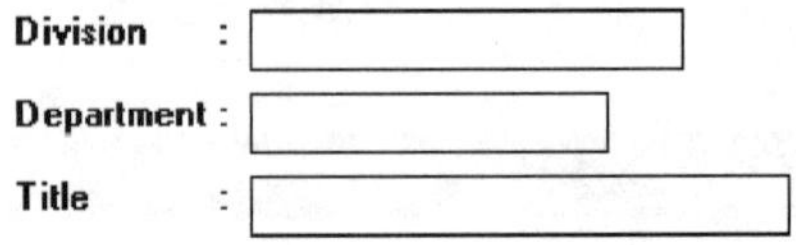

Division   :

Department :

Title   :

Figure 3.47

D. Right-justifying captions; left-justifying data fields.

Division:

Department:

Title:

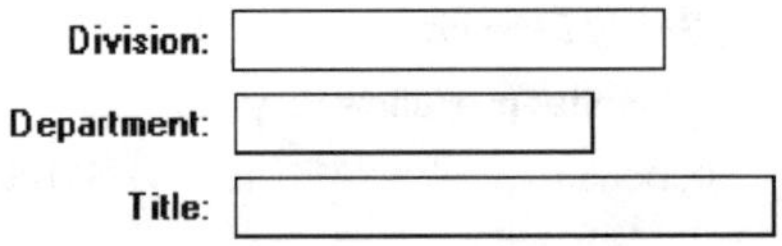

Figure 3.48

Alternatives A and C are not recommended. Alternative A, left-justified aligned captions with data fields immediately following, results in poor alignment of data fields and increases the screen's complexity. It is more difficult to find data when searching data fields. Alternative C, while structurally sound, associates the colon primarily with the data field. The strongest association of the colon should be with the caption.

The two most desirable alternatives are B and D. Alternative B, left-justified captions and data fields, is the first approach illustrated in these guidelines. Alternative D, right-justified captions and left-justified data fields, is the second approach illustrated in these guidelines.

Left-justified captions and data (B). A disadvantage to this approach is that the caption beginning point is usually farther from the entry field than the right-justified caption approach. A mix of caption sizes can cause some captions to be far removed from their corresponding data field, greatly increasing eye movements between the two and possibly making it difficult to accurately tie caption to data field. Tying the caption to the data field by a line of dots (. . . . .) solves the association problem but adds a great deal of noise to the screen. This does not solve the eye movement problem. Eye movement inefficiencies can be addressed by abbreviating the longer captions. The cost is reduced caption clarity.

An advantage to this approach is that section headings using location positioning as the key element in their identification do stand out nicely from the crisp left-justified captions.

Right-justified captions and left-justified entry fields (D). A disadvantage here is that section headings using location positioning as the identification element do not stand out as well. They tend to get lost in the ragged left edge of the captions.

Advantages are that captions are always positioned close to their related data fields, thereby minimizing eye movements between the two, and that the screen takes on a more balanced look.

There is no universal agreement as to which is the better approach. Experimental studies have not provided any answers, although most style guides recommend, and illustrate, the left-aligned caption approach. IBM's SAA CUA does discuss and permit both alignment styles.

Examples to follow in this and succeeding chapters reflect both styles. This is done to enable the reader to see and evaluate each. Whichever method is chosen, however, should be consistently followed, through a series of related screens.

MYTH **All we really have to do is make the interface look glitzy.**

Special Symbols

- Consider special symbols for emphasis.
- Separate symbols from words by a space.

Figure 3.49　　　　**DELEGATES >>**

Special symbols can be considered to emphasize or call attention to elements on a screen. An icon, for example, can precede an error message, or the greater than sign can be used to direct attention (DELEGATES >>). Symbols should be separated from words by one space.

Headings

Used with related controls, headings are primarily incorporated to create a common identity. In addition to providing meaning, they foster the concept of grouping, create visual appeal, and aid screen learning. Used with Web page text, headings are used to break up large textual blocks; they also create visual appeal and aid in page scanning. For controls, three kinds of headings may be incorporated on screens: section, subsection or row, and field group.

Control Section Headings

- Provide a meaningful heading that clearly describes the relationship of the grouped controls.
- Locate section headings above their related screen controls, separated by one space line.

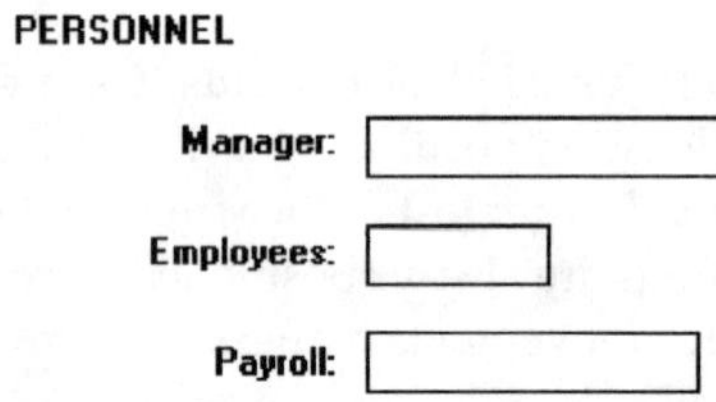

PERSONNEL

Manager:

Employees:

Figure 3.50 Payroll:

— Alternately, headings may be located within a border surrounding a grouping, justified to the upper-left corner.

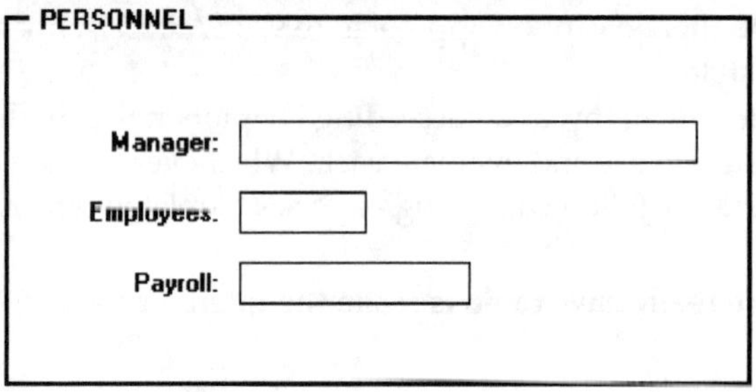

PERSONNEL

Manager:

Employees.

Payroll:

Figure 3.51

- Indent the control captions to the right of the start of the heading.
- Fully spell out in an uppercase font.
- Display in normal intensity.
  — Alternately, if a different font size or style exists, the heading may be displayed in mixed case, using the headline style.

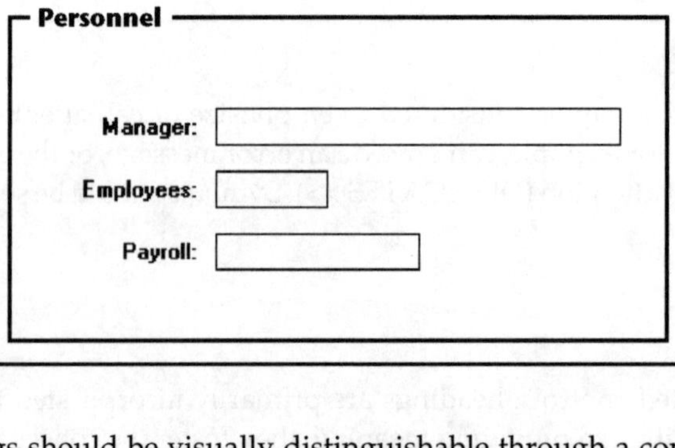

Personnel

Manager:

Employees:

Payroll:

Figure 3.52

Sections headings should be visually distinguishable through a combination of location and font style. They should not be overly emphasized, however. Displaying them in upper case and positioning them to the left will provide the moderate emphasis needed. Many products display headings in the same type size and style as control captions. This provides very poor differentiation between captions and headings, each equally competing for the viewer's attention. This should be avoided. IBM's SAA CUA gives visual emphasis to section headings through higher intensity in a mixed-case font. This is not recommended. Higher intensity should be reserved for the more important screen data.

If right-aligned or justified captions are used, an indention greater than five spaces may be necessary to set off the heading from the captions properly. Section headings may also be positioned to the right of a group of controls, as is illustrated in the following section, "Subsection or Row Headings."

Techniques other than positional cues may be used to set off section headings. Choices may include different kind of fonts, underlining, and so on. If this is done, the heading may be displayed in mixed case using the Headline style (capitalization of all significant words). The method employed should always permit easy, but subtle, discrimination of the section headings from other components of the screen. It should also be visually compatible with other screen components. Whatever styles are chosen, they should be consistently followed throughout a family of screens or a system.

Control Subsection or Row Headings

- Provide a meaningful heading that clearly describes the relationship of the grouped controls.
- Locate to the left of the:
  — Row of associated fields.
  — Topmost row of a group of associated fields.
- Separate from the adjacent caption through the use of a unique symbol, such as one or two greater than signs or a filled-in arrow.
- Separate the symbol from the heading by one space and from the caption by a minimum of three spaces.
- Subsection or row headings may be left- or right-aligned.
- Fully spell out in an uppercase font.
- Display in normal intensity.
  — Alternately, if a different font size or style exists, the heading may be displayed in mixed-case using the headline style.

Figure 3.53   AUTO >   Make: [   ]   Model: [   ]   Year: [   ]

Row or subsection headings may be positioned to the left of a group of related controls. A meaningful convention to designate subsection or row headings is a filled-in arrow or greater than sign. It directs the viewer's attention to the right and indicates that everything that follows refers to this category. Space lines should separate subsections. They may also be right-aligned instead of left-aligned, as shown in Figure 3.54.

AUTO >   AUTO >

REGISTRATION >   REGISTRATION >

DRIVER >   DRIVER >

Figure 3.54   Left-aligned and right-aligned row headings.

Field Group Headings

- Provide a meaningful heading that clearly describes the relationship of the grouped controls.
- Center the field group heading above the captions to which it applies.
- Relate it to the captions by a solid line.
- Fully spell it out in an uppercase font.
- Display it in normal intensity.
  - Alternately, if a different font size or style exists and is used, the heading may be displayed in mixed-case, using the headline style.

```
┌─────────────────── AUTOMOBILE ───────────────────┐
│                                                    │
│   Driver                        License Number     │
│   ┌──────────────────┐          ┌──────────────┐   │
│   └──────────────────┘          └──────────────┘   │
│   ┌──────────────────┐          ┌──────────────┐   │
│   └──────────────────┘          └──────────────┘   │
│   ┌──────────────────┐          ┌──────────────┐   │
│   └──────────────────┘          └──────────────┘   │
└────────────────────────────────────────────────────┘
```

Figure 3.55

Occasionally a group heading above a series of multiple-occurring captions may be needed. It should be centered above the captions to which it applies and related to them through a solid line extending to each end of the grouping. This will provide closure to the grouping.

Web Page Headings

- Control Headings:
  - For groupings of controls, follow the control heading guidelines.
- Page and Text Headings:
  - Provide a meaningful page heading that clearly describes the content and nature of the page that follows.
  - Provide meaningful text headings and subheadings that clearly describe the content and nature of the text that follows.
  - Establish a hierarchy of font styles, sizes, and weights dependent upon the organization created and the importance of the text content.
  - Settle on as few sizes and styles as necessary to communicate page content and organization to the user.
  - Do not randomly mix heading levels or skip heading levels.

Headings for controls positioned on Web pages will follow the guidelines for controls described above. Headings for pages and text should be meaningful, clearly describing the content that follows. The guidelines for creating meaningful heading text will be addressed in Step 8 "Writing Clear Text and Messages."

In general, the presentation of page and text headings on Web pages will follow the practices used for paper documents. A hierarchy of fonts styles, sizes, and weights will be developed based upon the Web page's organization and the contents' importance. The guidelines presented earlier in the "Typography" section can be used for this purpose. To avoid clutter, only use as few sizes and styles as necessary to communicate page content and organization to the user. Do not randomly mix or skip heading levels. The page's organization will be more difficult to ascertain, and user confusion may result.

Instructions

- Incorporate instructions on a screen, as necessary:
    — In a position just preceding the part, or parts, of a screen to which they apply.
    — In a manner that visually distinguishes them, such as:
        • Displaying them in a unique type style.
        • Displaying them in a unique color.
    — In a position that visually distinguishes them by:
        • Left-justifying the instruction and indenting the related field captions, headings, or text a minimum of three spaces to the right.
        • Leaving a space line, if possible, between the instructions and the related control, heading, or text.

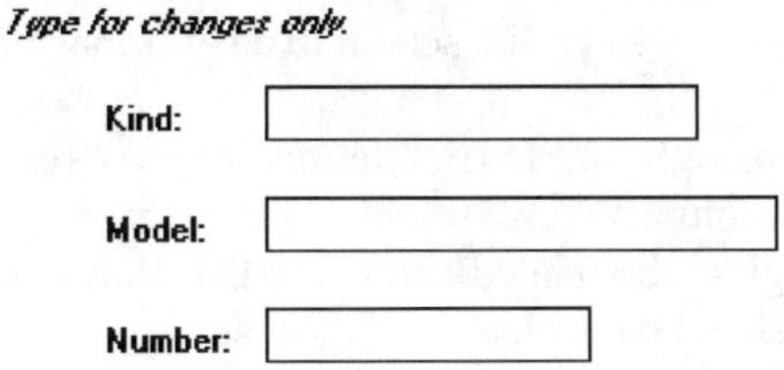

Type for changes only.

Kind: [   ]

Model: [   ]

Figure 3.56   Number: [   ]

— Using a mixed-case font.

Instructions to the screen user on what to do with, or how to work with, the screen presented are occasionally necessary. Whether or not to include them will be dependent upon the experience of the user, the frequency of screen use, and the nature of the information itself. Inexperienced or occasional users may need instructions; data that is complex or unfamiliar may also require them. For experienced and frequent screen users, instructions can quickly become visual noise. When you are deciding whether or not to include instructions on a screen, other techniques, such as using Help or the message area should also be considered.

When it is necessary to place instructions on a screen, they must be positioned at the screen point where they are applicable. Instructions placed at the bottom of a screen will probably not be seen. Instructions placed on one screen but applying to another will never be remembered.

When it is necessary to place instructions on a screen, they must be visually recognized as instructions. This will allow them to be easily ignored by the user when they are not needed. Therefore, some visual aspect of the instruction must indicate that it *is* an instruction. Designers of paper forms do this by presenting instructions in a different font kind or font style such as italics. The form user then immediately recognizes them as instructions, and they can be read or ignored as desired.

To make instructions immediately recognizable on a screen, they may also be presented in a unique font or color. If one of these methods is used, however, cautions concerning the excessive use of different font styles (and colors, as will be shown in Step 12) must be heeded. Another, but less visually strong, technique is to identify the technique simply by its location. Begin the instruction to the left of the screen elements to which it applies; the left-justification identifies it as an instruction.

Try to leave a space line between the instruction and the elements to which it relates, whenever possible. Screen space constraints may not always permit a space line, however. The instruction should be presented in the normal mixed-case sentence style. Guidelines for writing text, including instructions, will be found in Step 8.

Completion Aids

- Incorporate completion aids on a screen, as necessary:
  - In a position to the right of the text entry control to which they apply.
  - In a manner that visually distinguishes them, including:
    - Displaying them within a parentheses ( ).
    - Possibly displaying them in a unique font style.
  - If the controls are arrayed on the screen in a columnar format, position the completion aid, or aids:
    - Far enough to the right so as to not detract from the readability of the entry controls within the column.
    - But close enough to the related control so that they easily maintain an association with the related control.
  - Left-alignment of completion aids in a column of controls is desirable but not absolutely necessary.

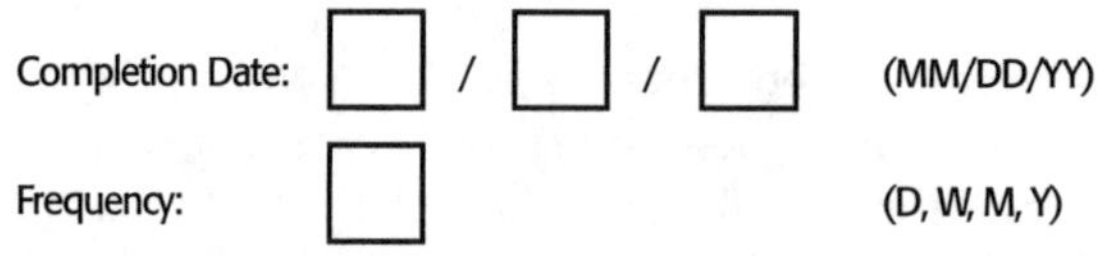

Figure 3.57

Completion aids are a form of instruction but they are directed to the contents of a specific entry field control and the content's format. A date, for example, may require entry of a specified number of characters in a specific order, and it may be necessary to present on the screen a reminder of this format for key entry.

As with instructions, the decision whether or not to include text entry control completion aids will be dependent upon the experience of the user, the frequency of screen use, and the nature of the information itself. Inexperienced or occasional users may need aids; data that is complex or unfamiliar may also require them. For experienced and frequent screen users, however, aids can quickly become visual noise. In deciding whether or not to include completion aids on a screen, other techniques, such as using Help or the message area should also be considered.

When it is necessary to place entry control completion aids on a screen, they must be recognized as such. This will allow them to be easily ignored when they are not needed. Therefore, some visual aspect of the completion aid must indicate that it is an aid.

To make completion aids immediately recognizable on a screen, display them within parentheses ( ). A distinguishing font may also be used but parentheses are visually strong enough to stand by themselves, providing an adequate indication that what is contained within is a completion aid.

The best location for a completion aid is to the right of the entry control that it applies to. Right positioning optimizes the screen layout for the expert user by placing the aid outside of the "working area" of a group of columnized controls. Alternate positioning, such as placing the aid within the caption itself, pushes the caption farther away from the entry control, and for the expert this is less efficient and also creates visual noise. Placing the aid above or below the entry control detracts from the readability of the entry control fields, creates an association problem (Is the aid related to the field above or below?), and yields a less efficient screen organization. For the novice or infrequent user, positioning the aid to the right of the entry field is less efficient because his or her eyes must move right to read it, but these kinds of users will be less efficient, anyway.

In a columnized group of controls, position completion aids far enough to the right so as not to detract from the readability of all the entry controls contained in the column. Positioning, however, must be close enough to the related control so that the aid easily maintains an association with its related control. Left-alignment of completion aids in a column of controls is desirable but not absolutely necessary, since the sizes of entry fields may vary significantly. Final positioning of the completion aid must balance all the above factors.

Keying Procedures

For large-volume data entry applications substantial keying may still be required. The following must be considered in establishing keying procedures.

Keystrokes

- Do not focus on minimizing keystrokes without considering other factors such as:
  — The keying rhythm.
  — The goals of the system.

A sought-after goal in many past data entry applications has always been to minimize keystrokes. Fewer keystrokes have been synonymous with faster keying speeds and greater productivity in the minds of many practitioners. But this is not always true. Fewer keystrokes may actually decrease keying speeds and reduce productivity in many cases.

One research study compared manual tabbing with auto skip in a data entry application. Auto skip, while requiring fewer keystrokes, was found to result in longer keying times and more errors than manual tabbing because it disrupted the keying rhythm. This study is described in more detail in the following section.

Another study, in an information retrieval task, compared input keystrokes to the time needed to evaluate the system output. They found that more keystrokes yielded more meaningful inputs. This yielded more precise and informative outputs, which resulted in faster problem-solving.

So the number of keystrokes, and selections, must be considered in light of keying rhythms and the objectives of the system. Fewer are not necessarily always better.

Tabbing

- Initially, position the cursor in the first field or control in which information can be entered.
- Tab in the order in which the screen's information is organized.

When a screen is first presented, the cursor must be positioned in the first field or control in which information can be entered. Tabbing order must then follow the flow of information as it is organized on the screen.

Manual Tab versus Auto Skip

- Define fields to permit manual tabbing.

Auto skip is a feature that causes a cursor to automatically move to the beginning of the next text entry control field once the previous field is completely filled. Auto skip obviates manual tabbing and requires fewer keystrokes to complete a screen. Theoretically, keying speeds should increase with auto skip. In practice, they do not always do so.

Rarely are many text entry screen fields completely filled to their maximum length with data. When an entry field is not full, the user must still press the tab key to move the cursor to the next entry field. Figure 3.58 illustrates auto skip functioning.

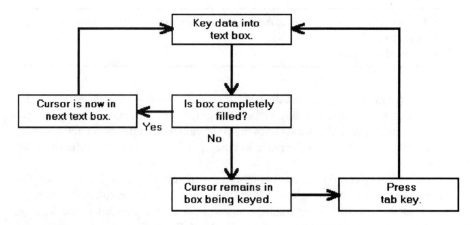

Figure 3.58   Text entry using auto skip.

Auto skip, therefore, imposes decision-making and learning requirements. After keying text into each field, one must determine where the cursor is and whether to press the tab key or not to go to the next field. Only then can the next keying action be performed. As illustrated in Figure 3.59, manual tabbing requires extra keystrokes but no decisions must be made. The keying task is rhythmic. One study, comparing auto skip with manual tabbing, found that manual tabbing resulted in faster keying performance and fewer keying errors.

Auto skip can delay detection of one particular kind of error. If an extra character is inadvertently keyed into a field, the cursor will automatically move to the next field while keying continues. The error may not be immediately detected, and spacing in subsequent fields may also be one position off, at least until the tab key is pressed. Were this situation to occur while using manual tabbing, the keyboard would lock as soon as the entry field was full. The error would be immediately detected.

Auto skip, despite its limitations, can be useful if a system's screens are easily learned or if all screen fields are always completely filled. Nevertheless, most large-volume data entry applications would not appear to meet this criterion.

Keying Rules

- Do not require recoding, changing, omitting, or including data based on special rules or logical transformations.

In large-volume entry applications, decisions that must be made during the keying process impose learning requirements and greatly slow down the entry process. The fewer rules and decisions involved in keying, the faster and more accurate entry will be. Coding, omitting, changing, and including data by special rules or transformations as a group represent probably the greatest single decrement to data entry speed.

Organization and Structure Guidelines

What follows is a series of organization and structure guidelines for specific kinds of screens. They are: Information Entry and Modification (Conversational), Entry from a Dedicated Source Document, and Display/Read-Only screens.

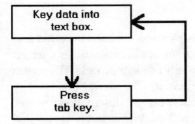

Figure 3.59 Text entry using manual tabbing.

Information Entry and Modification (Conversational) Screens

- Organization:
  - Logical and clear.
  - Most frequently used information:
    - On the earliest screens.
    - At the top of screens.
  - Required information:
    - On the earliest screens.
    - At the top of screens.
- Captions:
  - Meaningful.
  - Consistently positioned in relation to data field controls.
  - Left- or right-aligned.
  - Mixed case using headline style.
- Text boxes/selection controls:
  - Designate by boxes.
- Spacing and groupings:
  - Create logical groupings.
  - Make them medium in size, about 5 to 7 lines.
- Headings:
  - Upper case or headline-style mixed case.
  - Set off from related controls.
- Control arrangement:
  - Align into columns.
  - Organize for top-to-bottom completion.
- Required and optional input:
  - Consider distinguishing between required and optional data input through:
    - Placing required and optional information within different screens, windows, or groups.
    - Identifying information as required or optional in a completion aid.
    - Identifying required information with a unique font or symbol.
- Instructions and completion aids:
  - Include as necessary.
    - Position instructions before the controls to which they apply.
    - Position completion aids to the right of the controls to which they apply.

Information entry and modification (conversational) screens are used to collect and modify information, either by entry or selection. These screens are sometimes referred to as conversational screens. They guide a person through a task or process. The screen itself is the user's focal point for working with information. The viewer is driven by what is presented on the screen in the information collection and designation process. The information needed to complete a screen may be collected from, but is not limited to, these kinds of sources:

- A person being interviewed or queried at a desk or workstation.
- A person being queried or interviewed over a telephone.
- A collection of notes and written materials.
- An unstructured form.
- The mind of the user.

These guidelines, with the exception of "Required and optional input," have been presented earlier in this chapter.

Organization. Organize these screens logically and clearly, reflecting the exact information needs of the user for the task being performed. In general, place the most frequently used information, or required information, on the earliest screens and at the top of screens.

Captions. Provide meaningful captions, clearly identifying the information to be entered or selected. Use the headline style to display them (all significant words capitalized). Consistently position all captions in relation to their associated controls. They may be left- or right-aligned.

Text boxes/selection controls. Designate by boxes, using either a line border or polarity reversal.

Spacing and groupings. Create logical medium-size groupings of from 5 to 7 elements.

Headings. Provide headings to identify groupings. Set off from their related controls using upper case or mixed-case headline style.

Control arrangement. Align controls into columns. Maintain a top-to-bottom, then left-to-right arrangement.

Required and optional input. Distinguishing between required and optional data input may or may not be necessary on these screens. The decision on whether or not to distinguish these types of data should be based on the experience of the user doing the key entry, and the information's familiarity. When a technique to distinguish them is included on a screen, it is a form of completion aid so the arguments for and against completion aids are applicable here as well.

When it is necessary to differentiate required and optional data, consider the following alternatives. First, determine the feasibility of placing the two kinds of data on separate screens or within separate screen windows or groupings. This is the best and cleanest solution. If a meaningful screen organization of information will not permit this, then, describe the individual pieces of data as required or optional within a completion aid. The last choice is identify required information with a unique font or symbol. This alternative, however, requires the user to learn the convention in order to use it effectively. Displaying a unique font might also lead to screen clutter, if too many different fonts and styles are used on the screen.

Instructions and completion aids. Include these on screens as necessary. Locate instructions so they precede the controls to which they apply. Locate completion aids to the right of the controls to which they apply.

Grids

- Usage:
  — To enter large amounts of related data or information.
- Design guidelines:
  — Provide descriptive headings and, where appropriate, subheadings for columns and rows.
    • Do not include colons (:) after the headings.
  — Justify column headings according to the data presented in the table cells.
    • Left-justify headings for columns containing text.
    • Right-justify headings for columns containing numbers.
  — Left-justify row headings.
  — Organize the data or information to be entered logically and clearly.
    • Place similar information together.
    • Place most important or frequently used information at the top.
    • Arrange information chronologically or sequentially.
  — Use light backgrounds.
  — Provide consistent spacing between columns and rows.
  — If more than seven rows are presented, insert white space after every fifth row.

Usage. Large amounts of related data that must be entered can be collected in grids. Like a table, a grid is a matrix of entry fields arranged in columns and rows. Grids usually consume less screen space than do individual data elements.

Headings. Provide descriptive headings and, where necessary and appropriate, sub-headings for columns and rows. Do not include colons (:) after the headings. Justify column headings according to the data presented in the table cells. Use left-justification for columns containing text, right-justification for columns containing numbers. Row headings should be left-justified.

Organization. The organization of grid data or information will follow the same general organizational guidelines previously described. Organize table data logically and clearly. Place most important or frequently used information at the top and arrange it meaningfully.

Backgrounds. For legibility, present table data on light backgrounds, either off-white or light gray. Use black for the data or information.

Spacing. For balance, provide consistent spacing between columns and rows. For readability, if more than seven rows are presented, insert white space after every fifth row.

Text Entry from a Source Document

Occasionally, it may be necessary to key information directly from a source document or paper form into a screen. The document may take the form of an application for insurance, an application for a bank loan, a request for service, and so forth. The key issue for this function is that the document should be *dedicated* to the screen, and permit "head down" entry of data from the document to the screen, with the screen seldom being the point of the user's attention. An entire screen should be capable of being completed *without* the keyer ever looking at the screen. The design guidelines are based upon this assumption. Ideally, the document and screen should be created together so that a document-screen image relationship can be easily achieved. Creating them together permits trade-offs between the document and the screen to achieve this fit.

Sometimes, but not often, an existing document will allow the creation of a screen in its exact image. When this happens, this document can also be considered as dedicated and will follow these rules. Most documents, however, because they were not designed with a screen in mind, cannot be easily matched to a screen. In this case their corresponding screens should be considered as entry/modification (conversational) screens and should be designed accordingly because the screen will drive the keying process, not the document. The required information on the screen must be searched for and found on the form.

If an existing document or form is being converted to a screen format, and the existing document will no longer be used, its screens should also be designed following the entry/modification (conversational) guidelines. This is a much more effective approach for information collection, as discussed earlier in this chapter.

Dedicated Source Document Screens

- Organization:
  — Image of associated source document.
- Captions:
  — Abbreviations and contractions.
  — Consistently positioned in relation to data fields.
  — Right-aligned.
- Text boxes:
  — Designate by boxes.
- Spacing and grouping:
  — Logical groupings found on source document.
- Headings:
  — Include if on source document.
  — Upper case or headline-style mixed case.
  — Set off from related controls.
- Control arrangement:
  — As arranged on source document.
  — Left-to-right completion.
- Keying procedure:
  — Use manual tabbing.
- Required and optional input:
  — Not necessary to differentiate.
- Instructions and completion aids:
  — None needed.

For more detailed information concerning document screen design, see Galitz (1992).

Organization. The screen must be an exact image of its associated source document. Skipping around a source document to locate information adds a significant amount of time to the keying process. It also imposes a learning requirement on people, since the order and location of screen fields must be mastered. Having the source document and screen in the same image eliminates these problems. Cursor position on the screen is always known because it corresponds with a person's eye position on the source document.

Captions. To allow the screen to be in the image of a source document, screen captions usually must consist of abbreviations and contractions. The document will always be available to assist in identifying unclear captions. Because text boxes fit fairly tightly on these kinds of screens, captions must be right-aligned so they are associated with the proper box.

Text boxes. Designate by boxes, using either a line border or polarity reversal.

Spacing and grouping. Create the same groupings as exist on the document. Set off groupings as this is done on the form, through use of either white space and/or borders.

Headings. Include the same headings as are found on the source document. Capitalize or use mixed-case headline style (all significant words capitalized) to set them off from the remainder of the screen.

Control arrangement. Control positioning and alignment on the screen should match that of the source document. Position controls in the same manner, or as close to the same manner as possible, to facilitate eye movements between the document and screen. (A well-designed document should have aligned elements, too. If not, still follow the form alignment.) Maintain a left-to-right entry arrangement, if the form is organized for completion in this direction. If, per chance, the document is organized top-to-bottom, then follow this top-to-bottom scheme.

Keying procedure. Use manual tabbing, not auto skip, to permit a rhythmic keying process. Keying will be faster and less error prone.

Required and optional input. Distinguishing between required and optional data input is not necessary on these screens. This information will have been included within the source document design.

Instructions and completion aids. These will not be necessary. Instructions and completion aids will be located on the source document.

Display/Read-Only Screens

Display/read-only screens are used to display the results of an inquiry request or the contents of computer files. Their design objective is human ease in locating data or information. Thus, they should be developed to optimize human scanning. Scanning is made easier if eye movements are minimized, required eye movement direction is obvious, and a consistent viewing pattern is established. Next is a guideline summary.

- Organization:
  - — Logical and clear.
  - — Limit to what is necessary.
- Most frequently used information:
  - — On earliest screens.
  - — At the top of screens.
- Captions:
  - — Meaningful.
  - — Consistently positioned in relation to data fields.
  - — Left- or right-aligned.
- Text boxes:
  - — Do not include a surrounding border or box.
- Spacing and grouping:
  - — Create logical groupings.
  - — Make them medium-sized, about 5 to 7 lines.
- Headings:
  - — Upper case or headline-style mixed case.
  - — Set off from related controls.
- Data presentation:
  - — Visually emphasize the data.
  - — Give the data a meaningful structure.
- Data arrangement:
  - — Align into columns.
  - — Organize for top-to-bottom scanning.
- Data justification:
  - — For text and alphanumeric data, left-justify.
  - — For numeric data, right-justify.
  - — Create a data "ladder."
- Data display:
  - — Consider not displaying no, or null, data.
  - — Consider "data statements."

More detailed guidelines for screen organization, and data presentation, arrangement, justification, and display are included in the following discussion.

Organization

- Only display information necessary to perform actions, make decisions, or answer questions.
- Group information in a logical or orderly manner, with the most frequently requested information in the upper-left corner.
- For multiscreen functions, locate the most frequently requested information on the earliest screens.
- Do not pack the screen. Use spaces and lines to balance the screen perceptually.

Information contained on a display/read-only screen should consist of only what is relevant to the question for which an answer is sought. Forcing a person to wade through volumes of data is time consuming, costly, and error-prone. Unfortunately, relevance is most often situation-specific. An item that is relevant one time a screen is displayed may be irrelevant another time it is recalled.

Organization should be logical, orderly, and meaningful. When information is structured in a manner that is consistent with a person's organizational view of a topic, information is comprehended better and faster.

Finding information on a display/read-only screen can be speeded up by a number of factors. First, if information is never used, do not display it. Limit a screen to only what is necessary to perform actions, make decisions, or answer questions. Second, for multiple-window functions, locate the most frequently sought information on the earliest screens and the most frequently sought information on a screen in the upper-left corner. Never pack a display/read-only screen with information.

Captions. Provide meaningful captions clearly identifying the information displayed, unless the identity of data is obvious by its shape or structure (for example, an address). Use the headline style (all significant words capitalized), and consistently position all captions in relation to their associated data. Captions may be left- or right-aligned.

Text boxes. Do not place a border around display/read-only information; inscribe the data so that it appears on the normal window background. It will be much more readable presented in this manner.

Spacing and grouping. Provide easily scanned and identifiable logical groupings of information. Create groupings of a medium size (5 to 7 lines) and set them off through liberal use of white space and conservative use of line borders.

Headings. Provide headings to identify groupings. Set off from their related controls using upper case or mixed-case headline style.

Data Presentation

- Provide visual emphasis to the data.
- Give the data a meaningful structure.
  - Spell out any codes in full.
  - Include natural splits or predefined breaks in displaying data.

~~338302345~~	~~072179~~	~~162152~~
Figure 3.60 338-30-2245	07/21/79	16:21:52

- For data strings of five or more numbers or alphanumeric characters with no natural breaks, display in groups of three or four characters with a blank between each group.

Figure 3.61   ~~K349612094~~   K349 612 094

Data should be visually emphasized to attract attention. This will enable the viewer to quickly isolate the data and begin scanning the display for the needed information. A higher-intensity or brighter color is recommended to accomplish this. Also, fully spell out any codes and include natural splits or predefined breaks in displaying common pieces of data such as telephone numbers and dates.

A data display should also reinforce the human tendency to break things into groups. People handle information more easily when it is presented in chunks. Display data strings of five or more alphanumeric characters with no natural breaks in groups of three or four, with a blank space between each group.

Data Arrangement

- Align data into columns.
- Organize for top-to-bottom scanning.

To aid scanning, align data into columns with a top-to-bottom, left-to-right orientation. This means permitting the eye to move down a column from top to bottom, then move to another column located to the right, and again move from top to bottom. This also means, if the situation warrants it, permitting the eye to move easily left to right across the top of columns to the proper column, before beginning the vertical scanning movement.

Top-to-bottom scanning will minimize eye movements through the screen and enable human perceptual powers to be utilized to their fullest. Display/read-only screens are often visually scanned not through the captions but through the data fields themselves. A search for a customer name in a display of information frequently involves looking for a combination of characters that resembles the picture of a name that we have stored in our memory. The search task is to find a long string of alphabetic characters with one or two gaps (first name, middle initial, last name, perhaps). A date search might have the viewer seeking a numeric code broken up by slashes. Other kinds of information also have recognizable patterns and shapes. Control captions usually play a minor role in the process, being necessary only to differentiate similar-looking data fields, or for new screen users.

Vertical scanning has led to two key requirements in the design of display/read-only screens: call attention to data fields, and make the structural differences between data fields as obvious as possible. Differences are most noticeable in a columnar field structure, since it is easier to compare data when one piece is above the other.

Data Justification

- Left-justify text and alphanumeric formats.

	Name:	~~Bill Watters~~	Name:	Bill Watters
Figure 3.62	Street:	~~612 Hidden Valley~~	Street:	612 Hidden Valley

- Right-justify lists of numeric data.

Charge:	~~645,194.88~~	Charge:	645,194.88
Federal Tax:	~~19,235.16~~	Federal Tax:	19,235.16
State Tax:	~~5,204.03~~	State Tax:	5,204.03
Local Tax:	~~1.24~~	Local Tax:	1.24
Total Cost:	~~669,635.31~~	Total Cost:	669,635.31

Figure 3.63

- Create a data "ladder."

Tree:	~~Pine~~	Tree:	Pine
Age:	~~14~~	Age:	14
Number:	~~422,598~~	Number:	422,598
Class:	~~C~~	Class:	C
Location:	~~NW~~	Location:	NW

Figure 3.64

In general, columnized text and alphanumeric data should be left-justified, and numeric data should be right-justified. In aligning data fields, keep in mind how the pieces of data will look in relation to one another when they contain typical information. The visual scan should flow relatively straight from top to bottom. This may require that some data fields be right-justified in the column that is created, not left-justified, or vice versa. The objective is to create what looks like a ladder of data down the screen.

Data Display

- Consider not displaying data whose values are none, zero, or blank.

Elephants:	612	Elephants:	612
Lions:	123	Lions:	123
~~Hippos:~~	~~0~~	Giraffes:	361
Giraffes:	361		
~~Kudus:~~	~~0~~		

Figure 3.65

- Consider creating "data statements," in which the caption and data are combined.

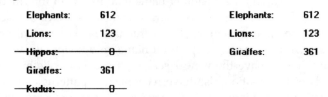

Elephants:	612	612 Elephants
Lions:	123	123 Lions
Giraffes:	361	361 Giraffes

Figure 3.66

Consider not displaying fields containing no data. When displayed on a display/read-only screen, some data fields may be blank or contain a value such as zero or none. In many situations it may not be important to the screen viewer to know that the field contains no data. In these cases consider not displaying these screen elements at all. Present on the screen only the fields containing data, thereby creating less cluttered screens.

If this alternative is chosen, space on the screen must be left for situations in which all fields contain data. In order to avoid large blank screen areas, a useful rule of thumb is to allow enough space to display clearly all data for about 90 percent of all possible screens. For situations in which screens must contain more data than this, going to an additional screen will be necessary.

This nondisplay alternative should *only* be considered if it is *not* important that the viewer know something is "not there." If it is important that the viewer know that the values in a field are zero or none, or that the field is blank, then the fields must be displayed on the screen.

You may also want to consider displaying data statements. The traditional way to display data on an inquiry screen is the "caption: data" format, for example, "Autos: 61." Another alternative is to create data statements where the caption and data are combined: "61 Autos." This format improves screen readability and slightly reduces a screen's density. If this data statement format is followed, consider the statement as data and highlight it entirely.

Tables

- Usage:
  — To present and/or compare large amounts of data or information.
- Design guidelines:
  — Provide descriptive headings and, where appropriate, subheadings for columns and rows.
    • Do not include colons (:) after the headings.
  — Justify column headings according to the data presented in the table cells.
    • Left-justify for columns containing text.
    • Right-justify for columns containing numbers.
  — Left-justify row headings.
  — Organize the presented data or information logically and clearly.
    • Place similar information together.
    • Place most important or frequently used at the top.
    • Arrange chronologically or sequentially.
  — Justify the data presented in a column according to its content.
    • Left-justify textual data.
    • Right-justify numeric data.
  — Length should not exceed the depth of a screen.
  — Use light backgrounds.
    • Highlight a particular cell, column, or row using a contrasting display technique.
  — Provide consistent spacing between columns and rows.
  — If more than seven rows are presented, insert white space after every fifth row.
  — Use caution in placing borders around cells.

Usage. Large amounts of information, or information that must be compared, can be arrayed in *tables*. Like a grid, a table is a matrix of information arranged in columns and rows. Tables usually consume less screen space than do individual data elements.

Headings. Provide descriptive headings and, where necessary and appropriate, subheadings for columns and rows. Do not include colons (:) after the headings. Justify column headings according to the data presented in the table cells. Use left-justification for columns containing text, right-justification for columns containing numbers. Row headings should be left-justified.

Organization and justification. Organization of table data or information will follow the general organization guidelines previously described. Organize table data logically and clearly so it can be quickly identified, scanned, and compared. Place most important or frequently used information at the top, place together information that must be directly compared, and arrange it chronologically or sequentially. Justify the data presented in a column according to its content. For textual data use left-justification, for numeric data, use right-justification.

Length. Avoid long vertical tables. A table should be entirely visible for readability and making data comparisons. Length should not exceed depth of a screen

Backgrounds. For legibility, present table data on light backgrounds, either off-white or light gray. Use black for the data or information. If highlighting a cell or cells is necessary, use a contrasting display technique that does not diminish the legibility of the displayed data.

Spacing. For balance, provide consistent spacing between columns and rows. For readability, if more than seven rows are presented, insert white space after every fifth row. Also, use caution in placing borders around table cells. Borders interfere scanning and readability.

Reading, Browsing, and Searching on the Web

The Web has an almost unlimited supply of information—for those who can find it. The dilemma for the user is how to navigate within the Web, deal with the overwhelming amount of information presented, and locate the elusive answer. The magnitude and structure of the Web seems to be creating a user interaction pattern with these characteristics:

- The most sought-after Web commodity is content.
- Behavior is often goal-driven.
- Reading is no longer a linear activity.
- Impatience.
- Frequent switching of purpose.

Web users access a site for different reasons: a focused search for a piece of information or an answer, a less focused browsing, or simply to surf. But content is what most users comes to see. High-tech capabilities, fancy graphics, and a rainbow of colors do not compensate for insufficient or poor content. All innovations are judged by how well they support the presented content. Users are also strongly goal-driven; often looking only for the thing they have in mind. In foraging through the Web, reading is no longer a linear activity, instead information is acquired in scattered bits and pieces. Easy content scanning is very important. The user is also impatient, with little time to waste. Things like a slow download, content that is not easily scannable, and confusing navigation will quickly drive users away from a site. The user also frequently switches purpose and direction, browsing one moment, searching the next, now in one site, then in another, then back again, and on and on. Design must accommodate people who change directions, and leave a site and return frequently to it.

Recently, the specific activities of Web users have come under closer scrutiny. Byrne, John, Wehrle, and Crow (1999) looked at what people do when browsing, Morrison, Pirolli, and Card (2001) analyzed the methods people reported they used to arrive at information they needed for important tasks, and their reasons for the use of the Web. The results are summarized in Table 3.1.

In the Byrne et al., study a significant amount of time was spent waiting and scrolling. This percentage was actually greater than reported above because waiting time between successive page presentations was not reported. In the Morrison et al. study, 96 percent of the activities were goal-driven, that is, users were addressing a specific need. It is also interesting to note that more than two-thirds of the time people were looking for multiple pieces of information, not single pieces. Browsing is now optimized for accessing information in single locations. As our experience with the Web continues, more useful usage information for design should continue to emerge.

Table 3.1   Reported User Web Activities

BROWSING ACTIVITIES (Byrne et al., 1999)	APPROXIMATE PERCENTAGES
Using information, including reading, printing, and downloading	58
Visually searching for information on pages	12
Providing requested information	18
Waiting or scrolling	12
PRIMARY REASONS FOR IMPORTANT USES OF THE WEB (Morrison et al., 2001)	
Evaluate multiple products or answers in order to make a decision (Comparing or Choosing)	51
Get a fact or document, find out something, or download something (Finding)	25
Gain understanding of some topic, including locating it (Understanding)	24
METHODS USED TO ARRIVE AT INFORMATION FOR IMPORTANT WEB USES (Morrison et al., 2001)	
Searching for multiple pieces of information, not looking for one particular answer (Collecting)	71
Searching for something specific (Finding)	25
Looking around or browsing without a particular goal (Exploring)	2
Visiting the same Web site looking for updated information (Monitoring)	2

Initial Focus of Attention

When a Web page is presented, like most screens, it will be scanned in a clockwise direction, people being influenced by its balance and the weight of its title, graphics, headings, and text. The page will be seen as large masses of shape, including its text and graphics, and color. Studies of Web users indicate that attention is then immediately directed to the page's content. Usually ignored are the peripheral parts of the screen, the navigation areas, logos, slogans, advertising, or anything else considered superfluous or fluff.

Page Perusal

Focusing on the page's content, the user's eyes are first drawn to the page's text, particularly headings, captions, summaries, and notes. Individual words and phrases are read for meaning and relevance. At this point the page's graphics are generally ignored. Studies find that the most frequent method used in perusing a page is scanning or skimming, concentrating less on detail and word for word reading. Three-quarters of Web page readers appear to prefer scanning to reading. Design features that enhance scanning are critically important in page design. As the scanning continues, the user's attention becomes progressively more detailed; page components begin to take on meaning. Shallow reading is combined with selective depth. Rarely are articles read fully. If page does not appear to be relevant to a user's needs or goals quickly, it will be removed.

Scanning Guidelines

- Organization:
  — Minimize eye movement.
  — Provide groupings of information.
  — Organize content in a logical and obvious way.
- Writing:
  — Provide a meaningful title.
  — Provide meaningful headings and subheadings.
  — Concisely write the text.
  — Write short paragraphs containing only one idea.
  — Use the inverted pyramid style of writing.
  — Use bulleted and numbered lists.
  — Array information in tables.
  — Provide concise summaries.
- Presentation:
  — Highlight:
    • Key information-carrying words or phrases.
    • Important concepts.

A Web page must be structured to facilitate scanning, its key points made very obvious. Use of the techniques described in this step, and in other steps (organization, layout, location, typography, color, and so forth), will serve to make the page easily scannable. Some important reminders, and several unique Web guidelines, follow.

Organization. Minimize eye movement through the page through alignment and columnizing of page elements. Order the page's content in an obvious way and provide a logical progression of links and pages. More easily learned pages will be easier to scan. Group information using white space as a primary grouping tool.

Writing. Provide a meaningful page *title*. The purpose and message of a page should be identifiable from its title. Provide meaningful *headings and subheadings*. Most users read headings, not all read further. Headings help users determine whether to continue or ignore large chunks of information. Headings should be simple, not clever or cute. Subheadings break up larger blocks of text, making it easier to find the portions of interest. Typeface variations should be used to establish a heading hierarchy.

- *Concisely write the page text.* Users prefer written text, says research, because words reduce one's cognitive load, resulting in faster and more efficient information processing. To aid scanning, Web page text should be very succinct, containing fewer words than conventional writing. Half the word count or less is recommended. Create narrow text columns that minimize the eye's horizontal scan. Write short paragraphs, restricting each to only one idea. People tend to skip additional important points in a paragraph as they scan, or if they are not caught by the first few words in paragraph. Also use the *inverted pyramid* style of writing. This style starts with the conclusion and follows with expanded detail, either within the paragraph or at the end of a link. The conclusion first allows the user to quickly determine whether it is worthwhile to continue reading.

- *Bulleted and numbered lists* break up long expanses of text. They also draw attention to important points that may be entirely missed if buried within a paragraph. Vertically align the lists so they are easy to skim. Lists also lend themselves to linking. Array information in *tables* for easier scanning, comprehension, and comparing. Provide concise content *summaries* to give the user a snapshot of the text content before reading. Link to full-length treatments where relevant and useful information can be presented.

Presentation. Important information-carrying words, phrases, or concepts should be *highlighted*. Keywords, words that differentiate a page from others, or words that symbolize what a page is all about are candidates for highlighting. About three times as many words as writing for print can usually be effectively highlighted on a Web page. Possible highlighting techniques include boldness, increased brightness, or a different color. The standard link designation, an underline, is considered a highlighting technique. Do not highlight entire sentences or long phrases. The eye picks up only 2 to 3 words at a time, and the screen may become too busy.

MAXIM   **When the visual design clarifies the functional intent . . . the interface becomes intuitive.**

Browsing

Web site browsing is analogous to shopping. A person walks into a store (Web site), looks around (the page), gets a feel for the place (presentation style, layout, and so on), looks for clues or signs of interest (headings, summaries, and so on), wanders at whim (follows a link), and then decides to stay and linger for a while, or leave. The person may leave empty-handed, or have picked up various products (or scattered bits and pieces of information) during these wanderings. Upon leaving, the person's destination may be another store (Web site) in the mall from which he or she may soon return after doing some "comparison shopping." In the shopping bag may now be other products (or scattered bits and pieces of information) that have been picked up. This sort of "interlaced" browsing behavior must be supported in Web site design.

Browsing Guidelines

- Facilitate scanning.
- Provide multiple layers of structure.
- Make navigation easy.
- Respect the user's desire to leave.
- Upon returning, help the users reorient themselves.

The *scanning* guidelines recently presented also facilitate browsing behavior. The organization of information and the writing and presentation of content are critical to the process. Provide *multiple layers of structure* with high-level summaries so users can decide if they want to browse deeper or simply move on. (Imagine a multilevel store without a floor layout sign with department locations.) Navigation through the structure must be very easy so the user can concentrate on content, not on how to get around and the frustrations resulting from being continually lost. (Now, imagine this multilevel store without elevators or escalators, only stairways.) Respect the user's *desire to leave*, even though you may want them to stay. (Imagine this multilevel store with only one exit on a single floor, an exit whose location is unknown to the shopper.) Now imagine this shopper getting very annoyed and never returning.

Should the user return (your Web site design will not have chased them away permanently, of course) provide guidance to help in *reorientation*. (Perhaps they also reentered on a different floor from which they last exited.) Never assume that the user will remember the entire previous browsing session. Provide signposts, meaningful page titles, headings, and summaries. Place keywords at the start of all page titles. This will help users pick out pages if they are minimized in the window task bar.

Provide consistency in all aspects of Web site design. Maintain the "viewed" link colors so pages already visited may be recognized. Use standard terms to minimize the need for users to switch context and try to remember what things are called.

Searching

People search on the Web when they have a specific goal or need for which they seek an answer. Their focus may be directed toward something specific, a fact, document, or product; toward gaining an understanding of some more general topic; or the search may be directed toward collecting multiple pieces of information (not necessarily looking for one particular piece), or to evaluate multiple products or answers in order to make a decision. The searching strategy a person employs may, based upon knowledge possessed, involve focused browsing, reviewing site maps and indexes, and reviewing and following site links. A person's strategy may also involve using a search engine.

Currently, the design of a Web site is the most effective searching tool, not a search facility itself. Experience and studies have shown that using a search engine can actually reduce a user's chance of success. Browsing and following links are more likely to lead to the desired result. Most users turn to a search facility only when all else fails. So, the first tool in facilitating user search is a well-designed site, one that is well organized, is easy to scan, and possesses clear navigation links, including a site map and links.

Problems with Search Facilities

Many sites seem to deal with their search facilities engines in a haphazard way. A survey has found that 71 percent of users are frustrated by Web searches, and 46 percent find them nerve-racking. Why? The answer can be gleamed from three search components: the user, the search formulation, and the presented search results.

> **Not understanding the user.** With so much variation among users there can never be a single ideal search interface. Too often, however, the level of searching expertise of the user is not determined. The nature of every possible query or the type of information being searched for is not anticipated. Not considered, as well, are some basic human traits. Few people read instructions, preferring to "try it." Instructions may not even be seen or simply ignored. People do not remember things very well. The existence of a search engine on another page, and/or the page's location is easily forgotten. Lots of people misspell words, 3 percent of all queries in one study contained misspellings, most off by only one letter. Misspelling may be caused by unfamiliarity with technical terms or the English language, by spelling difficulties, or simply by one's finger straying in the keying process. If the search engine does not accept misspelled variations, the chance of a search success is very slim.

> **Difficulties in formulating the search.** One study found that the average Web shopper does not know how to use a search function. Another study found that the users did not know what to type in or how to format the query. These problems can occur because of the diversity in user search needs. They may also occur due to numerous interface differences that create inconsistencies in layout and operation. Finally, too often the user is asked to think like the programming behind the search engine, a fruitless task. If the wrong search parameters are chosen, no results will appear.

> **Difficulties in presenting meaningful results.** Users are often frustrated with presented results because they do not know what the results mean, why they were presented, or what their relevance is to their query. If the chosen search parameters are too narrowly defined, no results or irrelevant results may appear. If too broadly defined, the user is inundated with results and the right answer is buried within. The user must then sift through all the useless data to try and determine where to go.

Users often cannot tell that a "No Matches Found" result occurred because of a simple keying typographical error. The wrong key was pressed. Result descriptions consisting of a few words often make no sense, as do URLs displayed in the results for novice users. Displayed search accuracy ratings are seldom relevant to any one particular user. Goal-oriented users don't care how relevant results are for someone else; their only concern is the information they need.

Search Facility Guidelines

Search services on the Web will be judged on how well they enable the user to easily find what is needed in the galaxy of information space. These services will also be judged on how well the user confusion and frustration existing in current the process is reduced. At this moment, human beings are better search instruments than machines.

The purpose of a search facility, then, is to bring back information, not data. Specifically, answers to questions, the shortest, clearest, possible are what really matter. It is currently recommended that large Web sites, those containing more than 100 pages, should have a local search facility.

The following sections address guidelines for a search facility. It begins with "Know Your User" and continues with "Expressing the Search," "Launching the Search," and "Presenting Meaningful Results." Guidelines for making pages "locatable" conclude the discussion.

Know Your Search User

- Identify the level of expertise of the user.
- Anticipate:
  — The nature of every possible query.
  — The kind of information desired.
  — The type of information being searched.
  — How much information will result from the search.
- Plan for the user's switching purposes during the search process.
- Plan for flexibility in the search process.

In designing search features, knowing your search users is just as important as it is in every other aspect of interface design. The more that is known about users, what they are looking for, and how they may search, the better the search facility can be designed to help them.

Expertise. Identify the level of the users' expertise in computer usage and in the function or application being designed. Do they need a simple or high-powered interface? A natural language or constrained and guided selection using check boxes and list boxes? Are they comfortable with Boolean operators? Will a help function be necessary?

Anticipate. Find out what the users' questions may be so every possible result can be included in the engine. Find out what kind of information is desired, a taste, a summary, or extensive detail. Present the proper amount in the results. Determine the type of information being searched, structured fields or full text, navigation pages or destination pages, so the searching function can be properly structured. Estimate how much information will result from the search. Will users be overwhelmed by the results? Should the search be qualified in more ways?

Switching purposes. Plan for the users' switching purposes during the search process. Searching may be a temporary interlude during a lengthy browsing process, or vice versa. What else might the users want to do coincidental with the search? Will it be easy to switch back and forth?

Flexibility. Searching strategies may vary. A person may want to search narrowly at one time, broadly the next. Can different user searching strategies be easily handled? Can changing the strategies also be easily handled?

Express the Search

- What:
  - — For insite facilities, structure the searching function to the Web site's information and the user's needs.
  - — Integrate searching and browsing.
- Where:
  - — Make the search facility prominent on the home page.
  - — Include a search facility on every page.
- How:
  - — Permit users to specify the extent of searches.
    - Within a section.
    - Across a site.
    - Within specified sources.
    - Globally.
  - — Provide methods of specifying search parameters, including:
    - Keywords.
      - – For large sites include an internal glossary of terms and a thesaurus.
    - Phrases.
    - Variants.
      - – Case insensitivity.
      - – Partial matches.
      - – Synonyms.
  - — Provide a spell checker.
  - — Provide search controls, including:
    - A text box
      - – Size: Large enough to enter a minimum of 20 characters.
      - – Font: Arial.
      - – Font size: 10 points.
    - Structured controls.
      - – Check boxes.
      - – List boxes or drop-down list boxes
    - A command button.
      - – Label: Search.

– Location: to right of search text box.
— Provide separate interfaces for simple and advanced search.
  • Place "Advanced Search" link under text search box.
— Provide guidance and assistance.
  • Present clear instructions.
  • Offer online help.
  • Offer a search wizard.

What. For insite facilities, structure the searching function to the Web site, the information it contains, and the user's anticipated needs. Don't use generic applications. A well-structured and organized content is a key factor in achieving good search results. Searching and browsing should also be closely integrated. Upon arriving a user may not know whether he or she wants to browse or search.

Where. Make the search option prominent on the home page. No matter how well one supports navigation, a user may still want to search immediately after accessing a site. Include a search facility on every page, as well. Where a user is when a decision is made to search can never be predicted. Also, permitting a search from any Web site point facilitates a new user, or a user who wanders into the Web site at that point. These users do not have to first learn the conceptual organization of the site before they find something of interest to them.

How. Studies show that users perform better and have higher subjective satisfaction when they can view and control a search (Koenemann and Belkin, 1996). Search options should be clear. Permit users to specify and control the *extent* of their searches, either confining them to within a section, across a site, within specified sources (such as libraries, educational institutions, particular kinds of businesses or industries, a particular language or geographical area, and so on), or globally across the Web. Specifying extent will also help the user maintain orientation. For insite facilities, the initial target should be the Web site's contents. Offer different ways to search, including by *parameters* such as keywords, phrases and variants. Do assist in identifying keywords in large sites and provide an internal glossary of terms and a thesaurus. Variants allow relaxation of or qualify search constraints, such as allowing case insensitivity, phonetic variations, abbreviations, or synonyms. Providing a *spell checker* will reduce typing and spelling errors that prevent matches from being found.

Provide search *controls*, including a text box, structured controls, and a command button. The search *text box* should be large enough to enter a minimum of 20 characters. Arial is the suggested font because it is narrow and permits entry of more characters. A 10-point size is best for entry legibility. Never, however, use a font smaller than 8 points. To constrain searches or designate variants use *structured* controls, including check boxes, list boxes, or drop-down list boxes. Default to the most likely selection. (Use of either list boxes or drop-down list boxes will be determined by screen space constraints, see Step 7.) Provide a *command button* labeled "Search" to the right of search text box. For a grouping of search controls, position the search command button at the end of the field completion sequence. (See Step 7 for detailed command button size and location guidelines.)

Provide *separate interfaces* for simple search and advanced search. A simple search will normally consist of a text box for entering keywords and phrases. If advanced search is included, place an "Advanced Search" link under the search box. Also provide *guidance and assistance.* Present clear instructions, offer online help, and offer a search wizard. Guidance and assistance are addressed in more detail in Step 9 "Provide Effective Feedback and Guidance and Assistance."

Progressive Search Refinement

- Allow the user to control the size of the result set by providing a simple mechanism to:
  — First perform a rapid rough search that reports only:
    • The number of items in the result set, or
    • A preliminary list of topical matches.
  — Then perform a refinement phase to narrow the search and retrieve the desired result set.

To help narrow the field for large searches, and avoid overwhelming the user with hundreds of items to search through, support progressive search refinement. A progressive search consists of two phases. The first is a quick search using specified criteria. For the second phase, two alternatives are possible. The first alternative is to simply report back the number of matches found based upon the search. For example, a message might say, "A search on 'Automobiles' found 977 matches." If the number is too large, the user can continue to refine the search until a manageable number is found. If too small, the search criteria can be relaxed. In the second alternative is to present a list of topical matches. The user can then select the relevant topic and continue further refinement. For example, the search may be for "automobiles." Returned topics may include such items as "New," "Used," "Purchase," or "Lease." Designating "New" might then result in "American," "European," or "Japanese."

Selection of variations and changing of parameters should be easy and convenient to do. Also, provide messages with suggestions to guide users in the refinement process. Suggesting possible similar words, or word spellings, would be helpful. So would guidance concerning whether the search involves looking for whole words such as "tire," or should include partial words such as "entire" or "tired." While the search parameters may allow specification of such criteria, the user may have neglected to set them properly.

Launch the Search

- Permit search activation by clicking on the command button or pressing the Return key.
- In search refinement, permit changes to a parameter to automatically produce a new set of results.

Activate the search with an explicit action—clicking the command button or pressing the return key. This will indicate that the parameter specification process is completed. In search refinement, permit changes to a parameter to automatically produce a new set of results. This will speed the refinement process.

Present Meaningful Results

- Goal:
  - — Provide exactly the information or answer the user is looking for.
  - — Present it in a language and format that is easy to understand and use.
- Criteria summary:
  - — Present a summary of the search criteria with the search results.
- Explanatory message:
  - — Provide a meaningful message to explain search outcomes.
  - — Indicate how many items compose the search result set.
- Results presentation:
  - Present a textual listing that is:
    - – Concise.
    - – Arrayed in order of relevance.
    - – Clear.
    - – Easily scannable.
- Permit the user to:
  - — Modify the result set sequencing.
  - — Cluster the result set by an attribute or value.
- For multipage listings, make obvious the link to the next search result page. For results with only one item, immediately present the result page.

Goal. In presenting meaningful results, the objective is to provide exactly the information or answer the user is looking for. Presenting information or data in great quantities will test the user's patience and likely "hide the tree in the forest." Presenting irrelevant results often leads to abandonment of the search. To speed the search results review process, present information in a language and format that is easy to understand and use.

Criteria summary. Present a summary of the search criteria with the search results. Never assume that the user will remember what the search parameters were.

Explanatory messages. Provide meaningful messages explaining search outcomes that aid progressive refinement. Include how many items compose the search result set.

Results set presentation. Result listings should be concise, arrayed in order of relevance, clear, and easily scannable. A *concise* listing is one that displays the least possible amount of descriptive information for determining that a match meets the user's search need. Display the results in the most useful way possible. A *relevance-ordered* list places exact or best matches first and follows with those less close. A relevance-ordered list may also be sorted by a criterion reflecting the users need—alphabetically, chronologically, by date, and so forth. A *clear* listing provides enough information for the user to determine whether to proceed. Textual listings are usually much clearer than graphical listings. Consider graphical listings, such as maps, however, if the information will be more clearly presented in a graphical format. While being concise, a 1 to 3 word description, in most cases, will not provide the necessary clarity. URLs should not be presented because they tend to confuse more than help. Page upload dates should be presented only if they are of relevance to the searching user. A news site date, for example, is usually important to the user. For most other kinds of sites, including the date would not be relevant. Present an easily scannable results listing. A vertical array with highlighted keywords is best.

Allow the user to *modify* the result set by changing its sequencing; from alphabetical to chronological, for example. Allow the user to *cluster* the result set by an attribute or value, or by presented topics. For *multiple-page* listings, the link to the next search page should be clearly presented at the end of the listing currently being displayed. This link should not be displayed when no more listing pages follow. For results that find only *one item* to link to, immediately present the item page instead of presenting a one-item listing.

Destination Pages

- Describe how the page relates to the search query.
  — Provide page summary.
  — Highlight keywords.

When linked to a page through a search facility, the user should know why the page was found. Start the page with summary of its contents. Also highlight the words in the page that were keywords used in the search.

Locatability

- Provide text-based content.
- Repeat keywords frequently throughout the text.
- Provide a page title:
  — That possesses meaningful keywords.
  — Whose first word is its most important descriptor.
  — That makes sense when viewed completely out of context.
  — Is different from other page titles.
  — Is written in mixed-case, headline style, with no highlighting.

A Web site must be easily found by search a facility. To ensure locatability, use the following guidelines.

Text content and keywords. *Text-based content is* easily accessible to search engines. Provide text-based content as much as possible. Include as *keywords* on the page all possible query terms that can be used to search for the topic presented on the page. Repeat the keywords frequently throughout the text. Do not add keywords only peripherally related to the page's contents. Consider using a professional indexer to create keywords for full-text searches.

Titles. Page titles must be carefully designed to provide useful information. They should contain as many keywords as possible. While a title may contain 60 characters, ensure that the first 40 characters adequately describe the page topic. Titles are often truncated in navigation menus and by search facilities. The title's first word should be its most important descriptor. This word is most easily noticed in the scanning of long lists. Never begin a title with a generic term such as "Welcome" or "Page," or with an article such as "The." Give different titles to different pages. If page titles addressing the same topic must begin with same word, end the title with words that explain the differences between them.

A title must also make sense when viewed completely out of context, with no supporting content, or arrayed in a listing with other titles. Write titles in mixed case using the headline style. Do not use highlighting for keywords. A single keyword might be emphasized by putting it in upper case, but be conservative in this regard. Never use upper case for the first word in a title, its position is sufficient emphasis.

Intranet Design Guidelines

- Provide a single home page containing at least:
  — A directory hierarchy.
  — A search facility.
  — Current news.
- Present a visual style that is:
  — Different.
  — Distinguishing.
  — Unified.
- Orient the intranet Web site toward tasks.
- Include many options and features.
- Develop a strong navigational system.

Intranets are internal closed systems that use the capabilities of the Internet. Most intranets suffer in comparison to their Internet siblings because of poor navigation and a lack of design standards (Nielsen, 1997a). Too many are chaotic collections of documents that cannot be navigated because the organization's departments essentially "do their own thing," and few organization-wide guidelines exist to create unity. Lack of usability for an intranet translates into a significant loss of employee productivity. Nielsen (1997b and 1999a) suggests the following intranet design guidelines:

Home page. Provide a single home page containing at least a directory hierarchy, a search facility, and a current news segment. The *directory* will provide a structured overview of the sites content. The *search facility* will provide a means of quickly accessing the site's index. Unlike a generic facility, this local facility can present information about the importance of the item or topic of interest to the organization. The *news* segment can include information about the company and things that are of interest to employees.

Visual style. Since the Internet and an intranet are different information spaces, a complementary but distinguishing look will quickly inform the users should they wander outside of the closed internal net to the public site. The style should also be unified and consistent throughout its entire structure.

Task-oriented. An intranet will be more task-oriented and less promotional.

Options and features. Since the site will be frequently used by employees, it will be understood and learned faster (if unified in design). More options and features can exist since feelings of intimidation and being overwhelmed are much less likely to occur.

Navigational system. A stronger navigational system will be necessary because the intranet will encompass a much larger amount of information. Movement between servers may be necessary.

Extranet Design Guidelines

- To distinguish the extranet from the Internet, provide a subtle difference in:
  — Visual style.
  — Navigation.
- Provide links to the public Internet site.

An *extranet* is part of an organization's intranet that may be accessed from the Internet. Since it is a mixture of the Internet and the intranet, its design should reflect this. Since its users will access it from the Internet, its visual style and navigation should be similar to the Internet site to indicate companionship but subtly different to connote its independence. Links to locations on the public Internet site may be included (Nielsen, 1997b).

Statistical Graphics

A *statistical graphic* is data presented in a graphical format. A well-designed statistical graphic, also referred to as a *chart* or *graph*, consists of complex ideas communicated with clarity, precision, and efficiency. It gives its viewer the greatest number of ideas, in the shortest time, and in the smallest space, and with least possible clutter. It will also induce the viewer to think of substance, not techniques or methodology. It will provide coherence to large amounts of information by tying them together in a meaningful way, and it will encourage data comparisons of its different pieces by the eye. A well-designed statistical graphic display also avoids distortions by telling the truth about the data. Much of this material on statistical graphics is based upon Tufte (1983), Smith and Mosier (1986), and Fowler and Stanwick (1995).

Use of Statistical Graphics

- Reserve for material that is rich, complex, or difficult.

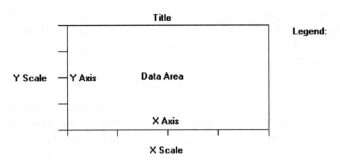

Figure 3.67   Components of a statistical graphic.

Statistical graphics should be reserved for large sets of data with real variability. The power of graphics should not be wasted on simple linear changes or situations in which one or two numbers would summarize the result better. Tufte (1983) says that tables usually outperform graphics on small data sets of 20 or fewer numbers, or when data sets are noncomparative or highly labeled. Tables are also better if the data must be studied or very specific information must be retrieved (Coll, Coll, and Thakur, 1994).

Components of a Statistical Graphic

Most statistical graphics have at least two axes, two scales, an area to present the data, a title, and sometimes a legend or key, as illustrated in Figure 3.67. Pie charts are the exception to this general rule. Guidelines for graphic components include the following.

Data Presentation

- Emphasize the data.
- Minimize the nondata elements.
- Minimize redundant data.
- Show data variation, not design variation.
- Provide the proper context for data interpretation.
- Restrict the number of information-carrying dimensions depicted to the number of data dimensions being illustrated.
- Employ data in multiple ways, whenever possible.
- Maximize data density.
- Employ simple data-coding schemes.
- Avoid unnecessary embellishment of:
  — Grids.
  — Vibration.
  — Ornamentation.
- Fill the graph's available area with data.

The most important part of a graphics display, as with an alphanumeric display, is the data itself.

Emphasize the data, minimize the nondata elements. A person's attention should be drawn to the measured quantities. The largest share of the graphic's "ink" should present data. Nondata elements—such as elaborate grid lines, gratuitous decoration, and extensive, detailed, and wordy labels—draw attention to themselves and mask the data. So, nondata elements should be minimized, or eliminated entirely.

Redundant data. Information that depicts the same value over and over should also be minimized or eliminated. Redundancy, on occasion, can be useful, however. It may aid in providing context and order, facilitating comparisons, and creating an aesthetic balance. Use redundancy only if necessary.

Data variation. Show data variation, not design variation. Each part of a graphic generates visual expectations about its other parts. The expectancies created in one part should be fulfilled in other parts so the viewer does not confuse changes in design with changes in data. Scales should move in regular intervals; proportions should be consistent for all design elements. If the viewer confuses changes in design with changes in data, ambiguity and deception result.

Proper context. Provide the proper context for data interpretation. Graphics often lie by omission. Data for making comparisons or establishing trends must always be included to provide a proper reference point. "Thin" data must be viewed with suspicion. The graphic in Figure 3.68, for example, might have a number of possible interpretations, as illustrated in Figure 3.69. All important questions must be foreseen and answered by the graphic.

Restrict information-carrying dimensions. Restrict the number of information-carrying dimensions depicted to the number of data dimensions being illustrated. Displaying one-dimensional data in a multidimensional format is perceptually ambiguous. With multidimensional data, changes in the physical area of the surface of the graphic do not produce an appropriate proportional change in the perceived area. Examples of multidimensional formats used to display one-dimensional data would be different-sized human bodies to indicate populations or different-sized automobiles to indicate the number of cars. Often the impression on the viewer is that the change is actually much greater than it really is. This problem can be avoided if the number of information-carrying dimensions on the graphic is restricted to the number of data dimensions being illustrated.

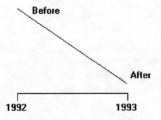

Figure 3.68 A change between 1992 and 1993 without proper context for interpretation.

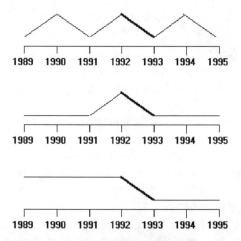

Figure 3.69 Changes between 1992 and 1993 with proper contexts for interpretation.

Employ data in multiple ways. Whenever possible, employ data in multiple ways. Parts of a graph can be designed to serve more than one purpose. A piece of data may at the same time convey information and also perform a design function usually left to a nondata element. Some examples are:

■ A grid to aid readability of a bar chart, instead of being inscribed on the graphic background, may be positioned within the bars themselves, as illustrated in Figure 3.70.

■ The size of what is being measured can be conveyed through the size of the graphical element, the intensity through color or level of shading.

Graphics can be designed to have multiple viewing depths. The top level provides an overall view, each succeeding level an ever-increasing closer view. They may be also designed to have different viewing angles or lines of sight.

The danger in employing data in multiple ways is that it can generate a graphical puzzle. A sign of a puzzle is that the graphic, instead of being interpreted visually, must be interpreted verbally. Symptoms of a puzzle are frequent references to a legend

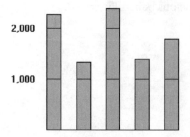

Figure 3.70 A piece of data (line in the bars) performing a nondata function.

to interpret what is presented and extensive memorization of design rules before one can comprehend what is presented. By contrast, a well-designed multiple-function graphic permits a quick and implicit transition of the visual to the verbal.

Maximize data density. In graphics more is better than less—the greater amount of information displayed, the larger the number of visual comparisons that can be made, improving comprehension. This is true because the eye can detect large amounts of information in a small space. Simple things belong in a table or in the text.

Data density of a graphic can be maximized in two ways: enlarging the data matrix or shrinking the graphic. Enlarging the data matrix involves displaying as much information as possible. If the graphic becomes overcrowded, techniques such as averaging, clustering, smoothing, or providing summaries can reduce the number of elements to be displayed. Shrinking the graphic means reducing it in size, but screen resolution may impose limitations on how much shrinking can be performed.

If visual differentiation in the types of data being displayed is necessary, use simple coding methods in the areas being depicted. Elaborate schemes or patterns can be eye straining and can actually impede the flow of information from the graphic to the viewer. Some possible coding alternatives include:

- Varying shades or densities.
- Labeling with words.
- Varying colors.

Avoid unnecessary embellishment. All pieces of a graphic must tell the viewer something new. An unnecessary embellishment is "chartjunk." It does not add anything new to the graphic's meaning. It is decoration or noise that hinders assimilation of the message being communicated. Nondata elements and redundant data are forms of chartjunk. Three other kinds are vibration, heavy grids, and ornamentation.

A grid carries no information, contributes noise, and focuses attention away from the data. An excessively heavy grid can even mask the data. Grids should be suppressed or eliminated so they do not compete with the data. When a grid serves as an aid in reading or extrapolating, it should, of course, be included. Its tendency to overwhelm can be reduced by constructing it with delicate lines or muted colors and placing it behind the data.

The eye is never absolutely still; it produces continuous slight tremors that aid visual acuity. The result is that, when small patterns lines, boxes, or dots are viewed, they shimmer or vibrate. This vibration can be distracting; examples are illustrated in Figure 3.71. Although eye-catching, vibrations can also strain the eye. Simple data-coding schemes, such as using shades of color, are much more effective.

When the graphic is overwhelmed by decoration, it is very ineffective. Ornamentation can take many forms: extensive use of color when it is not necessary; creating multidimensional graphics when single dimensional will do; pointless use of vibrating patterns, or forcing data into a graphic when a table would work

Figure 3.71 Examples of patterns creating vibrations.

much better. Ornamentation is more effective as a piece of art hanging on a wall. It is a symptom of "See what I can do with my computer" rather than an effort to provide the user with the data in the most comprehensible way possible. The best graphic display is the simplest graphic display.

Fill the display area. For ease of interpretation and efficiency, the graphic's data should fill up the entire display area within the axes. If it does not, the scale or the graphic is too large.

Axes

- Values on an axis should increase as they move away from the origin.
- Use the horizontal axis (X) to show time or cause of an event (the independent variable).
- Use the vertical axis (Y) to show a caused effect (the dependent variable).

Values on an axis should increase as they move away from the origin. If the numeric values displayed are positive, the origin point will be the lower-left point of the graphic. If the data includes negative values and the axes must extend in both directions from the zero point, position the origin in the center of the graph.

Use the horizontal axis (X) to show time or cause of an event (the independent variable). Use the vertical axis (Y) to show a caused effect (the dependent variable). When the X-axis plots time intervals, the labeled points should represent the end of each time interval. The X-axis may also be called *abscissa* or *category* axis, the Y-axis the *ordinal* or *value* axis. If the graphic possesses three dimensions, the third axis is called the Z-axis, reflecting the graph's plane.

Scales and Scaling

- Place ticks to marks scales on the outside edge of each axis.
- Employ a linear scale.
- Mark scales at standard or customary intervals.
- Start a numeric scale at zero (0).
- Keep the number of digits in a scale to a minimum.
- Display only a single scale on each axis.
- For large data matrices, consider displaying duplicate axes.
- Provide aids for scale interpretation.
- Provide scaling consistency across two or more related graphics.
- Clearly label each axis in a left-to-right reading orientation.

A scale is a set of measurement points or markers. Scaling is the positioning of data in relation to these points or markers. Choose an appropriate scale for both graph axes. If the scale is too expanded, the effect may be exaggerated, if too small, the effect may be underreported. Standard scaling practices are these:

Tick marks. Place ticks to mark scales on the outside edge of each axis. Placing them outside will prevent a tick from interfering with data located near the axis.

Linear scale. Employ a linear scale. Most people are more familiar with linear scales than with logarithmic or other nonlinear scales. These latter kinds are often interpreted inaccurately.

Scale markings. Mark scales at standard or customary intervals to aid comprehension. Familiar standard intervals are 1, 2, 5, 10, and multiples of 10. Familiar customary intervals include the days of the week and the months of the year.

Construct scales with tick marks at these intervals. To aid visual comprehension, it may be necessary to provide intermediate marks as well. Intermediate marks should be consistent with the scale intervals shown.

Start a numeric scale at zero. Start a numeric scale at zero. Using zero as the starting point on a scale aids visual comparisons since zero is an expected starting point. If a zero point is omitted because of the nature of the data, this omission should be clearly indicated in the graphic.

Minimization of scale digits. Keep the number of digits in a scale to a minimum. Smaller numbers aid understanding. Round off all numbers to two digits or less. However, place zeros in front of decimal numbers so the decimal point is not missed.

Single scale on each axis. Display only a single scale on each axis. Avoid multiple scales associated with a single axis. For all but the most experienced people, multiple scales can be confusing and can lead to interpretation errors. Meanings can also be greatly distorted. If multiscale graphs must be used, permit the user to select any data curve individually and have the computer highlight its corresponding scale.

Duplicate axes for large matrices. For large data matrices, consider displaying duplicate axes. The readability of large data matrices is improved if the X-axis scale appears at the top as well as the bottom of the graph, and the Y-axis scale at the right as well as the left side.

Scale interpretation. Provide aids for scale interpretation. When reading accuracy is extremely critical, provide computer aids for interpretation, such as the following:

- Displaying a fine grid upon request.
- Vertical and horizontal rules that the user can move to the intersection point.
- Letting the user point at a data item and having the computer then provide the exact values.

Consistency. Provide scaling consistency across two or more related graphics. If comparisons must be made between multiple graphs or charts, use the same scale for each. Data sets scaled differently lead to interpretation errors.

Labeling. Each scale axis should be clearly labeled in a conventional left-to-right reading orientation. A complete description of the values, with measurement units, should be provided.

Proportion

- Provide accurate proportion of the displayed surfaces to the data they represent.
- Provide proper proportion by:
  — Conforming to the shape of the data.
  — Making the width greater than the height.

The displayed surfaces on graphics should be directly proportional to the numeric qualities they represent. Failure to display the correct proportions can create false impressions of magnitudes of differences in sizes or changes. This kind of graphical distortion can be eliminated through clear, detailed, and thorough labeling, a topic to be addressed shortly.

Provide proper proportion. When the relative proportions of a graphic are in balance, it looks better. Graphics should tend toward the horizontal, assuming a greater length than height. There are a number of reasons for this recommendation. First, people prefer this shape. Second, it is easier to read words arrayed left-to-right. Third, many graphics plot cause and effect relationships, with effect on the vertical axis and cause on the horizontal. An elongated horizontal axis helps describe the causal variable in more detail. If, however, the data being displayed suggests a shape either square or higher than wide, conform to the shape suggested by the data.

Lines

- Data lines should be the heaviest.
- Axes lines should be of medium weight.
  — Extend the lines entirely around the graphic.
- Grid lines should be very thin or absent.

The most important part of the graphic is the data. Emphasize the data by making the data lines the heaviest. Of secondary importance are the axes lines. Display them in a medium thickness. Axes lines should be extended entirely around the graphic to create a rectangle (or box). This will define the graphic area and help focus attention on the data itself. Grid lines should be avoided if at all possible, unless absolutely needed for accurate data interpretation.

Labeling

- Employ clear, detailed and thorough labeling.
- Maintain a left-to-right reading orientation.
- Integrate the labeling with the drawing.
  — Do not curve letters to match the shape of curved lines.
- Use only one typeface, font, and weight.
  — For emphasis, use different type sizes.
- Do not separate labeling from the data through ruled lines.
- Provide information about the source of the data.
- Use a legend for complicated graphs.

Clear and detailed. Employ clear, detailed, and thorough labeling. Words should be fully spelled out. Follow standard capitalization schemes, using both upper and lower case, with lower case used for textual information. Use the simplest and shortest word forms possible.

Left-to-right. Maintain a left-to-right reading orientation. Display all labels horizontally. Avoid words that are organized vertically or words that run in different directions. Whereas non-horizontal words on hard-copy graphics can easily be read by turning the paper, this screen capability is not available, nor yet easy to accomplish.

Integrate. Integrate the labeling with the drawing. Explanations on graphics help the viewer and should be incorporated as much as possible. Words are data, and they can occupy space freed up by nondata elements or redundant data. Integrating words and captions with the graphic eliminates the need for a legend and the eye movements back and forth required to read it. Also, incorporate messages to explain the data, and label interesting or important points. Never curve letters to match the shape of curved lines. This is terribly distracting. Run all text horizontally.

One typeface. Use only one typeface, font, and weight. Using the same type style for graphics and text aids the visual integration of the two. If text needs to be emphasized, use different type sizes.

Separation. Do not separate labeling from the data through ruled lines. Again, this creates visual noise and impairs proper associations.

Source. Provide information about the source of the data. This information can be placed, in small type, below the X-axis label or in a caption. It can also be made available through online help.

Legends. If a graph is complicated, containing a lot of data and a lot of visual coding, use a legend. A legend, while not as easy to comprehend as integrated labeling, is better than cluttering up a graph with too much integrated labeling, or presenting illegible labels.

Title

- Create a short, simple, clear, and distinctive title describing the purpose of the graphic.
- Position the title above, centered, or left-aligned to the rectangle formed by the extended axes.
- Spell it out fully, using a mixed-case or uppercase font.

A title should be brief and descriptive of the graphic. A title may be centered or flush left to the rectangle formed by the extended axes. Marcus (1992) feels that left-aligning it yields a stronger composition. Titles should be spelled out fully, and may be displayed larger, bolder, and in mixed- or uppercase font.

Aiding Interpretation of Numbers

- Display a grid on request.
- Permit the viewer to click on a data point to display actual values.

- Show numeric values automatically for each point or bar.
- Permit the viewer to zoom in on an area of the graphic.
- Permit the user to change the scale values.
- Permit toggling between a graphic and a table.

Computer graphics, unlike paper graphics, can be easily manipulated. Fowler and Stanwick (1995) suggest that the interpretation of numbers in graphical displays can be aided by permitting the above actions.

Types of Statistical Graphics

Statistical graphics take many forms. There are curves and line graphs, surface charts, scatterplots, bar graphs, histograms, segmented or stacked bars, and pie charts.

Curve and Line Graphs

- Display data curves or lines that must be compared in a single graph.
- Display no more than four or five curves in a single graph.
- Identify each curve or line with an adjacent label whenever possible.
- If a legend must be included, order the legend to match the spatial ordering of the lines.
- For tightly packed curves or lines, provide data differentiation with a line-coding technique, such as different colors or different line composition types.
- Highlight curves or lines representing important or critical data.
- When comparing actual to projected data:
  — Use solid curves or lines for actual data.
  — Use broken curves or lines for projected data.
- Display a reference index if the displayed data must be compared to a standard or critical value.
- Display differences between two data sets as a curve or line itself.

Curves and line graphs can be used to show relationships between sets of data defined by two continuous variables. They are especially useful showing data changes over time, being superior to other graphic methods for speed and accuracy in determining data trends. With a curve, the data relations are summarized by a smoothed line. With a line, straight line segments connect the data plots. A line graph is illustrated in Figure 3.72. This kind of graph implies a continuous function. If the data point elements are discrete, it is better to use a bar graph.

Single graph. If several curves must be compared, display them in one combined graph to facilitate their comparison.

Four or five maximum. Display no more than four or five curves in a single graph. As more curves or lines are added to a graph, visually discriminating among them becomes more difficult. The maximum number of lines presented should be

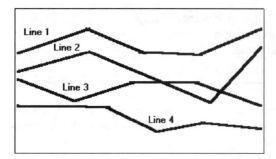

Figure 3.72   A line graph.

limited to four or five. If one particular curve or line must be compared to several others, consider multiple graphs where the line of interest is compared separately with each other line.

Label identification. Identify each curve or line with an adjacent label whenever possible. A label is preferable to a separate legend. If direct labeling is impossible due to the tightness of the lines, a legend may be the only alternative. If a legend is used, visually differentiate the lines (colors, line types, and so on), and include the coding scheme in the legend.

Legend. If a legend must be included, order the legend to match the spatial order-ing of the lines. If legends are to be used on a series of graphs, however, maintain one consistent order for the legends on all graphs.

Tightly packed curves or Lines. For tightly packed curves or lines, provide data dif-ferentiation through a line coding technique. Common coding techniques include different colors and line types. Do not exceed the maximum number of alterna-tives for the method selected, as shown in Table 11.1 in Step 11 "Create Meaning-ful Graphics, Icons, and Images." If color-coding is used, choose colors on the basis of the considerations described in Step 12 "Select the Proper Colors." Line width and dot size coding should be avoided because of their similarity to grids and scatterpoints. If a series of related graphs are line coded, be consistent in the selection of techniques for corresponding data.

Important or critical data. Highlight curves or lines representing important or criti-cal data. If one curve or line in a multiple-line graph is of particular significance, highlight that curve (high intensity, different color, and so on) to call attention to it. The coding scheme selected should be different from that used for spatial dif-ferentiation. Use solid curves or lines for actual data; use broken curves or lines for projected data.

Comparing actual and projected data. When a curve or line must be compared to a standard or critical value, display a reference curve or line reflecting that value.

Data differences. If the difference between two sets of data must be determined, dis-play the difference itself as a curve or line. This is preferable to requiring the user to visually compare the two values and calculate the difference between them. If the difference between the related curves is of interest, consider a band chart where both lines and curves are displayed and the area between them coded through use of a texture, shading, or color.

Surface Charts

- Order the data categories so that:
  — The least variable is at the bottom, and the most variable at the top.
  — The largest is at the bottom and the smallest at the top.
- Use different texture or shading coding schemes to differentiate the areas below each curve or line.
- Incorporate labels within the bands of data.

If the data being depicted by a curve or line represents all the parts of a whole, consider developing a *surface chart*, as illustrated in Figure 3.73. In this kind of graph, the curves or lines are stacked above one another to indicate individual amounts or aggregated amounts. Each boundary height is determined by the height of the line below it, and the area between each line or curve is differently coded, usually by textures or shading. A surface chart is similar to a segmented bar chart

Ordering. In ordering the data categories, place the least variable at the bottom and the most variable at the top. Irregularities in the bottom curve or line will affect those above it. This makes it difficult for a viewer to determine whether the irregularity in the upper curves reflect real data differences or is the result of this style of graph. Displaying the least variable data at the bottom will minimize this effect. Alternately, place the widest area at the bottom and the narrowest at the top. Wide bands look like they belong at the bottom, narrow at the top.

If the data itself implies that some logical organization must be followed, and the resulting organization creates confusing distortions in the curves, this kind of graph should not be used.

Coding schemes. Use different texture or shading coding schemes. Ensure that the coding scheme chosen for each area is visually distinguishable from all the others. Place darker shades or colors toward the bottom.

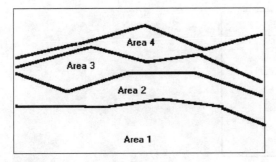

Figure 3.73 A surface chart.

Labels. Labels with a left-to-right reading orientation should be included within textured or shaded bands, if possible. Legends showing individual percentages, or cumulative percentages, should only be incorporated where space constraints exist within the bands.

Scatterplots

- Limit use to two-dimensional displays of data.
- Maintain consistent scale size intervals.
- Provide distinguishable, equal-sized plot points.
- If there is more than one set of data on the plot, use different symbols for each data set's points.
- Visually distinguish points of particular significance through a highlighting technique.

Scatterplots can be used to show relationships among individual data points in a two-dimensional array. A point is displayed on the plot where the X-axis and Y-axis variables intersect, as illustrated in Figure 3.74. Correlations and trends on scatterplots can be indicated by the superimposition of curves (thus combining the scatterplot with another kind of graphic display).

Two dimensions. Limit scatterplots to two dimensions. Three-dimensional scatterplots, while possible, do not yield clear, unambiguous displays.

Consistent intervals. Maintain consistent scale size intervals. Inconsistent spacing size between scale ticks on the two axes will distort the displayed data.

Distinguishable plots. Construct the plot points of distinguishable, equal-sized circles, squares, rectangles, or diamonds. These symbols may be filled in or empty. Color may also be used to designate the points. Keep in mind that, when using color, different colors can look different in size, and some people using the graphic may be colorblind.

Multiple data sets. If there is more than one set of data on the plot, use different symbols for each data set's points. Choose distinguishable symbols from those described above.

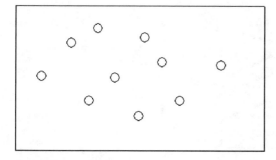

Figure 3.74   A scatterplot.

Significant points. Visually distinguish significant points. Points of particular significance on scatterplots can be made distinctive through highlighting techniques such as the use of high intensity, different colors, or different shapes.

Bar Graphs

- Orient bars consistently, either horizontally or vertically.
- Use vertical bars when the item being counted is of greatest interest.
- Use horizontal bars:
  — When the data labels are long.
  — To highlight the information rather than the count.
- Use a meaningful organizing principle.
  — If none exists, arrange the bars so that the length of bars is in ascending or descending order.
- Make the spacing between bars equal to one-half the width of the bars or less.
  — If groupings of bars are presented, leave space between the groupings only.
- If different kinds of bars must be easily distinguished, provide differentiation through a coding technique.
  — If possible, use a pattern or color that reinforces the data.
- Highlight bars representing important or critical data.
- Provide a consistent ordering for related groups of bars.
- Display a reference index if displayed data must be compared to a standard or critical value.
- Identify each bar with an adjacent label.
  — Place labels below, or to the left of, the baseline.
- When a great many pieces of data must be compared, consider using histograms or step charts.

Bar graphs can be used to show a few differences between separate entities or to show differences in a variable at a few discrete intervals. A bar graph consists of a series of bars extending from a common origin or baseline, as illustrated in Figure 3.75, or they may extend between separately plotted high and low points, as illustrated in Figure 3.76, having only one axis. Bar graphs may be arrayed horizontally or vertically. Vertical bar graphs are sometimes called *column charts*.

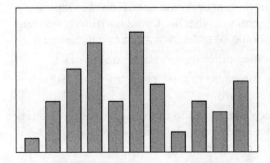

Figure 3.75 A bar graph with a common origin point.

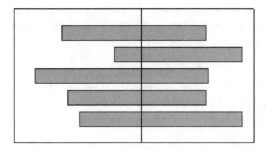

Figure 3.76 A bar graph with separately plotted high and low points.

Consistent orientation. While bars may be oriented either horizontally or vertically, a consistent orientation should be maintained for bars displaying similar information. In general, frequency counts are best displayed in vertical bars. Also, use vertical bars when the values or count being displayed are of greatest interest. Use horizontally arrayed bars for time durations. Also use this orientation when the data labels are long and room is needed to present them, and when the information categories must be highlighted, rather than the count.

Meaningful organization. Use a meaningful organizing principle, such as volumes, dates, or alphabetical. If no meaningful principle exists, arrange the bars so that the length of bars are in ascending or descending order. If the information is being compared to a baseline or other comparative data, place the baseline bar to the far left or at the top.

Bar spacing. Space the bars for ease of visual comparison. Comparison of bars should be accomplishable without eye movement. Generally, the spacing between bars should be one-half or less of the bar width. If many bars are to be displayed, the alternating pattern of bright and dark bands that results can be visually disturbing to some viewers. In this case it is better to completely eliminate the spacing between bars. (The graph is then called a *histogram*.) If groupings of bars are presented, leave the space between the groupings.

Differentiation. If different kinds of bars must be easily distinguished, provide differentiation through a coding technique such as the use of color, texture, or shading. If possible, use a meaningful pattern or color that reinforces the differences.

Important or critical data. Highlight important or critical data. If one bar represents data of unusual significance, call attention to that bar through a different coding technique. Related groups of bars should be ordered in a consistent manner.

Related bar ordering. Provide a consistent ordering for related groups of bars.

Reference index. When bars must be compared to some standard or critical value, display a reference line to aid that comparison.

Labeling. A label associated with each bar, in left-to-right reading orientation, is preferable to a separate legend. Place labels below, or to the left of, the baseline. If the labels on a horizontal bar chart are short, left-align them. If they are long, right-align them to the axis. If groups of bars are repeated, it is only necessary to label one group rather than all bars in all groups.

Figure 3.77   A histogram or step chart.

Histograms or step charts. When a great many pieces of data must be compared, consider histograms or step charts. These are bar graphs without spaces between each of the bars, as illustrated in Figure 3.77. The area of a bar in a histogram reflects the amount of the value; so all bars should be of equal width.

Segmented or Stacked Bars

- Order the data categories in the same sequence.
- Order the data categories so that:
  - The least variable is at the bottom.
  - The most variable is at the top.
- Limit the number of segments to those that are large enough to be seen and labeled.
- Use different texture or coding schemes to differentiate the areas within each bar.
- Clearly associate labels with bars or segments.
  - Place segment labels to the right on a vertical chart or above on a horizontal chart.

If both the total measure of a value and its component portions are of interest, consider using *segmented or stacked bars*. These bars are similar to bar graphs except that the bar is segmented into two or more pieces reflecting the component values, as illustrated in Figure 3.78. In this way they are similar to surface graphs and pie charts. Design guidelines are similar to stacked bars, except for the following:

Data category ordering. To provide consistency, order the data categories in the same sequence for all bars. Order data categories to show least variable at bottom and most variable at top. Irregularities in the bottom segment will affect those above it. This can make it difficult for a person to determine whether the irregularity in the upper segments reflects real data differences or is the result of this style of graph. Displaying least variable data at the bottom will minimize this effect. Also consider displaying the least variable values at the bottom, as is done with surface charts, unless the data itself dictates that some other logical organization must be followed.

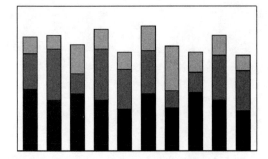

Figure 3.78 A segmented, or stacked, bar graph.

Large segments. Limit the number of segments to those that are big enough to be seen and labeled. If small segment components exist, group them into an "other" category.

Coding schemes. Use different texture or shading coding schemes. Ensure that the coding scheme chosen for each segment is visually distinguishable from all others. Place darker shades or colors toward the bottom or toward the left.

Labeling. Associate labels with bars and segments. Labels, with a left-to-right reading orientation, are preferable to legends. Do not place labels within segments, as they most often will not fit. Legends should only be used if space does not allow labels.

Pie Charts

- Pie charts should be used with caution.
- If pie charts are used:
  - They must add up to 100 percent.
  - Use five segments or fewer.
  - Each segment should take up at least 5 percent (18 degrees) of the circle.
  - Place the largest segment starting at 12:00.
  - Directly label each segment in the normal reading orientation.
    - If leaders for labels in small segments are necessary, orient them in as few angles as possible.
  - Include numbers with segment labels to indicate percentages of absolute values.
  - Texture- or color-coding selected for segments should not emphasize one segment over another (unless it is intended).
  - Highlight segments requiring particular emphasis through a contrasting display technique or by "exploding" it.
  - Never tilt a pie.

Figure 3.79   A pie chart.

Pie charts, a circle broken up into pie-shaped pieces, can be used to show an apportionment of a total into its component parts, as illustrated in Figure 3.79. Bar graphs, however, usually permit more accurate estimates of proportions. Experts caution against the use of pie charts because:

- They provide no means of absolute measurement.
- They cannot represent totals greater than 100 percent.
- They can only represent a fixed point in time.
- Human estimation of relationships is more accurate with linear than with angular representations.

If pie charts are used, the guidelines below should be followed.

Total 100 percent. The parts must add up to 100 percent. To convert from percentages to degrees, multiply the percentage by 3.6.

Five segments or fewer. To minimize confusion, restrict pies to five segments or fewer. This permits adequate differentiation of its pieces and accurate labeling.

Minimum five percent. Avoid very small segments. Segments should take up at least 5 percent (18 degrees) of the circle in order to provide adequate segment differentiation. If small portions exist, combine the pieces into an "other" category and list them in a caption or note.

Start at 12:00. Start with the largest wedge at 12:00 (or a quarter hour) and order from largest to smallest in a clockwise order.

Labeling. To provide maximum association of the label with data, and for reading clarity, use a left-to-right reading orientation. If it is impossible to include the label within the segment, it may be placed outside and tied to the segment with a leader line. Place the labels in one or two columns (one on each side). If multiple outside labels and leader lines are necessary, orient the lines in as few angles as possible.

Numbers with segment labels. Include numbers with the segment labels to indicate percentages or absolute values. Only by including numbers with segment labels can numeric values be accurately established. Alternately, make actual percentages available when requested.

Segment coding. The kinds of textures or colors selected for segments should not emphasize one segment over another, unless this emphasis is intended.

Highlighting. Highlight segments requiring emphasis. Use a contrasting display technique or *explode* segments requiring emphasis. Exploding is accomplished by slightly displacing a segment from the remainder of the pie.

Tilting. Never tilt a pie. Distortion will occur with tilting. Small wedges at the front will look larger than they actually are.

Choosing a Graph Type

- Determine what kind of information is most important for the viewer to extract.
- Choose the type of graph best suited for presenting that kind of information.

The types of graphics just described have rarely been experimentally studied to determine their most effective use. Some studies addressing this issue, however, are those of Hollands and Spence (1992) and Simkin and Hastie (1987). These researchers collected data on three tasks: (1) determining a proportion of a whole where the proportion *was* a part of the whole (proportion), (2) determining a proportion of a whole where the proportion *was not* a part of the whole (comparison), and (3) determining a change over time (change). The results are summarized in Table 3.2.

In estimating proportion, if a scale is not included on the graph, pie charts and segmented bars were found to be best. If a scale is included, line graphs and bar

Table 3.2 Tasks and Best Types of Graphs

	PROPORTION		COMPARISON	CHANGE
	WITH SCALE	**WITHOUT SCALE**	**COMPARISON**	**CHANGE**
Best	Line Graphs	Segmented Bars	Bar Graphs	Line Graphs
	Bar Graphs	Pie Charts	Segmented Bars	Bar Graphs
	Segmented Bars			
	Pie Charts			
Poorest	—	Bar Graphs	Pie Charts	Segmented Bars
	Line Graphs	Pie Charts		

Source: Spence (1992) and Simkin and Hastie (1987).

graphs are also usable, both actually having a slight edge in speed over pie charts and bar graphs. In the comparison task, bar graphs and segmented bars were superior to pie charts. In estimating change over time, line graphs and bar graphs were both very effective, and pie charts and segmented bars the poorest.

In choosing a graph to display information, the kind of information important to the viewer must always be determined first. This will point to the kind of graphic most effective for the task.

Flow Charts

- Displayed steps should be designed to:
  — Follow some logical order.
  — Minimize path link.
- Orient the chart following common flowchart reading conventions such as left-to-right and top-to-bottom.
- Follow common flowchart coding conventions to distinguish elements.
- Use arrows in conventional ways to indicate directional relationships.
- Highlight elements requiring particular attention through a contrasting display technique.
- Require only one decision at each step.
- Be consistent in all option ordering and wording.

If the data to be displayed flows in a complex, yet sequential, process, consider using a *flowchart* to schematically represent it. Flowcharts can also be used to aid problem solving in which a solution can be reached by answering a series of questions. They are not useful when trade-offs must be made.

Order of steps. One logical ordering scheme is to follow a sequence of operations or processes from start to finish. Other potential ordering schemes include placing the most important decisions first or the decisions that can be made with the most certainty. If no logical order is apparent, order the flowchart to minimize the length of the path through it. If some decision paths are more likely to occur than others, minimize the length of the most likely path.

Orientation. Follow a left-to-right and top-to-bottom orientation.

Coding conventions. Follow existing shape coding conventions for the kinds of boxes being displayed. Adhere to standards and people's expectations.

Arrows. Use arrows to indicate directional relations and sequential links.

Highlighting. Contrasting display techniques, such as high intensity or color, should be used to call attention to relevant paths or elements. Color is particularly effective in this regard.

Only one decision at each step. Multiple decisions reduce flowchart size. However, requiring multiple decisions such as "Is A true and B false?" can be confusing. Require that only single decisions be made.

Consistently order and word all choices. Consistency always aids learning.

Technological Considerations in Interface Design

Interface design is also affected by the physical characteristics of the display device itself and the characteristics of the interfaces controlling software.

Graphical Systems

- Screen design must be compatible with the capabilities of the system, including:
  — System power.
  — Screen size.
  — Screen resolution.
  — Display colors.
  — Other display features.
- Screen design must be compatible with the capabilities of the:
  — System platform being used.
  — Development and implementation tools being used.
  — Platform style guide being used.

Graphical system design must be compatible with the system's power, screen size, screen resolution, and displayable colors, fonts and other features. Designs for Web systems must also take into consideration the characteristics of the browsers being used and the bandwidth of the communication medium. The design must also be compatible with the system platform and any development and implementation tools being used. The design must also take into consideration any available platform style guide.

System Power

A slow processing speed and small memory may inhibit effective use of a system. Feedback and animation capabilities may be limited, reducing the system's usability. Slow responses can be error prone, grossly inefficient, and very aggravating. A slow screen refresh rate will increase the user's chances of perceiving screen flicker, which can be visually fatiguing. A system must be powerful enough to perform all necessary actions promptly, responsively, and meaningfully.

Screen Size

Through the years, the physical size of an available monitor's screen area has been gradually increasing. Current typical monitor sizes range from 13 to 21 inches (measured diagonally), with 17 inches being most common.

Many of today's screens are not large enough in size to take full advantage of windowing capabilities. As a result, many windows are still of Post-It dimensions. There is some evidence, from studies and personal observation, that many users of windowing systems expand their windows to cover a full screen. Either seeing all the contents of one window is preferable to seeing small parts of many windows, the operational complexity of multiple windows is not wanted, or visual noise is being eliminated. Whatever the case, these actions indicate a shortcoming in windowing systems, as they exist today.

Best monitor size was the focus of a study by Simmons and Manaham (1999). They compared monitors of 15, 17, 19, and 21 inches for search activities using Microsoft's Word and Excel, and for browsing the Web. The 21-inch monitor resulted in fastest task completion. Users, however, preferred using the 19-inch monitor. DiPierro, Nachman, and Raderman (2000) compared Web navigation performance using small, medium, and large screens. No performance difference was found between small and medium screens, but the large screen elicited a 26 percent faster performance.

Clearly, these studies point out that bigger screens may be better. One typical-sized screen today hardly approximates one standard-sized piece of paper. Comparisons between information contained on separate pieces of paper are still difficult using current monitor sizes. The answer to this problem may lie in providing multiple monitors for doing one's work or performing other activities. Multiple monitors reflect more closely the "cluttered desk" metaphor, for better or worse.

Continually expanding monitor and screen size as a solution, though, may create other problems. A large display area will require longer control movements to reach all locations on the screen, and more head and eye movements. Even with today's relatively small screens many activities in the peripheries of vision still go unnoticed. Larger screens will compound this problem. The effect on user's physical comfort, and the possibility of needing an expanded working area must be considered. Clearly, the screen size/multiple monitor usability trade-off must be studied further.

Screen Resolution

Screen resolution is the horizontal and vertical height of a screen in pixels. It is a function of the monitor's capabilities and its video card. Most common display resolutions currently are 640×480 (pixels width and height), 800×600, and 1024×768. Higher resolutions are also available. Poor screen resolution may deter effective use of a graphical system by not permitting sharp and realistic drawings and shapes. Window structure and icon design may be severely affected.

In a study mentioned previously, Ziefle (1998) evaluated reading performance, using both hard-copy paper documents and monitors at different resolutions. In the first study, she compared paper printed at 255 dots per inch (dpi) and monitors whose resolutions were 832×600 pixels (60 dpi) and 1664×1200 pixels (120 dpi). A 19-inch monitor showing black characters on a light background was used, and reading speeds and proofreading accuracy were compared. Ziefle found no difference in performance between the monitors with different resolutions. In the second Ziefle study, participants performed a continuous visual search task. Performance was compared using screens of lower resolution, 720×540 (62 dpi), and higher, 1024×768 (89 dpi). She found that the higher resolution screen was searched significantly faster. Using the lower resolution, she found that after 30 minutes the participants began to search more slowly, made more errors, and had more and longer eye fixations.

In conclusion, looking just at the differences between the monitors of different resolutions, both studies found advantages for the higher resolution screens in terms of both preference and performance. Adequate screen resolution then, is a necessity to achieve meaningful representations. Higher resolution screens also appear to be better for one's eyes.

Colors

The color palette must be of a variety large enough to permit establishment of a family of discriminable colors. The colors used must be accurately and clearly presented in all situations. The contextual effect of colors must also be considered, because hues may change based on factors such as size and one color's location in relation to other colors. Color is thoroughly discussed in Step 12.

Other Display Features

A wide range screen attributes or properties are available to aid the screen design process. Included are such techniques as higher brightness, reverse polarity, different font sizes and styles, underlining, blinking, line rules and boxes, color, and white space. Before beginning design, the designer must be aware of what capabilities exist, how they may be most effectively used, and what their limitations are. All of these techniques are described in other sections in this text.

The design must be compatible with the system platform and any development and implementation tools being used. The design may also take into consideration any available platform style guide. Finally, the design must effectively utilize the various available display features or attributes.

Platform Compatibility

The design must be compatible with the windowing platform being used—Apple Computer's Macintosh, Microsoft Windows or any other.

Development and Implementation Tool Compatibility

More that half of software code is now devoted to user interface design. To use a very old cliché, the tail is now beginning to wag the dog. Available tools include toolkits, interface builders, and user interface management systems.

A *toolkit* is a library of controls or widgets such as menus, buttons, and scroll bars. Toolkits have a programmatic interface and must be used by programmers. They are usually for a specific windowing platform. Examples of toolkits include those for Motif, OpenLook, and the Macintosh.

An *interface builder* is a graphical tool that helps a programmer create dialog boxes, menus, and other controls. It provides a palette to select and position controls, and to set properties. Interface builders are limited to use in laying out the static parts of the interface. They cannot handle the parts of the interface that involve graphical objects moving around. A *user interface management system* (UIMS) extends the features of a builder by also providing assistance with creating and managing the insides of windows. Examples include HyperCard and Visual Basic.

■ MAXIM ■ **Software should be seen and not heard.**

Style Guide Compatibility

A thrust for commonality in graphical system application design has emerged as providers have finally come to realize that design consistency is a virtue that has been ignored too long. To achieve this consistency in interface design, most providers have developed style guidelines for system developers. These guidelines specify the appearance and behavior of the user interface. They describe the windows, menus, and various controls available, including what they look like and how they work. They also provide some guidance on when to use the various components.

Examples of industry-produced guidelines include Apple's *Macintosh Human Interface Guidelines*, IBM's *System Application Architecture Common User Access (SAA CUA)* and Microsoft's *The Windows Interface Guidelines for Software Design.* Product style guides vary in their ability to control compliance with the guidelines they present. Some present strict requirements, leading to excellent consistency across applications; others provide little guideline compliance control. The design should comply with the relevant platform style guide.

Web Systems

- Understand the current level of Web technology.
- Design for system configuration used by most users.
- Refrain from haphazard use of leading-edge technology.

The Web is truly a Web, a Web of users whose only consistency is inconsistency in the variety of the technologies they possess. Old PCs with few features must coexist with new PCs possessing the latest technological advances. Monitors with small screens must coexist with large screens. Color must coexist with monochrome displays. High-resolution displays must coexist with those of low resolution. High-speed information transmission must coexist with low speed. New browsers that contain and support many different and desirable features must coexist with old browsers that support little. To make matters worse for the designer, users can reconfigure their own PCs, further changing some of its characteristics.

The designer must be capable of handling these various demands while creating usable Web pages accessible through different browsers, operating systems, and computer platforms. To do this requires having an awareness of system configurations that satisfy the needs of the majority of users, and then designing for these users. To utilize the Web's richest features, however, the designer must understand the current level of technology and apply it in a meaningful and usable way, especially for those users at the high end of the technological spectrum. The temptation, though, to apply technology simply for technology's sake must be resisted. The goal in design is to satisfy the user's need or want, not the designer's. The following sections address technological considerations affecting Web site design.

Browsers

- Compatibility:
  — Make the Web site accessible to all users' browsers.
  — Use browser defaults as much as possible.
- Monitor size and resolution:
  — Design within the boundaries of an image-safe area for all browsers.
  — Present images at a resolution appropriate for all users' monitors.
- Fonts:
  — Use fonts that can be displayed on a variety of browsers.
- Colors:
  — Use colors that succeed on a variety of browsers and platforms.
    • A palette of 216 colors.
- Bandwidth:
  — Design for the most commonly used bandwidth.
    • A 56-kbps modem is most common for home users.
- Versions
  — Create multiple versions that support multiple browsers.
    • Always provide a text-only version.
    • Make use of browser sniffers.

The pressure for lowest-common-denominator design is often outweighed by the designer's desire to create larger displays and employ the latest display and browser features. The needs of all users must be considered in design.

Compatibility

The entire Web page content should be accessible from the browsers of all users, presenting content as consistently and predictable as possible. Avoid fancy technology; many people still use old browsers that do not support such things as frames or JavaScript. Newer browsers will interpret Java applets. In general, use browser defaults as much as possible, designing for what everyone can see. Save the newer and more exotic features for supplements to the basic page content, or for another page version (see below).

Never assume that the designed page will look exactly the same to users as it does to the designer. Test the design on all browsers, operating systems, computer platforms, and all versions of the each.

Monitor Size and Resolution

Designed page content should always be restricted to the boundaries of an "image-safe" area horizontally, and perhaps vertically, depending upon whether vertical scrolling is determined as necessary to see the page's entire content. Exceeding the horizontal safe area will require horizontal scrolling to see the page's entire width. Because some information will not always be visible, content usability and interpretation will be severely degraded, and the user inconvenienced. Exceeding the safe area length will require vertical scrolling to see the entire page, and could push important information out of the user's view.

A display's safe area will be dependent upon the monitor's size and the resolution at which it is set. It must be established based upon the anticipated or known range of monitor sizes and their set resolutions. Current typical monitor sizes range from 13 to 21 inches (measured diagonally) with 17 inches being most common.

Most common display resolutions are 640×480 (pixels width and height), 800×600 pixels and 1024×768 pixels. Some users choose to use the highest resolution (1024×768) permitting more to be displayed on a screen. Users at 800×600 may maximize their browser to a full screen, but those displaying 640×480 may see additional scroll bars if the screen content does not fit.

The browser safe width for the 640×480 pixels screen is 600 pixels or less, the safe height about 350 pixels. An area of about 760×430 is safe for an 800×600 pixel screen. Smaller monitors will have smaller safe areas. Some browsers permit setting of an image as a percentage of the browser window, such as 80 percent for width. The height can also be set but it is best to leave this dimension unspecified. This scaling feature may also be used to establish safe areas. All browser elements, including scroll bars and command buttons, must be contained within this safe area

Few monitors display images at greater than 72 dots per inch (dpi). Because of this, the resolution of images displayed on screens should also be restricted to 72 dpi. Using a higher dpi ratio will not produce a better image, but will increase file size, causing longer download times. If higher-resolution monitors exist for most users, the dpi may be increased. Printable versions of page content may use a higher dpi, since most low-end printers are 300 dpi. A higher dpi means the printing will take longer, however.

Fonts

Not all browsers provide the same typographic operations. Different default font types and sizes may exist, depending on the type of browser, browser version, and operating system the browser runs on. If a page is designed using a font the user does not have installed, the browser displays its default fonts. Many older browsers support only two fonts, Times Roman and Courier. Newer browsers support more fonts but they must be installed on the machine doing the browsing. Default fonts may include Times New Roman, Arial, Helvetica, and Verdana. Type displayed on a Windows browser may look 2 to 3 points larger than that on a Macintosh.

It is best to stick with the default fonts installed on the user's computers. All available options must be known before beginning the design process. Then ensure that the text is readable and legible in all usage environments.

Color

The color palette must be of a variety large enough to permit establishment of a family of discriminable colors. The colors used must be accurately and clearly presented in all situations, but be aware that colors may appear slightly differently on different monitors, and all users may not default their palettes to high color settings. Use colors that will succeed on a variety of platforms and monitors. Design using a browser-safe, cross-platform palette of 216 colors. It is sometimes referred to as a "Web safe" color palette. Color is discussed in more detail in Step 12.

Bandwidth

The amount of data that can travel through a communication channel in a given amount of time is called bandwidth. Currently, the typical Web user is dialing in at 56 kilobytes per second (kbps) through a regular telephone line. Many users, however, are still dialing in at 28.8 kbps. While a cable modem is currently the most reliable high-speed connection to the Web for home users, only a small percentage of Americans have access to them. Other kinds of high-speed connection technologies include Integrated Services Digital Network (ISDN) and Digital Subscriber Line (DSL). ISDN offers good speed but is more common in urban areas. It is primarily used by business. DSL is also very fast but to work well, a local telephone switching office must be nearby.

At the other end of the bandwidth scale are users with low-cost devices, users wanting low-bandwidth wireless access, users with small personal display devices, and users in developing countries with poor communication infrastructures. All must be supported in Web page design.

In design, the bandwidths of users' devices must be considered. Now, as mentioned above, the typical Web user is dialing in at 56 kbps, with many still at 28.8 kbps. Failure to consider these modem speed limitations will lead to long download times and can result in user frustration and Web site avoidance. The biggest influence on download speed is the number and size of graphics on Web pages. Other speed-inhibiting factors will be described shortly in the section titled "Downloading."

If the site being designed possesses users with high bandwidth capabilities, an intranet site with ISDN, for example, large graphics can be used quite freely. Always test download speeds on the slowest communication channel available to the users.

Versions

To provide universal access to a Web site, provide multiple versions that support multiple browsers. To limit the site to one browser may deny access to, and alienate, users who do not have the proper one. Make use of browser "sniffers," programs on the server that detect the user's browser type and determine which version should then be downloaded.

Always provide a text-only version of the Web site. This will be necessary as long as users with small displays and low bandwidths exist. Vision-impaired users with readers will also require a text-only version, as will users with text-only browsers, and those who turn off image display.

Other Web Considerations

- Downloading:
  — Provide fast page download times, no more than 8 to 10 seconds per page.

- Minimize the use of design techniques that cause longer download times.
  - Long pages.
  - Large chunky headings.
  - Numerous or large graphics and images.
  - Animation.
  - Excessive amount of color.
  - Excess use of frames.
— Provide enough information to the user so that whether or not to request a download can be determined, including:
  - Program or document description.
  - Type of download.
  - Size of download.
  - Download version.
  - Estimated loading time.
  - Special operating requirements.
- Currency:
— Keep Web site information current.
- Page printing:
— Provide a means to print:
  - Groups of related pages.
  - Individual pages.
  - Sections of pages.
- Maintainability:
— Ensure easy Web site maintainability.

Downloading

Slow download speeds are an ongoing complaint of Web users. Download times of 8 to 10 seconds per page should not be exceeded, even for bandwidths of 28.8 kbps. In general, keep graphics and page size as small as possible. Specifically, use text instead of graphics whenever possible. When graphics are desirable, keep the graphic as small as possible. Also, repeatedly use a graphic so it may be stored in the browser's cache.

The cache is a temporary storage area for Web pages and images. There are two types: memory and hard drive. Once a graphic is downloaded, it is placed in the cache and remains there for a prescribed period of time. Download times, then, are longest when a site is visited and downloaded for the first time. After the first download, the graphic is in the cache. It is retrieved from there, reducing the time it takes to display the page.

In addition to graphics, other design elements that slow download times include large and chunky headings, the use of many colors, animation, excessive use of frames, and the use of Java and JavaScript. Limit the use of these elements that require a long time to download. Create graphics that load quickly. Limit an individual image to 5K, the images on a page to 20K. Use Graphics Interchange Format (GIF) files because they are smaller than Joint Photographic Experts Group (JPEG) files. GIFs and JPEGs are described more fully in Step 11.

Also, because few monitors display images at greater than 72 dpi, restrict the resolution of downloaded images to 72 dpi. Using a higher dpi ratio will not produce a better image, but will increase file size, causing longer download times. All images should also contain alternate text (alt text). This will give the user something to read while the image downloads, and is necessary for text-only viewers.

Always provide enough information to let the users know whether it is worth their time and trouble to download something of apparent interest described on a Web page. Provide a program or document description, type, size, version, estimated loading time, and any special operating requirements, including such things as hardware needed, the required operating system, special software needed, and memory requirements.

Currency

Update the Web site regularly to keep information current. The nature of the Web implies timeliness. Outdated information casts doubts on a Web site's credibility. Currency means trustworthiness to many users.

Page Printing

Some people prefer to read hard copy, especially anything longer than half a page. Make printing easy for users, including the capability to print sections, pages, or groups of related pages with minimal effort. Since most low-end printers print at 300 dpi, pages may be printed at this resolution. This higher resolution will result in a longer printing time, however.

Maintainability

Provide easy Web site maintainability to sustain its currency. Change must be easily accommodated as the Web site grows, evolves, and matures. Web site maintenance is, in reality, Web site enhancement. Remove outdated information and expired links, link old pages to those newly created. Properly designed, modular system pages covering specific topics can be updated quickly without needing to change and reformat large amounts of information.

The User Technology Profile Circa 2001

While a great variety does exist in the technological tools people use to interact with the Internet, the dominance of certain platforms and monitor characteristics is quite evident. Bailey (2001), in summarizing recently reported data (thecounter.com, 2001) says that the following operating systems, browsers, screen resolutions, and color depths each account for more than 90 percent of a user's technological capabilities.

OPERATING SYSTEMS

Windows 95	10%
Windows 98	72%
Windows 2000	6%
Windows NT	5%
	93%

BROWSERS

Internet Explorer 4	9%
Internet Explorer 5	77%
Netscape 4	<u>9%</u>
	95%

SCREEN RESOLUTION IN PIXELS

640×480	5%
800×600	53%
1024×768	31%
1280×1024	<u>3%</u>
	98%

COLOR IN BITS

8	5%
16	55%
24 and 32	<u>38%</u>
	92%

Assuming that these four elements are independent, the probability of a person having on his or her computer elements found in each listing above is .80. This means that designing for the above technological characteristics will satisfy the needs of four out of five Web users. Bailey suggests that when it is impossible to design for *all* users, because of cost, schedule, or personnel considerations, designing for the above computer characteristics will at least satisfy the needs of most users.

Examples of Screens

What follows are examples of poor and proper design. The problems of the poorly designed screens will be described in the discussion to follow. Redesigned versions of these poorly designed screens will be presented at the end of Step 8. Examples of other, properly designed, screens will also be presented as models of good design.

Example 1

Here are three information entry/modification dialog boxes from a popular drawing program, PRINT MERGE, PAGE SETUP, and EXPORT. Analyze them for problems, including inconsistencies between them.

Screen 1.1

The controls on the PRINT MERGE screen are very poorly aligned. The File text box is located quite far from its associated list box. What does the Up button do? It is actually related to the Directories list box. This is certainly not clear. Look at the required sequence of eye movements through this screen, as illustrated by the line drawn between successive controls. This is very inefficient.

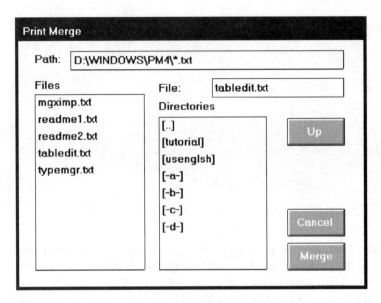

Screen 1.1A

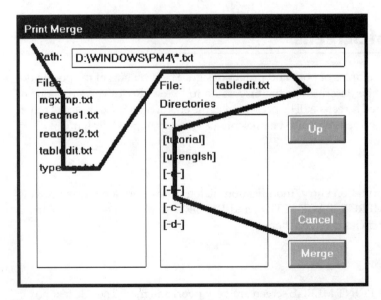

Screen 1.1B

Screen 1.2

The controls on the PAGE SETUP screen are very poorly grouped. Are the nine radio buttons beginning at the Page Size caption one or three groupings? The horizontal orientation of the radio buttons necessitates a less efficient horizontal scanning and makes visual comparison of the alternatives more difficult. Why is the Orientation caption not right-aligned with the other captions? What are the controls inscribed with Inches?

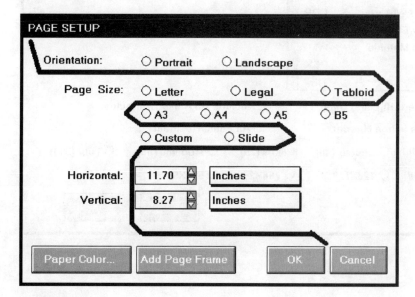

Screen 1.2A

Screen 1.2B

They are actually nonstandard controls but this is not clear until one discovers how to operate them (clicking on the rectangular bar changes the value [inches] now displayed). Nonstandard controls increase learning requirements and add to the complexity of the interface. Again, look at the required sequence of eye movements through this screen, as illustrated by the line drawn between successive controls. This is very inefficient.

Screen 1.3

The check boxes and radio buttons on the EXPORT screen are again very poorly grouped. Their horizontal orientation necessitates a less efficient horizontal scanning and makes visual comparison of the alternatives more difficult. Can the check boxes be grouped? The list box has no caption with it. Screen balance is also poor, with the large open area in the upper-right part of the screen. Again, look at the required eye scan through this screen.

Now, look at the inconsistencies between these three screens. The PRINT MERGE title is in mixed case; PAGE SETUP and EXPORT are capitalized. The PRINT MERGE command buttons are on the right side; the PAGE SETUP and EXPORT ones are on the bottom. PRINT MERGE uses the action being accomplished as the button label (Merge); the others use the standard OK. This will certainly cause user confusion. PRINT MERGE and EXPORT appear to use left-aligned captions, PAGE SETUP right-alignment.

Screen 1.3A

Screen 1.3B

Example 2

Two information entry/modification dialog boxes from a popular word-processing program, FOOTNOTE OPTIONS and LOCATION OF FILES. Some design enhancements are immediately obvious. The command buttons are consistently positioned in the lower-right corner and group boxes or borders are included to visually strengthen information groupings.

Screen 2.1

This screen's main problem is poor alignment of controls. The standalone check boxes tend to get lost. The centered headings in the group boxes are not a severe problem but they do somewhat compete with the control captions for the screen viewer's attention. The Position and Separator control borders are placed around single elements. This is not recommended but it does help to provide screen balance, which is quite good. The sequentiality of this screen, as illustrated by one's required eye scan, is quite poor, as illustrated.

Screen 2.1A

Screen 2.1B

Screen 2.2

Note the improved alignment of this screen's controls. It is excellent, except for the single check box in the lower-left corner. Again, this check box can get lost here. This screen does have two problems. First, the headings, in mixed case and centered in the group boxes, visually compete with the information within the boxes for the viewer's attention. It would be much better if they were positioned away from the important

Screen 2.2A

Screen 2.2B

screen information and capitalized to set them off visually from the captions and data. Second, for completeness and closure, a group box around the top five controls should also be included.

Example 3

This is an information entry/modification screen from a banking system. The major problem is very poor alignment of the controls, as illustrated by the eye scan require-

Screen 3.1A

Screen 3.1B

ments. There are some other problems. There are no groupings. Does the name control have a caption? Are the labels above the Name text box intended as captions? Are they intended as prompts? This is not clear. Is the prompt (dd/mm/yyyy) in the proper location? In its current position, it is set up as an aid to a novice or casual user of the system. For an expert user of the system, who does not need the prompt, it is positioned where it is visual noise. For the expert it should be to the right side of the text box.

Example 4

This is a properly designed information entry/modification screen. It contains groupings reinforced by group boxes, alignment of controls, right-alignment of all captions (in this case) located consistently to the left of each control, capitalized section headings aligned to the upper-right of the group boxes, and command buttons centered at the bottom. Scanning of the columns of information is simplified by the control alignment. Headings do not compete with control captions for the viewer's attention. The screen also possesses balance.

WEEKLY INCOME

┌─ BENEFITS BEGIN ─────────────
    Accident Day: [   ]

    Sickness Day: [   ]

    Period: ☐ First Day Hospital
             ☐ 24 Hour Coverage

┌─ COVERAGES ──────────────────
    Plan Choice: ○ I
                  ○ II
                  ○ III
                  ○ IV

    Maternity: ○ As Any Other
                ○ Exclude

┌─ MAXIMUM ────────────────────
    Coverage Period: [▼]
    Benefit Amount: [   ]

┌─ OTHER ──────────────────────
    Adjustment Factor: [   ]
    State/Municipal Tax: [   ]

[OK]   [Cancel]

Screen 4.1A

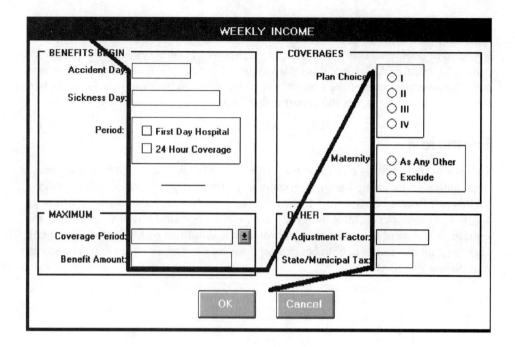

Screen 4.1B

Example 5

This is a read-only/display screen from the drawing program. It possesses good balance and nice groupings reinforced through use of group boxes. The problems are these: There are no colons with the captions. Other screens from this system have colons included with captions, violating the viewer's mental model of a caption possessing a colon. Which caption style is used, headline (all significant word initial caps) or sentence (capitalization of the first word only)? If you examine the screen you'll find many instances of both styles. The section headings are mixed case just like the control captions, competing with each other visually for the viewer's attention. The numeric data fields are not properly right-aligned although fairly good top-to-bottom scanning does exist. Units in the Image Size/Resolution groupings are at the bottom of listing. They would more appropriately be placed at the top because they appear to be column headings. In the Image Resolution grouping the use of "res" is redundant, since it already appears in the section heading.

```
                          walogo.tif Header Info.

  ┌TIFF File format──────────────┐   ┌Image size──────────────────────┐
  │  Version #              42    │   │  Horizontal      1888      6.3  │
  │  Byte order            I I    │   │  Vertical        1656      5.5  │
  │  NewSubFile Type        1     │   │  Units           Pixel     Inch │
  └──────────────────────────────┘   └─────────────────────────────────┘

  ┌Spatial Configuration─────────┐   ┌Image resolution────────────────┐
  │  Samples per pixel       1    │   │  Horizontal res.          300   │
  │  Bits per sample         1    │   │  Vertical res.            300   │
  │  Planar config.          1    │   │  Units                    dpi   │
  └──────────────────────────────┘   └─────────────────────────────────┘

                                      Palette: Red, Green, Blue
  ┌Photometric data──────────────┐   ┌─────────────────────────────────┐
  │  Photo Interpretation    1    │   │                                 │
  │  Resolution Unit      Inch    │   │                                 │
  │  Compression Type    PkBit    │   │                                 │
  └──────────────────────────────┘   │                                 │
                                      │                                 │
    ┌──────────┐   ┌──────────────┐   │                                 │
    │    OK     │   │ Display image │  │                                 │
    └──────────┘   └──────────────┘   └─────────────────────────────────┘
```

Screen 5.1

Example 6

Here is a pair of similar read-only/display screens from another system. Both are poorly aligned, the data getting buried among the captions. See the illustration of how TEXTBLOCK INFO will be scanned. Why abbreviate INFO; there is plenty of room to spell it out. The groupings are not very strong, either. Notice the inconsistencies in captions, Character count versus Char count, Area versus Total area, and Depth versus Total depth. Again, there is room to spell them out fully. Otherwise, the viewer has to establish two mental models for the same element. Why establish this learning requirement?

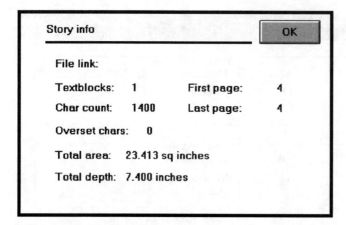

Screen 6.1A

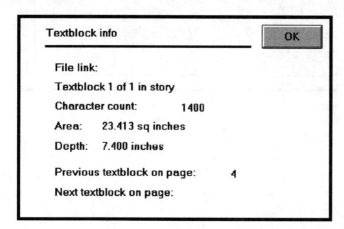

Screen 6.1B

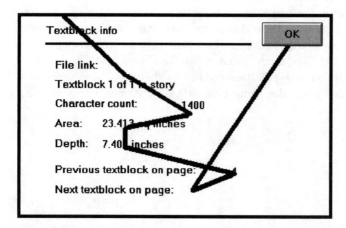

Screen 6.1C

Example 7

Here are two properly designed read-only/inquiry screens, both possessing good alignment, grouping, and balance. The data is displayed on the screen background for ease of identification and comprehension.

Screen 7.1

From an insurance system, this screen summarizes some of the most important kinds of information a policyholder would want to know about an insurance policy. Captions are omitted in the POLICY NUMBER/INSURED section at the top. Contextually, this information is self-explanatory. The information presented in the ENDORSEMENTS section reflects the principle of displaying something only if it is present or applicable. If one or more of these endorsements were not included with another similar policy, they would not be displayed at all. In that case, the applicable endorsements would fill this section beginning at its top. The descriptive information included with the top three endorsements reflects the conversion of the more customary "caption: data" format into simple data statements. The data statements are self-explanatory, captions are not required.

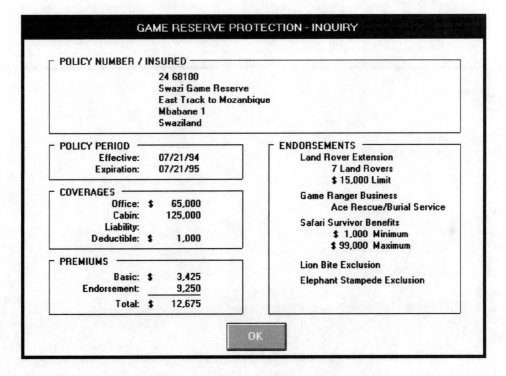

Screen 7.1

Screen 7.2

This screen from a shoe manufacturer is similar to the insurance screen in structure.

```
┌─────────────────────────────────────────────────────────────────────┐
│                     PRODUCT STYLE INQUIRY                             │
│                                                                       │
│  ┌─ STYLE ───────────────────────────────────────────────────────┐   │
│  │    Number:           4470                                       │   │
│  │    Name:             High Jumping                               │   │
│  └───────────────────────────────────────────────────────────────┘   │
│                                                                       │
│  ┌─ DESCRIPTION ─────────────────────┐  ┌─ UNITS ─────────────────┐  │
│  │    Identifying Color:   Blue        │ │  Unit/Measure:  01 Each │  │
│  │    Dimension Code:      00          │ │  Weight:          3.16  │  │
│  │    General Prod Class:  Footwear    │ │  Units/Case:      12    │  │
│  │    Short Name:          HJ          │ └─────────────────────────┘  │
│  │                                     │ ┌─ FLAGS ─────────────────┐  │
│  │    Gender Age:          Men         │ │  Technical Switch:  Yes │  │
│  │    Gender:              Male        │ │  Price by Flag:    Style│  │
│  │    Family:              N/A         │ │  Finish Good Flag: Finished│ │
│  │    Body Type:           Shoe        │ └─────────────────────────┘  │
│  │    Brand:               Airbourne   │ ┌─ SPECIAL FEATURES ──────┐  │
│  │    Warehouse Codes:                 │ │  1:  Air Bags           │  │
│  │                                     │ │  2:  Prime Tanning Leather│ │
│  │    Sport Activity:      Track       │ │                         │  │
│  │    Silhouette:          3/4 High    │ └─────────────────────────┘  │
│  └─────────────────────────────────────┘                             │
│                                                                       │
│                         [    OK    ]                                  │
│                                                                       │
└─────────────────────────────────────────────────────────────────────┘
```

Screen 7.2

Develop System Menus and Navigation Schemes

A system contains large amounts of information and performs a variety of functions. Regardless of its purpose, the system must provide some means to tell people about the information it possesses or the things it can do. This is accomplished by displaying listings of the choices or alternatives the user has at appropriate points while using the system, or creating a string of listings that lead a person from a series of general descriptors through increasingly specific categories on following listings until the lowest level listing is reached. This lowest level listing provides the desired choices. These listings of choices are commonly called menus. Menus are a major form of navigation through a system and, if properly designed, assist the user in developing a mental model of the system. In this step, the following menu topics will be addressed.

- The structures of menus.
- The functions of menus.
- The content of menus.
- Formatting menus.
- Writing menus.
- Navigation using menus.
- Web site navigation and links.
- Types of graphical menus.

Menus are effective because they utilize the more powerful human capability of recognition rather than the weaker capability of recall. Working with menus reminds people of available options and information that they may not be aware of or have forgotten.

Menus are not without problems, however. New and inexperienced system users might find learning large systems difficult. Menu information must often be remembered and integrated across a series of screens. If each menu is viewed in isolation, relationships between menus may be difficult to grasp. Words and phrases with multiple meanings may also be wrongly interpreted because of the user's inability to see relationships between menus. Ambiguities, also, may not be correctly resolved if the user makes incorrect assumptions about menu structure. The frequent result is that people make mistakes and can get lost in the hierarchical structure.

Experienced system users, while finding menus helpful at first, may find them tedious as they learn the system. Continually having to step through a series of menus to achieve the desired objective can be time-consuming and frustrating. Therefore, the design of menu systems must consider the conflicting needs of both inexperienced and experienced users.

Graphical and Web systems are heavily menu-oriented. They vary in form and are applied in diverse ways. In graphical systems they are used to designate commands, properties that apply to an object, documents, and windows. When selected, a graphical menu item may lead to another menu, cause a window to be displayed, or directly cause an action to be performed. To accomplish these goals, a graphical system presents a variety of menu styles to choose from. Included are entities commonly called menu bars, and menus called pull-downs, pop-ups, cascades, tearoffs, and iconic. In Web site design, common menus include textual links to other pages, command buttons, and both graphical and textual toolbars.

In this chapter, graphical and Web system menus will be addressed. It will begin with a description of the kinds of menu structures available and their content, and then present a series of general menu design guidelines for formatting, phrasing, selecting choices, and navigating menus. Next, Web-specific navigation issues and guidelines will be discussed. Finally, specific types of graphical menus will be described, recommendations for proper usage given, and relevant specific guidelines summarized.

Structures of Menus

Menus vary in form from very simple to very complex. They may range from small dialog boxes requesting the user to choose between one of two alternatives, to hierarchical tree schemes with many branches and level of depth. A menu's structure defines the amount of control given to the user in performing a task. The most common structures are the following.

Single Menus

In this simplest form of menu, a single screen or window is presented to seek the user's input or request an action to be performed, as illustrated in Figure 4.1. In using the Internet, for example, at a point in the dialog people may be asked if they wish to "Stay Connected" or "Disconnect." In playing a game, choices presented may be "novice," "intermediate," or "expert." Single menus conceptually require choices from this sin-

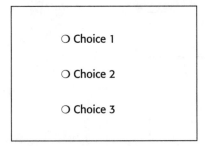

Figure 4.1 Single menu.

gle menu only, and no other menus will follow necessitating additional user choices. The user need only consider the immediate consequences of the item being chosen and need not be concerned with any other additional system menus. While other single menus may exist in the system and might be encountered later, these other menus are not perceived by the user as comprising a series of choices.

A single menu may be iterative if it requires data to be entered into it and this data input is subject to a validity check that fails. The menu will then be represented to the user with a message requesting reentry of valid data.

Sequential Linear Menus

Sequential linear menus are presented on a series of screens possessing only one path. The menu screens are presented in a preset order, and, generally, their objective is for specifying parameters or for entering data. The length of the path may be short, or long, depending upon the nature of the information being collected. All the menus are important to the process at hand and must be answered in some manner by the user. A sequential linear menu is illustrated in Figure 4.2.

Sequential path menus have several shortcomings. A long sequence may become tedious as menu after menu is presented. The user may not remember an answer to a previous question, a question important to the currently presented choices. The user may also want to return to a previous menu to change an answer or look at an answer, an awkward process that must be allowed. Finally, the user may, conceptually, want to complete the menus in a different order than which they are being presented.

Simultaneous Menus

Instead of being presented on separate screens, all menu options are available simultaneously, as illustrated in Figure 4.3. The menu may be completed in the order desired by the user, choices being skipped and returned to later. All alternatives are visible for reminding of choices, comparing choices, and changing answers. The tedium associated with a long series of sequential menus is greatly reduced.

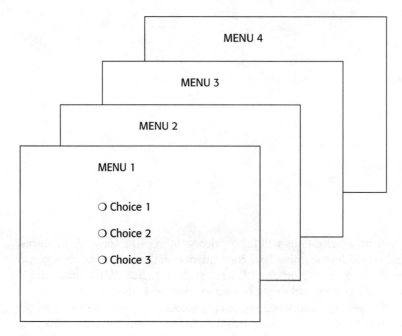

Figure 4.2   Sequential linear menus.

Problems with simultaneous menus are that for large collections of menu alternatives screen clutter can easily occur, and screen paging or scrolling may still be necessary to view all the choices. This type of menu must also clearly indicate menu choice relationships and dependencies, something better accomplished in a linear menu string, or a hierarchical menu described next. Presenting many menu dependencies and relationships on a screen, especially if poorly indicated, can also be very confusing for a novice user.

ALTERNATIVE 1	ALTERNATIVE 3
○ Choice 1	○ Choice 1
○ Choice 2	○ Choice 2
○ Choice 3	○ Choice 3
ALTERNATIVE 2	**ALTERNATIVE 4**
○ Choice 1	○ Choice 1
○ Choice 2	○ Choice 2
○ Choice 3	○ Choice 3
○ Choice 3	○ Choice 3

Figure 4.3   Simultaneous menus.

Hierarchical Menus

When many relationships exist between menu alternatives, and some menu options are only appropriate depending upon a previous menu selection, a hierarchical structure is the best solution. A hierarchical structure results in an increasing refinement of choice as menus are stepped through, for example, from options, to suboptions, from categories to subcategories, from pages to sections to subsections, and so on. A hierarchical structure can best be represented as an inverse tree, leading to more and more branches as one moves downward through it. Hierarchical structures are characterized by depth and breadth, depth being the number of choice levels one must traverse to reach the destination, breadth being the number of alternatives found at each level. Menu depth and breadth has been a well-researched topic and will be fully discussed in succeeding pages. Common examples of hierarchical design today are found in menu bars with their associated pull-downs, and in Web sites with their navigation links.

The order and structure of branching in a hierarchy is preset and the normal order of flow one-way, top down. A disadvantage of a hierarchical scheme is that the defined branching order may not fit the users conception of the task flow. If users are not familiar with the hierarchical menu, or are unable to predict what suboptions lie below a particular choice, they may go down wrong paths and find it necessary to go back up the tree to change a choice, or perhaps even return to the top-level menu. It is important, then, that hierarchies be consistent with user expectations, and that choice uncertainties be reduced as much as possible. It must also be easy to back upward through the tree to facilitate exploration of the tree.

A hierarchical menu is illustrated in Figure 4.4. Note that the top level of the tree is considered level 0 with subsequent levels numbered sequentially beginning with number 1. Starting at the top, level 0, two selections, or mouse clicks, are required to reach level 2.

Connected Menus

Connected menus are networks of menus all interconnected in some manner. Movement through a structure of menus is not restricted to a hierarchical tree, but is permitted between most or all menus in the network. From the user's perspective there is no top-down traversal of the menu system but an almost unhindered wandering between any two menus of interest. A connected menu system may be cyclical, with movement permitted in either direction between menus, or acyclical, with movement permitted in only one direction. These menus also vary in connectivity, the extent to which menus are linked by multiple paths. (In a hierarchical menu system, the ability to go back to a previous menu or to return to the top-level menu are also examples, although restricted, of connected menus.)

The biggest advantage of a connected menu network is that it gives the user full control over the navigation flow. Its disadvantage is its complexity, and its navigation may be daunting for an inexperienced user. An example connected menu structure is represented in Figure 4.5.

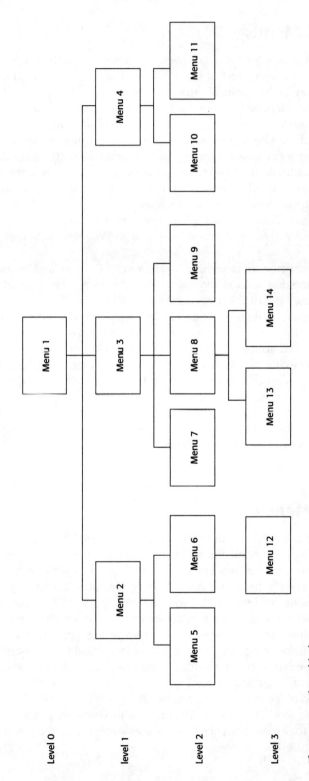

Figure 4.4 Hierarchical menus.

Level 0

level 1

Level 2

Level 3

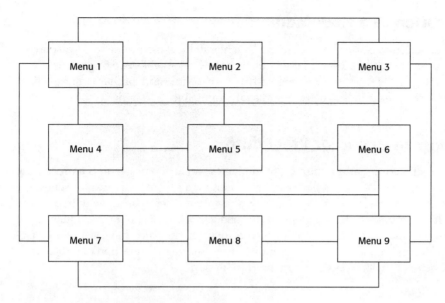

Figure 4.5 Connected menus.

Event-Trapping Menus

Event Trapping menus provide an ever-present background of control over the system's state and parameters while the user is working on a foreground task. They are, in essence, a set of simultaneous menus imposed on hierarchical menus. In a graphical system, for example, existing together are a simultaneous menu, the menu bar, and a hierarchy—the menu bar and its pull-downs. Event-trapping menus generally serve one of three functions. (1) They may immediately change some parameter in the current environment (bold a piece of text), (2) they may take the user out of the current environment to perform a function without leaving the current environment (perform a spell check), or (3) they may exit the current environment and allow the user to move to a totally new environment (Exit).

These menus can also change content based upon the system state, or an event, existing at that moment. A Paste option in a word-processing application, for example, will only function if there is something in a clipboard to paste. A Grid option on a pull-down, as another example, will toggle between a "Hide Grid" or "Show Grid" state, depending upon whether or not a grid is displayed on the screen at that moment. Event-Trapping menus such as menu bars are constantly available to aid in establishing a sense of context, or where one is, while things may be changing in the foreground.

Functions of Menus

From the user's perspective, a menu can be used to perform several functions, to *navigate* to a new menu, to *execute* an action or procedure, to *display* information, or to *input* data or parameters.

Navigation to a New Menu

Each user selection causes another menu in a hierarchical menu tree to be displayed. The purpose of each selection is to steer the user toward an objective or goal. Selection errors may lead the user down wrong paths, and cost time and, perhaps, aggravation, but these errors are nondestructive and usually undoable.

Execute an Action or Procedure

A user selection directs the computer to implement an action or perform a procedure. The action may be something like opening or closing a file, copying text, or sending a message. In some cases execution may only occur after a hierarchical menu tree is navigated. In other cases actions may be performed as successive hierarchical menus are encountered and traversed. Selection errors may or may not have serious consequences, depending upon the nature of the action. Accidental selection of critical irreversible actions must be prevented in interface design.

Displaying Information

The main purpose of selecting a menu choice may simply be to display information. The user may be searching for specific information in a database or browsing the Web. The user's focus is primarily on the information desired and less on the selection function. In many cases, information retrieval may occur only after a hierarchical menu tree is navigated. The content material and the user's interests will determine the paths followed. Users may spend considerable time and effort understanding and processing uncovered information in order to evaluate subsequently displayed menu choices. Wrong turns in the process will again cost time and perhaps aggravation, but these errors are nondestructive and usually undoable.

Data or Parameter Input

Each selection specifies a piece of input data for the system or provides a parameter value. Data or values may be input on a single menu or spread over a hierarchy of menus. The user's focus is primarily on the information being provided and, again, less on the selection function. Selection errors can easily be corrected if detected by the system.

Content of Menus

A menu consists of four elements, its *context*, its *title*, its *choice descriptions*, and its *completion instructions*. These concepts are introduced here and will be expanded in detailed guidelines to follow on succeeding pages.

Menu Context

A menu's context provides information to keep the user oriented. This kind of information is critical in complex or hierarchical menu systems, where loss of position or disorientation can easily occur. Feedback is necessary that tells users where they are in a process, what their past choices were, and possibly how much farther they still have to navigate. Human memory being what it is, where one is and how one got there all too easily slip from consciousness.

Verbal linkage, spatial linkage, or both may be used to provide navigation feedback. *Verbal linkage* involves providing, on the current menu screen, a listing of choices made on previous menus that have led to this position. It also involves assuring the user that the displayed menu is the menu desired. Its title should mirror the option selected on the previous menu, and its content should reflect its title. *Spatial linkage* can be accomplished by graphic methods. Each succeeding menu screen can be displayed overlapping the previous menu screen so a succession of choices can be seen in a single view. A sense of progress and distance can then be easily ascertained.

Menu Title

A menu's title provides the context for the current set of choices. The title must reflect the choice selected on the previously displayed menu.

Choice Descriptions

Choice descriptions are the alternatives available to the user. These descriptions can range from a mnemonic, numeric, or alphabetized listing of choices to single words or phrases to full sentences or more. The style chosen will reflect the experience of the user (novice or expert), the nature of the choices (well-learned alternatives or not), the nature of the selection mechanism (keyboard or mouse), and the nature of the system (business system application or Web page).

Completion Instructions

Completion instructions tell users how to indicate their choices. They may include the rationale for why the user is being asked to make this choice and the impact the choice will have on subsequent processes. Explicit instructions may be needed for first time or casual users of a system. Experienced users will find overly verbose instructions unnecessary. The needs of all system users, and the nature of the system, must again be considered in creating this kind of on-screen guidance.

Formatting of Menus

The human-computer interface has a rich history of experimental studies with menus, the results of which can and have been applied to graphical screen and Web page menu design and presentation. What follows is a series of guidelines for formatting menus.

Consistency

- Provide consistency with the user's expectations.
- Provide consistency in menu:
  - Formatting, including organization, presentation, and choice ordering.
  - Phrasing, including titles, choice descriptions, and instructions.
  - Choice selection methods.
  - Navigation schemes.

Like all aspects of screen design, menu design consistency is an integral component of system usability. Menu formatting, phrasing, choice selection, and navigation must be consistent throughout a graphical system or Web site.

Display

- If continual or frequent references to menu options are necessary, permanently display the menu in an area of the screen that will not obscure other screen data.
- If only occasional references to menu options are necessary, the menu may be presented on demand.
  - Critical options should be continuously displayed, however.

Whether to display a menu continually, or on demand, is determined by the menu's frequency of use. Always permanently display menus that are frequently referenced. This will provide memory support and immediate access to what is needed most. Occasionally needed menus may be presented on request via pop-ups or pull-downs. Critical options, however, should always be continuously displayed. Wright, Lickorish, and Milroy (1994) found superior performance for permanently displayed menus as opposed to menus that had to be retrieved through mouse clicks. They speculate that because retrieving a menu for display requires more actions, this may also impair people's memory for other tasks being performed.

Presentation

- Ensure that a menu and its choices are obvious to the user by presenting them with a unique and consistent structure, location, and/or display technique.
- Ensure that other system components do not possess the same visual qualities as menu choices.

A menu and its choices should be immediately recognizable by the user as being a menu of choices. This can be accomplished through giving the menu a distinctive and consistent structure and presenting it in a consistent screen or page location. Presentation techniques must, of course, be compatible with those used for other purposes on the remainder of the screen. A good way to set a menu off from the remainder of the screen is to enclose it in a box or display it using a background that contrasts with the remainder of the screen Techniques chosen should be consistent throughout the system. Web page navigation links, which may be scattered throughout a page, are displayed underlined and in a unique color to differentiate and identify them.

Ensure that other system elements do not possess qualities that allow users to confuse them with menu choices. In Web page design, for example, the underlining of any system component other than navigation links is not recommended because of the possibility that they may be confused with links.

Organization

- Provide a general or main menu.
- Display:
  — All relevant alternatives.
  — Only relevant alternatives.
    • Delete or gray-out inactive choices.
- Match the menu structure to the structure of the task.
  — Organization should reflect the most efficient sequence of steps to accomplish a person's most frequent or most likely goals.
- Minimize number of menu levels within limits of clarity.
  — For Web sites, restrict it to two levels (requiring two mouse clicks) for fastest performance.
- Be conservative in the number of menu choices presented on a screen:
  — Without logical groupings of elements, limit choices to 4 to 8.
  — With logical groupings of elements, limit choices to 18 to 24.
- Provide decreasing direction menus, if sensible.
- Never require menus to be scrolled.
- Provide users with an easy way to restructure a menu according to how work is accomplished.

In organizing a menu, the goal is to simply and effectively reveal its structure, while also reducing the number of actions needed to locate the target item.

General menu. The top-level menu in a hierarchical menu scheme should be a general or main menu, consisting of basic system options. This will provide a consistent starting point for all system activities and a "home base" to which the user may always return.

Relevant alternatives. A menu should provide all relevant alternatives, and only relevant alternatives, at the point at which it is displayed. Including irrelevant choices on a menu screen increases learning requirements and has been found to interfere with performance. There are two exceptions to this rule, however. Alternatives that are conditionally inactive may be displayed along with the conditionally active choices, if the active choices can be visually highlighted in some manner (such as through bolding or reverse video), or the inactive choices can be visually subdued (perhaps as through graying them out). One study, however, found that completely eliminating inactive alternatives on a menu resulted in faster choice access time, when compared to leaving inactive alternatives on a menu but displayed in a subdued manner. This study concludes that eliminating conditionally inactive choices from a menu appears to be the best approach. Mayhew (1992) suggests that while deletion does provide an advantage to expert users of keyboard-driven menus, graying out seems to be advantageous to novices in systems using pointer-driven selection devices. She concludes that since menus are geared toward novices, graying appears to be the best overall choice. In general, today's graphical systems follow the gray-out approach for inactive menu choices. Whatever method is chosen should be consistently followed throughout a system.

Options to be implemented in the future may also be displayed if they can be visually marked in some way (through a display technique or some other annotation).

Matching menu structure to the tasks. Menus should be organized according to how people structure their tasks. They should reflect the most efficient sequence of steps to accomplish a person's most frequent or likely goals.

Minimize number of levels. The issue that must be addressed in creating a multilevel menu structure is determining how many items will be placed on one menu (its breadth) and how many levels it will consume (its depth). In general, the more choices contained on a menu (greater breadth), the less will be its depth; the fewer choices on a menu (less breadth), the greater will be its depth.

The advantages of a menu system with greater *breadth* and less depth are:
- Fewer steps and shorter time to reach one's objective.
- Fewer opportunities to wander down wrong paths.
- Easier learning by allowing the user to see relationships of menu items.

A broad menu's disadvantages are:
- A more crowded menu that may reduce the clarity of the wording of choices.
- Increased likelihood of confusing similar choices because they are seen together.

The advantages of greater *depth* are:
- Less crowding on the menu.
- Fewer choices to be scanned.
- Easier hiding of inappropriate choices.
- Less likelihood of confusing similar choices since there is less likelihood that they will be seen together.

Greater depth disadvantages are:

- More steps and longer time to reach one's objective.
- More difficulties in learning since relationships between elements cannot always be seen.
- More difficulties in predicting what lies below, resulting in increased likelihood of going down wrong paths or getting lost.
- Higher error rates.

In text-based and graphical systems, a good number of studies have looked at the breadth-depth issue in recent years. Some have concluded that breadth is preferable to depth in terms of either greater speed or fewer errors, that a low number of levels (two to three) and an intermediate number of choices (4 to 8) results in faster, more accurate performance as opposed to fewer or greater numbers of levels and choices, and that 4 to 8 choices per menu screen is best. Another study found that one level was easiest to learn, and a couple of studies have concluded that a menu could contain up to 64 items if it were organized into logical groups. The least desirable alternative in almost all cases was deep-level menus that simply presented the user with a binary choice (select one of two alternatives) on each menu.

In Web site design, two recent studies have also looked at the breadth-depth issue (Zaphiris and Mtei, 1998; Larson and Czerwinski 1998). Both found that a two-level (two mouse click) Web site was searched faster than those containing more levels.

The conclusion that one might derive from these studies is this: Fewer levels of menus aid the decision-making process, but trying to put too many choices on a single menu also has a negative impact. The final solution is a compromise: Minimize the number of levels within limits of clarity. What is clarity? The studies seem to indicate that, if the choices to be displayed cannot be segmented into logical categories, then confine the number of alternatives displayed to 4 to 8 per menu. If logical categorization is possible, and meaningful, logical category names can be established, and then a larger number of choices can be presented. The maximum number of alternatives will, however, be dependent upon the size of the words needed to describe the alternatives to the user. Wordy captions will greatly restrict the number of alternatives capable of being displayed. There is one exception to these basic principles. Large linearly ordered, well-learned listings, such as months of the year, or numbers, would be better presented in a one-level menu, rather than by breaking them into multiple levels.

Limit the number of choices. Be conservative in the number of menu choices presented on a screen. If the choices cannot be logically grouped, restrict the number to 4 to 8. If the choices can be grouped, 18 to 24 can be displayed, with no more than 10 items within a group.

Mayhew (1992) suggests that if the menu choices are complex and/or there are no groupings of items, choices presented should be restricted to *10 or fewer*. This recommendation is similar to the eight or fewer recommendations above. If the menu choices are not complex, items on the menu can be grouped, and the users are infrequent or casual, she recommends *20 or fewer* choices. If the menu choices are not complex, items on the menu can be grouped, and the users are frequent or expert, she suggests *21 or more* choices can be provided.

MAXIM   **The best journey is the one with the fewest steps.**

Provide decreasing direction menus. In addition to breadth and depth, direction has been found to affect menu choice selection performance. In a multilevel menu, a *decreasing* direction structure presents successively fewer choices as each lower level is traversed. An *increasing* direction structure presents successively more choices as each lower level is traversed. Bishu and Zhan (1992) in a study of 16 and 32 item iconic menus found that decreasing direction menus were significantly faster and more accurate than increasing menus.

Scrolling. Never require menus to be scrolled. Keep all choices visible at all times.

Easy to restructure. Menus should be capable of being restructured by a user. Not everyone works the same way.

Complexity

- Provide both simple and complex menus.
- Simple: a minimal set of actions and menus.
- Complex: a complete set of actions and menus.

Providing two sets of menus will more effectively satisfy the differing needs of the novice and expert user. The novice or casual user often only requires a minimal set of actions and menus to accomplish tasks. The expert may prefer a full set of options. Make selection, and changing, between simple and complex menus easy to accomplish, preferably through a menu bar choice. IBM's SAA CUA refers to these menus as *short* and *full*

Item Arrangement

- Align alternatives or choices into single columns whenever possible.
  — Orient for top-to-bottom reading.
  — Left-justify descriptions.
- If a horizontal orientation of descriptions must be maintained:
  — Organize for left-to-right reading.

For scanning ease, menu choices should be left-justified and aligned vertically into columns. Research has found that columnar menus and listings are searched much faster than horizontally-oriented menus. Do not array a menu in multiple columns.

When menus are included on other screens, space constraints often exist, and the menu must be arrayed horizontally. If a single-row (horizontal) orientation is necessary organize for left-to-right reading. If two or more rows are available for displaying choices, organize for top-to-bottom, then left-to-right reading to facilitate visual scanning.

Ordering

- Order lists of choices by their natural order, or
- For lists associated with numbers, use numeric order.
- For textual lists with a small number of options (seven or less), order by:
  — Sequence of occurrence.
  — Frequency of occurrence.
  — Importance.
  — Semantic similarity.
- Use alphabetic order for:
  — Long lists (eight or more options).
  — Short lists with no obvious pattern or frequency.
- Separate potentially destructive actions from frequently chosen items.
- If option usage changes, do not reorder menus.
- Maintain a consistent ordering of options on all related menus.
  — For variable-length menus, maintain consistent relative positions.
  — For fixed-length menus, maintain consistent absolute positions.

Within information categories included on a menu, or in menus in which categories are not possible, options must be ordered in meaningful ways. When a menu contains multiple categories of information, the ordering of categories will follow these same principles. A meaningful ordering is necessary to:

- Facilitate search for an item.
- Provide information about the structure and relationships among items.
- Provide compatibility with the user's mental model of the item structure.
- Enhance the user's ability to anticipate a choice's location.

When items are organized along some dimension or characteristic, the user can use that information to locate items faster. An alphabetized list, for example, provides an indication of approximately where in the listing an item beginning with a particular letter will be found. Understanding structure and relationships, item similarities and dissimilarities, can also aid in focusing attention on that which is relevant. Any incompatibility with the user's mental model will disrupt searching as the user tries to make sense of something that had been well understood, but now is now being presented in a way that has not been well learned. Months of the year presented in alphabetic order, for example, would be very disrupting.

Experienced users often anticipate the location of a desired choice within a familiar menu. Hornof and Kieras (1999), in studying how items are selected from pull-down menus, found that people often make an initial eye and mouse-positioning movement toward the expected choice location before the pull-down even appeared on the screen. They also found that choices in the top three positions of the pull-down were selected faster then those in other positions. This may have been caused by users' ability to better predict a choice's location at the top, and/or the shorter mouse movement required from the menu bar to the pull-down. Observational studies also reveal that experienced users also anticipate the location of command buttons appearing within a window. While waiting for a window to appear upon which a command button will be immediately "clicked," the pointer is often positioned at the button's expected location before the window appears.

Another study, Byrne, John, Wehrle, and Crow, 1999, studied how people search unfamiliar pull-down menus. They found that the search primarily flowed from menu top to bottom, and that the initial eye fixation was usually the focused on the choice in the topmost menu position. Almost all recorded eye fixations were on one of the first three items.

Both of the studies point out the importance of presenting important menu items at the top of menu arrays, and providing consistency in menu organization schemes and menu locations. Common ordering schemes for menus, then, are the following:

Natural ordering. If items have a natural sequence, such as chapters in a book, days in a week, or months in the year, the ordering scheme should follow this natural sequence. The screen viewer will have learned these ordering schemes very well.

Numeric ordering. Use numeric ordering for choices associated with numbers, for example, type size, baud rate, or number of pixels.

Small number of options. For groupings with a small number of options (about seven or fewer), *sequence of use*, *frequency of use*, or *importance* are good ordering schemes. Also consider ordering by *semantic similarity*, along a semantic dimension such as impact, potency, or emphasis. Type style, for example, may be ordered by emphasis from least to most: regular, underlined, italicized, and bold.

Alphabetic order. For a large number of options, alphabetic ordering of alternatives is desirable. Alphabetic ordering is also recommended for small lists where no frequency or sequence pattern is obvious.

It has been found that alphabetically ordered menus can be searched much faster than randomly ordered menus. One study, for example, found that an 18-item alphabetic menu was visually searched four times faster than a randomly organized menu. Search time was a function of saccadic eye movements through the display. Search patterns were random, but fewer eye movements were required with the alphabetic arrangement. After 20 trials, however, only one eye movement was required for all conditions, and search time was the same. Another study has found that the longer the list, the greater the value of an alphabetic ordering scheme. As list length increased, the time to find items in longer random lists increased significantly faster than the time to find items in longer alphabetic lists.

Learning of a randomly ordered menu will eventually take place, but this learning will be greatly aided by a meaningful choice-ordering scheme.

Separate destructive choices. Destructive menu choices, such as delete or clear, should be positioned as far away from frequently chosen choices as possible to minimize the chance of accidental selection.

Do not reorder menus. Adaptivity is thought to be a desirable quality of a computer system. This may not be so for menu option ordering. A study compared static or fixed menus with dynamic menus whose options were continually reordered based upon the frequency in which they were chosen. Dynamic menus were slower to use and less preferred than static menus. The continual reordering interfered with menu order learning.

Consistency between menus. Options found on more than one menu should be consistently positioned on all menus. If menus are of variable length, maintain relative positioning of all item options (for example, always place Exit at the bottom or end of the list). If menus are of fixed length, place options in the same physical position within the list.

Groupings

- Create groupings of items that are logical, distinctive, meaningful, and mutually exclusive.
- Categorize them in such a way as to:
  — Maximize the similarity of items within a category.
  — Minimize the similarity of items across categories.
- Present no more than six or seven groupings on a screen.
- Order categorized groupings in a meaningful way.
- If meaningful categories cannot be developed and more than eight options must be displayed on a screen, create arbitrary visual groupings that:
  — Consist of about four or five but never more than seven options.
  — Are of equal size.
- Separate groupings created through either:
  — Wider spacing, or
  — A thin ruled line.
- Provide immediate access to critical or frequently chosen items.

Create groupings. Items displayed on menus should be logically grouped to aid learning and speed up the visual search process. Studies have demonstrated that logically categorized menus are easier to learn and result in faster and more accurate performance. Categorical organization may facilitate the transition from novice to expert user because information is visually represented in the way people think about it.

Categorizing. Groupings should also cover all the possibilities and contain items that are non-overlapping. While some collections of information will be easily partitioned into logical groups, others may be very difficult to partition. Some users may not understand the designer's organizational framework, and there may be differences among users based on experience. Thus, no perfect solution may exist for all, and extensive testing and refinement may be necessary to create the most natural and comprehensible solution.

Number. Limit the number of groupings on a screen to six or seven. The total number of items within all the groupings should not exceed about 18 to 24.

Ordering. Groupings of menu items may be ordered following the guidelines described in "Ordering" above. Ordering alternatives include alphabetic, sequence of use, frequency of use, importance, and semantic similarity.

Arbitrary visual groupings. Uncategorized menus should be broken in arbitrary visual groupings through the use of space or lines. Groups should be as equal in size as possible and consist of about four or five options. Groupings should never exceed more than seven options.

Separation. Perceptually separate groupings by a leaving a wider spacing between groupings, or by inscribing line separators between groupings. Guidelines for displaying line separators follow.

Critical choices. Choices that are critical or frequently chosen should be accessible as quickly and through as few steps as possible. Place them on the highest-level menu, whenever possible.

Line Separators

- Separate vertically arrayed groupings with subtle solid lines.
- Separate vertically arrayed subgroupings with subtle dotted or dashed lines.
- For subgroupings within a category:
  — Left-justify the lines under the first letter of the columnized choice descriptions.
  — Right-justify the lines under the last character of the longest choice description.
- For independent groupings:
  — Extend the line to the left and right menu borders.

Inscribing subtle solid or dashed lines between groupings can reinforce groupings and subgroupings of vertically arrayed related choices. For breaking subgroupings within one category, the line or lines should only extend from the first character of the descriptions to the end of the longest description, as shown in Figure 4.6. Many graphical platforms always extend the line from menu border to border, as illustrated in

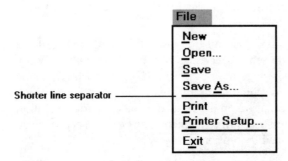

Figure 4.6 Partial line separators.

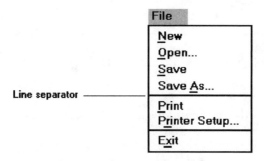

Line separator ———————

Figure 4.7   Extended line separators.

Figure 4.7. This extended line results in too strong a visual separation between what are related menu parts. Visual separation should exist, but it should not be too over-powering.

For independent groups of choices, extend the horizontal line from menu border to border. This will indicate to the user that the groupings are independent of one another. In summary, use a partial line for separating related choices; use an extended line for separating unrelated or independent choices.

Phrasing the Menu

A menu must communicate to the user information about:

- The nature and purpose of the menu itself.
- The nature and purpose of each presented choice.
- How the proper choice or choices may be selected.

Writing the content of menu components, the menu's title, the choice descriptions, and instructions, is often made difficult because of the varying experience levels of the menu users. At one extreme, there is the desire to explain, on the screen, everything in great detail. On the other hand, brevity is also important because of screen space constraints and limits on what people want to read. These conflicting goals often cause a trade-off between thoroughness and brevity. Also important in hierarchical menu systems is the role menus play in enabling a person to maintain a sense of place, or "Where am I now?" Also very important is a menu's ability to enable the user to accurately predict where a choice will lead, or what it will cause to happen, preventing user tedium and frustration. So, the menu content must be informative, but not intrusive. And it must balance the needs of all its expected users.

Following are guidelines for creating menu titles, choice descriptions, Web navigation links, and menu instructions. The standard graphical system conventions inscribed on menus, intent indicators, keyboard equivalents, and keyboard accelerators, are also described.

Menu Titles

- Main menu:
  — Create a short, simple, clear, and distinctive title, describing the purpose of the entire series of choices.
- Submenus:
  — Submenu titles must be worded exactly the same as the menu choice previously selected to display them.
- General:
  — Locate the title at the top of the listing of choices.
  — Spell out the title fully using either an:
    • Uppercase font.
    • Mixed-case font in the headline style.
  — Superfluous titles may be omitted.

A meaningful menu title aids in defining the context of the menu and increases menu comprehension. An experimental study has demonstrated the value of titles to comprehension. Study participants were presented the detailed steps to perform a function. A descriptive title for the steps was (A) not included, (B) presented at the start of the steps, and (C) presented at the end of the steps. Participants given a title at the start of the steps (B), reported higher comprehension and recalled twice as many items as those who were not given a title (A), or who were presented the title at the end (C). The title established the context of the task, and knowing this context greatly aided comprehension.

Main menu. The menu title should immediately orient the viewer to the menu's content and purpose. It should be a short, clear, distinctive, and descriptive title, representing the entire series of choices. It's an important contextual and navigation component. A title such as MAIN MENU OPTIONS provides no information except that the user is probably at the top of a hierarchical menu tree.

Submenus. Submenu titles must be worded exactly the same way as the menu choice previously selected to display them. This will provide structural continuity and assure users that they are progressing as expected through a menu hierarchy.

General. Locate the title at the top of a listing of choices, in the title bar if one is available. Display the title in uppercase or in a mixed-case font using the headline style of presentation. When using the headline style, capitalize the first letter of each significant title word. The case style chosen should be consistently used on all menus. Superfluous titles, titles that add nothing to the understanding of menu content and context, may be omitted. A pop-up menu requested during a text-editing task, for example, is displayed within the context of the task being performed. The presented choice descriptions by themselves (Copy, Font, and so on) provide the necessary context. Message windows do not need a title either; the text of the message provides the context.

Menu Choice Descriptions

- Create meaningful choice descriptions that are familiar, fully spelled out, concise, and distinctive.

- Descriptions may be single words, compound words, or multiple words or phrases.
  — Exception: Menu bar items should be a single word (if possible).

- Place the keyword first, usually a verb.

- Use the headline style, capitalizing the first letter of each significant word in the choice description.

- Use task-oriented not data-oriented wording.

- Use parallel construction.

- A menu choice must never have the same wording as its menu title.

- Identical choices on different menus should be worded identically.

- Choices should not be numbered.
  — Exception: If the listing is numeric in nature, graphic, or a list of varying items, it may be numbered.

- If menu options will be used in conjunction with a command language, the capitalization and syntax of the choices should be consistent with the command language.

- Word choices as commands to the computer.

Meaningful. Menu item descriptions should be composed of familiar and fully spelled out words. While abbreviations may occasionally be necessary, they should be kept to a minimum. If you are using an abbreviation, only use those that are standard or well known. Descriptions should also be concise, containing as few words as possible, and distinctive, constructed of words that make each choice clearly different from all others. Repeated use of the same word or words in multiple choice descriptions hinders distinctiveness and signals the necessity for creating a grouping whose title is based upon the repeated word.

Use high-imagery keywords, words that elicit a mental image of the object or action. Avoid low-imagery words that have more general connotations. For example, when obtaining a printout of a screen, the term "print" is much more descriptive than "list."

In creating menu item descriptions, never assume that the description chosen by the designer will have the same meaning to the user. A study has found that the probability of two people choosing the same name or description for something ranged from 8 to 18 percent. Names chosen by experts were no better than those chosen by nonexperts. Therefore, iteratively test and refine the choices to achieve as much agreement in meaning by users as possible.

Size. Item descriptions may be single words, compound words, multiple words, or phrases. Menu bar items should be a single word, if possible. If a menu bar item must be a multiple word, visually tie the two words together by incorporating a hyphen between them. Web page content links will typically be phrases. Link writing guidelines will be thoroughly described in Step 8.

Keyword first. Arrange multi-item descriptions so that the descriptive and unique words appear at its beginning. This optimizes scanning and recognition while the user is learning the menu. Description phrasing and wording should also be consistent across all menus to aid learning further.

Capitalization. Use the headline style of presentation. Capitalize the first letter of each significant choice description word.

Task-oriented wording. Task-oriented wording is preferable to data-oriented wording. Task-oriented wording usually positions a verb first, such as *Manage Customer Information*. An example of data-oriented wording would be to simply say *Customers*. What is being done with, for, or to customers is unclear in the latter.

Parallel construction. When choices are composed of phrases, use a parallel word construction in creating descriptions for related choices. Parallel construction would be: *Print* a File, *Execute* a Program, and *Eject* a Disk. An example of non-parallel construction is: *Print*; *Execute* a Program, and Disk *Eject*.

Relationship to title. A menu choice must never have the same wording as the title of the menu on which it is presented.

Consistency across menus. Identical choices on different menus should be worded the same.

Numbering. Items should not be numbered unless the listing is numeric in nature, graphic, or a list of varying items.

Command language. If menu options will be used in conjunction with a command language, the capitalization and syntax of the captions should be consistent with those of the command language.

Word as a command to computer. Phrase all menu choices as commands to the computer whenever possible. For example, say:

Choose one:

　Save and exit

　Exit without saving

rather than:

　Do you want to save and exit?
　- Yes
　- No

Wording a choice as a command to the computer more clearly describes the action of what the command accomplishes. The Yes/No alternatives shown above must be comprehended in conjunction with the question being asked. Wording a choice as a command also provides choice phrasing that is consistent with other system commands. A system, for example, often contains the standard commands *Save* and *Exit*. In addition, command wording enhances the learning of command mnemonics. Finally, this wording implies that the initiative is with the user in the dialog, not with the computer.

Menu Instructions

- For novice or inexperienced users, provide menu completion instructions.
  - Place the instructions in a position just preceding the part, or parts, of the menu to which they apply.
    - Left-justify the instruction and indent the related menu choice descriptions a minimum of three spaces to the right.
    - Leave a space line, if possible, between the instructions and the related menu choice descriptions.
  - Present instructions in a mixed-case font in sentence style.
- For expert users, make these instructions easy to ignore by:
  - Presenting them in a consistent location.
  - Displaying them in a unique type style and/or color.

People not familiar with a system and its menus may need guidance on how to complete a menu. Their needs may, however, have to be balanced against the needs of experienced users who may not want or desire such assistance. To satisfy the needs of all kinds of users at the same time necessitates that menu instructions be included on a menu, but that these instructions be easily ignored by those who do not need them.

Novice or inexperienced users. Provide explicit menu completion instructions for novice or inexperienced menu users. Place the instructions in a position just preceding the part, or parts, of the menu to which they apply. Left-justify the instruction and indent the related menu choice descriptions a minimum of three spaces to the right. Leave a space line, if possible, between the instructions and the choice descriptions. Present the instructions in a mixed-case, sentence-style font.

Expert users. When instructions are included on menus, they must be visually recognized as instructions. This will allow them to be easily ignored by the expert user when they are not needed, or no longer needed. Therefore, some visual aspect of the instruction must indicate that it *is* an instruction. As mentioned in Step 3 "Understand the Principles of Good Screen Design," designers of paper forms do this by presenting instructions in a different font or font style such as italics. The form user then immediately recognizes them as instructions, and they can be read or ignored as is desired.

To make instructions immediately recognizable as instructions on a menu, then, present them in a unique font or color. If one of these methods is used, however, cautions concerning the excessive use of different font styles (and colors, as will be shown in Step 12 "Choose the Proper Colors") must be heeded. Another, but less visually strong, technique is to identify the technique simply by its location. Begin the instruction to the left of the screen elements to which it applies, the left-justification identifying it as an instruction.

Try to leave a space line between the instruction and the elements to which it relates, whenever possible. Screen space constraints may not always permit a space line, however. Guidelines for writing text, including instructions, will be found in Step 8 "Writing Clear Text and Messages."

Intent Indicators

- Cascade indicator:
  - To indicate that selection of an item will lead to a submenu, place a triangle or right-pointing solid arrow following the choice.
  - A cascade indicator must designate every cascaded menu.

- To a window indicator:
  - For choices that result in displaying a window to collect more information, place an ellipsis (. . .) immediately following the choice.
    - Exceptions—do not use when an action:
      - Causes a warning window to be displayed.
      - May or may not lead to a window.

- Direct action items:
  - For choices that directly perform an action, no special indicator should be placed on the menu.

Providing an indication of what will happen when a menu item is selected can enhance predictability and exploration of a graphical system. If a choice leads to another lower-level menu, include a *cascade indicator*, a right-pointing arrow, following the item description. If a choice leads *to a window*, include an ellipsis following the item description. Items causing a direct action will have no indicator. These intent indicators are illustrated in Figure 4.8.

IBM's SAA CUA designates choices leading to submenus or windows as *routing* choices, and items causing direct actions as *action* choices. A Microsoft Windows *intent indicator* simply implies that additional information is needed. This additional infor-

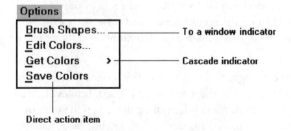

Figure 4.8   Intent indicators.

mation request is usually presented in a window, but it need not necessarily be restricted to a window.

Keyboard Equivalents

- To facilitate keyboard selection of a menu choice, each menu item should be assigned a keyboard equivalent mnemonic.
- The mnemonic should be the first character of the menu item's description.
    — If duplication exists in first characters, use another character in the duplicated item's description.
    — Preferably choose the first succeeding consonant.
- Designate the mnemonic character by underlining it.
- Use industry-standard keyboard access equivalents when they exist.

Keyboard selection. The ability to select a menu alternative through the keyboard should always be provided. This is accomplished by providing a keyboard *equivalent* for each menu alternative.

Mnemonics. Keyboard equivalents that have meaningful associations with their corresponding choices will be more easily learned and remembered. Studies have found that simple truncation is a good method for creating mnemonics. Therefore, the first letter of the item description is the recommended mnemonic. Unfortunately, in following this method, duplications easily occur, so an alternative principle must also be provided. A simple scheme is to use the second consonant for duplicate items. This duplication-breaking scheme need not always be faithfully followed, however. Occasionally another letter in the menu item may be more meaningful to the user. In these cases, it should be selected.

Designation. Mnemonic codes can be visually indicated in a number of ways. The recommended method is an underline beneath the proper character within the choice. Other methods—a different character color, different character intensity, or a contrasting color bar through the relevant character—are visually more complex and should be avoided. Underlined keyboard equivalents are illustrated in Figure 4.9.

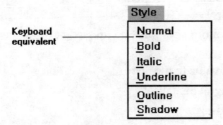

Figure 4.9 Keyboard equivalents.

Table 4.1 Standard Keyboard Equivalents

About	Help	Print	Send To
Apply	Help Topics	Print Preview	Show
Back	Insert	Properties	Size
Browse	Maximize	Redo	Split
Close	Minimize	Repeat	Stop
Copy	Move	Restore	Undo
Cut	New	Resume	View
Delete	Next	Retry	Yes
Edit	No	Rerun	
Exit	Open	Save	
File	Paste	Save As	
Find	Page Setup	Select All	

A great deal of commonality exists among these equivalents since they represent a wide variety of functions, many of which will rarely appear together on a single menu. If two actions with the same equivalents will be used within the same menu, one equivalent will have to be modified to make it unique.

> **Industry standards.** Standard industry keyboard equivalents have been established for many common system menu choices. Where these standard equivalents have been established, they should be followed. Microsoft Windows calls keyboard equivalents *access keys.* Standard keyboard equivalents are shown in Table 4.1.

Keyboard Accelerators

- For frequently used items, provide a keyboard accelerator to facilitate keyboard selection.
- The accelerator may be one function key or a combination of keys.
  — Function key shortcuts are easier to learn than modifier plus letter shortcuts.
- Pressing no more than two keys simultaneously is preferred.
  — Do not exceed three simultaneous keystrokes.
- Use a plus (+) sign to indicate that two or more keys must be pressed at the same time.
- Accelerators should have some associative value to the item.
- Identify the keys by their actual key top engraving.
- If keyboard terminology differences exist, use:
  — The most common keyboard terminology.
  — Terminology contained on the newest PCs.

- Separate the accelerator from the item description by three spaces.
- Right-align the key descriptions.
- Do not use accelerators for:
  — Menu items that have cascaded menus.
  — Pop-up menus.
- Use industry-standard keyboard accelerators when they exist.

Accelerators are keys, or combinations of keys, that invoke an action regardless of cursor or pointer position. They are most commonly used to activate a menu item without opening the menu. They are most useful for frequent activities performed by experienced users. IBM's SAA CUA and Microsoft Windows calls these keys *shortcut* keys. They may also be called *hot keys*. Many products have, within their guidelines, standard accelerator key recommendations as well as rules for creating new accelerator keys.

For frequently used items, assign a key, or combination of keys, to accomplish an action. Function key shortcuts are usually easier to learn than modifier plus letter shortcuts. Pressing no more than two keys simultaneously is preferred; three keystrokes is the maximum. Use a plus (+) sign to indicate on the screen menu that two or more keys must be pressed at the same time.

Accelerators should have some associative value to the item and be identified by their actual key-top engraving. In situations where multiple kinds of keyboards exist, and there are keyboard terminology differences, use the term most commonly found on the keyboards or use the term contained on the newest PC, if evolution to the new PCs is expected.

Display the accelerator right-aligned and enclosed in parentheses to the right of the choice. Incorporating these key names within parentheses indicates that they are prompts (which they actually are) and that they may easily be ignored when not being used. Most graphic systems do not place them within parentheses, giving them much too strong a visual emphasis. See Figure 4.10.

Do not use accelerators for menu items that lead to cascaded menus. Also, do not use accelerators on pop-up menus, because they are mouse driven. Use standard keyboard accelerators when they exist. Standard industry accelerators are shown in Table 4.2.

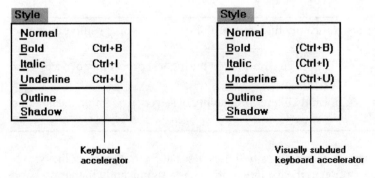

Figure 4.10 Keyboard accelerators.

Table 4.2 Standard Keyboard Accelerators

THIS ACCELERATOR:	DESIGNATES THIS ACTION:
Ctrl+C	Copy
Ctrl+N	New
Ctrl+O	Open
Ctrl+P	Print
Ctrl+S	Save
Ctrl+V	Paste
Ctrl+X	Cut
Ctrl+Z	Undo
F1	Display contextual help window
Shift+F1	Activate context-sensitive help
Shift+F10	Display pop-up menu
Spacebar	Select (single mouse click)
Esc	Cancel
Alt	Activate a menu bar

Selecting Menu Choices

Menu items can be selected by pointing at the choice with a mechanical pointer, by pointing at the choice through the keyboard, or by keying a value designating the choice.

Initial Cursor Positioning

- If one option has a significantly higher probability of selection, position the cursor at that option.
- If repeating the previously selected option has the highest probability of occurrence, position the cursor at this option.
- If no option has a significantly higher probability of selection, position the cursor at the first option.

When a menu is first displayed, position the cursor at the option most likely to be chosen, or at the first option in the list if no option has a significantly higher probability of selection. If repeating the previously selected option has the highest probability of occurrence, position the cursor at this option.

Choice Selection

- Pointers:
  - Select the choice by directly pointing at it with a mechanical device such as a mouse or trackball pointer, or light pen, or pointing with one's finger.
  - Visually indicate:
    - Which options can be selected.
    - When the option is directly under the pointer and can be selected.
  - Visually distinguish single- and multiple-choice menu alternatives.
  - If pointing with a mechanical device is the selection method used:
    - The selectable target area should be at least twice the size of the active area of the pointing device or displayed pointer. In no case should it be less than 6 millimeters square.
    - Adequate separation must be provided between adjacent target areas.
  - If finger pointing is the selection method used:
    - The touch area must be a minimum of 20 to 30 millimeters square.
    - The touch area must encompass the entire caption plus one character around it.
- Keyboard:
  - If moving the cursor to a menu choice:
    - The up and down arrow keys should move the cursor up or down vertically oriented menu options.
    - The left and right cursor keys should move the cursor left or right between horizontally oriented menu options.
  - If keying a choice identifier value within an entry field:
    - Locate the entry field at the bottom of the last choice in the array of choices.
    - Uppercase, lowercase, and mixed -case typed entries should all be acceptable.
- Selection/execution:
  - Provide separate actions for selecting and executing menu options.
  - Indicate the selected choice through either:
    - Highlighting it with a distinctive display technique.
    - Modifying the shape of the cursor.
  - Permit unselecting choice before execution.
    - If a menu is multiple choice, permit all options to be selected before execution.
- Combining techniques:
  - Permit alternative selection techniques, to provide flexibility.

Pointers. Items can be selected by being pointed at using a mechanical device such as a mouse, trackball, or light pen, or through touch pointing using one's finger (for touch-sensitive screens). Pressing a key, such as Transmit or Enter, or a mouse button, signals the choice to the computer. Always visually indicate in a distinctive manner which options are selectable and when the option is under the pointer and can be selected. Visually distinguish single- and multiple-choice arrays of menu choices.

An adequate pointing target area should be provided. This area should be at least twice the size of the active area of the displayed pointer of the pointing device. In no case should it be less than 6 millimeters square. To avoid unintended activation of the wrong option, provide adequate separation between selectable areas. Highlighting of the area when selected will also provide indication of an incorrect choice.

If finger pointing is the selection method used, an even larger touch area must be provided, a minimum of 20 to 30 millimeters. Single-character positions on a screen make poor targets for most fingers. Also, keep in mind that using a finger to signify a choice can be taxing on arm muscles, so this approach should only be used in casual or infrequent use situations.

Keyboard. If the user is moving the screen cursor to a menu choice, the up and down arrow keys should move the cursor up and down a vertical column of menu options. The left and right arrow keys should move the cursor left and right across a horizontal array of options. If the user is keying a choice identifier value within an entry field, locate the entry field at the bottom of the last choice in the array of choices. If the user is keying a mnemonic value, the entry should be acceptable in any case (upper, lower, and mixed).

Selection/execution. Provide separate actions for selecting and executing menu options. For example, require typing the mnemonic to select, and then a press of the *Enter* or *Return* key to execute. Or, with a mouse, require moving the pointer to the option to select, and then clicking to execute. Always permit erroneous selections to be unselected and, in a multiple-choice menu, permit all options to be selected before execution.

The item selected should be highlighted in some way through a distinctive display technique such as bolding or changing its color. An alternative is to change the shape of the pointer itself. These methods provide direct visual feedback that the proper choice has been selected, reducing the probability of errors in choice selection.

Combining techniques. Permit alternative selection techniques to provide flexibility. If a pointing method is used, also provide a keyboard alternative to accomplish the same task. Pointing will probably be easier for the novice, but many experts prefer the keyboard alternative.

Defaults

- Provide a default whenever possible.
- Display as bold text.

Defaults aid system learning and enhance efficiency. Provide as many as possible. Indicate a default by displaying it in a bold text.

Unavailable Choices

- Unavailable choices should be dimmed or "grayed out."
- Do not add or remove items from a menu unless the user takes explicit action to add or remove them through the application.

Choices not available to the user should be made visually distinctive by dimming them or graying them out. They must not compete with active items for the user's attention. Items should not be added or removed from a menu unless the user takes explicit action to do so. Allowing the system to change menu items takes control away from the user and can also lead to user confusion.

Mark Toggles or Settings

- Purpose:
  — Use to designate that an item or feature is active or inactive over a relatively long period of time.
  — Use to provide a reminder that an item or feature is active or inactive.
- Guidelines:
  — Position the indicator directly to the left of the option.
  — For situations where several nonexclusive choices may be selected, consider including one alternative that deselects all the items and reverts the state to the "normal" condition.

Purpose. Mark toggles or settings, illustrated in Figure 4.11, are menu items that toggle between active and not active. When it is active, an indicator is displayed adjacent to the item description. For nonexclusive choices, a check mark is displayed; for mutually exclusive choices, another distinctive symbol, such as a diamond or circle, is displayed. When the item is not active, no mark or symbol will appear.

Examples of items using mark toggles are: having a specific application automatically loaded after the system is loaded, having windows automatically reduced to icons when they are made inactive, or making a setting without requiring a dialog box. The purpose of mark toggles is to activate or deactivate an attribute by setting one menu item.

Advantages/disadvantages. Mark toggles provide a visual indication of the state of an item. They are accessed quickly but may not always be visible. Mark toggles are best suited to items or features that remain active or inactive over relatively long periods of time. They provide good reminders of the state that exists.

Regular	F5
√ Bold	Ctrl+B
√ Italic	Ctrl+I
Underline	Ctrl+U
Superscript	
Subscript	
Reduce Font	
Enlarge Font	
Fonts...	

Figure 4.11 Mark toggles.

Guidelines. Position the mark toggle indicator directly to the left of the menu option. In situations where several nonexclusive choices may be selected on one menu, consider including one alternative that deselects all the items and reverts the state to the normal condition, as illustrated by "Regular" in Figure 4.11.

Toggled Menu Items

- Purpose:
  — Use to designate two opposite commands that are accessed frequently.
  — Use when the menu item displayed will clearly indicate that the opposite condition currently exists.

- Guidelines:
  — Provide a meaningful, fully spelled-out description of the action.
  — Begin with a verb that unambiguously represents the outcome of the command.
  — Use mixed-case letters, with the first letter of each word capitalized.

Purpose. A toggled menu item is a one menu item command that toggles back and forth between the current state and its alternative state. When the menu item is first displayed, it reflects the alternative state to the condition that currently exists. For example, in Figure 4.12, if a background grid is currently being displayed, the menu item reads *Hide Grid*. When Hide Grid is selected, the grid is removed from the window, and the menu item dynamically changes to reflect the opposite action. It will now read *Show Grid*. When a grid is again requested, it will change back to Hide Grid. The purpose of toggled menu item is to use a single menu item to designate and activate the one, opposite, alternative of a two-state command setting.

Advantages/disadvantages. Toggled menu items shorten menus, decrease visual clutter, provide quicker access, and foster faster comprehension of the command action. When they are located on a pull-down menu, however, the actions themselves are not always visible. The opposite action reflecting the current state of the attribute, since it too is not visible, can cause uncertainty for novice users concerning what the state actually is. Toggled menu items are also limited in use to commands only.

Guidelines. Use toggled menu items to designate two opposite commands that are accessed frequently. The menu item displayed must be one that clearly indicates that the opposite condition currently exists. The menu captions should clearly state what would happen if the menu item action were requested. It is most meaningful to begin the command with a verb.

Figure 4.12 Toggled menu item.

Navigating Menus

Navigation, and an efficient navigational structure, is the most important element in system usability. A simple and clear navigational structure is the backbone upon which all system features are draped. In Web site design, the most successful sites have been found to be those with easy to use and understand navigational systems. No amount of graphical "sparkle" has yet been able to overcome a poor navigational design. A system's organizational structure and its navigational tools, including elements such as menus, links, toolbars, and command buttons influence the system's navigational ease of use. So, of course, does the size of the system, as well as the navigational aids available, including site maps and indexes. In Web site navigation design, the unique, often incompatible, relationship the browser has to the Web site application being presented can also strain navigation ease.

Web Site Navigation Problems

To fully understand what comprises good navigation, let's first look at some Web site navigational issues and problems, both technical and usage-related. The Web and its navigation is undoubtedly the most complex interface facing people today.

Technical issues. Unlike a graphical system application, whose screens tend to flow in an orderly and predictable manner, a Web application is composed of pages, each of which can, theoretically, be linked to any other page in the application. The graphical application user normally begins a process at a prescribed starting point and proceeds sequentially until a process or task is finished. Web users can perform tasks or satisfy needs at will, easily moving between most screens in the application "spider web" in any order desired, and even jumping to other spider webs when the urge arises. In an analogy to driving a car, the graphical system user is essentially following a freeway in Nevada. The Web user is wandering around in downtown Boston without a road map and, encountering a road link (a bridge over the Charles River), suddenly finds himself in Cambridge.

The graphical system user must deal with only one operating system whose navigational characteristics are standard and fairly consistent. The Web user must confront two navigational systems, that of the browser being used and that of the Web site being viewed. A click of the browser Back button, for example, simply redisplays the page that was previously displayed on the screen. This page may have been in another Web site, and the user is transported there. Neither Web site application is aware of this change. Nothing that might have been done on the page "moved back from" is changed. To move around within a Web site requires links within the Web site, either in the form of textual links or command buttons. The data must always be thought of as separate from the controls used to display it, not as being seamless, as occurs in graphical systems. Web users, especially novices, often do not recognize where the browser ends and the Web site application begins.

Another problem: Because of the rapidly evolving and expanding nature of the Web, Web sites also have a tendency to grow and grow. As more and more is added, what may have been initially a reasonable structure and menu scheme slowly dissolves into a confusing mass of listings and linked pages. The result is unrelated information that is presented in no particular order.

Usage problems. The two most serious user problems in Web navigation are the heavy mental loads imposed to use the Web and the feeling of spatial disorientation that often occurs. This problem may also occur in hierarchically structured graphical systems. The *cognitive or mental overhead* the user must expend in making decisions concerning which links to follow, or to abandon, can be overwhelming. Often, there are too many links presented on a page, many of whose meanings are not clear. Links frequently offer few clues to where they lead, how much information will be found at the other end, and how this information relates to the currently displayed page. For the user to reach a goal, each link's relevance to the task at hand must be determined. Another problem is that not all links on a page are always obvious. This often leads to much trial-and-error behavior; the user aimlessly clicking to see what happens.

Feelings of *disorientation* are easily experienced when one becomes "lost in Web space." Studies have shown that most people do not seem to become familiar with the layout of sites or develop useful mental models of their structure (Spool, Scanlon, Schroeder, Snyder, and DeAngelo, 1997). Many people also don't understand where they are in a Web site's information structure (Nielsen, 2000). A scrolling page can lead to loss of local context when the basic navigational elements, such as links to other local pages in the Web site disappear. There are then no familiar landmarks to then navigate by. Long chains of links to reach relevant material can be tedious and also lead to loss of context, and a "Where Am I?" reaction.

A recent research paper found that 39 percent of users of shopping sites failed in their buying attempts because the sites were too difficult to navigate. If people get buried in information, or lost on a side trip with no signposts or landmarks in sight, the most frequently implemented solution to the problem is to abandon the entire process.

Navigation Goals

A well-designed navigation system facilitates quick and easy navigation between components whose structure and relationship are easily comprehendible. For the user, answers to the following questions must be obvious at all times during an interaction:

- Where am I now?
- Where did I come from?
- Where can I go from here?
- How can I get there quickly?

Sometimes referred to as "wayfinding," a good navigational scheme, and the proper navigational tools, will minimize, if not eliminate, the problems associated with cognitive or mental overload and feelings of disorientation. General system navigation guidelines include the following.

Control

- For multilevel menus, provide one simple action to:
  — Return to the next higher-level menu.
  — Return to the main menu.
- Provide multiple pathways through a menu hierarchy whenever possible.

Navigation through menu levels should be accomplished through simple actions. It should always be very easy to return to the next higher-level menu and the main, general, or top menu. Provide multiple pathways, whenever possible, through a hierarchical menu structure.

Menu Navigation Aids

- To aid menu navigation and learning, provide an easily accessible:
  — Menu map or overview of the menu hierarchy.
  — A "look ahead" at the next level of choices, alternatives that will be presented when a currently viewed choice is selected.
  — Navigation history.

Menu maps. As has been discussed, as one wanders deeper into a multilevel menu system, it is increasingly difficult to maintain a sense of position or orientation The result is that getting lost in the menu maze is quite easy to do. The value of a menu map in reducing disorientation has been demonstrated in some studies. In these studies, providing a graphic representation of the menu structure in map form, either in hard copy or online, resulted in fewer errors or wrong choices, faster navigation, and greater user satisfaction when compared to providing no guides or simply providing indexes or narrative descriptions of the menu structure. So, menu maps or graphic representations of the menu structure are desirable and should be included on top-level menu screens. They should also be included in the system documentation where available, and through Help function.

Look-aheads. Menu navigation and learning will be assisted if a person is able to browse the next level of choices before the currently displayed choice is selected. As the cursor moves across a menu bar, for example, the pull-down menu may be automatically dropped, permitting review of the choices available if that menu bar item is selected. Such look-aheads are useful if ambiguity exists at higher-level choice points. They have been found to decrease errors and improve satisfaction. Menu search time may be longer, however.

Navigation history. It has been found that being able to view, on the screen, the path one is following improves learning and performance, and reduces feelings of disorientation. Provide a navigation history that summarizes the menu choices made leading to the currently displayed menu or screen.

Web Site Navigation

Understanding a Web site's navigational scheme is made more difficult because Web sites usually have much less *perceived* structure than typical graphical system applications. Web pages can be of any length and possess any number of links to any number of other pages. The user can wander at will or whim through multitudes of links, pages, and Web sites, and any meaningful structure a Web site design does possess can easily disappear from one's memory in the maze of directional twists and turns being made. The potential for getting lost is extremely high, unless numerous, obvious, and understandable landmarks are available as a guide.

The section focuses specifically on Web site navigation design. It will review typical Web site organizational schemes; the navigational components of a site, including the browser command buttons, links, Web site toolbars, and Web site command buttons; and the characteristics and components of a Web site that contribute to maintaining a "sense of place." In designing a Web site navigation scheme there are two things to always remember. Never assume that users know as much about a site as the site designers do (this has been said before), and, any page can be an entry point into the Web site.

Web Site Organization

- Divide content into logical fragments, units, or chunks.
- Establish a hierarchy of generality or importance.
- Structure the relationships among content fragments, units, or chunks.
  — Establish global or site-wide navigation requirements.
- Create a well-balanced hierarchical tree.
  — Restrict to two levels requiring no more than two clicks to reach deepest content, whenever possible.

It is easier to develop a clear and comprehendible navigation scheme if the Web site is organized and structured in a meaningful way. The design goal is a proper balance of menus and pages that can be easily and efficiently moved between.

Logical fragments, units, or chunks. Because of limitations in short-term human memory, smaller discrete fragments or chunks of information are often easier to navigate than long, undifferentiated units. The concept employed in Web site design, in reaction to this human memory frailty, is called *hypertext*. Hypertext is a nonlinear way of organizing information based upon the following principles:

- A large body of information exists that can be organized into fragments.
- The fragments relate to one another.
- The user needs only a small fraction of the fragments at any one time.

In organizing a Web site, information is first divided into logical fragments, units, or chunks. Coherent chunks that focus on a single topic is the desired goal.

These small chunks of related information are easier to organize into the modular groups of information that will compose the organization scheme, and form the basis for hypertext links to be described shortly. A design-organizing aid, card sorting, was described in Step 2 "Understanding the Business Function."

Hierarchy of generality or importance. Having identified the information units, information is now organized in according to importance or generality, from general to specific. A hierarchical tree is the most recommended organization scheme, Sun Microsystems (1998) suggests that whenever possible:

- State conclusions and link to supporting details.

- Enumerate categories of information and link them to detailed listings.

- Summarize information and link to full-length treatments.

A document organizational tree structure, (table of contents, chapters, sections, and subsections) is a good scheme, since people are very familiar with, and have an excellent mental model of this organization. Such a structure provides information about information sequence, information quantity, and the relationships existing between components. Other organizational schemes include topics followed by subtopics, or prioritization from most to least important. The objective is to allow the user to scan the page and then select relevant and useful content for further review. Excessive fragmentation of a long, sequential story, however, should be avoided. Reading will be impeded and printing made more difficult.

Structure the relationships. Identify the relationships that exist between various elements in the hierarchical tree. In a large Web site, two levels of navigation will exist. The first is movement within the subject area. This navigation includes moving *within a branch*—up to a parent page or down to a child page. It also involves navigating across branches to sibling pages or other sections of a site. What other points on other tree branches it will be beneficial to go directly to then, must be established. The second navigation type is *global or site-wide*. What other site features, such as search a facility, site maps, and other major content areas should be mentioned on each page? Do not mention all features on all pages. Restrict the number presented to the several most useful features.

To unveil the Web site's structure, use *progressive disclosure*. Heading levels, shown in varying type sizes (as on paper), will be helpful in aiding understanding of site organization.

Hierarchical tree. Web sites pages should be organized as offshoots of a single home page. If a site has a large number of information categories, and each category contains a lot of content, create submenus to aid navigation. The design goal: a well-balanced hierarchical tree that facilitates quick access to all information and also helps people understand how the site is organized. The so-called spoke design, where every page is linked to every other page, has been found to lead to lower usability.

Hierarchical breadth has been found by many research studies to be greatly preferable to hierarchy depth. A few menus with a larger number of choices are better than a large number of menus each with a smaller amount of choices.

When menu levels go to four, five, or more, the chance of users becoming lost or disoriented is greatly increased. As studies have found (Zaphiris and Mtei, 1998; Larson and Czerwinski, 1998), restrict, whenever possible, the hierarchical tree to two levels requiring no more than two clicks to reach the deepest content. A two-level structure encompasses a home page and two additional levels below it.

Components of a Web Navigation System

To move between Web site information fragments necessitates the creation of navigation *links*. They are contained within a framework of tools or controls, including the browser's command buttons, textual phrases, Web site navigation bars, and Web site command buttons. Collectively, these are all referred to as links. Links are one of the most discussed issues in Web site design.

A link functions as a menu choice that, when selected, results in the connected information being displayed, or results in a file being opened or downloaded. A movement link may transport the user to another location within a page, to a new site page, or to another Web site. Originally, due to the nature of technology at the time hypertext was employed in computer systems, links consisted of textual or binary files. Utilization of hypertext on the Web allowed links to by created using images as well as text, so the term *hypermedia* was coined to reflect this expanded nature.

In addition to being the critical component in Web navigation, links give the user an idea of what a Web site, document, or page is all about. The wording of a textual link should enable a person to predict what lies submerged below, or what will happen if it is activated. This lets the user determine whether a link should be followed, reading the page continued, reading the page ended, or a retreat to an earlier point initiated. This is a complex cost-benefit calculation that the user makes many times in a Web interaction session.

Providing an extensive collection of link navigation tools will focus the user on the Web site itself and its content, drawing attention away from the general-purpose browser links. Making these tools consistent and predictable will help the user create an understandable mental model of the site and its organization. To begin, several general link guidelines are:

- All navigation controls must:
  — Make sense in the absence of site context.
  — Be continually available.
  — Be obvious and distinctive.
  — Be consistent in appearance, function, and ordering.
  — Possess a textual label or description.
  — Offer multiple navigation paths.

Sensible. All navigation controls, in the absence of site context, must make sense to the user. The user may have "lost" the context, or the page or Web site may have been entered from almost anywhere.

Available. All navigational controls must be easy to access. If they are not readily available, the full advantages of hypermedia may not be achieved.

Obvious and distinctive. A navigation link or control must look like a navigation control. Its appearance to the user must immediately suggest that it is an entity to be clicked or otherwise selected. This is accomplished through a tool's appearance as well as its location. Non-obvious control choices lead to aimless and tedious page clicking and ultimately confusion and frustration. Conversely, do not make any other screen element look like a navigation tool if it is not one.

The obviousness of a link is called its *affordance*. A control with high affordance will be quickly identified as a control. Bailey (2000) in a study compared the link affordances of the home pages for two large Web sites. Each page contained 29 links. The link affordance rate for one site was 97 percent (participants, on the average, identified 28.2 page links). The rate for the other site was only 76 percent (the average link identification rate being 21.9 per page). This difference was statistically significant. Because of the non-obviousness of one-quarter of the poorer sites links, its users would have spent longer times searching for links, and would probably not have even discovered some links.

Techniques to create the necessary affordance and distinctiveness differ depending upon the kind of link. Guidelines enabling the various controls to achieve distinctiveness are described in the following control-specific sections.

Consistent. Like all elements of the interface, navigation links, toolbars, and command buttons must be consistent in appearance and behavior.

Textual. All navigation must have a textual label or description. Navigation using textual descriptions is much preferable to graphical-only navigation because the purpose and function of graphic images are often unclear. They also take longer to download. Textual links are also necessary for users who do not have graphics, or who have chosen not to display graphics.

Provide multiple navigation paths. Offer multiple paths or ways to move around the Web. Provide structural components such as site maps, a table of contents, and indexes to go directly to a point of interest, provide content links to move around nonsequentially, and provide command buttons, such as *Next* and *Previous*, to move sequentially.

Browser Command Buttons

- Hide the split between the browser and the Web site application by including navigational controls within the application.

The browser being used in interacting with the Web provides its own command buttons. As discussed earlier, pressing the browser *Back* and *Forward* buttons can create confusion because they can transport a user in and out of a Web site. Novice users often do not recognize where browser control ends and application control starts, and vice versa. Rather then relying on the browser's buttons, provide navigation controls within the application for movement within the application. They can take the form of links or command buttons such as *Next* and *Previous*.

Web Site Navigation Bars

- Provide a global navigation bar at the top of each page.
- Provide a local category or topical links navigation bar on the left side of a page.
- Place minor illustrative, parenthetical, or footnote links at the end of the page.
- For long pages, provide a navigation bar repeating important global or local links at the page bottom.

A Web site navigation bar is a menu, an array of textual phrases, graphical images or icons, or command buttons, as illustrated in Figures 4.13, 4.14, and 4.15. A Web site contains at least three levels of navigation links, *global,* or site-wide, links, indicating the site's total scope or categories of available information; *local* specific navigation links within the category or topical area being displayed; and *minor* illustrative, parenthetical, or footnote links. An evolving standard in design is to locate the global links at the page top, the categorical links in a columnar array down the pages left side, and the minor links at the page bottom. This structure, illustrated in Figure 4.16, separates navigation from content, making it easy for users to find each.

Locating the global links at the page top makes sense if one considers the logical flow of information through a screen. A selection from this global area eventually results in display of a page and its content, a top-to-bottom sequential eye flow. The left-justified category navigation area would, however, have been better positioned on the right. Given the common cultural left-to-right reading sequence, upon completion of reading of a page's content the eyes will be flowing right toward the right side of the screen. Finding the navigation links next needed would be more efficient. A right positioning of these links would also place them next to a scroll bar, a common focus of the user's attention on screens being scrolled. This vertically arrayed category navigation listing, while optimizing visual scanning of alternatives, is quite wasteful of screen space, consuming about 20 percent of a screen's pixels. Its space-consuming orientation is a usability trade-off, ease of scanning being enhanced at the expense of screen efficiency. All in all, navigation consistency reduces learning and avoids user confusion, so to now change its location would probably unleash greater problems.

For long scrolling pages, repeat important global or local links at the page bottom. When finishing a page, the user, then, will not have to scroll upward to locate important navigation links.

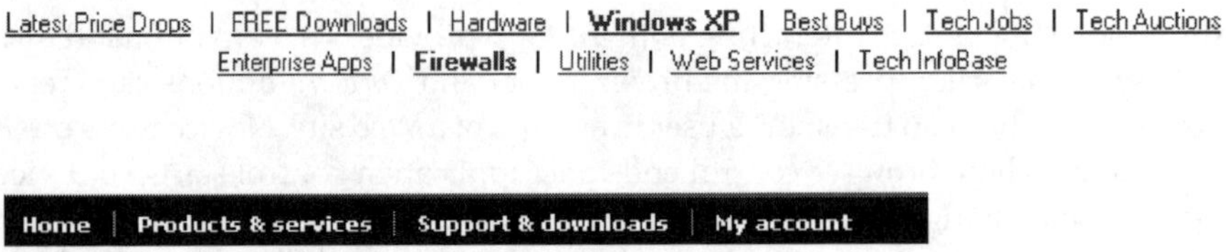

Latest Price Drops | FREE Downloads | Hardware | **Windows XP** | Best Buys | Tech Jobs | Tech Auctions
Enterprise Apps | **Firewalls** | Utilities | Web Services | Tech InfoBase

Home | Products & services | Support & downloads | My account

Figure 4.13 Textual explicit listing navigation bars.

Figure 4.14 Graphical or iconic navigation bars.

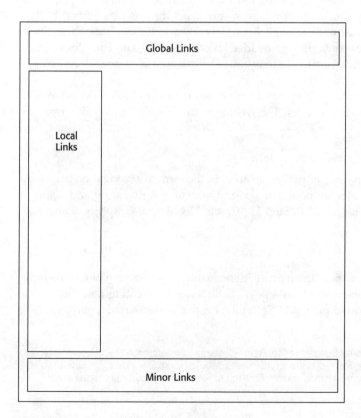

Figure 4.15 Command button navigation bar.

Figure 4.16 Web navigation component locations.

Textual Phrases

- Provide a mix of textual phrase links:
  — In explicit menus.
  — Embedded within page text.

Textual phrases are words, or short pieces of highlighted text, serving as links. Textual phrase links possess two distinct structures, explicit and embedded. An *explicit* menu is a listing of textual phrase links set apart from the main page content, often in a toolbar. These listings usually include links to various Web site topics, links to site global features such as the site map or search facility, and perhaps links to other related sites. These listings closely resemble typical screen menu arrays in their structure and presentation. A typical explicit menu is shown in Figure 4.13. An *embedded* menu is a link contained within the textual content of a page. Certain words or phrases are designated as links, highlighted, and when selected display the linked component for the user. An embedded menu is illustrated in Figure 4.17. Web sites usually contain both explicit link listings and embedded links in various mixes.

Lai and Waugh (1995) studied the effect of explicit listing hierarchical menus and embedded menus on a search task. They compared the three menu structures, menus composed solely of explicit listings, solely embedded menus, and mixed explicit and embedded menus. They found that the best menu structure was determined by the kind of search task performed. Explicit listings worked better for straightforward search tasks, while menus containing embedded links worked best for complex and not fully known searches. The embedded menus improved search accuracy but not search efficiency.

Providing a mix of explicit listings and embedded menus in Web site design will best satisfy the needs of all site users. The writing of meaningful links is described in Step 8.

Graphical Images or Icons

Graphical images or icons may appear in an array in the form of a navigation bar, or be individually located at relevant points in a page. Guidelines for creating and displaying graphics and icons are found in Step 11 "Create Meaningful Graphics, Icons, and Images."

Command Buttons

Command buttons may appear in an array in the form of a navigation bar, or be individually located at relevant points in a page. Guidelines for creating and displaying command buttons are found in Step 7 "Select the Proper Screen-Based Controls."

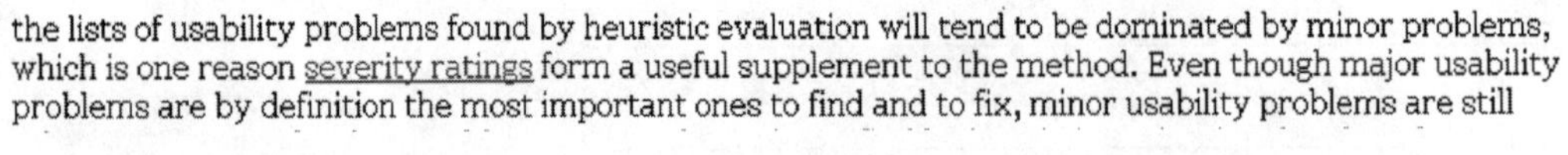

the lists of usability problems found by heuristic evaluation will tend to be dominated by minor problems, which is one reason severity ratings form a useful supplement to the method. Even though major usability problems are by definition the most important ones to find and to fix, minor usability problems are still

Figure 4.17   Embedded link menu.

Other Web Site Navigation Elements

In addition to Navigation bars, a number of other Web site elements are also important components of the Web navigation system. Among these are overviews, including executive summaries, site maps, indexes, and tables of contents. Other elements are historical trails and search engines.

Overviews

- Provide:
    - An executive summary that provides a preview of the site and contains links to all major concepts.
    - A site map illustrating the site's hierarchical structure and the relationships of components.
    - Both global and local maps.
    - An alphabetized site index.
    - A table of contents.
- Allow accessibility from any point in the Web site.

Overviews provide a top-level view of a site's organization and content. Having an understanding of how a site is organized, the landmarks available within it, and the content it contains, assists the navigation process. In driving an automobile, referring to a road map before embarking on trip usually results in reaching one's destination faster, easier recovery from inadvertent wrong turns, a better ability to handle any unexpected detours that may be encountered, and a less stressful trip.

Overviews are most useful if provided in several forms. They may be needed during a Web interaction as well as before starting into a site. A graphical system help function, for example, may be available in tutorial form, be accessible by topics, or be organized in alphabetic form for easy scanning. It is difficult to predict the user's exact need at any moment in a session.

An *executive summary* will provide an overview of the site in narrative form and contain links to all major concepts. A *site map* will illustrate the site's hierarchical structure in either graphical or textual form. These elements provide a prospective on one's position in the spatial hierarchy. Maps may be made available at both a global or local level within the site, depending upon the site's complexity. An alphabetized site *index* will permit quick access through keywords and specific topics. A *table of contents,* structured as in a printed book, will permit review of major topics and the subtopics within. All of a Web site's overview elements should be accessible from any point within the site.

Historical Trails

- Provide:
    - Breadcrumb Trails.
        - Locate at the top of the page below the navigation links.
    - History Lists.

— History Trees.
— Footprints.
— Bookmarks.

Historical navigation aids try to show the user's position in an information space by showing where they have come from, or where they have been. Seeing a navigation path enables a user to better understand the context of the currently displayed page. Displayed paths also provide a means to easily return to places of interest. A *bread-crumb trail* in a hierarchical Web site structure is a sequential textual listing of pages traversed from the parent page to the page currently being displayed. A trail, illustrated in Figure 4.18, is also a series of links that permit the user to go back to any page in the sequence with one click. At this moment no standard exists for how to separate the page names in a trail. Symbols used include an arrow (->), a colon (:), a greater than sign (>), and a slash (/). Until a standard evolves, any of the above symbols remain acceptable. Do not use anything else, however. Position a breadcrumb trail at the top of the page below any existing navigation links.

A *history list* is a sequential textual listing of sites or pages visited over a specific time period, a session, a day, or some other time period. A *history tree* is an overview map of a site's structure with pages already visited marked by an indicator such as a plus sign, check mark, or asterisk. The markings serve as *footprints*, guiding the user back to pages of interest, and/or signaling which have already been seen and may no longer be of interest. A *bookmark* is similar to a history list except that it is designated by the user to mark locations of continuing interest.

Search Facility

■ Provide a search facility.

Another form of navigation support is provided by a site search facility. Provide such a facility within larger sites. Search facilities were addressed in Step 3.

Web Site Navigation Guidelines

How many links should exist on a page? How should textual links be presented to make them obvious? What kinds of links should be included on a page? These and similar questions are addressed next.

useit.com → Papers and Essays → Heuristic Evaluation → List of Heuristics

IBM developerWorks : Web architecture : Web architecture articles

Weather > Pacific Rim > Australia > Sydney

Figure 4.18   Breadcrumb trails.

Scrolling

- Do not require scrolling of navigation-only pages.
- Minimize the need for scrolling to view all links on pages containing content.
- Never require horizontal scrolling.

Never require scrolling of navigation-only pages. Besides being tedious, not being able to see all links at the same time makes comparison of the alternatives for selection purposes much more difficult. For scrollable content pages, minimize the need to scroll to see all links. Also, ensure that all related links on a screen are seen together to facilitate comparison. Never require horizontal scrolling. It makes text reading difficult and users dislike it.

Number of Links

- Every page should contain at least one link.
- Be conservative in the total number of links presented on a screen:
  — Without logical groupings of elements, limit links to 4 to 8.
  — With logical groupings of elements, limit links to 18 to 24.
- Restrict embedded links to those most important, pertinent, and interesting.
  — Place less relevant links in a listing.

One link. At a minimum, every page should contain at least one link. To follow a path and then reach a dead end is frustrating. Also, a dead-end page, if accessed from another Web site, provides no means for the user to navigate to other site pages.

Conservative number. How many links presented on a page is ultimately determined by the complexity of the site and its content. Menu research indicates that without choice groupings, links should be limited to 4 to 8, with groupings, limited to 18 to 24. Some experts in Web design recommend even fewer, a maximum of 8 to 12 links. In general, the more links contained on a page, the more decisions concerning which link to follow are imposed on the user. Where any link ambiguity exists, the odds of guessing correctly which link to follow diminish. A smaller number of links also increases the likelihood that those being looked for will be noticed. It is not necessary to mention all features of a site on all pages. To reduce the number of links, restrict those presented to the most important site content or useful features.

Embedded links. The trade-off that must be addressed in creating embedded links is linkability versus readability. Embedded links can be a distraction and reduce page readability, especially if used in abundance. They may also be overlooked in text scanning, especially if the scanning is not carefully done. Embedded links, however, can provide more meaningful context, adjacent phrases or sentence words being useful in understanding the link's purpose. The best trade-off is to incorporate embedded links in moderation. Reserve them for the most important, pertinent, and interesting document points. If other relevant content exists, present it in an explicit link listing.

Presenting Links

- Link text:
    - Underline all link text, including that:
        - Embedded in page content.
        - Contained in explicit menu listings.
        - Contained in headings.
        - Used as graphical labels.
    - Distinguish between unselected/unvisited links and selected/visited links.
        - Make unselected/unvisited links blue.
        - Make selected/visited links purple.
- Kinds of links:
    - Distinguish links leading to different Web destinations through a differentiating symbol:
        - Precede links to content within the same page with a pound sign (#).
            - For links moving downward in the page, use: #The principles of design.
            - For links moving upward in the page use: #^ Principles introduction.
        - Precede links to external or foreign sites with another unique symbol such as an asterisk (*): * Additional information.
        - Do not precede links to other site pages with any symbol:
            - More principles of design.
    - Also distinguish links leading to different Web destinations by presenting them in consistent locations.
- Graphical links:
    - Distinguish graphical links from decorative graphics through:
        - Underlining graphical text labels.
- Links in toolbars:
    - Distinguish links contained in toolbars through:
        - Presenting in consistent locations.
        - Using different colored backgrounds.

Links must be easy to find. They must not be confused with other screen graphics or textual content. Having to search for links can be a tedious and frustrating process. Whether a link has been navigated before must also be obvious. When looking for something new, continually embarking down a path already traveled can also be frustrating.

Link text. To identify a link, the well-established convention is to *underline* the link text. All link text must be underlined, including that embedded in page content, that presented in explicit listings, that contained in headings, and that taking the form of labels in graphical images.

Unselected/unvisited links must be *distinguishable* from selected/visited links. The ability to understand what links have been followed is one of the few standard navigational aids available in browsers. Stick with the default colors of *blue* for links already followed and *purple* for links not yet ventured down. While the choice of blue as a text color was poor because of its degraded reading ability it is now well learned. Its use is recommended because it is now very familiar. Using nonstandard link colors can lead to severe problems. It is difficult to remember what color means what, increasing link selection errors. It can also lead to confusion with normal underlined text in a document.

Kinds of links. Visually distinguish links leading to different Web destinations. A link that simply moves within a page, if unknown to the user, can be confusing, leading people to follow a link prematurely. A link that moves to another Web site can be aggravating if the user was not ready to move on. A link's destination should be as predictable as the content at the other end. One way to distinguish these different kinds of links is to precede the link text with a unique symbol if it does not simply lead to a new page within a Web site being viewed. To create distinctiveness, precede links to content *within the same page* with a pound sign (#). For links moving to content downward in the page, use the pound sign by itself. For links moving to content upward in the page use, the pound sign with an upward pointing arrow (#^). For links to *external or foreign* sites, precede the text with another unique symbol such as an asterisk (*). For links to *other site pages*, do not adorn the text with any symbol. A destination convention has yet to be established in Web site design. When one is established, it should be applied.

Designation of different destinations can also be accomplished by grouping links by kind, giving them a descriptive heading, and placing them in unique and consistent *locations* on a page. In the margins, for example, or at the page's top or bottom. Locating within-page links at the page's top would make most sense; locating links to other or foreign sites at the page bottom would be the most logical choice.

Graphical links. If care is not exercised, graphical links may be confused with decorative graphics. A principle of graphical or icon design is to always provide a text label. (See Step 11.) Distinguish graphical links by underlining the graphical text labels, as is done with plain link text.

Links in toolbars. Distinguish links contained in toolbars from page content by presenting the toolbars in consistent locations, and/or displaying them in backgrounds of a contrasting color to the page content. Global toolbars, most often in iconic or button form, are becoming consistently arrayed across the top of a page. Category or topical toolbars are now commonly arrayed down the left side of the page. Toolbars containing textual listings that contrast less with textual page content, can be emphasized and differentiated through presenting them with a background that contrasts with the content.

Some kinds of links to avoid are summarized in Table 4.3.

Other Link Guidelines

In general, many of the principles in menu design presented earlier in this Step, and to be presented in Step 7, also apply to presenting and organizing links. These guidelines should be reviewed in conjunction with this brief summary that follows.

Table 4.3   Links to Avoid (or Links to Aggravate the User)

Orphan Link	A link leading to a page that does not possess any navigation options.
Boomerang Link	A links that returns to the exact same spot.
Gotcha Link	A link that leads to little or no content.
False Alarm Link	A warning to not follow a link you really should follow.
Mystery Link	A link that does not look like a link because it is not properly labeled or does not possess a raised appearance.
Link-mania	Linking every time the same keyword is mentioned in a page.
Link-drunk	A long succession of links that must be followed to reach the destination.
Stairmaster Links	No *Next* link in a series of pages, necessitating continual return to a table of contents.
Gratuitous Link	A link to other sites to return a favor.
Missed opportunities	For useful links.

- Writing:
  — Provide links to satisfy a range of user needs.
  — Create descriptive links clearly indicating their destination or resulting action.
- Grouping:
  — Group links by the most relevant menu-grouping scheme.
  — Separate visually the following types of navigation:
    - Upward to the immediate parent page.
    - Upward to the beginning of the section or category of information.
    - Across to main sections or categories of information.
    - To basic utilities.
- Ordering:
  — Order links by the most relevant menu choice-ordering scheme.
- Heading:
  — Where appropriate, provide a listing heading describing the organizing category, principle, or theme.
- Size:
  — Provide graphical images and command buttons of sufficient and equal size.
- Spacing:
  — Create equal spacing between choices graphical image and textual listing toolbars.
- Inapplicability:
  — Disable and display dimmed links conditionally not applicable.

Writing. People with a *broad range* of needs and interests will use Web sites. Create links to satisfy disparate goals. Redundant links (different links to the same page) may be useful in satisfying these varied needs. A link should be *descriptive*, clearly indicating its destination or resulting action. The success of the link will be dependent on how well the user can predict where the link will lead. Descriptiveness aids prediction. Complete guidelines for writing link text will be found in Step 8.

Grouping. Place links of a similar purpose and function together. Develop groupings using the most relevant grouping scheme. In Web navigation, it useful to visually separate the following types of links: upward to the immediate parent page, upward to the beginning of the presented section or category of information, across to main sections or categories of information, and to basic utilities. People make better link choices when they can readily eliminate wrong links. Grouping helps this process.

Ordering. Arrange the links by the most relevant menu-choice-ordering scheme, such as importance, frequency of use, or sequence of use, as previously described.

Headings. When appropriate, provide an introductory word or phrase at top of the link list as a heading. Inform viewers about the list's organizing category, principle, or theme. Establishing list context will aid users in selecting the correct link.

Size. To achieve balance, create a visually pleasing composition, make all links readily identifiable as links, create icons and command buttons of equal size. The size of any text inscribed on icons or buttons should also be consistent in size. In addition, explicit listings of textual links should be of the same size.

Spacing. To also achieve balance, and a visually pleasing composition, all groups of links composed of icons, command buttons, listings of textual links should be equally spaced.

Inapplicability. Links that are irrelevant in a given situation should be disabled and displayed dimmed out.

Kinds of Links

- Within a page:
  — For long pages, include links to internal page content.
- Within a Web site:
  — On all pages include links to:
    - The Web site home page.
    - Global Web site features.
    - Other main pages, navigation points, or categories.
    - The likely Web site starting point.
    - Main pages with links to the page.
  — On sequential pages, include links to the:
    - Next page.
    - Previous page.
  — Also consider including links to:
    - Places of related interest.
    - Important pages.

- Background or explanatory information.
- Supplemental information.
- New or changed content.
- Web site Quit or Exit.

■ External links:
— Most appropriate for informational sites.
— Provide links to relevant information on other Web sites.
  - Related content.
  - Reference information.
  - Background reading.
— Place external links on a separate page.
— Provide an indication when a link goes outside the current site.

Within a page. For long pages, include links to for important content within the page. Place these links at the top of the page and identify them, by a heading or symbol (see discussion above), as internal links.

Within a Web site, on all pages include the following links:

Home page. A home link will transport the user directly to the site's home page, a stable and safe anchor point to escape to in times of difficulty. Easy access is also achieved when the user is ready to start over, or ready to commence a new navigation. A home link eliminates the necessity for sequential backward movement up through a series of pages.

Global features. Provides links to a site's global features, including the highest level of information categories and utilities such as the Search facility.

Other main pages, navigation points, sections, or categories. Do not link to all sections of the site from all pages; to do so will be overwhelming. To provide easy navigation throughout a site, provide links to a site's major navigation points, sections, or categories of information. Pages linked to must possess substantive content.

MYTH **Why do users need a road map of a Web site. They'll know where to go.**

The likely Web site starting point. Provide links to the site's likely starting point, the home page, a site map, or an index.

Main pages with links to page. Provide links back to the main pages that have links to the displayed page. A return link describing the page one is going back to provides better predictability and much clearer context. It also provides escapability. While the browser's Back button will accomplish the same thing, it does not say what it is going back too, in case the user has forgotten where arrival was from. It also keeps navigation within the application itself (as opposed to the browser).

For *sequential* pages, provide easily accessible links to adjacent pages:

Next. To allow sequential movement downward through pages, place a Next link at the end of each page. Explain, whenever possible, what will happen or where one will go when the link is selected. Without this link, the user will have to continually refer to a table of contents or menu listing to continue navigation. This link will also allow users, should they choose, to leaf through the site as they would a printed book.

Previous. Also include Previous link returning the user to the prior page in the Web site structure, thereby reversing direction in screen navigation. The browser Back button will only return the user to the last page *viewed*. This will facilitate movement through a site for those entering from another Web site into the page. Leafing backward through the page hierarchy will also be easy. Locate this link at the end of the page. For long pages, also include a Previous link at the page top.

Also consider including links such as the following:

Places of related interest. Provide links to other pages with related content. Wherever the user's attention is likely to be captured, provide a direct link to related places. Also, during a search, especially when using a search facility, people rarely land directly on the desired page. Often, however, they get close. Provide links to the answers they are most likely looking for.

Important pages. Provide links to important or high-priority areas or pages you want to make sure the user sees.

Background or explanatory information. Provide links to background or explanatory information to aid users who do not have the necessary knowledge to understand or use the page. Every page must be considered independent, and its content must be understood based upon the assumption that the user has seen no other related pages.

Supplemental information. Use links to provide supplemental information like definitions of terms and abbreviations

New or changed content. Draw attention to new or changed content by making it easy to notice and go directly to. A prominently placed *What's New?* link can be used for this purpose.

Quit or Exit. The Web has no way to stop running an application without closing the browser or leaving by a link. Non-Web platforms have clearly marked exit paths, including a *Quit* or *Exit* on the File Menu. Provide this command so the users can confirm that an application is finished and any entered data should be saved. This command may be included on a special exit page showing external links and other useful information.

Provide *external* links to other relevant Web sites and information sources. There is some evidence that the inclusion of outbound links increases a site's credibility. It indicates that the site authors have done their homework, and they are not afraid to let users visit other sites.

Informational sites. Links to external or foreign sites are most appropriate for informational sites, where browsing is a primary usage purpose. In applications, where a task must be completed, focusing on the task is the most important aspect of design.

Related content. Provide links to relevant information on other Web sites, including sites with similar content to that mentioned in your Web site. Also provide links to other resources, repositories, reference information, and background reading.

Separate page. Whenever possible, locate links that go outside of the Web site on a separate page. To accomplish this, use a *See Also* link to this additional page. Placing these links on a separate page will not disrupt the flow of the displayed pages, and not tempt people to leave the site before they have adequately reviewed it.

Outside indication. Identify links leading away from the site by a heading or a unique symbol (see discussion above). Also inform users that they are leaving the displayed site for another Web site.

Link Maintenance

- Maintain correct internal links.
- Frequently check and correct external links.

As sites are modified, internal links may have to be revised. Carefully check sequential pages if *Next* and *Previous* links are used within the site. External links should also be checked and corrected frequently. Due to the volatile nature of the Web, a linked site's content may change, its location may change, or a site may cease to exist. The credibility of a site's entire content suffers if it is not properly maintained.

Maintaining a Sense of Place

As has been said several times, a sense of place—where one currently is in the labyrinth of the Web—is often difficult to maintain. A site's organizational structure is often complex, and the boundaries between sites often seem nonexistent. Navigation links can transport a person from anywhere to anywhere, as does the *Star Trek* spaceship transporter machine. (While this machine moves humanoids to a new environment, the Web moves the new environment to the humanoid.) These radical shifts in context created by jumping around information space through links can be extremely confusing. It is important that one's location be continually reinforced, because people desire stability and assurance that they are where they think they are. They also need a sense of exactly where they can go from their current location.

Paper documents create a sense of where one is located through a mixture of graphical and textual cues supplied by the design of the book, including the varying fonts and images used. Cues are also provided by the organizational scheme outlined in the table of contents, and the physical sensation of the entire book itself. Looking at where a bookmark is placed in a novel provides an excellent indication of one's location in the reading space. The answers to questions like "Can I finish before the aircraft lands and the business conference starts?" are capable of being predicted with some reliability. Electronic documents provide few of these physical cues. To provide a sense of place, plentiful and explicit cues relating to site context and organization must be provided. These cues are provided by the site's overall design characteristics and the specific orientation elements included within the Web site.

Design Characteristics That Aid in Maintaining a Sense of Place

- To assist maintaining a sense of place within a Web site:
  — Provide a simple hierarchical tree structure.
  — Provide ease of movement to important site features.
- To assist maintaining a sense of place across multiple Web sites:
  — Provide consistency in all Web site design elements, including:
    • Graphical identity schemes.
    • Component presentation.
    • Component organization and location.

Within a Web site. A simple hierarchical tree structure with obvious and linked major categories is an easily understood organization scheme. Easy identification of important site features, and ease of movement to them, is also important.

Across multiple Web sites. Design consistency contributes significantly to maintaining one's sense of place when one is moving between multiple sites. Design consistency gives a site a unique look and feel that becomes obvious as links are followed within it. Moving to a new site will be clearly evident when the design scheme changes. Consistency in the graphical identity scheme, use of colors, patterns, graphics, font styles, and so forth, will be the most noticeable aspects. Consistency in component presentation, organization, and location are also very important.

Design Elements That Aid in Maintaining a Sense of Place

- Provide a home base.
- Use recurring navigation tools on all pages.
- Use recurring elements on all pages.
- Provide page numbers for sequential pages.
- Provide ongoing feedback that shows where users are in a site.
- Provide on-demand aids that illustrate the user's location within a site.
  — Site maps.
  — Table of contents.
- Provide clearly written link labels.

Home base. As previously mentioned, a site's home page is a stable, concrete, and safe anchor point to escape to in times of difficulty.

Recurring navigation tools. Standard navigation tools should appear on every page. In addition to creating uniformity in sight appearance, recurring tools create a more stable page environment, enhance navigation learning, and increase the user's control of the dialog.

Recurring page elements. Repeated page elements, such as titles, banners, logos, and icons, also create site uniformity. Omanson, Cline, Kilpatrick, and Dunkerton (1998) found that the page element that most significantly aided user orientation was the site logo.

Page numbers. For a long series of sequential pages provide page numbers on each page to indicate where in the page string one is located. Another useful feature is to convert page numbers into links and present them on each page. A search, for example, may return a dozen pages of matches. At the bottom of each page inscribe, in link form, page numbers, as follows:

1   2   3   4   5   6   7   8   9   10   11   12

An estimation of document length is obtained, and the pages need not be viewed in sequential order.

Ongoing feedback showing location in Web site. Provide an historical trail, such as a breadcrumb trail, that shows where the user is located within a branch of a site. In addition to providing context for the displayed page, the trail permits easy return to any page up the trail.

On-demand aids illustrating location. Navigation aids, such as a site map or table of contents, when retrieved should show exactly where the user's current location fits within the structure of the site. The current position should be highlighted within the presented information structure. Ideally, in a site map, the complete navigation path from the home page through intermediate pages to the current page should be presented.

Clearly written links. Labels that clearly indicate the function of the link, its destination, or its resulting action, reduce disorientation. Bad links are less likely to be followed and aimless wandering reduced.

Kinds of Graphical Menus

Providing the proper kinds of graphical menus to perform system tasks is also critical to system success. The best kind of menu to use in each situation depends on several factors. The following must be considered:

- The number of items to be presented in the menu.
- How often the menu is used.
- How often the menu contents may change.

Each kind of common graphical menu will be described in terms of purpose, advantages, disadvantages, and suggested proper usage. Design guidelines for each kind are also presented. A proper usage summary for the various kinds of menus will be found in Table 4.4 at the end of the menu discussion.

Menu Bar

- Proper usage:
  — To identify and provide access to common and frequently used application actions that take place in a wide variety of different windows.
  — A menu bar choice by itself should not initiate an action.

The highest-level graphical system menu is commonly called the menu bar. A menu bar consists of a collection of descriptions that serve as headings or titles for a series of actions on an associated pull-down menu. A menu bar choice by itself should not initiate an action.

The menu is typically arrayed in a horizontal row at the top of a window. Occasionally a menu bar is referred to as a collection of menu *titles*. In reality it is a menu in itself, and it is appropriate to simply refer to it as a *menu*. A menu bar is the starting point for many dialogs. Consistency in menu bar design and use will present to the user a stable, familiar, and comfortable starting point for all interactions. Menu bars are most effectively used for presenting common, frequent, or critical actions used on many windows in a variety of circumstances.

Menu bars often consist of a series of textual words, as represented in Figure 4.19. Macintosh, Presentation Manager, and Microsoft Windows illustrate examples of this textual approach. Some products have placed the choices within buttons, as represented in Figure 4.20. An example of this approach is Sun Microsystems' Open Look, which calls them *menu buttons*. There are also combinations of both. OSF/Motif presents a list of textual choices, but when one is selected, it resembles a button. Motif refers to these as *cascade buttons*.

Each menu bar item is the top level of a hierarchical menu. It will have a pull-down menu associated with it, detailing the specific actions that may be performed. Some products have tried to circumvent this pull-down rule and have included items in menu bars that are direct actions themselves. These direct action items have frequently been designated by an exclamation point (!) following the menu bar description. The inclusion of direct items in a menu bar should be avoided. It creates inconsistency in menu bar use and may easily cause an action to be erroneously selected. Menu bars should always possess an associated pull-down menu.

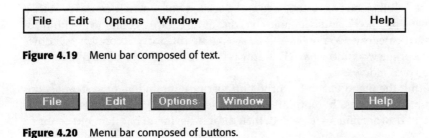

| File | Edit | Options | Window | | Help |

Figure 4.19   Menu bar composed of text.

Figure 4.20   Menu bar composed of buttons.

Menu bars are used to present application alternatives or choices to the screen user. Typically, each system provides a default set of menu bar commands (for example, File, Edit, View, Window, Help).

The *advantages* of menu bars are that they:

- Are always visible, reminding the user of their existence.
- Are easy to browse through.
- Are easy to locate consistently on the screen.
- Usually do not obscure the screen working area.
- Usually are not obscured by windows and dialog boxes.
- Allow for use of keyboard equivalents.

The *disadvantages* of menu bars are that:

- They consume a full row of screen space.
- They require looking away from the main working area to find.
- They require moving pointer from the main working area to select.
- The menu options are smaller than full-size buttons, slowing selection time.
- Their horizontal orientation is less efficient for scanning.
- Their horizontal orientation limits number of choices that can be displayed.

Display

- All primary windows must have a menu bar.
- All menu bars must have an associated pull-down menu containing at least two choices.
- Do not allow the user to turn off the display of the menu bar.
- If all the items in its associated pull-down menu are disabled, then disable the menu bar item.
  — Display the disabled item in a visually subdued manner.
  — However, the disabled pull-down menu must always be capable of being pulled-down so that the choices may be seen.

All primary windows must have a menu bar. Because a menu bar choice should not initiate an action, all menu bars must have an associated pull-down menu with at least two choices. If a planned menu bar choice has one or no choices, combine it within another menu bar category. Do not leave it as a separate category. Secondary windows may use their primary window bar. (Window types are described in Step 5 "Select the Proper Kinds of Windows.")

Never permit the menu bar to be turned off, because reminders of system actions will be eliminated and possibly forgotten by inexperienced users. If all the items in its associated pull-down menu are disabled, then disable the menu bar item but continue to display it in a visually subdued manner. The disabled pull-down menu must always be capable of being pulled down so that the choices may be seen. This will facilitate system exploration and learning.

Location

- Position choices horizontally over the entire row at the top of the screen, just below the screen title.
- A large number of choices may necessitate display over two rows.

Choices should be positioned horizontally across the top of the screen below the screen title. A typical bar is composed of no more than about seven or eight choices. Due to screen space constraints, and limitations in human information-processing capabilities, a maximum of seven or eight is reasonable. In the event that more are needed, a second line of choices may be added. Try to avoid a second line, however.

Title

- The window title will be the menu bar title.

The window title will serve as the menu bar title.

Item Descriptions

- The menu item descriptions must clearly reflect the kinds of choices available in the associated pull-down menus.
- Menu item descriptions will be the "titles" for pull-down menus associated with them.
- Use mixed-case letters to describe choices.
- Use single-word choices whenever possible.
- Do not display choices that are never available to the user.

The menu item descriptions must clearly reflect alternatives available in the associated pull-down menus. Choices should be composed of mixed-case single words. Typically, only the first letter of the choice is capitalized. Acronyms, abbreviations, or proper nouns that are normally capitalized may be capitalized. Choices should never be numbered.

If a multiple-word item must be used for clarity, consider including a hyphen between the multiple words to associate the words and differentiate them from other items. Do not display choices that are never available to the user.

Organization

- Follow standard platform ordering schemes where they exist.
  — Place application-specific choices where they fit best.

- Order choices left-to-right with:
  — Most frequent choices to the left.
  — Related information grouped together.
- Choices found on more than one menu bar should be consistently positioned.
- Left-justify choices within the line.
- When choices can be logically grouped, provide visual logical groupings, if possible.
- Help, when included, should be located at the right side of the bar.

Figure 4.21

File Edit Options Window	Help

Follow standard platform ordering schemes where they exist. Place application-specific choices where they fit best. Order all choices left-to-right, with the most frequently elected choices to the left and related information grouped together. Choices found on more than one menu bar should be consistently positioned.

Left-justify all choices within the line (as opposed to centering them when there are not enough choices to completely fill the line). However, always locate Help, when included, at the far right side. Right side positioning will always keep Help in a consistent location within the bar. Also, provide visual groupings of all related choices, if space on the bar permits.

Layout

- Indent the first choice one space from the left margin.
- Leave at least three spaces between each of the succeeding choices (except for Help which will be right-justified).
- Leave one space between the final choice and the right margin.

Figure 4.22

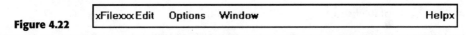

xFilexxxEdit Options Window	Helpx

The spacing recommendations above are intended to provide clear delineation of choices, leave ample room for the selection cursor, provide a legible selected choice, and provide efficiency in bar design.

Separation

- Separate the bar from the remainder of the screen by:
  — A different background, or
  — Solid lines above and below.

In addition to being identified by its location at the top, the bar should be identifiable by a contrasting display technique. The most effective way to do this is through the use of a different background, either reversed polarity (black on white for the bar, con-trasted with white on black for the screen body), or a color different from the adjacent title and screen body. When a color is used, it must be chosen in conjunction with good color principles in Step 12. Affecting the background color choice will be the fore-ground or choice description color, the selection indicator to be described next, and the screen body background color. The contrast of the bar to the remainder of the screen should be moderate, neither too vivid nor too subtle.

Other Components

- Keyboard equivalent mnemonics should be included on menu bars.
- Keyboard accelerators, to a window indicators, and cascade indicators need not be included.

While keyboard mnemonics should be included on menu bars, keyboard accelera-tors and other intent indicators should not because a menu bar selection will always lead to a pull-down menu.

Selection Indication

- Keyboard cursor:
  — Use a reverse video, or reverse color, selection cursor to surround the choice.
  — Cover the entire choice, including one blank space before and after the choice word.

File	Edit	Options	Window		Help

Figure 4.23

- Pointer:
  — Use reverse video, or reverse color, to highlight the selected choice.

When using the keyboard, the selection cursor should be indicated by a contrasting reverse video or reverse color bar surrounding the choice. The cursor should extend at least one space to each side of the choice word. When using a pointer, use a reverse video or reverse color to highlight the choice when it is selected.

The recommended reverse color combination is simply to reverse the foreground and background colors of the unselected choices. Colors chosen must be those that are completely legible in either polarity. Some good combinations would include: black-white, blue-white, and black-cyan. Other contrasting color combinations may, of course, also be used. Since limitations exist in the number of colors that may be used on a screen, however, the colors chosen for menu bars must be selected in conjunction with the colors of other screen components. Since a menu bar can be identified by its lo-cation, the use of a completely different color to identify it can be redundant and un-necessary. It is more practical to reserve the use of color for other less identifiable screen components.

Pull-Down Menu

■ Proper usage:
— To initiate frequently used application actions that take place on a wide variety of different windows.
— A small number of items.
— Items best represented textually.
— Items whose content rarely changes.

Selection of an alternative from the menu bar results in the display of the exact actions available to the user. These choices are displayed in a vertically arrayed listing that appears to pull down from the bar. Hence, these listings, as illustrated in Figure 4.24, are typically referred to as *pull-downs*. Other identification terms may be used, such as *drop-downs*.

Pull-downs are first-level menus used to provide access to common and frequently used application actions that take place on a wide variety of different windows. They are most useful for a small number of rarely changing items, usually about 5 to 10. Larger numbers of choices become awkward to use, being best handled by incorporating cascade menus (see discussion that follows). Pull-downs are best suited for items represented textually, but graphical presentations, such as colors, patterns, and shades, may also be used.

The *advantages* of pull-down menus are:

■ The menu bar cues a reminder of their existence.

■ They may be located relatively consistently on the screen.

■ No window space is consumed when they are not used.

■ They are easy to browse through.

■ Their vertical orientation is most efficient for scanning.

■ Their vertical orientation is most efficient for grouping.

■ Their vertical orientation permits more choices to be displayed.

■ They allow for display of both keyboard equivalents and accelerators.

The *disadvantages* of pull-down menus are:

■ They require searching and selecting from another menu before seeing options.

■ They require looking away from main working area to read.

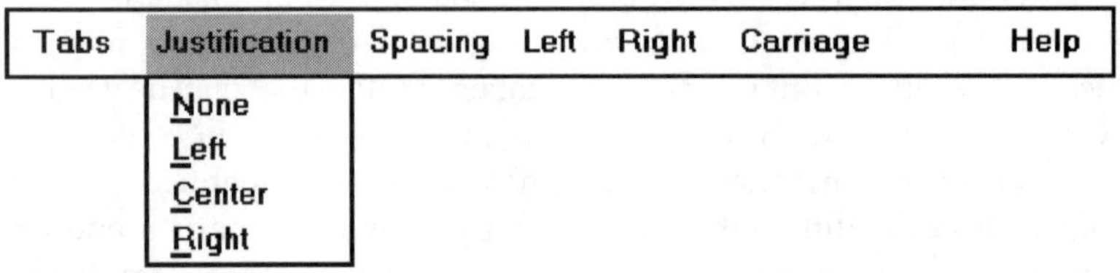

Tabs	Justification	Spacing	Left	Right	Carriage	Help
	None					
	Left					
	Center					
	Right					

Figure 4.24   Menu bar pull-down.

- The require moving the pointer out of working area to select (unless using keyboard equivalents).
- The items are smaller than full-size buttons, slowing selection time.
- The may obscure the screen working area.

Display

- Display all possible alternatives.
- Gray-out or dim items that cannot be chosen due to the current state of an application.

Display all possible alternatives on a pull-down. Gray-out or dim items that cannot be chosen due to the current state of an application. If all items are, at any one point, not applicable, they must still be capable of being retrieved for perusal through the menu bar.

Location

- Position the pull-down directly below the selected menu bar choice.

The pull-down will be located directly below the menu bar choice by which it is selected.

Size

- Must contain a minimum of two choices.
- Restrict to no more than 5 to 10 choices, preferably 8 or less.

A typical pull-down consists of about 5 to 10 choices, although more or less are sometimes seen. A pull-down should always contain more than one choice. Because of their vertical orientation, there is space for more choices containing longer descriptions than on a menu bar, and they can easily be positioned on one screen.

Title

- Not necessary on a pull-down menu. The title will be the name of the menu bar item chosen.

The name of the item chosen on the menu bar serves as the title of a pull-down menu.

Item Descriptions

- Use mixed-case, headline-style words to describe choices.
  - If the choices can be displayed graphically, for example, as fill-in patterns, shades, or colors, textual descriptions are not necessary.
- Do not:
  - Identify a menu item by the same wording as its menu title.
  - Change the meaning of menu items through use of the Shift key.
  - Use scrolling in pull-downs.
  - Place instructions in pull-downs.

Choices should be composed of mixed-case, headline-style words. For multiword choice descriptions, capitalize the first letter of each significant word. Acronyms, abbreviations, or proper nouns that are normally capitalized may be capitalized. If the choices can be displayed graphically, such as fill-in patterns, shades, or colors, textual descriptions are not necessary.

Never identify a pull-down menu item by the same wording as its menu bar title. The menu bar title must reflect all the items within the pull-down. Never change the meaning of items through use of the Shift key. Shift key activations are extremely error-prone, and their use should be reserved for key accelerators. Also, do not use scrolling in, or place instructions within, a pull-down.

Organization

- Follow standard platform ordering schemes when they exist.
  - Place application-specific choices where they fit best.
- Place frequent or critical items at the top.
- Separate destructive choices from other choices.
- Align choices into columns, with:
  - Most frequent choices toward the top.
  - Related choices grouped together.
  - Choices found on more than one pull-down consistently positioned.
- Left-align choice descriptions.
- Multicolumn menus are not desirable. If necessary, organize top-to-bottom, then left-to-right.

Follow standard platform ordering schemes when they exist. Place application-specific choices where they fit best. Place frequent or critical items at the top of the listing, and separate destructive choices from other choices. Align all pull-down choices into columns with their descriptions left-aligned. Locate most frequently chosen alternatives toward the top, and group related choices together. Choices found on more than one pull-down should be consistently positioned. Multicolumn menus are not desirable; if necessary, organize pull-downs from top-to-bottom, then left-to-right.

Layout

- Leave the menu bar choice leading to the pull-down highlighted in the selected manner (reverse video or reverse color).
- Physically, the pull-down menu must be wide enough to accommodate the longest menu item description and its cascade or accelerator indicator.
- Align the first character of the pull-down descriptions under the second character of the applicable menu bar choice.
- Horizontally, separate the pull-down choice descriptions from the pull-down borders by two spaces on the left side and at least two spaces on the right side.
  — The left-side border will align with the left side of the highlighted menu bar choice.
  — The right-side border should extend, at minimum, to the right side of its highlighted menu bar choice.

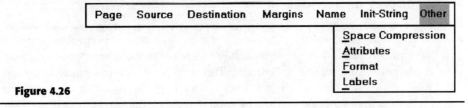

Tabs	Justification	Spacing	Left	Right	Carriage	Help
	None					
	Left					
	Center					
	Right					

Figure 4.25

  — Pull-downs for choices on the far right side of the menu bar, or long pull-down descriptions, may require alignment to the left of their menu bar choice to maintain visibility and clarity.

Page	Source	Destination	Margins	Name	Init-String	Other
						Space Compression
						Attributes
						Format
						Labels

Figure 4.26

The menu bar choice leading to the pull-down should remain highlighted in the selected manner. Columnized pull-down descriptions should be aligned beginning under the second character position of the applicable bar choice. Pull-down borders should be positioned for balance and for maximum legibility and clarity of the choice descriptions. Leave two spaces to the left of the descriptions to align the left pull-down border with the left border of the selected menu bar choice. Leave a minimum of two spaces after the longest description and the right pull-down border. At the minimum, the right pull-down border should extend to the right border of the highlighted menu bar choice. Menu bar choices located at the far right, or long pull-down choice descriptions, may require alignment to the left of the applicable choice, however.

Groupings

- Provide groupings of related pull-down choices:
  - — Incorporate a solid line between major groupings.
  - — Incorporate a dotted or dashed line between subgroups.
  - — Left-justify the lines under the first letter of the columnized choice descriptions.
  - — Right-justify the lines under the last character of the longest choice description.
  - — Display the solid line in the same color as the choice descriptions.

Figure 4.27

Indicate groupings of related choices by inscribing a line between each group. The line, or lines, should only extend from the first character of the descriptions to the end of the longest description, as shown above.

Some common style guides recommend that the line extend from pull-down border to border. Many other system pull-downs also follow this border-to-border approach. This extended line, however, results in too strong a visual separation between pull-down parts. The parts should be separated but not too strongly.

Mark Toggles or Settings

- If a menu item establishes or changes the attributes of data or properties of the interface, mark the pull-down choice or choices whose state is current or active "on."
  - — For nonexclusive items, display a check mark to the left of the item description.
    - • If the two states of a setting are not obvious opposites, a pair of alternating menu item descriptions should be used to indicate the two states.
  - — For exclusive choices, precede the choice with a contrasting symbol such as a diamond or circle.

If a menu item is made permanently active or "on" when selected, this can be made clear to the user by providing a mark by the item. For nonexclusive or independent items, display a check mark to the left of the item description. For exclusive or interdependent choices, precede the choice with a different and contrasting symbol such as a diamond or circle. Microsoft Windows indicates active choices of this nature with an *option button mark.*

If a setting containing two states does not consist of clear and obvious opposites, a pair of alternating menu item descriptions should be used to indicate the two states.

Pull-Downs Leading to Another Pull-Down

■ If a pull-down choice leads to another pull-down, provide a cascade indicator as fol-
lows:
— Place an arrow or right-pointing triangle after the choice description.
— Align the triangles to the right side of the pull-down.
— Display the triangle in the same color as the choice descriptions.

Figure 4.28

Occasionally a secondary or second level pull-down (or cascading pull-down, as it
is frequently called) may be desirable if the first pull-down leads to another short series
of choices. Or, it may be desirable if the first pull-down has a large number of choices
that are capable of being logically grouped. The existence of this second-level, hidden
pull-down should be indicated to the user on the first pull-down in a consistent manner. A simple way to do this is to include a right-pointing triangle to the right of the applicable choice description. These triangles should be aligned to the right side of the
pull-down.

Pull-Downs Leading to a Window

■ For pull-down choices leading to a window:
— Place an ellipsis (three dots) after the choice description.
— Do not separate the dots from the description by a space.
— Display the ellipsis in the same color as the choice descriptions.

Figure 4.29

When a window results from the selection of a pull-down choice, a visual indication
of this fact is desirable. An ellipsis inscribed after the choice description is a good indicator that a window will appear.

Keyboard Equivalents and Accelerators

■ Provide unique mnemonic codes by which choices may be selected through the
typewriter keyboard.
— Indicate the mnemonic code by underlining the proper character.

■ Provide key accelerators for choice selection.
   — Identify the keys by their actual key-top engravings.
   — Use a plus (+) sign to indicate that two or more keys must be pressed at the same time.
   — Enclose the key names within parentheses ( ).
   — Right-align the key names, beginning at least three spaces to the right of the longest choice description.
   — Display the key alternatives in the same color as the choice descriptions.

<u>F</u>ind...	(Ctrl+F)
Find <u>N</u>ext	(F3)
Find Pre<u>v</u>ious	(Shift+F3)
<u>R</u>eplace...	(Ctrl+R)

Figure 4.30

Enabling the user to select pull-down choices through the keyboard provides flexibility and efficiency in the dialogue. One method of doing this is to provide single-character mnemonic codes that, when typed, will also cause the choice to be invoked. Mnemonic codes can be visually indicated in a number of ways. The recommended method is an underline beneath the proper character within the choice. Standard mnemonic codes for common commands were listed in Table 4.1.

Another method is to assign accelerators (one key, or a combination of keys) to accomplish the action. Identify these keys exactly as they are engraved on the keyboard; indicate simultaneous depression through use of a plus sign, and right-align the accelerator description and position it to the right of the choice description. Accelerators should be reserved for the most common commands. Standard accelerators are listed in Table 4.2.

Separation

■ Separate the pull-down from the remainder of the screen, but visually relate it to the menu bar by:
   — Using a background color the same as the menu bar.
   — Displaying choice descriptions in the same color as the menu bar.
   — Incorporating a solid-line border completely around the pull-down in the same color as the choice descriptions.
■ A drop shadow (a heavier shaded line along two borders that meet) may also be included.

In addition to being identified by its position below the menu bar, the pull-down should visually relate to the menu bar and also visually contrast with the screen body. The most effective way to do this is to use the same foreground and background colors that are used on the menu bar but ensure that these colors adequately contrast with the screen body background. Because good contrasting background colors are often limited, a solid-line border of the same color as the choice descriptions will clearly delineate the pull-down border. A drop shadow, when included, will give the pull-down a three-dimensional effect.

Selection Cursor

■ Use a reverse video, or reverse color, selection cursor the same color as the menu bar to surround the choice.

■ Create a consistently sized cursor as wide as the pull-down menu.

Figure 4.31

The selection cursor should be a contrasting reverse video or reverse color bar of a consistent size encompassing the selected choice. The reverse color combination should be the same as the one that appears within the menu bar. Create a consistently sized cursor as wide as the pull-down menu.

Cascading Menus

■ Proper usage:
  — To reduce the number of choices presented together for selection (reduce menu breadth).
  — When a menu specifies many alternatives and the alternatives can be grouped in meaningful related sets on a lower-level menu.
  — When a choice leads to a short, fixed list of single-choice properties.
  — When there are several fixed sets of related options.
  — To simplify a menu.
  — Avoid using for frequent, repetitive commands.

A cascading menu is a submenu derived from a higher-level menu, most typically a pull-down. Cascades may also be attached to other cascades or pop-up menus, however. Cascading menus are located to the right of the menu item on the previous menu to which they are related, as illustrated in Figure 4.32. Menu items that lead to cascading menus are typically indicated by a right-pointing triangle.

Cascading menus are developed to simplify menus by reducing the number of choices that appear together on one menu. Cascades can be used when many alternatives exist that can be grouped meaningfully. The top-level menu may contain the grouping category headings and the cascaded menu the items in each group. Any menu choices with a fixed set of related options may utilize cascades.

The *advantages* of cascading menus are that:

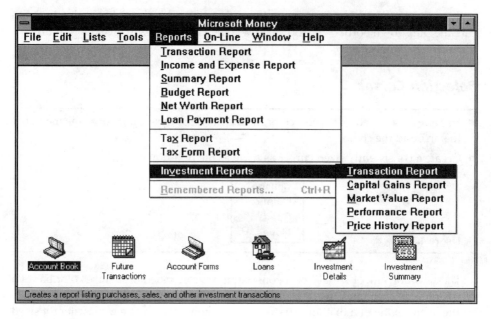

Figure 4.32 Cascading menu.

- The top-level menus are simplified because some choices are hidden.
- More first-letter mnemonics are available because menus possess fewer alternatives.
- High-level command browsing is easier because subtopics are hidden.

The *disadvantages* of cascading menus are:

- Access to submenu items requires more steps.
- Access to submenu items requires a change in pointer movement direction.
- Exhaustive browsing is more difficult; some alternatives remain hidden as pull-downs become visible.

Changing pointer movement from a vertically oriented menu such as a pull-down to an adjacent cascade is an error-prone manual movement. Sliding the mouse and its pointer horizontally is not a very precise hand movement. As the pointer moves horizontally across the menu from which the cascade is selected it has a tendency to move vertically as well, sometimes exiting the menu over an item above or below the desired choice. When this occurs in Microsoft Windows the cascade displayed is not the one desired, but the cascade for the adjacent choice over which the pointer exited. The wrong cascade is then presented to the user, and the selection process must be repeated. Apple minimizes this problem by presenting a movement "cone" for the selected choice. This cone gradually widens as it approaches the cascade, extending somewhat over the adjacent choices. If the mouse and pointer exit the menu within an adjacent choice, but still within this cone, the originally designated cascade is still presented. The Apple solution is much more understanding of human motor limitations.

Cascade Indicator

- Place an arrow or right-pointing triangle to the right of each menu choice description leading to a cascade menu.
- Separate the indicator from the choice description by one space.
- Display the indicator in the same color as the choice descriptions.

Figure 4.33

To indicate that another lower-level menu will appear when a menu item is selected, place an arrow or right-pointing triangle immediately to its right. Display the cascade indicator in the same color as the choice descriptions.

Location

- Position the first choice in the cascading menu immediately to the right of the selected choice.
- Leave the choice leading to the cascading menu highlighted.

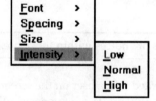

Figure 4.34

Cascading menus should be positioned so that the first choice in the cascading menu is immediately to the right of the selected choice. The choice leading to the cascade should remain highlighted in some way so that the cascade path is obvious.

Levels

- Do not exceed three menu levels (two cascades).
  — Only one cascading menu is preferred.

Each additional cascade level presented reduces ease of access and increases visual clutter. The number of cascade levels presented should represent a balance between menu simplification, ease in menu comprehension, and ease in item selection. Whenever possible, do not exceed three levels of menus (original and two cascades). Try to limit cascades to one. If too many cascade levels are derived, create additional pull-down menus, or provide a window for some alternatives. A window is useful for establishing independent settings or the setting of multiple options. A toolbar may also be used to eliminate the necessity for traversing cascades.

Title

- Not necessary on the cascading menu.
  — The title will be the name of the higher-level menu item chosen.

The title of the cascading menu will be the choice selected on the menu from which it cascades.

Other Guidelines

- Follow the organization, content, layout, separation, and selection cursor guidelines for the kind of menu from which the menu cascades.

The design of a cascade menu should follow all relevant guidelines for the family of menus to which it belongs. Included are organization, content, layout, and selection cursor.

Pop-up Menus

- Use to present alternatives or choices within the context of the task.

Choices may also be presented to the user on the screen through *pop-up* menus, vertically arrayed listings that only appear when specifically requested. Pop-up menus may be requested when the mouse pointer is positioned over a designated or *hot* area of the screen (a window border or text, for example) or over a designated icon. In look, they usually resemble pull-down menus, as shown in Figure 4.35.

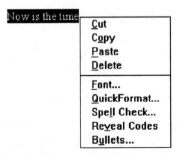

Figure 4.35 Pop-up menu.

The kinds of choices displayed in pop-up menus are context sensitive, depending on where the pointer is positioned when the request is made. They are most useful for presenting alternatives within the context of the user's immediate task. If positioned over text, for example, a pop-up might include text-specific commands.

The *advantages* of pop-up menus are:

- They appear in the working area.
- They do not use window space when not displayed.
- No pointer movement is needed if selected by button.
- Their vertical orientation is most efficient scanning.
- Their vertical orientation most efficient for grouping.
- Their vertical orientation allows more choices to be displayed.
- They may be able to remain showing ("pinned") when used frequently.
- They allow for display of both keyboard equivalents and accelerators.

The *disadvantages* of pop-up menus are:

- Their existence must be learned and remembered.
- Means for selecting them must be learned and remembered.
- They require a special action to see the menu (mouse click).
- Items are smaller than full-size buttons, slowing selection time.
- They may obscure the screen working area.
- Their display locations may not be consistent.

For experienced users, pop-up menus are an alternative to retrieve frequently used contextual choices in pull-down menus. Choices should be limited in number and stable or infrequently changing in content.

Windows contains many contextual pop-up menus. They are also referred to as *context menus* or *shortcut menus*. Examples include the *window pop-up* and an *icon pop-up*, which presents operations of the objects represented by icons.

Display

- Provide a pop-up menu for common, frequent, contextual actions.
  - If the pointer is positioned over an object possessing more than one quality (for example, both text and graphics), at minimum present actions common to all object qualities.
- Items that cannot be chosen due to the current state of an application should not be displayed.
- Continue to display a pop-up until:
  - A choice is selected.
  - An action outside the pop-up is initiated.
  - The user removes the pop-up.

Provide a pop-up menu for common, frequent, contextual actions. If the pointer is positioned over an object possessing more than one quality (for example, both text and graphics), at minimum present actions common to all object qualities. Items that cannot be chosen due to the current state of an application should not be displayed.

Continue to display a pop-up until the user selects a choice, initiates an action outside the pop-up, or requests that the pop-up be removed.

Location

- Position the pop-up:
  - Centered and to the right of the object from which it was requested.
  - Close enough to the pointer so that the pointer can be easily moved onto the menu.
  - But not so close that the pointer is positioned on an item, possibly leading to accidental selection.
- If the pointer is positioned in such a manner that the pop-up would appear off-screen or clipped, position the menu:
  - As close as possible to the object, but not covering the object.
  - So that it appears fully on the screen.

Position a pop-up menu in a consistent location relative to the object from which it is requested. The preferable location is centered to the right. Locate the pop-up close enough to the pointer so that the pointer can be easily moved onto the menu. Positioning of the pointer on the menu itself could lead to accidental selection of an action.

If the pointer is positioned in such a manner that a right-centered position would force the pop-up partially or fully off the screen, locate the pop-up fully on the screen as close as possible to the object. Do not move the pointer to make a menu fit in the most desirable location.

Size

- Restrict the pop-up to no more than 5 to 10 choices, preferably 8 or less.

Limit pop-up menus to about eight choices or fewer. If a large number of choices are needed, consider creating cascading menus. Minimize the number of levels of cascades, however, to provide ease of access and prevent visual clutter.

Title

- Not necessary on a pop-up menu.
- If included, clearly describe the menu's purpose.
- Locate in a centered position at the top.

- Display in uppercase or mixed-case letters.
- Separate it from the menu items by a line extending from the left menu border to the right border.

A title is not necessary on a pop-up menu, since it is an expert feature. Some graphical platforms include titles, others do not. Microsoft Windows does not. If a title is included, it should clearly reflect the menu's purpose. This will avoid any possible confusion that may occur if the wrong menu is accidentally selected and displayed. The title should be set off from the item descriptions by using uppercase letters or mixed-case letters in the headline style.

Other Guidelines

- Arrange logically organized and grouped choices into columns.
- If items are also contained in pull-down menus, organize pop-up menus in the same manner.
- Left-align choice descriptions.
- Use mixed-case headline-style words to describe choices.
- Separate groups with a solid line the length of the longest choice description.
- If the choice leads to a pop-up window, place an ellipsis after the choice description.
- To separate the pop-up from the screen background:
  — Use a contrasting, but complementary background.
  — Incorporate a solid line border around the pull-down.

Follow the same menu guidelines as for pull-down menus regarding organization, content, layout, separation, and selection cursor.

Tear-off Menus

- Follow all relevant guidelines for pull-down menus.

A tear-off menu is a pull-down menu that can be positioned anywhere on the screen for constant referral. As such, it possesses all the characteristics of a pull-down. It may also be called a *pushpin, detachable,* or *roll-up* menu. Its purpose is to present alternatives or choices to the screen user that are needed infrequently at some times and heavily at other times.

Advantages/disadvantages. No space is consumed on the screen when the menu is not needed. When needed, it can remain continuously displayed. It does require extra steps to retrieve, and it may obscure the screen working area.

Tear-off menus are most useful for expert users. Use these menus in situations where the items are sometimes frequently selected and other times infrequently selected. Items

Figure 4.36   Iconic menu (from Microsoft Windows).

should be small in number and rarely change in content. A typical use would be to detach and permanently leave displayed a pull-down menu when it must be frequently used.

Since a tear-off menu is a pull-down style, all pull-down guidelines should be followed.

Iconic Menus

- Use to remind users of the functions, commands, attributes, or application choices available.
- Create icons that:
  — Help enhance recognition and hasten option selection.
  — Are concrete and meaningful.
  — Clearly represent choices.

An iconic menu is the portrayal of menu items or objects in a graphic or pictorial form, as illustrated in Figure 4.36.

The purpose of an iconic menu is to remind users of the functions, commands, attributes, or application choices available.

Advantages/disadvantages. Pictures help facilitate memory of applications, and their larger size increases speed of selection. Pictures do, however, consume considerably more screen space than text, and they are difficult to organize for scanning efficiency. To create meaningful icons requires special skills and an extended amount of time. Iconic menus should be used to designate applications or special functions within an application. Icons must be meaningful and clear. They should help enhance recognition and hasten option selection. See Step 11 for a complete review of icon design guidelines.

Pie Menus

- Consider using for:
  — Mouse-driven selections, with one- or two-level hierarchies, short lists, and choices conducive to the format.

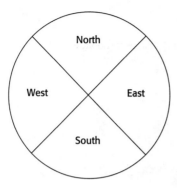

Figure 4.37 Pie menu.

A pie menu is a circular representation of menu items, as illustrated in Figure 4.37, that can be used as an alternative to a pull-down or pop-up menu. Research has found that this style of menu yields higher performance than the typical vertical array, especially when the menu tasks are unrelated. Their basic advantage is that, when presented with the mouse pointer positioned in the pie's center, average movement to any pie wedge is shorter. Mayhew (1992) concludes that pie menus might work well for mouse-driven selections with one- or two-level hierarchies, short choice listings, and data conducive to the format. Performance advantages for keyboard selection are doubtful, however.

Default Menu Items

Every system will provide a set of standard menu items. Using the default items will reduce design time and encourage interface consistency. System learning time will also be reduced. Microsoft Windows, for example, provides the following standard and optional menu bar items and pull-down actions. Always follow industry standards for naming, menu bar choices, ordering, and keyboard equivalents and accelerators.

File

A standard element, the File menu provides all the commands needed to open, create, and save files. Some standard File functions are:

- New
- Open
- Close
- Save
- Save As
- Print Preview
- Print
- Exit

Edit

A standard element, the Edit menu provides commands that affect the state of selected objects. Some standard Edit functions are:

- Undo
- Cut
- Copy
- Paste
- Select All
- Find
- Replace

View

An optional element, the View menu provides commands that affect the perspective, details, and appearance of the application. They affect the view, not the data itself. The view functions are application-specific and include the following:

- Toolbars
- Status Bar
- Magnify
- Zoom In
- Zoom Out
- Grid Points

Window

The Window menu, an optional element, provides commands to manipulate entire windows. Included are items such as:

- New Window
- Arrange All
- Hide
- Show

Help

The Help menu, a standard element, provides Help commands, including:

- Contents
- Search for Help On
- How to Use Help
- About (Application)

Table 4.4 Menu Proper Usage Summary

Menu Bar	To identify and provide access to: • Common and frequently used application actions. • Actions that take place in a wide variety of different windows.
Pull-Down Menu	For frequently used application actions that take place in a wide variety of different windows: • A small number of items (5–10). • Items rarely changing in content.
Cascading Menu	To simplify a higher-level menu. To provide easier browsing of a higher-level menu. For mutually exclusive choices. Restrict to 1–2 cascades.
Pop-Up Menu	For: • Frequent users. • Frequently used contextual commands. • A small number of items (5–10). • Items rarely changing in content. • Items that require a small amount of screen space.
Tear-Off Menu	For items: • Sometimes frequently selected. • Sometimes infrequently selected. • Small in number (5–10). • Rarely changing in content.
Iconic Menu	To designate applications available. To designate special functions within an application.

These standard menu items also have a prescribed order on the menu bar: File, Edit, View, Window, and Help. Items on their related pull-down menus also follow standard orders.

Standard menus and items should always be used when creating an application. Refer to a system's design documentation for exact details concerning what menu items are available and how they are used.

Functions Not Represented by Default Items

Having established the usability of the standard menu functions, additional system functions must be identified. Commands to accomplish these functions must be created and added to the pertinent menus. Command design guidelines include the following.

Labels

- General:
  - Provide a label for each command.
  - Use labels that indicate:
    - The purpose of the command, or
    - The result of what happens when the command is selected.
  - Use familiar, short, clear, concise words.
  - Use distinctive wording.
  - Use mixed case, with the first letter capitalized.
  - Begin commands with verbs or adjectives, not nouns.
  - Preferably, use only one word.
    - If multiple words are required for clarity, capitalize the first letter of each significant word.
    - Do not use sentences as labels.
  - Provide an ellipsis (. . .) to indicate that another window will result from selection of a command.
    - Do not use the ellipsis when the following window is a confirmation or warning.
- Dynamic labels:
  - As contexts change, dynamically change the label wording to make its meaning clearer in the new context.
    - For example, after a cut operation, Undo may be changed to Undo Cut.

Provide a clear label for each command, indicating the purpose of the command or the result of what happens when the command is selected. Preferably, use single-word commands. If multiple words are required for clarity, capitalize the first letter of each significant word. Provide an ellipsis to indicate that another window will result from selection of a command, but do not use the ellipsis when the resulting window is a confirmation or warning. As contexts change, the label wording may be dynamically changed to make its meaning clearer in the new context. For example, after a cut operation, Undo may be changed to Undo Cut. This is called a *toggled menu item* and was previously described.

Disabled Commands

- When a command is not available, indicate its disabled status by displaying it grayed out or subdued.
- If selection of a disabled command is attempted, provide a message in the information area that the "Help" function will explain why it is disabled.

When a command is not available, indicate its disabled status by displaying it grayed out or subdued. If selection of a disabled command is attempted, provide a message in the information area that the Help function will explain why it is disabled. Help, of course, must provide the proper explanation.

Navigation and Selection

- General:
  — Permit multiple methods for selecting commands.
- Keyboard equivalents:
  — Assign a mnemonic for each command.
  — A mnemonic should be as meaningful as possible. Use:
    • The first letter of the command, or if duplications exist,
    • The first letter of another word in the command, or
    • Another significant consonant in the command.
  — For standard commands, use mnemonics provided by the tool set.
- Keyboard accelerators:
  — Assign keyboard accelerators for frequently used commands.
  — For standard commands, use keyboard accelerators provided by the tool set.

Permit commands to be implemented through the keyboard as well. Provide keyboard equivalents or accelerators. Finally, the menus needed must be designed following principles of effective menu design earlier in this chapter.

Graphical Menu Examples

What follows are examples of poor and proper menu design.

Example 1

An improperly presented menu bar and pull-down.

Menu 1.1

What are the problems in the way this menu bar and pull-down menu are presented? (1) Keyboard mnemonics are designated by capital letters. Note the uncommon shape of "foRmat," "cuT," and "clEar" when the mnemonic is not the first letter of the word. (2) Item groupings do not exist in the pull-down. The differences in basic functions are not obvious, and the more destructive operations (Undo, Clear, and Delete) are positioned close to standard actions, increasing the potential for accidental selection. (3) The keyboard accelerators are adjacent to the choice descriptions and not set off in any way. Therefore, these alternate, and supplemental, actions visually compete with choice descriptions for the viewer's attention.

```
                    OFFICE SYSTEM
  File    Edit    foRmat    View    Options                Help
          Undo      Ctrl+Z

          cuT       Ctrl+X
          Copy      Ctrl+C
          Paste     Ctrl+V
          clEar
          Delete    Del
```

Menu 1.1

Menu 1.2

Keyboard mnemonics are designated by underlines, not capital letters. Choice descriptions now assume more common and recognizable shapes. Groupings, through use of white space, are established for choices in the pull-down. The different functions are much more obvious and separation is provided for the destructive actions. The different groupings are visually reinforced through use of separating lines. The lines are not extended to the pull-down border so as not to completely disassociate the choices. Keyboard alternatives are right-aligned to move them further from the choice descriptions. They are also enclosed in parentheses to visually deemphasize them, thereby reducing their visual competition with the choices. Choice descriptions are now more obvious.

```
                    OFFICE SYSTEM
  File    Edit    Format    View    Options                Help
          Undo      (Ctrl+Z)

          Cut       (Ctrl+X)
          Copy      (Ctrl+C)
          Paste     (Ctrl+V)

          Clear
          Delete    (Del)
```

Menu 1.2

Example 2

An improperly organized menu bar and pull-down.

Menu 2.1

A very poor menu bar—all alternatives are presented creating a very crowded series of choices in a difficult-to-scan horizontal array. No groupings are provided and an alphabetic order causes intermixing of what appear to be different functions. While menu breadth is preferred to excessive menu depth, too many choices are presented here.

OFFICE SYSTEM				
Address Book	Calendar	Communications	Copy File	Database
Delete File	Exit	Memo Pad	Help	Move File	New File	Open File
Spreadsheet	Telephone Book	Word Processor	World Clock	

Menu 2.1

Menus 2.2 and 2.3

A better, but still poor menu bar—while File, Function, and Help are now presented separately, the cascading Function menu requires an excessive number of steps to complete selection. Note the number of levels needed to access the Address or Telephone book. Excessive levels of depth are difficult to scan and lead to one's getting lost. Some have referred to this problem as cascade confusion.

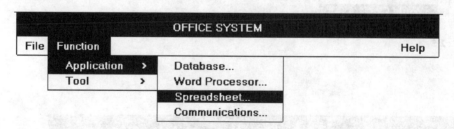

Menu 2.2

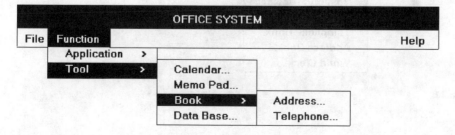

Menu 2.3

Menus 2.4, 2.5, and 2.6

A much more reasonable solution—Application and Tool menu bar items are created and all alternatives now exist on one pull-down menu. The number of steps necessary to reach any alternative is minimized and easier scanning of all items is permitted.

Menu 2.4

Menu 2.5

Menu 2.6

Menu 2.7A through 2.7J

Illustrated is a collection of textual Web site global navigation bars showing various presentation styles. Menu A is horizontally arrayed with good separation between alternate choices. No delimiters between the choices are included. Menu B uses the symbol >> to designate the choices. Menus C, D, E, and F use a vertical line to separate the choices, a very common technique used today in textual navigation presentation. All choices are arrayed horizontally, with Menu F comprising two lines. Menu G is composed of four columns. This menu would be scanned horizontally between columns and vertically within a column. Spacing and choice content make this obvious. Menus H and I are composed of fewer choices than Menu G and are arrayed for vertical scanning.

The vertical menu arrangements do make scanning of the choices much easier. Whenever possible, orient menus in the manner illustrated by Menus G, H, and I. If a horizontal array is used, a separation delimiter is recommended. A vertical line separator is recommended. This will give the choices a more "button-like" appearance, and this style commonly appears on Web pages.

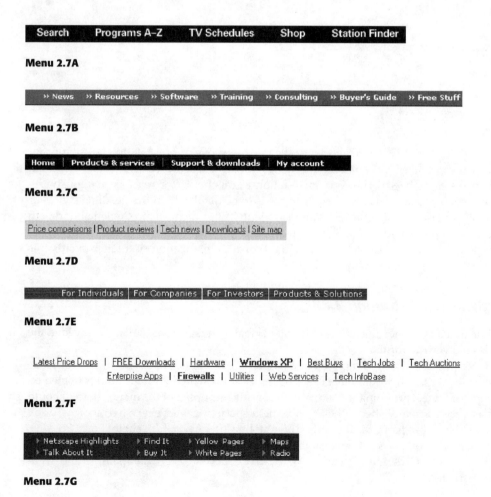

Menu 2.7A

Menu 2.7B

Menu 2.7C

Menu 2.7D

Menu 2.7E

Menu 2.7F

Menu 2.7G

Home
Dictionary
Site Map
FAQs

Menu 2.7H

Business Services
Catalogue
Press Area
Recruitment
Contact us

Menu 2.7I

Ease of use > Design > Web guidelines > Design >

Menu 2.7J

Menus A, B, E, F, G, H, and I, use the headline style of presentation (all significant words capitalized). The remaining menus (C, D) use sentence style (only the initial word is capitalized). The recommendation in this book, for reasons previously described, is for captions and menu choices is to be displayed in the headline style. For another reason, look at the illustration in Menu 2.7J. A menu choice, when underlined, can have letters with descenders degraded, destroying the shape of the word. This is especially critical if the letter is the first word. Capitalization of a letter avoids this problem.

Menus 2.8A through 2.8E

Illustrated is a collection of local Web site global navigation bars. All are arrayed in the desired vertical format.

Menu A is a listing comprised of 20 choices. While it is alphabetized, no groupings of choices exist. It would have been much better presented with groupings related by topic. If topical grouping was not possible, visual grouping of the menu choices should have been accomplished either by leaving a space line after every five choices, or by providing a bolder or distinctively different line after every fifth choice.

Menu B, composed of nine choices, is grouped, with separation of groups by horizontal lines. Ordering appears to be by frequency of use. It is a simple and well-constructed menu.

Autos
Browser Central
Business
Careers
Computing
Entertainment
Games
Health
House & Home
International
Lifestyles
Local Guide
Music
News
Personal Finance
Research & Learn
Shopping
Small Business
Sports
Travel

Menu 2.8A

Check Mail

Compose

⊞ Folders

Addresses

Search

Options

Mail Add-ons

Help Desk

Sign Out

Menu 2.8B

MARKETS
News
Columns
Movers by Exchange
World Indices
Stocks on the Move
Earnings Center
Tech Stocks
IPO Center
U.S. Treasuries
Currencies
Currency Calculator
Commodities

MONEY
Mutual Funds
Portfolio
Mortgage Calculator
Retirement

Menu 2.8C

Action to Take

In **City of London**

See Information

- Information about the
  Town/Village
- Weather

Prepare an Itinerary

- To this location
- From this location

Search for
in the map

- Hotels
- Restaurants
- Tourist Attractions

To export the map

- Add the map to My
  Selections
- Save Location
- Send by e-mail
- Print the map

- Display a new map

Menu 2.8D

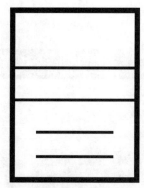

Menu 2.8E

Menu C is composed of two groups, with headings for each group. The headings, being capitalized, stand out well. The orderings schemes within groupings are not immediately obvious, however. In the *MARKETS* section, subgroupings of choices are desirable.

Menu D contains a heading (*In City of London*) with five subheadings. A larger size makes the heading stand out, and boldness makes all headings stand out. Sections are grouped and visually separated. Why, however, is the subheading "Search for in the map" positioned over two lines? It would appear to easily fit on one line. What is the purpose of the horizontal lines separating the bottom three groupings? Since these groupings all relate to "map" perhaps it was to separate the three map components. The horizontal line extending to each end of the box implies too great a separation and no relationship, however. It would have been better to inscribe a shorter line extending no wider than the choices themselves.

Also worth considering, if these lines were shortened, would be to include two lines the entire width of the box to separate the three major menu sections. This recommendation is illustrated in Menu 2.8E.

Menus 2.9A through 2.9C

Illustrated is a collection of global navigation bars containing icons.

Do these icons add to screen usability? When searching through these menu arrays do you look at the icons or words? Menu C is particularly wasteful of screen space, forcing below the screen and out of sight content that might otherwise be visible if the navigation bar were more reasonably sized.

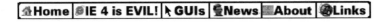

Menu 2.9A

Menu 2.9B

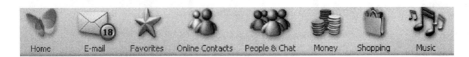

Menu 2.9C

Menu 2.10

Menu 2.10 is an interesting menu, combining a two-level menu with an historical trail. The top level, *individual pages*, has led to the selection of *layout* on the submenu. The path followed exists within the displayed menu. All lowercase letters for menu choices is *not* recommended, however. Headline-style presentation would have been much better.

Menu 2.10

Select the Proper Kinds
of Windows

A window is an area of the screen, usually rectangular in shape, defined by a border that contains a particular view of some area of the computer or some portion of a person's dialog with the computer. It can be moved and rendered independently on the screen. A window may be small, containing a short message or a single field, or it may be large, consuming most or all of the available display space. A display may contain one, two, or more windows within its boundaries. In this step the following is addressed:

- A window's characteristics.
- A window's components.
- A window's presentation styles.
- The types of windows available.
- Organizing window system functions.
- A window's operations.
- Web system frames and pop-up windows.

Window Characteristics

A window is seen to possess the following characteristics:

- A name or title, allowing it to be identified.
- A size in height and width (which can vary).

- A state, accessible or active, or not accessible. (Only active windows can have their contents altered.)
- Visibility—the portion that can be seen. (A window may be partially or fully hidden behind another window, or the information within a window may extend beyond the window's display area.)
- A location, relative to the display boundary.
- Presentation, that is, its arrangement in relation to other windows. It may be tiled, overlapping, or cascading.
- Management capabilities, methods for manipulation of the window on the screen.
- Its highlight, that is, the part that is selected.
- The function, task, or application to which it is dedicated.

The Attraction of Windows

The value of windowing is best seen in the context of a task or job. A person performs a variety of tasks, often in a fairly unstructured manner. A person is asked to monitor and manipulate data from a variety of sources, synthesize information, summarize information, and reorganize information. Things are seldom completed in a continuous time frame. Outside events such as telephone calls, supervisor or customer requests, and deadlines force shifts in emphasis and focus. Tasks start, stop, and start again. Materials used in dealing with the tasks are usually scattered about one's desk, being strategically positioned in the workspace to make handling the task as efficient as possible. This spatial mapping of tools helps people organize their work and provides reminders of uncompleted tasks. As work progresses and priorities change, materials are reorganized to reflect the changes.

Single-screen technology supports this work structure very poorly. Since only one screen of information can be viewed at one time, comparing or integrating information from different sources and on different screens often requires extensive use of one's memory. To support memory, a person is often forced to write notes or obtain printed copies of screens. Switching between tasks is difficult and disruptive, and later returning to a task requires an extensive and costly restructuring of the work environment.

The appeal of windowing is that it allows the display workspace to mirror the desk workspace much more closely. This dramatically reduces one's short-term memory load. One's ability to do mental calculations is limited by how well one keeps track of one's place, one's interim conclusions and products, and, finally, the results. Windows act as external memories that are an extension of one's internal memory. Windows also make it much easier to switch between tasks and to maintain one's context, since one does not have to reestablish one's place continually. In addition, Windows provide access to more information than would normally be available on a single display of the same size. Overwriting, or placing more important information on top of that of less importance at that moment, does this.

While all the advantages and disadvantages of windows are still not completely understood, windows do seem to be useful in the following ways.

Presentation of Different Levels of Information

Information can be examined in increasing levels of detail. A document table of contents can be presented in a window. A chapter or topic selected from this window can be simultaneously displayed in more detail in an adjoining window. Deeper levels are also possible in additional windows.

Presentation of Multiple Kinds of Information

Variable information needed to complete a task can be displayed simultaneously in adjacent windows. An order-processing system window could collect a customer account number in one window and retrieve the customer's name and shipping address in another window. A third window could collect details of the order, after which another window could present factory availability of and shipping dates for the desired items. Significant windows could remain displayed so that details may be modified as needed prior to order completion. Low inventory levels or delayed shipping dates might require changing the order.

Sequential Presentation of Levels or Kinds of Information

Steps to accomplish a task can be sequentially presented through windows. Successive windows are presented until all the required details are collected. Key windows may remain displayed, but others appear and disappear as necessary. This sequential preparation is especially useful if the information-collection process leads down various paths. An insurance application, for example, will include different types of coverage. A requested type of coverage might necessitate the collection of specific details about that type of coverage. This information can be entered into a window presented to collect the unique data. The windows disappear after data entry, and additional windows appear when needed.

Access to Different Sources of Information

Independent sources of information may have to be accessed at the same time. This information may reside in different host computers, operating systems, applications, files, or areas of the same file. It may be presented on the screen alongside the problem, greatly facilitating its solution. For instance, a writer may have to refer to several parts of a text being written at the same time. Or, a travel agent may have to compare several travel destinations for a particularly demanding client.

Combining Multiple Sources of Information

Text from several documents may have to be reviewed and combined into one. Pertinent information is selected from one window and copied into another.

Performing More Than One Task

More than one task can be performed at one time. While waiting for a long, complex procedure to finish, another can be performed. Tasks of higher priority can interrupt less important ones. The interrupted task can then be resumed without the necessity to "close down" and "restart."

Reminding

Windows can be used to remind the viewer of things likely to be of use in the near future. Examples might be menus of choices available, a history of the path followed or the command choices to that point, or the time of an important meeting.

Monitoring

Changes, both internal and external, can be monitored. Data in one window can be modified and its effect on data in another window can be studied. External events, such as changes in stock prices, out of normal range conditions, or system messages can be watched while another major activity is carried out.

Multiple Representations of the Same Task

The same thing can be looked at in several ways—for example, alternate drafts of a speech, different versions of a screen, or different graphical representations of the same data. A maintenance procedure may be presented in the form of textual steps and illustrated graphically at the same time.

Constraints in Window System Design

Windowing systems, in spite of their appeal and obvious benefits, have failed to completely live up to their expectations. In the past, a windows user interface has been described as "chaotic" because of the great amount of time users must spend doing such things as pointing at tiny boxes in window borders, resizing windows, moving windows, closing windows, and so forth. The problems with windowing systems can be attributed to three factors: historical considerations, hardware limitations, and human limitations.

Historical Considerations

Historically, system developers have been much more interested in solving hardware problems than in user considerations. Since technical issues abound, they have received the most attention. There has been very little research addressing design issues and their impact on the usability of window systems. Therefore, there are few concrete window design guidelines to aid designers.

This lack of guidelines makes it difficult to develop acceptable and agreeable window standards. While many companies have developed style guides, they are very general and limited in scope to their products. Standardization is also made more difficult by the complexity and range of alternatives available to the designer. Without user performance data, it is difficult to compare realistically the different alternatives, and design choices become a matter of preference.

Standardization of the interface is also inhibited by other factors. Some software developers, who are proud of their originality, see standards as a threat to creativity and its perceived monetary rewards. Some companies are wary of standards because they fear that other companies are promoting standards that reflect their own approach. Finally, some companies have threatened, or brought, legal action against anyone who adopts an approach similar to their own.

The result is that developers of new systems create another new variation each time they design a product, and users must cope with a new interface each time they encounter a new windowing system.

Hardware Limitations

Many of today's screens are not large enough to take full advantage of windowing capabilities. As a result, many windows are still of "Post-It" dimensions. As already mentioned, there is some evidence that many users of personal computers expand their windows to cover a full screen. Either seeing all the contents of one window is preferable to seeing small parts of many windows or the operational and visual complexity of multiple windows is not wanted.

Also, the slower processing speeds and smaller memory sizes of some computers may inhibit the use of windows. A drain on the computer's resources may limit feedback and animation capabilities, thereby reducing the system's usability. Poor screen resolution and graphics capability may also deter effective use of windows by not permitting sharp and realistic drawings and shapes.

Human Limitations

A windowing system, because it is more complex, requires the learning and using of more operations. Much practice is needed to master them. These window management operations are placed on top of other system operations, and window management can become an end in itself. This can severely detract from the task at hand. In one study comparing full screens with screens containing overlapping windows, task completion times were longer with the window screens, but the non-window screens generated more user errors. After eliminating screen arrangement time, however, task solution times were shorter with windows. The results suggest that advantages for windows do exist, but they can be negated by excessive window manipulation requirements.

It is also suggested that to be truly effective, window manipulation must occur implicitly as a result of user task actions, not as a result of explicit window management actions by the user.

Other Limitations

Other possible window problems include the necessity for window borders to consume valuable screen space, and that small windows providing access to large amounts of information can lead to excessive, bothersome scrolling.

Where To?

In spite of their problems, windows do have enormous benefits and are here to stay. So, we must cope with their constraints for now and, in the meantime, enjoy the benefits they possess.

Components of a Window

A typical window may be composed of up to a dozen or so elements. Some appear on all windows; others only on certain kinds of windows, or under certain conditions. For consistency purposes, these elements should always be located in the same position within a window. Most windowing systems provide consistent locations for elements in their own windows. Some inconsistencies do exist in element locations between different systems, however, as do some differences in what the elements are named, or what graphic images or icons are chosen to identify them. What follows is a description of typical window components and their purposes, with emphasis on the most popular windowing system, *Microsoft Windows*. Specifically reviewed will be primary windows, secondary windows, and a form of secondary window called the dialog box. An illustration of a primary window is found in Figure 5.1. Illustrations of secondary

Figure 5.1 Microsoft Windows primary window.

windows and dialog boxes are illustrated in Figures 5.8 and 5.13. How these different types of windows are used will be described in a later section in this chapter. A summary of window components for these types of windows is also found in Table 5.1.

Frame

A window will have a frame or border, usually rectangular in shape, to define its boundaries and distinguish it from other windows. While a border need not be rectangular, this shape is a preferred shape for most people. Also, textual materials, which are usually read from left to right, fit most efficiently within this structure. The border comprises a line of variable thickness and color. This variation can be used as an aid in identifying the type of window being displayed. Windows filling an entire screen may use the screen edge as the border. If a window is resizable, it may contain control points for sizing it. If the window cannot be resized, the border coincides with the edge of the window.

Title Bar

The title bar is the top edge of the window, inside its border and extending its entire width. This title bar is also referred to by some platforms as the *caption, caption bar*, or *title area*. The title bar contains a descriptive title identifying the purpose or content of the window. In Microsoft Windows, the title bar may also possess, at the extreme left and right ends, control buttons (described below) for retrieving the system menu and performing window resizing. The title bar also serves as a control point for moving the window and as an access point for commands that apply to a window. For example, as an access point, when a user clicks on the title bar using the secondary mouse button, the pop-up or shortcut menu for the window appears. Pressing the Alt-Spacebar key combination also displays the shortcut menu for the window. Title bars are included on all primary and secondary windows. Title bar text writing guidelines are described in Step 8 "Write Clear Text and Messages."

Microsoft recommends that one never place application commands or other controls in the title bar. Doing so may conflict with the special user controls Windows adds for configurations that support multiple languages.

Title Bar Icon

Located at the left corner of the title bar in a primary window, this button is used in Windows to retrieve a pull-down menu of commands that apply to the object in the window. It is 16 × 16 version of the icon of the object being viewed. When clicked with the secondary mouse button, the commands applying to the object are presented. Microsoft suggests that:

- If the window contains a tool or utility (that is, an application that does not create, load, and save its own data files), a small version of the application's icon should be placed there instead.

Table 5.1 Microsoft Windows Components

COMPONENT	WINDOWS CONTAINING COMPONENT		
	PRIMARY	**SECONDARY**	**DIALOG BOX**
Frame or Border • Boundary to define shape. • If sizable, contains control points for resizing.	X	X	X
Title Bar Text • Name of object being viewed in window. • Control point for moving window.	X	X	X

Title Bar Icon
• Small version of icon for object
  being viewed.
• Access point for commands that apply
  to the object.
	X		

Title Bar Buttons • Shortcuts to specific commands.	X	X	X
Close	X	X	X
Minimize/Maximize/Restore	X		

What's This?
— Displays context-sensitive
  Help about any object displayed
  on window.
		X	X

Menu Bar • Provides basic and common application commands.	X		

Status Bar
• An area used to display status
  information about what is displayed
  in window.
	X		

Scroll Bar • Standard control to support scrolling.	X		
Size Grip • Control to resize window, located at right side of status bar.	X		

- If the application creates, loads, and saves documents or data files and the window represents the view of one of its files, a small version of the icon that represents its document or data file type should be placed there.

- Even if the user has not yet saved the file, display the data file icon rather than the application icon, and again display the data file icon after the user saves the file.

Window Sizing Buttons

Located at the right corner of the title bar, these buttons are used to manipulate the size of a window. The leftmost button, the *minimize* button— inscribed with a short horizontal line toward the bottom of the button—is used to reduce a window to its minimum size, usually an icon. It also hides all associated windows. The *maximize* button—typically inscribed with a large box—enlarges a window to its maximum size, usually the entire screen. When a screen is maximized, the *restore* button replaces the maximize button, since the window can no longer be increased in size. The restore button—typically inscribed with a pair overlapping boxes—returns a window to the size it had before a minimize or maximize action was performed. A *close* button—typically inscribed with an X—closes the window. Minimize, maximize, and close buttons are shown in Figure 5.1. These command buttons are graphical equivalents to the actions available through the Title Bar icon.

Sizing buttons are included on primary windows only. All buttons on a primary window's title bar must have equivalent commands on the pop-up or shortcut menu for that window.

When these buttons are displayed, use the following guidelines:

- When a window does not support a command, do not display its command button.

- The *Close* button always appears as the rightmost button. Leave a gap between it and any other buttons.

- The *Minimize* button always precedes the *Maximize* button.

- The *Restore* button always replaces the *Maximize* button or the *Minimize* button when that command is carried out.

What's This? Button

The *What's This?* Button, which appears on secondary windows and dialog boxes, is used to invoke the What's This? Windows command to provide contextual Help about objects displayed within a secondary window. When provided, it is located in the upper-right corner of the title bar, just to the left of the close button. It is inscribed with a question mark, as illustrated in Figure 5.2.

On a primary window this command is accessed from the Help drop-down menu. This command may also be included as a button on a toolbar or as a command on a pop-up menu for a specific object. This command is described more fully in Step 9 "Provide Effective Feedback and Guidance and Assistance."

Figure 5.2 What's This? button.

Menu Bar

A menu bar is used to organize and provide access to actions. It is located horizontally at the top of the window, just below the title bar. A menu bar contains a list of topics or items that, when selected, are displayed on a pull-down menu beneath the choice. A system will typically provide a default set of menu actions that can be augmented by an application. In the past, some platforms have called the menu bar an *action bar*. Menu bar design guidelines were presented in Step 4 "Develop System Menus and Navigation Schemes." The contents of the menu bar and its pull-downs are determined by the application's functionality and the context in which the user is interacting with it.

Status Bar

Information of use to the user can be displayed in a designated screen area or areas. They may be located at the top of the screen in some platforms and called a *status area*, or at the screen's bottom. Microsoft recommends the bottom location and refers to this area as the *status bar*. It is also referred to by other platforms as a *message area* or *message bar*.

Microsoft Windows suggests using the status bar to display information about the current state of what is being viewed in the window, descriptive messages about a selected menu or toolbar button, or other noninteractive information. It may also be used to explain menu and control bar items as the items are highlighted by the user.

Scroll Bars

When all display information cannot be presented in a window, the additional information must be found and made visible. This is accomplished by scrolling the display's contents through use of a scroll bar. A scroll bar is an elongated rectangular container consisting of a scroll area or shaft, a slider box or elevator, and arrows or anchors at each end. For vertical scrolling, the scroll bar is positioned at the far right side of the work area, extending its entire length. Horizontal scrolling is accomplished through a scroll bar located at the bottom of the work area. Scroll bars are more fully described in Step 7 "Choose the Proper Screen-Based Controls."

Split Box

A window can be split into two or more pieces or panes by manipulating a *split box* located above a vertical scroll bar or to the left of a horizontal scroll bar. A split box is sometimes referred to as a *split bar*. A window can be split into two or more separate viewing areas that are called *panes*. Splitting a window permits multiple views of an object. A split window allows the user to:

- Examine two parts of a document at the same time.
- Display different, yet simultaneous, views of the same information.

To support the splitting of a window that is not presplit by design, include a split box. The split box should be just large enough for the user to successfully target it with the pointer; the default size of a size handle, such as the window's sizing border, is a good guideline.

Toolbar

Toolbars, illustrated in Figure 5.3, are permanently displayed panels or arrays of choices or commands that must be accessed quickly. They are sometimes called *command bars*. Toolbars are designed to provide quick access to specific commands or options. Specialized toolbars are sometimes referred to as *ribbons, toolboxes, rulers,* or *palettes.* Each toolbar band includes a single-grip handle to enable the user to resize or rearrange the toolbars. When the user moves the pointer over the grip, it changes to a two-headed arrow. When the user drags the grip, the pointer changes to a split move pointer. To resize the toolbar to its maximum or minimum size, the user clicks the grip.

Toolbars may occupy a fixed position or be movable. The design of toolbars is discussed in Step 7.

Command Area

In situations where it is useful for a command to be typed into a screen, a command area can be provided. The desired location of the command area is at the bottom of the window. If a horizontal scroll bar is included in the window, position the command area just below it. If a message area is included on the screen, locate the command area just above it.

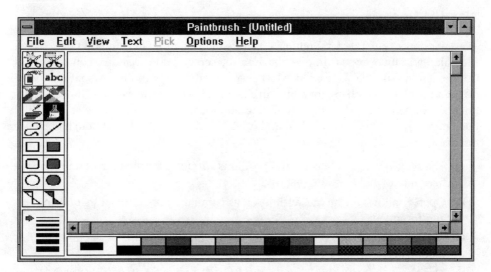

Figure 5.3 Toolbars.

Size Grip

A size grip is a Microsoft Windows special handle included in a window to permit it to be resized. When the grip is dragged the window resizes, following the same conventions as the sizing border. Three angled parallel lines in the lower-right corner of a window designate the size grip. If the window possesses a status bar, the grip is positioned at the bar's right end. Otherwise, it is located at the bottom of a vertical scroll bar, the right side of a horizontal scroll bar, or the junction point of the two bars. A size grip is shown in the lower-right corner of Figure 5.2.

Work Area

The work area is the portion of the screen where the user performs tasks. It is the open area inside the window's border and contains relevant peripheral screen components such as the menu bar, scroll bars, or message bars. The work area may consist of an open area for typing, or it may contain controls (such as text boxes and list boxes) or customized forms (such as spreadsheets). The work area may also be referred to as the *client area*.

Window Presentation Styles

The presentation style of a window refers to its spatial relationship to other windows. There are two basic styles, commonly called tiled or overlapping. In early windowing days, most systems commonly used one or the other style exclusively, seldom using both at the same time. Now, the user is usually permitted to select the style to be presented on the display.

Tiled Windows

Tiled windows, illustrated in Figure 5.4, derive their name from common floor or wall tile. Tiled windows appear in one plane on the screen and expand or contract to fill up the display surface, as needed. Most systems provide two-dimensional tiled windows, adjustable in both height and width. Some less-powerful systems, however, are only one-dimensional, the windows being adjustable in only one manner (typically the height). Tiled windows, the first and oldest kind of window, are felt to have these advantages:

- The system usually allocates and positions windows for the user, eliminating the necessity to make positioning decisions.
- Open windows are always visible, eliminating the possibility of them being lost and forgotten.
- Every window is always completely visible, eliminating the possibility of information being hidden.
- They are perceived as less complex than overlapping windows, possibly because there are fewer management operations or they seem less "magical."

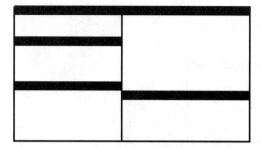

Figure 5.4 Tiled windows.

- They are easier, according to studies, for novice or inexperienced people to learn and use.
- They yield better user performance for tasks where the data requires little window manipulation to complete the task.

Perceived disadvantages include the following:

- Only a limited number can be displayed in the screen area available.
- As windows are opened or closed, existing windows change in size. This can be annoying.
- As windows change in size or position, the movement can be disconcerting.
- As the number of displayed windows increases, each window can get very tiny.
- The changes in sizes and locations made by the system are difficult to predict.
- The configuration of windows provided by the system may not meet the user's needs.
- They are perceived as crowded and more visually complex because window borders are flush against one another, and they fill up the whole screen. Crowding is accentuated if borders contain scroll bars or control icons. Viewer attention may be drawn to the border, not the data.
- They permit less user control because the system actively manages the windows.

Overlapping Windows

Overlapping windows, illustrated in Figure 5.5, may be placed on top of one another like papers on a desk. They possess a three-dimensional quality, appearing to lie on different planes. Users can control the location of these windows, as well as the plane in which they appear. The sizes of some types of windows may also be changed. Most systems today normally use this style of window. They have the following advantages:

- Visually, their look is three-dimensional, resembling the desktop that is familiar to the user.
- Greater control allows the user to organize the windows to meet his or her needs.
- Windows can maintain larger sizes.

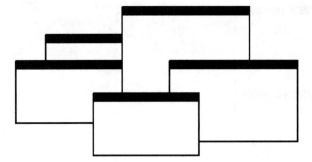

Figure 5.5   Overlapping windows.

- Windows can maintain consistent sizes.
- Windows can maintain consistent positions.
- Screen space conservation is not a problem, because windows can be placed on top of one another.
- There is less pressure to close or delete windows no longer needed.
- The possibility exists for less visual crowding and complexity. Larger borders can be maintained around window information, and the window is more clearly set off against its background. Windows can also be expanded to fill the entire display.
- They yield better user performance for tasks where the data requires much window manipulation to complete the task.

Disadvantages include the following:

- They are operationally much more complex than tiled windows. More control functions require greater user attention and manipulation.
- Information in windows can be obscured behind other windows.
- Windows themselves can be lost behind other windows and be presumed not to exist.
- That overlapping windows represent a three-dimensional space is not always realized by the user.
- Control freedom increases the possibility for greater visual complexity and crowding. Too many windows, or improper offsetting, can be visually overwhelming.

Cascading Windows

A special type of overlapping window has the windows automatically arranged in a regular progression. Each window is slightly offset from others, as illustrated in Figure 5.6. Advantages of this approach include the following:

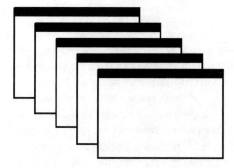

Figure 5.6 Cascading windows.

- No window is ever completely hidden.
- Bringing any window to the front is easier.
- It provides simplicity in visual presentation and cleanness.

Picking a Presentation Style

- Use tiled windows for:
  — Single-task activities.
  — Data that needs to be seen simultaneously.
  — Tasks requiring little window manipulation.
  — Novice or inexperienced users.
- Use overlapping windows for:
  — Switching between tasks.
  — Tasks necessitating a greater amount of window manipulation.
  — Expert or experienced users.
  — Unpredictable display contents.

Tiled windows. Tiled windows seem to be better for single-task activities and data that must be seen simultaneously. A study found that tasks requiring little window manipulation were carried out faster using tiled windows. They also found that novice users performed better with tiled windows, regardless of the task.

Overlapping windows. Overlapping windows seem to be better for situations that necessitate switching between tasks. A research study concluded that tasks requiring much window manipulation could be performed faster with overlapping windows but only if user window expertise existed. For novice users, tasks requiring much window manipulation were carried out faster with tiled windows. Therefore, the advantage to overlapping windows comes only after a certain level of expertise is achieved. Overlapping windows are the preferred presentation scheme.

Types of Windows

People's tasks must be structured into a series of windows. The type of window used will depend on the nature and flow of the task. Defining standard window types is again difficult across platforms because of the varying terminology and definitions used by different windowing systems, and changes in terminology for new versions of systems. For simplicity, the Microsoft Windows windowing scheme will be described. Summarized are a description of the window, its purpose, and its proper usage. Any other platform's windows may not behave exactly as presented, and some platform windows may exhibit characteristics common to more than one of the described window types.

Primary Window

- Proper usage:
  - Should represent an independent function or application.
  - Use to present constantly used window components and controls.
    - Menu bar items that are:
      - Used frequently.
      - Used by most, or all, primary or secondary windows.
    - Controls used by dependent windows.
  - Use for presenting information that is continually updated.
    - For example, date and time.
  - Use for providing context for dependent windows to be created.
  - Do not:
    - Divide an independent function into two or more primary windows.
    - Present unrelated functions in one primary window.

The *primary* window is the first one that appears on a screen when an activity or action is started. It is required for every function or application, possessing a menu bar and some basic action controls, as previously described. It should present the framework for the function's commands and data, and provide top-level context for dependent windows. It has also been variously referred to as the *application* window or the *main* window. In addition, it may be referred to as the *parent* window if one or more *child* windows exist. A Microsoft Windows primary window is shown in Figure 5.7.

The primary window is the main focal point of the user's activities and should represent an independent function. Avoid dividing an independent function into two or more primary windows, and avoid presenting unrelated functions in a single primary window. This tends to confuse people.

Independent functions should begin in a primary window. A primary window should contain constantly used window components such as frequently used menu bar items and controls (for example, control bars) used by dependent windows. Also include in a primary window continually updated information such as the date and time. The components of a primary window are summarized in Table 5.2.

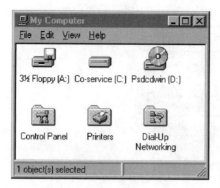

Figure 5.7   Microsoft Windows primary window.

Secondary Windows

- Proper usage:
  - For performing subordinate, supplemental, or ancillary actions that are:
    - Extended or more complex in nature.
    - Related to objects in the primary window.
  - For presenting frequently or occasionally used window components.
- Important guidelines:
  - Should typically not appear as an entry on the taskbar.
  - A secondary window should not be larger than 263 dialog units x 263 dialog units.

Secondary windows are supplemental windows. Secondary windows may be dependent upon a primary window or displayed independently of the primary window. They structurally resemble a primary window, possessing some of the same action controls (Close button) and possibly a What's This? button.

A *dependent* secondary window is one common type. It can only be displayed from a command on the interface of its primary window. It is typically associated with a single data object, and appears on top of the active window when requested. It is movable, and scrollable. If necessary, it uses the primary window's menu bar. Most systems permit the use of multiple secondary windows to complete a task. In general, dependent secondary windows are closed when the primary window closes, and hidden when their primary window is hidden or minimized.

An *independent* secondary window can be opened independently of a primary window—for example, a property sheet displayed when the user clicks the Properties command on the menu of a desktop icon. An independent secondary window can typically be closed without regard to the state of any primary window unless there is an obvious relationship to the primary window.

A Microsoft Windows secondary Window is illustrated in Figure 5.8.

Proper usage. Although secondary windows share many characteristics with primary windows, they also differ from primary windows in behavior and use. Secondary

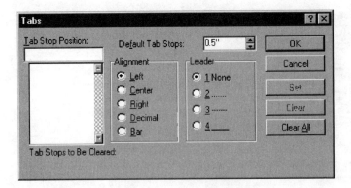

Figure 5.8 Microsoft Windows secondary window.

windows are used to perform supplemental or subordinate tasks, or tasks that are extended in nature. Frequently and occasionally used window components should also be presented in secondary windows. Microsoft Windows possesses several types of secondary windows called *dialog boxes, property sheets, property inspectors, message boxes, palette windows,* and *pop-up* windows.

Guidelines. A secondary window should typically not appear as an entry on the taskbar. Secondary windows obtain or display supplemental information that is usually related to the objects that appear in a primary window.

A secondary window is typically smaller than its associated primary window and smaller than the minimum display resolution. Microsoft recommends not displaying any secondary window larger than 263 dialog units × 263 dialog units. Microsoft defines size and location of user-interface elements not in pixels but in *dialog units* (DLUs), a device-independent unit of measure.

- One horizontal DLU is equal to one-fourth of the average character width for the current system font.
- One vertical DLU is equal to one-eighth of the average character height for the current system font.

These sizes keep the window from becoming too large to display at most resolutions. However, they still provide reasonable space to display supportive information, such as Help information, that applies.

The components of a secondary window are summarized in Table 5.2.

Modal and Modeless

- Modal:
  — Use when interaction with any other window must not be permitted.
  — Use for:
    - Presenting information.
      — For example, messages (sometimes called a message box).

- Receiving user input.
  — For example, data or information (sometimes called a prompt box).
- Asking questions.
  — For example, data, information, or directions (sometimes called a question box).
— Use carefully because it constrains what the user can do.

- Modeless:
  — Use when interaction with other windows must be permitted.
  — Use when interaction with other windows must be repeated.

A secondary window can be modal or modeless.

Modal. Most secondary windows will be *modal*. Modal windows will not permit interaction with another window until the current dialog is completed. It remains displayed until the appropriate action is taken, after which it is removed from the screen. Modal dialog boxes typically request critical information or actions that must be reacted to before the dialog can continue. Since modal dialog boxes constrain what the user can do, limit their use to situations in which additional information is required to complete a command or when it is important to prevent any further interaction until satisfying a condition.

Modeless. A *modeless* dialog box permits the user to engage in parallel dialogs. Switching between the box and its associated window is permitted. Other tasks may be performed while a modeless dialog box is displayed, and it may be left on the screen after a response has been made to it. Actions leading to a modeless dialog box can be canceled, causing the box to be removed from the screen.

Use a modeless dialog box when interaction with a primary window or another secondary window must be permitted, for example, during the accessing of the Help function. Also, use a modeless dialog box when interaction with other windows must be repeated; for example, in a word search operation.

Cascading and Unfolding

- Cascading:
  — Purpose:
    - To provide advanced options at a lower level in a complex dialog.
  — Guidelines:
    - Provide a command button leading to the next dialog box with a "To a Window" indicator, an ellipsis (. . .).
    - Present the additional dialog box in cascaded form.
    - Provide no more than two cascades in a given path.
    - Do not cover previous critical information.
      — Title Bar.
      — Relevant displayed information.
    - If independent, close the secondary window from which it was opened.

■ Unfolding:
  — Purpose:
    • To provide advanced options at the same level in a complex dialog.
  — Guidelines:
    • Provide a command button with an expanding dialog symbol (>>).
    • Expand to right or downward.

Access to additional options can be accomplished by inclusion of a command button that opens another secondary window. These multiple secondary windows needed to complete a task may be presented in two forms, cascading or expanding.

Cascading. A *cascading* window keeps the original window displayed, with the dependent window displayed on top, offset slightly to the right and below the original secondary window. A cascade, illustrated in Figures 5.9 and 5.10, is generally used when advanced options at a lower level in a complex dialog must be presented. An indication that the dialog will be cascading is signaled by an ellipsis placed in the command button used to display the additional dialog box. Because of the confusion that can develop with too many cascades, restrict the number of

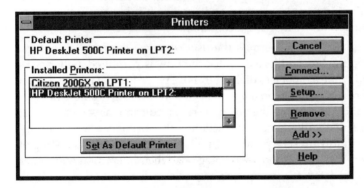

Figure 5.9   Printers secondary window with Connect... cascade button.

Figure 5.10   Cascading Connect secondary window.

cascades to no more than two in a given path. Do not cover information on the upper-level dialog boxes that may have to be referred to, such as box title bars and other critical or relevant information. If the cascaded window is independent in its operation, close the secondary window from which it was opened and display only the new window.

Unfolding. An *unfolding* secondary window expands to reveal additional options, a form of progressive disclosure. Unfolding windows, sometimes called *expanding* windows, are generally used to provide advanced options at the same level in a complex dialog. They are good alternatives when the interface contains a fixed set of options or controls that seldom need to be accessed. An unfolding window is illustrated in Figures 5.11 and 5.12. An indication that the dialog will be expanding is signaled by a double arrow (>>) placed in the command button used to display

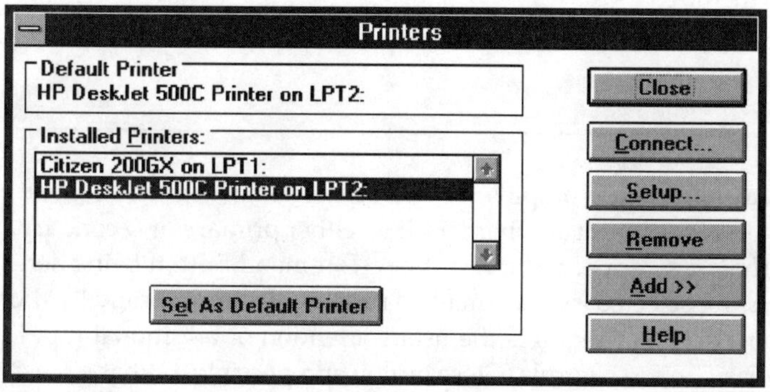

Figure 5.11 Printers secondary window with *Add* >> unfolding button.

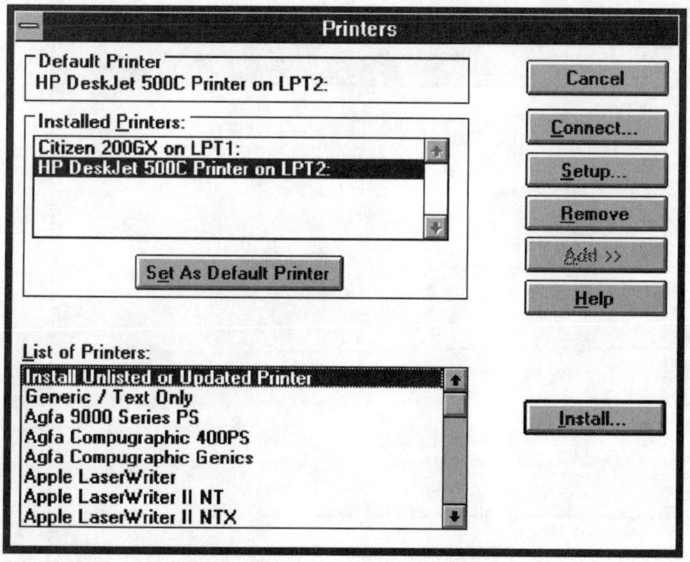

Figure 5.12 Unfolded Printers secondary window.

the additional dialog box. Expand the box to right, preferably, or downward if screen space constraints exist. As an option, the same button can be used to "refold" the additional part of the window.

Dialog Boxes

- Use for presenting brief messages.
- Use for requesting specific, transient actions.
- Use for performing actions that:
  — Take a short time to complete.
  — Are not frequently changed.
- Command buttons to include:
  — OK.
  — Cancel.
  — Others as necessary.

Dialog boxes are used to extend and complete an interaction within a limited context. Dialog boxes are always displayed from another window, either primary or secondary, or another dialog box. They may appear as a result of a command button being activated or a menu choice being selected, or they may be presented automatically by the system when a condition exists that requires the user's attention or additional input. They may possess some basic action controls (Close button and possibly a What's This? button), but do not have a menu bar. A Microsoft Windows dialog box is illustrated in Figure 5.13.

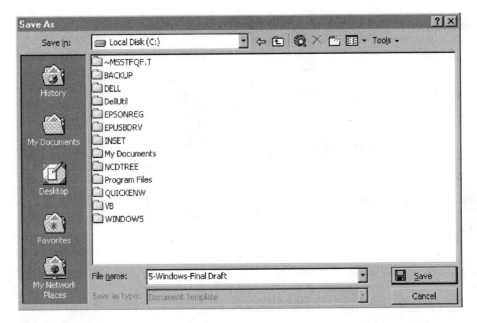

Figure 5.13 Microsoft Windows dialog box.

Most windowing systems provide standard dialog boxes for common functions, some examples being *Open, Save As*, and *Print.* Many platforms also recommend a set of standard command buttons for use in the various kinds of dialog boxes, such as OK, Cancel, and so on. Dialog boxes are of two types, modal and modeless, as recently described. They may also cascade or unfold.

Uses. Dialog boxes are used for presenting brief amounts of information or to request specific transient actions. Dialog box actions will usually be those that do not occur frequently.

Command buttons. Dialog boxes commonly include OK and Cancel command buttons. OK and Cancel buttons work best in dialog boxes that allow the user to set the parameters for a particular command. OK is typically defined as the default command button when the dialog box window opens. Other command buttons may be included in a dialog box in addition to or instead of the OK and Cancel buttons. Follow the design conventions for command buttons found in Step 7.

Property Sheets and Property Inspectors

The properties of an object in an interface can be displayed in a variety of ways. For example, the image and name of an icon on the desktop reflect specific properties of that object, as do other interface components such as toolbars, status bars, and even scroll bars. Secondary windows provide two other techniques for displaying properties, *property sheets* and *property inspectors.*

Property Sheets

- Use for presenting the complete set of properties for an object.
- Categorize and group within property pages, as necessary.
  - Use tabbed property pages for grouping peer-related property sets.
  - The recommended sizes for property sheets are:
    - 252 DLUs wide x 218 DLUs high
    - 227 DLUs wide x 215 DLUs high
    - 212 DLUs wide x 188 DLUs high
  - Command buttons to include:
    - OK.
    - Cancel.
    - Apply.
    - Reset.
    - Others as necessary.
  - For single property sheets, place the commands on the sheet.
  - For tabbed property pages, place the commands outside the tabbed pages.

Use. A property sheet is the most common way to present an object's complete set of properties in a secondary window. A property sheet is a modeless secondary window that displays the user-accessible properties of an object, properties that may be viewed but not necessarily edited. A single page property sheet is illustrated in Figure 5.14.

Property pages. Because there can be many properties for an object and the object's context, the categorization and grouping of properties within sets may be necessary. A technique for supporting navigation to groups of properties in a property sheet is a tabbed *property page,* where each set of properties is presented within the window as a separate page. Each page tab is labeled with the name of the set, as shown in Figure 5.15. Use tabbed property pages for grouping peer-related property sets, tabs are described in Step 7.

Size. The sizes recommended for property sheets by Microsoft are shown above. These will create a window smaller than its associated window and smaller than the minimum display resolution.

Command buttons. Property sheets typically allow the values for a property to be changed, and then applied. Include the following common command buttons for handling the application of property changes. For common property sheet transaction buttons, use OK, Cancel, and Apply. A Reset command button to cancel pending changes without closing the window can also be included. Other command buttons can be included in property sheets. Avoid including a Help command button. If a Help button seems necessary, the best solution is to simplify the window.

Command buttons on *tabbed property pages* should be located outside of the tabbed page but still within the window. Buttons placed on a page imply that the action being performed applies *only* to that page. Buttons outside the pages imply

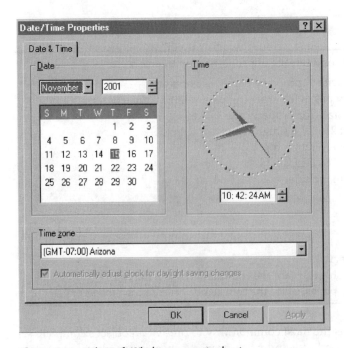

Figure 5.14 Microsoft Windows property sheet.

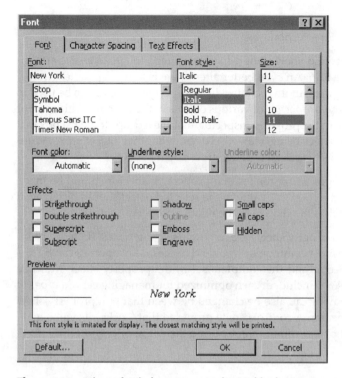

Figure 5.15 Microsoft Windows property sheet tabbed pages.

the action performed applies to *all* pages. This is the desired positioning because, most often, the tabs are considered by the user as simple grouping or navigation techniques. If the properties are to be applied on a page-by-page basis, however, then place the command and buttons on the property pages, and always in the same location on each page. When the user switches pages without selecting a command button, any property value changes for that page are applied. In these situations, it is useful to prompt the user by displaying a message box that asks whether to apply or discard any changes made.

Property Inspectors

- Use for displaying only the most common or frequently accessed object properties.
- Make changes dynamically.

Use. Display only the most common or frequently accessed properties in a property inspector. Properties of an object are displayed by using a dynamic viewer or browser that reflects the properties of the current selection. A property inspector differs from a property sheet. Even when a property sheet window is modeless, the window is typically modal with respect to the object for the properties being displayed. If the user selects another object, the property sheet continues to display the properties of the original object. A property inspector, on the other hand, always reflects the current selection.

A palette window (described shortly) or a toolbar is used to create a property inspector, as shown in Figure 5.16. An even better alternative is to use a palette window that the user can also configure. Another control in a property inspector can be used to enable the user to display the properties of various objects in the primary window. For example, as the first control in the property inspector, include a drop-down list box that displays the name of the object being viewed. To view another object's properties within the inspector, the object is selected in the drop-down list box.

Dynamic changes. Changes a user makes in a property inspector should be made dynamically. That is, the property value in the selected object should be changed as soon as the user makes the change in the related property control.

Property inspectors and property sheets are not exclusive interfaces. Both can be included in an interface. The most common or frequently accessed properties can be displayed in a property inspector and the complete set in the property sheet. Multiple property inspectors can also be included, each optimized for managing certain types of objects. An interface's behavior can also be changed between that of a property sheet and that of a property inspector. A control can be provided that "locks" its view, making it modal to the current object, rather than tracking the entire selection.

Message Boxes

- Use for displaying a message about a particular situation or condition.
- Command buttons to include:
  — OK.
  — Cancel.
  — Help.
  — Yes and No.
  — Stop.
  — Buttons to correct the action that caused the message box to be displayed.
- Enable the title bar close box only if the message includes a cancel button.
- Designate the most frequent or least destructive option as the default command button.

Use. A message box, as illustrated in Figure 5.17, is a secondary window that displays a message about a particular situation or condition.

Figure 5.16   Microsoft Windows property inspector.

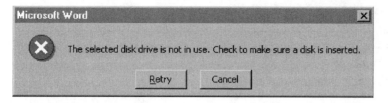

Figure 5.17 Microsoft Windows message box.

Command buttons. Typically, message boxes contain only command buttons with the appropriate responses or choices offered to the user. The command buttons used should allow the message box interaction to be simple and efficient. Microsoft suggests providing the following:

- If a message requires no choices to be made but only acknowledgment, include an OK button and, optionally, a Help button.
- If the message requires the user to make a choice, include a command button for each option.
- Include OK and Cancel buttons only when the user has the option of continuing or stopping the action.
- Use Yes and No buttons when the user must decide how to continue.
- If these choices are too ambiguous, label the command buttons with the names of specific actions, for example, *Save* and *Delete.*

Command buttons to correct the action that caused the message box to be displayed can also be included in a message box. For example, if the message box indicates that the user must switch to another application window to take corrective action, a button that opens that application window can also be included.

Stop. If Cancel is used as a command button in a message box, remember that to users, cancel implies that the state of the process or task that started the message is being restored. If you use Cancel to interrupt a process and the state cannot be restored, use *Stop* instead.

Help. A Help button can be included in a message box for messages needing more detail. This allows the message text to be more succinct.

If other command buttons are needed, consider the potential increase in complexity that their inclusion will cause.

Close box. Enable the title bar Close box only if the message includes a Cancel button. Otherwise, the meaning of the Close operation may be ambiguous.

Default. Designate the most frequent or least destructive option as the default command button.

A definition of message types, and guidelines for writing message, are found in Step 8.

Palette Windows

- Use to present a set of controls.
- Design as resizable.
  — Alternately, design them as fixed in size.

Use. Palette windows are modeless secondary windows that present a set of controls, as shown in Figure 5.18. Palette windows are distinguished by their visual appearance, a collection of images, colors or patterns. The title bar for a palette window is shorter and includes only a *close* button.

Sizing. A palette window can be defined as fixed in size, or, more typically, resizable by the user. Two techniques should indicate when the window is resizable, changing the pointer image to the size pointer, and placing a *size* command in the window's shortcut menu. Preserve the window's size and position so the window can be restored if it, or its associated primary window, is closed and then reopened.

Pop-up Windows

- Use pop-up windows to display:
  — Additional information when an abbreviated form of the information is the main presentation.
  — Textual labels for graphical controls.
  — Context-sensitive Help information.

Pop-up windows can be used to display additional information when an abbreviated form of the information is the main presentation technique, as illustrated in Figure 5.19. Other examples of pop-up windows used to display contextual information are *ToolTips* and *balloon tips* that provide the names for controls in graphical toolbars. Pop-up windows are also used to provide context-sensitive Help information. Pop-up windows do not contain standard secondary window components such as a title bar and close button.

Figure 5.18 Microsoft Windows palette window.

Figure 5.19   Microsoft Windows pop-up window.

Table 5.2   Microsoft Windows Window Types and Components

PRIMARY WINDOW	
Purpose:	To perform a major interaction.
Components:	Frame or border.
	Title bar.
	—Access point for commands that apply to the window, with commands displayed in a pop-up menu.
	Title Bar icon.
	—Small version of the icon of the object being viewed.
	—Access point for commands that apply to the object being displayed in the window, with commands displayed in a pop-up window.
	Title bar text.
	Title bar buttons to: close/minimize/maximize /restore a window.
	Menu bar.
	Status bar.
	Scroll bar.
	Size grip.
SECONDARY WINDOWS	
Purpose:	To obtain or display supplemental information related to the objects in the primary window.
Components:	Frame or border.
	Title bar.
	Title bar text.
	Close button.
	What's This? button.
	—Context-sensitive Help about components displayed in the window; this is optional.
Kinds:	Modal and modeless.

(continues)

Table 5.2 Continued

SECONDARY WINDOWS	
Dialog Boxes	
Purpose:	To obtain additional information needed to carry out a particular command or task.
Description:	Secondary window. Contains the following common dialog box interfaces: — Open/Replace/Find. — Save As /Print/Print Setup. — Page Setup/Font/Color.
Property Inspectors	
Purpose:	To display the most common or frequently accessed properties of a current selection, usually of a particular type of object.
Description:	A modeless secondary window. Typically modal with respect to the object for which it displays properties.
Usage:	Displayed when requested from selected object.
Property Sheets	
Purpose:	For presenting the complete set of properties for an object.
Description:	A modeless secondary window. Typically modal with respect to the object for which it displays properties.
Usage:	Displayed when requested from selected object.
Message Boxes	
Purpose:	To provide information about a particular situation or condition.
Description:	Secondary window. Types of message boxes: — Information/Warning/Critical.
Palette Windows	
Purpose:	To present a set of controls such as palettes or toolbars.
Description:	Modeless secondary window.

Table 5.2   Continued

SECONDARY WINDOWS	
Pop-Up Windows	
Purpose:	To display additional information when an abbreviated form of the information is the main presentation.
Description:	Secondary window. Does not contain standard secondary window components such as title bar and close button. Example: ToolTip.

Window Management

Microsoft Windows also provides several window management schemes, a *single-document interface, a multiple-document interface, workbooks*, and *projects*. To choose the right scheme to present an application's collection of related tasks or processes, consider a number of design factors, including: the intended users and their skill level, the application and its objects or tasks, and the most effective use of display space. These window management schemes are not exclusive design techniques. They may be combined, or others developed. These techniques, however, are the most frequently used schemes. Each is briefly described below. For greater detail, see Microsoft (2001).

Single-Document Interface

- Description:
  - A single primary window with a set of secondary windows.
- Proper usage:
  - Where object and window have a simple, one-to-one relationship.
  - Where the object's primary presentation or use is as a single unit.
  - To support alternate views with a control that allows the view to be changed.
  - To support simultaneous views by splitting the window into panes.
- Advantages:
  - Most common usage.
  - Window manipulation is easier and less confusing.
  - Data-centered approach.
- Disadvantage:
  - Information is displayed or edited in separate windows.

Often, the window interface can be established using a single primary window. A single-document window design is sufficient when the object's primary presentation or use is as a single unit, such as a folder or document, even when the object contains different types. In a single-document window design, the primary window provides the primary view or work area. Secondary windows can be used for supplemental forms of input, and to view information about objects presented in the primary window.

Multiple-Document Interface

- Description:
  - A technique for managing a set of windows where documents are opened into windows.
  - Contains:
    - A single primary window, called the parent.
    - A set of related document or child windows, each also essentially a primary window.
  - Each child window is constrained to appear only within the parent window.
  - The child windows share the parent window's operational elements.
  - The parent window's elements can be dynamically changed to reflect the requirements of the active child window.
- Proper usage:
  - To present multiple occurrences of an object.
  - To compare data within two or more windows.
  - To present multiple parts of an application.
  - Best suited for viewing homogeneous object types.
  - To clearly segregate the objects and their windows used in a task.
- Advantages:
  - The child windows share the parent window's interface components (menus, toolbars, and status bars), making it a very space-efficient interface.
  - Useful for managing a set of objects.
  - Provides a grouping and focus for a set of activities within the larger environment of the desktop.
- Disadvantages:
  - Reinforces an application as the primary focus.
  - Containment for secondary windows within child windows does not exist, obscuring window relationships and possibly creating confusion.
  - Because the parent window does not actually contain objects, context cannot always be maintained on closing and opening.
  - The relationship between files and their windows is abstract, making an MDI application more challenging for beginning users to learn.
  - Confining child windows to the parent window can be inconvenient or inappropriate for some tasks.
  - The nested nature of child windows may make it difficult for the user to distinguish a child window in a parent window from a primary window that is a peer with the parent window but is positioned on top.

A multiple-document interface (MDI) may be used when multiple views of an object, or multiple documents, must be looked at simultaneously. The purpose of this scheme of windows is to provide multiple views of the same object, to permit comparisons among related objects, and to present multiple parts of an application. An MDI interface consists of multiple document windows that are easy to move between, essentially primary windows constrained to appear only within the parent windows boundary (instead of on the desktop). These windows may be referred to by a name that describes their contents, such as "Main" in Windows Program Manager. When minimized, they are displayed at the bottom of their parent window in iconic form. They are also resizable, movable, and scrollable. The primary window menu bar content may change dynamically, depending on the MDI window with the focus.

MAXIM   **The information to make a decision *must be there* when the decision is needed.**

With MDI, the parent window provides a visual and operational framework for its child windows. Child windows typically share the menu bar of the parent window and can also share other parts of the parent's interface, such as a toolbar or status bar. These components can be changed to reflect the commands and attributes of the child window active at that moment. Secondary windows displayed as a result of interaction within the MDI parent or child window (dialog boxes, message boxes, or property sheets, for example), typically are not contained or clipped by the parent window. These windows should activate and display content according to the conventions for secondary windows associated with a primary window.

If an MDI document is opened, the MDI parent window opens first, and then the child window for the document opens within it. When the user closes the parent window, all of its child windows are closed. Where possible, the state of a child window, such as its size and position within the parent window, should be preserved and restored when the user reopens the file.

Workbooks

- Description:
  - A window or task management technique that consists of a set of views organized like a tabbed notebook.
  - It is based upon the metaphor of a book or notebook.
  - Views of objects are presented as sections within the workbook's primary windows; child windows do not exist.
  - Each section represents a view of data.
  - Tabs can be included and used to navigate between sections.
  - Otherwise, its characteristics and behavior are similar to those of the multiple-document interface with all child windows maximized.
- Proper usage:
  - To manage a set of views of an object.
  - To optimize quick navigation of multiple views.
  - For content where the order of the sections is significant.

- ■ Advantages:
  - — Provides a grouping and focus for a set of activities within the larger environment of the desktop.
  - — Conserves screen real estate.
  - — Provides the greater simplicity of the single-document window interface.
  - — Provides greater simplicity by eliminating child window management.
  - — Preserves some management capabilities of the multiple-document interface.
- ■ Disadvantage:
  - — Cannot present simultaneous views.

A workbook is a scheme for managing a set of views that uses the metaphor of a book or notebook. Within the workbook, views of objects, in the form of sections, are presented within the workbook's primary window, rather than in individual child windows. Tabs are used as a navigational interface to move between different sections. (Tabs are described in Step 7.) Order the tabs to fit the content and organization of the presented information. Each tabbed section represents a view of data. One section can be used to list the workbook's table of contents.

Projects

- ■ Description:
  - — A technique that consists of a container: a project window holding a set of objects.
  - — The objects being held within the project window can be opened in primary windows that are peers with the project window.
  - — Visual containment of the peer windows within the project window is not necessary.
  - — Each opened peer window must possess its own menu bar and other interface elements.
  - — Each opened peer window can have its own entry on the task bar.
  - — When a project window is closed, all the peer windows of objects also close.
  - — When the project window is opened, the peer windows of the contained objects are restored to their former positions.
  - — Peer windows of a project may be restored without the project window itself being restored.
- ■ Proper usage:
  - — To manage a set of objects that do not necessarily need to be contained.
  - — When child windows are not to be constrained.
- ■ Advantages:
  - — Provides a grouping and focus for a set of activities within the larger environment of the desktop.
  - — Preserves some management capabilities of the multiple document interface.
  - — Provides the greatest flexibility in the placement and arrangement of windows.

- Disadvantage:
  — Increased complexity due to difficulty in differentiating peer primary windows of the project from windows of other applications.

A project is similar to a multiple-document interface (MDI), but does not visually contain the child windows. Objects represented by icons contained within it can be opened into primary windows that are peers with the parent window. Opened peer windows in the project do not share the menu bar or other areas contained with the parent window. Each opened peer window within the project must possess its own menu bar and other interface elements. (A palette window can be developed for sharing by all project windows, however.) Each peer child window can have its own entry on the taskbar.

Organizing Window Functions

Information and functions must be presented to people when and where they need them. Proper organization and support of tasks by windows will only be derived through a thorough and clear analysis of user tasks.

Window Organization

- Organize windows to support user tasks.
- Support the most common tasks in the most efficient sequence of steps.
- Use primary windows to:
  — Begin an interaction and provide a top-level context for dependent windows.
  — Perform a major interaction.
- Use secondary windows to:
  — Extend the interaction.
  — Obtain or display supplemental information related to the primary window.
- Use dialog boxes for:
  — Infrequently used or needed information.
  — "Nice-to-know" information.

People most often think in terms of tasks, not functions or applications. Windows must be organized to support this thinking. The design goal is to support the most common user tasks in the most efficient manner or fewest steps. Less frequently performed tasks are candidates for less efficiency or more steps.

Mayhew (1992) suggests that poor functional organization usually occurs because of one of, or a combination of, these factors:

- Emphasis on technical ease of implementation rather than proper analysis of user tasks.

- Focus on applications, features, functions, or data types instead of tasks.
- Organization of the design team into applications, with little cross-team communication.
- Blindly mimicking the manual world and carrying over manual inefficiencies to the computer system.

Emphasis on implementation ease puts the needs of the designer before the needs of the customer. Focusing on tasks conforms to the model of how people think. Application orientation imposes an unnatural boundary between functions, and lack of cross-team communication seldom yields consistent task procedures. Mimicking "what is" will never permit the capabilities of the computer system to be properly exploited.

Recommended usages for the various window types are summarized in the above guidelines. These recommendations were discussed more fully earlier in this chapter.

Number of Windows

- Minimize the number of windows needed to accomplish an objective.

A person does not work with windows simply for the joy of working with windows. Windows are a means to an end, a method of accomplishing something. Multiple windows on a display, as discussed elsewhere in this text, can be confusing, can increase the load on the human visual system, or may be too small to effectively present what needs to be contained within them.

Guidelines that appeared in early stages of window evolution concerning the maximum number of windows that a person could deal with were quite generous, a limit of seven or eight being suggested. As experience with windows has increased, these numbers have gradually fallen. One study found the mean number of windows maintained for experienced users was 3.7. Today, based on expressions of window users, a recommendation of displaying no more than two or three at one time seems most realistic. The guidelines on limitations for items like cascades (1–2) reflect today's feelings. The exact number of windows a person can effectively deal with at one time will ultimately depend on both the capabilities of the user and the characteristics of the task. Some users and situations may permit handling of more than three windows; for other users and situations, three windows may be two too many.

The general rule: Minimize the number of windows used to accomplish an objective. Use a single window whenever possible. Consider, however, the user's task. Don't clutter up a single window with rarely used information when it can be placed on a second, infrequently used, window.

Window Operations

Guidelines for windows operations are still evolving. Because of the paucity of published research data, many of the guidelines are still more anecdotal and intuitive than scientific. Guidelines will continue to develop and change as our understanding of, and experiences with, the windows interface continue to increase. Today, the following operational guidelines seem appropriate.

Active Window

- A window should be made active with as few steps as possible.
- Visually differentiate the active window from other windows.

While a system supports the display of multiple windows, the user generally works within a single window at one. This window, called the active window, may be designated either by the system or the user. Many systems make a window active when it is the object of another windowing operation. It is assumed that if users wish to change one aspect of a window's structure, they also wish to change its contents. They should also be permitted to move to and make any window active with as few steps as possible. This can be accomplished by simply allowing the user to move the selection cursor to the window's interior and then signal by pressing a key or button. For hidden windows, a menu of open windows might be presented from which the user selects a new open window.

In some situations, it may be desirable to allow multiple open windows. One research study compared a single open window with multiple open windows in performing queries and found that multiple open windows were described by people as more "natural." Performance was slower with multiple open windows, however. The study concluded that if user acceptance is important, multiple open windows might be the better alternative. If speed of task handling is critical, a single active window is more desirable.

Visually differentiate the active window from other windows. It is important that the user be able to quickly identify the active window. Methods to do this include a contrasting window title bar, border, or background color. An "active" indicator in the window border, which is turned on or off, may also be used. A combination of two or more of these visual cues may be used as well. The visual cue selected should be of moderate intensity, neither too powerful nor too subtle. Powerful cues will be distracting; subtle cues will be easily overlooked.

General Guidelines

- Design easy to use and learn windowing operations.
  - Direct manipulation seems to be a faster and more intuitive interaction style than indirect manipulation for many windowing operations.
- Minimize the number of window operations necessary to achieve a desired effect.
- Make navigating between windows particularly easy and efficient to do.
- Make the setting up of windows particularly easy to remember.
- In overlapping systems, provide powerful commands for arranging windows on the screen in user-tailorable configurations.

Easy to use. Design easy to use and learn window operations. The complexity of a windowing system should not cancel out its potential advantages. Operations must be carefully designed to achieve simplicity. As has been suggested, the ideal is that window manipulations should occur *implicitly* as a result of the user's task actions, not as a result of explicit, conscious, window management actions.

Minimize number. Minimize the number of window operations needed to achieve a desired effect. Establish the kinds of window operations that people are likely to want, and minimize the number of operations that must be performed to attain these configurations.

Easy navigation. Make navigating between windows easy and efficient. A study found that navigation between windows was the most frequent manipulation activity performed. High-frequency operations should always be easy to do.

Setting up. Make the process of setting up windows easy to remember. A study found that window arrangement (opening, resizing, moving, and so on) was a less frequent activity. Low-frequency operations should always be easy to learn.

User-tailorable configurations. In overlapping systems, provide powerful commands for arranging windows in user-tailorable configurations. When an overlapping window system is used, provide easy operations to achieve desired windowing configurations. Specific configurations should be capable of being created, named, and recalled.

Opening a Window

- Provide an iconic representation or textual list of available windows.
  — If opening with an expansion of an icon, animate the icon expansion.
- When opening a window:
  — Position the opening window in the most forward plane of the screen.
  — Adapt the window to the size and shape of the monitor on which it will be presented.
  — Designate it as the active window.
  — Set it off against a neutral background.
  — Ensure that its title bar is visible.
- When a primary window is opened or restored, position it on top.
  — Restore all secondary windows to the states that existed when the primary window was closed.
- When a dependent secondary window is opened, position it on top of its associated primary window.
  — Position a secondary window with peer windows on top of its peers.
  — Present layered or cascaded windows with any related peer secondary windows.
- When a dependent secondary window is activated, its primary window and related peer windows should also be positioned at the top.
- If more than one object is selected and opened, display each object in a separate window. Designate the last window selected as the active window.

- Display a window in the same state as when it was last accessed.
  — If the task, however, requires a particular sequence of windows, use a fixed or consistent presentation sequence.
- With tiled windows, provide an easy way to resize and move newly opened windows.

Typically, when windows are opened, they are designated as active and positioned in the most forward plane of the screen so that they can be used immediately. When opening a window one should not assume a fixed monitor size, but reflect the size of the monitor on which the window will actually be displayed. The window's title bar must be visible. To focus attention on the newly opened window, display the screen background behind the window in a neutral or subdued manner. When opening windows from an iconic representation, gradually expand the window so that the movement is visible. This will aid association of the icon with the window in the mind of the viewer.

When a primary window is opened or restored, position it at the top. Restore all secondary windows to the states that existed when the primary window was closed. When a dependent secondary window is opened, position it on top of its associated primary window. If a secondary windows has peers, position it on top of its peers. Present layered or cascaded windows with any related peer secondary windows.

When a dependent secondary window is activated, its primary window and related peer windows should also be positioned at the top. If more than one object is selected and opened, display each object in a separate window. Designate the last window selected as the active window. Always display a window in the same state as when it was last accessed. If the task, however, requires a particular sequence of windows, use a fixed or consistent presentation sequence.

The first opened tiled window will consume the entire screen. Subsequent windows are usually positioned by defaults in the system. The system positioning of these subsequent windows may not always be consistent with the user's needs. The system should allow the user to change the default positions, or provide a way for the user to move and resize the system-provided windows easily.

Sizing Windows

- Provide large-enough windows to:
  — Present all relevant and expected information for the task.
  — Avoid hiding important information.
  — Avoid crowding or visual confusion.
  — Minimize the need for scrolling.
    • But use less than the full size of the entire screen.
- If a window is too large, determine:
  — Is all the information needed?
  — Is all the information related?
- Otherwise, make the window as small as possible.
  — Optimum window sizes:

- For text, about 12 lines.
- For alphanumeric information, about seven lines.

Larger windows seem to have these advantages:

- They permit displaying of more information.
- They facilitate learning: Data relationships and groupings are more obvious.
- Less window manipulation requirements exist.
- Breadth is preferred to depth (based on menu research).
- More efficient data validation and data correction can be performed.

Disadvantages include:

- Longer pointer movements are required.
- Windows are more crowded.
- More visual scanning is required.
- Other windows more easily obscure parts of the window.
- It is not as easy to hide inappropriate data.

Always provide large enough windows to present all the relevant and expected information for the task. Never hide important or critical information, and minimize the need for scrolling. A study has found that very small windows requiring a significant amount of scrolling appear to increase decision-making time. Scrolling is also a cumbersome operation. To avoid scrolling, consider using unfolding dialog boxes, cascading windows, or a tab control. Avoid, however, making a window's default size the full size of the display. Doing so leads to any underlying windows being completely hidden from the user's view. The option to maximize primary and secondary windows always exists.

If, through analysis and design, a window appears to be too large, determine:

- Is all the information needed?
- Is all the information related?

Important, critical, or frequently used information must be maintained on a screen, but perhaps information exists that is needed or used infrequently, for example. only 10 to 20 percent of the time. This kind of information is a good candidate for placement on another window or dialog box. Perhaps information is included on a screen that is not related to the task being performed. This kind of information should be located with the information to which it is related. As a last resort, consider shortening some window control captions or other included window text to achieve a proper fit.

At least two studies have looked at optimum window sizes. Procedural text in window sizes of 6, 12, and 24 lines were evaluated by one study. Fastest and most accurate completion occurred with the 12-line window. The retrieval of alphanumeric information was compared in 7-, 13-, and 19-line windows in another study. A seven-line window was found to be more than adequate.

Window Placement

- Considerations:
  - In placing a window on the display, consider:
    - The use of the window.
    - The overall display dimensions.
    - The reason for the window's appearance.
- General:
  - Position the window so it is entirely visible.
  - If the window is being restored, place the window where it last appeared.
  - If the window is new, and a location has not yet been established, place it:
    - At the point of the viewer's attention, usually the location of the pointer or cursor.
    - In a position convenient to navigate to.
    - So that it is not obscuring important or related underlying window information.
  - For multiple windows, give each additional window its own unique and discernible location.
    - A cascading presentation is recommended.
  - In a multiple-monitor configuration, display the secondary window on the same monitor as its primary window.
  - If none of the above location considerations apply, then:
    - Horizontally center a secondary window within its primary window just below the title bar, menu bar, and any docked toolbars.
  - If the user then moves the window, display it at this new location the next time the user opens the window.
    - Adjust it as necessary to the current display configuration.
  - Do not let the user move a window to a position where it cannot be easily repositioned.
- Dialog boxes:
  - If the dialog box relates to the entire system, center it on screen.
  - Keep key information on the underlying screen visible.
  - If one dialog box calls another, make the new one movable whenever possible.

Considerations. In placing a window on the display, consider how the window is used in relation to other windows, the overall dimensions of the display, and the reason that the window is being presented.

General. First, locate the window so it is fully visible. If the window is being restored, locate it where it last appeared. If the window is new and the location has not yet been established, place it at the point of the viewer's attention. This will usually be the location of the pointer or cursor. Also, place the window in a position where it will be convenient to navigate to, and where it will not obscure important underlying screen information. Preferred positions are essentially below and right. The suggested order of placement is below right, below, right, top right, below left, top, left, top left.

In a multiple-monitor configuration, display the secondary window on the same monitor as its primary window. If none of these situations applies, horizontally center a secondary window within the primary window, just below the title bar, menu bar, and any docked toolbars. Give each additional window its own unique location. A cascading presentation, from upper left to lower right is recommended. If the user then moves the window, display it at this new location the next time the user opens the window, adjusted as necessary for the current display configuration. Do not let the user move a window to a position where it cannot be easily repositioned.

Dialog boxes. If a dialog box relates to the entire system, center it on display, keeping key information on an underlying window visible. If one dialog box calls another, make the new one movable whenever possible.

Window Separation

- Crisply, clearly, and pleasingly demarcate a window from the background of the screen on which it appears.
  — Provide a surrounding solid line border for the window.
  — Provide a window background that sets the window off well against the overall screen background.
  — Consider incorporating a drop shadow beneath the window.

Component separation is especially critical in a graphics environment because of the spatial layering that can occur. All windows must be clearly set off from the underlying screen or windows. The demarcation must be crisp and visually pleasing. A solid single-line border is recommended for this purpose. Also provide a window background that sets the window off well against the overall screen background. If color is used, exercise caution and choose compatible colors. (See Step 12 "Choose the Proper Colors.") Another alternative is to use for the window a lighter shade of the color used for the screen background. Changes in the density of shades are often more visually pleasing than different colors. To emphasize the three-dimensional aspects of graphic windows, incorporate a drop shadow beneath each window.

Moving a Window

- Permit the user to change the position of all windows.
- Change the pointer shape to indicate that the move selection is successful.
- Move the entire window as the pointer moves.
  — If it is impossible to move the entire window, move the window outline while leaving the window displayed in its original position.
- Permit the moving of a window without its being active.

An indication that the move operation has been successfully selected and that the move may begin should be indicated to the user by changing the pointer's shape. This will provide feedback indicating that it is safe to begin the move operation and will avoid false starts. Ideally, the entire window should move along with the pointer. If the entire window cannot be moved, move the window outline while leaving the full window displayed on the screen. Displaying only the window's outline during the move operation, and not the window itself, may make it harder for the user to decide when the window has been repositioned correctly. It may be necessary for a window to be moved without being active. This should be possible. The action of moving the window may implicitly activate it, however.

Resizing a Window

- Permit the user to change the size of primary windows.
  - Unless the information displayed in the window is fixed or cannot be scaled to provide more information.
- Change the pointer shape to indicate that the resizing selection is successful.
- The simplest operation is to anchor the upper-left corner and resize from the lower-right corner.
  - Also permit resizing from any point on the window.
- Show the changing window as the pointer moves.
  - If it is impossible to show the entire window being resized, show the window's outline while leaving the window displayed in its original position.
- When window size changes and content remains the same:
  - Change image size proportionally as window size changes.
- If resizing creates a window or image too small for easy use, do one of the following:
  - Clip (truncate) information arranged in some logical structure or layout when minimum size is attained, or
  - When no layout considerations exist, format (restructure) information as size is reduced, or
  - Remove less useful information (if it can be determined), or
  - When minimum size is attained, replace information with a message that indicates that the minimum size has been reached and that the window must be enlarged to continue working.
- Permit resizing a window without its being active.

Make your primary windows resizable unless the information displayed in the window is fixed or cannot be scaled to provide the user with more information. (For example, a calculator window.)

An indication that the resize operation has been successfully selected, and that the move may begin, should be indicated to the user by changing the pointer's shape. This will provide the necessary feedback that it is safe to begin the resizing and will avoid false starts. The simplest operation for the user, conceptually, is always to resize from the lower-right corner and anchor the window in the upper-left corner. Flexibility can be provided by permitting resizing to occur from any point on the border (the anchor is always opposite the pulling point), but conceptually this is more complex. Some people may have difficulty predicting which window sides or corners will be resized from specific pulling points.

Ideally, the entire window should move along with the pointer. If the entire window cannot be moved, move the window outline while leaving the full window displayed on the screen. Displaying only the window's outline during the move operation, and not the window itself, may make it harder for the user to decide when the window has been repositioned correctly.

The effect of a resizing operation on the window's contents usually depends on the application. In enlarging, more data may be displayed, a larger image may be created, or blank space may be added around the image. In reducing, less data may be displayed, the image may be made smaller, blank space may be eliminated, or the data may be reformatted. If resizing creates a window or image too small for easy use, clip or truncate information arranged in some logical structure, format, or layout. When no layout considerations exist, as is the case for text, format or restructure the displayed information. Also consider removing less useful information, if it can be determined. When the minimum size has been attained and any additional attempts to reduce window size occur, replace the information with a message that indicates that the minimum size has been reached and that the window must be enlarged to continue working.

It may be necessary for a window to be resized without being active. This should be possible. The action of moving the window may implicitly activate it, however.

Other Operations

- Permit primary windows to be maximized, minimized, and restored.

Maximizing. Maximizing a window increases the size of the window to its largest optimum size. The system default setting for the maximum size is as large as the display. This should be adjustable, as necessary.

Minimizing. Minimizing a window reduces it to its smallest size.

Restoring. Restoring returns a window to its previous size and position after the user has maximized or minimized it.

Window Shuffling

- Window shuffling must be easy to accomplish.

Window shuffling should be easy to perform in as few steps as possible. One method is to permit the toggling of the two most recently displayed windows. Another is to permit rapid window shuffling and the swapping of the front window and the second or back window.

Keyboard Control/Mouseless Operation

- Window actions should be capable of being performed through the keyboard as well as with a mouse.

- Keyboard alternatives should be designated through use of mnemonic codes as much as possible.
- Keyboard designations should be capable of being modified by the user.

All window actions should be capable of being performed using the keyboard as well as the mouse. This will provide a more efficient alternative for applications that contain tasks that are primarily keyboard-oriented, for users skilled in touch typing, and for any other situations in which frequent movement between keyboard and mouse may be required. The use of mnemonic codes to reflect window mouse actions will greatly aid user learning of the keyboard alternatives. To provide the user flexibility, all keyboard designations should be capable of being user modified.

Closing a Window

- Close a window when:
  — The user requests that it be closed.
  — The user performs the action required in the window.
  — The window has no further relevance.
- If a primary window is closed, also close all of its secondary windows.
- When a window is closed, save its current state, including size and position, for use when the window is opened again.

Close a window when the user requests it to be closed, when the action required in the window is performed, or when the window has no further relevance to the task being performed. If the closed window is a primary window, also close its associated secondary windows. When a window is closed, it is important that its current state, including size and position, be saved for use when the window is again opened.

Web Systems

Web systems have limited windowing capabilities. The *frame* concept does provide window-like ability, and JavaScript does provide *pop-up* windows.

Frames

- Description:
  — Multiple Web screen panes that permit the displaying of multiple documents on a page.
  — These documents can be independently viewed, scrolled, and updated.
  — The documents are presented in a tiled format.
- Proper usage:
  — For content expected to change frequently.
  — To allow users to change partial screen content.
  — To permit users to compare multiple pieces of information.

■ Guidelines:
— Use only a few frames (three or less) at a given time.
— Choose sizes based upon the type of information to be presented.
— Never force viewers to resize frames to see information.
— Never use more than one scrolling region on a page.

Description. The Web is, historically, essentially a single page (or, by analogy, a single window) entity. While providing significant interface benefits, it is also a reversal of the interface evolution process that led from single-screen technology to windowing. To counteract this shortcoming, *frames* were created. A frame is an independent pane of information presented in a Web page, or, again by analogy, as multiple windows. Frames, however, are presented as tiled, with no overlapping capability. The interaction richness, support, and contextual cues provided by overlapping windows are lacking. Frames, then, allow the displaying of multiple documents on a single Web page. These multiple documents can be independently viewed, scrolled, and updated.

Proper usage. Frames are useful in situations where portions of the page content are expected to change frequently. The volatile information can be separated from other page content and placed within a frame, thereby requiring only a portion of the page's content to be modified. Frames are also useful for allowing the user to change page content; navigation links can be placed in one frame and the resulting content displayed within another frame. As different links are selected, the content in the related frame changes. Finally, frames more effectively allow users to compare multiple pieces of related information displayed within the different frames.

Advantages and disadvantages. Frames, like most interface entities, have advantages and disadvantages. At this moment in their existence, the disadvantages seem to outweigh the advantages. These disadvantages, however, are being whittled away as Web technology advances.

Frames *advantages* mostly cluster around their ability to reduce the user's content comprehension mental load. These include the following:

■ They decrease the user's need to jump back and forth between screens, thereby reducing navigation-related cognitive overhead.

■ They increase the user's opportunity to request, view, and compare multiple sources of information.

■ They allow content pages to be developed independently of navigation pages.

The *disadvantages* mostly cluster around navigational shortcomings, including:

■ The difference between a single Web page and a page with frames is not always obvious to the user.

■ They suffer some of the shortcomings of tiled screens:
— Only a limited number can be displayed in the available screen area.
— They are perceived as crowded and more visually complex because frame borders are flush against one another and they fill up the whole screen.

Crowding is accentuated if the borders contain scroll bars and/or control icons. Viewer attention may be drawn to the border, not the data.

- Frames-based pages behave differently from regular Web pages.
  — Page-printing difficulties and problems can exist.
  — Page interaction can be clumsy.
  — URLs cannot be e-mailed to other users.
- Frames will not work on older browsers.

Past problems, now being addressed and mostly solved, have included difficulties in bookmarking pages, difficulties in creating browser history lists, and inconsistencies in behavior of the browser's Back button. So, while no longer an interface disaster, frames do make a page clumsy to work with. One study has found that well-designed frames didn't hinder users, but they didn't help, either. A review of the top 100 Web sites (in 1999) found that one common characteristic they all shared was no use of frames.

Guidelines. Guidelines to consider in using frames are the following: Use no more than three frames at a time. Using more will shrink each frame's usable area to the point where little space will be available for presenting content. Then, users will not be able to see much and be forced to scroll. Choose frame sizes based upon the type of information you want to present. Navigational links, for example, should be presented in a small frame and the corresponding information in a larger adjacent frame. Never force people to resize frames to see information. If people feel they must resize frames, the page design is poor. Finally, do not use more than one scrolling region in frames contained on a page. This may be confusing to many users.

Technological advances in frames will continue to occur. Knowledge related to frame usability will also advance. Always be aware of the latest developments.

Pop-Up Windows

- Be extremely cautious in the use of pop-up windows.

JavaScript pop-up windows began appearing on the Web in 1996. Their use is multiplying and, in the view of almost all Web users, polluting screens. Because they are most frequently used in advertising, they have become a source of great aggravation to almost every user. Anecdotal evidence suggests that when a pop-up window begins to appear, most people close them before they are rendered. So, if a pop-up window is used, it may never be completely seen or read by the user. Use them with extreme caution.

Select the Proper Device-Based Controls

Device-based controls, often called input devices, are the mechanisms through which people communicate their desires to the system. The evolution of graphical systems has seen a whole new family of devices provided to assist and enhance this communication. These new mechanisms are most commonly referred to as pointing devices. In this step, we will:

- Identify the characteristics and capabilities of various device-based controls:
  - Trackball
  - Joystick
  - Graphic tablet
  - Light pen
  - Touch screen
  - Voice
  - Mouse
  - Keyboard
- Select the proper controls for the user and tasks.

For years the device of choice in display-based systems was the standard keyboard and some human-engineered variations. As graphical systems evolved, emphasis shifted to another device, the mouse and some of its cousins: the trackball and joystick. A few other devices have also been around and have seen extended service through the years: the light pen and the graphic tablet. Some uniquely human devices also exist, touch and voice. A finger has been used in conjunction with touch-sensitive screens. Our vocal chords are being harnessed to speak meaningfully to the computer, not simply to shout words of exasperation. These various alternatives have both strengths and weaknesses. Selecting the proper device-based control to do the required job is critical to system success. A good fit between user and control will lead to fast, accurate performance. A poor fit will result in lower productivity, produce more errors, and increase user fatigue.

We'll begin by reviewing the kinds of tasks being performed using graphical systems. We'll discuss each device and identify its advantages and disadvantages. Then, we'll focus on the most popular control, the mouse, describing it in more detail and presenting a series of design guidelines for its use. The keyboard, because of its versatility and usefulness for text entry tasks, will also be examined in more detail. Finally, pertinent research will be reviewed and guidelines presented to aid in selecting the proper device.

Characteristics of Device-Based Controls

Several specific tasks are performed using graphical systems.

- To point at an object on the screen.
- To select the object or identify it as the focus of attention.
- To drag an object across the screen.
- To draw something free form on the screen.
- To track or follow a moving object.
- To orient or position an object.
- To enter or manipulate data or information.

The various devices vary in how well they can perform these actions. Among the considerations to be reviewed are two very important factors. First, is the mechanism a direct or indirect pointing device? *Direct* devices are operated on the screen itself. Examples include the light pen, the finger, and voice. *Indirect* devices are operated in a location other than the screen, most often on the desktop. Examples include the mouse, trackball, and keyboard. The psychomotor skills involved in learning to use, and using, a direct device are much simpler than those required for an indirect device. Most of these direct device skills were instilled in our formative years.

Second, in terms of *direction, distance,* and *speed,* what is the relationship between movement of the hand-operated device and the corresponding pointer movement on the screen? Does the pointer movement track control movement exactly or does it not? The mouse achieves a coupled relationship in all three aspects of direction, distance, and speed: The pointer on the screen moves in the direction the mouse is pushed, at the speed the mouse is pushed, and the distance the mouse is pushed (there may be some ratios applied). A trackball does not achieve this relationship in all three aspects. The pointer moves the direction the trackball is turned and the speed the ball is turned, but not the distance the ball is moved because the ball does not move forward or backwards; its socket is stationary. Devices possessing coupled relationships in these three aspects require less psychomotor skill learning than those not possessing a coupled relationship in all three aspects.

Trackball

- Description:
  — A spherical object (ball) that rotates freely in all directions in its socket.
  — Direction and speed is tracked and translated into cursor movement.
- Advantages:
  — Direct relationship between hand and pointer movement in terms of direction and speed.
  — Does not obscure vision of screen.
  — Does not require additional desk space (if mounted on keyboard).
- Disadvantages:
  — Movement is indirect, in a plane different from the screen.
  — No direct relationship exists between hand and pointer movement in terms of distance.
  — Requires a degree of eye-hand coordination.
  — Requires hand to be removed from keyboard keys.
  — Requires different hand movements.
  — Requires hand to be removed from keyboard (if not mounted on keyboard).
  — Requires additional desk space (if not mounted on keyboard).
  — May be difficult to control.
  — May be fatiguing to use over extended time.

Description. Commonly used with notebook PCs, the trackball is a ball that rotates freely in all directions in its socket. The ball is rotated with one's fingertips, and its direction and speed are tracked and translated into equivalent screen cursor movement. Trackballs are well suited for navigational control, as in video games or exploration of 3-D environments. In these tasks, smooth movement is more important than fine target acquisition.

Advantages. In terms of direction and speed, a trackball possesses a direct relationship between how it is rolled and how the cursor moves on the screen. The cursor moves in the same direction and speed ratio as the ball is rotated. Many trackballs are mounted on the keyboard itself, permitting the user's hands to remain close to the keys. Trackballs on the keyboard do not require additional desk space, although the keyboard must often be expanded to allow for their inclusion.

Disadvantages. Trackballs share a common problem with several other controls: control movement is in a different plane from the screen, or indirect. The cursor, or pointer, is separated from the control itself—the pointer being on the screen, the control on the keyboard. To effectively use a trackball requires learning the proper psychomotor skills, fine finger movements for accurate pointing, and gross hand movements for moving longer distances. The fine finger movements necessary to use them can be difficult to perform. Over longer periods of use, they can be fatiguing. When paired with keyboard tasks, they require a shift in motor activity from keystrokes to finger/hand movement.

Joystick

- ■ Description:
  - — A stick or bat-shaped device anchored at the bottom.
  - — Variable in size, smaller ones being operated by fingers, larger ones requiring the whole hand.
  - — Variable in cursor direction movement method, force joysticks respond to pressure, movable ones respond to movement.
  - — Variable in degree of movement allowed, from horizontal-vertical only to continuous.
- ■ Advantages:
  - — Direct relationship between hand and pointer movement in terms of direction.
  - — Does not obscure vision of screen.
  - — Does not require additional desk space (if mounted on keyboard).
- ■ Disadvantages:
  - — Movement indirect, in plane different from screen.
  - — Indirect relationship between hand and pointer in terms of speed and distance.
  - — Requires a degree of eye-hand coordination.
  - — Requires hand to be removed from keyboard keys.
  - — Requires different hand movements to use.
  - — Requires hand to be removed from keyboard (if not mounted on keyboard).
  - — Requires additional desk space (if not mounted on keyboard).
  - — May be fatiguing to use over extended time.
  - — May be slow and inaccurate.

Description. A joystick, like its aircraft namesake, is a stick or bat-shaped device usually anchored at the bottom. They come in variable sizes, smaller ones being operated by fingers, larger ones requiring the whole hand. The smaller joysticks require fine motor coordination, the larger ones more gross coordination. Some, called *force* joysticks, are immovable, responding to pressure exerted against them. The direction and amount of pressure is translated into pointer movement direction and speed. Others, called *movable* joysticks, can be moved within a dish-shaped area. The direction and distance of the movements create a similar pointer movement on the screen. Some kinds of joysticks permit continuous movements, others only horizontal and vertical movements. Joysticks may also be mounted on the keyboard. Joysticks are also well suited for navigational control where smooth movement is most important.

Advantages. Joysticks typically possess a direct relationship between hand and cursor movement in terms of direction. They do not obscure vision of the screen and, when mounted on the keyboard, do not require additional desk space.

Disadvantages. Joysticks are also indirect devices, the control and its result being located in different planes. They require developing a skill to use and can be slow and inaccurate. Use over extended time, they may also be fatiguing. When paired with keyboard tasks, they require a shift in motor activity from keystrokes to finger/hand movement.

Graphic Tablet

- Description:
  — Pressure-, heat-, light-, or light-blockage-sensitive horizontal surfaces that lie on the desktop or keyboard.
  — May be operated with fingers, light pen, or objects like a stylus or pencil.
  — Pointer imitates movements on tablet.
- Advantages:
  — Direct relationship between touch movements and pointer movements in terms of direction, distance, and speed.
  — More comfortable horizontal operating plane.
  — Does not obscure vision of screen.
- Disadvantages:
  — Movement is indirect, in a plane different from screen.
  — Requires hand to be removed from keyboard.
  — Requires hand to be removed from keyboard keys.
  — Requires different hand movements to use.
  — Requires additional desk space.
  — Finger may be too large for accuracy with small objects

Description. A graphic tablet, also called a *touch* tablet, is a device with a horizontal surface sensitive to pressure, heat, light, or the blockage of light. It may lie on the desk or may be incorporated on a keyboard, and it is operated with fingers, light pen, or objects like a pencil or stylus. The screen pointer imitates movement on the tablet.

Advantages. With graphic tablets, a direct relationship exists between touch movements and pointer movements in terms of direction, distance, and speed. The screen mimics the tablet. When used with objects like styluses, light pens, or pencils, the operational angle, horizontal, is more comfortable than those vertically oriented.

Disadvantages. Tablets are also indirect controls, creating coordination problems. To use them requires moving one's hand from the keyboard and, if using another device, picking it up. If the finger is the tablet-activation object, accuracy with small objects is difficult. Tablets also require desk space.

Touch Screen

- Description:
  — A special surface on the screen sensitive to finger or stylus touch.

- Advantages:
  — Direct relationship between hand and pointer location in terms of direction, distance, and speed.
  — Movement is direct, in the same plane as screen.
  — Requires no additional desk space.
  — Stands up well in high-use environments.
- Disadvantages:
  — Finger may obscure part of screen.
  — Finger may be too large for accuracy with small objects.
  — Requires moving the hand far from the keyboard to use.
  — Very fatiguing to use for extended period of time.
  — May soil or damage the screen.
- Design Guidelines:
  — Screen objects should be at least 3/4" × 3/4" in size.
  — Object separation should be at least 1/8".
  — Provide visual feedback in response to activation. Auditory feedback may also be appropriate.
  — When the consequences are destructive, require confirmation after selection to eliminate inadvertent selection.
  — Provide an instructional invitation to begin using.

Description. A touch screen is a screen that consists of a special surface sensitive to finger or stylus touch. Objects on the screen are pointed to and touched to select them.

Advantages. Touch screens possess a direct relationship between hand and pointer movement in terms of direction, distance, and speed. This relationship is direct, not indirect, because the control (finger or stylus) is on the same plane as the pointer. Another significant advantage of a touch screen is that it does not require any additional desk space.

Disadvantages. A disadvantage of touch screens is that they are fatiguing to use over an extended period of time. If a finger is the touch mechanism, it may obscure part of the screen and be too large to be accurate with small objects. A stylus is usually more accurate than the finger. Fingers may also soil the screen, and a stylus may damage it. Both finger and stylus require moving a hand from the keyboard, and if a stylus is used, it must also be picked up.

Guidelines. When using touch screens, larger screen objects should always be provided to foster accuracy in use. Objects should be 3/4" square at a minimum and separated by at least 1/8". Visual, and perhaps auditory, feedback should be provided in response to activation. When the consequences of selection are destructive, require a confirmation to avoid inadvertent selection. Observational research indicates that touch screen devices placed in public places, for use by the general public, should possess an instructional invitation to begin their use.

Today, other forms of touch screen devices are being used. One type allows placement of a finger on the screen without item selection, selection being accomplished by lifting the finger off the screen. This may allow more accurate item selection. Another method involves placing a cursor on the screen directly above one's finger and moving the cursor as the finger is moved. The cursor permits better target visibility, as well as the detection of smaller targets.

Light Pen

- Description:
  — A special surface on a screen sensitive to the touch of a special stylus or pen.
- Advantages:
  — Direct relationship between hand and pointer movement in terms of direction, distance, and speed.
  — Movement is direct, in the same plane as screen.
  — Requires minimal additional desk space.
  — Stands up well in high-use environments.
  — More accurate than finger touching.
- Disadvantages:
  — Hand may obscure part of screen.
  — Requires picking it up to use.
  — Requires moving the hand far from the keyboard to use.
  — Very fatiguing to use for extended period of time.

Description. A light pen also utilizes a touch screen, but one that is sensitive in a specific way to one kind of pen or stylus. Advantages and disadvantages are similar to those of the touch screen.

Advantages. Light pens possess a direct relationship between hand and pointer movement in terms of direction, distance, and speed, and are also classified as direct pointing devices because the control (pen or stylus) is on the same plane as the pointer. Another advantage of a light pen is that it does not require any additional desk space, except for a place for the pen to rest. A light pen is usually more accurate than the finger.

Disadvantages. A disadvantage is that they are also fatiguing to use over an extended period of time. Light pens require moving a hand from the keyboard to pick up and use.

Voice

- Description:
  — Automatic speech recognition by the computer.
- Advantages:
  — Simple and direct.
  — Useful for people who cannot use a keyboard.
  — Useful when the user's hands are occupied.

- Disadvantages:
  — High error rates due to difficulties in:
    • Recognizing boundaries between spoken words.
    • Blurred word boundaries due to normal speech patterns.
  — Slower throughput than with typing.
  — Difficult to use in noisy environments.
  — Impractical to use in quiet environments.

Description. Automatic speech recognition technology has been under development for more than a quarter of a century. Its progress has been hindered by the disadvantages listed below.

Advantages. Speech is a simple and direct communication medium. It is very useful for people who cannot use a keyboard, or whose hands are otherwise occupied.

Disadvantages. Speech recognition errors are fundamentally different from keying errors. Most keying errors result from a user's inability to always press the correct key. Most speech recognition errors result from the computer speech recognizers' inability to correctly recognize words. People can dictate to a computer at a fairly fast rate, about 105 words per minute (Karat, Halverson, Horn, & Karat, 1999 and Lewis, 1999). After making the required corrections, the input rate becomes about 25 words per minute when transcribing the input. New users had even lower transcribing rates. As summarized in Step 2 "Understand the User or Client," typists, even those of the two-finger variety, have much higher keying rates. Error correction also takes much longer with a speech recognition system. The most commonly used correction methods are: deleting and repeating the last phrase, deleting and repeating a specific word, deleting and selecting a correct word from a list of alternative words, and retyping the selection.

Several research studies have shown that correcting voice recognition errors using a method other than additional voice recognition speeds up the correction process. Suhm, Myers, and Waibel (1999) found that fast typists made almost three times more corrections per minute than people who made corrections by voice only. Lewis (1999) and Karat et al. (1999) uncovered very similar results.

Speech recognition is also, of course, difficult to utilize in an improper environment. Noise can hinder the process, and it is very impractical, and disturbing, to try and use it in a very quiet location such as a library.

Mouse

- Description:
  — A rectangular or dome-shaped, movable, desktop control containing from one to three buttons used to manipulate objects and information on the screen.
  — Movement of screen pointer mimics the mouse movement.
- Advantages:
  — Direct relationship between hand and pointer movement in terms of direction, distance, and speed.

— Permits a comfortable hand resting position
— Selection mechanisms are included on mouse.
— Does not obscure vision of the screen.

- Disadvantages:
  — Movement is indirect, in a plane different from screen.
  — Requires hand to be removed from keyboard.
  — Requires additional desk space.
  — May require long movement distances.
  — Requires a degree of eye-hand coordination.

Description. A mouse is a rectangular or dome-shaped, movable, desktop control containing from one to three buttons used to manipulate objects and information on the screen. The movement of the screen pointer mimics the mouse movement. In 1968, Doug Engelbart, a researcher at the Stanford Research Institute, invented what became the mouse. While using a trackball, he was inspired to turn it upside down and let the ball become the bottom of a control that, attached to a cord, was moved across the desk. It was patented as the "x-y position indicator," and finally christened the "mouse" by a colleague of Engelbart's (a colleague whose name is lost in time). In 1997, Engelbart was at long last rewarded for his invention when he received the annual Lemelson-Mit Prize for American Innovation, including a well-deserved and very substantial monetary reward (cnn.com, 1997).

Advantages. There is a direct relationship between hand and pointer movement in terms of direction, distance, and speed. The mouse itself contains some basic controls (buttons) useful for manipulating screen objects. The hand position when using the mouse is generally fairly comfortable, and the mouse does not obscure the screen.

Disadvantages. Disadvantages are that they are also indirect devices, the control and its result being located in different planes. They require developing a skill to use and, when paired with keyboard tasks, they require movement away from the keyboard and a shift in motor activity from keystrokes to finger/hand movement. The mouse also requires extensive additional desk space and long positioning movements. The mouse comes in a variety of configurations, performs some basic functions, and is operated in several ways.

Configurations. A mouse may possess one, two, or three buttons. Most, but not all, windowing systems permit operation using all configurations. Buttons are used to perform three functions to be described. When three mouse buttons are not available, the pointer location or keyboard qualifiers must be used to determine the function to be performed. A multibutton mouse permits a more efficient operation, but a person must remember which button to use to perform each function. A multibutton mouse may usually be configured for left- or right-hand use.

Functions. The functions performed by a mouse are Select, Menu, and Adjust. The Select function is used to manipulate controls, to select alternatives and data, and to select objects that will be affected by actions that follow. *Select* is a mouse's most important function and is the function assigned to a one-button mouse. For a multibutton mouse, it is usually assigned to the leftmost button (assuming a right-handed operation).

The *Menu* function is typically used to request and display a pop-up menu on a screen. A menu appears when the button is depressed within a particular defined area of the screen. This area may be, for example, the entire screen, within a window, or on a window border. This button eliminates the need for a control icon, which must be pointed at and selected. The user, however, must remember that a menu is available. The *Adjust* function extends or reduces the number of items selected. It is the least used of the three functions and is usually assigned last and given the least prominent location on a mouse.

Operations. Several operations can be performed with a mouse. The first, *point*, is the movement and positioning of the mouse pointer over the desired screen object. It prepares for a selection or control operation. To press is to hold the button down without releasing it. It identifies the object to be selected.

To *click* is to press and immediately release a button without moving the mouse. This operation typically selects an item or insertion point, operates a control, or activates an inactive window or control. To *double-click* is to perform two clicks within a predefined time limit without moving the mouse. It is used as a shortcut for common operations such as activating an icon or opening a file.

To *drag* is to press and hold the button down, and then move the pointer in the appropriate direction. It identifies a range of objects or moves or resizes items. To *double-drag* is to perform two clicks and hold the button down, and then move the pointer in the appropriate direction. It identifies a selection by a larger unit, such as a group of words.

Mouse Usage Guidelines

- Provide a "hot zone" around small or thin objects that might require extremely fine mouse positioning.
- Never use double-clicks or double-drags as the only means of carrying out essential operations.
- Do not use mouse plus keystroke combinations.
- Do not require a person to point at a moving target.

If an object is very small and might require fine mouse positioning, provide a large "hot zone" around it. This will increase target size and speed selection. Do not require double-clicks or double-drags as the only way to carry out essential operations. Rapid double-pressing is difficult for some people. Do not use mouse plus keystroke combinations to accomplish actions. This can be awkward. One exception: multiple selections of items in a list. Do not require a person to point at a moving target, except, of course, for a game.

Keyboard

- Description:
  — Standard typewriter keyboard and cursor movement keys.
- Advantages:
  — Familiar.
  — Accurate.
  — Does not take up additional desk space.
  — Very useful for:
    • Entering text and alphanumeric data.
    • Inserting in text and alphanumeric data.
    • Keyed shortcuts—accelerators.
    • Keyboard mnemonics—equivalents.
  — Advantageous for:
    • Performing actions when less than three mouse buttons exist.
    • Use with very large screens.
    • Touch typists.
- Disadvantages:
  — Slow for non-touch-typists.
  — Slower than other devices in pointing.
  — Requires discrete actions to operate.
  — No direct relationship between finger or hand movement on the keys and cursor movement on screen in terms of speed and distance.

Description. Christopher Latham Sholes invented the standard typewriter keyboard in 1870. Commonly called the QWERTY layout, Sholes' placement of letters was intended to slow down a typist's keying movements so that the potential for key jams was minimized. From a strictly human-engineering perspective, its layout inadequacies included a dominance of the left hand in making keystrokes, frequent successive keystrokes with the same hand, frequent movement between keyboard key rows, and frequently used letter pairs being placed far from each other. In 1936, August Dvorak created a revised and well-human-engineered keyboard that overcame many of these deficiencies. The advantages of the DVORAK layout, as it came to be called, included a right-hand dominance in keying, much less frequent row changes, and more systematic alternation between the right and left hand. With this new layout, finger travel distances were reduced by at least one order of magnitude. Acceptance of this new keyboard was, and continues, to be slow. Most users have seemed unwilling to invest the time and effort to change.

In the 1980s, IBM performed a series of studies comparing the QWERTY keyboard with various sequential key layouts such as ABCDEF or JIHGFE (starting from the upper left or QWERTY location). IBM wanted to determine if a sequential layout was better for users who professed to be non-touch-typists. Their findings were surprising. Non-touch-typist performance results were as good, or better, using the QWERTY layout as using the various systematic layouts. IBM's conclusion: Why change? So they didn't. IBM researchers could only speculate as to why the new systematic layouts fared so poorly. Perhaps, they said, while non-touch-typists profess no knowledge of the QWERTY layout, through experience they have learned the layout, at least well enough to permit effective two-finger typing to be accomplished. Another possibility, they said, was that perhaps some characteristic of the QWERTY layout makes it easy to scan and find needed keys. Speculation number one seems to be the most reasonable explanation, but we may never know for sure.

Advantages. The standard keyboard is familiar, accurate, and does not consume additional desk space. It is useful and efficient for entering or inserting text or alphanumeric data. For tasks requiring heavy text or data entry, shifting the hands between a keyboard and an alternative control, such as a mouse, can be time-consuming and inefficient, especially for a touch typist. The keyboard is flexible enough to accept keyed shortcuts, either keyboard accelerators or mnemonic equivalents. Some systems also permit navigation across a screen through use of keyboard keys such as the space bar, arrows, Tab, and Enter.

Inefficiencies in using other graphical device-based controls can occur, making it advantageous to use a keyboard. A mouse with a limited number of buttons will require use of the keyboard to accomplish some functions, possibly causing frequent shifting between devices. When operations are being performed on very large screens, the user may also find keyboard window management preferable to the long mouse movements frequently required. Therefore, to compensate for these possible inefficiencies, many windowing systems provide alternative keyboard operations for mouse tasks.

Disadvantages. Disadvantages of a keyboard include its requiring discrete finger actions to operate instead of the more fine positioning movements. As a result, no direct relationship exists in terms of speed and distance between finger or hand movement on the keys and cursor movement on the screen. Depending on the layout of the keyboard cursor control keys, direct-relationship direction problems may also exist, because fingers may not move in the same direction as the cursor. Keyboards will also be slower for non-touch-typists and slower than other controls in pointing tasks.

Keyboard Guidelines

- Provide keyboard accelerators.
  - Assign single keys for frequently performed, small-scale tasks.
  - Use standard platform accelerators.
  - Assign Shift-*key* combinations for actions that extend or are complementary to the actions of the key or key combination used without the Shift-*key*.
  - Assign Ctrl-*key* combinations for:
    - Infrequent actions.
    - Tasks that represent larger-scale versions of the task assigned to the unmodified key.
- Provide keyboard equivalents.
  - Use standard platform equivalents.

— Use the first letter of the item description.
— If first letter conflicts exist, use:
  • Another distinctive consonant in the item description.
  • A vowel in the item description.
- Provide window navigation through use of keyboard keys.

Keyboard accelerators. Accelerators provide a way to access menu elements without displaying a menu. They are useful for frequent tasks performed by experienced users. Keys assigned for accelerators should foster efficient performance and be meaningful and conceptually consistent to aid learning. Use standard accelerators as shown in Table 4.7 in Step 4 "Develop System Menus and Navigation Schemes."

Microsoft suggests that frequently performed, small-scale tasks should be assigned single keys as the keyboard alternative. Actions that extend or are complementary to the actions of a key (or key combination) should be assigned a Shift key in conjunction with the original action. Microsoft, for example, uses a single key, F6, as the key to move clockwise to the next pane of an active window. To move counterclockwise to the next pane, use Shift-F6.

Infrequent actions, or tasks that represent larger-scale versions of the task assigned to the unmodified key, should be assigned Ctrl-*key* combinations. The left arrow key in Microsoft Windows, for example, moves the cursor one character; Ctrl-left arrow moves it one word.

Keyboard equivalents. Keyboard mnemonics enable the selection of a menu choice through the keyboard instead of by pointing. This enables a person's hands to remain on the keyboard during extensive keying tasks. Keyboard mnemonics should be chosen in a meaningful way to aid memorability and foster predictability of those things that may be forgotten. Mnemonics need only be unique within a menu. A simple rule is always to use the first letter of a menu item description. If the first letter of one item conflicts with that of another, choose another distinctive consonant in the item description, preferably, but not always necessarily, the second in the item word (occasionally another consonant may be more meaningful). The last choice would be a vowel in the item description. If standard platform equivalents are available, use them. Standard equivalents were shown in Table 4.6 in Step 4.

Window navigation. Also provide ways of navigating through windows by the use of keyboard keys.

Selecting the Proper Device-Based Controls

A number of studies have been performed comparing the various controls for assorted office tasks. Significant findings include the following.

Keyboard versus Mouse

Why do many skilled typists prefer a keyboard to a mouse? Speed is obviously one reason. An experienced typist, through kinesthetic memory, has memorized the location of keyboard keys. The keying process becomes exceptionally fast and well learned. The mouse is slower, and it has a tendency to move about the desk. Its location cannot be memorized. The keyboard keys always remain in the same spot.

Consider the following: When using the mouse, the time to move one's hand from the keyboard, grasp the mouse, and point at a screen object ranges from 1.5 to 2 seconds. A very skilled typist can type 13 to 15 characters in that amount of time; an average typist can type 4 to 6 characters. No wonder the keyboard is often preferred.

Control Research

Which devices work better for which tasks and under what conditions has been addressed by a number of investigators. A survey of the research literature comparing and evaluating different devices yields the following summarization concerning tasks involving pointing and dragging:

- The fastest tools for pointing at stationary targets on screens are the devices that permit direct pointing: the touch screen and light pen. This is most likely due to their high level of eye-hand coordination and because they use an action familiar to people.

- In terms of positioning speed and accuracy for stationary targets, the indirect pointing devices—the mouse, trackball, and graphic tablet, do not differ greatly from one another. The joystick is the slowest, although it is as accurate as the others. Of most importance in selecting one of these devices will be its fit to the user's task and working environment.

- A separate confirmation action that must follow pointer positioning increases pointing accuracy but reduces speed. The mouse offers a very effective design configuration for tasks requiring this confirmation.

- For tracking small, slowly moving targets, the mouse, trackball, and graphic tablet are preferred to the touch screen and light pen because the latter may obscure the user's view of the target.

Another common manipulation task is dragging an object across the screen. Using a mouse, graphic tablet, and trackball for this task, as well as pointing, was studied by MacKenzie, Sellen, and Buxton (1991). They report the following:

- The graphic tablet yielded best performance during pointing.

- The mouse yielded best performance during dragging.

- The trackball was a poor performer for both pointing and dragging, and it had a very high error rate in dragging.

Guidelines for Selecting the Proper Device-Based Control

- Consider the characteristics of the task.
  - Provide keyboards for tasks involving:
    - Heavy text entry and manipulation.
    - Movement through structured arrays consisting of a few discrete objects.

— Provide an alternative pointing device for graphical or drawing tasks. The following are some suggested best uses:
- Mouse—pointing, selecting, drawing, and dragging.
- Joystick—selecting and tracking.
- Trackball—pointing, selecting and tracking.
- Touch screen—pointing and selecting.
- Graphic tablet—pointing, selecting, drawing, and dragging.

— Provide touch screens under the following conditions:
- The opportunity for training is minimal.
- Targets are large, discrete, and spread out.
- Frequency of use is low.
- Desk space is at a premium.
- Little or no text input requirement exists.

- Consider user characteristics and preferences.
  — Provide keyboards for touch typists.
- Consider the characteristics of the environment.
- Consider the characteristics of the hardware.
- Consider the characteristics of the device in relation to the application.
- Provide flexibility.
- Minimize eye and hand movements between devices.

Selection of the proper device for an application, then, depends on a host of factors.

Task characteristics. Is the device suited to the task? Standard typewriter keyboards are always necessary for tasks requiring text entry and manipulation; Keyboards (cursor control keys) are usually faster when moving through structured arrays consisting of a few discrete objects.

For graphical and drawing tasks, alternative pointing devices are easier and faster. Use a mouse, joystick, trackball, or graphic tablet for pointing, selecting, drawing, dragging, or tracking. The devices best suited for each kind of task are summarized above.

Provide touch screens when the opportunity for training is minimal; targets are large, discrete, and spread out; frequency of use is low; desk space is at a premium; and little or no text input requirement exists. Touch screens also work well when the usage environment is dirty.

User characteristics and preferences. Will the user be able to easily and comfortably operate the control? Are the fine motor movements required by some devices capable of being performed? Is the user familiar with the standard keyboard? What are the user's preferences? While preferences do not always correspond to performance, it is important that the user be comfortable with the selected device.

Environmental characteristics. Will the device fit easily into the work environment? If desk space is necessary, does it exist and is it large enough?

Hardware characteristics. Is the device itself of a quality that permits easy performance of all the necessary tasks? Joysticks, for example, are quite variable in their movement capabilities.

The device in relation to the application. Is the device satisfactory for the application?

Flexibility. Often task and user needs will vary within an application. Providing more than one kind of device will give the user choices in how to most efficiently accomplish whatever tasks must be performed. A keyboard paired with another kind of pointing device is almost always necessary.

Minimizing eye and hand movements. When multiple devices are used, eye and hand movements between them must be minimized. Structure the task, if possible, to permit the user to stay in one working area. If shifts must be made, they should be as infrequent as possible. It is estimated that, for a good typist, it costs 3 to 8 keystrokes for each jump between the keyboard and a mouse. The general rule is that more than 80 percent of the tasks should be doable using only one device.

Pointer Guidelines

- The pointer:
  — Should be visible at all times.
  — Should contrast well with its background.
  — Should maintain its size across all screen locations and during movement.
  — The hotspot should be easy to locate and see.
  — Location should not warp (change position).
- The user should always position the pointer.
- The shape of a pointer:
  — Should clearly indicate its purpose and meaning.
  — Should be constructed of already defined shapes.
  — Should not be used for any other purpose other than its already defined meaning.
  — Do not create new shapes for already defined standard functions.
- Use only as many shapes as necessary to inform the user about current location and status. Too many shapes can confuse a person.
- Be conservative in making changes as the pointer moves across the screen.
  — Provide a short "time-out" before making noncritical changes on the screen.
- Animation should not:
  — Distract.
  — Restrict one's ability to interact.

Pointer. The focus of the user's attention in most device operations is most often the pointer. Therefore, the pointer image should be used to provide feedback concerning the function being performed, the mode of operation, and the state of the system. For example, the pointer shape image can be changed when it is positioned over a selectable object, signaling to the user that a button action may be performed. When an action is being performed, the pointer can assume the shape of a progress indicator such as a sand timer, providing an indication of processing status.

A pointer should contrast well with its background and be visible at all times. The user should always be in control of its location on the screen. The shape of a pointer should clearly indicate its purpose and meaning. Always use predefined shapes provided by graphical systems. Microsoft Windows, for example, provides about two dozen standard shapes. To aid learning and avoid user confusion, never create new shapes for already defined standard functions or use a shape for any purpose other than its previously defined meaning. Also, use only as many shapes as absolutely necessary to keep the user informed about current position and status. Too many shapes can also confuse a person.

Be conservative in making changes as the pointer moves across the screen. Excessive changes can be distracting to a person. To avoid frequent changes while crossing the screen, establish a short time-out before making noncritical pointer changes. Any pointer animation should not distract the viewer or restrict one's ability to interact with the system.

Choose the Proper Screen-Based Controls

Screen-based controls, often simply called *controls* and sometimes called *widgets*, are the elements of a screen that constitute its body. By definition, they are graphic objects that represent the properties or operations of other objects. A control may:

- Permit the entry or selection of a particular value.
- Permit the changing or editing of a particular value.
- Display only a particular piece of text, value, or graphic.
- Cause a command to be performed.
- Possess a contextual pop-up window.

In the last decade, some platforms have expanded the definition of a control to include all specifiable aspects of a screen, including screen text, headings, and group boxes. For the purposes of this discussion, this broader definition of a screen-based control will be assumed. In this step we will:

- Identify the characteristics and capabilities of the various screen-based controls, including:
  - Buttons.
  - Text entry/read-only controls.
  - Selection controls.
  - Combination entry/selection controls.
  - Specialized operable controls.
  - Custom controls.

- Presentation controls.
- Web controls.

■ Select the proper controls for the user and tasks.

The screen designer is presented with an array of screen-based controls to choose from. Selecting the right one for the user and the task is often difficult. But, as with device-based controls, making the right choice is critical to system success. A proper fit between user and control will lead to fast, accurate performance. A poor fit will result in lower productivity, more errors, and dissatisfaction.

We'll start by describing the types of controls and identifying their advantages, disadvantages, and proper usage. Relevant control design guidelines will also be presented. Not all toolkits or platforms will necessarily possess all the kinds of controls to be described. After describing the controls, we'll look at several research studies addressing the way to choose the best control or controls for particular situations. By the time we look at these studies, their findings will have been incorporated into the control usage and design guidelines already presented. This organization has been chosen because it is more meaningful to first clearly describe each control before discussing it in a research context. We'll finish by providing some general guidance in choosing the proper kind of control to enable tasks to be performed quickly and efficiently by the user.

In describing the controls, we'll break them down into categories that reflect the way they are used. We'll begin with operable controls, those that are manipulable, changeable, or settable. We'll then review presentation controls, those used to inscribe permanent information on a screen or used to give the screen structure. Before starting this review, three extremely important principles regarding controls should be noted:

■ A control must:
  - Look the way it works.
  - Work the way it looks.
■ A control must be used exactly as its design intended.
■ A control must be presented in a standard manner.

The look of a control should make it obvious that it is a control. Its design characteristics should signal "enterability" or "clickability." Microsoft Windows, for example, presents the following simple rules:

■ Raised elements can be pressed.
■ Recessed elements cannot be pressed.
■ Elements on a flat white background can be opened, edited, or moved.

A control must also be presented in a standard and consistent manner, and used exactly as its design intended. The nonstandard design use of controls destroys consistency and aggravates and frustrates users, who have developed expectations based upon their past experiences. Using standard controls allows people to focus on their tasks or the content of the screens with which they are interacting, instead of having to figure out what to do.

Web page design has unleashed and exposed thousands of instances where these basic principles (and others to be described) have been violated. Page designers, all to often it seems, have been placing greater value on personal creativity than on interface usability. Some examples will be presented throughout the following pages.

Operable Controls

Operable controls are those that permit the entry, selection, changing, or editing of a particular value, or cause a command to be performed. Classes include buttons, text entry/read-only, selection, combination entry/selection, and other specialized controls.

Buttons

- Description:
  — A square or rectangular-shaped control with a label inside that indicates action to be accomplished.
  — The label may consist of text, graphics, or both.
- Purpose:
  — To start actions.
  — To change properties.
  — To display a pop-up menu.
- Advantages:
  — Always visible, reminding one of the choices available.
  — Convenient.
  — Can be logically organized in the work area.
  — Can provide meaningful descriptions of the actions that will be performed.
  — Larger size generally provides faster selection target.
  — Can possess 3-D appearance:
    • Adds an aesthetically pleasing style to the screen.
    • Provides visual feedback through button movement when activated.
  — May permit use of keyboard equivalents and accelerators.
  — Faster than using a two-step menu bar/pull-down sequence.
- Disadvantages:
  — Consumes screen space.
  — Size limits the number that may be displayed.
  — Requires looking away from main working area to activate.
  — Requires moving the pointer to select.
- Proper usage:
  — Use for frequently used actions that are specific to a window.
    • To cause something to happen immediately.
    • To display another window.
    • To display a menu of options.
    • To set a mode or property value.

A button comes in three styles. The first resembles the control commonly found on electrical or mechanical devices and is sometimes called a pushbutton. These are most often rectangular, with text that indicates the action to be taken when they are selected or pressed. These buttons are usually placed within a window, and activating them causes the action or command described on them to be performed immediately. This kind of button may take a variety of forms, some of which are illustrated in Figure 7.1. They are often referred to as *command buttons*.

The second style is square or rectangular in shape with an icon or graphic inside. It may have an associated label. This kind of button is illustrated in Figure 7.2. The label may be permanently affixed to the screen within the button, adjacent to it, or only appear when the pointer is moved to the button (called ToolTip, to be discussed). These buttons may appear singly or be placed in groupings commonly called *button bars* or *toolbars*. We'll refer to them as toolbars in this text. They are most frequently used to quickly access commands, many of which are normally accessed through the menu bar, or to initiate other actions or functions. These button groupings are usually placed at the screen's top or side. They are usually relocatable and removable by the user.

The third style is square or rectangular in shape with a symbol inscribed inside, as illustrated in Figure 7.3. The symbol, when learned, identifies the button and the action to be performed when the button is selected. These buttons, specific to a platform and provided by it, are located in the borders of windows and are used to do such things as obtaining a system menu or resizing a window. They have already been described in more detail in Step 5 "Select the Proper Kinds of Windows" and will not be addressed in this Step. This chapter will focus on *command* and *toolbar* buttons.

Command button advantages. An advantage of a command button is that it is always visible, providing a reminder of its existence. Command buttons are conveniently and logically located in the work area and can be inscribed with meaningful descriptions of what they do. Their ability to assume a fairly large size speeds selection, and their three-dimensional appearance is aesthetically pleasing. Buttons can also provide meaningful visual feedback through the movement of the button when activated. Their activation is much easier and faster than using a two-step menu bar/pull-down sequence.

Figure 7.1   Command buttons.

Figure 7.2   Toolbar buttons without labels.

Figure 7.3   A symbol button.

Command button disadvantages. Among the disadvantages of command buttons is their larger size, which consumes considerable screen space and limits the number that can be displayed.

Toolbar advantages. Advantages of toolbar buttons include their continuous visibility and ease and speed of use. They also, individually, consume a relatively small amount of space.

Toolbar disadvantages. Disadvantages include their location being away from the main work area and their small size, which slows down selection. Another disadvantage is that when a large number of buttons are grouped in a bar, they consume a great deal of screen space, and they can easily create screen clutter. In circumstances where they do not possess a label, the necessity of learning and remembering what they are used for can also cause problems.

Proper usage. Buttons are best for frequently used actions in a window. They can be used to cause actions to occur immediately, such as saving a document, quitting a system, or deleting text. They can be used to display a menu of options, such as colors or fonts. Windows calls a button that leads to a menu a *menu button*. Buttons can also be used to display other secondary windows or dialog boxes, and to expand the dialog or invoke dialog features. Windows calls a button that expands the dialog an *unfolding* button. Buttons may also be used to reflect a mode or property value setting similarly to the use of radio buttons or check boxes. In some kinds of windows, command buttons may be the only command method available to the user.

Web browsers also provide a series of command and toolbar buttons that vary from platform to platform. These buttons are not addressed in this Step.

Command Buttons

Command button guidelines include the following.

Usage

- For windows with a menu bar:
  — Use to provide fast access to frequently used or critical commands.
- For windows without a menu bar:
  — Use to provide access to all necessary commands.

For fast access to commands contained in a menu bar, especially those frequently used or critical, also provide access by command buttons. Buttons must also be provided for situations where a command is not available through the menu bar. For windows without menu bars, buttons must be provided to provide access to all window commands.

Structure

- Provide a rectangular shape with the label inscribed within it.
- Give the button a raised appearance.
- Maintain consistency in style throughout an application.

The shape of a button can vary. Generally, rectangular-shaped buttons are preferred because they provide the best fit for horizontally arrayed textual captions. Square-cornered rectangles are found in some platforms including Microsoft Windows, while rounded-corner rectangles are found in others. The button style chosen must reflect the three cornerstone principles presented at the beginning of this Step, including giving it a raised appearance to make it obvious that it is a command button. To do this, drop shadows are used in some platforms, beveled edges in others. "Invisible" buttons must never exist. Web command button styles are noted for their variety in shape and size. The button style chosen is mostly a matter of preference. Web-specific button styles should be consistently designed and maintained throughout the Web site.

Labels

- Use standard button labels when available.
- Provide meaningful descriptions of the actions that will be performed.
- Use single-word labels whenever possible.
  — Use two-three words for clarity, if necessary.
- Use mixed-case letters with the first letter of each significant label word capitalized.
- Display labels:
  — In the regular system font.
  — In the same size font.
- Do not number labels.
- Center the label within the button borders, leaving at least two pixels between the text and the button border.
- Provide consistency in button labeling across all screens.

Labels. Button labels should be clearly spelled out, with meaningful descriptions of the actions they will cause to be performed. Choices should be composed of mixed-case single words. Multiple words are preferred, however, to single words lacking clarity in their intent. If multiple-word labels are used, capitalize the first letter of each word (headline style). Use the same size and style of font in all buttons. The regular system font is preferred. Never change font style or size within buttons; these kinds of changes can be very distracting to the viewer. Center each label within the button borders, leaving at least two pixels between the text and the border.

Common button functions should have standard names and uses. Microsoft windows, for example, provides these standard names and definitions:

OK—Any changed information in the window is accepted and the window is closed.

Cancel—Closes window without implementing unsubmitted changes.

Reset—Resets defaults and cancels any changed information that has not been submitted.

Apply—Any changed information in the window is accepted and again displayed in the window that remains open.

Close—Closes the window.

Help—Opens online Help.

Always follow all platform presentation and usage guidelines for standard button functions.

Size

- Provide as large a button as feasible.
- Maintain consistent button heights and widths.
- Exception: Buttons containing excessively long labels may be wider.

Provide as large a button as possible, consistent with Fitts' Law (see Step 1 "Know Your User or Client "). Buttons must, at minimum, be wide enough to accommodate the longest label. Leave at least two pixels between labels and button borders. A command button's minimum height should be 25 pixels. Create, however, standard, equal-sized buttons encompassing the majority of system functions. When a button's label will not fit within the standard size, expand the button's size to achieve a proper label fit. Never reduce the font size of some labels to create equal-sized buttons. In this case, buttons of different widths are preferable. Also, do not create an unnecessarily wide button for aesthetic balance purposes, as illustrated by the Color Palette button in Figure 7.4. The perceptual model we possess in our memory for a button will be lost.

Number

- Restrict the number of buttons on a window to six or fewer.

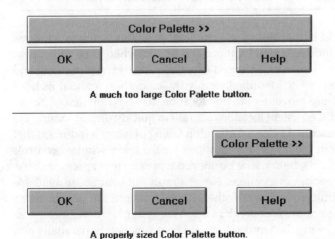

A much too large Color Palette button.

A properly sized Color Palette button.

Figure 7.4   Improper and proper button sizes.

The maximum number of buttons on a window must reflect a balance between effectiveness, real estate efficiency, and operational simplicity. Having no more than six buttons per window or dialog box seems to appropriately balance these issues. If an extra button or two is necessary and space is available, they may be included.

Location and Layout

- Maintain consistency in button location between windows.
- Never simply "fit" buttons in available space.
- If buttons are for exiting the dialog:
  — Position them centered and aligned horizontally at the bottom.
- If buttons are used for invoking a dialog feature or expanding the dialog:
  — Position them centered and aligned vertically on the right side.
- If a button has a contingent relationship to another control:
  — Position it adjacent to the related control.
- If a button has a contingent relationship to a group of controls:
  — Position it at the bottom or to right of related controls.
- If, due to space constraints, exiting and expanding/invoking feature buttons must be placed together:
  — If at the bottom, place exiting buttons to the right, separating the groupings by one button's width.
  — If along the right side, place exiting buttons at the bottom, separating the groupings by one button's height.
- For exiting and expanding/invoking feature buttons, do not:
  — Align with the other screen controls.
  — Present displayed within a line border.
- Provide equal and adequate spacing between adjacent buttons.
- Provide adequate spacing between buttons and the screen body controls.

Command buttons should be positioned in consistent positions within a window. This enables a person to memorize button locations and predict where they will appear when a window is presented. For an experienced user this permits faster pointing and activation because a button may be identified simply by its location without its label having to be read, and a mouse movement to that location may be commenced before a window is even displayed. Consistent locations also aid in quickly discriminating the different kinds of buttons described below. A common failing of many windows is that buttons are positioned within windows *after* locations for the other window controls are established. When this occurs, buttons are positioned where there is space available. The result is usually a hodgepodge of locations. Never simply "fit" buttons in available space. Allocate a space for buttons before the other control locations are established.

Button location within a window is dependent upon the type of button. Buttons *exiting* a dialog, and usually closing the window, should be positioned horizontally and centered across the lower part of the window. This positioning places the buttons at the end of the dialog. A study of Web pages (Spool et al., 1997) found that people preferred to scroll to the bottom of a page to press the final buttons. If a button *invokes* a dialog feature or *expands* the dialog, position it centered and aligned vertically along the right side of the window. Maintaining these consistent locations will enable a person to quickly identify what general kind of button it is, and what kind of action will occur if the button is activated. The location of the exiting buttons across the bottom will also allow more efficient use of window real estate when invoking/expanding buttons are not included within a window. Exiting and expanding/invoking feature button locations are illustrated in Figure 7.5. If, due to screen space constraints, exiting and expanding/ invoking feature buttons must be positioned together at the screen bottom, place the exiting buttons to the right, separating the groupings by one standard button's width. If they are located together along the right side, place exiting buttons at the bottom, separating the groupings by one button's height.

If a button has a *contingent* relationship to another control, position it adjacent to the related control in the order in which the controls are usually operated, as illustrated in Figure 7.6. If a button possesses a contingent relationship to a group of controls, position it at the bottom or to the right of the grouping, again in logical flow order, as illustrated in Figure 7.7.

For exiting and expanding/invoking feature buttons, do not provide alignment with the other screen controls. Maintain alignment and spacing only within the buttons themselves. Trying to align the buttons to other screen controls will most often create variable spacing between the buttons themselves, which is visually distracting. Also, do not display buttons within a line border; instead present them on the background of the window itself. The unique physical look of the buttons is strong enough for them to create their own visual grouping. Reserve line borders for individual controls or groups of controls that are in greater need of closure. Too many borders can also create visual clutter.

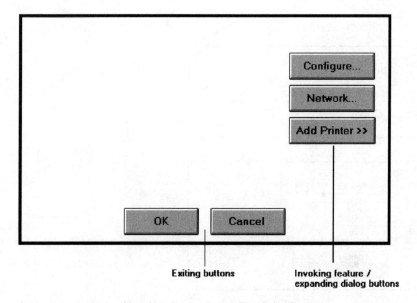

Figure 7.5 Exiting and invoking feature/expanding dialog buttons.

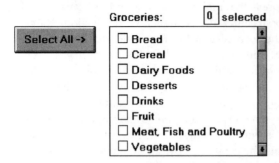

Figure 7.6 Button with contingent relationship to a control.

Provide equal and consistent spacing between adjacent buttons, and groups of buttons. Also, maintain adequate separation between screen buttons and other screen controls.

Organization

- Organize standard buttons in the manner recommended by the platform being used.
- For other buttons, organize them in common and customary grouping schemes.
  — For buttons ordered left to right, place those for most frequent actions to the left.
  — For buttons ordered top to bottom, place those for most frequent actions at the top.
- Keep related buttons grouped together.
- Separate potentially destructive buttons from frequently chosen selections.

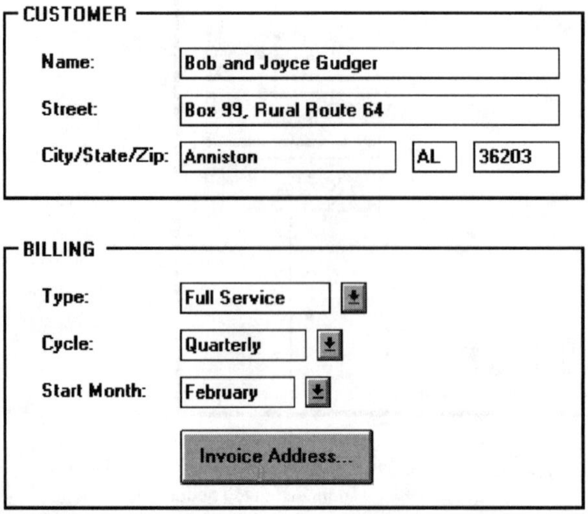

Figure 7.7 Button with contingent relationship to a grouping.

- Buttons found on more than one window should be consistently positioned.
- The order should never change.
- For mutually exclusive actions, use two buttons; do not dynamically change the text.

Follow the standard, consistent ordering schemes recommended by the platform being used. Windows recommends the following:

- An affirmative action to the left (or above).
- The default first.
- OK and Cancel next to each other.
- Help last, if supported.

Other platforms may suggest a different ordering. If differences exist, and people may be using more than one platform, some organizational compromises may be necessary.

Buttons should be ordered logically, such as by frequency of use, sequence of use, or importance. For buttons arrayed left to right, start the ordering from left to right. For buttons arrayed top to bottom, start the ordering from top to bottom.

Keep related buttons grouped together. Separate potentially destructive buttons from frequently chosen selections to avoid inadvertent activation and potentially catastrophic results. Always locate the same buttons that appear on different windows in consistent positions. For mutually exclusive actions, avoid using one button that toggles changing text. This can be confusing. Use two buttons with labels that clearly describe the two actions.

Intent Indicators

- When a button causes an action to be immediately performed, no intent indicator is necessary.

Figure 7.8

- When a button leads to a cascading dialog, include an ellipsis (...) after the label.

Figure 7.9

- When a button leads to a menu, include a triangle pointing in the direction the menu will appear after the label.

Figure 7.10

- When a button leads to an expanding dialog, include a double arrow (>>) with the label.

Figure 7.11

- When a button has a contingent relationship to another control that must be indicated, include a single arrow (->) pointing at the control.

Figure 7.12

Button intent indicators will follow, where applicable, the same conventions used for menu items. When a button causes a command to be performed immediately, no special intent indicator is necessary on the button. When a button leads to a cascading dialog box, include an *ellipsis* with the label. When a button leads to a menu of choices, include a *triangle* after the label; point the triangle in the direction the menu will appear. If a button expands the dialog, include a *double arrow* with the label. When a button has a contingent relationship to another control, include a *single arrow* pointing at the control. Intent indicators are very useful because they enable the user to predict the consequences of an intended action.

Expansion Buttons

- Gray them out after expansion.
- Provide a contraction button, if necessary.
  — Locate it beneath, or to right of, the expansion button.
  — Gray it out when not applicable.

When a button that expands a dialog is activated, and the dialog is expanded, display the button dimmed or grayed out. If the dialog can again be contracted, provide a contraction button beneath the expansion button or to the right of it. Gray this button out when the dialog is contracted; display it at normal intensity when the dialog is expanded.

Defaults

- Intent:
  — When a window is first displayed, provide a default action, if practical.
- Selection:
  — A default should be the most likely action:
    • A confirmation.
    • An application of the activity being performed.
    • A positive action such as OK, unless the result is catastrophic.
  — If a destructive action is performed (such as a deletion), the default should be Cancel.
- Presentation:
  — Indicate the default action by displaying the button with a bold or double border.
- Procedures:
  — The default can be changed as the user interacts with the window.
  — When the user navigates to a button, it can temporarily become the default.

— Use the Enter key to activate a default button.

— If another control requires use of the Enter key, temporarily disable the default while the focus is on the other control.

— Permit double-clicking on a single selection control in a window to also carry out the default command.

When a window with buttons is first displayed, provide a default action whenever practical. The default action should be the most likely action within the window. It may be a confirmation, an application of the activity being performed, or a positive response such as OK. If the default is irreversible or destructive (such as Delete), the default should be Cancel, requiring a person to change the selection in order to perform the destructive action. If none of the buttons is destructive in nature, the default button should be the one most frequently selected.

The default can be changed as the user interacts with a window. When the user navigates to a button, it can temporarily become the default. Return the button to its original state when the focus leaves a button. Permit use of the Enter key to activate a default button. If another control requires use of the Enter key, temporarily disable the default while the focus is on the other control. Permit double-clicking on a single selection control in a window to also carry out the default command.

Unavailable Choices

■ Temporarily unavailable choices should be dimmed or grayed out.

A button should visually indicate whether it is available for activation. Dim or gray-out buttons for actions that are not available.

Keyboard Equivalents and Accelerators

■ Equivalents:
— Assign a keyboard equivalent mnemonic to each button to facilitate keyboard selection.
— The mnemonic should be the first character of the button's label.
• If duplication exists in first characters, for duplicate items, use another character in the label.
• Preferably, choose the first succeeding consonant.
— Designate the mnemonic character by underlining it.
— Maintain the same mnemonic on all identical buttons on other screens.

Figure 7.13

| <u>A</u>pply |

■ Accelerators:
— Assign a keyboard accelerator to each button to facilitate keyboard selection.

Enabling the user to select button actions through the typewriter keyboard provides flexibility and efficiency in the dialog. To do this, provide keyboard equivalent, single-character mnemonic codes that, when typed, will cause the action to be performed. The suggested method is to indicate the accelerator by underlining the proper character in the button label.

Keyboard accelerators, a keyboard key or combination of keys, may also be assigned to buttons to facilitate keyboard activation.

Keyboard equivalents and accelerators, including Microsoft Windows standard ones, were more fully described in Step 4 "Develop Navigation Schemes and Menus."

Scrolling

- If a window can be scrolled, do not scroll the command buttons.
  — Exception: if the screen cannot scroll independently of the buttons.
- Use buttons to move between multipage forms, not scroll bars.
  — Label buttons Next and Previous.

If scrolling the contents of a window, never scroll the buttons. They should be available at all times. Web page screens, whose content cannot be scrolled independently of buttons, are exceptions to this rule at the moment. Use buttons to move between multipage forms, not scroll bars. Paging is, conceptually, easier for people to use and understand, and was discussed in detail in Step 3 "Understand the Principles of Good Screen Design." Label the buttons Next and Previous.

Button Activation

- Pointing:
  — Highlight the button in some visually distinctive manner when the pointer is resting on it and the button is available for selection.
- Activation:
  — Call attention to the button in another visually distinctive manner when it has been activated or pressed.
  — If a button can be pressed continuously, permit the user to hold the mouse button down and repeat the action.

Highlight the button in some visually distinctive manner when the pointer is resting on it and it is available for selection. This will provide the user with feedback indicating that the selection process may be performed. Some platforms display a brighter button.

Highlight the button in another visually distinctive manner when it has been activated or pressed, to indicate that the action is successful. One platform subdues or grays out the button. Another has raised beveled buttons that appear to sink into the screen when selected. Another alternative is to move the button slightly as if it has been depressed.

If a button can be pressed continuously, permit the mouse button to be held down and the action repeated.

Toolbars

Toolbars are compilations of commands, actions, or functions, usually graphical in structure but sometimes textual, grouped together for speedy access. Microsoft Windows defines a toolbar as a panel that contains a *set* of controls. Toolbars may also be called *button bars*, *control bars*, or *access bars*. Specialized toolbars may also be referred to as *ribbons*, *toolboxes*, or *palettes*. Toolbars may also appear in palette windows.

Usage

- To provide easy and fast access to most frequently used commands or options across multiple screens.
- To invoke a subapplication within an application.
- To use in place of certain menu items.

Provide toolbars to allow fast and easy access to a system's most frequently used commands, functions, or options. Also provide toolbars for easily invoking subapplications within an application. Toolbars are considered "fast paths" or expert aids. All toolbar functions must also be obtainable by normal textual menu means, including through use of the menu bar. One exception: if menu text cannot clearly explain an item and a graphical toolbar representation can, the toolbar item may replace the menu item.

Structure

- Images:
    - Provide buttons of equal size.
    - Create a meaningful and unique icon.
        - Design them using icon design guidelines.
    - Center the image within the button.
    - Give the button a raised appearance.
    - Ensure that toolbar images are discernible from Web page graphical images.
- Text:
    - Create a meaningful label, adhering to label guidelines for command buttons.
    - Create toolbar buttons of equal size, following the size guidelines recently described.
- Consistency:
    - Use the same icon throughout an application and between applications.

Create meaningful and unique images and icons utilizing the icon design guidelines in Step 11 "Create Meaningful Graphics, Icons, and Images." Center the image within the button and provide an associated textual label. A label is always necessary to ensure button comprehensibility. One study has found that placing graphics *and* words on buttons, makes them more usable than including graphics only. Create the label following the guidelines for command buttons. The label may be located within the button, positioned beneath it, or presented on demand through a ToolTip control. Labels beneath toolbar button images will provide a larger pointing target. If the label is located within the button and the system will be translated into one or more other languages, allow extra space for the label. See *International Translation* in Step 10 "Provide Effective Internationalization and Accessibility" for further important considerations. A ToolTip control is discussed later in this chapter. Give the button a raised appearance to convey that it is a screen navigation element to be pressed. Ensure that toolbar images are discernible from all Web page graphical images.

For text-only toolbar buttons, create a meaningful label, adhering to the label guidelines for command buttons. Provide consistent icons throughout all applications.

Size

- Button:
  - 24 (w) by 22 (h) pixels, including border.
  - 32 (w) by 30 (h) pixels, including border.
  - Larger buttons can be used on high-resolution displays.
- Label:
  - 16 (w) by 16 (h) pixels.
  - 14 (w) by 24 (h) pixels.
- Default:
  - Provide the smaller size as the default size with a user option to change it.
- Image:
  - Center the image in the button.

A toolbar button should be large but not too large because of the number that may need to be displayed. Microsoft provides the above guidelines. Other sizing guidelines and much more detailed image guidelines are presented in Step 11.

Organization

- Order the buttons based on common and customary grouping schemes.
  - For buttons ordered left to right, place those for the most frequently used actions to the left.
  - For buttons ordered top to bottom, place those for the most frequently used actions at the top.
- Keep related buttons grouped together.
- Separate potentially destructive buttons from frequently chosen selections.
- Permit user reconfiguration of button organization.

Toolbar buttons should be ordered logically, such as by frequency of use, sequence of use, or importance. If the buttons reflect a quality on a continuum such as colors or shades, follow standard and expected ordering schemes. For buttons arrayed left to right, start the ordering from left to right. For buttons arrayed top to bottom, start the ordering from top to bottom.

Keep related buttons grouped together. Separate potentially destructive buttons from frequently chosen selections to avoid inadvertent activation and potentially catastrophic results. Permit the user to reconfigure the button organizational structure to better meet his or her unique needs.

Location

- Position main features and functions bar horizontally across top of window just below menu bar.
- Position subtask and subfeatures bars along sides of window.
- Permit the location of the bar to be changed by the user.
- Permit display of the bar to be turned on or off by the user.
  — Also provide access through standard menus.

Locate the main features and functions tool bar horizontally across the top of the window just below the menu bar. Locate subtask and subfeature tool bars along sides of window. Permit the location of the toolbar to be changed by the user. Since a toolbar can create visual noise, permit its display to be turned on or off. Always also provide access to the toolbar actions through standard menus.

Active Items

- Make only currently available toolbar items available.
- Temporarily not available items may be displayed grayed out.

As the user moves around through an application, items at various points that are not applicable do not have to be displayed. Temporarily unavailable items may be grayed out.

Customization

- Permit toolbars to be turned off by the user.
- Allow the customizing of toolbars.
  — Provide a default, however.

Permit the toolbars to be turned off by the user, should their use not be necessary or should more screen space be desired. Also, allow users to customize the toolbar, determining what they would like to add or remove. Many users do not customize them, however, so a default set should always be provided.

Keyboard Equivalents and Accelerators

- Equivalents:
  - — Assign keyboard equivalents to facilitate keyboard selection.
  - — Maintain the same mnemonic on all identical buttons on all screens.
- Accelerators:
  - — Assign a keyboard accelerator to facilitate keyboard selection.

Provide keyboard equivalents and accelerators to facilitate keyboard selection. Maintain the same mnemonic on all identical buttons on all screens. One caution, if a particular mnemonic is being used somewhere else in the window; it may not be available for use on the toolbar.

Button Activation

- Pointing:
  - — Highlight the button in some visually distinctive manner when the pointer is resting on it and the button is available for selection.
- Activation:
  - — Call attention to the button in another visually distinctive manner when it has been activated or pressed.

Highlight the button in some visually distinctive manner when the pointer is resting on it and the button is available for selection. This will provide the user with feedback indicating that the selection process may be performed. Highlight the button in another visually distinctive manner when it has been activated or pressed, to indicate that the action is successful.

Text Entry/Read-Only Controls

A Text Entry/Read-Only control contains text that is exclusively entered or modified through the keyboard. It may also contain entered text being presented for reading or display purposes only.

Text Boxes

- Description:
  - — A control, usually rectangular in shape, in which:
    - Text may be entered or edited.
    - Text may be displayed for read-only purposes.
  - — Usually possesses a caption describing the kind of information contained within it.
  - — An outline field border:
    - Is included for enterable/editable text boxes.
    - Is not included for read-only text boxes.

— Two types exist:
- Single line.
- Multiple line.

— When first displayed, the box may be blank or contain an initial value.

■ Purpose:
- To permit the display, entering, or editing of textual information.
- To display read-only information.

■ Advantages:
- Very flexible.
- Familiar.
- Consumes little screen space.

■ Disadvantages:
- Requires use of typewriter keyboard.
- Requires user to remember what must be keyed.

■ Proper usage:
- Most useful for data that is:
  - Unlimited in scope.
  - Difficult to categorize.
  - Of a variety of different lengths.
- When using a selection list is not possible.

Two types of *text boxes* exist. One consists of a rectangular box into which information is typed. It may also be referred to as an *edit* control. The second is also rectangular in shape but contains text displayed purely for read-only purposes. The former type has historically been referred to as an *entry field*, the latter as an *inquiry* or *display field*. While display-only text boxes are not operable in the true sense of the word, the information contained within them is capable of being modified by other controls. Hence, they will be reviewed as an operable control since their characteristics, and the characteristics of an entry field, are very similar. Some platforms classify both as text boxes. Text boxes almost always possess a separate caption describing the kind of information to be keyed. An enterable text box is visually presented on the screen, its shape being defined by an outline border, a reversal in screen polarity, a white background, or various combinations of these features. The information in a read-only text field is most effectively displayed on the screen background, not in a box. Therefore, a box does not surround the information contained in read-only text boxes.

Single-Line and Multiple-Line Text Boxes

■ Single line:
- Description:
  - A control consisting of no more than one line of text.
- Purpose:
  - To make textual entries when the information can be contained within one line of the screen.

— Typical uses:
  - Typing the name of a file to save.
  - Typing the path of a file to copy.
  - Typing variable data on a form.
  - Typing a command.
- Multiple line:
  — Description:
    - A control consisting of a multiline rectangular box for multiple lines of text.
  — Purpose:
    - To type, edit, and read passages of text.
  — Typical uses:
    - Creating or reading an electronic mail message.
    - Displaying and editing text files.

Text boxes exist in two forms: *single line* and *multiple line*. A single-line box is used when the information contained within it can be confined to one screen line. Multiple-line boxes are used when the information exceeds a single line. When first displayed, a text box may be blank or contain an initial value. Text boxes are illustrated in Figure 7.14.

Text boxes are familiar, flexible, and consume little screen space. They do require a typewriter keyboard, which, depending upon one's skill with a keyboard may be an advantage or a disadvantage. A disadvantage to all is that what is keyed into an entry field must often be remembered. They are most useful for data that is difficult to categorize or unlimited in scope, or when use of a selection field is not possible.

Captions

- Structure and size:
  — Provide a descriptive caption to identify the kind of information to be typed, or contained within, the text box.
  — Use a mixed-case font.
  — Display the caption in normal intensity or in a color of moderate brightness.

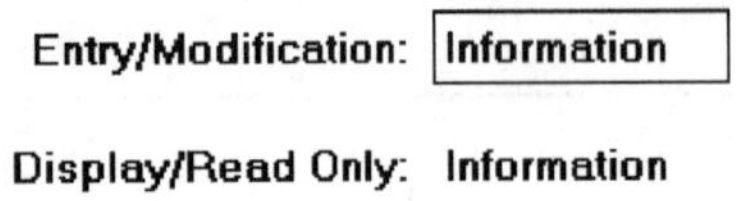

Entry/Modification: | Information |

Display/Read Only: Information

Figure 7.14   Text boxes.

- Formatting:
  — Single fields:
  - Position the field caption to the left of the text box.
    — Place a colon (:) immediately following the caption.
    — Separate the colon from the text box by one space.

Figure 7.15   **Composition:** [   ]

  - Alternately, the caption may be placed above the text box.
    — Place a colon (:) immediately following the caption.
    — Position above the upper-left corner of the box, flush with the left edge.

                              Composition:
                              [   ]
Figure 7.16

  — Multiple occurrence fields:
  - For entry/modification text boxes:
    — Position the caption left-justified one line above the column of entry fields.

                    Offices:
                    [   ]
                    [   ]
Figure 7.17   [   ]

  - For display/read-only boxes:
    — If the data field is long and fixed-length, or the displayed data is about the same length, center the caption above the displayed text box data.

                              Date:
                              | 07/17/94 |
                              | 07/21/94 |
                              | 01/26/95 |
                              | 08/21/95 |
Figure 7.18 | 11/18/96 |

    — If the data displayed is alphanumeric, short, or quite variable in length, left-justify the caption above the displayed text box data.

                    Location:
                    | Alice Springs |
                    | Kakadu National Park |
                    | Traralgon |
                    | Wagga Wagga |
Figure 7.19 | Whyalla |

— If the data field is numeric and variable in length, right-justify the caption above the displayed text box data.

Balances:

12,642,123.05
53.98
355,125.44
199.13
612.01

Figure 7.20

Structure and size. Captions are usually added to text boxes using *static text* fields, to be described shortly. Many toolsets do not include captions with text box controls. Captions must be understandable and fully spelled out in a language meaningful to the user. In general, abbreviations and contractions should not be used. To achieve the alignment recommendations (to be discussed shortly), however, an occasional abbreviation or contraction may be necessary. If so, choose those that are common in the everyday language of the user or those that are meaningful or easily learned. Use mixed-case text in the headline style, capitalizing only the first letter of each word (except for articles, conjunctions, and prepositions— a, the, and, for, and so on). Acronyms, abbreviations, or proper nouns that are normally capitalized, however, may be capitalized. If the caption is of a sentence-style nature, sentence-style capitalization should be followed. In this case, capitalize only the first letter of the first word of the caption.

In relation to the text box, the caption should be of normal intensity or consist of a moderately bright color. Visual emphasis should always be given to the information in the text box.

Single fields. For single fields, it is recommended that the caption precede the text box. Place a colon (:) directly following the caption to visually separate the caption from the data; separate the colon from the text box by one space.

Multiple occurrence fields. For multiple-occurrence fields, the caption should be positioned above the columnized text boxes. The exact location of the caption will depend on the kind of screen and the kind of data displayed. For entry screens, the caption should be left-justified above the columnized entry fields. This will signal the starting point of the text box and ensure that the caption is positioned directly above the keyed data.

For display/read-only or inquiry screens in which text box information already exists, the positioning of the caption depends on the kind of information displayed within the box. The objective is to center the caption over the information. If the box is fixed-length, or the information to be displayed within it usually fills, or almost fills, the box, center the caption above the data. If the information is alphanumeric and can be quite variable in length, left-justify the caption. This will keep the caption directly above the data when it appears in the box. Similarly, for numeric fields, right-justify the caption to keep it above the data that will be right-justified when it appears.

Fields

- Structure:
  - — Identify entry/modification text boxes with a line border or reverse polarity rectangular box.
    - • To visually indicate that it is an enterable field, present the box in a recessed manner.

Figure 7.21   Account: | Savings |

- • Present display/read-only text boxes on the window background.

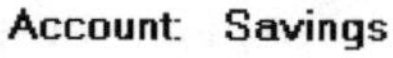

Figure 7.22   Account: Savings

  - — Break up long text boxes through incorporation of slashes (/), dashes (-), spaces, or other common delimiters.

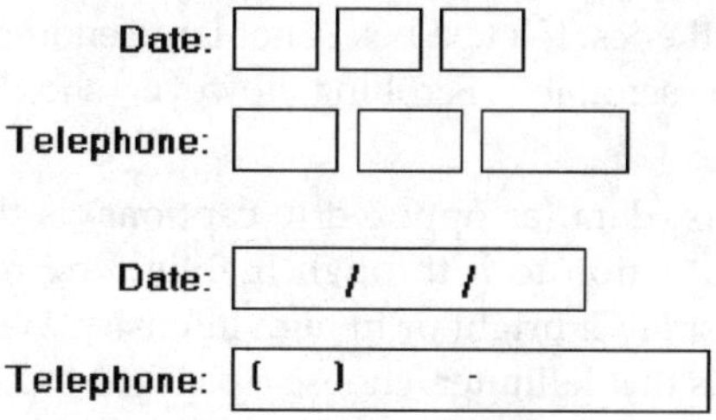

Date: ☐ ☐ ☐

Telephone: ☐ ☐ ☐

Date: | / / |

Figure 7.23   Telephone: | ( ) - |

- Size:
  - — Size to indicate the approximate length of the field.
  - — Text boxes for fixed-length data must be large enough to contain the entire entry.
  - — Text boxes for variable-length data must be large enough to contain the majority of the entries.
  - — Where entries may be larger than the entry field, scrolling must be provided to permit keying into, or viewing, the entire field.
  - — Employ word wrapping for continuous text in multiple-line text boxes.
- Highlighting:
  - — Call attention to text box data through a highlighting technique.
    - • Higher intensity.
    - • If color is used, choose one that both complements the screen background and contrasts well with it.
- Unavailable fields:
  - — Gray-out temporarily unavailable text boxes.
- Fonts:
  - — To support multiple fonts, use a *Rich-Text Box*.

Structure. A text box should attract attention, but not detract from the legibility of the data contained within it, be capable of allowing an indication of the structure of the data contained within it, and indicate the appropriate number of characters to be keyed into it. An early study found that, in meeting these objectives, a broken underscore and an outlined box were the best delimiters for screen entry fields. The older text-based screens traditionally have used the underscore as the delimiter; graphical screens, the outlined box. Interestingly, both resemble the coding areas most frequently found on paper forms. To visually indicate that it is an enterable field, present the box in a recessed manner, as is done by Microsoft Windows.

Present display/read-only text boxes on the window background. To make text boxes more readable, it is desirable to break them up into logical pieces. Slashes, dashes, and spaces should be inserted into the entry fields as illustrated.

Size. The size of a field must give an approximate indication of the data length. Text boxes for fixed-length data must be long enough to contain the entry. Variable-length text boxes should be large enough to contain the majority of the entries. The size of a variable-length text box will be dependent on field alignment, space utilization, and aesthetics. If a text box is not large enough to key or view the entire entry, it must be scrollable. Scrolling, however, should be avoided whenever possible.

Highlighting. Text box data (as opposed to captions) is the most important part of a screen. Call attention to it through highlighting techniques. With monochrome screens, display it bright or in high intensity. With color, use the brightest colors. If a box is the delimiter, choose a background color that complements the screen body background and provides good contrast with the color chosen for the data.

Temporarily unavailable. For fields temporarily unavailable for entry, gray-out the box and its associated label. This temporary graying out implies, however, that the user can perform some action that will again make the field enterable.

Rich-Text Boxes. Most text boxes typically support only the standard system font. A Microsoft Windows rich-text box is similar to a text box but provides, in addition, font properties, such as typeface, size, color, bold, and italics. It also supports character and paragraph alignment, tabs, indents, and numbering, as well as printing.

Selection Controls

A selection control presents on the screen all the possible alternatives, conditions, or choices that may exist for an entity, property, or value. The relevant item or items are selected from those displayed. Some selection controls present all the alternatives together, visibly on a screen; others may require an action to retrieve the entire listing and/or scrolling to view all the alternatives. Selection controls include radio buttons, check boxes, list boxes, drop-down/pop-up list boxes, and palettes.

Radio Buttons

- Description:
  - A two-part control consisting of the following:
    - Small circles, diamonds, or rectangles.
    - Choice descriptions.
  - When a choice is selected:
    - The option is highlighted.
    - Any existing choice is automatically unhighlighted and deselected.

- Purpose:
  - To set one item from a small set of mutually exclusive options (2 to 8).

- Advantages:
  - Easy-to-access choices.
  - Easy-to-compare choices.
  - Preferred by users.

- Disadvantages:
  - Consume screen space.
  - Limited number of choices.

- Proper usage:
  - For setting attributes, properties, or values.
  - For mutually exclusive choices (that is, only one can be selected).
  - Where adequate screen space is available.
  - Most useful for data and choices that are:
    - Discrete.
    - Small and fixed in number.
    - Not easily remembered.
    - In need of a textual description to meaningfully describe the alternatives.
    - Most easily understood when the alternatives can be seen together and compared to one another.
    - Never changed in content.
  - Do not use:
    - For commands.
    - Singly to indicate the presence or absence of a state.

Structure. Controls of this type take several different physical forms. They are most often called *radio buttons* because of their resemblance to similar controls on radios. Microsoft Windows, however, refers to these controls as *option buttons*. One common display method consists of a circle associated with each choice description. When an alternative is selected, the center of the circle is partially or fully filled in to provide a visual indication that it is the active choice. Other styles of radio buttons have also been implemented. Microsoft Windows uses a small depressed circle that contains a small dot when selected. Other presentation methods include small circular buttons that look recessed when not selected and are raised when selected, and small diamond-shaped buttons that look raised when

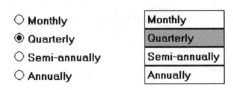

Figure 7.24   Radio buttons.   **Figure 7.25**   Radio buttons.

not selected and depressed when selected. Another method for presenting exclusive choices is the butted box or button where the alternatives are inscribed in horizontally arrayed adjoining rectangles resembling command buttons. The selected alternative is highlighted in some way. Examples of radio buttons are illustrated in Figures 7.24 and 7.25. Deciding on which style to use seems to be more a matter of preference than performance. No published comparison studies are available for guidance.

Purpose. Radio buttons are used to designate one of a small set of options, no more than about eight. As with a radio, the choices are mutually exclusive, only one frequency or setting is permitted at one time in the presented array.

Advantages/disadvantages. With radio buttons, all alternatives are always visible. Therefore, it is easy to access and compare choices. Two recent studies (Johnsgard, Page, Wilson, and Zeno, 1995; Tullis and Kodimer, 1992) have found radio buttons a preferred and very effective control for presenting mutually exclusive choices. These studies will be described later in this chapter. On the negative side, radio buttons do consume a certain amount of screen real estate, limiting the number of alternatives that can reasonably be displayed.

Proper usage. Radio buttons are useful for setting attributes, properties, or values where adequate screen space is available. The alternatives should be discrete, small in number, and in need of a textual description to identify them meaningfully. Radio buttons are helpful in situations where the alternatives cannot always be easily remembered or where displaying the alternatives together facilitates understanding and selecting the proper choice. The radio button choices displayed should be stable, never changing in content.

Never use radio buttons for implementing commands, such as causing a dialog box to immediately appear based upon a button setting. Commands to the system should result from direct user command actions, such as pressing a command button. This allows control to remain with the user. Unfortunately, use of a radio button to perform an action is a common Web page design problem. Also, do not use one radio button by itself to indicate the presence or absence of a state. A single check box is recommended for this purpose.

Choice Descriptions

- Provide meaningful, fully spelled-out choice descriptions clearly describing the values or effects set by the radio buttons.

- Display in a single line of text.
- Display using mixed-case letters, using the sentence style.
- Position descriptions to the right of the button. Separate them by at least one space from the button.
- When a choice is conditionally unavailable for selection, display the choice description grayed out or dimmed.
- Include a None choice if it adds clarity.

Choice descriptions must be clear, meaningful, fully spelled out, and displayed in a mixed-case text. For multiword descriptions, capitalize the first letter of the description and use the sentence style for the remainder of the description. Small button-type indicators should be located to the left of the choice description; rectangular boxes that resemble a command button will find the description within the box. Small buttons associated with text are advantageous when the choice description must be lengthy. Descriptions in boxes impose restrictions on the number of words that can be inscribed within them. When a choice is unavailable for selection in the present condition, display the choice selection grayed out or dimmed. Where a "None" alternative clarifies the alternatives presented, provide it in the listing.

Size

- Show a minimum of two choices, a maximum of eight.

Generally, selection fields of this style should not present more than eight choices. Displaying more than eight is usually not efficient, wasting screen space. If the number of choices exceeds this maximum, consider using a single selection list box or a drop-down list box. Johnsgard, Page, Wilson and Zeno (1995) have found, however, that even for as many as thirty choices, radio buttons were preferred by users, and performed better, than these other controls.

Defaults

- When the control possesses a state or affect that has been predetermined to have a higher probability of selection than the others, designate it as the default and display its button filled in.
- When the control includes choices whose states cannot be predetermined, display all the buttons without setting a dot, or in the *indeterminate* state.
- When a multiple selection includes choices whose states vary, display the buttons in another unique manner, or in the *mixed value* state.

Provide a default setting for a radio button whenever possible. In some situations, however, a default setting may be difficult to predetermine, or inappropriate to predetermine (sex: male or female?). Microsoft Windows provides for additional settings called the *indeterminate* or *mixed value* states. When a default setting cannot be preestablished because of the nature of the information, leave all the buttons blank or not filled in. If a multiple selection on an object is performed and the values in the selection are mixed or differ, display the applicable radio buttons in another distinctive manner, such as a gray shadow.

Structure

- A columnar orientation is the preferred manner of presentation.
- Left-align the buttons and choice descriptions.

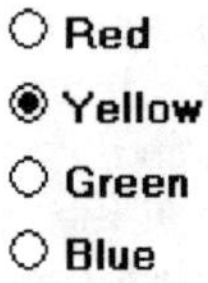

          ○ Red

          ◉ Yellow

          ○ Green

Figure 7.26   ○ Blue

- If vertical space on the screen is limited, orient the buttons horizontally.
- Provide adequate separation between choices so that the buttons are associated with the proper description.
  — A distance equal to three spaces is usually sufficient.

Figure 7.27   ◉ Green   ○ Blue   ○ Yellow   ○ Red

- Enclose the buttons in a border to visually strengthen the relationship they possess.

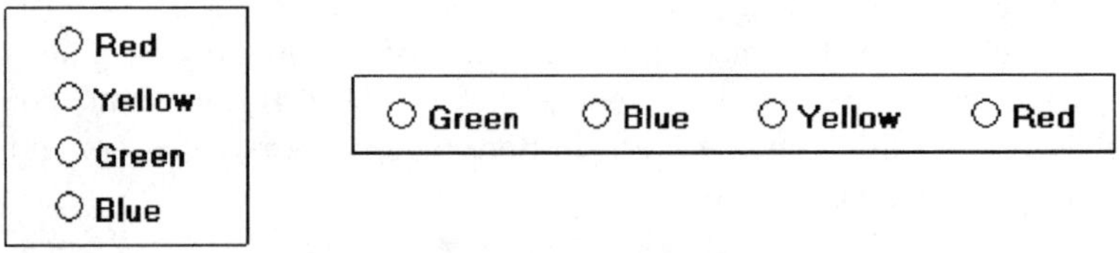

     ┌─────────┐

     │ ○ Red   │

     │ ○ Yellow   │   ┌─────────────────────────────────────┐

     │ ○ Green   │   │ ○ Green   ○ Blue   ○ Yellow   ○ Red │

     │ ○ Blue   │   └─────────────────────────────────────┘

Figure 7.28   └─────────┘

The preferred orientation of radio buttons is columnar. This aids visual scanning and choice comparison. Controls with small button indicators usually fit best in this manner because choice descriptions do not have to be restricted in size. Left-align the buttons and choice descriptions. Provide adequate separation—about three spaces—between choices if they must be presented horizontally. Enclose the buttons in a border. Rectangular boxes should be of equal height and/or width and be butted up against one another. This will distinguish them from nonexclusive choice fields (check boxes) that will be separated from one another. Figure 7.29 illustrates the best ways to, and not to, present radio buttons.

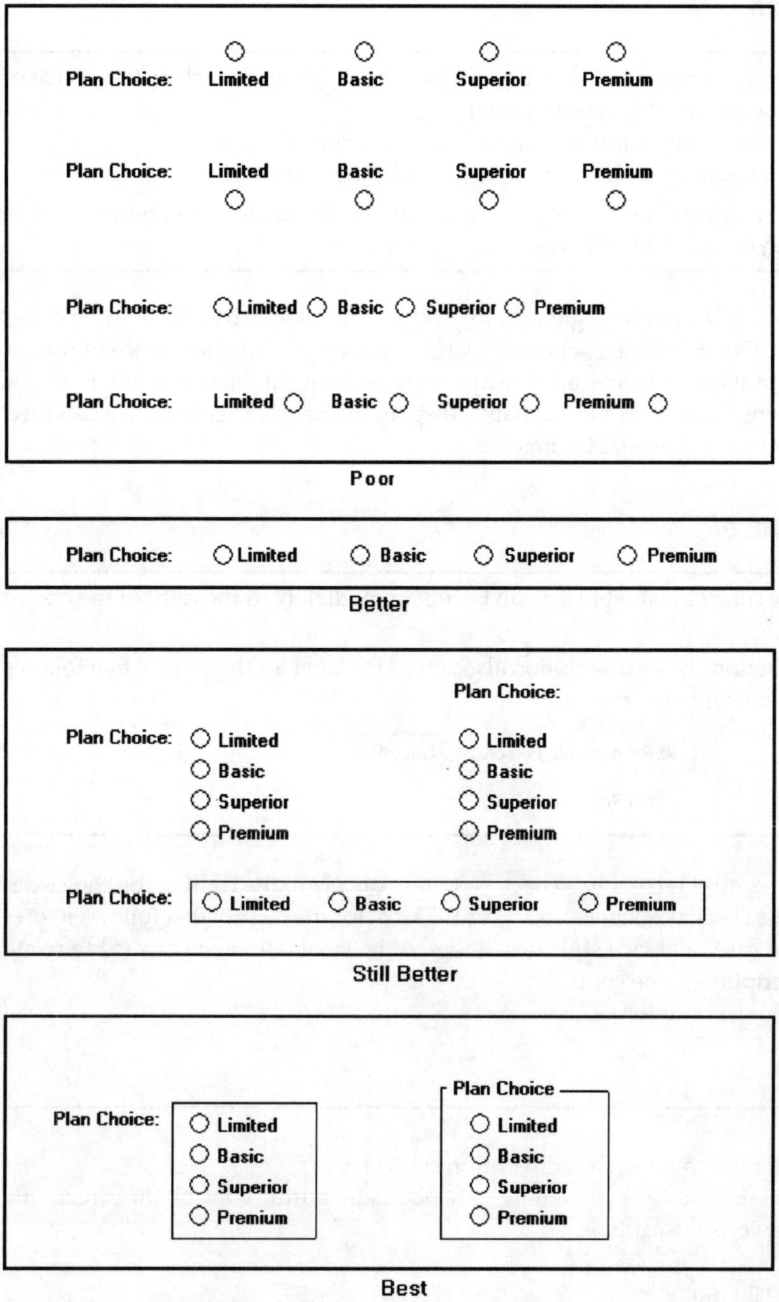

Figure 7.29 Ways to, and not to, present radio buttons.

Organization

- Arrange selections in expected order or follow other patterns such as frequency of occurrence, sequence of use, or importance.
  — For selections arrayed top to bottom, begin ordering at the top.
  — For selections arrayed left to right, begin ordering at the left.
- If, under certain conditions, a choice is not available, display it subdued or less brightly than the available choices.

Selection choices should be organized logically. If the alternatives have an expected order, follow it. Other ordering schemes such as frequency of use, sequence of use, or importance may also be considered. Always begin ordering at the top or left. If, under certain conditions, a choice is not available, display the nonselectable choice subdued or less brightly than the available choices.

Related Control

- Position any control related to a radio button immediately to the right of the choice description.
- If the radio button choice description also acts as the label for the control that follows it, end the label with an arrow (>).

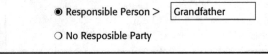

Figure 7.30

Position any control related to a check box immediately to the right of the choice description. If a check box label also acts as the label for the control that follows it, present it in mixed case, sentence style text, and end the label with an arrow (>) to relate the choice description to the control.

Captions

- Structure:
  — Provide a caption for each radio button control.
    • Exception: In screens containing only one radio button control, the screen title may serve as the caption.
- Display:
  — Fully spelled out.
  — In mixed-case letters, capitalizing the first letter of all significant words.
- Columnar orientation:
  — With a control border, position the caption:
    • Upper-left-justified within the border.

Color
Red
Yellow
Green
Blue

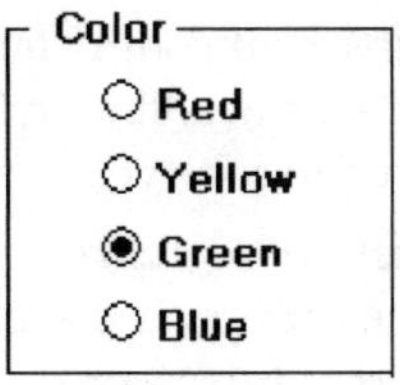

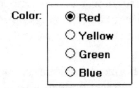

Figure 7.31

• Alternately, the caption may be located to the left of the topmost choice description.

Color:
Red
Yellow
Green
Blue

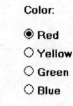

Figure 7.32

— Without an enclosing control border, position the caption:

• Left-justified above the choice descriptions, separated by one space line.

Color:
Red
Yellow
Green
Blue

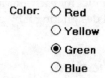

Figure 7.33

• Alternately, the caption may be located to the left of the topmost choice description.

Color:
Red
Yellow
Green
Blue

Figure 7.34

■ Horizontal orientation:

— Position the caption to the left of the choice descriptions.

Figure 7.35

Color:
Green
Blue
Yellow
Red

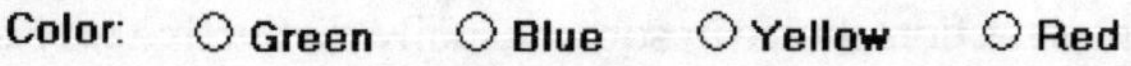

• Alternately, with an enclosing control border, left-justified within the border.

Color
Green
Blue
Yellow
Red

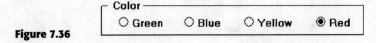

Figure 7.36

— Be consistent in caption style and orientation within a screen.

Structure. Using a *static text* or *group box* control field, display the caption fully spelled out, using mixed-case letters in the headline style. Some occasional common abbreviations may be used, however, to achieve the alignment goals to be specified.

Columnar orientation. The preferred location of a radio button control caption within a screen can vary. Ideally, the caption is placed upper-left-justified within a line border or group box that surrounds columnar-oriented radio buttons, as shown in the example in the above guideline summary. If other controls on a screen possess captions positioned to the left, and the radio button control is aligned with these controls, position the caption to the left of the control. This will help achieve screen efficiency, minimize viewer eye movements, and provide caption and choice distinctiveness. Without an enclosing control border, position the caption left-justified above the choice descriptions, or to the left of the topmost choice description.

Horizontal orientation. In a horizontal orientation, position the caption to the left of the choice descriptions, or left-justified within an enclosing control border. If the screen contains only one radio button control, the screen title may serve as the control caption. Be consistent in caption style and orientation within a screen.

Keyboard Equivalents

- Assign a keyboard mnemonic to each choice description.
- Designate the mnemonic by underlining the applicable letter in the choice description.

Figure 7.37   ⊙ <u>R</u>ed

Assign unique keyboard mnemonics for each alternative in the standard way, choosing the first letter (or another) and designating it by character underlining.

Selection Method and Indication

- Pointing:
    — The selection target area should be as large as possible.
        • Include the button and the choice description text.
    — Highlight the selection choice in some visually distinctive way when the cursor's resting on it and the choice is available for selection.
        • This cursor should be as long as the longest choice description plus one space at each end. Do not place the cursor over the small button.

○ Red

○ Yellow

○ Green

○ ⌐Blue ⌐

Figure 7.38

- Activation:
  - When a choice is selected, distinguish it visually from the unselected choices.
    - A radio button should be filled in with a solid dark dot or made to look depressed or higher through use of a shadow.
  - When a choice is selected, any other selected choice must be deselected.
- Defaults:
  - If a radio button control is displayed that contains a choice previously selected or a default choice, display the selected choice as set in the control

Pointing. The selection target area should be as large as possible in order to make it easy to move to. If a small button is the selection indication method used, the target area should include the button and the choice description text. If the rectangular box selection method is used, the entire box should be the target. Highlight the selection choice in some visually distinctive way when the pointer is resting on it and the choice is available for selection. If a small button is the selection indication method used, a distinctive reverse video, reverse color, or dotted or dashed box selection cursor or bar may be used to surround the selected choice description. This cursor should be as long as the longest description plus one space at each end. The cursor should not cover the small button.

Activation. When a choice is selected, distinguish it visually from the unselected choices. A radio button should be filled in with a solid dark dot or other similar marking (for example, making the button look depressed or higher than the others through the use of a drop shadow). A rectangular box can be highlighted in a manner different from when it is pointed at, or a bolder border can be drawn around it. When a choice is selected, any other selected choice must be deselected or made inactive.

Defaults. If a selection field is displayed with a choice previously selected or a default choice, display the currently active choice in the same manner as when it is selected.

MYTH   **Our software is highly usable—it includes all the latest interface widgets.**

Check Boxes

- Description:
  - A two-part control consisting of a square box and choice description.
  - Each option acts as a switch and can be either "on" or "off."
    - When an option is selected (on), a mark such as an "X" or "check" appears within the square box, or the box is highlighted in some other manner.
    - Otherwise the square box is unselected or empty (off).
  - Each box can be:
    - Switched on or off independently.
    - Used alone or grouped in sets.

- Purpose:
  — To set one or more options as either on or off.
- Advantages
  — Easy-to-access choices.
  — Easy-to-compare choices.
  — Preferred by users.
- Disadvantages:
  — Consume screen space.
  — Limited number of choices.
  — Single check boxes difficult to align with other screen controls.
- Proper usage:
  — For setting attributes, properties, or values.
  — For nonexclusive choices (that is, more than one can be selected).
  — Where adequate screen space is available.
  — Most useful for data and choices that are:
    • Discrete.
    • Small and fixed in number.
    • Not easily remembered.
    • In need of a textual description to describe meaningfully.
    • Most easily understood when the alternatives can be seen together and compared to one another.
    • Never changed in content.
  — Can be used to affect other controls.
  — Use only when both states of a choice are clearly opposite and unambiguous.

Description. *Check box* controls differ from radio buttons in that they permit selection of more than one alternative. Each option acts as a switch and can be either "on" or "off." When an option is selected (on), an X or check appears within the square box, or it is highlighted in some other manner. When not selected, the square box is unselected or empty (off). Each box can be switched on or off independently. Check boxes may be used alone or grouped in sets.

Check boxes, too, may take different physical forms and be called by different names. The most common name is *check boxes*, the name used by Microsoft Windows. Others names include: *toggle buttons*, *switches*, and *two state nonexclusive settings*. Not only their names differ; differences also exist in the way these fields are presented on screens. One very common display method is a check box, which, resembling its namesake, consists of a square placed adjacent to each alternative. When the choice is selected, some systems place an X in the square to provide a visual indication that it is active. Others, including Microsoft Windows, place a check mark in the square, or fill in the selected square or make it look depressed when selected.

Interestingly, in the past decade, Microsoft Windows and others have switched from Xs to checks as the "on" mark in a check box. This has occurred because of possible confusion concerning Xs that have existed in some using communities. In an engineering environment, for example, an X marked in a box means not applicable or not set, while a check mark customarily means active or set. Internationally, also, an X is not universally recognized. (This control is called a check box, isn't it?)

Another style for this type of field is a button or box with the choice description inscribed inside. When selected, the alternative is highlighted in some way. To distinguish these fields visually from similarly constructed fields presenting mutually exclusive choices, the buttons are not adjacent to, or butted up against, one another. Check boxes are illustrated in Figures 7.39 and 7.40. Again, deciding on which style to use seems to be more a matter of preference than performance (other than for the possible confusion of Xs and checks). No published comparison studies are available for guidance.

Purpose. The purpose of a check box, then, is to set one or more options either on or off.

Advantages/disadvantages. With check boxes, all alternatives are always visible. Therefore, it is easy to access and compare choices. Like radio buttons, check boxes were the preferred, and fastest to use, controls in the Johnsgard et al. (1995) study. One disadvantage is the large amount of screen real estate they consume, limiting the number of alternatives that can be efficiently displayed. Another potential disadvantage is that it can be difficult to align a single check box with other arrayed screen controls because they often possess long descriptions for clarity purposes.

Proper usage. Check boxes are useful for setting attributes, properties, or values where adequate screen space is available. The alternatives should be discrete, small in number, and in need of a textual description to identify meaningfully. Check boxes are helpful in situations where the alternatives cannot always be easily remembered and the displaying of the alternatives together aids in understanding and

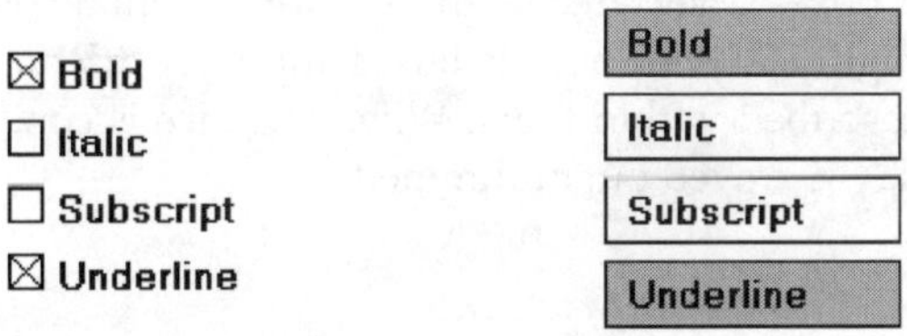

Figure 7.39   Check boxes.

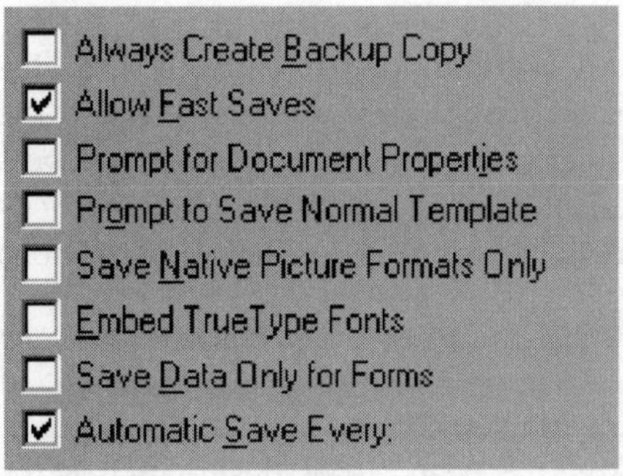

Figure 7.40   Check boxes.

selecting the proper choice. The choices displayed should be stable, never changing in content.

Check boxes can be used to affect other controls. The contents of a list can, for example, be filtered by setting check boxes. Use a check box only when both states of a choice are clearly opposite and unambiguous. If opposite states are not clear, use two radio buttons, clearly stating the opposite states.

Choice Descriptions

- Provide meaningful, fully spelled-out choice descriptions clearly describing the values or effects set by the check boxes.
- Display them in a single line of text.
- Display them using mixed-case letters in sentence style.
- Position descriptions to the right of the check box. Separate by at least one space from the box.
- When a choice is unavailable for selection under a certain condition, display the choice description visually dimmed.

Choice descriptions must be clear, meaningful, fully spelled out, and displayed in a mixed-case text. For multiword descriptions, capitalize the first letter and present the description in the sentence style. Small box-type indicators should be located to the left of the choice description; rectangular boxes that resemble a command button will find the description within the box. Small boxes associated with text are advantageous when the choice description must be lengthy. Descriptions in boxes impose restrictions on the number of words that can be inscribed within them. When a choice is conditionally unavailable for selection, display it grayed out or dimmed.

Size

- Show a minimum of one choice, a maximum of eight.

Generally, selection fields of this style should not offer more than eight choices. Displaying more than eight is usually not efficient because it wastes screen space. If the number of choices exceeds this maximum, consider using a multiple selection list box. Johnsgard et al. (1995) have found, however, that even for as many as 30 choices, check boxes were preferred by users and performed better than other nonexclusive controls.

Defaults

- When the control possesses a state or affect that has been preset, designate it as the default and display its check box marked.

■ When a multiple selection includes choices whose states vary, display the buttons in another unique manner, or the *mixed value* state.

Provide a default setting for a check box whenever possible. If a multiple selection is performed and the values in the selection differ, display the applicable check boxes in the *mixed value* state, or in another distinctive manner such as with a gray shadow.

Structure

■ Provide groupings of related check boxes.
■ A columnar orientation is the preferred manner of presentation for multiple related check boxes.
■ Left-align the check boxes and choice descriptions.

Figure 7.41

☒ Bold
☐ Italic
☐ Underline

■ If vertical space on the screen is limited, orient the boxes horizontally.
■ Provide adequate separation between boxes so that the buttons are associated with the proper description.
  — A distance equal to three spaces is usually sufficient.

Figure 7.42   ☒ Bold   ☐ Italic   ☐ Underline

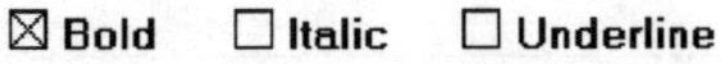

■ Enclose the boxes in a border to visually strengthen the relationship they possess.

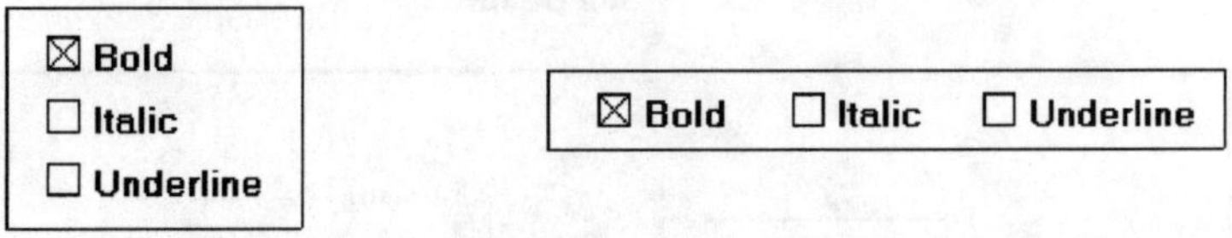

☒ Bold
☐ Italic
☐ Underline

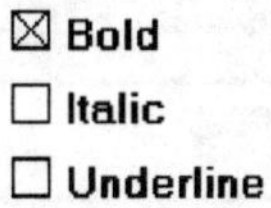

☒ Bold   ☐ Italic   ☐ Underline

Figure 7.43

Provide groupings of related check boxes. The preferred check box orientation is columnar. This aids scanning and choice comparison. Controls with small box indicators usually fit best in this manner because choice descriptions are not restricted in size. Left-align the check boxes and choice descriptions. Rectangular boxes should be of equal width and separated from one another by small and equidistant spaces. This will distinguish them from mutually exclusive choices that will be butted up against one another. If the boxes must be horizontally oriented, provide adequate separation between them. Enclose the boxes in a border to emphasize their relationship. Figure 7.44 illustrates ways to, and not to, present groupings of check boxes.

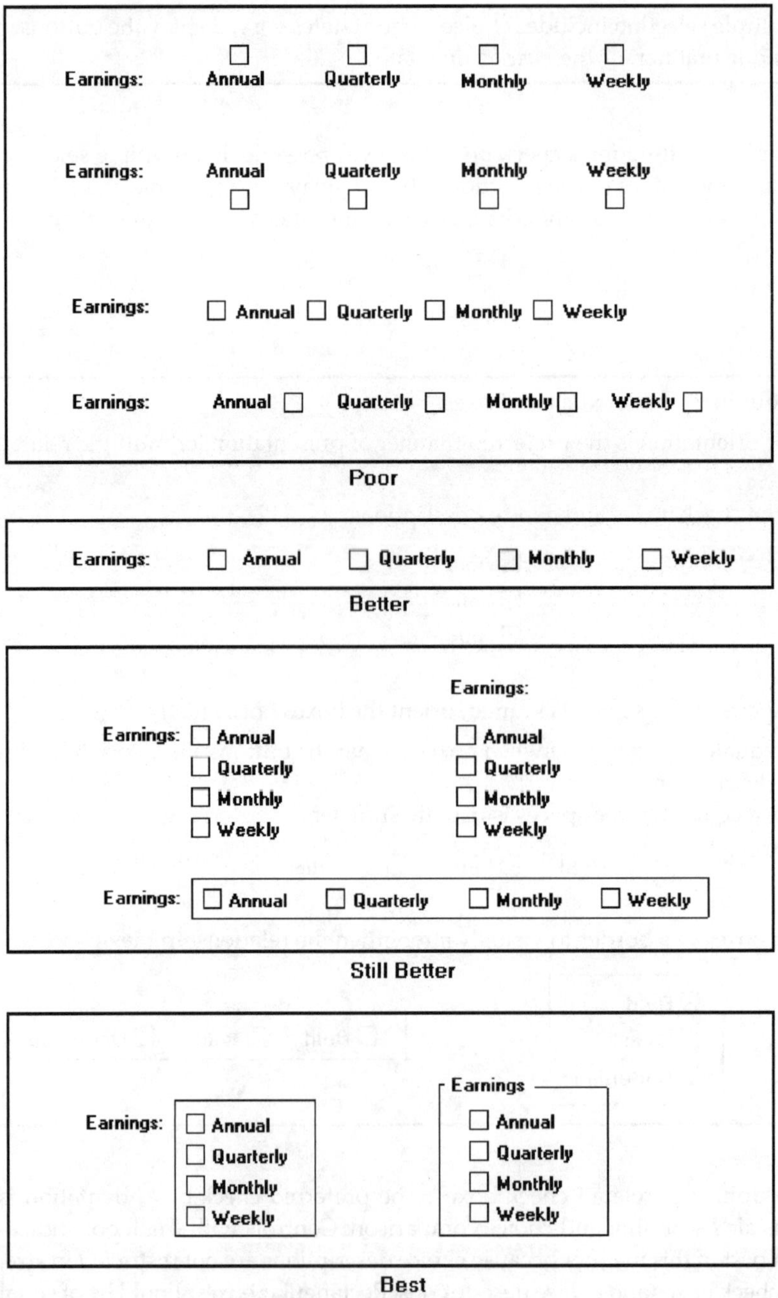

Figure 7.44 Ways to, and not to, present check boxes.

Organization

- Arrange selections in logical order or follow other patterns such as frequency of occurrence, sequence of use, or importance.
  - For selections arrayed top to bottom, begin ordering at the top.
  - For selections arrayed left to right, begin ordering at the left.
- If, under certain conditions, a choice is not available, display it subdued or less brightly than the available choices.

Selection choices should be organized logically. If the alternatives have an expected order, follow it. Other ordering schemes such as frequency of use, sequence of use, or importance may also be considered. Always begin the ordering at the top or left. If, under certain conditions, a choice is not available, display the unavailable choice subdued or less brightly than the available choices.

Related Control

- Position any control related to a check box immediately to the right of the choice description.
  - If a the check box choice description also acts as the label for the control that follows it , end the label with an arrow (>).

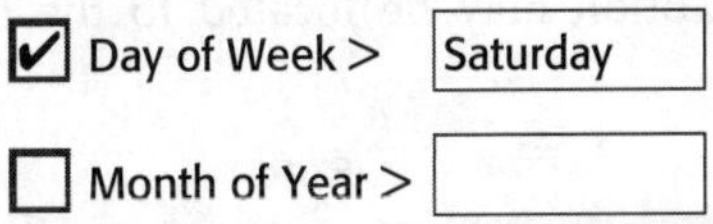

☑ Day of Week > | Saturday |

Figure 7.45   ☐ Month of Year > | |

Position any control related to a check box immediately to the right of the choice description. If a the check box label also acts as the label for the control that follows it, present it mixed case, sentence style text and end the label with an arrow (>) to relate the choice description to the control.

Captions

- Structure:
  - Provide a caption for each grouping of related check boxes.
    - Exception: In screens containing only one check box grouping, the screen title may serve as the caption.
  - Display:
    - Fully spelled out.
    - In mixed-case letters capitalizing the first letter of all significant words.
- Columnar orientation:
  - With a control border, position the caption:
    - Upper-left-justified within the border.

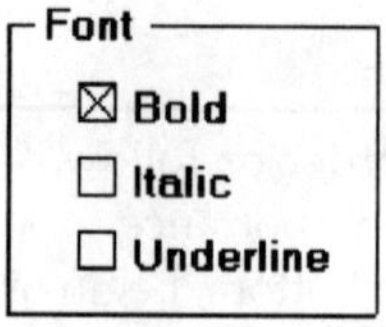

```
┌ Font ──────────┐
│  ☒ Bold        │
│  ☐ Italic      │
│  ☐ Underline   │
└────────────────┘
```

Figure 7.46

- Alternately, the caption may be located to the left of the topmost choice description.

```
              ┌─────────────┐
Font:         │ ☒ Bold      │
              │ ☐ Italic    │
              │ ☐ Underline │
              └─────────────┘
```

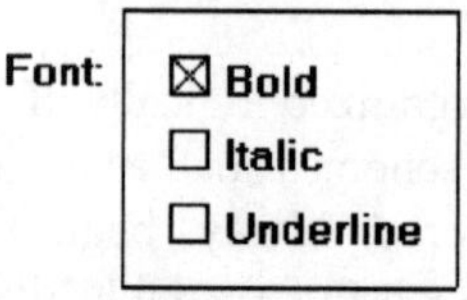

Figure 7.47

— Without an enclosing control border, position the caption:
  - Left-justified above the choice descriptions separated by one space line.

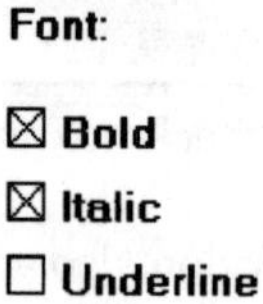

Font:

☒ Bold

☒ Italic

Figure 7.48   ☐ Underline

- Alternately, the caption may be located to the left of the topmost choice description.

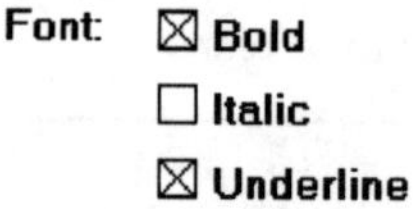

Font: ☒ Bold

             ☐ Italic

Figure 7.49   ☒ Underline

■ Horizontal orientation
  — Position the caption to the left of the choice descriptions.

Font: ☒ Bold   ☐ Italic   ☐ Underline

```
Font: │ ☒ Bold    ☐ Italic    ☐ Underline │
```

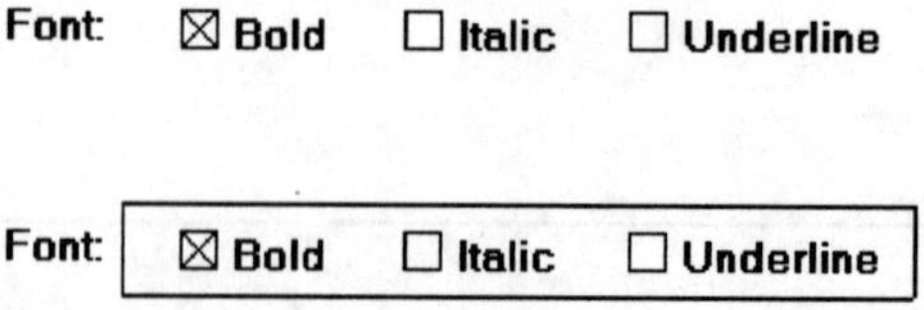

Figure 7.50

- Alternately, with an enclosing control border, it should be left-justified within the border.

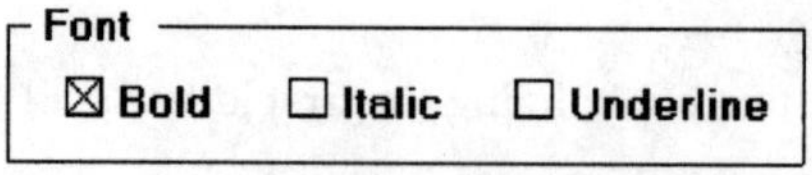

```
┌ Font ─────────────────────────────────┐
│  ☒ Bold    ☐ Italic    ☐ Underline    │
└───────────────────────────────────────┘
```

Figure 7.51

— Be consistent in caption style and orientation within a screen.

Structure. Using a *static text* or *group box* control, provide a caption for each grouping of related check boxes. Display the caption fully spelled out using mixed-case letters. Some occasional common abbreviations may be used, however, to achieve the alignment goals to be specified.

Columnar orientation. The preferred location of a check box control caption within a screen can vary. Ideally, the caption is placed upper-left-justified within a line border, or group box, surrounding columnar-oriented check boxes as shown in the first example in the above guideline summary. If other controls on a screen possess captions positioned to the left, and the check box control is aligned with these controls, position the caption to the left of the control. This is the second example illustrated above. This will help achieve screen efficiency, minimize viewer eye movements, and provide caption and choice distinctiveness. Without an enclosing border, position the caption left-justified above the choice descriptions, or to the left of the topmost choice.

Horizontal orientation. If horizontal orientation is necessary, position the caption to the left of the choice descriptions, or left-justified within an enclosing control border. If the screen contains only one related grouping of check boxes, the screen title may serve as the control caption. Be consistent in caption style and orientation within a screen.

Keyboard Equivalents

- Assign a keyboard mnemonic to each check box.
- Designate the mnemonic by underlining the applicable letter in the choice description.

Figure 7.52 ☐ <u>U</u>nderline

Assign unique keyboard mnemonics for each check box in the standard way, choosing the first letter (or another) and designating it by character underlining.

Selection Method and Indication

- Pointing:
  - The selection target area should be as large as possible.
    - Include the check box and the choice description text.
  - Highlight the selection choice in some visually distinctive way when the cursor's resting on it and the choice is available for selection.
    - This cursor should be as long as the longest choice description plus one space at each end. Do not place the cursor over the check box.

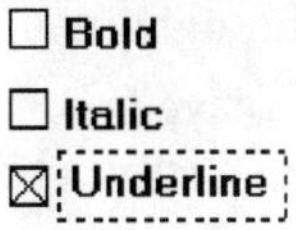

☐ **Bold**
☐ **Italic**
☒ **Underline**

Figure 7.53

- Activation:
  — When a choice is selected, distinguish it visually from the non-selected choices.
    • A check box should be filled in or made to look depressed or higher through use of a shadow.
- Defaults:
  — If a check box is displayed that contains a choice previously selected or default choice, display the selected choice as set in the control.
- Select/deselect all:
  — Do not use *Select All* and *Deselect All* check boxes.
- Mixed-value state:
  — When a check box represents a value, and a multiple selection encompasses multiple value occurrences set in both the on and off state, display the check box in a *mixed value* state.
    • Fill the check box with another easily differentiable symbol or pattern.

■ **Bold**

☐ **Italic**

Figure 7.54   ☐ **Underline**

  — Toggle the check box as follows:
    • Selection 1: Set the associated value for all elements. Fill the check box with an "X" or "check."
    • Selection 2: Unset the value for all associated elements. Blank-out the check box.
    • Selection 3: Return all elements to their original state. Fill the check box with the mixed value symbol or pattern.

Pointing. The selection target area should be as large as possible in order to make it easy to move to. If a small check box is the selection indication method used, the target area should include the box and the choice description text. If the rectangular box selection method is used, the entire box should be the target. Highlight the selection choice in some visually distinctive way when the pointer is resting on it and the choice is available for selection. If a check box is the selection indication method used, a distinctive reverse video, reverse color, or dotted or dashed box selection cursor or bar may be used to surround the selected choice description. This cursor should be as long as the longest description plus one space at each end. The cursor should not cover the check box.

Activation. When a choice is selected, distinguish it visually from the unselected choices. A check box may be marked with an X or check or filled in. Other methods include making the button look depressed or raised through appropriate use of drop shadows. A rectangular box can be highlighted in a manner different from when it is pointed at, or a bolder border can be drawn around it. The style chosen must be consistently applied throughout an application or system.

Defaults. If a selection field is displayed with a choice previously selected or a default choice, display the currently active choice in the same manner as when it is selected.

Select/deselect all. Do not use *Select All* and *Deselect All* check boxes. If this option is necessary, consider using a multiple selection list box with command buttons to accomplish these actions.

Mixed-value state. A check box can have three states.

- Checked—the associated property or value is set.
- Cleared—the associated value or property is not set.
- Mixed value—the associated value is set for some, but not all elements of the selection.

An example of the mixed value state would be when a sentence is selected and the selected text is partly bold and partly normal. So, when a check box represents a value, and a selection encompasses multiple value occurrences set in both the on and off state, display the check box in the *mixed value* state. Fill the check box with another easily differentiable symbol or pattern. Toggle the check box through clicking as described in the above guidelines.

Palettes

- Description:
  - A control consisting of a series of graphical alternatives. The choices themselves are descriptive, being composed of colors, patterns, or images.
  - In addition to being a standard screen control, a palette may also be presented on a pull-down or pop-up menu or a toolbar.
- Purpose:
  - To set one of a series of mutually exclusive options presented graphically or pictorially.
- Advantages:
  - Pictures aid comprehension.
  - Easy-to-compare choices.
  - Usually consume less screen space than textual equivalents.
- Disadvantages:
  - A limited number of choices can be displayed.
  - Difficult to organize for scanning efficiency.
  - Requires skill and time to design meaningful and attractive graphical representations.
- Proper usage:
  - For setting attributes, properties, or values.
  - For mutually exclusive choices (that is, only one can be selected).
  - Where adequate screen space is available.
  - Most useful for data and choices that are:
    - Discrete.
    - Frequently selected.
    - Limited in number.
    - Variable in number.

- Not easily remembered.
- Most easily understood when the alternatives may be seen together and compared to one another.
- Most meaningfully represented pictorially or by example.
- Can be clearly represented pictorially.
- Rarely changed in content.
— Do not use:
- Where the alternatives cannot be meaningfully and clearly represented pictorially.
- Where words are clearer than images.
- Where the choices are going to change.

Description. Like radio buttons, *palettes* can also be used to present two or more mutually exclusive alternatives. The choices presented, however, are visually descriptive within themselves, no choice descriptions being needed to identify them. Examples of palettes might be fill-in colors, patterns, or different shades of a color. A palette may also be referred to as *value set* or *well*. A palette is illustrated in Figure 7.55. In addition to being a standard screen control, a palette may also be presented on a pull-down or pop-up menu, included in a toolbar, or be contained in a Palette window.

Purpose. A palette's purpose is to set one of a series of mutually exclusive options presented in a graphic or pictorial form.

Advantages/disadvantages. Palettes are preferable to radio buttons in that they take up less space and allow the viewer to focus on the visual characteristics of the choice itself, instead of having to read the choice text and cross-reference it to a radio button. Some qualities, such as colors, patterns, and shades, are much more easily comprehended when they are actually seen. While a larger number of choices can be presented than with radio buttons, there is still a limit to how many can be practically displayed. Because of their larger size, palettes are also more difficult to organize for scanning efficiency. Palettes also require skill and time to design meaningful and attractive graphical representations.

Proper usage. Palettes are used for setting attributes, properties, or values of mutually exclusive choices where adequate screen space is available. Consider using a palette when the choices have qualities that can be best described by actual illustration. They are useful for data and choices that are discrete and limited in number. They are most useful when the choices' being seen together and compared to

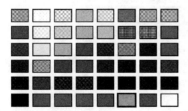

Figure 7.55 Palette.

one another aids identification and selection of the proper alternative. They are also most useful when the alternatives can be meaningfully and clearly represented pictorially or by example. Palettes should rarely change in content.

Palettes should be displayed in the proper manner. If the attributes on a palette must be available at all times, place them on a standard control or fixed palette. If the attributes on the palette are sometimes used frequently and other times used infrequently, place them on a pop-up or tear-off menu. Do not place frequently used palettes on pull-down menus.

Also, from a presentation perspective, do not use a palette if the alternatives cannot be meaningfully and clearly represented pictorially. In addition, do not use one where words are clearer than images, or in situations where the choices are going to change.

Graphical Representations

- Provide meaningful, accurate, and clear illustrations or representations of choices.
- Create images large enough to:
  - Clearly illustrate the available alternatives.
  - Permit ease in pointing and selecting.
- Create images of equal size.
- Always test illustrations before implementing them.

Provide meaningful, accurate, and clear illustrations of alternative choices. Create equal size images large enough to illustrate clearly the available alternatives and permit ease in pointing and selecting. Always test illustrations with users before implementing them, to ensure that they will work satisfactorily. While most palettes will not possess textual choice descriptions, under certain circumstances textual descriptions may be needed. For example, a choice might require selection of a style of font. The palette may contain the names of the available styles (such as Roman) with the text displayed as the font style would actually appear.

Size

- Present all available alternatives within the limits imposed by:
  - The size of the graphical representations.
  - The screen display's capabilities.

Since palettes will consume less screen space, more choices can be displayed in a given area of a screen than can be displayed when using textual descriptions. Present all available alternatives within the limits imposed by how big the graphical representations must be and the capabilities of the display hardware in creating clear illustrations. Limitations in people's ability to accurately differentiate the kinds of graphical representations being presented must also be considered.

Layout

- Create boxes large enough to:
  — Effectively illustrate the available alternatives.
  — Permit ease in pointing and selecting.
- Create boxes of equal size.
- Position the boxes adjacent to, or butted up against, one another.
- A columnar orientation is the preferred manner.
- If vertical space on the screen is limited, orient the choices horizontally.

Palette boxes must be large enough to illustrate effectively the available alternatives and to maximize ease in selecting. Created boxes should be of equal size and positioned adjacent to, or butted up against one another, since they are mutually exclusive choices. Columns are preferred, but horizontal rows can be used if space constraints exist on the screen.

Organization

- Arrange palettes in expected or normal order.
  — For palettes arrayed top to bottom, begin ordering at the top.
  — For palettes arrayed left to right, begin ordering at the left.
- If an expected or normal order does not exist, arrange choices by frequency of occurrence, sequence of use, importance, or alphabetically (if textual).
- If, under certain conditions, a choice is not available, display it subdued or less brightly than the other choices.

Palettes should be organized logically. If the alternatives have an expected order, follow it. Colors, for example, should be ordered from the right or top by their spectral position: red, orange, yellow, green, blue, indigo, and violet. If an expected or normal order does not exist, arrange choices by frequency of occurrence, sequence of use, or importance. Palettes with text may be arranged alphabetically. If, under certain conditions, a choice is not available, display the unavailable choice subdued or less brightly than the available choices.

Captions

- Provide a caption for each palette.
  — On screens containing only one palette, the screen title may serve as the caption.
- Display the caption fully spelled out using mixed-case letters.
- Columnar orientation:
  — The field caption may be positioned left-aligned above the palette.

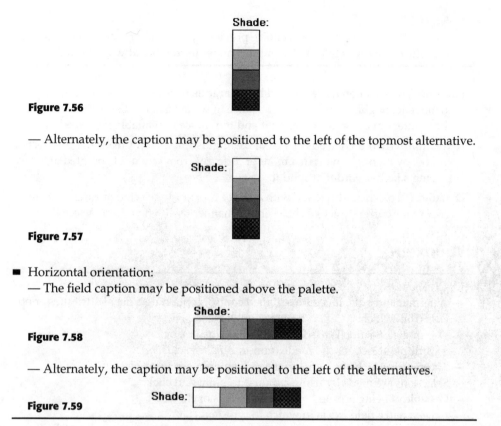

Figure 7.56

— Alternately, the caption may be positioned to the left of the topmost alternative.

Figure 7.57

- Horizontal orientation:
  — The field caption may be positioned above the palette.

Figure 7.58

— Alternately, the caption may be positioned to the left of the alternatives.

Figure 7.59

Using a *static text* control, provide a caption for each palette. In screens containing only one palette, the screen title may serve as the caption. Display the caption fully spelled out using mixed-case letters, although some abbreviations may be used to achieve the alignment goals to be specified. Captions may be located above or to the left of the palette, as shown above. With a horizontal orientation, the caption may be positioned above the palette or to the left of the alternatives. Positioning on any one screen will be dependent on other caption-control relationships within the screen.

Selection Method and Indication

- Pointing:
  — Highlight the choice in some visually distinctive way when the pointer or cursor is resting on it and the choice is available for selection.
- Activation:
  — When a choice is selected, distinguish it visually from the unselected choices by highlighting it in a manner different from when it is pointed at, or by placing a bold border around it.

- Defaults:
  — If a palette is displayed with a choice previously selected or a default choice, display the currently active choice in the manner used when it was selected.

Pointing. The selection target should be as large as possible in order to make it easy to move to. Highlight the selection choice in some visually distinctive way when the pointer or cursor is resting on it and the choice is available for selection.

Activation. When a choice is selected, distinguish it visually from the unselected choices by highlighting it in a manner different from when it is pointed at, or by placing a bolder border around it.

Defaults. If a palette is displayed with a choice previously selected or a default choice, display the currently active choice in the manner used when it was selected.

List Boxes

- Description:
  — A permanently displayed box-shaped control containing a list of attributes or objects from which:
    - A single selection is made (mutually exclusive), or
    - Multiple selections are made (non-mutually-exclusive).
  — The choice may be text, pictorial representations, or graphics.
  — Selections are made by using a mouse to point and click.
  — Capable of being scrolled to view large lists of choices.
  — No text entry field exists in which to type text.
  — A list box may be may be associated with a *summary list box* control, which allows the selected choice to be displayed or an item added to the list.

- Purpose:
  — To display a collection of items containing:
    - Mutually exclusive options.
    - Non-mutually-exclusive options.

- Advantages:
  — Unlimited number of choices.
  — Reminds users of available options.
  — Box always visible.

- Disadvantages:
  — Consumes screen space.
  — Often requires an action (scrolling) to see all list choices.
  — The list content may change, making it hard to find items.
  — The list may be ordered in an unpredictable way, making it hard to find items.

- Proper usage:
  — For selecting values or setting attributes.
  — For choices that are:
    - Mutually exclusive (only one can be selected).
    - Non-mutually-exclusive (one or more may be selected).

— Where screen space is available.
— For data and choices that are:
  • Best represented textually.
  • Not frequently selected.
  • Not well known, easily learned, or remembered.
  • Ordered in an unpredictable fashion.
  • Frequently changed.
  • Large in number.
  • Fixed or variable in list length.
— When screen space or layout considerations make radio buttons or check boxes impractical.

Description. A *list box* is a permanently displayed rectangular box control that contains a list of values or attributes from which single or multiple selections are made. It can also be referred to as a *fixed list box* because it is fixed on the screen. In Java, they are called *lists*, and in HTML, *selection lists/scrolling lists*. The choices are usually text, but they may be pictorial representations or graphics as well. A list box may be scrollable to view large lists, and the user uses a mouse to point and click to make selections. No text entry field exists in which to type text, but a single-selection list box may be associated with a text box where the selected choice is displayed or an item may be added to the list. Examples of single-selection list boxes are illustrated in Figure 7.60.

Purpose. The purpose of a list box is display a collection of items. The choices may be mutually exclusive (single-selection) or not mutually exclusive (multiple-selection).

Advantages/disadvantages. List boxes are always visible, reminding users of the choices available. They permit an unlimited number of options to be displayed. Among their disadvantages are the excessive screen space they consume and the possible necessity for time-consuming scrolling to see all items. Since the list content can change, and items can be ordered in an unpredictable way, it can be hard to find items.

Proper usage. List boxes are used for selecting objects or values or setting attributes, either mutually exclusive or not, where sufficient screen space is available to display 6 to 8 choices. Their best use is for data and choices that are textual; large in number; fixed or variable in list length; not well known, easily learned or

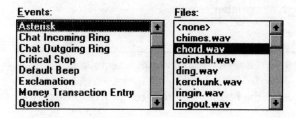

Figure 7.60 List boxes.

remembered; and ordered in an unpredictable fashion. List box items should not have to be selected or changed frequently. List boxes may be used when screen space, list size, and data volatility considerations make use of radio buttons and check boxes impractical. The content of a list box is easier to change than that of radio buttons and check boxes.

List Box General Guidelines

First, general list box guidelines will be presented. Then, specific guidelines for single- and multiple-selection lists will be reviewed.

Selection Descriptions

- Clearly and meaningfully describe the choices available. Spell them out as fully as possible.
  — Graphical representations must clearly represent the options.
- Present in mixed case, using the sentence style structure.
- Left-align into columns.

Selection descriptions will reflect the selection alternatives available. They should be meaningful, fully spelled out, and follow the sentence style of presentation. Array the descriptions into columns. Meaningful ordering schemes include logical order, frequency of use, sequence of use, and importance. If no such pattern exists, arrange the list alphabetically. Display the list of choices using mixed-case letters.

List Size

- Not actual limit in size.
- Present all available alternatives.
- Require no more than 40 page-downs to search a list.
  — If more are required, provide a method for using search criteria or scoping the options.

A list being displayed in a fixed list box has no actual size limit. All available alternatives should be capable of being displayed. Searching a very long list, however, can be very time-consuming. A list should not require more than 40 page-downs to completely search it. If more are necessary, provide a method for using search criteria or scoping the options, perhaps through a first-letter search.

Box Size

- Must be long enough to display 6 to 8 choices without requiring scrolling.
  — Exceptions:
    - If screen space constraints exist, the box may be reduced in size to display at least three items.
    - If it is the major control within a window, the box may be larger.

— If more items are available than are visible in the box, provide vertical scrolling to display all items.

■ Must be wide enough to display the longest possible choice.

Figure 7.61

— When box cannot be made wide enough to display the longest entry:
  • Make it wide enough to permit entries to be distinguishable, or,
  • Break the long entries with an ellipsis (...) in the middle, or,
  • Provide horizontal scrolling.

The exact size of a fixed list box will depend on its function and screen space constraints. Generally, boxes should be restricted to displaying no more than eight choices at one time. Slightly larger boxes that eliminate the need for scrolling, however, are preferable to list boxes that require a little scrolling. If screen space constraints exist, the box may be reduced in size to display at least three items. If scrolling is necessary, include a scroll bar on the right side of the box.

The list box should be wide enough to display fully all item wording. When a box cannot be made wide enough to display the longest entry, make it wide enough to permit entries to be distinguishable, or, break the long entries with an ellipsis in the middle. If breaking long entries, preserve the important characteristics needed to distinguish them. When shortening an item's name in this way, include a *ToolTip* that displays the item's full name.

As a last resort, provide horizontal scrolling and a scroll bar at the bottom of the list box. Many people dislike horizontal scrolling, however.

Organization

■ Order in a logical and meaningful way to permit easy browsing.
  — Consider using separate controls to enable the user to change the sort order or filter items displayed in the list.

■ If a particular choice is not available in the current context, omit it from the list.
  — Exception: If it is important that the existence and unavailability of a particular list item be communicated, display the choice dimmed or grayed out instead of deleting it.

Choices should be organized logically to permit easy browsing. If the alternatives have an expected order, follow it. Other ordering schemes such as frequency of use, sequence of use, or importance may also be considered. When no obvious scheme exists, use alphabetic order. You can provide separate controls to enable the user to change the sort order or filter items displayed in the list.

If a particular choice is not available in the current context, it should be omitted from the list. If it is important that the existence and unavailability of a list item be communicated, however, display the choice dimmed or grayed out instead of deleting it.

Layout and Separation

- Enclose the choices in a box with a solid border.
  — The border should be the same color as the choice descriptions.
- Leave one blank character position between the choice descriptions and the left border.
- Leave one blank character position between the longest choice description in the list and the right border, if possible.

Enclose the box in a solid border in the color of the choice descriptions. To provide adequate legibility, leave one space between the choice descriptions and the left border, and one space between the longest choice description and the right border.

Captions

- Use mixed-case letters.
- The preferred position of the control caption is above the upper-left corner of the list box.

Figure 7.62

- Alternately, the caption may be located to the left of the topmost choice description.

Figure 7.63

- Be consistent in caption style and orientation within a screen, and related screens.

To identify the list box, a field caption in mixed-case letters, with each significant word capitalized is necessary. A list box does not have a caption, so create one using a *static text* control. Place this caption either above the upper-left corner of the box or to the left of the first choice description. The caption style chosen will again be dependent upon caption-control relationships in other controls included within the screen. It should be consistently oriented with the other control captions.

Disabling

- When a list box is disabled, display its caption and show its entries as grayed out or dimmed.

Display a list box's caption and entries as dimmed or grayed when the list box is entirely disabled.

Selection Method and Indication

- Pointing:
  — Highlight the selection choice in some visually distinctive way when the pointer or cursor is resting on it and the choice is available for selection.
- Selection:
  — Use a reverse video or reverse color bar to surround the choice description when it is selected.
  — The cursor should be as wide as the box itself.

Figure 7.64

  — Mark the selected choice in a distinguishing way.
- Activation:
  — Require the pressing of a command button when an item, or items, is selected.

Pointing. Highlight the selection choice in some visually distinctive way when the pointer or cursor is resting on it and the choice is available for selection. One method used for this is to place a bold border around the choice.

Selection. Indicate the selected choice through use of a reverse video or reverse color bar, as wide as the box itself. Visually differentiate multiple-choice (nonexclusive) from single-choice (mutually exclusive) fixed list boxes, as described in the following sections.

Activation. Require the pressing of a command button when an item, or items, is selected. Double-clicking is difficult for many people. Always provide for a single click followed by a button press.

Single-Selection List Boxes

- Purpose:
  — To permit selection of only one item from a large listing.
- Design guidelines:
  — Related text box
    • If presented with an associated text box control:
      — Position the list box below and as close as possible to the text box.
      — The list box caption should be worded similarly to the text box caption.

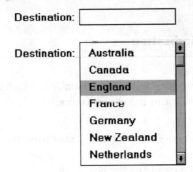

Figure 7.65

  — If the related text box and the list box are very close in proximity, the caption may be omitted from the list box.

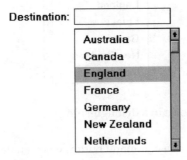

Figure 7.66

  — Use the same background color for the text box as is used in the list box.
  — Defaults:
    • When the list box is first displayed:
      — Present the currently active choice highlighted or marked with a circle or diamond to the left of the entry.
      — If a choice has not been previously selected, provide a default choice and display it in the same manner that is used in selecting it.

— If the list represents mixed values for a multiple selection, do not highlight an entry.
— Other:
  • Follow other relevant list box guidelines.

Purpose. A *single-selection* list box is used for selecting only one item in a list. It provides a mutually exclusive operation similar to a group of radio or option buttons. This kind of list box, however, can handle a large number of items more efficiently.

Related text box. If the list box is associated with a text field, position the list box below and as close as possible to the related text box. If this cannot be accomplished, position the text box to the left. Captions of related text boxes and list boxes must be worded similarly. If, however, the text box and the list box are located in close physical proximity, the caption may be omitted from the list box. Visually relate a list box to a text box by using the same background color for both boxes.

For single-selection fixed list boxes, indicate an active choice by highlighting it or marking it with a circle or diamond to the left of the choice description. If the list represents mixed values for a multiple selection, do not highlight any entry.

Extended and Multiple-Selection List Boxes

■ Purpose:
— To permit selection of more than one item in a long listing.
  • Extended list box: Optimized for individual item or range selection.
  • Multiple-selection list box: Optimized for independent item selection.
■ Design guidelines:
— Selection indication:
  • Mark the selected choice with an X or check mark to the left of the entry.

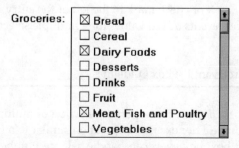

Figure 7.67

  • Consider providing a *summary list box*.
    — Position it to the right of the list box.
    — Use the same colors for the summary list box as are used in the list box.

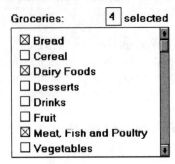

Groceries:

☒ Bread
☐ Cereal
☒ Dairy Foods
☐ Desserts
☐ Drinks
☐ Fruit
☒ Meat, Fish and Poultry
☐ Vegetables

Groceries Selected:

Bread
Dairy Foods
Meat, Fish and Poultry

Figure 7.68

    — Provide command buttons to *Add* (one item) or *Add All* (items) to the summary list box, and *Remove* (one item) or *Remove All* (items) from the summary list box.
- Consider providing a display-only text control indicating how many choices have been selected.
    — Position it justified upper-right above the list box.

Groceries: `4` selected

☒ Bread
☐ Cereal
☒ Dairy Foods
☐ Desserts
☐ Drinks
☐ Fruit
☒ Meat, Fish and Poultry
☐ Vegetables

Figure 7.69

— Select All and Deselect All buttons
- Provide command buttons to accomplish fast *Select All* and *Deselect All* actions, when these actions must be frequently or quickly performed.
— Defaults:
- When the list box is first displayed:
    — Display the currently active choices highlighted.
    — Mark with an X or check mark to the left of the entry.
    — If the list represents mixed values for a multiple selection, do not highlight an entry.
— Other:
- Follow other relevant list box guidelines.

Purpose. *Multiple-selection* list boxes permit selection of multiple items from a long listing. They provide a nonexclusive operation similar to a group of check boxes. This kind of list box, however, can handle a large number of items more efficiently. *Extended list* boxes are optimized for individual item or range selection. *Multiple-selection* list boxes are optimized for independent item selection.

Selection indication. For choice selections, mark them with an X or check mark to the left of the entry. Also consider providing a *summary list* box, another list box containing a compilation of the active selections from the multiple-selection list box. This will permit quick scanning and comparison of these active choices and greatly reduce the need for scrolling if the selectable list is lengthy. The summary list box can be made scrollable, if necessary. Position the summary list adjacent to, and to the right of, the multiple-selection list box. Use the same colors for the summary list box and the multiple-selection list box. Include command buttons to *Add* (one item) or *Add All* (items) to the summary list box, and *Remove* (one item) or *Remove All* (items) from the summary list box.

Also consider providing a *display-only text box* control indicating how many choices have been selected in the multiple-selection list box. This text box can be associated with either the multiple-selection or summary list box. It is useful in situations where the multiple selections may be numerous and all the choices cannot be seen without scrolling. It is also useful when the user must know exactly how many choices have been selected. Position this text box justified upper-right above the list box.

Select All and Deselect buttons. Provide command buttons to accomplish fast "select all" and "deselect" actions, when these actions must be frequently or quickly performed.

Defaults. When the list box is first displayed, the active selection will depend on previous activities. If a choice has been previously selected, display the currently active choice in the same manner used when it was selected. If the list represents mixed values for a multiple selection, do not highlight any list entries.

List View Controls

- Description:
  - A special extended-selection list box that displays a collection of items, consisting of an icon and a label.
  - The contents can be displayed in four different views:
    - Large Icon: Items appear as a full-sized icon with a label below.
    - Small Icon: Items appear as a small icon with label to the right.
    - List: Items appear as a small icon with label to the right.
      - Arrayed in a columnar, sorted layout.
    - Report: Items appear as a line in a multicolumn format.
      - Leftmost column includes icon and its label.
      - Subsequent columns include application-specific information.
- Purpose and usage:
  - Where the representation of objects as icons is appropriate.
  - To represent items with multiple columns of information.

Description. A *list view* control is a special extended-selection list box that displays a collection of items, each consisting of an icon and a label. List view controls can display content in four different views, *large icon, small icon, list,* and *report.* The control also supports options for aligning, selecting, and sorting icons, and for editing icon labels.

Purpose and usage. Use list views when the representation of objects as icons is appropriate, or to represent items with multiple columns of information.

Drop-down/Pop-up List Boxes

- Description
  - A single rectangular control that shows one item with a small button to the right side.
    - The button provides a visual cue that an associated selection box is available but hidden.
  - When the button is selected, a larger associated box appears, containing a list of choices from which one may be selected.
  - Selections are made by using the mouse to point and click.
  - Text may not be typed into the control.
- Purpose:
  - To select one item from a large list of mutually exclusive options when screen space is limited.
- Advantages:
  - Unlimited number of choices.
  - Reminds users of available options.
  - Conserves screen space.
- Disadvantages:
  - Requires an extra action to display the list of choices.
  - When displayed, all choices may not always be visible, requiring scrolling.
  - The list may be ordered in an unpredictable way, making it hard to find items.
- Proper usage:
  - For selecting values or setting attributes.
  - For choices that are mutually exclusive (only one can be selected).
  - Where screen space is limited.
  - For data and choices that are:
    - Best represented textually.
    - Infrequently selected.
    - Not well known, easily learned, or remembered.
    - Ordered in a unpredictable fashion.
    - Large in number.
    - Variable or fixed in list length.
  - Use drop-down/pop-up lists when:
    - Screen space or layout considerations make radio buttons or single-selection list boxes impractical.
    - The first, or displayed, item will be selected most of the time.
  - Do not use a drop-down list if it important that all options be seen together.

Description. A *drop-down/pop-up list box* is a single rectangular field with a small button to the side and an associated hidden list of options. In Java, they are called *choice/pop-up lists*, in HTML, *selection lists/pop-up menus*. The button provides a visual cue to the user that an associated selection box of choices is hidden but available on demand. When requested, a larger associated rectangular box appears containing a scrollable list of choices from which one is selected. Selections are made by using the mouse to point and click. No text field exists in which to type text.

Fields of this nature go by many different names. They are called *drop-down lists* because they appear to drop down from the single-selection field. Microsoft Windows calls them *drop-down list boxes*. Other common names are *pull-down lists, option menus,* and simply *list boxes*. Other list boxes of this type seem to *pop-up* on the screen, either next to or over the selection field. Even a Microsoft Windows "drop-down" will "pop-up" if it is opened near the bottom of the screen. In this discussion, these variously named controls will be given the generic name of *drop-down/pop-up list boxes*. A drop-down list is illustrated in Figures 7.70 and 7.71. Figure 7.72 shows a pop-up list.

Purpose. The purpose of these list boxes is to permit selection from a large set of mutually exclusive choices when screen space is scarce.

Country:	United States
Language:	English (American)
Keyboard Layout:	US
Measurement:	English

Figure 7.70 Drop-down list boxes. There are four unopened boxes, Country, Language, Keyboard Layout, and Measurement.

Country:	Canada (French)
Language:	Canada (English)
	Canada (French)
	Denmark
	Finland
Keyboard Layout:	France
	Germany
Measurement:	Iceland
	Ireland

Figure 7.71 Drop-down list box opened for Country.

Horizontal:	Left

	Set
	Right
Horizontal:	Centered
	Left
	Full

Figure 7.72 Pop-up list box, closed and opened.

Advantages/disadvantages. The most useful feature of drop-down/pop-up list boxes is that they conserve screen space. They may be retrieved on demand, reminding users of the choices available. They permit an unlimited number of options to be displayed.

A significant disadvantage of these lists is that they necessitate an extra step to display the available options. Scrolling may also be necessary to see all items. Since items can be ordered in an unpredictable way, they can be hard to find occasionally. Generally, drop-down/pop-up list boxes require more work on the part of the user than many other screen-based controls because of the activation step and the possible need for scrolling. A study comparing drop-down/pop-up lists to other similar controls will be described later in this Step.

Proper usage. Drop-down/pop-up list boxes are used much like regular list boxes, except that the choices are not visible at all times. They are used for selecting values or setting attributes when sufficient screen space is not available to display the choices permanently. Their best use is for data and choices that are textual; large in number; fixed or variable in list length; not well known, easily learned or remembered; and ordered in an unpredictable fashion. Items should not have to be selected frequently.

Drop-down/ pop-up lists are most useful when screen space or layout considerations make radio buttons or single-selection list boxes impractical. It is also desirable that most users select the first, or displayed, item in the listing so the box does not have to be opened. Never use a drop-down/pop-up list if it is important that all options be seen together at one time.

Prompt Button

- Provide a visual cue that a box is hidden by including a downward pointing arrow, or other meaningful image, to the right side of the selection field.
  — Position the button directly against, or within, the selection field.

Figure 7.73   Sport: [_____] **∨**

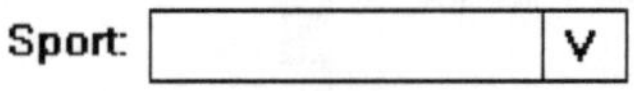

Most systems indicate the presence of a drop-down or pop-up list by associating a meaningful icon with the applicable field. This icon can be seen positioned to the left of the selection field, within the selection field as is done by Microsoft Windows, or to the right of the selection field. Other platforms do not provide any visual indication that a hidden list is available. An indication to the user that a drop-down or pop-up list is available should be indicated on the screen. This is especially critical if not all fields have associated hidden lists. The best location is to the right of the selection field where it is out of the way until needed. To visually differentiate it from another control—the drop-down/pop-up combination box—position the button abutting or within the selection field. (A drop-down/pop-up combination box button will be separated by a space.) The indicator should be large enough to provide a good pointing target.

Selection Descriptions

- Clearly and meaningfully describe the choices available. Spell them out as fully as possible.
  - Graphical representations must clearly represent the options.
  - Left-align them in columns.
  - Display the descriptions using mixed-case letters.

Selection descriptions will reflect what choices exist in the control. They should be meaningful, fully spelled out, and organized in columns. Display the list of choices using mixed-case letters. Box descriptions should be displayed in the same color as the selection field text. If a particular choice is not available in the current context, it should be omitted from the list.

List Size

- Not limited in size.
- Present all available alternatives.

A list being displayed in a drop-down/pop-up list box has no size limit. All available alternatives should be capable of being displayed. It would seem practical that for large scrollable lists, the same rules as presented for list boxes should also be applied. Restrict page-downs to no more than 40 and provide a method to scope actions.

Box Size

- Long enough to display 6 to 8 choices without scrolling.
  - If more than eight choices are available, provide vertical scrolling to display all items.
- Wide enough to display the longest possible choice.
- When a box cannot be made wide enough to display the longest entry:
  - Make it wide enough to permit entries to be distinguishable, or,
  - Break long entries with ellipses (...) in the middle, or,
  - Provide horizontal scrolling.

Drop-down/pop-up list boxes should be restricted to eight or fewer choices. If more must be displayed, permit scrolling and include a scroll bar on the right side of the box. The list box should be wide enough to fully display all selection choice wording. When a box cannot be made wide enough to display the longest entry, make it wide enough to permit entries to be distinguishable, or break the long entries, inserting an ellipsis in the middle. If breaking entries, preserve the important characteristics needed to distinguish them. When shortening an item's name in this way, include a *ToolTip* that displays the item's full name. As a last resort, provide horizontal scrolling and a scroll bar at the bottom of the list box. Avoid horizontal scrolling whenever possible, however.

Organization

- Order in a logical and meaningful way to permit easy browsing.
- If a particular choice is not available in the current context, omit it from the list.
  - Exception: If it is important that the existence and unavailability of a particular list item be communicated, display the choice dimmed or grayed out instead of deleting it.

Selection choices should be organized logically. If the alternatives have an expected order, follow it. Other ordering schemes such as frequency of use, sequence of use, or importance, may also be considered. Always begin ordering at the top or left. If, under certain conditions, a choice is not available, display the unavailable choice subdued or less brightly than the available choices.

Layout and Separation

- Enclose the choices in a box composed of a solid line border.
  - The border should be the same color as the choice descriptions.
  - Leave one blank character position between the choices and the left border.
  - Leave one blank character position between the longest choice description in the list and the right border, if possible.

To provide adequate legibility, leave one space between the choice descriptions and the left border, and one space between the longest choice description and the right border. Extending the listing box to the right edge of the prompt button allows the user to move easily from the button to the list. To set off the box from the screen body background, use the same color background for the box as is used in the entry field. Also incorporate a solid line border around the box in the same color as the choice descriptions.

Captions

- Display using mixed-case letters.
- Position the caption to the left of the box.
  - Alternately, it may be positioned left-justified above the box.

To identify the drop-down/pop-up list box, a field caption in mixed-case letters, with each significant word capitalized is necessary. Use a *static text* control to create the caption. The recommended position is to the box's left. Select a positioning consistent with other controls presented on the window.

Defaults

- When the drop-down/pop-up listing is first presented, display the currently set value.
- If a choice has not been previously selected, provide a default choice.

When the drop-down/pop-up listing is first presented, display the currently set value. If a choice has not been previously selected, provide a default choice. The list must be opened to change the choice.

Disabling

- When a drop-down/pop-up list box is disabled, display its caption and entries as disabled or dimmed.

Display a drop-down/pop-up list box's caption and entries as dimmed or grayed out when the list box is entirely disabled.

Selection Method and Indication

- Pointing:
  — Highlight the selection choice in some visually distinctive way when the pointer or cursor is resting on it and the choice is available for selection.
- Activation:
  — Close the drop-down/pop-up list box when an item is selected.

Highlight the selection choice in some visually distinctive way when the pointer or cursor is resting on it and the choice is available for selection. Close the listing when an item is selected.

Combination Entry/Selection Controls

It is possible for a control to possess the characteristics of both a text field and a selection field. In this type of control, information may either be keyed into the field or selected and placed within it. The types of combination entry/selection fields are spin boxes, attached combination boxes, and drop-down/pop-up combination boxes.

Spin Boxes

- Description:
  — A single-line field followed by two small, vertically arranged buttons.
    - The top button has an arrow pointing up.
    - The bottom button has an arrow pointing down.
  — Selection/entry is made by:
    - Using the mouse to point at one of the directional buttons and clicking. Items will change by one unit or step with each click.
    - Keying a value directly into the field itself.

- Purpose:
  — To make a selection by either scrolling through a small set of meaningful predefined choices or typing text.
- Advantages:
  — Consumes little screen space.
  — Flexible, permitting selection or typed entry.
- Disadvantages:
  — Difficult to compare choices.
  — Can be awkward to operate.
  — Useful only for certain kinds of data.
- Proper usage:
  — For setting attributes, properties, or values.
  — For mutually exclusive choices (only one can be selected).
  — When the task requires the option of either key entry or selection from a list.
  — When the user prefers the option of either key entry or selection from a list.
  — Where screen space is limited.
  — Most useful for data and choices that are:
    • Discrete.
    • Infrequently selected.
    • Well known, easily learned or remembered, and meaningful.
    • Ordered in a predictable, customary, or consecutive fashion.
    • Infrequently changed.
    • Small in number.
    • Fixed or variable in list length.

Description. A *spin box,* also called a *spin button,* is a single-line field followed by two small, vertically arranged buttons inscribed with up and down arrows. These buttons may also be referred to as *up-down* buttons. Selection of an item is accomplished using the mouse to point at one of the buttons and clicking. Items in a listing in the display field will change by one unit or step in the direction selected with each click. The list is searched as the ring or circle of alternatives "spins" by. Keying a value directly into the field itself may also complete a spin box. A spin box is illustrated in Figure 7.74.

Advantages/disadvantages. Spin boxes are flexible, permitting either selection or typed entry. They also consume little screen space. On the other hand, spin boxes are useful only for certain kinds of data, that which is predictable or consecutive. Because only one item is displayed at a time, it is difficult to compare choices. Spin

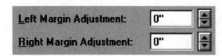

Figure 7.74 Spin boxes.

boxes may also be awkward to operate, often requiring several back and forth iterations to bring the desired value into view.

Proper usage. Spin boxes are used for setting attributes, properties, or values that are mutually exclusive. They are useful when the task requires, or the user prefers, the option of either key entry or selection from a list. Spin boxes are useful for data and choices that are discrete and small in number. The choices themselves should be well known, easily learned or remembered, and meaningful. Choices should be ordered in a predictable, customary, or consecutive fashion so people can anticipate the next not-yet-visible choice. Items in spin boxes should not require frequent selection, and the array of items listed should be stable.

List Size

- Keep the list of items relatively short.
- To reduce the size of potentially long lists, break the listing into subcomponents, if possible.

Since the list must be manipulated to display its contents, it should be as short as feasible. To reduce the size of potentially long lists, break the listing into subcomponents whenever possible. A date, for example, may be broken into its components of month, day, and year.

List Organization

- Order the list in the customary, consecutive, or expected order of the information contained within it.
  — Ensure that the user can always anticipate the next (not-yet-visible) choice.
- When first displayed, present a default choice in the box.

Spin boxes are most effective when the values they contain have a customary or consecutive order that is predictable. Information can be letters or numbers. Examples are days of the week, months of the year, shoe sizes, and so on. The user must always be able to anticipate the next choice before it is displayed. The control should always contain a default value when first displayed.

Other Spin Box Guidelines

- Box size:
  — The spin box should be wide enough to display the longest entry or choice.
- Caption:
  — Display it using mixed-case letters.
  — Position the caption to the left of the box.
    • Alternately, it may be positioned left-justified above the box.

- Entry and selection methods:
  - Permit completion by:
    - Typing directly into the box.
    - Scrolling and selecting with a mouse.
    - Scrolling and selecting with the up/down arrow keys.
  - For alphabetical values:
    - Move down the order using the down arrow.
    - Move up the order using the up arrow.
  - For numeric values or magnitudes:
    - Show a larger value using the up arrow.
    - Show a smaller value using the down arrow.

Box size. Fully display all alternatives within the spin box. The box should be wide enough to display the longest entry or choice.

Caption. To identify the spin box, use a static text field to provide a field caption in mixed-case letters, with each significant word capitalized. The recommended position is to the box's left. Select a positioning consistent with other controls presented on the window.

Entry and selection. Spin box completion should be possible by typing directly into the field or by scrolling and selecting options with a mouse or keyboard keys. When spinning alphabetical values, move down the order using the down arrow and up the order using the up arrow. For numeric values or magnitudes, display a larger value using the up arrow and a smaller value using the down arrow.

Combo Boxes

- Description:
  - A single rectangular text box entry field, beneath which is a larger rectangular list box (resembling a drop-down list box) displaying a list of options.
  - The text box permits a choice to be keyed within it.
  - The larger box contains a list of mutually exclusive choices from which one may be selected for placement in the entry field.
    - Selections are made by using a mouse to point and click.
  - As text is typed into the text box, the list scrolls to the nearest match.
  - When an item in the list box is selected, it is placed into the text box, replacing the existing content.
  - Information keyed may not necessarily have to match the list items.
- Purpose:
  - To allow either typed entry in a text box or selection from a list of options in a permanently displayed list box attached to the text box.
- Advantages:
  - Unlimited number of entries and choices.
  - Reminds users of available options.
  - Flexible, permitting selection or typed entry.

— Entries not necessarily restricted to items selectable from list box.
— List box always visible.

- Disadvantages:
— Consumes some screen space.
— All list box choices not always visible, requiring scrolling.
— Users may have difficulty recalling sufficient information to type entry, making text box unusable.
— The list may be ordered in an unpredictable way, making it hard to find items.

- Proper usage:
— For entering or selecting objects or values or setting attributes.
— For information that is mutually exclusive (only one can be entered or selected).
— When users may find it practical to, or prefer to, type information rather than selecting it from a list.
— When users can recall and type information faster than selecting it from a list.
— When it is useful to provide the users a reminder of the choices available.
— Where data must be entered that is not contained in the selection list.
— Where screen space is available.
— For data and choices that are:
  • Best represented textually.
  • Somewhat familiar or known.
  • Ordered in an unpredictable fashion.
  • Frequently changed.
  • Large in number.
  • Variable or fixed in list length.

Description. A *combo box*, also known as an *attached combination box*, is a single rectangular entry field, beneath which is a larger rectangular box (resembling a drop-down list box) displaying a list of options. In Java combo boxes are called *editable choice pop-up lists*. The entry field permits a choice to be keyed within it, while the larger box contains a list of mutually exclusive choices, from which one may be selected for placement in the entry field. A combo box combines the capabilities of both a text box and a list box. It visually resembles a drop-down list box or drop-down combo box (to be described). The text box and its associated list box have a dependent relationship. As text is typed into the text box, the list scrolls to the nearest match. Also, when an item in the list box is selected, that item is placed within the text box, replacing the existing content. When typing into the field, the information keyed does not have to match the list items. Combo boxes are illustrated in Figure 7.75.

Advantages/disadvantages. Combo boxes are flexible, permitting selection or typed entry. Alternatives are always visible, or retrievable, reminding people of the available options. An unlimited variety of entries and choices are possible. Entries are not necessarily restricted to items selectable from a box.

Combo boxes do consume quite a bit of screen space. Because all box choices may not be visible, some scrolling may be required. It is always possible that people may have difficulty recalling sufficient information to type, making the text

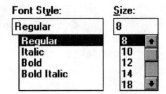

Figure 7.75 Combo boxes.

box unusable. The list may also be ordered in an unpredictable way, making it hard to find items. Additional work is required of the user if selection scrolling must be performed.

Proper usage. Combo boxes are useful for entering or selecting objects or values or setting attributes that are mutually exclusive. They are most valuable when users may find it practical to, or prefer to, type information rather than selecting it from a list, but where reminders of alternatives available must occasionally be provided. They are also useful when the listings are dynamic and changeable, permitting the user to key items not contained on the list in the box. They do require that screen space be available to display them, but they eliminate the extra steps involved in retrieving drop-down lists.

Combo boxes are useful for textual data and choices that are frequently changed and somewhat familiar or known, fostering keyed entry. The lists may be long, variable, and ordered in an unpredictable fashion.

Combo Box Guidelines

For the text box entry field, see "Text Box/Single Line" guidelines. For the list box, see "Drop-down/Pop-up List Box" guidelines.

Drop-down/Pop-up Combo Boxes

- Description:
  - A single rectangular text box with a small button to the side and an associated hidden list of options.
    - The button provides a visual cue that an associated selection box is available but hidden.
  - When requested, a larger associated rectangular box appears, containing a scrollable list of choices from which one is selected.
  - Selections are made by using the mouse to point and click.
  - Information may also be keyed into the field.
  - As text is typed into the text box, the list scrolls to the nearest match.
  - When an item in the list box is selected, it is placed into the text box, replacing the existing content.
  - The information keyed does not necessarily have to match list items.
  - Combines the capabilities of both a text box and a drop-down/pop-up list box.

- Purpose:
  — To allow either typed entry or selection from a list of options in a list box that may be closed and retrieved as needed.

- Advantages:
  — Unlimited number of entries and choices.
  — Reminds users of available options.
  — Flexible, permitting selection or typed entry.
  — Entries not restricted to items selectable from list box.
  — Conserves screen space.

- Disadvantages:
  — Requires an extra step to display the list of choices.
  — When displayed, all box choices may not always be visible, requiring scrolling.
  — User may have difficulty in recalling what to type.
  — The list content may change, making it hard to find items.
  — The list may be ordered in an unpredictable way, making it hard to find items.

- Proper usage:
  — For entering or selecting objects or values or setting attributes.
  — For information that is mutually exclusive (only one can be entered or selected).
  — When users may find it practical to, or prefer to, type information rather than selecting it from a list.
  — When users can recall and type information faster than selecting from a list.
  — When it is useful to provide the users with an occasional reminder of the choices available.
  — Where data must be entered that is not contained in the selection list.
  — Where screen space is limited.
  — For data and choices that are:
    • Best represented textually.
    • Somewhat familiar or known.
    • Ordered in an unpredictable fashion.
    • Frequently changed.
    • Large in number.
    • Variable or fixed in list length.

Description. A *drop-down/pop-up combo box* is a single rectangular field with a small button to the side and an associated hidden list of options. The button provides a visual cue to the user that an associated selection box of choices is available but hidden. When requested, a larger associated rectangular box appears, containing a scrollable list of choices from which one can be selected. One makes selections by using the mouse to point and click. The text box and its associated list box have a dependent relationship. As text is typed into the text box, the list scrolls to the nearest match. Also, when an item in the list box is selected, that item is placed within the text box, replacing the existing content. It closely resembles a drop-down/pop-up list box.

Information, however, may also be keyed into the field. The information keyed does not necessarily have to match items in the list. A drop-down/pop-up

Baud Rate: 9600   ±

Figure 7.76   Windows 3.1 Drop-down combo box, closed.

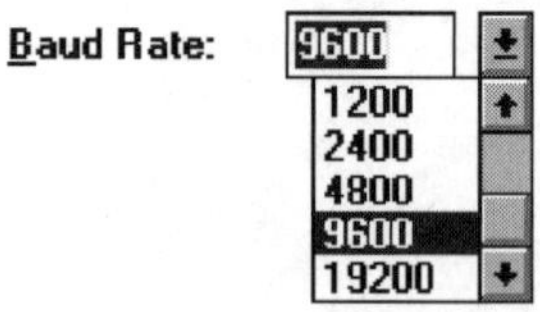

Baud Rate: 9600
              1200
              2400
              4800
              9600
              19200

Figure 7.77   Windows 3.1 Drop-down combo box, opened.

combination box, therefore, combines the capabilities of both a text box and a selection field. A drop-down combo box is illustrated in Figures 7.76 and 7.77.

Advantages/disadvantages. Drop-down/pop-up combo boxes are flexible, permitting selection or typed entry. They conserve screen space, but alternatives are always retrievable, reminding people of the available options. An unlimited variety of entries and choices are possible. Entries are not restricted to items selectable from a box.

In terms of disadvantages, they necessitate an extra step to display the available options. Scrolling may also be necessary to see all items. Since the list content can change, and items can be ordered in an unpredictable way, it can be hard to find items. It is always possible also that people may have difficulty recalling sufficient information to type, making the entry field unusable. Generally drop-down/pop-up combination boxes require more work on the part of the user than many other screen-based controls.

Proper usage. Drop-down/pop-up combo boxes are useful for entering or selecting objects or values or setting attributes that are mutually exclusive. They are most valuable when users may find it practical to, or prefer to, type information rather than selecting from a list but where reminders of alternatives available must occasionally be provided. The box may only be retrieved as needed, thereby conserving screen space. They are also useful when the listings are dynamic and changeable, permitting the user to key items not contained on the list in the box.

Drop-down/pop-up combo boxes are useful for textual data and choices that are frequently changed and somewhat familiar or known, fostering keyed entry. The list may be long, variable, and ordered in an unpredictable fashion.

Prompt Button

- Provide a visual cue that a list box is hidden by including a downward-pointing arrow to the right of the text box.
- Separate the button from the text box by a small space.

Figure 7.78   Sport: [   ]   ±

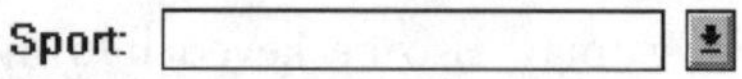

Provide a visual cue that a list box is hidden by including a downward-pointing arrow to the right of the entry field. Unfortunately, Microsoft Windows has provided drop-down list boxes and combo boxes that are visually almost identical. The only way to differentiate the two types is to click and see whether a box can be typed into. This is extremely poor design. Each unique control should be identifiable by the way it looks so trial and error behavior can be avoided. Microsoft, in Windows 3.1, did provide this distinction. The prompt button was slightly separated from the text box, as shown in Figures 7.76 and 7.77. Ideally, then, position the prompt button separated by a space from the associated text box.

Other Guidelines

For the text box entry field, see the "Text Box/Single Line" guidelines. For the box and selection components, see the "Drop-down/Pop-up List Box" guidelines.

Other Operable Controls

Other more specialized operable controls also exist. Among them are sliders, tabs, date-pickers, and scroll bars.

Slider

- Description:
  - A scale exhibiting degrees of a quality on a continuum.
  - Includes the following:
    - A shaft or bar.
    - A range of values with appropriate labels.
    - An arm indicating relative setting through its location on the shaft.
    - Optionally, a pair of buttons to permit incremental movement of the slider arm.
    - Optionally, a text box for typing or displaying an exact value.
    - Optionally, a detent position for special values.
  - May be oriented vertically or horizontally.
  - Selected by using the mouse to:
    - Drag a slider across the scale until the desired value is reached.
    - Point at the buttons at one end of the scale and clicking to change the value.
    - Keying a value in the associated text box.
- Purpose:
  - To make a setting when a continuous qualitative adjustment is acceptable, it is useful to see the current value relative to the range of possible values.
- Advantages:
  - Spatial representation of relative setting.
  - Visually distinctive.

- Disadvantages:
  - — Not as precise as an alphanumeric indication.
  - — Consumes screen space.
  - — Usually more complex than other controls.
- Proper usage:
  - — To set an attribute.
  - — For mutually exclusive choices.
  - — When an object has a limited range of possible settings.
  - — When the range of values is continuous.
  - — When graduations are relatively fine.
  - — When the choices can increase or decrease in some well-known, predictable, and easily understood way.
  - — When a spatial representation enhances comprehension and interpretation.
  - — When using a slider provides sufficient accuracy.

Description. A *slider* is a scale that exhibits the amount or degree of a quantity or quality on a continuum (see Figure 7.79). It is sometimes called a track bar control. A slider incorporates the range of possible values and includes a shaft or bar representing the range, the values themselves with appropriate labels, and a visual indication of the relative setting through the location of a sliding arm. Optionally, sliders also may include a pair of buttons to permit incremental movement of the slider arm, an entry/display text box for typing and displaying an exact value, and a detent position for special values. A slider may be oriented vertically or horizontally.

Slider values can be set by using the mouse to drag a slider across the scale until the desired value is reached. A visual indication of the relative setting is seen as the setting movement is made. In addition, some sliders may also be set by pointing at slider buttons located at one end of the scale and incrementally moving the arm through button clicks. Finally, keying a value in an associated text box may also set some sliders.

A slider is used to make a setting when a continuous qualitative adjustment is acceptable, and it is advantageous to see the current value relative to all possible values.

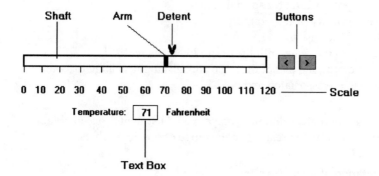

Figure 7.79 Slider.

Advantages/disadvantages. A slider displays a spatial representation of a relative setting, providing an excellent indication of where a value exists within a range of values. They are also visually distinctive and very recognizable. Sliders, however, are not as precise as an alphanumeric indication, unless a display field is provided. They also consume more screen space than other kinds of fields, and they can be more complex to operate.

Proper usage. Sliders are used to set an attribute when a limited range of continuous, relatively fine, possible settings exist. The choices must increase or decrease in some well-known, predictable, and easily understood way. Spatial representation of the attribute should enhance comprehension and interpretation and be sufficiently accurate.

General

- Use standard sliders whenever available.

Use of standard system sliders will speed learning

Caption and Labels

- Caption:
  — Provide meaningful, clear, and consistent captions.
  — Display them using mixed-case letters.
  — Position the caption to the left of the box.
    • Alternately, it may be positioned left-justified above the slider.
- Labels:
  — Provide meaningful and descriptive labels to aid in interpreting the scale.

Caption. The slider caption must clearly reflect the quality being displayed. Use a *static text* or *group box* control to provide a field caption in mixed-case letters with each significant word capitalized. Use a static text field; the recommended position is to the box's left. Alternately, captions may be positioned above the slider, aligned with the left edge. Select a positioning consistent with other controls presented in the window.

Labels. Provide meaningful and descriptive labels to aid in interpreting the scale. A temperature slider will necessitate the inclusion of numeric temperature values. A volume slider may be labeled *low* and *high*. Create the labels using *static* text fields.

Scale

- Show a complete range of choices.
- Mark the low, intermediate, and high ends of the scale.
- Provide scale interval markings, where possible.

- Provide consistent increments.
- Permit the user to change the units of measure.
- If the precise value of a quantity represented is important, display the value set in an adjacent text box.

Provide a complete range of choices on the scale. Mark the low, intermediate, and high ends of the scale. For example, volumes may be indicated by low and high. Provide scale interval markings at consistent increments. Allow the user to change the units of measure, for example, changing a temperature from Fahrenheit to centigrade. If the precise value of a quantity represented is critical, display the set value in an adjacent entry/display text box control. This will also permit typed entry of the desired value.

Slider Arm

- If the user cannot change the value shown in a slider, do not display a slider arm.

Do not display a slider arm if the user cannot change the value shown in a slider. Fill in the shaft in a distinctive way to indicate the relative setting, as illustrated in the guideline for proportions.

Slider Buttons

- Provide slider buttons to permit movement by the smallest increment.
- If the user cannot change the value shown in a slider, do not display slider buttons.

Provide slider buttons to permit movement by the smallest increment. Movement is achieved by pointing and clicking. If the user cannot change the value shown in a slider, do not display slider buttons.

Detents

- Provide detents to set values that have special meaning.
- Permit the user to change the detent value.

For values that have special meaning, provide detents that can be changed by the user.

Proportions

- To indicate the proportion of a value being displayed, fill the slider shaft in some visually distinctive way.
  — Fill horizontal sliders from left to right.
  — Fill vertical sliders from bottom to top.

When the proportion of a value is also important, provide proportional indicators by filling in the slider shaft in a distinctive way. Fill it from left to right and bottom to top.

Tabs

- Description:
  — A window containing tabbed dividers that create pages or sections.
  — Navigation is permitted between the pages or sections.
- Purpose:
  — To present information that can be logically organized into pages or sections within the same window.
- Advantages:
  — Resembles their paper-based cousins.
  — Visually distinctive.
  — Effectively organize repetitive, related information.
- Disadvantages:
  — Visually complex.
- Proper usage:
  — To present discrete, logically structured, related, information.
  — To present the setting choices that can be applied to an object.
  — When a short tab label can meaningfully describe the tab's contents.
  — When the order of information use varies.

Description. A *tab* control is a window containing tabbed dividers that create pages or sections. Also referred to as a *notebook*, the tabs are analogous to dividers in a file cabinet or notebook. Navigation is permitted between the tabbed pages or sections. Microsoft Windows has a window organization scheme called a *workbook* (See Step 4) that is similar to the notebook control. Tabs from Microsoft Windows are illustrated in Figure 7.80.

Advantages/disadvantages. Tabs resemble their paper-based cousins, entities that are familiar to almost everyone. They are very meaningful electronic metaphors. Tabs are visually distinctive, and they permit effective organization of repetitive and related information. One drawback: They may result in a visually more complex screen.

Proper usage. Tabs can be used to present data that can be logically structured into discrete and meaningful pages or sections. They are most useful for presenting the choices that can be applied to an object, for example, a person and the person's descriptive data such as address, employment, family, and so forth. When the information on one tab is heavily dependent on information found on another tab, tabs are a poor choice because the user will have to keep flipping between tabs. Tabs are useful only if a brief tab label can identify their contents. Tabs are also useful when the order in which information is used varies.

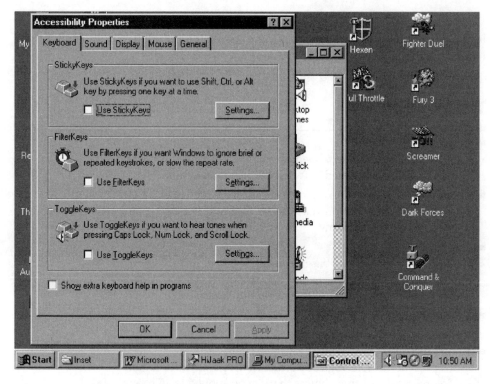

Figure 7.80 Tabs from Microsoft Windows.

Sections and Pages

- Place related information within a page or section.
- Order them meaningfully.
- Arrange pages so they appear to go deeper, left to right and top to bottom.
- Provide pages of equal size.

Place related information within a page or section. Order the pages in a meaningful way, based upon the window's content. Arrange the pages so they appear to go deeper, left to right and top to bottom. Provide pages of equal size.

Location, Size, and Labels

- Place the tabs at the top of the page or section.
- Provide fixed-width tabs for pages or sections of related information.
- Provide textual labels.
  — Use system fonts.
  — Keep information brief and the same general length.
    • Nouns are usually better than verbs.

— Use mixed case, capitalizing each significant word.

— Assign a keyboard equivalent for keyboard access.

- Center the labels within the tabs.
- Restrict tabs to only one row.
- Arrange tabs so that they appear to go deeper, left to right and top to bottom.

Place tabs at the top of the page or section. This is the most customary location. Tabs may be capable of being located at all four points of the compass but these positions are not as common. Left and right tabs will provide label readability problems. Fixed-width tabs are preferred but variable-width tabs may be used if screen space constraints exist. For labels, use the standard system fonts in mixed case, capitalizing each significant word. Keep tab text labels brief and of the same general length. Nouns are usually better than verbs. Assign each tab a keyboard equivalent to facilitate keyboard access. Center the labels within the tabs and restrict them to only one row.

Avoid multiple rows of tab or scrolling a single row of tabs. This adds complexity to the interface and makes it harder for the user to read and access a particular tab. As an alternative, consider separating the tabbed pages into sets and using another control to move between sets, or use subordinate dialog boxes. Arrange tabs so that they appear to go deeper, left to right and top to bottom.

Command Buttons

- If they affect only a page or section, locate the buttons on the page or section.
- If they affect the entire tabbed control, locate the buttons outside the tabbed pages.

For command buttons that affect only the tabbed page being displayed, locate the buttons on that page. If they affect the entire tabbed control, position the buttons outside the pages but within the window holding the pages. Tab users often have trouble understanding that command buttons actions within a tab page only affect that page, but that command buttons outside all the pages affect the entire tab window. The users may not always be aware that when the window is closed, actions taken within a window are not "activated" until the *window's* OK button is pressed. Guidance may have to be provided to the users to ensure that all expected user actions are actually performed. Alternatives include providing instructions on the window or providing a confirming message box if the window is closed.

Date-Picker

- Description:
    - A drop-down list box that displays a 1-month calendar in the drop-down list box.
    - The displayed month can be changed through pressing command buttons with left- and right-pointing arrows.

- The left arrow moves backward through the monthly calendars.
- The right arrow moves forward through the monthly calendars.
— A date for the list box can be selected from the drop-down calendar.

■ Purpose:
— To select a date for inscribing in a drop-down list box.

■ Advantages:
— Provides a representation of a physical calendar, a meaningful entity.
— The calendar listing is ordered in a predictable way.
— Visually distinctive.

■ Disadvantages:
— Requires an extra step to display the calendar.
— When displayed, all month choices are not visible, requiring a form of scrolling to access the desired choice.

■ Proper usage:
— To select and display a single date in close monthly proximity to the default month presented on the drop-down list box.

A *date-picker*, illustrated in Figure 7.81, is a drop-down list box that displays a 1-month calendar in the drop-down. The displayed month can be changed by pressing command buttons with left- and right-pointing arrows. A relevant date to be entered in the list box is selected from the calendar drop-down list box. Advantages and disadvantages are similar to drop-down list boxes. Its structure as a calendar is a meaningful representation for most users. Like drop-down list boxes, the date-picker requires exposing the list before the date can be chosen. If the date desired as not within the default month's calendar presented, the calendar must be scrolled to the proper month. If the date is far away in time, excessive scrolling may be required to obtain it. Therefore, it is most useful for dates close in time to the default month presented. A wide range of dates would best be collected through a text box.

Figure 7.81 A date-picker control.

Tree View

■ Description:
— A special list box control that displays a set of objects as an indented outline, based on the objects' logical hierarchical relationship.
— Includes, optionally, buttons that expand and collapse the outline.
  • A button inscribed with a plus (+) expands the outline.
  • A button inscribed with a minus (-) collapses the outline.
— Elements that can optionally be displayed are:
  • Icons.
  • Graphics, such as a check box.
  • Lines to illustrate hierarchical relationships.

■ Purpose and proper usage:
— To display a set of objects as an indented outline to illustrate their logical hierarchical relationship.

A *tree view* control, as illustrated in Figure 7.82, is a special list box control that displays a set of objects as an indented outline, based on their logical hierarchical relationship. The control is used to display the relationship between a set of containers or other hierarchical elements, and, optionally, includes buttons to expand or collapse the

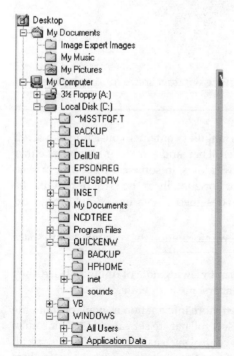

Figure 7.82   A tree view control.

hierarchy. Icons can be included with the text label for each item in the tree. Different icons can be displayed when the tree expands or collapses. A graphic, such as a check box, can be used to reflect state information about the item. The tree view control also supports an optional display of lines to illustrate the hierarchical relationship of the items in the list.

Scroll Bars

- Description:
  - An elongated rectangular container consisting of:
    - A scroll area.
    - A slider box or elevator inside.
    - Arrows or anchors at either end.
  - Available, if needed, in primary and secondary windows, some controls, and Web pages.
  - May be oriented vertically or horizontally at the window or page edge.
- Purpose:
  - To find and view information that takes more space than the allotted display space.
- Advantages:
  - Permits viewing data of unlimited size.
- Disadvantages:
  - Consumes screen space.
  - Can be cumbersome to operate.
- Proper use:
  - When more information is available than the window space for displaying it.
  - Do not use to set values.

Description. A *scroll bar* is an elongated rectangular container consisting of a scroll area, a slider box, or elevator inside the scroll bar, and arrows or anchors at either end. They may be placed, if needed, in windows, in some controls, and in Web pages. They may be oriented vertically or horizontally at the right or bottom of a screen. Historically, scroll bars have been designed in a variety of styles; a typical one is illustrated in Figure 7.83.

Purpose. Scroll bars are used to find and view information that occupies more space than the allotted display space.

Advantages/disadvantages. While they permit viewing data of unlimited size, they do consume screen space and can be cumbersome to operate.

Proper usage. Use a scroll bar, or bars, when more information is available than the window space for displaying it. Do not use scroll bars to set values. If a value must be set or adjusted, use a *slider* or another control such as a *spin box*. Because scroll bars are designed for scrolling through information, using a scroll bar to set values may confuse the user about the purpose or interaction of the control.

Figure 7.83   Scroll bar.

Scroll Bar Design Guidelines

- General:
  — Provide a scroll bar when invisible information must be seen.
- Scroll area or container:
  — To indicate that scrolling is available, a scroll area or container should be provided.
    • Construct it of a filled-in bar displayed in a technique that visually contrasts with the window and screen body background.
- Scroll slider box or handle:
  — To indicate the location and amount of information being viewed, provide a slider box or handle.
    • Constructed of a movable and sizable open area of the scroll area, displayed in a technique that contrasts with the scroll area.
    • By its position, spatially indicate the relative location in the file of the information being viewed.
    • By its size, indicate, proportionately, the percentage of the available information in the file being viewed.
- Scroll directional arrows:
  — To indicate the direction in which scrolling may be performed, directional arrows should be provided.
    • Construct them as arrows in small boxes, with backgrounds that contrast with the scroll area.
- Selection:
  — When the slider box/handle has been selected, highlight it in some visually distinctive way.
- Location:
  — Position a vertical (top-to-bottom) scroll bar to the right of the window.
  — Position a horizontal (left-to-right) scroll bar at the bottom of the window.
- Size:
  — A vertical scroll bar should be the height of the scrollable portion of the window body.
  — A horizontal scroll bar should be at least one-half the width of the scrollable portion of the window body.
- Current state indication:
  — Whenever the window's size or the position of the information changes, the scroll bar components must also change, reflecting the current state.

— Include scroll bars in all sizable windows.
  • If no information is currently available by scrolling in a particular direction, the relevant directional arrow should be subdued or grayed out.

General. A *scroll bar* provides a method to permit the displaying of information that may not always fit within a window on a screen. A scroll bar should only be included when scrolling may be necessary.

In today's systems, scroll bars come in a variety of styles. Scroll bars consist of three elements: a scroll area or container, a slider box or handle that moves within a track made by the scroll area/container, and directional or scroll arrows.

Scroll area or container. The scroll area or, as it is sometimes called, the scroll container, is an elongated rectangular-shaped bar. Its presence indicates scrolling is available. It usually is constructed of a filled-in area displayed in a technique that visually contrasts with the window and screen body background. The chosen display technique should be of moderate intensity, neither too powerful nor too subtle. A powerful technique will be distracting; a subtle technique may be overlooked.

Slider box or handle. To indicate the location and amount of information being viewed, a slider box or, as it is sometimes called, a scroll handle, is included within the scroll area/container. It is constructed of a movable and sizable portion of the scroll area displayed in a technique that contrasts with the scroll area. It should indicate, by its position, the relative spatial location in the file of the information being viewed. It should indicate by its size, proportionately, the percentage of the available information in the file being viewed. Displaying, within a scrollable screen, the page number of page-organized material being viewed can further enhance the usability of the slider box or handle.

Directional or scroll arrows. To indicate the direction in which scrolling may be performed, directional or scroll arrows are also included. They are constructed of variously shaped arrows in small boxes with backgrounds that contrast with the scroll area/container. They are most often located at each end of the scroll bar, but some systems locate them adjacent to one another within the scroll area/container itself.

Placing directional arrows at opposite ends of the scroll bar is conceptually the clearest. The mouse pointer is moved in the same direction, away from the current position, when either the scroll arrow or scroll handle is manipulated. The distance that the directional arrows are separated by, however, causes increased effort when a window's contents must be adjusted by scrolling in opposite directions.

One platform solved the direction-switching problem by positioning the directional arrows adjacent to one another at one end of the scroll bar. While the forward-backward scrolling is made more efficient, the spatial correspondence between the beginning, middle, and end of the data is lost.

Another platform took another approach, placing the directional arrows at opposite ends of the slider box/handle to maintain the desirable spatial correspondence while at the same time minimizing their separation. Since during a continuous scrolling operation the directional arrows move as the slider box/handle moves, this platform automatically moves the mouse pointer to keep it aligned with the scroll arrow. This eliminates the need for the user to move the pointer during the continuous scrolling operation, but it requires that the user relinquish control of the mouse operation, and may be disorienting.

Using a scroll bar, the scrolling movement can be performed in several ways. The most common actions involve grabbing the slider box/handle and moving it in the desired direction, or selecting the proper directional arrow. Clicking a mouse button while selecting a directional arrow moves the contents of a window one line. Pressing the mouse button scrolls the window's contents continuously until the button is released. One platform provides another more efficient process. A region of the scroll area/container can also be selected, automatically moving the slider box/handle to that point and displaying the proper window contents.

Based upon early scrolling research (Bury, Boyle, Evey, and Neal, 1982), movement of the window data usually follows the window-up or telescope approach, whereby the window moves around over data that appears fixed in location. This causes the data in a window to move in the direction opposite the one indicated by the directional arrow or the direction of movement of the scroll container/handle. Scrolling using window systems, however, seems to be especially mistake-prone, users often assuming the arrows will move the data in the same direction as the directional arrow or scroll container/handle. In other words, it is sensed that the data moves under the window, not the window over the data (Billingsley, 1988). Why this happens is open to conjecture. Billingsley speculates that, because windows seem to move on screens, when data scrolls or moves in a window, people may conclude the data must be moving because the window remains still during the scrolling operation. Or, because of the close physical proximity of the directional arrows in scroll bars to the data, people may feel that the arrows are acting on the data, not the window. The implication is that the scrolling procedure should be rethought and restudied. Some recent applications have devised scrolling methods through actually point at the window data.

Selection. When the slider box/handle has been selected, highlight it in some visually distinctive way. Most systems do provide some visual feedback of this kind.

Location. While, again, no universal agreement exists, the majority of systems locate the vertical (top-to-bottom) scroll bar to the right of the window and the horizontal (left-to-right) scroll bar at the bottom of the window.

Size. A vertical scroll bar should be the height of the scrollable portion of the window body. A horizontal scroll bar should be at least one-half the width of the scrollable portion of the window body.

Current state indication. Whenever the window's size or the position of information changes, the scroll bar components must also change, reflecting the current state of the scrolling process. Providing accurate information about the scrolling location facilitates user navigation and makes it easier to reposition the slider box/container. Include scroll bars in all sizable windows.

If scrolling cannot be performed in a particular direction, the relevant arrow box should be reduced in contrast or grayed out. If all the information in a window is displayed and no information is available for scrolling, both directional arrows should be reduced in contrast or grayed out.

Scroll Bar Usage Guidelines

- Scroll bar style:
  — Stick with standard, proven design styles.
- Directional preference:
  — Use vertical (top-to-bottom) scrolling.
  — Avoid horizontal (left-to-right) scrolling.

Style. The standard, well-known, proven design style used in graphical systems works best. A scroll bar is complex enough that presenting a new style to the user will focus attention away from the screen content as the user struggles to learn how to deal with the new style. This is a form of "senseless" learning and must be avoided.

Directional preferences. Where the choice exists, people prefer and deal better with vertical (top-to-bottom) scrolling rather than horizontal (left-to-right) scrolling. Avoid horizontal scrolling whenever possible.

The usability aspects of scrolling, and paging were thoroughly reviewed in Step 3 "Understand the Principles of Good Screen Design."

Media Controls

- For all playable files provide the following controls.
  — Play.
  — Pause/Resume.
  — Stop.
  — Rewind.
  — Fast Forward.
  — Volume.

Some media products provide their own controls. For others, controls may have to be designed. Always provide the above standard media controls.

Custom Controls

- Implement custom controls with caution.
- If used, make the look and behavior of custom controls different from that of standard controls.

Many toolkits and interface builders provide the ability to create custom controls; implement them with caution. The user is currently presented with a multitude of controls whose usage and operation must be learned and remembered. The addition of custom controls adds to this learning and increases system complexity. If custom controls must be developed and implemented, make their look and behavior as different as possible from the standard controls. This will avoid confusion between the various controls.

MAXIM   **Fewer is usually better.**

Presentation Controls

Presentation controls are purely informational. They provide details about other screen elements or controls, or assist in giving the screen structure. Common presentation controls are *static text fields, group boxes column headings, ToolTips, balloon tips,* and *progress indicators.*

Static Text Fields

- Description:
  — Read-only textual information.
- Purpose:
  — To identify a control by displaying a control caption.
  — To clarify a screen by providing instructional or prompting information.
  — To present descriptive information.
- Proper usage:
  — To display a control caption.
  — To display instructional or prompting information.
  — To display descriptive information.

Description. A *static text field*, as illustrated in Figure 7.84, provides read-only textual information. It is a standard Microsoft Windows control.

Purpose/proper usage. Use static text fields to create and present read-only information, including all control captions. Also using static text fields clarify screen usage by providing prompting or instructional information. Other descriptive screen information can also be provided through static text fields. Examples are headings, subheadings, slider scales, progress indicator text, and so on. In Microsoft Windows, static text cannot be selected, so avoid using it for any text the user might want to copy to the clipboard.

Caption:

HEADING

This message is **very important!**

Figure 7.84   Static text field.

Static Text Field Guidelines

- Captions:
  - Include a colon (:) as part of the caption.
  - Include a mnemonic for keyboard access.
  - When the associated control is disabled, display it dimmed.
  - Follow all other presented guidelines for caption presentation and layout.
- Instructional or prompting information:
  - Display it in a unique and consistent font style for easy recognition and differentiation.
  - Follow all other presented guidelines for prompting and instructional information.
- Descriptive information:
  - Follow all other guidelines for required screen or control descriptive information.

Captions. Always include a colon as part of the caption. The colon immediately identifies the element as a caption. In Microsoft Windows the colon is also used by screen review utilities. Include a keyboard equivalent (mnemonic) for all captions to provide keyboard access to its associated control. Captions may also provide a means of indicating that their associated controls are disabled. Follow all the rules for caption display presented throughout these guidelines.

Instructional or prompting information. Display in a unique and consistent font style for easy recognition and differentiation. Follow all other presented guidelines for prompting and instructional information. Guidelines for writing instructional or prompting information are found in Step 8 "Write Clear Text and Messages."

Descriptive information. Other descriptive information includes headings, subheadings, slider scales, progress indicator text, and so forth. Also, follow all the rules for these other kinds of screen information presented throughout these guidelines.

Group Boxes

- Description:
  - A rectangular frame that surrounds a control or group of controls.
  - An optional caption may be included in the frame's upper-left corner.
- Purpose:
  - To visually relate the elements of a control.
  - To visually relate a group of related controls.
- Proper usage:
  - To provide a border around radio button or check box controls.
  - To provide a border around two or more functionally related controls.
- Guidelines:
  - Label or heading:
    - Typically, use a noun or noun phrase for the label or heading.
    - Provide a brief label or heading, preferably one or two words.

- Relate label or heading's content to the group box's content.
- Capitalize the first letter of each significant word.
- Do not include and ending colon (:).
— Follow all other guidelines presented for control and section borders.

Description. A *group box is* a standardized rectangular frame that surrounds a control or group of controls. An optional caption may be included in the frame's upper-left corner. Standard Microsoft Windows Group boxes are illustrated in Figure 7.85.

Purpose/proper usage. The purpose of a group box is to visually relate the elements of a single control or a grouping of related controls. Group boxes should be used to provide a border around a radio button control, a grouping of related check boxes, or two or more functionally related controls.

Guidelines. Typically, use a noun or noun phrase for group box labels or headings. Keep the text brief, one or two words. Consider the group box content and relate the control captions inside the group box to the label or heading being created. Use headline-style capitalization, but do not include any ending colon. Refer to all the guidelines presented for control and section borders, in designing group boxes.

Column Headings

- Description:
  — Read-only textual information that serves as a heading above columns of text or numbers.
  — Can be divided into two or more parts.

- Purpose:
  — To identify a column of information contained in a table.

- Proper usage:
  — To display a heading above a column of information contained in a table.

- Guidelines:
  — Heading:
    - Provide a brief heading.
    - Can include text and a graphic image.
    - Capitalize the first letter of each significant word.
    - Do not include an ending colon (:).
  — The width of the column should fit the average size of the column entries.
  — Does not support keyboard access.

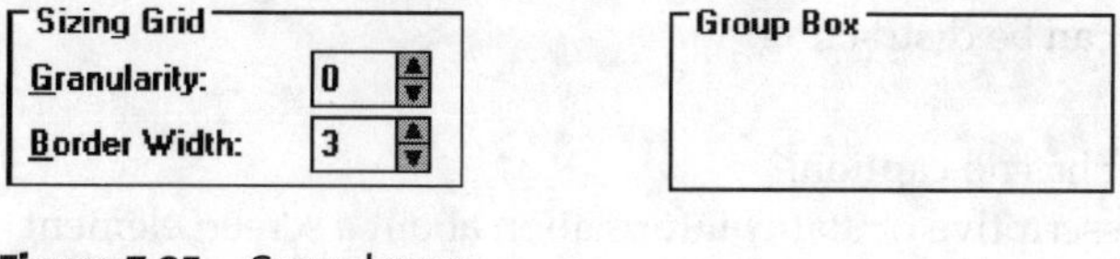

Figure 7.85 Group boxes.

Column heading

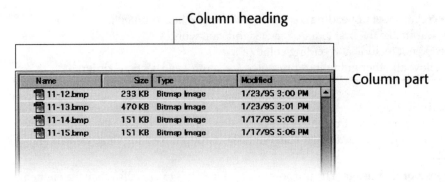

Column part

Figure 7.86 Column heading control.

Description. A *column heading control*, also known as a *header control*, is used to display a heading above columns of text or numbers. A column heading is illustrated in Figure 7.86. It can be divided into two or more parts.

Purpose/proper usage. To identify and display a heading above a column of information contained in a table.

Guidelines. Provide a brief heading. Headings can include text as well as a graphic image. Use the headline style of capitalization, without an ending colon. The width of each column should fit the average size of the column entries. Column heading controls do not support keyboard access.

ToolTips

- Description:
  — A small pop-up window containing descriptive text that appears when a pointer is moved over a control or element either:
    - Not possessing a label.
    - In need of additional descriptive or status information.
- Purpose:
  — To provide descriptive information about a control or screen element.
- Advantages:
  — Identifies an otherwise unidentified control.
  — Reduces possible screen clutter caused by control captions and descriptive information.
  — Enables control size to be reduced.
- Disadvantages:
  — Not obvious, must be discovered.
  — Inadvertent appearance can be distracting.
- Proper usage:
  — To identify a control that has no caption.
  — To provide additional descriptive or status information about a screen element.

Description. A *ToolTip*, sometimes called a Screen Tip, is a standard Microsoft Windows control, a small pop-up window that displays descriptive text when the pointer is moved over a control that does not possess a caption, or that possesses only an abbreviated caption. A ToolTip is illustrated in Figure 7.87.

Purpose/proper usage. The purpose of a ToolTip is to simply provide thorough descriptive information about a control when its function must be quickly identified. It is also used to provide additional descriptive or status information about a screen element.

Advantages/disadvantages. A ToolTip provides an easy way to identify an otherwise unidentifiable control, or a control with a cryptic caption. It reduces possible screen clutter caused by control captions, enabling the control size to be reduced. A ToolTip, however, is not obvious and must be discovered. Its appearance when the pointer is positioned incorrectly, or is slowly passing over it, can be distracting to the screen viewer.

ToolTip Guidelines

- Display after a short time-out.
- For toolbars, provide a brief word as a label.
  — Use mixed case in the headline style of presentation with no ending punctuation.
- For other elements, provide a brief phrase presenting descriptive or status information.
  — Use mixed case in the sentence style of presentation.
- Present ToolTips at the lower-right edge of the pointer.
  — Display them fully on the screen.
  — For text boxes, display ToolTips centered under the control.
- Display them in the standard system ToolTip colors.
- Remove the ToolTip when the control is activated or the pointer is moved away.
- Don't substitute ToolTips for good design.

Display the ToolTip on the screen after a short pause, ideally three-quarters of a second. This avoids its appearing briefly as the pointer is just being moved over a control or element that possesses a ToolTip. When used to provide descriptions of toolbar buttons, keep ToolTips brief, usually one or two words that identify the button's action. Use the headline style of capitalization with no ending punctuation. For other elements,

Figure 7.87 ToolTip

descriptive or status information may be provided. In this case, use a short phrase, in sentence-style capitalization, which briefly describes the item or status. Position the ToolTip to the lower-right of the pointer, but fully on the screen. Always adjust the location for a full fit. For text boxes, present the ToolTip centered under the control it relates to. Display it in the system's standard ToolTip colors so it will be immediately recognized as a ToolTip. Remove the ToolTip when the control is clicked or the pointer is moved away.

Don't substitute ToolTips for good design. Presented screen elements should always be designed for maximum comprehension. ToolTips are supplements.

Balloon Tips

- Description:
  - A small pop-up window that contains information in a word balloon.
  - Components can include:
    - Title.
    - Body text.
    - Message Icons.
  - Appear adjacent to the item to which they apply, generally above or to left.
  - Only one tip, the last posted, is visible at any time.
  - Tips are removed after a specified time period.

- Purpose:
  - To provide additional descriptive or status information about a screen element.

- Advantages:
  - Provides useful reminder and status information.

- Disadvantages:
  - If overused they lose their attention-getting value.
  - If overused in situations the user considers not very important, their continual appearance can be aggravating.

- Proper usage:
  - To display noncritical:
    - Reminder information.
    - Notification information.
  - Do not use tips to display critical information.

Description. A *balloon tip*, illustrated in Figure 7.88, is a small pop-up window that contains information presented in a word balloon. Its components can include a title, body text, and informational, warning, or critical icons. (These icons are described in the Step 8.) Custom icons are not supported. Balloon tips appear adjacent to the item to which they apply, generally, above or to the left of the item. However, the system automatically adjusts their position so they remain on-screen. Although a tip can be posted at any time, only one, the last posted, will be visible at any time. Balloon tips used for the taskbar are presented for a specified, within minimum and maximum limits.

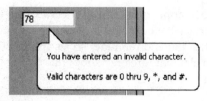

Figure 7.88 Balloon tip.

Purpose. To provide additional descriptive or status information about a screen element.

Advantages/disadvantages. Balloon tips can provide useful reminder and status information to the user. Their sudden appearance can at some times be distracting, and perhaps aggravating, however, especially if overused in situations the user considers not very important. If overused the also lose their attention-getting value.

Proper usage. For noncritical reminder or notification information, special conditions, or status information that would otherwise require a message box. They are very useful for informing the user of unexpected system behaviors. Due to their brief nature and frequent out-of-the-way location, never rely on balloon tips to display critical information.

Balloon Tip Guidelines

- General:
  — Use a notification tip to inform the user about state changes.
  — Use a reminder tip for state changes that the user might not usually notice.
  — Point the tip of the balloon to the item it references.
  — Do not use them to replace ToolTips.
  — Do not overuse balloon tips.

- Content:
  — Restrict them to a length of 100 characters, including title and body text.
  — Title text should:
    • If the tip refers to an icon or other image representing a specific object, include:
      — The object's name, using its normal capitalization.
      — The object's status, using sentence-style presentation without ending punctuation.
    • Be presented in bold.
  — Body text should:
    • Include a description of the situation in one or two brief sentences.
    • Include a brief suggestion for correcting the situation.
    • Be presented using mixed-case in the sentence style.

General. Balloon tips can provide either notifications or reminders. The notification balloon is displayed and then times out. This tip style should be used to notify the user about state changes. The reminder balloon appears at regular intervals. The default interval is 60 minutes. Use the reminder balloon only for state changes that the user might not usually notice. Notification and reminder styles are supported for taskbar components. Other screen elements are only supported by the notification style. Tips are automatically removed when the user clicks it or clicks elsewhere.

Always point the tip of the balloon to the item it references. Balloon tips are not intended to replace standard ToolTips. ToolTips and balloon tips are mutually exclusive; if a ToolTip is currently displayed and a balloon tip is presented, the balloon tip will automatically cause the ToolTip to be removed. ToolTips will not appear until the balloon tip is dismissed. Finally, be careful not to overuse balloon tips. The user may ignore them if they appear too frequently.

Content. The notification balloon tip has a maximum length of 100 characters, including the title and body text. Title text automatically appears as bold text. Body text uses the text style and size of standard ToolTips. For the title text, if the balloon tip refers to an icon or other image representing a specific object, include the object's name using its normal capitalization and its status using sentence-style capitalization without ending punctuation. Otherwise, just display the status text. The body text should include a statement of the problem in one or two brief sentences, followed by a brief suggestion for correcting the problem. Use sentence-style capitalization and appropriate punctuation.

Progress Indicators

- Description:
  - A rectangular bar that fills as a process is being performed, indicating the percentage of the process that has been completed.
- Purpose:
  - To provide feedback concerning the completion of a lengthy operation.
- Proper usage:
  - To provide an indication of the proportion of a process completed.

A *progress indicator* is a rectangular bar that fills as a process is being performed. The filled-in area indicates the percentage of a process that has been completed. A progress indicator, sometimes called a *progress bar*, is illustrated in Figure 7.89.

Progress Indicator Guidelines

- When filling the indicator:
  - If horizontally arrayed, fill it from left to right.
  - If vertically arrayed, fill it from bottom to top.
- Fill it with a color or a shade of gray.
- Include descriptive text for the process, as necessary.
- Place text outside of the control.

> RECORDS
>
> Updating...
>
> 80% Complete
>
> Stop

Figure 7.89   Progress indicator.

Fill horizontally arrayed progress indicators from left to right; fill vertically arrayed progress indicators from bottom to top. Fill them with a color or a shade of gray. Create necessary descriptive text using a *static text* control. Position the text outside of the control. Progress indicators are also discussed in the Step 9 "Provide Effective Feedback and Guidance and Assistance."

Sample Box

- Description:
  — A box illustrating what will show up on the screen based upon the parameter or parameters selected.
  — May include text, graphics, or both.
- Purpose:
  — To provide a representation of actual screen content based upon the parameter or parameters selected.
- Guidelines:
  — Include a brief label.
  — Use mixed case in the headline style.
  — Locate it adjacent to the controls upon which it is dependent.

Description. A *sample box* is a box illustrating what will show up on the screen based upon the parameter or parameters currently selected. A common example, shown in Figure 7.90, illustrates a font selected for display on a screen. Sample boxes may include text, graphics, or both.

Purpose. To provide a representation of actual screen content based upon the parameter or parameters selected so that the choice may actually be seen.

Figure 7.90   Sample box.

Guidelines. Include a brief label using mixed case in the headline style. Position the sample box immediately adjacent to the control or controls affecting its content.

Scrolling Tickers

- Description:
  — Text that scrolls horizontally through a container window.
- Advantages:
  — Consume less screen space than full text.
- Disadvantages:
  — Hard to read.
  — Time-consuming to interpret.
  — Distracting.
- Guideline:
  — Do not use.

Description. A *scrolling ticker* is a window that contains text scrolling horizontally.

Advantages/disadvantages. The biggest advantage of a scrolling ticker is its efficient use of screen space. Disadvantages include scrolling text being hard to read and time-consuming to interpret. Human memory being what it is, information scrolled out of sight is difficult to remember, and longer messages may not be understood. Scrolling screen elements are also visually distracting.

Guideline. The most prudent guideline at the moment is: do not use scrolling tickers.

Selecting the Proper Controls

Providing the proper control, or mix of controls, is critical to a system's success. The proper control will enable a person to make needed selections, entries, and changes quickly, efficiently, and with fewer mistakes. Improper selection most often leads to the opposite result.

This section will begin with a survey of several research studies addressing control selection. Studies such as these, while few in number, appear in the research literature. The results of these studies have already been incorporated within the control usage guidelines just discussed. Next, the criteria that must be considered in control selection will be summarized. Finally, some selection guidelines will be presented.

Entry versus Selection—A Comparison

The first studies to be described are a series performed by IBM. These studies (Gould, Boies, Meluson, Rasamny, and Vosburgh, 1988; Greene, Gould, Boies, Meluson, and Rasamny, 1988; Greene, Gould, Boies, Rasamny, and Meluson, 1992) looked at the advantages and disadvantages of using either entry fields or selection fields for data collection. Entry involved keying text; selection was performed by pointing at a choice

SOME THOUGHTS ON POOR SCREEN DESIGN

Following is a collection of control design inadequacies whose most endearing qualities are they *really, really aggravate* the author.

Why do interface designers insist on collecting state codes through drop-down list boxes when all other name and address details are collected through text boxes?

I'm merrily typing away my "mentally programmed" name and address when I encounter the state field and come to a screeching halt. Do I reach for the mouse? Open the drop-down list box with the keyboard? I stumble, grumble, open the drop-down list box, find my home state, Arizona, and select it, thinking all the while how glad I am I live in a state whose name is near the top of the alphabetized list. My condolences go out to friends in places like Illinois and Texas who'll have to scroll to their state name. I return my hands to the keyboard and forge ahead to zip code. Why, I'm now thinking, do they need my zip code? They now have enough information to determine it—but that's another story.

Why am I often penalized by American systems for living in the United States?

Back to the name and address again; now I must indicate country. Can I type USA? Nope, back to a drop-down list box. Opening it, I stare at an alphabetized list of countries within which, I quickly realize, the United States of America lies well submerged. I look at the system's owner (a large hotel chain) and, since 95 percent of their hotels are in the USA, I estimate that the overwhelming majority of guests must be American. Have these people ever thought of another sequence like, perhaps, frequency of use? Or a combination of frequency and alphabetical with the several most frequent possibilities at the top? I guess not, I think, wondering if I should move to Australia to avoid this nonsense. "They're getting even with you for living in Arizona," you may be thinking, and this may be true. My friends in Illinois and Texas are double-whammed, however.

Why do they clear one critical piece of information when they re-present a screen?

With another hotel system, I encounter a "sorry, no room at this inn" for the days I'd like to be there. I select a different hotel and glance at the booking screen. The dates I previously entered are still there as well as well as the room type. I click "send." You didn't tell us whether your trip was for business or pleasure, their error message sternly advises. (Can't I also have pleasure on a business trip, I wonder?) I glance at the top of the screen. The radio buttons designating business or pleasure have magically been cleared, but nothing else on the reservation screen has changed. If I'm looking for another hotel on the same dates as just a moment ago, would I now be doing it for business instead of pleasure (or vice versa), I wonder. Perhaps some hotels are only for business, others only for pleasure—a worthwhile subject for usability research…

Why do they give me a small command button and surround it by acres of white space?

Are they afraid it might be too easy to find? Don't they really want it pressed? Are they testing my perceptual-motors skills? Is an anorexic button beautiful? Have they ever heard of Fitts' Law? Undoubtedly not!

through the keyboard using the cursor control keys (not a mouse). The information compared was of three kinds: dates, text, and data. The first conclusion:

Choosing a Type of Control

- For familiar, meaningful data choose the technique that, in theory, requires the fewest number of keystrokes to complete.
- If the data is unfamiliar or prone to typing errors, choose a selection technique.

The studies found that if the data to be entered was familiar, the technique that required the minimum theoretical number of keystrokes to complete the task was the fastest. Theoretical keystrokes are the minimum number possible, excluding mis-keys, and erroneous cursor or selection movements. However, as the information became less familiar or became subject to spelling or typing errors, the minimum keystroke principle broke down. Selection techniques, and the reminders and structure they provide for unfamiliar items, hard to spell words, and items prone to typing errors becomes advantageous. The point at which the changeover occurs is not known. It would be influenced by the nature of the task and the nature of the user.

These studies point out the advantages of the techniques that permit both typed entry and selection to enter the data (spin box, drop-down/pop-up combination box, and attached combination box).

Aided versus Unaided Entry

- Provide aided entry whenever possible.
  - Absorb any extra and unnecessary keystrokes.
  - Provide an auditory signal that autocompletion has been performed.

The studies also compared unaided typed entry (the entire field had to be keyed) with aided entry (the system automatically and immediately completed the field when enough characters were keyed to make the desired data known). They found that aided entry, also known as autocompletion, was preferred over unaided entry methods, and it was also the fastest. Autocompletion was also preferable to, and faster than, many selection methods. Greene et al. (1992) found that, for keying of difficult to spell words, aided entry was much faster, and significantly reduced errors, when compared to unaided entry.

The result is that, when possible, autocompletion of text entry fields should be provided. Autocompletion will minimize the user's effort by reducing input time and keystrokes. It should also enhance the user's opinion of the system. If aided entry is provided, extra keystrokes must be absorbed by the system. The software will finish spelling a word much faster than a person's fingers are capable of stopping movement. Also, provide some kind of auditory signal that autocompletion has begun. A person may not be looking directly at the control when the completion is performed.

Comparison of GUI Controls

Tullis and Kodimer (1992) compared seven controls used for direct manipulation, selection, and data entry. The task was to reorder four items in a table (Filename, Number, Size, and Date). The controls studied were the following. Complete descriptions of control usage methods are summarized in Table 7.1.

- Direct Manipulation.
    1. Drag and drop on.
    2. Drag and drop between.
- Selection.
    3. Icons.
    4. Radio buttons.
    5. Menus (drop-down list boxes).
- Entry.
    6. One entry area.
    7. Four entry areas.

The direct manipulation methods reflected the perceived strength of graphical systems, namely manipulation of objects on the screen. The selection methods utilized indirect manipulation and illustrated the types of controls available in graphical screen design. The entry methods are a carryover from text-based screens, the only way the task could be accomplished for many years. Study participants were experienced Microsoft Windows users. No instructions were provided on how to carry out the item reorganization tasks. Users had to rely on their experience.

The two fastest methods were radio buttons and the one entry field. The methods most preferred by participants were radio buttons, drop-down list boxes, and one entry field. The direct manipulation methods fared rather poorly, ending midlist in the speed and preference rankings. The surprise, perhaps, was the good showing of an old control: the one entry field, or text box.

Tullis (1993) performed a follow-up to this study by asking a group of programmers to predict the study results (without, of course, being privy to its results). For both reordering speeds and subjective preferences, their predictions were way off the mark. They anticipated that the direct manipulation methods would be the fastest and most preferred. This, of course, was not at all the case. They predicted that radio buttons would be midway in the speed and preference ordering and that one entry field would be near the bottom. Again, they were quite mistaken. The correlation between their predictions and actual reordering speed was a dismal .07. They did slightly better on predicting preferences, the correlation being .31.

Based on these studies, Tullis concludes that control selection decisions made according to convention and intuition may not necessarily yield the best results. We might modify that conclusion to say, with a great deal of justification, that such decisions made using *common sense* may not even yield *good* results. Just because a control or process is new does not necessarily make it better. Just because the control has been around a long time does not necessarily make it poorer. Controls should be selected on the basis

Table 7.1 Controls Evaluated by Tullis and Kodimer (1992)

DIRECT MANIPULATION

1. Drag and Drop On
   - The items are arrayed horizontally. An item is dragged to a new location above another item and released. The item in that position moves to the old location of the arriving item.

2. Drag and Drop Between
   - The items are arrayed horizontally. An item is dragged to a new location between two other items and released. The items are readjusted into new positions, including, when necessary, automatic wrap-around for items located at the end of the line.

SELECTION

3. Icons
   - The items are arrayed horizontally. Icons are positioned between each pair of items. Selecting an icon switches the positions of each adjacent item.

4. Radio Buttons
   - The items are presented in a matrix, item name along the left side, item position numbers across the top. Radio buttons in the matrix are selected to represent each item's position.

5. Menus (Drop-down List Boxes)
   - Items are positioned horizontally. A drop-down listing is activated, and the item for that location selected.

ENTRY

6. One Entry Area
   - A single text entry field is provided. A one-character mnemonic (F,N,S,D) is provided for each choice. The mnemonics are keyed in the order in which the items are to be arrayed.

7. Four Entry Areas
   - Four text entry fields, labeled with the item names are arranged vertically. A number (1-4) is keyed into each field, indicating the manner in which the items are to be ordered.

of the objectives they are to achieve, and they should be subjected to the same rigorous testing as all other parts of the system.

Another control comparison study was conducted by Johnsgard et al. (1995). They evaluated a variety of controls including check boxes, drop-down list boxes, drop-down combination boxes, text boxes, list boxes, radio buttons, sliders, and spin boxes. Speeds, errors, and preferences were obtained for the various controls under various conditions.

Mutually Exclusive Choice Controls

For a small set of options (5), a medium set (12), and a large set (30), radio buttons were significantly faster than the other mutually exclusive controls. They were also the most accurate and most preferred by the study participants. This result is consistent with the results of the Tullis and Kodimer (1992) study. Among other findings: as control set sizes increased, control activation speeds significantly increased (took longer), and sets organized in a meaningful way were searched significantly faster than those in random orders.

The medium and large set sizes (12 and 30) are larger than generally recommended for radio buttons (8 or less). The results indicate that radio buttons may effectively be used for these larger quantities, if sufficient screen space exists for their presentation. Controls requiring scrolling to see all the choices, or require an action to display a listing of choices (drop-downs), seem to significantly impede selection speeds.

Nonexclusive Choice Controls

For a small set of options (5) with two selected choices, a medium set (12) with three selected choices, and a large set (30) with eight selected choices, check boxes were significantly faster than the other nonexclusive controls. Check boxes were also the most preferred by the study participants. Among other findings: like radio buttons, as control set sizes increased, control activation speeds increased (took longer), and sets organized in a meaningful way were searched significantly faster than those in random order.

The medium and large set sizes (12 and 30) are also larger than generally recommended for check boxes (8 or less). The results also seem to indicate that check boxes may effectively be used for these larger quantities, if sufficient screen space exists for their presentation. Again scrolling and retrieving lists slow one down.

Combination Selection and Entry Controls

Two controls were compared: a drop-down combination box and an array of radio buttons, including an "other" choice with an associated text entry field for keying the "other" value. The fastest, most accurate, and preferred: radio buttons with the text entry field.

Controls for Selecting a Value within a Range

Setting range values included indicating a time, a percentage, or the transmission frequency of a radio station. Controls evaluated were the spin button, text entry field, and the slider. The spin button was the most accurate, and the text entry field fastest and most preferred. The slider finished last in all three measurement categories.

The study's general conclusions are:

- Making all options always visible will enhance performance.
- Requiring additional actions to make further options visible slows performance.
- For longer lists, scrolling tends to degrade performance more than the action associated with retrieving a hidden list.

As set size increases, performance times increase more for controls that require scrolling than for those that do not. For a large set size (30 options) scrolling slowed performance more than the action to retrieve a list.

Control Selection Criteria

Selection of the proper control, then, depends on several factors. The first is the structure and characteristics of the property or data itself. Other considerations include the nature of the task, the nature of the user, and the limitations of the display screen itself.

Property or data considerations reflect the characteristics of the data itself. Some kinds of controls are very restrictive in that they permit only specific kinds of information with specific qualities to be presented within them. Other kinds of controls may not be as restrictive concerning a data's qualities, but they are not well suited to the kind of data being used. Data considerations include the following:

- Is the property or data *mutually exclusive* or *nonexclusive*? Does entry/selection require single or multiple items?
- Is the property or data *discrete* or *continuous*? Discrete data can be meaningfully specified and categorized, while continuous data cannot.
- Is the property or data *limited* or *unlimited* in scope? If limited, how many items will the data normally not exceed?
- Is the property or data *fixed* or *variable* in list length? Are there always a fixed number of items, or will it vary?
- Is the property or data ordered in a *predictable* or *unpredictable* fashion? If predictable, will the user be able to anticipate the next, unseen, item?
- Can the property or data be *represented pictorially*? Will a picture or graphic be as meaningful as a textual description?

Task considerations reflect the nature of the job. Considerations include the following:

- *How often* is an item *entered* or *selected*?
- *How often* is an item *changed*?
- How *precisely* must the item be entered or selected?

User considerations reflect the characteristics of the user. Important considerations:

- How much *training* in control operation will be provided?
- How *meaningful* or *known* is the property or data to the user?
- How *easily remembered or learned* by the user is the property or data?
- How *frequently used* will the system be?
- Is the user an *experienced typist*?

Display considerations reflect the characteristics of the screen and hardware.

- How much *screen space* is available to display the various controls?

Choosing a Control Form

In light of the above research and considerations, and the known characteristics of the various controls, some guidance in control selection can be presented.

When to Permit Text Entry

■ Permit text entry if any of the following questions can be answered *Yes*:
  — Is the data unlimited in size and scope?
  — Is the data familiar?
  — Is the data *not* conducive to typing errors?
  — Will typing be faster than choice selection?
  — Is the user an experienced typist?

Permit text entry when any of the above conditions exist. The use of combination controls is almost always the best alternative, permitting the user to *choose* when to type and when to point and select.

What Kind of Control to Choose

Next are two tables providing some control recommendations based upon a control's known advantages, disadvantages, and proper usage characteristics. Table 7.2 is a simple decision chart for small listings, based upon Johnsgard et al. (1995). Table 7.3 is more thorough and is based upon the known characteristics of the controls described in this chapter.

The recommendations presented by Johnsgard et al., in these tables are based upon their research study. The names of some controls have been modified to reflect the control classification scheme found in this text. It would seem worth considering for controls containing a small number of choices. All controls in their study, except *setting a value within a range*, were limited to 30 options. For more than 30 choices, the use of radio buttons or check boxes still seems inappropriate at this time. More research is needed in this area.

Table 7.2   Best Controls for Certain Tasks and Screen Conditions

TASK	BEST CONTROL	IF SCREEN SPACE CONSTRAINTS EXIST
Mutually Exclusive	Radio Buttons	Drop-down/Pop-up List Box
Not Mutually Exclusive	Check Boxes	Multiple-Selection List Box
Select or Type a Value Text Entry Field	Radio Buttons with "Other"	Drop-down Combo Box
Setting a Value within a Range	Spin Button	Text Box

From Johnsgard et al., 1995

Table 7.3 Suggested Uses for Graphical Controls

1. IF:	USE:
• *Mutually exclusive* alternatives. • Discrete data. • Best represented verbally. • Very limited in number (2 to 8).	
AND: • Typed entry is never necessary. • Content can never change. • Adequate screen space is available.	Radio Buttons
OR: • Typed entry is never necessary. • Content can never change. • Adequate screen space is not available.	Drop-down/Pop-up List Box
OR: • Typed entry may be necessary. • Content can change. • Adequate screen space is available.	Combo box
OR: • Typed entry may be necessary. • Content can change. • Adequate screen space is not available.	Drop-down/Pop-up Combo Box

2. IF:	USE:
• *Mutually exclusive* alternatives. • Discrete data. • Best represented verbally. • Potentially large in number (9 or more).	
AND: • Typed entry is never necessary. • Content can never change. • Adequate screen space is available.	Single-Selection List Box
OR: • Typed entry is never necessary. • Content can never change. • Adequate screen space is not available.	Drop-down/Pop-up List Box
OR: • Typed entry may be necessary. • Content can change. • Adequate screen space is available.	Combo Box
OR: • Typed entry may be necessary. • Content can change. • Adequate screen space is not available.	Drop-down/Pop-up Combo Box

Table 7.3 Continued

3. IF:	USE:

- *Mutually exclusive* alternatives.   Palette
- Discrete data.
- Best represented graphically.
- Content rarely changes.
- Small or large number of items.

4. IF:	USE:

- *Mutually exclusive* alternatives.
- Not frequently selected.
- Content does not change.
- Well-known, easily remembered data.
- Predictable, consecutive data.
- Typed entry sometimes desirable.

AND:
- Adequate screen space is not available.   Spin Box

OR:
- Adequate screen space is available.   Combo Box

5. IF:	USE:

- *Mutually exclusive* alternatives.   Slider
- Continuous data with a limited range
  of settings.
- Value increases/decreases in a well-known,
  predictable way.
- Spatial representation enhances comprehension.

6. IF:	USE:

- *Nonexclusive* alternatives.
- Discrete data.
- Best represented verbally.
- Typed entry is never necessary.
- Content can never change.
- Adequate screen space is available.

AND:
- Very limited in number (2 to 8).   Check Boxes

OR:
- Potentially large in number (9 or more).   Multiple-Selection List Box

Table 7.4   Choosing a Command Form

IF THE COMMANDS:	USE:
Are standard commands provided by a tool set.	Commands provided by the tool set
Total seven or more, and can be arranged hierarchically into groups.	Menu bar and pull-downs
Total six or fewer, are selected frequently, and affect an entire window.	Buttons in a window
Total seven or more, are selected frequently, and affect an entire window.	Buttons in a toolbar
Are used with other controls, or are complicated commands and need to be simplified.	Buttons in a dialog box
Are sometimes used frequently and are sometimes used infrequently.	Buttons in a dialog box
Are frequently accessed and have only two conditions.	Toggled menu item

Choosing between Buttons and Menus for Commands

Determining the proper way to present a command also depends on several factors. The following considerations are involved in choosing the correct command form:

- Whether or not the command part of a *standard tool set*.
- The total *number* of commands in the application.
- The *complexity* of the commands.
- The *frequency* with which commands are used.
- Whether or not the command is used in association *with another control*.

Guidelines for choosing the proper command form are presented in Table 7.4.

Examples

Improper and proper usage of several controls are illustrated and discussed.

Example 1

This is an instance of improper and proper presentation of command buttons.

Screen 1.1

Here the design and display of buttons is poor. Problems include: (1) The buttons are split between the left and right side of the screen, causing a wide separation. Positioning buttons to the left, from a screen usage and flow standpoint, is illogical. (2) Differences in sizes exist between buttons. OK, a very frequently used button is the smallest, slowing down selection speed if a pointer is used. (3) Different size labels also exist (OK and Search). (4) There appears to be redundancy in button use and purpose. How does OK differ from Save? What does Edit do? (5) From an organization standpoint, standard and application buttons appear to be intermixed. (6) The Back and Next actions are widely separated, making fast reversal of actions more difficult.

Screen 1.2

This shows a much better button design and presentation. Enhancements include: (1) The buttons are located at the bottom of the screen, in a position following the screen usage flow. (2) Button size is standardized, presenting generally larger targets. (3) Button label size is standardized. (4) The seemingly redundant buttons are eliminated. (5) Function-specific buttons are grouped separately from standard buttons, and button groupings are created through a larger spacing between Print and OK. (6) Back, now called Previous, and Next are positioned together for fast paging reversal.

Screen 1.1

Screen 1.2

Example 2

Here we are dealing with inconsistent location of command buttons.

Screens 2.1 to 2.4

These are the button locations found on four windows within a graphical system. Positions include spread out across the window's bottom (Screen 2.1), left-justified at the bottom (Screen 2.2), centered along the right side (Screen 2.3), and top-justified along the right side (Screen 2.4). Memorization and prediction of button location will be very difficult, slowing down the experienced user.

Screen 2.5

Proper positioning would have found *all* the command buttons consistently positioned, as at the bottom center as illustrated in Screen 2.5.

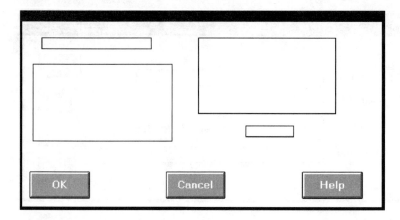

Screen 2.1

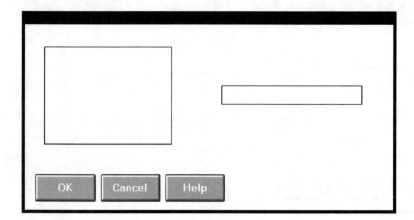

Screen 2.2

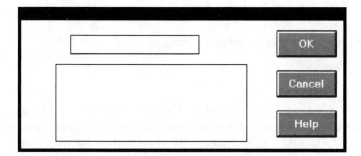

Screen 2.3

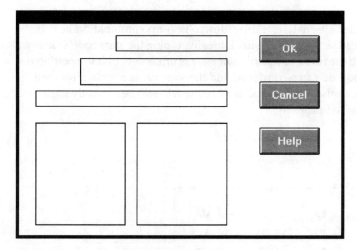

Screen 2.4

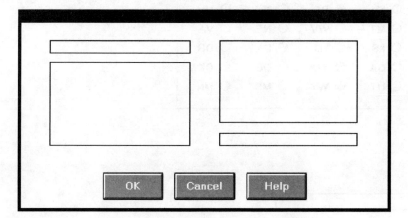

Screen 2.5

Example 3

This is an example of improper and proper use of a control.

Control 3.1

The names of states must be selected using radio buttons. Problems include: (1) The large number of choices presented makes scanning very difficult. (2) Are all the state abbreviations familiar to you, and all users? (3) The organization of states must have been established by a lottery. The name of the state I want is Mississippi. How do I find it in the array?

Control 3.2

This shows a much better alternative, a drop-down/pop-up combination box. If the state name is known, it can be typed in the field. Ideally, typing the state code, if known, will also be acceptable. If the name of a particular state is unknown, or if its spelling unclear, the drop-down/pop-up can be retrieved and the state name selected from the list presented. Ideally, also, a misspelled keyed state name will still be correctly identified by the system and displayed properly.

```
┌─ State ──────────────────────────────────────────┐
│                                                   │
│   ○ ME     ○ NH     ○ LA     ○ WA     ○ MA        │
│   ○ AK     ○ MI     ○ ID     ○ IN     ○ AL        │
│   ○ HI     ○ IL     ○ NC     ○ TX     ○ MO        │
│   ○ NY     ○ VT     ○ CA     ○ WI     ○ ND        │
│   ○ IA     ○ MD     ○ CT     ○ AR     ○ OH        │
│   ○ FL     ○ KY     ◉ SC     ○ NV     ○ NM        │
│   ○ AZ     ○ MT     ○ WV     ○ NE     ○ VA        │
│   ○ CO     ○ KS     ○ NJ     ○ PA     ○ OR        │
│   ○ SD     ○ GA     ○ TN     ○ DE     ○ OK        │
│   ○ RI     ○ UT     ○ WY     ○ MS     ○ MN        │
│                                                   │
└───────────────────────────────────────────────────┘
```

Control 3.1

State: [_____] ⬇

Control 3.2

Example 4

Here is another instance of improper and proper use of a control.

Screen 4.1

A listing of names is being collected. A courtesy title is selected through list box; last name, first name, and middle initial are typed. The problem: The task is heavily keyboard intensive. To select a title requires shifting to an alternative device control, such as a mouse, or tabbing through the list box listing to find the proper title. This slows down the keying process and may be awkward. The list box also consumes a great deal of space on the screen.

Screen 4.2

A solution: Collect the courtesy title using a pop-up/drop-down combination box. Familiar titles may be quickly typed, along with the remainder of the name data. Rare or unusual titles may be identified by selecting, displaying, and searching the listing of all alternatives. The title may then be entered in the field by selecting from the list or keying it into the field.

Screen 4.1

NAME

Title:

Last:

First:

Middle Initial:

OK   Apply   Cancel

Screen 4.2

Example 5

Again, improper and proper use of controls.

Screen 5.1

A collection of seashells is being cataloged by class and order. Text boxes are provided for the task. The catalog process includes typing words such as "Cephalopoda" and "Eulamellibranchia." The process is slow and conducive to spelling errors.

Screen 5.2

A solution: Present Class and Order in list boxes from which the proper varieties are selected. This will speed up the cataloguing process and eliminate the possibility of spelling errors. To make the entire procedure a selection task, also make Item Number a selectable and incrementable spin box.

SEASHELLS

Item Number:

Class:

Order:

OK   Apply   Cancel

Screen 5.1

SEASHELLS

Item Number:

Class:
Amphineura
Cephalopoda
Gastropoda
Pelecypoda
Scaphopoda

Order:
Eulamellibranchia
Filibranchia
Palaeoconcha
Protobranchia
Septibranchia

OK   Apply   Cancel

Screen 5.2

Example 6

Again, improper and proper use of a control.

Screen 6.1

An international corporation is setting up a worldwide account database. Names from dozens of different countries are added each day. Country is collected though a spin box. Is this proper usage for a spin box?

ACCOUNT

Name:

Street:

City/State/Post Cd:

Country:

OK   Apply   Cancel

Screen 6.1

Screens 6.2 and 6.3

With a spin box, the next unseen choice must be capable of being anticipated. If not, tedious clicking and searching to find the correct choice might have to be performed. (What country follows Greece in the worldwide alphabetical listing of countries today? Guatemala—at least at this writing.) The data in spin boxes should be stable, not often changing. This quality does not accurately reflect the state of countries in the world today.

The best choice would really depend on the variability of the information being collected. If the account information being collected tended to be quite variable in flow, that is, successive account entries were usually from different countries, a better choice would be a combo box (Screen 6.2). Well-known country names can be typed and less well-known ones found in the listing. Because of the dynamic nature of country names, frequent reference to the list can be expected. Permanently displaying the list avoids the step of retrieving it when needed. The attached listing also permits scanning several names at one time, alleviating the predictability problem. Names can also be easily added or changed as needed. The combo box is also at the bottom of the window where it tends to be out of the way.

If successive account entries tended to be from the same country, that is, the information is batched, a pop-up/drop-down combination would be more appropriate (Screen 6.3). The box can remain closed through successive same country entries and only need be opened occasionally when actually needed.

Screen 6.2

Screen 6.3

Write Clear Text and Messages

The wording of the interface and its screens is the basic form of communication with the user. Clear and meaningfully crafted words, messages, and text lead to greatly enhanced system usability and minimize user confusion that leads to errors and possibly even system rejection. In this step, general guidelines for choosing the proper words and writing clear messages and text will be presented. These general guidelines will be followed by a discussion of some Web-specific guidelines.

Words, Sentences, Messages, and Text

All communications should simply, clearly, and politely provide the information one must have to effectively use a system. The design of these communications must take into account the user's experience and knowledge of the system topic, and how much information the user actually needs to efficiently interact with the system. Like all aspects of interface design, knowing the user is the first step in choosing the proper words and creating acceptable messages and text.

Words

■ Do not use:
  — Jargon, words, or terms:
    • Unique to the computer profession.
    • With different meanings outside of the computer profession.
    • Made up to describe special functions or conditions.

— Abbreviations or acronyms.
  • Unless the abbreviation or acronym is as familiar as a full word or phrase.
— Word contractions, suffixes, and prefixes.

■ Use:
— Short, familiar words.
— Standard alphabetic characters.
— Complete words.
— Positive terms.
— Simple action words; avoid noun strings.
— The "more" dimension when comparing.
— Consistent words.

■ Do not:
— Stack words.
— Hyphenate words.
— Include punctuation for abbreviations, mnemonics, and acronyms.

Jargon. Jargon may take several forms. It may be words or terms that are unique to the computer profession such as *filespec, abend,* or *spool*; words with different meaning outside of information systems such as *boot* or *abort*; or made-up words used to describe special functions or actions such as *ungroup* or *dearchive*. Avoid jargon because it will have to be learned, and it may be interpreted incorrectly.

Abbreviations or acronyms. Avoid using abbreviations and acronyms unless they are as familiar as the fully spelled-out word or phrase. (An example of a familiar acronym is IBM for International Business Machines.) The reason again, it must be understood and learned. Familiar abbreviations and acronyms, if legal to use, may be used following these guidelines:

■ **Always use the fully spelled-out form the first time it is encountered in the interface.** Present the abbreviation or acronym in parentheses following the fully spelled-out form.

■ **Use the abbreviation or acronym in any subsequent locations in the dialog reached directly, and only directly, from the place where it is defined.** If these subsequent locations can be reached from places in the dialog other than the location where the abbreviation or acronym was defined (as in Web page design), then do not use the abbreviation or acronym alone.

Contractions or short forms. While contractions (*won't* instead of *will not*) save space and lend an informal tone to the interface, be cautious in their use. Never form a contraction from a subject and it's verb, *he'll* instead of *he will*. Words can also be more difficult to understand if they contain prefixes and suffixes, like "un-," or "-ness." A study found that word comprehension often involves a person decomposing more complex terms to establish their basic root meaning and then modifying the meaning to account for the various prefixes and suffixes. Structural complexity hinders comprehension.

Short, familiar words. Shorter words tend to be used more often in everyday conversation, so they are more familiar and easier to understand. The most important factor, however, is familiarity, not length. A longer but familiar word is better than a short, unfamiliar word.

Standard alphabetic characters. Standard alphabetic characters are most familiar to screen viewers. Never use restricted alphabetic sets. Symbols should be used only if they are familiar to all who are using the screen. Common symbols that may be considered as substitutes for alphabetic characters are # for number, % for percent, and $ for dollar. Again, all potential screen users must be familiar with a symbol if it is used as a substitute for alphabet characters.

Complete words. Instead of contractions or short forms, use complete words. Complete words are understood better and faster.

Positive terms. It is generally easier to understand positive, affirmative information than the same information expressed in a negative way. Therefore, avoid the prefixes "ir-," "in-," "dis-," and "un-." Implicitly negative terms, such as "decrease," should be replaced with positive terms, such as "increase."

Simple action words. Replace noun strings with simple action words. Instead of saying, for example, "Project Status Listing" say *List* Project Status."

"More" dimension. When using comparative terms, the "more" dimension is easier to deal with. The opposite of the "more" is usually considered the "negative." So, use "longer" rather than "shorter," "bigger" rather than "smaller."

Consistency. Words chosen for use in an interface should be used consistently throughout the interface. Never use different words to describe identical functions.

Stacking words. Multiple-word phrases are more readable if the entire phrase is on one line, not stacked vertically.

Hyphenating words. Again, for better readability, never break a word between two lines. Hyphenation was created for ease in production, not ease in comprehension.

Punctuation. Abbreviations, mnemonics, and acronyms should not include punctuation. This permits better readability and avoids confusion between the punctuation and other screen elements.

Some words to forget. Words should be meaningful to, understandable by, and acceptable to, all users. As mentioned above, words perceived as "computerese" may confuse or place an unnecessary intellectual demands on the user. Other words may have a particularly harsh meaning or invoke unpleasant associations (abort, execute, kill), or have vague meanings (abend, boot). These problem words, summarized in Table 8.1, should be avoided in communications whenever possible. Suggested alternative words are presented.

Sentences and Messages

- Sentences and messages must be:
  — Brief and simple.
  — Directly and immediately usable.
  — An affirmative statement.
  — In an active voice.

— In the temporal sequence of events.
— Structured so that the main topic is near the beginning.
— Of parallel construction.

■ Sentences and messages must be of the proper tone:
— Nonauthoritarian.
— Nonthreatening.
— Nonanthropomorphic.
— Nonpatronizing.
— Nonpunishing.
— Cautious in the use of humor.

A sentence, and a message, must minimize ambiguity and confusion, allowing easy, correct, and fast interpretation. It must also have the proper tone, reflecting the needs of the users. Threatening, rude, or impolite messages most often evoke negative responses. The following guidelines will lead to easy, correct, and fast message interpretation and acceptance. A study restructuring error messages along such guidelines has found higher success rates in problem resolution, lower error rates, and improved user satisfaction.

Brief and simple. A message that has to be explained does not communicate. It fails as a message. Brief, simple sentences are more readily understood than longer sen-

Table 8.1   Some Words to Forget

AVOID	USE
Abend	End, Cancel, Stop
Abort	End, Cancel, Stop
Access	Get, Ready, Display
Available	Ready
Boot	Start, Run
Error	—
Execute	Complete
Hit	Press, Depress
Implement	Do, Use, Put Into
Invalid	Not Correct, Not Good, Not Valid
Key	Type, Enter
Kill	End, Cancel
Output	Report, List, Display
Return Key	Enter, Transmit
Terminate	End, Exit

tences containing multiple clauses. Research indicates that sentences over 20 words in length cause a loss in reading comprehension with each additional sentence word. Another research study created messages at three levels of reading ability (fifth, tenth, and fifteenth grade) and tested them on people of varying verbal abilities. The fifth-grade version was found to be best for all levels. People of high verbal ability did not perceive the fifth-grade version as insulting, as some had feared. So, break long sentences into two or more simple sentences if this can be done without changing the meaning. Always write at the eighth grade level, or less.

Directly and immediately usable. Searching through reference material to translate a message is unacceptable, as are requirements for transposing, computing, interpolating, or mentally translating messages into other units.

Affirmative statement. Affirmative statements are easier to understand than negative statements. For example, *"Complete entry before returning to menu."* is easier to grasp than *"Do not return to menu before completing entry."* Tell a person what to do rather than what to avoid. There is an exception, of course. The user may be told how to avoid a situation with disastrous consequences.

Active voice. The active voice is usually easier to understand than passive voice. For example, *"Send the message by depressing TRANSMIT"* is more understandable than *"The message is sent by depressing TRANSMIT."*

Temporal sequence. If a sentence describes a temporal sequence of events, the order of words should correspond to this sequence. A prompt should say, *"Complete address and page forward"* rather than *"Page forward after completing address."*

Main topic at beginning. Information that must be remembered should be placed at the beginning of a message or sentence. A person can remember something longer if it appears at the start. Items in the middle of a sentence or message are hardest to remember.

Parallel construction. Use the same grammatical structure for elements of sentences or messages that provide the same kind of information. For example, say, *"Use this control to select one choice"* and *"Use this menu to select one option."* Not, *"To select one choice use this control,"* and *"This menu is used to select one option."*

Nonauthoritarian. Imply that the system is awaiting the user's direction, not that the system is directing the user. For example, phrase a message as *"Ready for the next command,"* not *"Enter the next command."*

Nonthreatening. Negative tones or actions, or threats, are not very friendly. Since errors are often the result of a failure to understand, mistakes, or trial-and-error behavior, the user may feel confused, inadequate, or anxious. Blaming the user for problems can heighten anxiety, making error correction more difficult and increasing the chance of more errors. Therefore, harsh words like "illegal," "bad," or "fatal" should be avoided.

Also, avoid using the word "error" in messages when it implies a user error. "Error" tends to focus the attention on the person involved rather than on the problem. For example, instead of saying *"Error—Numbers are illegal,"* say, *"Months must be entered by name."* Since the computer does not have an ego to be bruised, an excellent design approach would be to have it assume the blame for all miscommunications.

Nonanthropomorphic. Having the computer "talk" like a person should be avoided for several reasons. An attribution of knowledge or intelligence will, first, imply a much higher level of computer "knowledge" than actually exists, creating shattered user expectations. Second, this attribute eliminates the distinction that actually exists between people and computers. People "control" computers; they "respect the desires" of other human beings. Third, many people express anxiety about using computers by saying things like "they make you feel dumb." The feeling of interacting with another person who is evaluating your proficiency can heighten this anxiety. There is also some research evidence that a nonanthropomorphic approach is best, being seen as more honest, preferred, and easier to use.

The best advice at this moment is do not give a human personality to a machine. Imply that the system is awaiting the user's direction, not vice versa. Say, for example, *"What do you need?"* not *"How can I help you?"*

Nonpatronizing. Patronizing messages can be embarrassing. *"Very good, you did it right"* may thrill a fourth-grader, but would be somewhat less than thrilling to an adult. Being told *"You forgot again"* once may be acceptable, but being told three or four times in one minute is another story. In a commonly available video golf game, after a player makes a high score on a golf hole, the program returns with the suggestion to the player to *"Try another sport."* A golf professional that played this game took great offense to this advice and walked away. Would Tiger Woods appreciate this kind of suggestion? A person may disagree with patronizing conclusions, so why risk the offense?

Punishment and humor. Until an optimal computer personality is developed, messages should remain factual and informative, and should not attempt humor or punishment. Humor is a transitory and changeable thing. What is funny today may not be funny tomorrow, and what is funny to some may not be to others. Punishment is never a desirable way to force a change in behavior, especially among adults.

Messages

Messages are communications provided on the screen to the screen viewer. Several different types of messages exist, and they may be displayed in different forms and locations. A message should possess the proper tone and style and be consistent within itself and with other messages.

Screen messages fall into two broad categories: system and instructional. *System* messages are generated by the system to keep the user informed of the system's state and activities. They are customarily presented within message boxes. They reflect the system state, as it exists at that moment in time. *Instructional* messages, sometimes referred to as *prompting* messages, are messages that tell the user how to work with, or complete, the screen displayed. They may be provided in messages boxes and also within the screen itself.

System messages. System messages are of several types, each reflecting a different purpose. The various platforms have developed standard message boxes, with standard components, for these different types. Message box elements include a standard icon to assist in fast recognition of message kind, the message itself, and standard command buttons. The types of message boxes in Microsoft Windows are illustrated in Figures 8.1, 8.2, and 8.3.

Common message types are:

Status messages. A status message is used for providing information concerning the progress of a lengthy operation. It usually contains a progress indicator and a short message describing the kind of operation being performed. It typically only possesses a *Cancel* button, to stop the operation being performed. *Pause* and *Resume* buttons may also be included, if desired.

Informational messages. Informational messages, also called *notification* messages, provide information about the state of the system when it is not immediately obvious to the user. They may confirm that non-obvious processing is taking place or is completed. They may also be used to provide intermediate feedback when normal feedback is delayed. This kind of message is usually identified by an "I" icon to the left of the message. In Microsoft Windows "I" is in a balloon. No user actions are normally necessary with these kinds of messages, although confirmation that the message has been seen can be requested. A Microsoft Windows informational message box is illustrated in Figure 8.1

Warning messages. Warning messages call attention to a situation that may be undesirable. They are usually identified by an "!" icon to the left of the message. The user must determine whether the situation is in fact a problem and may be asked to advise the system whether or not to proceed. A deletion request by a user is an action that commonly generates a warning message. When a user requests a deletion, a message asking for confirmation of the deletion is usually presented. A warning message can also be used for field edit error messages. A Microsoft Windows warning message box is illustrated in Figure 8.2

Figure 8.1 Informational message box from Microsoft Windows with icon, text, and button.

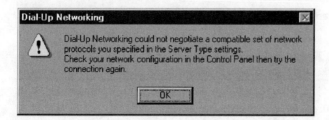

Figure 8.2 Warning message box from Microsoft Windows with icon, text, and button.

Figure 8.3   Critical message box from Microsoft Windows with icon, text, and button.

Critical messages. Critical messages, sometimes called *action* messages, call attention to conditions that require a user action before the system can proceed. A message describing an erroneous situation is usually presented as a critical message. Some inconsistency currently exists in the icons used to designate this kind of message. Some products use a "Do Not" symbol while others use a "Stop" sign. An X in a circle is used by Microsoft Windows. Additionally, one platform provides the option of using a "?" icon if the user's attention to the problem may not be immediately needed (for example, Printer is out of paper). Critical messages require a user action to continue. A Microsoft Windows critical message box is illustrated in Figure 8.3.

Question messages. Question messages are another kind of message type sometimes seen. A question message asks a question and offers a choice of options for selection. It is designated by a "?" icon preceding the message text. This type may be used when there is a question to be asked and the message does not appear to be suited to the above types. Before using a question message, remember that one platform uses the "?" icon for certain kinds of critical messages. Also, Microsoft Windows no longer recommends the "?" icon because of possible confusion with help dialogs.

Messages that are too generic or poorly written frustrate users, increase support costs, and ultimately reflect poorly on the quality of the product. Therefore, it is worthwhile to design effective message boxes. It is even better to avoid creating situations that require displaying such a message. For example, if the user does not have sufficient disk space to perform an operation, check for available disk space before the user attempts the operation and disable the command if necessary. A balloon tip or status bar message can be used to notify the user about why the command is unavailable.

MYTH   **If the users need an explanation they'll always read the documentation.**

Writing Message Box Text

- Title bar:
  — Clearly identify the source of the message.
    • The name of the object to which it refers.
    • The name of the application to which it refers.

- — Do not include an indication of message type.
- — Use mixed case in the headline style.
- Message box:
  - — Provide a clear and concise description of the condition causing the message box to be displayed.
    - Use complete sentences with ending punctuation.
    - State the problem, its probable cause (if known), and what the user can do about it.
    - Avoid contractions.
    - Avoid technical jargon and system-oriented information.
    - Provide only as much background information as necessary for the message to be understood.
    - Show only one message box about the cause of condition in a single message.
    - Make the solution an option offered in the message.
    - Avoid multistep solutions.
    - Use consistent words and phrasing for similar situations.
    - Use the word "please" conservatively.
  - — Do not exceed two or three lines.
  - — Include the relevant icon identifying the type of message to the left of the text.
  - — Center the message text in window.

Microsoft recommends these message box guidelines.

Title Bar Text

Clearly identify the source of the message in the message box title bar. This may be the name of the object to which it refers, or the name of the application to which it refers. A clear title is particularly important in the Windows multitasking environment because message boxes that appear might not always be the result of current user interaction. In addition, because objects supported by different applications can be embedded in the same document, different application code may be running when the user activates the object for editing. Therefore, the title of a message box plays a vital role in communicating the source of a message.

Do not include in the title an indication of message type. (*Warning* or *caution*, for example.) The icon contained within the message box conveys the nature of the message. Never include the word "error" in the title, for reasons previously mentioned. Use mixed case in the headline style to present the message box title.

Message Box Text

Provide a clear and concise description of the condition causing the message box to be displayed, in terminology the user understands. Use complete sentences with ending punctuation. State the problem, its probable cause (if known), and what the user can do about it, no matter how obvious the solution. To aid user comprehension, avoid contractions, technical jargon, and system-oriented information.

Provide only as much background information as necessary for the message to be understood. To supplement the amount of information in the message box text, include a *Help* button to access more complete descriptive information.

Make messages as specific as possible. Show only one message box regarding a condition in a single message; avoid combining two or more conditions in a single message. For example, if something cannot be done for several reasons, provide a specific message describing each reason.

Make the solution an option offered in the message. For example, if an object such as a string of text will not fit within a certain boundary, and another boundary is available within which it will fit, provide the option to switch to the larger boundary. Do not simply say "The text will not fit."

Avoid multistep solutions. People have difficulty remembering more than two or three simple steps after a message box closes. If multiple steps are necessary, provide general instructions or add a Help button that displays a relevant Help topic. Always present the steps in the order they should be completed. Use consistent words and phrasing for similar situations.

Use the word *please* conservatively. Overuse will diminish its effectiveness. Consider using it in the following situations:

- When the user is asked to wait while the program completes an action.

- When the user is asked to retype information that is required before the user can continue.

- When the user is inconvenienced in some other way.

Do not exceed two or three lines of text. Include the relevant icon identifying the type of message to the left of the text, and center the message text in window.

Message Box Controls

- Command buttons:
  - If a message requires no choices to be made but only acknowledgment:
    - Include an *OK* button.
  - If a message requires a choice be made, provide a command button for each option:
    - Include *OK* and *Cancel* buttons only when the user has the option of continuing or stopping the action.
    - Include *Yes* and *No* buttons when the user must decide how to continue.
    - If these choices are too ambiguous, label the command buttons with the names of specific actions.
  - If a message allows initiation of an action to correct the situation described:
    - Include a properly labeled button initiating the corrective action.
  - If a message describes an interrupted process whose state cannot be restored:
    - Provide a *Stop* button.
  - If a message offers an opportunity to cancel a process as well as to perform or not perform an action:
    - Provide a *Cancel* button.
  - If more details about a message topic must be presented:
    - Provide a *Help* button.
  - Designate the most frequent or least destructive option as the default.

— Display a message box only when the window of an application is active.
— Display only one message box for a specific condition.
- Close box:
— Enable the title bar *Close* box only if the message includes a Cancel button.

Command buttons. A user response to a message box is usually accomplished though a command button. The kind, or kinds, of command buttons included depend upon the reason the message box was presented. If a message requires no user choices to be made but only an acknowledgment of the message, include an *OK* button. If the message requires the user to make a choice, include a command button for each option. Include *OK* and *Cancel* buttons only when the user has the option of continuing or stopping the action. Use *Yes* and *No* buttons when the user must decide how to continue. If these choices are too ambiguous, label the command buttons with the names of specific actions to be performed, *Save* and *Delete* for example.

If a message allows initiation of a user action to correct the situation described, include a properly labeled button initiating the corrective action. If, for example, the message indicates that the user must switch to another application window to take corrective action, include a button that opens that application window. Be sure to clearly label the button and the results the user can expect from pressing it. If a message describes an interrupted process whose state cannot be restored, provide a *Stop* button. (Cancel implies restoring the state of the process or task that initiated the message.) If a message offers an opportunity to cancel a process as well as to perform or not perform an action, provide a *Cancel* button. Clearly label the button and the results the user can expect from selecting it. If more details about a message topic must be presented, provide a *Help* button. This enables the message text to be succinctly presented.

Designate the most frequent or least destructive command option as the default. Because a message box disrupts the user's current task, it is best to display a message box only when the window of the application to which the message refers is active. If the application's window is not active, use the application's button entry on the taskbar to alert the user. After the user activates the application, the message box can be displayed. Display only one message box for a specific condition. Displaying a sequential set of message boxes tends to confuse users.

Command buttons allow the message box interaction to be simple and efficient. If other types of controls are considered, always be aware of the potential increase in interface complexity.

Close box. Enable the title bar *Close* box only if the message includes a Cancel button. To leave it available in other situations can confuse users.

Message Location

- Use the message line for messages that must not interfere with screen information.
- Pop-up windows may be used for all kinds of messages, if available.
- Pop-up windows should always be used for critical messages.

Messages may also be displayed either in the message line as well as within pop-up windows, with pop-up windows being recommended location. All critical messages should be displayed in a pop-up window. A research study compared locating messages in pop-up windows with messages presented in permanently displayed fixed locations, such as at the screen's bottom or top. The study found pop-up windows were detected more often, and faster, than those permanently affixed in standard locations on the screen.

Other Message Considerations

- Abbreviated, more concise versions of messages should be available.
- Something that must be remembered should be at the beginning of the text.
- Do not include code numbers with messages.

Abbreviated versions. People are impatient with uninformative or redundant computer messages. A problem, however, is that the degree of computer-to-person message redundancy depends on the person's experience with the system. And it may vary with different parts of a system. So the availability of abbreviated and detailed messages allows the tailoring of the system to the needs of each user. During system training and early implementation stages, detailed versions can be used. Individuals can switch to abbreviated versions as their familiarity with the system increases. People using abbreviated messages should, however, be able to request detailed messages at any time.

Important at beginning of text. One can remember something longer if it appears at the beginning of a message. Items in the middle of a message are hardest to remember.

Code numbers. Messages that begin with a strange code number do not meet the user's needs. A code number, if needed at all, is only necessary after reading the message and should, therefore, be placed in parentheses at the end of the message.

Instructional Messages

- Provide instructional information at the depth of detail needed by the user.
- Locate it at strategic positions on the screen.
- Display it in a manner that visually differentiates it from other screen elements.
- In writing, follow all relevant writing guidelines for words, sentences, and messages.

The second categories of messages, *instructional* or prompting messages, are guidance messages that tell the user how to work with, or complete, the screen displayed. They may be permanently affixed to a screen, or they may appear as the result of a help request.

Depth of detail. Instructional messages are of most benefit to the novice or casual system user. Instructions for these kinds of users must be more detailed than for experienced users. Experienced users usually require only cryptic reminders. To balance the needs of a wide range of users with varying experience levels, accessing instructions through a *Help* function is the best solution.

Location. Locate instructions at strategic points on screens. They should be placed at spots just preceding the controls or elements to which they apply. Never, however, place an instruction on one screen that applies to elements on a following screen. They will not be remembered.

Visual differentiation. Display instructions in a manner that visually differentiates them from all other screen elements. This will allow them to be easily ignored by users who do not need them.

Writing. In writing instructions, follow all relevant writing guidelines recently described for words, sentences, and messages. Also refer to Table 8.2 for the proper terms to use when interacting with a screen control. Guidelines for instruction presentation on a screen were also outlined in Step 3 "Understand the Principles of Good Screen Design."

In conclusion, the following "error message" was recently encountered using the Web site of a popular cable TV channel:

> ERROR!
> PLEASE HIT YOUR BACK BUTTON AND ENTER A SEARCH.

In this brief 10-word message, the message writer managed to use three nonrecommended words (error, hit, and enter). Wouldn't the following have been much more agreeable?

> THE SEARCH FIELD DID NOT CONTAIN AN ENTRY.
> PLEASE CLICK THE BACK BUTTON AND TYPE A SEARCH VALUE.

The original message writer gets one point for including *Please*, however.

Table 8.2   Instructional Interaction Terms

TO INTERACT WITH THIS CONTROL:	USE THIS TERM:
For a command button, to activate.	Click
For a text box, to type or paste information.	Type
For a list box, to select an item, or items.	Select
To either type or select an option.	Enter

For a check box:
    To add a component.
    To clear a component.
	
	Select
	Clear

For a radio button.	Select
For a slider interaction.	Move
For a tab interaction.	Click

Text

Text, by a very general definition, is any textual element that appears on a screen, including field captions, headings, words, sentences, messages, and instructions. Text, in the following discussion, refers to *body* text, a large compilation of words whose smallest element is a paragraph and whose maximum length is unlimited, its size being governed by the reason for its existence.

Presenting Text

- Fonts:
  - — Use plain and simple fonts.
  - — Choose a minimum point size of 12 to 14.
  - — Use proportional fonts.
- Width:
  - — Include no more than 40 to 60 characters on each line.
    - • A double column of 30 to 35 characters separated by five spaces is also acceptable.
  - — Do not right-justify.
  - Do not hyphenate words.
- Content:
  - — Use headings to introduce a new topic.
  - — Separate paragraphs by at least one blank line.
  - — Start a fresh topic on a new page.
  - — Use lists to present facts.
  - — Emphasize important things by:
    - • Positioning.
    - • Boxes.
    - • Bold typefaces.
    - • Indented margins.
- Miscellaneous:
  - — Use paging (not scrolling).
  - — Provide a screen design philosophy consistent with other parts of the system.

Fonts. Fonts chosen for text should be plain and simple and of adequate size for easy reading, either 12 or 14 points. Proportional spacing (width governed by actual letter size, when an *l* is narrower than an *m*) is preferred to nonproportional spacing.

Width. A typical screen is a little too wide for comfortable reading of text. It is difficult for the eye to keep its place as it moves from the end of one line to the beginning of the next line. Studies find that a line of text should contain no more than 40 to 60 characters, or be confined to 1.5 lowercase alphabets or 39 characters. For greater screen efficiency, consider using two columns of text, each about 30 or 35 characters wide. Confine double-columns to one screen of information, however. Never require scrolling up and down multiple times to read all the text.

Studies also find that non-right-justified (or ragged-right edge) text lines are just as legible as justified text lines. Large spaces left in right-justified text interrupt eye movement and impede reading. The reading speed of right-justified text was actually found to be 8 to 10 percent slower than non-right-justified text in one study. Non-right-justified text has another advantage in that word hyphenation is not required. Experts also say that non-right-justified text creates more visual interest, and is best for very narrow columns of text. Full left- and right-justification, may be considered for long works that require continuous reading and concentration, such as long text, newspapers, and novels.

Content. Headings to introduce new topics provide breaks or pause points for the reader. They provide obvious closure points. Starting new topics on new pages reinforces the needed breaks. Separating paragraphs by a blank line will result in more cohesive groupings and alleviate the impression of a dense screen.

Use lists to present facts. Lists are convenient, simple, and uncluttered and can effectively break up long strings of text. Designate items in a list with a "bullet" or other simple symbol. Emphasize important points by placing them in unusual places, drawing boxes around them, using bold typefaces, or providing indented left and right margins. In addition to their emphasizing capabilities, they also make the screen more visually interesting.

Miscellaneous. Paging through screens, rather than scrolling, has been found to yield better performance and to be preferred by many system users, as was discussed in Step 3. A severe disadvantage of scrolling for novices is loss of orientation. While experts can handle scrolling, the best choice if all users are considered is paging.

If scrolling is going to be used, the preferred approach is *telescoping*, in which the window moves around the data. This method is more natural and causes fewer errors than the *microscope* approach, in which the data appears to move under a fixed viewing window. These concepts were also discussed in Step 3.

MAXIM   **Clear communication is not shouting VERY, VERY LOUD.**

Writing Text

- Sentences and paragraphs:
  — Use short sentences composed of familiar, personal words.
    • Cut the excess words.
    • Try to keep the number of words in a sentence to 20 or less.
  — Cut the number of sentences.
  — Use separate sentences for separate ideas.
  — Keep the paragraphs short.
  — Restrict a paragraph to only one idea.
- Style:
  — Use the active writing style.
  — Use the personal writing style, if appropriate.

— Write as you talk.
— Use subjective opinion.
— Use specific examples.
— Read it out loud.

Sentences and paragraphs. Simple words and short sentences are the cornerstones of good writing. As mentioned above, research indicates that sentences over 20 words in length cause a loss in reading comprehension with each additional sentence word. Long sentences often result from trying to express more than one idea in the sentence, or from using unnecessary words. Table 8.3, derived from Microsoft (2001), lists some common "wordy" phrases to avoid and their replacement words. It also describes some redundant word pairings to avoid. These redundancies are also known as *baby puppies,* a concept that was graciously explained to me by the editor of my first book many years ago. Use separate sentences for separate ideas. Place multiple items in a list format, and delete all unnecessary words. Short paragraphs are less threatening to the user and more frequently read. They also provide visual breaking points in a screen or page.

Style. The style chosen should reflect the needs and characteristics of the user. The style will affect the readability and comprehensibility of the text. The active writing style is easier to read and understand. It almost always uses fewer words and leaves no unanswered questions (contrast the passive "The customer name should be typed" with the active "Type the customer name"). The personal style, the use of "you" and "I" ("Now you must press the Enter key"), keeps the writing active, makes writing directly relevant to the reader, and is more interesting. Materials read by a wide variety of people for informational purposes only, however, should not use the personal style.

Write in the way you would say something to the reader. Also, use subjective opinion ("This screen is not used very often") to reinforce the users' understanding of what they are reading. It does not tell anything specific, but reinforces facts already read or about to be read. Do not overuse subjective opinion, however, and make sure it is correct. Overuse makes facts harder to find, and an incorrect opinion casts suspicion on all the facts being presented.

The best way to explain a general rule is to show how it applies through examples. Examples should be short, relevant, and easy for the reader to relate to. They should also be made visually different from the main text, either through indentation, boxing, or some other technique. Finally, read what you have written out loud to yourself. If it sounds wordy, stilted, or difficult, it will sound this way to the reader, too. Rewrite it.

Window Title

- All windows must have a title located in a centered position at the top.
  — Exception: Windows containing messages.
- Clearly and concisely describe the purpose of the window.
- Spell it out fully using an uppercase or mixed-case font.

- If title truncation is necessary, truncate it from right to left.
- If presented above a menu bar, display it with a background that contrasts with the bar.

The window title should be positioned at the top center and fully spelled out using either uppercase letters or mixed case in the headline style. Using an uppercase font will give it the needed moderate emphasis, aiding in setting it off from the screen body (IBM's SAA CUA and Microsoft's Windows guidelines display the title, like all screen components, in mixed-case letters). Windows containing messages, however, need not have a title. The title should clearly and concisely describe the screen's purpose. If the window appears as a result of a previous selection, the title should clearly reflect the wording of the selection made to retrieve it. For small windows, where title truncation is necessary, truncate from right to left.

If the title appears above the menu bar, the title's background should contrast with that of the bar. A recommendation is to use the same background color and caption color as the screen body. A title can always be identified by its topmost location on the screen, so using a color different from other screen components may add to visual confusion.

Conventions

- Establish conventions for referring to:
  — Individual keyboard keys.
  — Keys to be pressed at the same time.
  — Field captions.
  — Names supplied by users or defined by the system.
  — Commands and actions.

Table 8.3 Wordy Phrases and Word Redundancies

INSTEAD OF THIS PHRASE:	SAY THIS:	WORD REDUNDANCIES
By means of	By	Surrounding Environment
For the purposes of	For	Absolutely Complete
In many cases	Often	Exactly identical
In the event that	If	Repeat again
Is able to	Can	Final conclusion
The way in which	The way, how	Knowledge and awareness
In order to	To	Each and every
Prior to	Before	Complete overview
Is required to	Must	Advance planning
		Full and complete

Derived from Microsoft (2001)

In messages and text it is often necessary to refer to keyboard keys, field captions, filenames, commands, or actions. These components should be described in the same manner whenever referenced. Keyboard keys should always be referenced as they are inscribed on the keyboard. (They usually appear in a mixed-case text format.) A useful convention for referring to keys that should be pressed at the same time is a plus (+) sign between the key descriptions (Alt+F10). Names may be enclosed in quotes ("Pending").

Sequence Control Guidance

- Consider providing a guidance message telling how to continue at points in the dialog when:
  — A decision must be made.
  — A response needs to be made to continue.
- Consider indicating what control options exist at points in the dialog where several alternatives may be available.
- Permit these prompts to be turned on or off by the user.

Consider providing prompts telling the user how to continue when a decision and response must be made to continue. For example, it might be indicated that:

INFORMATION IS CURRENT THROUGH AUGUST 26, 2001.
PRESS ENTER TO CONTINUE.

Where several control options exist, consider providing a prompt such as:

PRESS S TO SAVE, D TO DELETE, OR P TO PRINT.
TYPE C TO CREATE A NEW FILE, OR E TO EDIT A NEW FILE: _

For experienced users, these kinds of prompts can become visual noise. Allow users to turn them on or off as needed.

Text for Web Pages

Text for Web pages will generally follow the aforementioned guidelines for words, sentences, messages, instructions, and text. The unique characteristics of the Web, however, require a separate set of supplemental guidelines for several Web topics, including, word usage, error message presentation, and text, heading, and title writing. Additionally, the writing of links must be addressed. This section focuses on these topics.

Words

- Minimize the use of words that call attention to the Web.

Generally, avoid using words that are specific to the Web. A few Web-specific terms are "This Web site," "Click here," and "Follow this link." A good test of this guideline is to print out a page, read it, and see if it makes as much sense on paper as it does on the screen.

Error Messages

- Provide helpful error messages for:
  — Incomplete or incorrectly keyed, entered, or selected data.
  — Requests for documents that do not exist or cannot be found.
- Redisplay a message on the page to which it relates.
- Present them in a visually distinctive and noticeable manner.

Provide helpful error messages for data that has been incompletely or incorrectly entered. Also provide messages for requested documents that do not exist or cannot be found. In a graphical interface, an error message is displayed in a message box overlaying the error-causing screen. The underlying screen is visible and can be viewed in conjunction with the error-correction instructions. The message box remains displayed until the user acknowledges its presence. In Web page design, displaying the error message on a separate page is accomplished at the expense of the error-causing page disappearing from view. Human memory being what it is, a possible solution now exists to a problem whose details are now vague. Problem resolution typically involves paging back and forth between the error message and the related Web page, an inefficient operation.

The alternate solution is to present the error message on the page where the error exists. This is the recommended choice. Context is maintained, and both elements can be viewed in fairly close proximity to each other. The error message must be displayed in a visually distinctive manner as close to the problem as possible. Visual distinctiveness can be achieved through displaying the message in a larger, bolder, and distinctive font. The user's attention will probably be directed to the part of the page on which actions can be performed, so the message should be made as obvious as possible. A message in the same font style as the page will be less likely to be noticed.

Keep in mind, however, that it is better to prevent errors than handle them. This topic will be addressed next in Step 9 "Provide Effective Feedback and Guidance and Assistance."

Instructions

- Do not use phrasing that indicates a certain page order or flow.
- Explain where "Up" leads too.
- Phrase them in a browser-independent manner.
- Minimize "Click here" instructions.
  — Say "Select this link."

Do not use phrasing that indicates a certain page order or flow. How the visitor arrived at the site is unknown. Do not use "Return to" instructions; it cannot be assumed that the term is meaningful in the new context. Describe where an "Up" button leads, where the user will go, and what will be found there. Make sure instructions are detailed enough to be understood without being specific to one browser version or brand. Don't use the phrase "click here." Some users will not use a mouse and may feel alienated. A more proper instruction for all users is "Select this link."

Text

Web page text must be legible and properly written for the medium.

Presentation

- Provide text that contrasts highly with the background.

Text legibility can be a severe problem if insufficient contrast exists between the text and its background. Patterned backgrounds can severely impact legibility, as do many colors. A common characteristic of the best Web sites is they contain text highly contrasting with its background. Overall, the best combination is black text on a white background.

Writing

- Style:
  — Use a style reflecting the needs of the site users.
  — Write objectively.
  — Use the inverted pyramid organization.
  — Be concise, using only about half the number of words of conventional text.
  — Each paragraph should:
    • Be short.
    • Contain only one main idea.
- Links:
  — Minimize within-text links.
  — Place them at the beginning or end of paragraphs or sections of text.
- Scanning:
  — Make text scannable by using:
    • Bulleted listings.
    • Tables.
    • Headings.
    • Bold type.
- Testing:
  — Test for legibility and readability.

Style. Web users can be characterized as being multicultural with multi-interests, multi-needs, and multi-just about everything else. Writing styles will vary, depending on the needs of the target audience. Establishing the proper style depends on who the viewers are, what they know, where they normally get similar information, and the nature of the material. A business application will be written differently than an entertainment site. A product sales site differently than that of a business application or entertainment site. Writing style depends less on medium differences than on answers to the above questions. Writing style, then, should reflect the tone of similar copy published for the target audience in other media. Generally speaking, writing that strays too far from what is conventional for the target audience draws attention to itself at the expense of content. If Web writing does have one quality that sets it apart from print writing, however, it is its informality. Users seem to prefer a more informal writing style.

Users also prefer writing, says research, that is *objective* rather than filled with overly hyped or boastful promotional claims or sprinkled with "marketese-isms." Subjective adjectives, such as outstanding, experienced, reliable, and dynamic, have been shown to inspire mistrust on the part of the user, and also to increase the user's cognitive load as the "irrelevant stuff " must first be comprehended and then discarded. So, always be objective in writing style.

The *inverted pyramid* organization starts with a conclusion or summary of key points and follows with the supporting details or background information. This organization scheme, also commonly found in newspaper articles, lets the user quickly identify an article's content and assess whether continued reading is warranted.

Be *concise,* succinct, and to the point, using only about half the number of words of conventional text. Pack the maximum meaning into minimum text, so users will get the message in the shortest possible time. Keep the writing tight and nonverbose. Use short sentences and the shortest form of a word or an idea. Minimize "fluff," useless, and inessential information, or words that do not add meaning to what is being said. Avoid words with three syllables. Research shows that concise and short writing reduces the user's cognitive load, resulting in faster and more efficient information processing.

Each *paragraph* should contain only one main thought. Make the paragraph's intentions plain in the first sentence. For additional ideas or points use additional paragraphs. Users tend to skip over more than one point or ideas in a paragraph as they scan. Keep paragraphs short, no longer than five sentences encompassing no more than 75 words. Provide clear paragraph breaks.

Links. Too many links embedded within text can disrupt reading continuity and content understanding. Minimize within-text links and, where possible and appropriate, place them at the beginning or end of paragraphs or sections of text.

Scanning. Make texts more scannable by using bulleted listings, tables, headings, and bold type. Key information will be found faster.

Testing. Test for readability. Print out text to carefully proofread it; errors will be more easily caught. Also, write and edit with international readers in mind.

Links

- Create wording that makes links:
  - Descriptive.
  - Differentiable.
  - Predictive.
- Create concisely worded links.
- Integrate embedded links smoothly into the text.
  - Make only a few words the active link.
  - Do not spread links over two lines.
- Standalone links should not exceed one sentence in length.

Descriptive, differentiable, and predictive. The success of a link is determined by how well the user can predict where the link leads. Link differentiability and descriptiveness aids prediction. Understanding of a link's purpose reduces disorientation, because irrelevant links are less likely to be followed. Link text should clearly communicate the link's nature and purpose, and contain enough information to let users decide whether or not to follow it. The links of the best-rated Web sites are textual and descriptive, letting the user know what to expect

Concise. Create links that are brief and to the point, avoiding wordiness. Generally, a link has to strike a proper balance between enough words to make it descriptive and differentiable, and few enough words to make it most easily readable and legible. Underlining does slow reading of text.

Embedded links. Write text containing embedded links as if there were no links in it. The links must integrate smoothly and continuously into the text. Choose the most relevant words or phrase as the active link. Embedded links must not be continued over two lines. They may be mistaken for two links.

Standalone links. Standalone links should not exceed one sentence in length.

Examples of proper link writing are shown in Figure 8.4. Placing links in headings always make them easier to find.

POOR >   <u>Paragraphs with embedded links are sometimes useful for a variety of reasons.</u>

BETTER >   Paragraphs with <u>embedded links</u> are sometimes useful for a variety of reasons.

BEST >   <u>**Embedded Links**</u>

Paragraphs with embedded links are sometimes useful for a variety of reasons.

Figure 8.4   Writing links.

Link Titles

- Provide link titles that describe:
  — The name of site the link will lead to (if different from current site).
  — The name of subsection the link will lead to (if staying within current site).
  — The kind of information to be found at the destination.
  — How the linked information relates to the anchor link and the current page content.
  — How large the linked information is.
  — Warnings about possible problems to be encountered at the other end.
- Restrict them to no more than 60 characters.

Some Web browsers have added the ability to pop up a short explanation of a link before the user selects the link. This explanation, called a *link title*, gives a more thorough preview of where the link goes, greatly enhancing predictiveness. Types of information that may be included in a link title are summarized above. Link titles should be reserved for supplementary information to help clarify the link's purpose. They do not eliminate need for a link and its surrounding text to be understandable. Generally, a link title should not exceed 60 characters in length.

Page Title

- Provide a page title:
  — That possesses meaningful keywords.
  — Whose first word is its most important descriptor.
  — That makes sense when viewed completely out of context.
  — That is different from other page titles.
  — Is written in mixed case using the headline style.
- Do not highlight keywords.

Page titles must be carefully designed to provide useful information. They should contain as many keywords as possible. While a title may contain 60 characters, ensure that the first 40 characters adequately describe the page topic. Titles are often truncated in navigation menus and by search facilities. The title's first word should be its most important descriptor. This word is most easily noticed in the scanning of long lists. Never begin a title with a generic term such as "Welcome" or "Page," or with an article such as "The." Give different titles to different pages. If page titles addressing the same topic must begin with same word, end the title with words that explain the differences between them.

A title must also make sense when viewed completely out of context, with no supporting content or arrayed in a listing with other titles. Write titles in mixed case using the headline style. Do not use highlighting for keywords. A single keyword might be emphasized through putting it in upper case, but be conservative in this regard. Never use upper case for the first word in a title; its position is sufficient emphasis.

Headings and Headlines

- Create meaningful headings and headlines that quickly communicate the content of what follows.
  - Make the first word an important information-carrying one.
  - Skip leading articles (the and a).
- Create meaningful subheadings to break up large blocks of text.

Headings and headlines are often scanned to find screen content of interest. Their wording must provide a strong clue as to the content they relate to. Headings should be descriptive and straightforward. Headlines must often be made sense of out of context. Clever, cute or funny headlines or headings, or teasers to entice, should be avoided. A study has found that users prefer straightforward headlines to funny or cute ones. The first word in a heading or headline is the most important information-carrying one. Make it as distinctive as possible, especially if the heading or headline will be contained in an alphabetized listing. Skip leading articles (the and a) to also achieve distinctiveness. Distinctive first words will be easier to find in scanning. Use subheads to break up large blocks of text for visual appeal and ease of scanning.

Provide Effective Feedback and Guidance and Assistance

All user actions must be reacted to in some way. Feedback, as has been noted, shapes human performance. Without it, we cannot learn. To aid user learning and avoid frustration, it is also important to provide thorough and timely guidance and assistance. In this step, the following feedback topics are addressed:

- Acceptable response times.
- Dealing with time delays.
- Blinking for attention.
- The use of sound.

This will be followed by a review of guidance and assistance, including:

- Preventing errors and problem management.
- The types of guidance and assistance to provide.
  - Instructions or prompting.
  - A Help facility.
  - Contextual Help.
  - Task-oriented Help.
  - Reference Help.
  - Wizards.
  - Hints or tips.

Providing the Proper Feedback

To be effective, feedback to the user for an action must occur within certain time limits. Excessive delays can be annoying, interrupt concentration, cause the user concern, and impair productivity as one's memory limitations begin to be tested.

Response Time

- System responsiveness should match the speed and flow of human thought processes.
    - If continuity of thinking is required and information must be remembered throughout several responses, response time should be less than one or two seconds.
    - If human task closures exist, high levels of concentration are not necessary, and moderate short-term memory requirements are imposed; response times of 2 to 4 seconds are acceptable.
    - If major task closures exist, minimal short-term memory requirements are imposed; responses within 4 to 15 seconds are acceptable.
    - When the user is free to do other things and return when convenient, response time can be greater than 15 seconds.
- Constant delays are preferable to variable delays.

What the ideal system response time is has been the subject of numerous studies. Unfortunately, there still does not exist definitive time or times that are acceptable under all conditions. What is clear is that dissatisfaction with response time is very dependent on user expectations. It is also clear that expectations can vary, depending on the task as well as the situation. The ideal condition is one in which a person perceives no delays. Generally, a response time is too long for a person when one *notices* that something is taking too long. The following paragraphs summarize some study conclusions and some tentative findings.

> **The optimum response time is dependent upon the task.** There is an optimum work pace that depends on the task being performed. Longer or shorter response times than the optimum lead to more errors. In general, response times should be geared to the user's short-term memory load and to the way he or she has grouped the activities being performed. Intense short-term memory loads necessitate short response times. While completing chunks of work at task closures, users can withstand longer response delays.
>
> The human *now*, or psychological present, is under 2 to 3 seconds. This is why continuity of thinking requires a response time within this limit. Research indicates that for many creative tasks, response times under one second, in the range of four-tenths to nine-tenths of a second, can yield dramatic increases in productivity, even greater in proportion to the decrease in response time. The probable reason is the elimination of restrictions caused by short-term memory limitations. For data entry tasks, research has found no advantages for having response times less than 1 second.

If human task closures exist, high levels of concentration are not necessary, and moderate short-term memory requirements are imposed; response times of two to four seconds are acceptable. If major task closures exist, minimal short-term memory requirements are imposed, and responses within 4 to 15 seconds are acceptable. As the response-time interval increases beyond 10 to 15 seconds, however, continuity of thought becomes increasingly difficult to maintain. It has been suggested that this happens because the sequence of actions stored in short-term memory becomes badly disrupted and must be reloaded.

The response time guidelines above, then, relate to the general tasks being performed. Their applicability to every situation can never be guaranteed.

Satisfaction with response time is a function of expectations. Expectations are based, in part, on past experiences. These experiences may be derived from working with a computer, from the world in general, or from the perceived complexity of the task the computer is performing. These expectations vary enormously across individuals and tasks.

Dissatisfaction with response time is a function of one's uncertainty about delay. The degree of frustration with delay may depend on such psychological factors as a person's uncertainty concerning how long the delay will be, the extent to which the actual delay contradicts those expectations, and what the person thinks is causing the delay. Such uncertainty concerning how long a wait there will be for a computer's response may in some cases be a greater source of annoyance and frustration than the delay itself.

People will change work habits to conform to response time. As response time increases, so does think time. People also work more carefully with longer response times because the time penalty for each error made increases. In some cases, more errors have been found with very short response times. This may not necessarily be bad if the errors are the result of trial-and-error learning that is enhanced by very fast response times.

Constant delays are preferable to variable delays. It is the variability of delays, not their length, that most frequently distresses people. From a consistency standpoint, a good rule of thumb is that response-time deviations should never exceed half the mean response time. For example, if the mean response time is 4 seconds, a 2-second deviation is permissible. Variations should range from 3 to 5 seconds. Variation should never exceed 20 percent, however, because lower response time variability has been found to yield better performance, but small variations may be tolerated.

More experienced people prefer shorter response times. People work faster as they gain experience, a fact that leads Shneiderman (1987) to conclude that it may be useful to let people set their own pace of interaction. He also suggests that in the absence of cost or technical feasibility constraints, people will eventually force response time to well under 1 second. In general, the longer people interact with a system, the less delay they will tolerate.

Very fast or slow response times can lead to symptoms of stress. There is a point at which a person can be overwhelmed by information presented more quickly than it can be comprehended. There is also some evidence indicating that when a system responds too quickly, there is subconscious pressure on users to respond quickly also, possibly threatening their overall comfort, increasing their blood pressure, or causing them to exhibit other signs of anxious behavior. Symptoms of job burnout have been reported after substantial reductions in response time.

Slow and variable response times have also been shown to lead to a significant build-up of mood disturbances and somatic discomfort over time, culminating in symptoms of work stress, including frustration, impatience, and irritation.

Web response time. Bouch, Kuchinsky, and Bhatti (2000) performed three related studies. Web pages were presented at preestablished delays ranging from 2 to 73 seconds. Delay was defined as the time between a page's request and its complete displaying on the screen. Test participants rated the response times with the following results:

- *High (Good):* Up to 5 seconds.
- *Average:* From 6 to 10 seconds.
- *Low (Poor):* Over 10 seconds.

In the second study, test participants were presented a button labeled "Increase Quality" and asked to press it when response time became unacceptable. The average button-pressing time was 8.6 seconds. In the third study, the Web pages were loaded incrementally, the banner first, the text second, and the graphics last. The test participants were much more tolerant of delays under these conditions. Response times up to 39 seconds were rated as "good," and response times over 56 seconds were rated as "poor."

Selvidge, Chaparro, and Bender (2000) studied the effect of downloading delays on user performance. For delays of 1, 30, and 60 seconds they examined task success, task efficiency, and participant frustration. They found that participants were less frustrated with the 1-second delay, but task success and efficiency were not affected by any of the response times. Ramsay, Barbesi, and Preece (1998) evaluated people's reactions to a Web page's quality in relation to downloading times ranging between 2 and 120 seconds. Pages with longer delays, over 41 seconds, were rated as less interesting and more difficult to scan.

In general, these studies seem to indicate that the same factors affecting optimum computer response times in general also operate in the world of the Web, although longer downloading times may be more readily accepted due to the graphical nature of the Web's content. Slower response times, from a practical standpoint, however, would appear to reduce the amount of work that can be performed, and probably lead to increased user frustration.

Dealing with Time Delays

- Button click acknowledgement:
  - Acknowledge all button clicks by visual or aural feedback within one-tenth of a second.

- Waits up to 10 seconds:
  - If an operation takes 10 seconds or less to complete, present a "busy" signal until the operation is complete.
    - Display, for example, an animated hourglass pointer.
- Waits of 10 seconds to 1 minute:
  - If an operation takes longer than 10 seconds to complete, display:
    - A rolling barber's pole or other large animated object.
    - Additionally, a progress indicator, percent complete message, or elapsed time message.
- Waits over 1 minute:
  - Present an estimate of the length of the wait.
  - Display a progress indicator, percent complete message, or elapsed time message.
  - When a long operation is completed, present an acknowledgment that it is completed.
    - A significantly changed screen appearance.
    - An auditory tone.
  - If an operation is very time-consuming:
    - Consider breaking the operation into subtasks and providing progress indicators for each subtask.
    - Allow users to start a new activity while waiting.
- Long, invisible operations:
  - When an operation not visible to the user is completed, present an acknowledgment that it is completed.
    - A message.
    - An auditory tone.
- Progress indicator:
  - A long rectangular bar that is initially empty but filled as the operation proceeds.
    - Dynamically fill the bar.
    - Fill it with a color or shade of gray.
    - Fill it from left to right or bottom to top.
- Percent complete message:
  - A message that indicates the percent of the operation that is complete.
  - Useful if a progress indicator takes too long to update.
- Elapsed time message:
  - A message that shows the amount of elapsed time that the operation is consuming.
  - Useful if:
    - The length of the operation is not known in advance.
    - A particular part of the operation will take an unusually long time to complete.
- Web page downloads:
  - For pages requiring download times greater that 5 seconds, give the user something to do while waiting.
    - Quickly present, at the top of the downloading page, some text or links.

Elapsing time is in the eye of the beholder. What is important is *perceived* passing time, not actual time as measured by a clock. Dealing with time delays involves providing feedback that the system is truly working, and that the system's processing will be completed at some foreseeable and predictable time. Dealing with time delays also involves diverting people's attention away from a delay by engaging them in some meaningful interim activities.

Button clicks. Acknowledge all button clicks by visual or aural feedback within one-tenth of a second. This assures the user that a requested action has been received by the system.

Waits up to 10 seconds. If an operation takes 10 seconds or less to complete, present a "busy" signal until the operation is finished. An hourglass pointer is the customary signal. A "Please wait..." message can be presented to indicate that more complex processing is occurring or has been delayed. When the process is finished, provide an indication that the user may precede.

Waits of 10 seconds to 1 minute. If an operation takes longer than 10 seconds to complete, display a rolling barber's pole or other large animated object. Additionally, present a progress indicator, percent complete message, or elapsed time message. When the process is finished, provide an indication that the user may precede.

Waits over 1 minute. For waits exceeding one minute, present an estimate of the length of the wait. If the length is unknown, an educated guess is better than a "Don't Know" or no estimate at all. A time estimate allows the user to decide what to do next—wait, go to lunch, or start some other task. For these waits, display a progress indicator, percent complete message, or elapsed time message. If an operation is very time-consuming, consider breaking the operation into subtasks and providing progress indicators for each subtask. Also allow users to start a new activity while waiting so a delay will not be unproductive. Also, consider offering engaging text messages to keep users informed and entertained while they are waiting for process completion. Provide a clear indication of when the process is finished, significantly changing the screen's appearance so the change may be recognized from some distance away. Also include an auditory tone to attract the user's attention back to the screen.

Long, invisible operations. When a long operation not visible to the user is completed, present an acknowledgment message that it is completed. For example, upon completion of a search with no positive results, "Search complete, Jones not found" might be displayed. Also provide an auditory signal, since the user's attention may be directed to another part of the screen, or entirely away from the screen.

Progress indicator. A *progress indicator* is a long rectangular bar that is initially empty but filled as the operation proceeds. Dynamically fill the bar with a color or shade of gray. Fill all bars from left to right or bottom to top. A progress indicator is illustrated in Figure 9.1.

Percent complete message. A *percent complete* message provides an indication of the percent of an operation that is complete. It is useful if a progress indicator takes too long to update. An indication of the percentage of processing that has been ac-

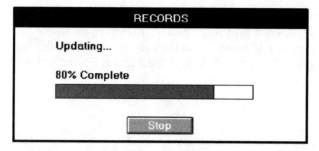

Figure 9.1   Processing progress indicator.

complished can also be given through a message such as "22 of 27 transactions have been processed."

Elapsed time message. An *elapsed time* message shows the amount of elapsed time the operation has consumed. It is useful if the length of the operation is not known in advance, or if a particular part of the operation will take an unusually long time to complete.

Web page downloads. For pages requiring download times greater that 5 seconds, give the user something to do while waiting. Quickly provide at the downloading page top some text to hold one's interest, or some links to act upon. These diversions will reduce impatience while images load.

Blinking for Attention

- Attract attention by flashing an indicator when an application is inactive but must display a message to the user.
  — If a window, flash the title bar.
  — If minimized, flash its icon.
- To provide an additional message indication, also provide an auditory signal (one or two beeps).
  — Very useful if:
    • The window or icon is hidden.
    • The user's attention is frequently directed away from the screen.
- Display the message:
  — When the application is activated.
  — When requested by the user.

Attention. Flashing an element on the screen will usually capture a person's attention. If a window is displayed on the screen, flash its title bar. If the window is minimized, flash its icon.

Auditory signal. To provide an additional indication that a message is waiting, also provide an auditory signal (one or two beeps). This will be useful if the window or icon is hidden or the user's attention is frequently directed away from the screen.

Message display. Display the message when an application is activated or when the user requests it. Displaying it when the user requests it preserves the user's control over the work environment and ensures that the message is not accidentally closed through an inadvertent key press. Finally, blinking is annoying to many people, so it should not be overused on a screen.

Use of Sound

- Always use in conjunction with a visual indication.
- Use no more than six different tones.
  — Ensure that people can discriminate among them.
- Do not use:
  — Jingles or tunes.
  — Loud signals.
- Use tones consistently.
  — Provide unique but similar tones for similar situations.
- Provide signal frequencies between 500 and 1,000 Hz.
- Allow the user to adjust the volume or turn the sound off altogether.
- Test the sounds with users over extended trial periods.
- Use sounds sparingly because they:
  — Are annoying to many people, including other users and nonusers in the vicinity.
  — Can easily be overused, increasing the possibility that they will be ignored.
  — Are not reliable because:
    • Some people are hard of hearing.
    • If they are not heard, they leave no permanent record of having occurred.
    • The user can turn them off.

Sounds, sometimes called *earcons*, are useful for alerting the user:

- To minor and obvious mistakes.
- When something unexpected happens.
- Where visual attention is directed away from the screen and immediate attention is required.
- When a long process is finished.

Tones used must be discriminable, nonannoying, and consistently used. Therefore, they must be thoroughly tested for discrimination and effectiveness. Brewster, Wright, and Edwards (1993) have found that high levels of recognition can be achieved by careful use of earcon pitch, rhythm, and timbre. They recommend:

- Timbre: Use synthesized musical instrument timbres, where possible with multiple harmonics.
- Pitch: Do not use on its own unless there are very big differences between the pitches used.

- Register: Acceptable to use alone to differentiate earcons; otherwise large differences of three or more octaves should be used.

- Rhythm: Make rhythms as different as possible. Including a different number of notes in each rhythm is very effective.

- Intensity: 10dB to 20dB above threshold. Since sound level will be under control of the user, it should be kept in a close range.

- Combinations: Leave a delay of 0.01 second between successively played earcons.

Since sounds can be annoying to some people, they should be capable of being turned down or off by the user. Playing jingles or tunes, or loud sounds, focuses attention on the sound itself, which is distracting. Loud sounds can also be irritating, especially to those with sensitive hearing.

Never consider sounds reliable; because they can be turned off, they leave no permanent record of their existence, and not all users will be able to hear all tones because of hearing defects. Sounds should always be used in conjunction with a visual indication of some kind.

Guidance and Assistance

We'll begin by first looking at ways to prevent errors from occurring in the first place. Then, we will look at how to gracefully handle them when they do occur. Finally, we'll look at guidance and assistance and its components, including the various forms of Help typically available in a system.

Preventing Errors

In spite of our lofty design goals, people will make errors using even the most well-designed system. When errors occur they must be properly managed. The magnitude of errors in computer systems is astounding. Studies have found error rates in commands, tasks, or transactions as high as 46 percent. In addition to stranding the user and wasting time, errors interrupt planning and cause deep frustration.

Errors can be classified as slips or mistakes. A *slip* is automatic behavior gone awry. One's hands navigate the keyboard improperly and the wrong key is accidentally pressed. The wrong menu bar item is chosen because of inattentiveness. An inference error is made due to carelessness. A person often detects a slip because it is usually noticeable. The wrong letter appears within a word or the expected action is not performed. Slips are usually, but not always, corrected fairly easily. Slips can be reduced through proper application of human factors in design (for example, by providing adequate separation between elements to be selected).

A *mistake* results from forming a wrong model or goal and then acting on it. A mistake may not be easily detected because the action may be proper for the perceived goal—it is the goal that is wrong. Anticipating a mistake in design is also more difficult. Mistakes can be reduced, however, by eliminating ambiguity from design. Doing usability testing and watching for nonsensical (to the designer) requests and actions can also detect mistake-conducive situations.

Some experts have argued that there is no such thing as an "error" in using a system; they are simply iterations toward a goal. There is much truth to that statement. It is also said "to err is human." The corollary to that statement, at least in computer systems, might be, ". . . to forgive is good design." Whatever we call them, errors will occur. People should be able to correct them as soon as they are detected, as simply and easily as they were made.

MAXIM **Everyone makes mistakes, so every mistake should be fixable.**

Problem Management

- Prevention:
    - Disable inapplicable choices.
    - Use selection instead of entry controls.
    - Use aided entry.
    - Accept common misspellings, whenever possible.
    - Before an action is performed:
        - Permit it to be reviewed.
        - Permit it to be changed or undone.
    - Provide a common action mechanism.
    - Force confirmation of destructive actions.
        - Let expert users disable this.
    - Provide an automatic and continuous Save function.

- Detection:
    - For conversational dialogs, validate entries as close to point of entry as possible.
        - At character level.
        - At control level.
        - When the transaction is completed or the window closed.
    - For high speed, head-down data entry.
        - When the transaction is completed or the window closed.
    - Leave window open.
    - Maintain the item in error on the screen.
    - Visually highlight the item in error.
    - Display an error message in a window.
        - Do not obscure item in error.
    - Handle errors as gracefully as possible.
        - The greater the error, the more dramatic should be the warning.
    - Use auditory signals conservatively.

- Correction:
    - Preserve as much of the user's work as possible.
    - At window-level validation, use a modeless dialog box to display an error list.
        - Highlight first error in the list.
        - Place cursor at first control with error.
        - Permit fixing one error and continuing to next error.
    - Always give a person something to do when an error occurs.

- Something to enter/save/reverse.
- A Help button.
- Someone to call.
— Provide a constructive correction message saying:
  - What problem was detected.
  - Which items are in error.
  - What corrective action is necessary.
— Initiate a clarification dialog if necessary.

Preventing, detecting, and correcting errors involves doing the following.

Prevention. It is always better to prevent errors than handle them. Errors can be reduced in a number of ways. First, disable all choices that are not applicable at any one moment. Make improper alternatives impossible to select or activate. Next, after considering the task and user, if practical, design screens using selection instead of entry controls. Selection error rates tend to be lower than entry error rates. Use aided entry if at all possible. The computer has been found to be a better speller than most people. When entry is performed, human misspellings of commands and requests should be accepted by the system. Person-to-person communication does not require perfection. Person-to-computer communication should impose no more rigor than that imposed between people. Use of the Shift key should also be discouraged, since it is such a large cause of keying errors. Actions about to be performed should also be reviewable and changeable. Keying or selection slips will occasionally occur.

A common send mechanism should be provided to transmit an action to the system. The existence of two or more keys to accomplish the same purpose, especially if their use is mandated by different conditions, can be confusing and more prone to error. Finally, if an action causes an irreversible change and the change is critical, the user should be requested to confirm the change. A separate key should be used for this purpose, not the Send key. Let expert users disable the confirmation request, if the action is recoverable. Finally, provide an automatic continuous *Save* function so that users never lose their work due to a system (or user) malfunction.

Detection. Errors should be detected quickly, but without disrupting a person's thought patterns and actions if this can be avoided. Generally, the longer the wait before editing is performed, the longer the time to accomplish the editing. So, validate according to how important accuracy is to the user, and the characteristics of the task being performed. It is also preferable to wait for a closure point in the dialog. For conversational dialogs, accuracy is usually more important than speed, actions are slower paced, and more closure points usually exist. In these situations, validate as close to the point of input as possible: at the character level or at the control level, and when the transaction is completed or the window closed. High-speed, head-down data entry is generally fast paced. Constant interruptions for errors can be a great speed detriment. In this situation, validate when the transaction is completed or the window closed. This is usually the only task closure point.

All errors should be maintained on the screen and identified to the user through a highlighting display technique (for example, high intensity or contrasting color). Display an error message in a dialog box and position it on the screen so it does not obscure the item in error. Handle all errors as gracefully as possible, avoiding discouraging, embarrassing, or alarming words. Words with such intent can compound the frustration a person already feels in having made an error. For minor problems, provide less intrusive warnings. The greater the error, the more dramatic may be the warning.

Be cautious in using auditory signals to notify of an error. Many people, especially those with status or position, do not want their inefficiencies advertised, especially to peers and subordinates.

Correction. Preserve as much of the user's work as possible. It can be irritating to have to reenter an entire screen when only one field is in error. At the window level of validation, use a modeless dialog box to display a list of errors. Highlight the first error in the list and place the cursor at the first control with error. Permit fixing one error, and then continuing on to the next error. If multiple errors occur, and it is impossible to display messages about all of them at one time, provide an indication that there are additional messages. Say, for example, "+ 2 other problems." Also, provide a distinct visual difference if the same error message is displayed more than once, because the first attempt to correct the problem failed. A person may not notice a repeated message that looks identical to the previous one. Always give a person something to do when an error occurs: something to enter, save, or reverse, or someone to call. Also provide a Help button. The Help button *must* be helpful, though.

Explicit and constructive error messages should be provided. These messages should describe what error occurred, and how it should be corrected. Corrective actions will be clearer if phrased with words like "must be" or "must have." A study addressing restructuring messages following guidelines such as these, and others previously described, found improved success rates in fixing errors, lower overall error rates, and improved user satisfaction.

Any error ambiguities should be resolved by having the system query the user. Errors should be corrected with minimal typing. Another important error control measure is to have the system identify and store errors. This will allow tracking of common errors so that appropriate prevention programs can be implemented.

Providing Guidance and Assistance

New users must go through a learning process that involves developing a conceptual or mental model to explain the system's behavior and the task being performed. Guidance in the form of the system's hard-copy, online documentation, computer-based training, instructional or prompting messages, and system messages serves as a cognitive development tool to aid this process. So does assistance provided by another form of online documentation, the Help function. Broadly speaking, online documentation is *every* communication provided online to help people to do their work effectively.

While it is desirable that the human-computer interface be so "self-evident" and "intelligent" that people never experience difficulties, this goal will not be achieved in the foreseeable future. So a great deal of emphasis should be placed on creating good guidance and assistance, and managing the trouble that does occur. Indeed one survey found that documentation was the second most important factor influencing the decision to purchase something. (Quality was first.)

Useful guidance and assistance answers the following questions:

- What is this?
- What does it do?
- How do I make it do it?
- What is its role in the overall scheme of things?

Technical information, unlike works of fiction, is seldom read for pleasure. People turn to it only when a question has to be answered. Failure to provide the guidance and assistance needed in learning, answering questions, and problem solving makes it very difficult for the user to recover from trouble on his or her own and to avoid future trouble by learning from his or her mistakes. The result is most often more errors and great frustration.

Problems with Documentation

Wright (1991) feels that poor documentation is usually not the result of stupid and careless writing. Most writers, professional or not, she says, try to communicate their ideas as well as they can. Poor products, however, suggest that being a native speaker of the language is not a sufficient qualification to ensure communicative success. Rather, four other factors contribute to bad design.

Organizational factors. First are organizational factors including management decisions concerning who does the writing: product developers or specialist technical authors. Product developers, by their nature, are more interested in the technical aspects and seldom have time to focus on writing. Another organizational factor is the frequency and nature of the contact between writers and developers. Successful writing requires that frequent contact be maintained between writers and developers. If not, modifications may go undocumented, and functionality may occur that is difficult to explain.

Time scale. Second is the time scale allocated for the writing process. Successful writing also involves detailed early planning, drafting, testing, and considerable revising. Without adequate time being made available for the writing process, the planning, testing, and revising processes are limited, thereby increasing the potential for a mismatch between the final product and its documentation.

Theoretical rationale. Third, there is not yet a clear theoretical rationale about what content should be included in documentation and how this information should be presented. Until this is developed, one cannot be sure that the documentation being developed is the most effective that it can be.

Resources. Finally, Wright concludes, there are the resources. Adequate resources are needed to include people with different skills in the documentation development process. Required are people good at visual layout, writing, and test and evaluation. Rarely does the same person possess more than one of these skills. Without the proper expertise, documentation will also suffer.

Another problem with documentation is created by the need for translation in our shrinking world. The following is found in a current user guide: "The color deviation from the original is thus resulted." (KYE Systems, 1995) The product manufacturer is guilty of Wright's sins number two and four above. International considerations will be presented in detail in Step 10 "Provide Effective Internationalization and Accessibility."

How Users Interact with Documentation

There are three broad stages through which a reader interacts with documentation: finding information that is relevant, understanding what the documentation says, and applying that understanding to the current task in order to solve the problem that prompted turning to the documentation in the first place.

Finding information is enhanced through use of contents pages and index lists. It is also enhanced if browsing is made easy through clearly visible page headings and sub-headings. Pictures and symbols can also be used to draw the reader's attention to particular kinds of information. Understanding information is achieved through a variety of factors. Included are following good writing principles. Understanding can also be maximized through testing and revision of materials as necessary.

Instructions or Prompting

Instructional or prompting information is placed *within the body* of a screen. It may take the form of messages or other advice, such as the values to be keyed into a field. Prompting is provided to assist a person in providing what is necessary to complete a screen.

Inexperienced users find prompting a valuable aid in learning a system. Experienced users, however, often find prompting undesirable. It slows them down, then adds "noise" to the screen, and may reduce the amount of working information that can be displayed at one time.

Since instructions or prompting can easily create screen noise, be cautious in placing it on a screen. Use it only if all screen usage will be casual or infrequent. If people with a wide range of experience will be using a screen, it should be selectable, capable of being turned on or off as needed. As an alternative, two separate sets of screens could be made available, one with prompts and the other without. Guidelines for writing instructions and prompts were covered in Step 8 "Write Clear Text and Messages."

Help Facility

The most common form of online documentation is the Help system. The overall objective of a Help facility is to assist people in remembering what to do. Its benefits include improving the usability of a system, providing insurance against design flaws that may develop, and accommodating user differences that may exist (novice versus expert). Typical methods of invoking Help include: through a typed command, by pressing a Help key or button, or by selecting a Help option from a multiple-item menu. Help may also automatically appear on the screen.

Some studies have found a Help system can aid performance, others have concluded that a Help function can impair performance if it is not task-oriented, and if it makes the interface more complex. One potential danger of the Help facility, as one study found, is that a person's recall of command operations is related to frequency of Help facility access; fewer Help requests were associated with better command recall. The researchers speculate that the availability of Help may become a crutch and lead to less effective retention. People may implement a passive cognitive strategy. A Help facility, then, may influence performance in systematic and subtle ways.

The specific design characteristics that enhance an online Help are still being identified. Three broad areas of Help that must be addressed in creating Help are: its content, its presentation, and its access mechanisms. Of these, presentation and access are best understood.

Elkerton and Palmiter (1991) propose that the content (and structure) of an effective online Help can be specified using the GOMS (goals, operators, methods, selection rules) model (Card, Moran, and Newell, 1983). Using GOMS, information is provided to the user on *goals* for meaningful tasks, on *operators* for actions required to be performed, on *methods* for accomplishing the goals, and where multiple interface methods exist, and on *selection rules* for choosing a specific method. Gugerty, Halgren, Gosbee, and Rudisill (1991) found that this structure was useful in remembering medical procedures. Elkerton (1988) presents a set of suggested principles for online assistance (which he calls *online aiding*). These principles are reproduced in Table 9.1.

Next, we'll look at some general Help guidelines. Then, we'll address some specific considerations for contextual Help, task-oriented Help, reference Help, and wizards.

Help Facility Guidelines

- Kind:
  — Collect data to determine what types of Help are needed.
- Training:
  — Inform users of availability and purpose of Help.
- Availability:
  — Provide availability throughout the dialog.
  — If no Help is available for a specific situation, inform the user of this and provide directions to where relevant Help may exist.
- Structure:
  — Make them as specific as possible.
  — Provide a hierarchical framework.
    • Brief operational definitions and input rules.
    • Summary explanations in text.
    • Typical task-oriented examples.
- Interaction:
  — Provide easy accessibility.

Table 9.1 Suggested Design Principles for Providing Online Advice Based on the GOMS Model

USE *GOALS* IN ONLINE AIDING TO DO THE FOLLOWING:

1. Describe what can be done in task-oriented terms (interface actions and objects) for improved initial skill learning.

2. Provide an adjustable level of detail on interface procedures for accommodating the information needs of a wide range of users.

3. Provide procedurally incomplete advice so that users can actively learn for improved long-term performance with and understanding of the interface.

4. Provide feedback to users that may help in reminding them of appropriate procedures to use, particularly when recovering from errors.

5. Develop modular assistance and instructional dialogs that can be used to describe similar and dissimilar procedural elements of the interface.

USE *OPERATORS* IN ONLINE AIDING TO DO THE FOLLOWING:

1. Describe simple actions, such as pressing specific keys or finding specific objects on the display, that are common to many interface procedures, to assist the user in current task performance.

2. Provide detailed information on interface procedures that inexperienced users can actively learn and that more skilled users can combine with other procedural knowledge to improve long-term performance and understanding of the interface.

3. Monitor users' actions to provide context-sensitive Help or to diagnose user problems actively.

USE *METHODS* IN ONLINE AIDING TO DO THE FOLLOWING:

1. Present step-by-step interface procedures to assist the user with specific problems.

2. Improve user understanding and acceptance of online advice.

3. Decrease the cognitive load of users who are learning a new interface task by providing an explicit procedure for users to follow.

4. Provide procedural demonstrations of interface procedures so that users can quickly learn simple operations.

5. Map sequences of users' actions to a reduced set of interface goals to help provide context-sensitive advice to users.

USE *SELECTION RULES* IN ONLINE AIDING TO DO THE FOLLOWING:

1. Help users choose between multiple interface methods.

2. Provide users with an understanding of representative tasks to increase their knowledge of when to apply specific interface skills.

From Elkerton (1988)

— Leave the Help displayed until:
  • The user exits.
  • The action eliminating the need for Help is performed.
— Provide instructions for exiting.
— Return to original position in dialog when Help is completed.

■ Location:
— Minimize the obscuring of screen content.
— If in a window, position priorities are: right, left, above, and below.

■ Content:
— Minimize the Help's length.
— Develop modular dialogs that can be used to describe similar and dissimilar procedural elements of the interface.
— Provide step-by-step interface procedures to assist the user with specific problems.
— Provide procedural demonstrations of interface procedures to aid quick learning of simple operations.
— Provide information to help users select between multiple interface methods.
— Provide users with an understanding of representative tasks to increase their knowledge of when to apply specific skills.

■ Style:
— Provide easy browsing and a distinctive format.
  • Contents screens and indexes.
  • Screen headings and subheadings.
  • Location indicators.
  • Descriptive words in the margin.
  • Visual differentiation of screen components.
  • Emphasized critical information.
— Use concise, familiar, action-oriented wording.
— Refer to other materials, when necessary.
— Never use Help to compensate for poor interface design.

■ Consistency:
— Provide a design philosophy consistent with other parts of the system.

■ Title:
— Place the word "Help" in all Help screen titles.

Kind. The two most common reasons people use Help are: (1) Confusion exists about something located on the screen, and (2) information about a specific function is needed. All system usability problems should be systematically identified through testing and evaluation. Monitoring users' actions can also be a useful tool in identifying user problems. Online Help can then be developed to address these problems.

Training. Inform users of the availability and purpose of various types of Help. Never assume that this will be obvious.

Availability. Make Help available at all points in the dialog. It is especially critical that Help be available consistently in all similar situations. For example, if one particular system menu has Help, ensure that all menus provide Help. If no Help is available for a specific situation, inform the user of this and provide directions to where relevant Help may exist, including hard-copy materials.

Structure. The Help response should be as specific as possible, tailored to the task and the user's current position. When accessed, the Help facility should be aware of the kind of difficulties a person is having and respond with relevant information. Only the information necessary to solve the immediate problem or to answer the immediate question should be presented. If the Help facility is unsure of the request, it should work with the user through prompts and questions to resolve the problem.

A Help facility should be multilevel, proceeding from very general to successively more detailed and specific explanations to accommodate a wide range of users. The first level should provide brief definitions and rules, simple reminders, and memory joggers sufficient for skilled users. The second level should incorporate more detailed explanations in a textual format. The final, and deepest, level should provide guidance in the form of task-oriented examples.

Interaction. A Help facility should be retrievable simply, quickly, and consistently by a key action, selection, or command. Leave the Help displayed until the user explicitly exits the Help, or performs the action eliminating the need for Help. Instructions for exiting the Help process should always be provided. These may take the form of displayed pushbuttons, function keys, or something similar.

Help should not disrupt processing. Easy return to the point of the problem should be permitted. Ideally, the problem or work should be retained on the screen when Help is accessed, but this will not always be possible unless the system provides a windowing capability.

Location. When Help is displayed, minimize the obscuring of relevant screen content. If Help is displayed within a window, position priorities are right, left, above, and below.

Content. Minimize the Help's length, whenever possible. Carroll, Smith-Kerker, Ford, and Mazur (1986) recommend the development of Help text in the form of "minimal manuals." These manuals are explicit and focus on real tasks and activities, and they have been found to be significantly better than traditional Help texts (Black, Carroll, and McGuigan, 1987; Carroll, et al., 1986).

Elkerton (1988) suggests that few Help users want detailed, fact-oriented knowledge such as a hierarchical list showing the syntax of a command. Instead, they want to know the methods to complete a task. Without knowledge of how to do things, users are left to browse through a wealth of information with little understanding of what may be useful. Hence, he recommends, among other things, providing the following:

- Step-by-step interface procedures to assist the user with specific problems.
- Procedural demonstrations of interface procedures to aid quick learning of simple operations.
- Information to help users choose between multiple interface methods.
- Users with an understanding of representative tasks to increase their knowledge of when to apply specific skills.

When procedural steps are presented, consecutive numbering will make them easy to follow.

Style. Provide easy browsing and a distinctive format. Often the exact location of information needed to answer a question cannot be definitely established. Providing information in a format that can be easily skimmed aids the search process and also helps the user become familiar with the information being presented. The following techniques enhance the skimming process:

- Contents screens and indexes.
- Screen headings and subheadings.
- Location indicators.
- Descriptive words in the margin.
- Visual differentiation of screen components.
- Emphasized critical information.

An index has been found to be one of the first place users turn when they have a problem. Help wording should also be concise, familiar, and action oriented. Reference to outside material may be included in the Help text, especially if the Help information cannot be provided in a concise way. Never use Help to compensate for poor interface design.

Consistency. The Help design philosophy should be consistent with the philosophy used in other parts of the system. This includes presentation techniques, style, procedures, and all other aspects.

Title. For easy identification, place the word "Help" in all Help screen titles.

Contextual Help

Contextual Help provides information within the context of a task being performed, or about a specific object being operated upon. Common kinds of contextual Help include Help command buttons, status bar messages, and ToolTips. Microsoft Windows has also introduced what is called the What's This? Command.

Help Command Button

- Description:
  — A command button.
- Purpose:
  — To provide an overview of, summary assistance for, or explanatory information about the purpose or contents of a window being displayed.
- Design guidelines:
  — Present the Help in a secondary window or dialog box.

Description and purpose. The proper usage of a command button labeled Help, illustrated in Figure 9.2, is to provide supplemental Help for a secondary window,

Figure 9.2 Help command button.

dialog box, or message box. It should provide an overview of, summary assistance for, or explanatory information about, the purpose or contents of a window.

Design guideline. Present this form of Help in a secondary window or dialog box. Microsoft Windows considers this Help an optional secondary form of contextual assistance, and not a substitute for the *What's This?* command to be described shortly. The guidance and assistance provided by a Help command button differs from the "What's This?" In that more general assistance is provided rather than information specific to the control that has the current input focus.

Status Bar Message

- Description:
  — An abbreviated, context-sensitive message related to the screen item with the focus.
  — Appears in window's status bar when the primary mouse button is pressed over an item (or keyboard focus is achieved).
- Purpose:
  — To provide explanatory information about the object with the focus.
  — Use to:
    • Describe the use of a control, menu item, button, or toolbar.
    • Provide the context of activity within a window.
    • Present a progress indicator or other forms of feedback when the view of a window must not be obscured.
  — Do not use for information or access to functions essential to basic system operations unless another form of Help is provided elsewhere in the Help system.
  — If extended Help is available and must be presented, place "Press F1 for Help" in bar.
- Writing guidelines:
  — Be constructive, not simply descriptive.
  — Be brief, but not cryptic.
  — Begin with a verb in the present tense.
  — If a command has multiple functions, summarize them.
  — If a command is disabled, explain why.

Description. An abbreviated, context-sensitive message related to the screen item with focus. The message appears in the screen's status bar, as shown in Figure 9.3 when the primary mouse button is pressed over an item (or keyboard focus achieved).

Purpose. A status bar message's purpose is to provide explanatory information about the screen object with focus. Because the user may not always notice a mes-

Figure 9.3 Status bar message.

sage displayed in the bar, or the bar may be turned off and not displayed, it must be considered a form of secondary or supplemental assistance.

Use a status bar message to provide context for the activity being performed in window, or to describe the use of toolbars, menu items, or buttons being displayed. When the primary mouse button is clicked over one of these items (or keyboard focus achieved) display a short message describing the use of the associated command.

The bar may also be used for presentation of a progress indicator, or other forms of feedback, when the view of a window must not be obscured. Never use the bar for information or access to functions essential to basic system operations, unless another form of Help for this operation is provided elsewhere in the interface. If extended Help must be provided, and displaying it in the bar is not possible, place "Press F1 for Help" in the bar.

Writing. Do not simply describe something but explain it in a constructive manner Be as brief as possible so the text can be read easily, but do not make the text so short that it is cryptic Begin all messages with a verb in the present tense. If a command with multiple functions has focus, summarize its multiple uses. If a command is disabled, explain why.

ToolTip

- Description:
  — A small pop-up window that appears adjacent to control.
  — Presented when the pointer remains over a control a short period of time.
- Purpose:
  — Use to display the name of a control when the control has no text label.
- Design guidelines:
  — Make application-specific ToolTips consistent with system-supplied ToolTips.
  — Use system color setting for ToolTips above to distinguish them.

Description. A ToolTip is a small pop-up window with a label that appears adjacent to a control without a label (such as a toolbar) when the pointer is positioned over the control. It is displayed after the pointer remains over the control for a short period of time. This avoids the distracting effect of a ToolTip appearing when a pointer is simply being moved past a control.

Purpose. To display the name of a control when the control has no text label.

Design guidelines. Make application-specific ToolTips consistent in size and structure with system-supplied ToolTips, including using the system's color setting to distinguish them. ToolTips were also described in Step 7 "Choose the Proper Screen-Based Controls."

What's This? Command

- Description:
  — A command located on the Help drop-down menu on a primary window.
  — A button on the title bar of a secondary window.
  — A command on a pop-up menu for a specific object.
  — A button on a toolbar.
- Purpose:
  — Use to provide contextual information about any screen object.
- Design guidelines:
  — Phrase to answer the question "What is this?"
  — Indicate the action associated with the item.
  — Begin the description with a verb.
  — Include "why," if helpful.
  — Include "how to," if task requires multiple steps.
  — For command buttons, use an imperative form: "Click this to...."

Description and purpose. A *What's This* command may take the form of a command in a menu or a button, as summarized above. It's purpose is to provide contextual information about any screen object, including controls, dialog boxes, and property sheets.

Design guidelines. Phrase the label or caption to answer the question "What is this?" Indicate the action associated with the item and begin description with a verb. If helpful, include an answer to "Why?" as well. Include a "how to" if the task requires multiple steps. For command buttons, use an imperative form, "Click this to...."

The guidance and assistance provided by "What's This? differs from that of a command button. With command button Help, more general assistance is provided rather than information specific to the control that has the current input focus.

Task-Oriented Help

- Description:
  — A primary window typically accessed through the Help Topics browser.
  — Includes a set of command buttons at the top; at minimum:
    • A button to display the Help Topics browser dialog box.
    • A Back button to return to the previous topic.
    • Buttons that provide access to other functions such as Copy or Print.

- Purpose:
  - — To describe the procedural steps for carrying out a task.
  - — Focuses on *how* to do something.

- Design guidelines:
  - — Provide one procedure to complete a task, the simplest and most common.
  - — Provide an explanation of the task's goals and organizational structure at the start.
  - — Divide procedural instructions into small steps.
  - — Present each step in the order to be executed.
  - — Label each step.
  - — Explicitly state information necessary to complete each step.
  - — Provide visuals that accurately depict the procedural steps.
  - — Accompany visuals with some form of written or spoken instructions.
  - — Begin any spoken instructions simultaneously with or slightly after a visual is presented.
  - — Segment any animation to focus attention on specific parts.
  - — Segment instructions.
  - — Delay the opportunity to perform the procedure until all the procedure's steps have been illustrated.

- Presentation guidelines:
  - — The window should consume a minimum amount of screen space, but be large enough to present the information without scrolling.
  - — Normally, do not exceed four steps per window.
  - — Use a different window color to distinguish task-oriented Help windows from other windows.

- Writing guidelines:
  - — Write simply and clearly, following all previously presented guidelines.
  - — Focus on *how* information, rather than *what* or *why*.
  - — Do not include introductory, conceptual, or reference material.
  - — Limit steps to four or fewer to avoid scrolling or multiple windows.
  - — If a control is referred to by its label, bold the label to set it off.
  - — Include the topic title as part of the body.

Description. *Task-oriented Help*, sometimes called *procedural Help* is presented on a primary window accessed through the Help Topics browser dialog box in Microsoft Windows. It includes a set of command buttons at the top, minimally, a button to display the Help Topics browser dialog box, a Back button to return to the previous topic. And buttons that provide access to other functions such as Copy or Print.

Purpose. Task-oriented Help details the procedural steps for carrying out a task. People prefer task-oriented Help to product-oriented Help, and research evidence shows a productivity gain using it. It is not surprising that task-oriented Help has such a preference and benefits, because people think in terms of tasks, not functions. This form of Help focuses on *how* to do something, rather than the *what* or *why*. Its purpose is not to document everything there is to know about a subject.

Design guidelines. The following guidelines are mostly derived from Harrison (1995). First, present only one procedure to complete a task, the simplest and most common. (If information about alternate methods is included, place it in a Notes or Related Topic section.)

At the beginning, provide an explanation of the task's goals and organizational structure. Divide procedural instructions into small steps and present them in the order they are to be executed. Clearly label each step. Explicitly state what information is necessary in order to complete each step, presenting the most important information first.

Provide visuals that accurately depict the procedural steps. People prefer to follow visual examples rather than instructions, and visuals minimize orientation errors. Accompany the visuals with some form of written or, if possible, spoken instructions. Instructions provide cues as to most important aspects of the procedure. Begin any spoken instructions simultaneously with or slightly after a visual is presented. If animation is included, segment it to focus attention on specific parts. Segment the instructions to reinforce the concept of chunks or steps. Finally, delay the opportunity to perform the procedure until all the procedure's steps have been illustrated.

Presentation guidelines. A task-oriented Help window should consume a minimum amount of screen space, but be large enough to cover all the necessary information without requiring cumbersome scrolling. Normally, this means do not exceed four steps per window. To distinguish task-oriented Help windows from other windows, use a different window color to present them.

Writing guidelines. Write simply and clearly, following all previously presented text guidelines. Focus on *how* information, rather than *what* or *why*. Do not include introductory, conceptual, or reference material. If a control is referred to by its label, bold the label to set it off. Include the topic title as part of the body.

Reference Help

- Description:
  — An online reference book.
  — Typically accessed through a:
    • Command in a Help drop-down menu.
    • Toolbar button.
- Purpose:
  — To present reference Help information, either:
    • Reference oriented.
    • User guide oriented.
- Design guidelines:
  — Provide a consistent presentation style, following all previously presented guidelines.
  — Include a combination of contextual Help, and task-oriented Help, as necessary.
  — Include text, graphics, animation, video, and audio effects, as necessary.
  — Make displayed toolbar buttons contextual to the topic being viewed.

— Provide jumps, a button or interactive area that triggers an event when it is selected, such as:
- Moving from one topic to another.
- Displaying a pop-up window.
- Carrying out a command.
— Visually distinguish a jump by:
- Displaying it as a button.
- Using a distinguishing color or font to identify it.
- Changing the pointer image when it is over it.

- Presentation guidelines:
— Provide a nonscrolling region for long topics to keep the topic title and other key information visible.

- Writing guidelines:
— Write simply and clearly, following all previously presented guidelines.
— Provide meaningful topic titles.

Description and purpose. *Reference Help* is another form of online documentation. Its purpose is to present Help information that may be reference-oriented, documenting the features of a product, or it may serve as a user's guide to a product. It is typically accessed through a command in a Help drop-down menu, or a toolbar button. Reference-oriented Help is usually organized by functions and features and includes more text than other types of Help. User-guide-oriented Help is usually organized by tasks and may include more illustrations than other types of Help.

Design guidelines. Provide a consistent presentation style, following all previously presented guidelines. Include a combination of contextual Help, and task-oriented Help, as necessary. Include text, graphics, animation, video, and audio effects, as necessary and as available. Make toolbar buttons contextual to the topic being viewed in the Help window.

Provide *jumps*, a button or interactive area that triggers an event when it is selected. The action may be to move from one topic to another, to display a pop-up window, or to carry out a command. Jumps, when in button form are called *shortcut buttons* in Microsoft Windows. They automatically perform a task, thereby providing efficiency by reducing the amount of information necessary to present for reading by the viewer. Do not use a jump, however, if the goal is to enable the user to perform the task. Consider a balance for common tasks. Provide information that explains how to perform a task and also provide a shortcut button to accomplish the task, making stepping through the task easier. Visually distinguish a jump by displaying it as a unique style button or using a distinguishing color or font to identify it. The system default for a textual jump in Microsoft Windows is green underlined text. Also, change the pointer image when the pointer is positioned over the jump.

Presentation guidelines. If scrolling is necessary, provide a nonscrolling region for long topics to keep the topic title and other key information visible.

Writing guidelines. Write simply and clearly, following all previously presented guidelines. Also, provide meaningful topic titles.

Wizards

- Description:
  - A series of presentation pages displayed in a secondary window.
  - Include:
    - Controls to collect input.
    - Navigation command buttons.
  - Typically accessed through:
    - Toolbar buttons.
    - Icons.

- Purpose:
  - To perform a complex series of steps.
  - To perform a task that requires making several critical decisions.
  - To enter critical data and for use when the cost of errors is high.
  - To perform an infrequently accomplished task.
  - The necessary knowledge or experience to perform a task is lacking.
  - Not suited to teaching how to do something.

- Design guidelines:
  - Provide a greater number of simple screens with fewer choices, rather than a smaller number of more complex screens with too many options or too much text.
  - Provide screens of the exact same size.
  - Include on the first page:
    - A graphic on the left side to establish a reference point or theme.
    - A welcoming paragraph on the right side to explain what the wizard does.
  - Include on subsequent pages:
    - A graphic for consistency.
    - Instructional text.
    - Controls for user input.
  - Maintain consistent the locations for all elements.
  - Make it visually clear that the graphic is not interactive.
    - Vary from normal size or render it as an abstract representation.
  - Include default values or settings for all controls when possible.
  - For frequently used wizards, place a check box with the text "Do not show this Welcome page again" at the bottom of the Welcome page.
  - Include a Finish button at the point where the task can be completed.
  - Do not require the user to leave a wizard to complete a task.
  - Make sure the design alternatives offered yield positive results.
  - Make certain it is obvious how to proceed when the wizard has completed its process.

- Presentation guidelines:
  - Display the wizard window so it is immediately recognized as the primary point of input.
  - Present a single window at one time.
  - Do not advance pages automatically.

■ Writing guidelines:
— Clearly identify the wizard's purpose in title bar.
— At the top right of the wizard window, title the Welcome page "Welcome to the *Wizard Name* Wizard."
  • Use mixed case in headline style and no ending punctuation.
— Write simply, concisely, and clearly, following all previously presented guidelines.
— Use a conversational rather than instructional style.
— Use words like "you" and "your."
— Start most questions with phrases like "Which option do you want . . ." or "Would you like . . ."

Description. A *Wizard* is a structured set of screens that guides the user through a decision-making or data entry process. Wizards are displayed in a secondary window. The screens include controls to collect input, and navigation command buttons located at the page bottom (Back, Next, Finish, and Cancel). A wizard is typically accessed through toolbar buttons or icons.

Purpose. A wizard's purpose is to assist a user by automating a task and walking the user through the process. It may not appear as an explicit part of the Help interface. Wizards are useful for complex or infrequently occurring tasks that people may have difficulty learning or doing. Wizards are designed to hide many of the steps and much of the complexity in doing something. They are not suited to teaching how to do something, and should be considered a supplement to the actual performance of the task. An experienced user who knows a process will usually find a wizard inefficient or lacking access to all necessary functionality. A wizard can be accessed through toolbar buttons or icons. Microsoft (2001) suggests the following guidelines.

Design guidelines. Provide a greater number of simple pages with fewer choices, rather than a smaller number of more complex pages with too many options or too much text. Fewer pages will make it easier to understand the wizard and the process. Create screens of the exact same size. Include on the first page a graphic on the left side to establish a reference point or theme and a welcoming paragraph on the right side to explain what the wizard does. The graphic's purpose is to establish a reference point, or theme, or present a preview of the wizard's result. Include on subsequent pages a graphic for consistency, instructional text, and the necessary controls for user input. (If screen space is critical, graphics on subsequent pages may be omitted.)

Make it visually clear that the graphic is not interactive by varying it from normal size or rendering it as an abstract representation. Do not require the user to leave a wizard to complete a task. The user, often a novice, may lose context if asked to leave. Everything must be done from within the wizard. Make sure the design alternatives offered to the user yield positive results.

For frequently used wizards, place a check box with the text "Do not show this Welcome page again" at the bottom of the Welcome page. Include a Finish button at the point where the task can be completed. Make certain it is obvious how to proceed when the wizard has completed its process by including proper closing text on the last page.

Presentation guidelines. Display the wizard window so it is immediately recognized as the primary point of input. Present a single window at one time, overlaying underlying windows so they are not visible. Do not advance pages automatically. The viewer may be unable to read all the information, and control of the dialog is removed from the user and placed in the hands of the computer.

Writing guidelines. Clearly identify the wizard's purpose in the title bar. At the top right of the wizard window, title the Welcome page "Welcome to the *Wizard Name* Wizard." Use mixed case in the headline style of presentation, and no ending punctuation. Write simply, concisely, and clearly, following all previously presented guidelines. Use a conversational rather than instructional style, and words like "you" and "your." Start most questions with phrases like "Which option do you want?" or "Would you like . . .?" People react better to phrasing that implies they are in control, rather than phrasing telling them what to do.

Hints or Tips

- Description:
  — A command button labeled Hints or Tips.
- Purpose:
  — To provide a few important contextual, but specific, items of information related to a displayed screen.
- Design guidelines:
  — Provide guidance on only two or three important points.
  — Locate the button near where its guidance applies.
  — Write concisely and to the point.

Description. A *Hint* or *Tip* is a command button placed on a screen and labeled as such.

Purpose. To provide a few important contextual, but specific, items of information related to a displayed screen. It is a supplement to the standard Help facility, but more easily accessible and relevant to the current situation. The objective is to quickly get the user back on track when disorientation or confusion occurs.

Design guidelines. Provide guidance on only two or three important points. Locate the button near the location where its guidance applies and write concisely and to the point.

For more information on Hints and Tips, see User Interface Engineering (2001).

Provide Effective Internationalization and Accessibility

Today the Internet and the market for software are global. It crosses endless cultural and language boundaries, each with its own requirements, conventions, customs, and definitions of acceptability. To be accepted, and used, a screen's text and images must reflect the needs and sensibility of each partner in the worldwide community where it is used. To make a product acceptable worldwide, it must be internationalized. A system must also be designed to be usable by an almost unlimited range of people, being accessible to anyone who desires to use it. The design concepts used to achieve these goals are called internationalization and accessibility. This step addresses these design issues.

International Considerations

To create a product for use internationally may involve two steps, *internationalization* and *localization* (Russo and Boor, 1993). Internationalization is the process of isolating culturally specific elements from a product. The German text of a program developed in Germany, for example, is isolated from the program itself. This occurs in the country where the product is developed. Localization is the process of infusing a specific cultural context into a previously internationalized product. Translating German screen components and messages into English for American users is an example of localization.

Creating a product that has been properly localized and speaks fluently to another culture requires addressing a number of factors. These include text; formats for elements such as number, date, and time; images; symbols; colors; flow; and functionality.

Localization

■ When to do it:
  — When the market includes few or no English speakers.
  — When translation is required by law or by custom.
  — When the widest possible market is desired.

■ When not to do it:
  — When the audience already reads English.
  — When the cost of retrofitting or rewriting the software is prohibitive.

This discussion of when, and when not, to internationalize and localize a product, is mostly based on Fowler and Stanwick (1995). Considerations include the prospective users and their English capabilities, local laws and customs, and costs associated with translation.

English is the most widely used language in the world. The current estimate for its speakers ranges from 700 million to 2 billion (Tripathi, 1992). Although many speakers of English have been taught it as a second language and may not all be facile readers and writers, they can communicate using it. The first consideration, then, is the English capabilities of the prospective user. This must be ascertained. Toward this end, both IBM (National Language Technical Center, 1991) and Apple (1992a) have documents listing the official language requirements of countries, and regions or political divisions. In addition, within some international business and scientific communities, English is the accepted language of communication. For example, the air transportation industry uses English as the language of communication between airline pilots and flight controllers worldwide. Scientists and engineers in Japan also prefer to communicate their research findings in English because of its greater precision (Kohl, Barclay, Pinelli, Keene, and Kennedy, 1993). If English is accepted in the using body, then concerns are only cultural.

Legal requirements may also mandate translation. For example, Canada, being composed of both English and French speakers, requires bilingual materials. The European Economic Community (ECC) will, at some point, mandate that all documentation shipped with imported products be written in all of the ECC languages. Whether the product will actually be used in all the countries will be immaterial.

Cost will also, of course, dictate whether a translation can, or will, be performed. Software translation rates can range from $40–80 dollars an hour or more, documentation translation $50–150 or more per page. These rates are presented for illustrative purposes only. Actual costs will be driven by many factors, including the local cost of living. For readers in need of a translation, one will be best served by getting a quote reflecting the time and locale of the translation. A translation performed in the target country often results in better quality than a translation by those who are native speakers of the producing country.

Words and Text

- Use very simple English.
  — Develop a restricted vocabulary.
  — Restrict the sentence structure using: noun-verb-object.
- Avoid:
  — Acronyms and abbreviations.
  — Stringing three nouns together.
  — Local or computer jargon.
  — A telegraphic writing style.
  — An over-friendly writing style.
  — Culturally specific examples.
  — References to national, racial, religious, and sexist stereotypes.
- Adhere to local user language idioms and cultural contexts.
- Keep the original term for words that cannot be translated.
- Allow additional screen space for the translation.
  — Horizontally, using Table 10.1.
  — Vertically.
- When translating to other languages, first do:
  — European: German.
  — Middle East: Arabic.
  — Far East: Japanese.
- Position icon captions outside of the graphic.
- Modify mnemonics for keyboard access.
- Adhere to local formats for date, time, money, measurements, addresses, and telephone numbers.

Text translation is simplified, and user interpretation errors reduced, if these guidelines, many of which are derived from del Galdo (1990), Russo and Boor (1993) and Fowler and Stanwick (1995) are followed.

Simple English. Simple English text will be easier and less expensive to translate. Simple English is achieved by using a restricted vocabulary. Create a dictionary of approved terms and prohibit all synonyms, and different meanings for the same word as well. A restricted sentence structure is also necessary. Sentences meaning the same thing can be written in many ways in English. This makes text more interesting to look at and read. In other languages, however, word order affects the meaning. Multiple structures cause translation problems and foster errors. Follow a *noun-verb-object* structure. Another benefit of simple English: translation may not always be necessary. The number of non-native English-speaking people capable of understanding the language will increase as screen English is simplified.

Avoid. Do not use acronyms and abbreviations. They are difficult, and often confusing, to translate. A translated acronym may not be as concise, or may possess negative associations. Abbreviations may also not be as concise, and they may not be understandable.

Avoid stringing three nouns together. Relationships between nouns become very explicit in many other languages, and it is difficult to determine what terms are modifying one another when three are strung together. The use of prepositions, such as *at*, *in*, *by*, and *on*, can help to clarify nouns' relationships. Avoid local or computer jargon. Jargon is not universal and probably will not be understood.

Do not use telegraphic writing. This means a terse style where words such as, "and," "the," and "is" are left out. Again, translation problems can easily occur. An overly friendly style, in which the reader is addressed in the first person or in a childish manner, should also be avoided. It can be considered condescending and irritating to readers in non-English-speaking countries. Finally, avoid references to national, racial, religious, and sexist stereotypes and do not use culturally specific examples. The latter must be recreated by the translator so they are suitable for the language and culture.

Local Language's Idioms. Adhere to local language's idioms and cultural contexts. Some words have different meanings in other languages. This is of special concern for product names. Automakers have been particular victims of this problem. Italy's Fiat had an auto named "Uno." They could not sell it by that name in Finland because uno in Finnish means "garbage." England's Rolls Royce planned to name a new car "Silver Mist." Then, someone discovered that mist in German means "manure" (Taylor, 1992). Proper attention to localization can avoid some embarrassing, and costly, problems.

Some languages are not read from left to right, as English is. Arabic, for example, is read from right to left. Chinese is read from top to bottom, right to left.

Original Terms. Keep the original terms for words that cannot be translated. Some words do not exist in other languages. "Disk drive" and "zooming" do not exist in Thai, for example. It has been found that people often prefer the original term to a created word. Never invent words; keep the original term for nontranslatable words (Sukaviriya and Moran, 1990).

Additional Screen Space. Allow additional screen space for the translation. English is very concise. It usually takes less space to communicate the same word, phrase, or text than most other languages. Listed below are words with the same meaning from four languages. Can you translate them?

Besturingselement	(Dutch)
Olvadaci prvek	(Czech)
Ohjausobjekti	(Finnish)
Steuerelement	(German)

Here is a clue. This word in English is seven characters long and has already been mentioned many, many times in this book. The Dutch version is 17 characters in length, or 143 per cent longer than the English version. The others are composed of 13 characters and are 85 per cent longer. The answer will follow shortly.

Objects whose sizes are affected by translation include captions, entry areas, menu options, prompting message boxes, areas of text, and icon labels. Expansion room must be allowed for translation. Generally, the shorter the text the more additional room is needed. Table 10.1 (National Language Technical Center, 1991) provides some additional horizontal space guidelines. Extra vertical spacing may also have to be allowed. In many languages, accents and descenders fall above and below the usual ascender and descender lines. What is the English version of the above words? *Control*. Were you able to translate one or more of them?

Translating. When translating, start from a translator's point of view. The language world is divided into three parts: Europe, the Middle East, and the Far East. Fowler and Stanwick (1995) report that Microsoft addresses translation in the following manner. In Europe, where problems involve changes in words caused by gender, accented letters, and text expansion, translation begins with German. This is done because German solves for accent, gender, and expansion issues. In the Middle East difficulties in translation include bidirectional and cursive letters. To address these, Microsoft recommends starting with Arabic. When this is done, localization is accomplished for Hebrew, Farsi, Dari Persian, Pashto, and the Indian languages Sindhi and Urdu. In the Far East the main difficulty is doublebyte character sets. One of the most difficult Asian languages, with ten thousand ideograms divided into four character sets, is Japanese. So Microsoft starts with it.

Icon Captions. Place icon captions outside of the graphic. Text placed within an icon may cause the icon to have to be redrawn when translation occurs. Text positioned outside the icon will negate the need for redrawing.

Table 10.1 Translation Expansion Requirements

NUMBER OF CHARACTERS IN TEXT	ADDITIONAL SPACE
Field labels and menu options	
Up to 10	100–200%
11–20	80–100%
Messages and on-screen instructions	
21–30	60–80%
31–50	40–60%
Online help and documentation	
51–70	31–40%
Over 70	30%

From National Language Technical Center, IBM (1991)

Mnemonics. Modify mnemonics used for keyboard access. Because mnemonics are established for ease of memorization, and because they are based upon a letter in a text object, when the text changes, so must the mnemonic. Attempting to create unique mnemonics may constrain the translation, but this must be addressed. Maintaining the old mnemonics will severely affect users' ability to learn them. They will no longer be mnemonics.

Local Formats. Adhere to local formats for date, time, money, measurements, addresses, and telephone numbers. A nearly infinite variety of these various units exist worldwide. They must also be localized to the exact needs of the user.

Images and Symbols

- Adhere to local cultural and social norms.
- Use internationally accepted symbols.
- Develop generic images.
- Be particularly careful with:
  — Religious symbols (crosses and stars).
  — The human body.
  — Women.
  — Hand gestures.
  — Flags.
  — The cross and check for check boxes.
- Review proposed graphical images early in the design cycle.

Images are the visible language of a culture and must be recognizable, meaningful, and acceptable. Like text, improper use of images, symbols, and icons can create problems internationally. Social norms vary, so great variations exist in what is recognizable and acceptable throughout the world. What one culture recognizes may have no meaning in another. What is acceptable in one country may not be in another. The images created for graphical interfaces are particularly susceptible to these problems. To be successful internationally, images must be carefully selected and designed. The following guidelines are also derived from del Galdo (1990), Russo and Boor (1993), and Fowler and Stanwick (1995).

Local Norms. Adhere to local cultural and social norms. Few world travelers have not suffered embarrassment caused by failure to understand, and adhere to, local customs and mores. On an early trip to Australia, I pulled in to a service station to replenish my auto's "petrol." I communicated my need to the attendant through a "thumbs-up" sign, an American convention (when there were still attendants) meaning "fill-it-up." The Australian attendant's response was a stunned look and a frown. Sensing something was wrong, I hastily lowered the window and communicated my need verbally. He smiled, replying, "Ah, you're

American, eh, OK." It wasn't until much later I discovered I had made a gesture considered obscene in Australia.

Examples abound in the computer literature of images that have created problems internationally. The mailbox and trashcan are two examples of objects whose shape, and resulting recognizability, vary substantially around the world. A cocktail glass used to signify an after-work appointment is a poor image to use in countries where alcohol is not associated with social activities. In the United States, a black cat is usually associated with bad luck; in the United Kingdom it means good luck. In the United States, the number 13 is considered unlucky; in Japan the number 4 is.

Images that are culturally specific must be isolated during the internationalization process. Then, proper images must be developed for use in the culture where the product will be used.

Internationally Accepted Symbols. Use internationally accepted symbols. Before developing an image, first determine if any international images have already been created by trade or standards organizations. The ISO (International Standards Organization), for example, has developed standard shapes for a variety of purposes. Always consult all relevant reference books before inventing new images or modifying existing ones.

Generic Images. Whenever possible, create generic images that are usable in multiple cultures. Having different images can confuse people who may use more than one language version of a product.

Where Caution Is Necessary. Some topics are more susceptible to acceptability problems than others. Inappropriate presentation can result in the viewer's being offended or insulted. Be particularly careful when using religious symbols such as crosses or stars. Also be wary of images depicting a human body, particularly the female. In some cultures simply revealing a woman's arms and legs is unacceptable. During the World Cup soccer tournament in the United States in 1994, one Middle East country televised the soccer games using a several-second tape delay. This was done so that stadium crowd pictures potentially containing pictures of women dressed to accommodate the USA's summer heat would not be shown on local television. What crowd scenes were substituted instead? Pictures of people attending an American football game in December in a northern city (like Green Bay, Wisconsin) when the temperature hovered around zero degrees Fahrenheit. Needless to say, *all* the fans were well covered from toes to top of head. While television viewers in this middle-eastern country saw spectators with skin barely visible, the soccer players cavorted in shorts and jerseys.

Also, be wary of hand gestures, as my Australian experience illustrates. Actually, I'm in pretty good company in committing this kind of faux pas. A former American president departed Air Force One on a visit to Germany exhibiting his customary hand wave to the welcoming people. Unfortunately, his Protocol Officer neglected to inform him that his wave had a vulgar connotation in Germany. We can only hope that German viewers of this action interpreted what he felt in is heart, not what he indicated with his hands. Also exercise caution in using a country's flag for a language icon. Many countries are multilingual, Canada, South Africa, and Switzerland, for example. Their flags may not be associated with any one language. Be more generic in nature, a word (such as French, Spanish, Italian) encompasses many countries and cultures.

Last, the X and check mark used for check boxes do not have meaning universally. It has also been found that they do not have universal meaning in the United States. In recent years, various graphical systems have moved away from X to the check mark as the symbol to indicate an active or set check box control. Why? In an engineering environment an X in a check box means the choice is not applicable or not set, a check means it is applicable, or it is set. Thus, an "X" was found to be confusing to some people when it meant active or set. Research has also indicated that when people complete a form with check boxes, the symbol most often used is the check mark.

MAXIM   **Perception = Reality!**

Review Images Early. Review proposed graphical images early in the design cycle. Creating acceptable images can be a time-consuming process. Start developing them early so ample time exists for extensive testing and modification.

Color, Sequence, and Functionality

- Adhere to local color connotations and conventions.
- Provide the proper information sequence.
- Provide the proper functionality.
- Remove all references to features not supported.

Other international considerations include the following.

Local Color Connotations. Color associations also differ among cultures. In the United States mailboxes are blue; in England they are red; in Greece they are yellow. In the United States red is associated with danger or stop, green with OK or go. This red-green association does not exist everywhere in the world. Table 10.2, derived from Russo and Boor (1993), lists some common cultural color associations. Colors used on screens must also reflect the color expectancies of its viewers.

Information Sequence. Information within a screen will be arranged to reflect the logical flow of information. In many cultures, including those we are most familiar with, it will be from left to right for text and from top to bottom, left to right for ease of scanning. Some cultures, however, read from right to left. For these, information sequence must be reorganized to reflect this right-to-left sequence. Similarly, cascaded windows for left-to-right readers are usually presented in an upper-left to lower-right structure. These will have to be reorganized to reflect different reading patterns.

Table 10.2   Some Cultural Color Associations

	RED	YELLOW	GREEN	BLUE	WHITE
China	Happiness	Birth Wealth Power	Ming Dynasty Heavens Clouds	Heavens Clouds	Death Purity
Egypt	Death	Happiness Prosperity	Fertility Strength	Virtue Faith Truth	Joy
France	Aristocracy	Temporary	Criminality	Freedom Peace	Neutrality
India	Life Creativity	Success	Prosperity Fertility		Death Purity
Japan	Anger Danger	Grace Nobility	Future Youth Energy	Villainy	Death
United States	Danger Stop	Cowardice Caution	Safety Go	Masculinity	Purity

Proper Functionality. Product features developed for one culture may not be appropriate for all cultures. Nielsen (1990), for example, describes a school hypertext product developed in France. During requirements determination it was established that only the schoolteacher should be able to add comments and viewpoints to the screens, not the students. This was a socially acceptable practice in France. Later, when the product was marketed in Sweden this aspect created problems. In Sweden independent discovery is greatly valued, and the inability of the students to add comments and viewpoints was unacceptable. All international products have to be reviewed for functionality as well and may require multiple versions to reflect the individual needs of cultures.

Features Not Supported. All aspects of a product not supported internationally should be removed from the system. Any references to features not supported should also be eliminated from all documentation. To leave this information in creates visual noise and will be confusing.

Requirements Determination and Testing

- Establish international requirements at the beginning of product development.
- Establish a relationship within the target culture.
- Test the product as if it were new.

When a product is translated for a new culture, it becomes a new product. Russo and Boor (1993) suggest the following should be accomplished.

Establish Requirements at Beginning. Developers must establish in what cultures the product will be used in at the start of the development cycle. Then, differing product requirements must be established, reflecting the differing needs of the various users. This permits localization issues to be addressed throughout the development process.

Relationship with Target Culture. A close working relationship with *natives* from all using cultures during requirements and development will permit local, culturally specific feedback to be obtained in a timely manner. A close working relationship will also educate the designers about the culture where their product will be used.

Testing. When a product is translated for a new culture, it is a new product and it should be subjected to a normal testing during the development cycle. If international testing is delayed until after the product is released to the domestic market, problems may be difficult, if not impossible, to address.

Accessibility

Accessibility, in a general sense, means a system must be designed to be usable by an almost unlimited range of people, essentially anyone who desires to use it. In a narrower sense, accessibility can be defined as providing easy access to a system for people with disabilities. We'll focus on this aspect of accessibility in the following paragraphs. Design objectives in creating accessibility for users with disabilities are:

- Minimize all barriers that make a system difficult, or impossible, to use.
- Provide compatibility with installed accessibility utilities.

Many governments have passed laws requiring that most employers provide reasonable accommodation for workers with disabilities. In the United States, one piece of legislation with this intent is the Americans with Disabilities Act. Accessible system design, then, seeks to ensure that no one with a disability is denied access to computer technology.

Types of Disabilities

Worldwide, a significant number of people have disabilities of one form or another. Disabilities may be temporary or permanent, or simply the result of aging. Disabilities can be grouped into several broad categories: visual, hearing, physical movement, speech or language impairments, cognitive disorders, and seizure disorders.

Visual disabilities can range from slightly reduced visual acuity to total blindness. *Hearing* disabilities range from an inability to detect certain sounds to total deafness.

Physical movement disabilities include difficulties in, or an inability to, perform certain physical tasks such as moving a mouse, pressing two keyboard keys simultaneously, or accurately striking a single keyboard key. People with *speech or language* disabilities may find it difficult to read and write (as with dyslexia). *Cognitive* disabilities include memory impairments and perceptual problems. People with *seizure* disorders are sensitive to visual flash rates, certain rates triggering seizures.

Accessibility Design

- Consider accessibility issues during system planning, design, and testing.
- Provide compatibility with installed accessibility utilities.
- Provide a customizable interface.
- Follow standard Windows conventions.
- Use standard Windows controls.

Accessibility issues should be considered throughout the entire system development cycle. Costs of retrofitting after the design is completed are always much higher than costs associated proper design itself. Unlike internationalization, where design costs are weighed against potential benefits, designing for accessibility may be required because of federal laws. All accessibility issues and requirements must be understood in system planning so that they may be incorporated within the design and testing processes.

Provide compatibility with accessibility utilities installed by users (screen review and voice input, for example). Also provide a customizable interface to accommodate the widest variety of user needs and preferences. Users are then free to choose an array of properties most satisfying to their viewing and usage needs. Whenever possible follow standard Windows conventions and use standard Windows controls in design. Most accessibility aids work best with applications that follow standard system conventions. Custom controls may not be usable by screen-review utilities.

Visual Disabilities

- Utilities:
  - Ensure compatibility with screen-review utilities.
  - Ensure compatibility with screen-enlargement utilities.
- Screen components:
  - Include meaningful screen and window titles.
  - Provide associated captions or labels for all controls, objects, icons, and graphics.
    - Including graphical menu choices.
  - Provide a textual summary for each statistical graphic.
  - Allow for screen element scalability.

— Support system settings for high contrast for all user interface controls and client area content.
  • When a "high contrast" setting is established, hide any images drawn behind the text to maintain screen information legibility.
— Avoid displaying or hiding information based on the movement of the pointer.
  • Exception: Unless it's part of the standard interface (Example: ToolTips).

■ Keyboard:
— Provide a complete keyboard interface.
— Provide a logical order of screen navigation.

■ Color:
— Use color as an enhancing design characteristic.
— Provide a variety of color selections capable of producing a range of contrast levels.
  • Create the color combinations based on the system colors for window components.
  • Do not define specific colors.

Visual disabilities range from impaired visual acuity, often resulting from aging; decreased sensitivity to a specific color or colors; partial blindness, or total blindness. Moderately impaired vision may simply require the availability of larger fonts or restrictions in the use of colors. Severe impairments, such as blindness, may require compatibility with speech or Braille utilities.

Utilities. For people who cannot use a screen's visual content, a *screen-review* utility will be necessary. These utilities, also called *screen-reader* programs or *speech access* utilities, take the displayed information being focused on and direct it through another medium. Alternate media include synthesized speech and refreshable Braille displays. *Screen enlargement* utilities enable the user to enlarge a portion of the screen, the monitor becoming a viewport that displays only a section of an enlarged display. These programs, also referred to as *screen magnification* utilities or *large-print* programs, track the user's use of a keyboard or mouse, moving the viewport to different areas of the screen as the user navigates within it.

Screen components. Meaningful, specific, and unique screen and window *titles* will assist the user in differentiating between these, especially when using a screen-review review utility. When using a reader, content must be addressed separately, so it will not be available with the title to aid in comprehension of what is presented. Provide associated *labels or captions* for all controls, objects, icons, and graphics, since all screen information must be presented as text by a screen reviewer. These labels must also be located in close proximity to the screen elements they refer to. A screen reviewer will relate the label to its associated screen element by its physical proximity, if it is not related programmatically. In rare situations, where the caption may be visually distracting (display-only data on inquiry screens, for example), provide a label but do not make it visible. Follow all the conventions presented in Step 3 "Understand the Principles of Good Screen

Design" for caption and label placement. *Graphical menu* choices, such as illustrated colors, shades, and patterns, must also possess textual labels.

Also provide a textual summary for each *statistical graphic*. Statistical graphics are images containing detailed information and, because of their graphic nature, their contents cannot be conveyed by a screen reader. The textual summary should include all information available to a sighted user.

Support screen element *scalability*, the presentation of larger text and graphics for people with only slight or moderate vision impairment. Also consider providing a "Zoom" command that scales the information displayed within a window. Support system settings for *high contrast* for all user interface controls and client area content. Users with visual impairments require a high contrast between foreground and background elements for best text legibility. Poor contrasts may result severely degraded legibility because the background may "bleed" into the foreground. When a "high contrast" setting is established, hide any images drawn behind text (watermarks, logos, patterns, and so on) to maintain screen information legibility. Monochrome versions of graphics and icons can also be presented using an appropriate foreground color for the displayed background color. In general, use black text on a white background to achieve the best foreground-background contrast. While some softer colors may be more attractive to look at, black on white always yields the best legibility.

Finally, avoid displaying or hiding information based on the movement of the pointer, unless it is part of the standard interface (a ToolTip, for example). These techniques may not be available to screen-review utilities. If these techniques are used, however, allow them to be turned on or off if a screen-review utility is used.

Keyboard. Provide a thorough and *complete keyboard interface*. Blind users cannot use a mouse to navigate because the pointer's location is unknown. All mouse actions, therefore, must be available through the keyboard using keyboard equivalents and keyboard accelerators. A logical order of screen *element navigation* is also a requirement for blind users. While this principle is standard for all screen users, a failure to adhere to it can be especially confusing for the blind because, when using a screen-review utility, they must navigate a screen sequentially in the predetermined navigation order. Their ability to scan the entire contents of a control or screen to establish context is simply not possible.

Color. Color must always be used as a supplemental or *enhancing* design characteristic. Users with a color-viewing deficiency may not be able to discriminate certain colors, and, consequently, they may be unable to understand that an action is required if the action is based upon an element's color alone. Provide a *variety* of color selections capable of producing a range of contrast levels. Create these combinations based on the system colors for window components. Never define and use specific colors. With a selection variety, the user may then customize the interface, choosing the best combination for his or her visual needs. Use of color is much more thoroughly described in Step 12 "Select the Proper Colors."

Hearing Disabilities

- Provide captions or transcripts of important audio content.
- Provide an option to display a visual cue for all audio alerts.
- Provide an option to adjust the volume.
- Use audio as an enhancing design characteristic.
- Provide a spell-check or grammar-check utility.

Hearing disabilities range from an inability to detect or interpret auditory output at normal or maximum levels certain sounds, to total deafness. A noisy work environment may also disrupt hearing, or sound may be turned off to avoid annoying neighboring workers.

Because audio may be missed or not understood, provide *captions or transcripts* of all important audio content. Also provide an option to display a *visual cue* for all audio alerts. Methods include displaying the alert in a message box or within the status bar. Provide an option to *adjust the volume* so that auditory content may be turned louder or off as necessary. A volume control may also benefit the vision-impaired user, who relies on a speech access utility to understand the screen. Like color, always use audio as an *enhancing* design characteristic; never rely on it as the sole means of communicating with the user.

Many people who are deaf, and whose language is American Sign Language, can be helped by a *spell-* or *grammar-check* utility. Uses of and problems with sound were described more fully in Step 9 "Provide Effective Feedback and Guidance and Assistance."

Physical Movement Disabilities

- Provide voice-input systems.
- Provide a complete and simple keyboard interface.
- Provide a simple mouse interface.
- Provide on-screen keyboards.
- Provide keyboard filters.

Voice input. People who have difficulty typing should have the option of using a voice-input system. Voice-input systems, also called *speech recognition* systems, permit the user to control software by voice instead of by mouse or keyboard. In a voice-input system, captions or labels are used to identify manipulable screen objects. Speaking the object's label then activates the object.

Keyboard interface. People with limited use of their hands may not be able to effectively use a mouse because of the fine motor movements necessary to control it. All mouse actions, therefore, must also be available through the keyboard using keyboard equivalents and keyboard accelerators for people with this physical movement disability. Accessibility Options in the Windows Control Panel also provide a setting to allow the mouse pointer to be controlled through the numeric keypad. Some people may have difficulty pressing two keys at the same time. This can be remedied by ensuring that the keyboard interface is simple.

Mouse interface. Pointing devices may actually be more efficient for some users with physical movement disabilities. Therefore, a simple mouse interface is also important. As is done for the entire range of system users, do not require basic system functions to be performed through double-clicks, drag-and-drop manipulation, and keyboard-modified mouse actions. These are shortcut techniques for advanced users.

On-screen keyboards. Some people cannot even use a standard keyboard. Keyboards can be presented on the screen and activated through special switches, a special mouse, or a headpointer, a device used to manipulate a pointer through head motion.

Keyboard filters. People with erratic motion, tremors, or slow responses often make incorrect keystrokes. Keyboard filters can be used to ignore brief or repeated keystrokes. Accessibility Options in the Windows Control Panel provide a range of keyboard filtering options.

Speech or Language Disabilities

- Provide a spell-check or grammar-check utility.
- Limit the use of time-based interfaces.
  - Never briefly display critical feedback or messages and then automatically remove them.
  - Provide an option to permit the user to adjust the length of the time-out.

Spell-checker. People with language disabilities, such as dyslexia, find it difficult to read and write. A spell-checker or grammar-checker can help these users, as well as or people with writing impairments, and people whose first language is not English.

Time-based interfaces. Limit the use of interface techniques that "time-out" and are removed after a prescribed period of time. People with some speech and language disabilities may not be able to react, either by reading text or pressing keys, within the allotted time period. Again, it is helpful to provide an option to permit the user to adjust and extend the time-out period.

Cognitive Disabilities

- Permit modification and simplification of the interface.
- Limit the use of time-based interfaces.
  - Do not briefly display critical feedback or messages and then automatically remove them.
  - Provide an option to permit the user to adjust the length of the time-out.

Interface modification and simplification. People with memory or perceptual problems can often be aided by a simplified interface. Allowing modification of the interface, customization of menus, customization of dialog boxes, or hiding graphics, for example, should be permitted. Conversely, some people with cognitive difficulties can be assisted by more extensive use of icons and graphics to illustrate objects and choices. Permitting modifications of this sort is also beneficial.

Time-based interfaces. People with cognitive impairments may also not be able to react to some situations in a timely manner. Again, for these people limit use of interface techniques that "time-out" and are removed after a prescribed period of time. It is also helpful to provide an option to permit the user to adjust and extend the time-out period.

Seizure Disorders

- Use elements that do not blink or flicker at rates between frequency ranges of 2 Hz and 55 Hz.
- Minimize the area of the screen that is flashing.
- Avoid flashing that has a high level of contrast between states.
- Provide an option to enable users to slow down or disable screen flashing.

People with seizure disorders may experience photosensitive epileptic seizures when exposed to certain visual flicker or flash rates of screen elements. In general, the higher the intensity of the flash, the larger area of the flash, or the faster the frequency of the flash, the greater the problem may be. Screen elements particularly susceptible to this phenomenon are flashing text, graphics that repeatedly turn on and off, and screen images that repeatedly change.

2Hz to 55Hz flicker. Use screen elements that do not blink or flicker at rates between 2Hz and 55Hz.

Flashing area. Smaller areas of flicker are less likely to cause seizures than larger areas. Minimize the area of the screen that is flashing.

High contrast. Avoid flashing that has a high level of contrast between states. Some people are more susceptible to high-intensity flashing.

Slow down or disable. Provide an option to enable users to slow down or disable screen flashing. In Windows, the Keyboard option in the Control Panel permits adjustment of the cursor blink rate. When set to slow, the cursor will flash 1.2 times per second. The rate increases 100 milliseconds for each notch up to a maximum of five times per second.

Web Page Accessibility Design

- Provide a "Skip to Main Content" link at the top of each page.
- Structure articles with two or three levels of headings.

- For all images provide associated text.
  — For lengthy descriptions, provide a link to a separate page.
- For all audio content include one or more of the following:
  — A caption or pop-up text window.
  — A textual transcript.
  — A textual description.
    • For lengthy transcripts or descriptions, provide a link to a separate page.
- For all video content include one or more of the following in both a textual and audio format:
  — A transcript.
  — A description.
    • For lengthy transcripts or descriptions, provide a link to a separate page.
- For image maps, provide equivalent text menus.
- Provide alternate ways to access items contained within tables.
- For online forms that cannot be read by screen utilities, provide alternate methods of communication.
- Provide an option to display animation in a nonanimated presentation mode.
- If accessibility cannot be accomplished in any other way, provide a text-only page with equivalent information and functionality.
- Follow the standards set by the World Wide Web Consortium for accessibility of Web content.

In addition to the previously described guidelines, Web applications require some additional considerations.

Skip to Main Content link. When a navigation bar is located at the top or left side of a page, a user using speech synthesis must listen to all navigation links before arriving at the main page content. This can become especially cumbersome if the links are consistently repeated on successive pages. (A sighted user can easily ignore the links.) To by-pass these links, and other elements such as tables of contents, provide a "Skip to Main Content" link attached to an unimportant image at the beginning of each page. The user can activate this link when it is presented, and the focus will move directly to the start of the page's content. (The user always has the choice to pass over this link and continue through the navigation links.)

Headings. Structure articles with two or three levels of headings. Nested headings facilitate access using screen-review utilities.

Images. Screen-review utilities cannot reveal images to visually impaired users. Therefore it is important to associate text with active images, particularly links or command buttons. When an image is not active, whether to provide associated text must be determined based upon the situation. The visually impaired user will not be able to ignore this audio text as a sighted user can if text is included. Include, then, short textual description for all important images. To include a lengthy text description, provide a link to a separate page that contains a complete description.

Audio. For hearing-impaired users, include one of the following textual alternatives. For short audio pieces, provide a *caption or small pop-up* window describing the audio. For longer audio, consider providing a *textual transcript,* an exact word-for-word version of the audio. Give the user the choice of reading the transcript, listening to the audio, or both reading and listening. Also consider a *textual description,* a longer and more extensive audio presentation than a transcript. This kind of description can be both subjective and artistic, depending on the needs of the use. Governmental legislation in some countries requires that these textual alternatives be synchronized with the audio presentation. For a very lengthy transcript or description, consider providing a link to a separate page containing a complete transcript or description.

Video. For all video content include a transcript or description in both a textual and audio format. As mentioned above, a *transcript is* an exact word-for-word version of the video. A *description,* also both subjective and artistic, is a longer and more extensive summarization of the video. It generally includes actions, settings, body language, and scene changes necessary to fully understand the video. Again, governmental legislation in some countries requires that these alternatives be synchronized with the video presentation.

Image maps. For content embedded in image maps provide equivalent textual menus because their content may not be accessible to screen-review utilities.

Tables. For tables, provide alternate ways to access their content. It may be difficult for sight-impaired users to navigate within a table using screen-review utilities.

Online forms. For online forms that cannot be read by screen utilities, provide alternate methods of communication. For example, provide instructions for supplying needed information by telephone, regular mail, or e-mail.

Animation. Screen reviewers cannot read information that is animated. Provide an option that enables users to stop animation. Also, ensure that the information conveyed by the animation is available in an alternate format.

Text-only pages. If accessibility cannot be accomplished in any other way, provide a text-only page with equivalent information and functionality. These pages must be maintained and updated in conjunction with the primary Web page.

WWW Consortium. The World Wide Web Consortium (www.w3.org) is establishing guidelines for Web content accessibility. Follow the existing guidelines, and new guidelines as they are approved and become available.

Other useful and thorough references for creating accessible systems are found in the Web sites of Microsoft (www.msdn.microsoft.com/library/books) and IBM (www-3.ibm.com).

Documentation

- Provide documentation on all accessible features.
- Provide documentation in alternate formats.
- Provide online documentation for people who have difficulty reading or handling printed material.

All accessibility features must be documented for the user. Much standard documentation does not address keyboard access as thoroughly as is required by disabled people. Also, some people have difficulties in reading or handling printed material. Documentation in alternate formats, such as audio or Braille, may be required.

Testing

- Test all aspects of accessibility as part of the normal system testing process.

Testing for accessibility must be part of the normal testing process. Test is reviewed in Step 14 "Test, Test, and Retest."

Create Meaningful Graphics, Icons and Images

The graphics era in interface and screen design began with the Xerox Star computer in the 1970s and fully blossomed with the advent of Apple's Lisa and Macintosh in the mid-1980s. GUI systems rapidly began to supplement the earlier text-based systems that had been in existence for three decades. When Microsoft finally entered the picture with their Windows system, GUI systems quickly became the dominant user interface. The significant graphical feature of a GUI system is the use of *icons* (the symbolic representation of objects, such as applications, office tools, and storage locations) and the symbolic representation of actions that could be applied to objects. The faces of many 1990s and beyond GUI screens scarcely resembled their older text-based siblings of the mid- to late-twentieth century.

The graphical evolution in interface design was further expanded in the 1990s with the maturing of the World Wide Web. The Web permitted easy inclusion of other media on a screen, including images, photographs, video, diagrams, drawings, and spoken audio. Since these media, including icons, could be combined in various ways, the term *multimedia* was coined to describe these combinations. A Web interface, then, has its foundation in GUI systems, but it has added its own unique elements to screen design.

Screen graphics, if used properly, can be a powerful communication and attention-getting technique. They can hold the user's attention, add interest to a screen, and quickly convey information. Improperly used graphics, however, can confuse the user, lead to navigation inefficiencies, and be distracting. Screen graphics must always serve a useful purpose.

This step will provide design guidelines for the various graphical techniques available in GUI and Web screen design. It will begin with a discussion of icons, the kinds available, their characteristics, and their usability influences. It will then address how icons are chosen and the icon design process. Finally, design guidelines for the various other graphical media will be presented.

Icons

Icons are most often used to represent objects and actions with which users can interact with or that they can manipulate. These types of icons may stand alone on a desktop or in a window, or be grouped together in a toolbar. A secondary use of an icon is to reinforce important information, a warning icon in a dialog message box, for example.

Kinds of Icons

The use of icons to reflect objects, ideas, and actions is not new to mankind. We've been there before. Early humans (100,000 years or so ago) used pictographs and then ideographs to communicate. Some of these early communications can still be found today on rock walls and in caves around the world. Until recent times, this was also the only way to communicate in some cultures (Native Americans and Australian aborigines, for example).

Word writing is traced back to Chinese writing from about 6000 BC and Egyptian hieroglyphics from about 3000 BC. This was followed by cuneiform (Babylonia and Assyria) from about 1900 BC, and the contemporary Chinese vocabulary (numbering about 50,000) around 1500 BC. In 1000 BC the Phoenicians developed a 22-sign alphabet that the Greeks adopted about 800–600 BC. The Greeks passed this alphabet on to the Romans about 400 BC, who then developed a 23-character alphabet. This alphabet has been modified and embellished but has remained essentially the same for the last 2000 years.

Pictorial representations, then, have played a prominent role in mankind's history. Word writing, however, unleashed much more flexibility and richness in communication. This has caused some skeptics to wonder why, after taking 2500 years to get rid of iconic shapes, we have now revived them on screens.

Whatever the past, today, objects or actions *are* depicted on screens by icons. The term icon by itself, however, is not very specific and can actually represent very different things. An attempt has been made by some to define the actual types of icons that do exist. Marcus (1984) suggests icons fall into these categories:

Icon. Something that looks like what it means.

Index. A sign that was caused by the thing to which it refers.

Symbol. A sign that may be completely arbitrary in appearance.

He states that what are commonly referred to as icons may really be indexes or symbols. A true icon is something that looks like what it means. It is representational and easy to understand. A picture of a telephone or a clock on a screen is a true icon. An index is a sign caused by the thing to which it refers. An open door with a broken window indicates the possible presence of a burglar. The meaning of an index may or may not be clear, depending upon one's past experiences. A symbol is a sign that may be completely arbitrary in appearance and whose meaning must be learned. The menu and sizing icons on screens are examples of symbols. From this perspective, strictly speaking, so-called icons on screens are probably a mixture of true icons, signs, and indexes.

Rogers (1989) provided an expanded definition for icon kinds.

- Resemblance—An image that looks like what it means.
- Symbolic—An abstract image representing something.
- Exemplar—An image illustrating an example or characteristic of something.
- Arbitrary—An image completely arbitrary in appearance whose meaning must be learned.
- Analogy—An image physically or semantically associated with something.

She suggests that an icon is *used* in a number of different ways: for *objects* such as a document, *object attributes* such as a color or fill pattern, *actions* such as to paste, *system states* such as ready or busy, and *message types* like critical or warning.

The different ways icons are used may then be represented by different design schemes. A *resemblance* icon is an image that looks like what it means—a book, for example, to represent a dictionary. This is equivalent to Marcus's icon. A *symbolic* icon is an abstract image that represents something. A cracked glass, for example, can represent something fragile. Marcus's symbol would be similar. An *exemplar* icon represents an example or characteristic of something. A sign at a freeway exit picturing a knife and fork has come to indicate a restaurant. An *arbitrary* icon is not directly related in any way and must be learned. Marcus's symbol would be an equivalent. Finally, an *analogy* icon is an image physically or semantically associated with something—a wheelbarrow full of bricks for the move command, for example. Marcus's symbol would also be similar.

In a study looking at various kinds of icons, Rogers found that those depicting both an action and an object were quite effective. For example, a drawing of a page and an arrow pointing up means "go to the top of the page." She also found that arbitrary icons were only meaningful in very small sets, and that icons based on analogies were relatively ineffective.

Characteristics of Icons

An icon possesses the technical qualities of syntactics, semantics, and pragmatics (Marcus, 1984). *Syntactics* refers to an icon's physical structure. Is it square, round, red, green, big, small? Are the similarities and differences obvious? Similar shapes and colors can be used to classify a group of related icons, communicating a common relationship. *Semantics* is the icon's meaning. To what does it refer—a file, a wastebasket, or some other object? Is this clear? *Pragmatics* is how the icons are physically produced and depicted. Is the screen resolution sufficient to illustrate the icon clearly? Syntactics, semantics, and pragmatics determine an icon's effectiveness and usability.

Influences on Icon Usability

Simply providing an icon on a screen does the user no particular favor, unless it is carefully designed to present a natural and meaningful association between the icon itself and what it stands for. Unfortunately, a sampling of many current systems finds icons that do not achieve this objective. Icons are included because "this is the thing to do" in a graphical system today. Little concern is given to effectiveness. The result is too often a cluttered and confusing screen that is visually overwhelming. So, proper icon design is important from an acceptance, learning, and productivity perspective. The following factors influence an icon's usability:

- Provide icons that are:
  - Familiar.
  - Clear and Legible.
  - Simple.
  - Consistent.
  - Direct.
  - Efficient.
  - Discriminable.
- Also consider the:
  - Context in which the icon is used.
  - Expectancies of users.
  - Complexity of task.

Familiarity. How familiar is the object being depicted? Familiarity will reduce learning time. How familiar are the commonly seen icons in Figure 11.1? Lack of familiarity requires learning the icons' meanings. Very unfamiliar icons require a great deal of learning.

Experience often makes words and numbers more familiar to a person than symbols. Confusion matrices have been developed through extensive research for alphanumeric data (0 versus O, 1 versus I). Graphic symbols may be more visually similar to each other.

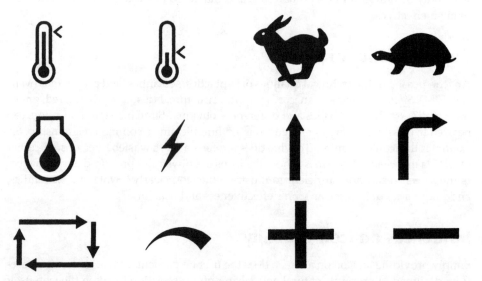

Figure 11.1   Some common icons. What do they stand for? Answers are on the next page.

From Micro Switch (1984)

The icons depicted in Figure 11.1 have the following meanings:

Hot	Cold	Fast	Slow
Engine Oil	Ammeter/Generator	Straight	Turn
Automatic	Variable Regulation (Increase/Decrease)	Plus/Positive	Minus/Negative

Clarity. Is the icon legible? Does the shape, structure, and formation technique on the screen permit a clear and unambiguous depiction of what it is? Screen resolution should be sufficiently fine to establish clear differences of form at the normal working distance. The resolution and pixel shapes for screens differ from one another. Icons must appear correctly and consistently no matter what kind of screen is used. If color is used, it should contrast well with the background. Poor clarity will lead to identification errors and slower performance.

Simplicity. Is the icon simple? Is the shape clean and devoid of unnecessary embellishments? Too many parts will only confuse the screen viewer.

Consistency. Are families of icons consistent in structure and shape? Are the same icons displayed on different screens consistent in shape and structure? Are the same icons displayed in different sizes also consistent in structure and shape?

Directness. How "sign-like" is the icon; how well does it convey its intended meaning? For concrete objects and actions, direct links are more easily established. Adjectives, adverbs, conjunctions, and prepositions can cause problems, however. Also, how does one easily convey concepts such as bigger, smaller, wider, or narrower?

Efficiency. In some situations, a graphics screen may be less efficient, consuming more screen display space than a word or requiring more physical actions by the user than text. A telephone directory of 50 names and numbers listed on an alphanumeric screen may consume the same screen space required for, and manipulation of, 15 file cards. Raising an arm or moving a mouse may be slower than simply typing. In other situations, icons can be more effective than words in communicating concepts in a smaller area of space. Icons' strength lies in situations where this occurs.

Discriminability. The symbols chosen must be visually distinguishable from other symbols. A person's powers of differentiation for shapes and other forms of codes have been experimentally determined over the years. The maximum number of codes that can be effectively differentiated by a human being, including geometric shapes, is summarized in Table 11.1. A person's ability to discriminate alphabetic or alphanumeric information is much more potent.

Context. The context of a symbol may change its meaning. Does the rabbit symbol illustrated in Figure 11.1, if seen on a road sign in a national park, mean, "go faster"? From this contextual perspective, icons are similar to words.

Expectancies. The symbol may be comprehended, but a false conclusion may be reached about the desired action because of an incorrect expectancy. A study of international road signs found that eight percent of all drivers never saw the "do not do" slash through a symbol on a road sign. Their expectancy was that they could do it, not "not do it."

Table 11.1 Maximum Number of Codes for Effective Human Differentiation

ENCODING METHOD	RECOMMENDED MAXIMUM	COMMENTS
Alphanumerics	Unlimited	Highly versatile. Meaning usually self-evident. Location time may be longer than for graphic coding.
Geometric Shapes	10–20	High mnemonic value. Very effective if shape relates to object or operation being represented.
Size	3–5	Fair. Considerable space required. Location time longer than for colors and shapes.
Line Length	3–4	Will clutter the display if many are used.
Line Width	2–3	Good.
Line Style	5–9	Good.
Line Angle	8–11	Good in special cases (such as wind direction).
Solid and Broken Lines	3–4	Good.
Number of Dots or Marks	5	Minimize number for quick assimilation.
Brightness	2–3	Creates problems on screens with poor contrast.
Flashing/Blinking	2–3	Confusing for general encoding but the best way to attract attention. Interacts poorly with other codes. Annoying if overused. Limit to small fields.
Underlining	No data	Useful but can reduce text legibility.
Reverse Video	No data	Effective for making data stand out. Flicker easily perceived in large areas, however.
Orientation (location on display surface)	4–8	—
Color	6–8	Attractive and efficient. Short location time. Excessive use confusing. Poor for the color blind.
Combinations of Codes	Unlimited	Can reinforce coding but complex combinations can be confusing.

Data derived from Martin, 1973; Barmack and Sinaiko, 1966; Mallory et al., 1980; Damodaran et al., 1980; and Maguire, 1985.

Complexity of task. The more abstract or complex the symbol, the more difficult it is to extract or interpret its intended meaning. It has been found that more concrete graphic messages are easier to comprehend than the more abstract. Icons, therefore, cannot completely replace words in more complex situations.

Choosing Icons

Icon design is an important process. Meaningful and recognizable icons will speed learning and recall and yield a much more effective system. Poor design will lead to errors, delays, and confusion. While the art of icon design is still evolving, it is agreed that the usability of a system is aided by adhering to the following icon design guidelines.

A Successful Icon

- Looks different from all other icons.
- Is obvious what it does or represents.
- Is recognizable when no larger than 16 pixels square.
- Looks as good in black and white as in color.

Fowler and Stanwick (1995) provide these general guidelines. An icon must look different from all other product icons, making it discriminable and differentiable. What it does or represents must also be obvious so it is interpretable. It must be recognizable when no larger than 16 pixels square. Finally, it must look as good in black and white as in color. Color is always an enhancing quality of an icon.

Size

- Supply in all standard sizes.
  - 16 × 16 pixels.
    - 16- and 256-color versions.
  - 32 × 32 pixels
    - 16- and 256-color versions.
    - Effective: 24 × 24 or 26 × 26 in 32 × 32 icon.
  - 48 × 48 pixels
    - 16- and 256-color versions.
- Use colors from the system palette.
- Use an odd number of pixels along each side.
  - Provides center pixel around which to focus design.
- Minimum sizes for easy selection:
  - With stylus or pen: 15 pixels square.
  - With mouse: 20 pixels square.
  - With finger: 40 pixels square.
- Provide as large a hot zone as possible.

Size. Typically, icons come in three standard sizes, 16, 32 and 48 pixels square. For clarity, 16 x 16 should be an icon's minimum size. An effective combination for an image is a 24 × 24 or 26 × 26 in a 32-pixel square icon.

Colors. Microsoft suggests that while 256 colors may be used in the smaller sizes than 48 × 48 pixels, to do so increases icon storage requirements, and they may not be displayable on all computer configurations. If 256 colors are used for icons, they suggest that the standard 16-color format should *always* be provided. Also, use colors from the system palette to ensure that the icons look correct in all color configurations.

Odd number of pixels. Horton (1994) recommends using an odd number of pixels along each side of the matrix. This provides a center pixel around which to focus, thus simplifying the design process.

Icon selection. For easy selection the following are minimum icon sizes: with a stylus or pen, 15 pixels square; with a mouse, 20 pixels square; with one's finger, 40 pixels square.

Hot zone. An icon's hot zone, the area within it that allows it to be selected, should be as large as possible, preferably the entire size of the icon. This allows easier selection.

Choosing Images

- Use existing icons when available.
- Use images for nouns, not verbs.
- Use traditional images.
- Consider user cultural and social norms.

Existing icons. Many standard icons have already been developed for graphical systems. Use these standard icons where they are available. This will promote consistency across systems, yielding all the performance benefits that consistency provides. Where standard icons are not available, determine if any applicable icons have already been developed by industries and trade or standards organizations. The International Standards Organization (ISO), for example, has developed standard shapes for a variety of purposes. Always consult all relevant reference books before inventing new symbols or modifying existing ones.

Nouns. An object, or noun, is much easier to represent pictorially than an action or verb. Choose nouns for icons whenever possible.

Traditional images. Old-fashioned, traditional images often work better than newer ones. They have been around longer, and more people recognize them.

Cultural and social norms. Consider users' cultural and social norms. Improper design of icons can create problems internationally. Social norms vary, so great variations exist in what is recognizable and acceptable throughout the world. What one culture recognizes may have no meaning in another. What is acceptable in one country may not be in another. International considerations were thoroughly described in Step 10 "Provide Acceptable Internationalization and Accessibility."

Creating Images

- Create familiar and concrete shapes.
- Create visually and conceptually distinct shapes.
  — Incorporate unique features of an object.
  — Do not display within a border.
- Clearly reflect objects represented.
- Simply reflect objects represented, avoiding excessive detail.
- Create as a set, communicating relationships to one another through common shapes.
- Provide consistency in icon type.
- Create shapes of the proper emotional tone.

Concrete and familiar shapes. Ideally, an icon's meaning should be self-evident. This is enhanced when concrete shapes are provided, those that look like what they are. An icon should also be intuitive or obvious, based upon a person's preexisting knowledge. Familiar shapes are those images that are well learned. Figure 11.2 illustrates concrete and familiar icons for a file folder, book, and telephone as well as images for the same objects that are more abstract and unfamiliar. A study found that concrete, familiar icons were preferred to abstract, unfamiliar ones.

Keep in mind, however that familiarity is in the eye of the viewer. The concrete images pictured may be familiar to us, readers of this book, but not to a tribal chief living in a remote area of the world where these objects do not exist. Similarly, items familiar to those working on the factory floor may not be at all familiar in the office or in the home, and vice versa. Mayhew (1992) also cautions that some

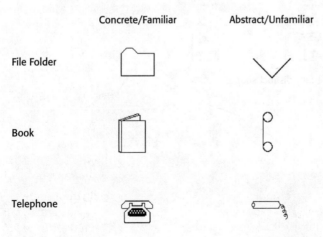

Figure 11.2 Concrete and familiar shapes.

abstract images should not be discounted because they have become familiar, in spite of their being abstract. On a road sign, for example, an angled red bar inscribed over an object means do not do what is pictured beneath (at least to most people, as described earlier). While abstract, it is a very familiar shape today. If an abstract image must be used, it should be capable of being learned quickly and easily recalled. Familiarity can only be determined through knowing one's user.

Visually and conceptually distinct shapes. It must be easy to tell icons apart so the chances of confusing them are minimized. Differentiation is aided when icons are visually different from one another. It is also aided when icons are conceptually different—that is, when they portray specific features of an object that are relatively unique within the entire set of objects to be displayed. Figure 11.3, based upon Mayhew (1992), illustrates how distinctiveness may be achieved for two similar items, a dictionary and a telephone book. Visual distinctiveness is achieved by incorporating unique features of each: for the dictionary, it is its content of letters and words, for the telephone book, numbers and the telephone bell.

Visual distinctiveness is degraded when borders are placed around icons, as illustrated in Figure 11.4. Borders tend to obscure the shape of the object being displayed.

Clearly reflect objects. The characteristics of the display itself should permit drawings of adequate quality. Poorly formed or fuzzy shapes will inhibit recognition.

DICTIONARY   TELEPHONE BOOK

Conceptually	Visually		
Similar	Distinct		
Distinct	Similar		
Distinct	Distinct		

Figure 11.3   Visually and conceptually distinct shapes.

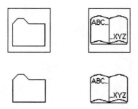

Figure 11.4   Borders degrading icon distinctiveness.

Simply reflect objects. Construct icons with as few graphical components as necessary, using no more than two or three, if possible. Also, use simple, clean lines, avoiding ornamentation. Byrne (1993) found that simple icons, icons containing fewer graphical elements, were located faster in a visual search task than complex icons, icons with more components. He concluded that complex icons seemed to clutter a screen with information that people were unable to employ to their advantage. Too much detail inhibits rather than facilitates perception, as illustrated in Figure 11.5. For real-world objects, use only enough detail to permit recognition and recall.

Design as a set. Do not design icons in isolation, but as a family considering their relationships to each other and the user's tasks. Provide a common style. When icons are part of an overall related set, create shapes that visually communicate these relationships. Objects within a class, for example, may possess the same overall shape but vary in their other design details, as illustrated in Figure 11.6. Color may also be used to achieve this design goal. In creating sets, always avoid repeating unrelated elements.

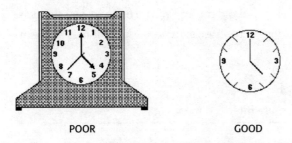

POOR   GOOD

Figure 11.5   Avoid excessive detail in icon design.

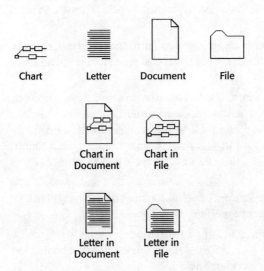

Chart   Letter   Document   File

Chart in   Chart in
Document   File

Letter in   Letter in
Document   File

Figure 11.6   Communication relationships in icons.

Consistency in icon type. As previously noted, there are many different kinds of design schemes for icons (resemblance, symbolic, arbitrary, and so on). All these schemes might be used to create a meaningful family of icons for an application. Learning the meaning of icons and searching for the right icon, however, will be aided if the same design scheme is used for all icons within a family. In presenting a series of icons for actions such as paint, cut, and so on, one could, for example, (1) depict a before-after representation of the action, (2) depict the action itself being performed, or (3) picture the tool to perform the action. While a series of meaningful icons could be developed using each scheme, the best approach would be to use only one of these schemes to develop the entire family of icons.

Proper emotional tone. The icon should appropriately reflect the environment in which it is used. A sewage disposal system would be an inappropriate metaphor for an electronic mail system wastebasket.

Drawing Images

- Provide consistency in shape over varying sizes.
- Do not use triangular arrows in design to avoid confusion with other system symbols.
- When icons are used to reflect varying attributes, express these attributes as meaningfully as possible.
- Provide proper scale and orientation.
- Use perspective and dimension whenever possible.
- Accompany icon with a label to assure intended meaning.

Consistency. When drawing images, create consistency in shapes for identical icons of differing sizing. Preserve the general shape and any distinctive detail. Consistency is achieved through limiting the variations of angles, line thicknesses, shapes, and amount of empty space.

Triangular arrows. Avoid using a triangular graphic similar to that used as a cascade symbol for menus, a drop-down button for controls, and scroll arrows. The similarity may cause confusion.

Meaningful attributes. When an icon is also used to express an attribute of an object, do this as meaningfully as possible. The status of a document, for example, might be represented by displaying it in a different shade, but would be more effectively illustrated by filling it in, as illustrated in Figure 11.7. Shading requires remembering what each specific type of shading stands for; the filled-in proportion is more intuitively obvious.

Scale and orientation. Ensure that the size and orientation are consistent with other related objects. Also ensure that they fit well on the screen.

Perspective and dimension. Use lighting and shadow to more accurately reflect the real-world experiences of people. When a light source is used, it must be located upper left, as is done with other screen elements.

POOR   GOOD

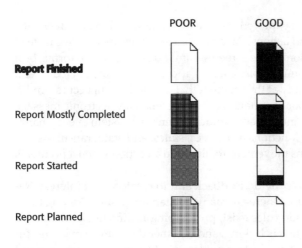

Figure 11.7 Expressing attributes in icon design.

Caption or label. Since icons may not be used often, the ability to comprehend, learn, and recall an icon's meaning can be greatly improved by attaching textual captions or labels to them The preferred label location is directly beneath the icon, not within it, because of the international considerations discussed in Step 10. Labels beneath the icon also provide a larger target, speeding selection. Labels should always be related to icons in a consistent positional way. "Mystery icons," icons with no caption or label to explain them, lead to a user guessing game and many errors. While ToolTips can be used to present labels, they are time-consuming to present, taking about two-thirds of a second to appear and be comprehended. Scanning an entire row of 15 icons with ToolTips, therefore, will consume about 10 extra seconds.

MAXIM   **If people must remember hieroglyphics, they won't stick around long.**

Icon Animation and Audition

- Animation:
  - Use:
    - To provide feedback.
    - For visual interest.
  - Make it interruptible or independent of user's primary interaction.
  - Do not use it for decoration.
  - Permit it to be turned off by the user.
  - For fluid animation, present images at 16 or more frames per second.

- Audition:
  - Consider auditory icons.

Animation. Recent research has explored the use of bringing to life on screens the icons representing objects and actions. An animated icon appears to move instead of maintaining a static position on the screen. Animation can take two forms, best described as static and dynamic. A *static* icon's appearance is unchanged over a period of time and changes only at the moment that a system event occurs. An example would be the open door of a mailbox shutting when an electronic message is received. A *dynamic* icon's movement is independent of a system event, changing appearance to represent functions, processes, states, and state transitions. An example is an icon that begins movement to illustrate an action when a pointer is moved close to it.

Animation can be used to provide feedback and to create visual interest. Researchers caution, however, that there are many outstanding issues. Among them are that few animation creation rules exist, prototyping is difficult, a scheme for how they fit into a larger system is lacking, and whether they can be made useful for more complex and abstract concepts is not known. Morimoto, Kurokawa, and Nishimura, (1993) found that dynamic animation of the type in the example above did not increase the comprehensibility of icons. Its only advantage was its entertainment value.

Some general guidelines, however, seem appropriate. First, do not prevent the user from interacting with the system while the animation is performed. Unless the animation is part of a process, it should be independent of what the user is doing. It should also be interruptible. Be conservative in its use; do not use animation simply for decoration. It can be very distracting or annoying. Finally, provide the user with the option of turning it on or off, as desired

Microsoft recommends that to achieve fluidity in movement, images should be presented at a speed of at least 16 frames per second. The reader interested in more information on animation is referred to Baecker and Small (1990).

Audition. Objects make sounds as they are touched, dragged, bumped against one another, opened, activated, and thrown away. Auditory icons are computer sounds replicating everyday sound-producing events. When a printer near one's desk begins printing, the sound of the printing mechanism is heard. This provides auditory feedback that a print operation one has just asked for has successfully started. An auditory icon would be the same sound, generated by the computer. Another example would be to convey information about an object's dimensions. If a file is large, it can sound large. If an object is dragged over a new surface, the new surface is heard. If an ongoing process starts running more quickly, it sounds quicker.

Sounds can convey information about many events in computer systems, permitting people to listen to computers as we do in the everyday world. It may be well suited to providing information:

- About previous and possible interactions.
- Indicating ongoing processes and modes.
- Useful for navigation.
- To support collaboration.

Auditory icons are distinct from *earcons*, abstract synthetic tones used in structured combinations to create sound messages. Auditory icons may also be susceptible to the distracting influences that sounds can cause to listeners, especially others. The use of sound was more fully discussed in Step 9 "Provide Effective Feedback and Guidance and Assistance." The reader in need of more information on auditory icons is referred to Garver (1993).

The Design Process

- Define the icon's purpose and use.
- Collect, evaluate, and sketch ideas.
- Draw in black and white.
- Draw using an icon-editing utility or drawing package.
- Test for user:
  — Expectations.
  — Recognition.
  — Learning.
- Test for legibility.
- Register new icons in the system's registry.

Define purpose. To begin the design process, first define the icon's purpose and use. Have the design team brainstorm about possible ideas, considering real-world metaphors. Simple metaphors, analogies, or models with a minimal set of concepts are the best places to start in developing icons.

Collect, evaluate, and sketch ideas. Start by designing on paper, not on the computer (Fowler and Stanwick, 1995). Ask everyone to sketch his or her ideas. Do not worry about too much detail; exact pixel requirements are not necessary at this time.

Draw in black and white. Many icons will be displayed in monochrome. Color is an enhancing property; consider it as such.

Test for expectation, recognition, and learning. Choosing the objects and actions, and the icons to represent them, is not a precise process, and will not be easy. So, as in any screen design activity, adequate testing and possible refinement of developed images must be built into the design process. Icon recognition and learning should both be measured as part of the normal testing process.

Test for legibility. Verify the legibility and clarity of the icons in general. Also, verify the legibility of the icons on the screen backgrounds chosen. White or gray backgrounds may create difficulties. An icon mapped in color, then displayed on a monochrome screen, may not present itself satisfactorily. Be prepared to redraw it in black and white, if necessary.

Register new icons in the system's registry. Create and maintain a registry of all system icons. Provide a detailed and distinctive description of all new icons.

Screen Presentation

- Follow all relevant general guidelines for screen design.
- Limit the number of symbols to 12, if possible, and at most 20.
- Arrange icons:
  — In a meaningful way, reflecting the organization of the real world.
  — To facilitate visual scanning.
  — Consistently.
- Place object and action icons in different groups.
- Present an interactive icon as a raised screen element.
- Ensure that a selected icon is differentiable from unselected icons.
- Permit arrangement of icons by the user.
- Permit the user to choose between iconic and text display of objects and actions.

In designing, or establishing, screen layout rules; adhere to the following presentation rules.

General guidelines. Follow all relevant general guidelines for screen design. Icons are but one part of a larger picture.

Number of icons. A person's ability to identify shapes is limited (see Figure 11.1). A literature review, suggest using no more than eight to twelve or so functions that require icons at one time. At most, present no more than 20. If labels are attached to icons, however, the meaning of the icon is greatly clarified. Too many icons on a screen, though, will greatly increase screen clutter and create confusion. In general, fewer are better.

Arranging icons. Organize icons in a way that reflects the *real-world* organization of the user. Place object icons and action icons within different groupings. *Visual scanning* studies, in a non-iconic world, universally find that a top-to-bottom scan of columnar-oriented information is fastest. Generalization of these findings to an icon screen may not necessarily be warranted if icons have attached labels. Columnar orientation icons (with labels below the icons) will separate the labels from one another by the icons themselves. The labels will be farther apart and fewer icons will fit in a column than in a horizontal or row orientation. A row orientation would seem to be more efficient in many cases, as adjacent icons will be in closer physical proximity. Until research evidence is established to the contrary, organizing icons either in a column or a row seems appropriate. In either case, a *consistent* straight eye movement must be maintained through the icons.

Object and action icons. Conceptually similar items should always be arrayed together. Locating them will be easier.

Interactive icons. To provide a visual indication that an icon is interactive or "clickable," present it in a three-dimensional state raised from the screen background.

Selected icon. Ensure a selected icon is visually differentiable from unselected icons. One common method to achieve this is to present the selected icon in a three-dimensional "pressed" state.

User arrangement. Allow the user to arrange the icons in a manner that is meaningful for the task. A default arrangement should be provided, however.

Iconic or text display. In some situations, and for some users, pure text labels may be more meaningful than icons. The option to display text only should always be provided.

Multimedia

The graphical flexibility of the Web permits inclusion of other media on a screen, including images, photographs, video, diagrams, drawings, and spoken audio. The availability of these additional interface elements has, however, been a double-edged sword. On the one hand, the various media can be powerful communication and attention-getting techniques. Multimedia can hold the user's attention, add interest to a screen, entertain, and quickly convey information that is more difficult to present textually. It can also make the Web much more accessible to people with disabilities. On the other hand, effective use of multimedia in design has been hindered by a lack of knowledge concerning how the various media may best be used, and a scarcity of applied design guidelines. (GUI guidelines relevant to Web page design have been available for years, but their existence was either unknown or ignored.) Effective multimedia use has also been hindered by the "let's use it because we have it" attitude exhibited by many designers. (To be fair, early GUI design has suffered from the same problem.) The resulting usability problems, user confusion and frustration, poor screen legibility, and slow downloads, and so on have created situations where the user was too often denied an efficient and meaningful Web experience.

As a result, recent studies (Spool et al., 1997, for example) have found that the most difficult to use Web sites were those that were graphically intense, and the top Web sites were characterized by little, if any, multimedia. Studies have also found that for users, text is currently a much more important Web site component than graphics. (At least at this stage in Web evolution.) Today, consequently, good interface design employs multimedia in a conservative and appropriate manner. The objective is good interaction design, not "sparkle." In the future, experts say, multimedia elements will be much better integrated with browsers, alleviating many of today's usability problems.

Graphics

- Use graphics to:
  — Supplement the textual content, not as a substitute for it.
  — Convey information that can't be effectively accomplished using text.

— Enhance navigation through:
- Presenting a site overview
- Identifying site pages.
- Identifying content areas.

■ Limit the use of graphics that take a long time to load.

■ Coordinate the graphics with all other page elements.

Graphics contained in Web pages serve several distinct purposes, which can be classified as follows:

Navigational. To identify links that may be followed.

Representational. To illustrate items mentioned in the text.

Organizational. To depict relationships among items mentioned in text.

Explanative. To show how things or processes work.

Decorative. To provide visual appeal and emphasis.

Graphics must always be used for a specific purpose. This purpose must be determined before designing or choosing the graphic itself. Graphics should only be used when they add to a Web site's message. Graphics that do not relate to a Web site's purpose, and do not strengthen the Web site's message should never be used.

Supplement textual content. Use graphics to supplement text, not as a substitute for it. Graphics are not easily accessible to search facilities and screen reviewers, and are slower to download than text. As studies have shown, people prefer textual page content to graphical content. So, never use graphics when text will do the job. If a graphic will help people understand the text they are reading, then certainly use it.

Convey information not possible using text. Use graphics to convey information that can't be effectively conveyed using text. In some cases the old adage "a picture is worth a thousand words" is indeed true. Photographs, for example, can be used to communicate the exact appearance of objects. Video is useful for showing objects or things that move. Diagrams can be used to present an object's structure. Drawings are useful when selected parts of an object need to be emphasized or represented. If a graphic does a better job of communicating an idea or concept than text, then use it. (Remember, however, text descriptions or transcripts of the graphic will always be necessary for accessibility reasons.)

Enhance navigation. Graphics can be used to enhance navigation. A graphical *overview* of a site's organizational scheme will enable the user to conceptualize and learn the site's structure faster than can be done through textual overviews. *Site pages* can be related through a consistent graphical theme carried from page to page. This will reinforce the browsing user's sense of place. Graphics can also be used to identify and represent major site *content areas*. The experienced user will locate and identify the content areas faster using meaningful graphical identifiers rather than text.

Limit long-loading graphics. Limit the use of graphics that take a long time to load In general, all graphics must be smaller on the Web than on the printed page. Large graphics take longer to download testing the user's patience. If a large graphic is needed, present a small version and link it to a page containing the large version. Richly colored graphics and pages containing numerous graphics are also slower to load.

Coordinate graphics. Graphics are only one component of a Web page. The graphics must fit in with the style of typography used, the colors used, and the page layout itself. Use of plain and simple fonts are best coordinated with simple graphics. Realistic graphics work best with elements like three-dimensional effects and more complex typography.

Images

- General:
  - Use standard images.
  - Use images consistently.
  - Produce legible images.
  - Provide descriptive text or labels with all images.
  - Distinguish navigational images from decorative images.
  - Minimize:
    - The number of presented images.
    - The size of presented images.
      - Restrict single images to 5K.
      - Restrict page images to 20K.
      - Provide thumbnail size images.
    - Image animation.
  - Avoid extraneous or gratuitous images.
- Color:
  - Minimize the number of colors in an image.
- Format:
  - Produce images in the most appropriate format.
    - GIF.
    - JPEG.
- Internationalization:
  - Provide for image internationalization.
- Screen design:
  - Reuse images on multiple pages.

Standard images. Whenever possible, use standard images that have already been developed and tested. This will promote consistency across systems, yielding all the performance benefits that consistency provides. These standard images may be found in guideline books, company or organizational documentation, or in industry, trade, or standards organizations' documentation. The International Standards Organization (ISO), for example, has developed standard image shapes for a variety of purposes. Always consult all relevant reference books before inventing new images or modifying existing ones.

Consistency. Use an image consistently throughout an application or Web site. Multiple images with the same meaning will be difficult to learn.

Legibility. Create legible images, images that are easy to identify from a variety of viewing distances and angles. Legibility is affected by a number of factors, including contrast with the background, image complexity, and image size. Images with a minimum amount of detail are usually easier to comprehend and faster to load. If an image with more detail is needed, provide a link to a page containing the detailed version. An image that is perfectly legible when it is drawn or rendered large may, when shrunk for placing on a page, become incomprehensible.

Descriptive text or labels. Many images are not immediately clear, even if well designed. The ability to comprehend, learn, and recall an image's meaning, especially if it is used for navigation, can be greatly improved by providing images with descriptive text or labels. Also, many people browse the Web with their graphics turned off. Without alternate, text an image's purpose and function will not be known. Alternate text for an image also provides the following benefits:

- It provides vision-impaired users with access to content through a screen-review utility.
- It helps sighted users determine whether they want to wait for the image to fully load.
- It enables users to read a description of a linked image and activate the link before image fully loads.

Navigational and decorative images. Clearly indicate which graphical images on the screen are used for navigation by providing a visual indication that an image is interactive or "clickable." Possibilities include giving the image a raised or three-dimensional appearance (like a navigational icon) or underlining any descriptive text contained within it (like a textual link). Navigational images that cannot be distinguished from decorative images force users to "mouse over" each image to determine which are interactive. (Once they are over their initial state of confusion.) This is time-consuming, and important navigation links may be missed.

Minimize number of images. The more images presented on a Web page, the slower the download time. Use text whenever possible

Minimize size of images. Oversized images also take a long time to load. Slow-loading graphics rarely add value to text, and people often don't bother to stick around for them. The design goal is to produce images that load quickly. Make the graphic as small as possible while still retaining sufficient image quality. In general, restrict *single images* to 5K, *page images* to no more than 20K. A 200K file can take several minutes to load. Never put borders around an image with a drawing program because this also adds to the file size.

Thumbnail size. A thumbnail is a small version of an image, usually fairly low in quality. This small image will load quickly because of its small file size. Link this thumbnail image to a large high-quality version of the image. Users can then decide whether or not they want to retrieve and view the full-size version. Always let the user know the size of the full-size image. Thumbnails are especially useful when several images, or a collection of images, must be displayed on a Web page.

Minimize animation. Animated images take a long time to load and are distracting to many people. Only use animation when it serves a useful purpose.

Extraneous or gratuitous images. Similarly, do not present extraneous or gratuitous images. Images take longer to load than text, and Web users prefer text. Images must always serve a useful purpose.

Minimize the number of colors. To reduce the size of image files, reduce the size of the color palette and the number of colors in the image. Color-rich images tend to be large. If the image color palette is too small, however, the image will be degraded. The objective is to retain sufficient image quality while making the file as small as possible. To create images of sufficient color quality while at the same time reducing file size, begin with a high-quality image and create versions using successively smaller color palettes. Stop when the image degradation becomes apparent. (Guidelines for the use of color in screen design are addressed in Step 12 "Choose the Proper Colors.")

Appropriate format. Produce images in the most appropriate format, GIF or JPEG. CompuServe developed the GIF format (Graphics Interchange Format) in 1987. The JPEG (Joint Photographic Experts Group) was developed for the transfer of photographic images over the Internet.

GIF. Most Web color images and backgrounds are GIF files. They are usually smaller and load faster than JPEGs. They are particularly useful for images that contain flat areas of color. Since GIFs are limited to 256 colors, they are ideal for graphics that use only a few colors. GIFs exist in either a *dithered* or *nondithered* format. Dithering is the color-mixing process a computer goes through when it encounters a color not in its palette. In this process palette colors are mixed to approximate the appearance of the desired color. The resulting color may be grainy or unacceptable. The dithering will be most apparent in gradations, shadows, and feathered edges. A nondithered GIF attempts to match the closest colors from the palette to the image. This is referred to as *banding*. This banding may also create an unacceptable image.

One way to control the dithering process is to create images that only use nondithering colors. The 216 colors that are shared by PCs and Macintoshes are called the Web palette or browser-safe colors. These colors display properly across all platforms without dithering.

GIFs may also be *interlaced*. Interlacing is the gradual display of an image in a series of passes on the screen. The first pass displays a low-resolution out-of-focus image and each succeeding pass creates a clearer view until finally a complete image is displayed. With interlacing, users see a complete, although not clear, image much more quickly. An impression that the image is loading much faster is achieved, and users can quickly determine if they are interested in the image. With a *noninterlaced* GIF, the graphic unfolds more slowly one row at a time. Use interlaced GIFs to give users a preview of graphics while they unfold.

Most Web servers call up to four GIFs at a time for display. Limiting GIF images on a page to four will allow pages to load much faster.

JPEG. JPEG formats are superior for images such as photographs that contain numerous changes in color tonality. They look best on monitors capable of displaying 16 million colors. A JEPG's range of colors cannot be produced in monitors displaying 256 or fewer colors. Images that contain flat areas of color may also find that JEPGs introduce unwanted artifacts. JPEGs usually take longer to download than GIFs.

JPEGs may be displayed as progressive or standard. *Progressive* images gradually fade into view like interlaced GIFs, each pass an increasingly higher quality scan. *Standard* images are drawn from top to bottom like noninterlaced GIFs. Use progressive JPEGs to give users a preview of the graphics while they are unloaded.

Internationalization. When designing for international or multilingual users, using images may eliminate the need for translating words. All images, however, must comply with the internationalization design guidelines covered in Step 10.

Reuse images. Repeat the same images on multiple pages. Repeated images will be stored in a *cache*, the browser's temporary storage area. Loading an image from cache significantly reduces an image's downloading time.

Image Maps

- Use:
  — To provide navigation links to other content.
- Advantages:
  — Can be arrayed in a meaningful and obvious structure.
  — Faster to load than separate images.
- Disadvantages:
  — Consume a significant amount of screen space.
  — "Hot spots" not always obvious.
  — One's location within image map is not always obvious.
- Guidelines:
  — Use with caution.
  — Provide effective visual cues and emphasis to make it easy to identify link boundaries.
  — Ensure image maps are accessible to the vision impaired.

Use. An *image map* is a complete image containing individual segments with navigation links to other content. It primary use is to present a meaningfully structured image within which the links are contained.

Advantages/disadvantages. An *advantage* of an image map is its meaningful and obvious structure. It can reflect the user's mental model of an object, minimizing organizational learning requirements. An image map may be a map of a country, for example, with areas reflecting regions that can be selected as links to more detailed content. An image map can also be an image reflecting a site's organization. Image maps, because of their graphical nature, can aid conceptualization of a Web site and how it is organized. Another image map advantage is that they are faster to load than individual images, at least for users accessing the Web through a modem.

There are several *disadvantages* of image maps. First, they are quite wasteful of screen space. Providing large enough "hot spots" or "clickable" areas for each element often necessitates creating very large maps. Within the maps, clickable regions are also not always obvious because they cannot be seen. Whether to click on the map, or where to click, is not always known. This can be confusing for the new user. Unclear or poorly designed image maps can cost users a great deal of time when they make erroneous navigation selections. Selected image map links are also not obvious to the user. A link just selected may be again selected, directing the user right back to the page displayed with no indication that anything has changed. User confusion can again exist. Another disadvantage is that search facilities may not be able to index an image map.

> **MYTH** **Cool = Usable**

Guidelines. Because of these disadvantages, be cautious in the use of image maps. Some experts recommend not using them at all. If used, provide effective visual cues and emphasis to make it easy to identify individual selectable segments and where link boundaries exist. Consider supplementing the image map graphic with text to inform users what they will see when they select a particular area. Finally, ensure that image maps are accessible to vision-impaired users.

Photographs/Pictures

- Use:
  — When every aspect of the image is relevant.
- Guidelines:
  — Use JPEG format.
  — On the initial page:
    - Display a small version.
      — A thumbnail size image.
      — Zoom-in on most relevant detail.
    - Link to larger photos showing as much detail as needed.

Use. When every aspect of an image or object is relevant, present a picture or photograph of it. A photo or picture will capture all visible aspects.

Guidelines. The *JPEG* format was developed for presenting photographs that contain numerous changes in color tonality. Pictures or photos look best on monitors capable of displaying 16 million colors.

A large photo will have an excessively long downloading time. To minimize this time, on the initial page display a small version of the photo and provide a link to a larger, high-quality, complete photo on another page. The small version may be a *thumbnail* image, a complete miniature photograph, usually fairly low in quality. Because of the complexity of a photographic image, a thumbnail may not always be legible. When legibility is a problem, instead of resizing the image to a miniature photo, provide a *zoom-in* on the most relevant photo detail, cropping and resizing as necessary to provide a meaningful and legible image.

For linked full-size photographs provide as much detail as the users need and always inform the users of the image's size. Also, if necessary, provide a zoom or rotation capability for the photograph on the linked page.

Video

- Uses:
  — To show things that move or change over time.
  — To show the proper way to perform a task.
  — To provide a personal message.
  — To grab attention.
- Disadvantages:
  — Expensive to produce.
  — Slow to download.
  — Small and difficult to discern detail.
- Guidelines:
  — Never automatically download a video into a page.
  — Create short segments.
  — Provide controls, including those for playing, pausing, and stopping.
  — Consider using:
    • Existing video.
    • Audio only.
    • A slide show with audio.

Uses. Video is especially suited to showing things that move or change over time. Examples include product demonstrations, how to repair a piece of equipment, or how to perform a dance step. Videos can also be used to present personal messages, although the speaker's "presence" may not always have the desired emotional effect. Because of their animation, videos can also be used to grab attention.

Disadvantages. Videos are expensive to produce and slow to download and play. They are also small and limited in the detail they can present. Always inform the user of a video's size so a choice of whether or not to download it can be made. Depending on a video's purpose, its animation may also be distracting to the user.

Guidelines. Do not *automatically download* a video into a loading Web page. Create *short segments*. There are many distractions people may encounter while using a video (the telephone or interruptions by people, and so on), so long segments should be avoided. A 60 to 90 second video is considered long so keep a video's length well within these limits. For all playable files provide the following *controls*: Play, Pause/Resume, Stop, Rewind, Fast Forward, and Volume.

Because of a video's disadvantages consider using existing videos, audio alone, or a slide show with audio. Reusing an *existing video* will save production time and money. A new voice-over may be all that is necessary. *Audio alone* may be as powerful a tool as a video, since the human voice is an important aspect of all videos. Determine whether audio alone will accomplish the video's objectives. An *audio slide show* may also be a good substitute for a video. The impression of movement is still achieved as the slides change, but they are quicker and easier to create and download.

Diagrams

- Uses:
  — To show the structure of objects.
  — To show the relationship of objects.
  — To show the flow of a process or task.
  — To reveal a temporal or spatial order.
- Guidelines:
  — Provide simple diagrams.
  — Provide cutaway diagrams or exploded views to illustrate key points.

Uses. Diagrams are useful for illustrating the structure of an object, its key parts and how they are related to each other. Diagrams are also useful for illustrating the relationships of objects, the structure of an organization, or the structure of a Web site. Other uses are to illustrate the flow of a process or task, a software program, or an airline passenger check-in sequence, for example. (Guidelines for displaying flow charts were presented in Step 3 "Understand the Principles of Good Screen Design.") Diagrams can also be used to reveal temporal or spatial order, including activities such as the sequence in which an object's parts should be assembled.

Guidelines. Provide simple diagrams showing only as much detail as necessary to clearly illustrate the diagram's objective. Simpler diagrams will also load faster on a Web page. To illustrate key points, provide cutaway diagrams or exploded diagram views.

Drawings

- Use:
  — When selective parts need to be emphasized or represented.
- Guidelines:
  — Provide simple drawings showing minimal detail.
  — Provide a link to a complete drawing.

Use. Use a drawing when only certain parts of an image are of relevance, and these parts must be emphasized or clearly represented. If the working of a specific object is to be described, a diagram illustrating its relevant parts should be used.

Guidelines. Provide simple drawings showing minimal detail. They are easier to view and understand and they also load more quickly. Photographs are likely to be less effective since they contain information that is not relevant, they lack clarity, and they take longer to load on a Web page. If the user is also in need of a detailed drawing, provide a link to a page containing a complete drawing.

Animation

- Uses:
  - To explain ideas involving a change in:
    - Time.
    - Position.
  - To illustrate the location or state of a process.
  - To show continuity in transitions.
  - To enrich graphical representations.
  - To aid visualization of three-dimensional structures.
  - To attract attention.

- Disadvantages:
  - Very distracting.
  - Slow loading.

- Guidelines:
  - Use only when an integral part of the content.
  - Create short segments.
  - Provide a freeze frame and stop mode.
  - Avoid distracting animation.

Uses. Only use animation when it serves a useful purpose. Animations can be used to enhance textual explanations of objects changing over *time*. A map illustrating population growth can be animated to illustrate population densities and patterns over a sequence of years or centuries. Proper sequential body *positions* needed to skillfully perform a sport can also be illustrated as they are textually described. The current *location* within, or the state of, a process can be highlighted through animating flow arrows or process steps.

Continuity in transitions can also be illustrated. The changing of states of an element with two or more states will be easier to understand if the transitions are animated instead of being instantaneous. In Windows, actually seeing an icon moving as it is dragged from a desktop to the Recycle Bin or the My Documents file strengthens one's understanding of the task and the results. *Graphical representations* can also be enriched. Some kinds of information are easier to visualize with movement rather than with still pictures. *Visualization* of three-dimensional structures can also be aided. While a two-dimensional screen can never provide a full understanding of a three-dimensional element, animating the element by slowly turning it aids in understanding its structure. Animation can also be used to *attract attention*. The user's attention can be directed to an important screen element or alerted to an important condition.

MAXIM   *Content* **is always more important than graphics.**

Disadvantages. Any discussion of screen image animation includes a strong caution concerning animation's side effects. Screen animation is difficult to ignore, often overpowering a person's peripheral vision. As was discussed in Step 1 "Know Your User or Client," peripheral vision competes with foveal vision for a person's attention. That sensed in the periphery is passed on to our information-processing system along with what is actively being viewed foveally. It is, in a sense, visual noise. Mori and Hayashi (1993) experimentally evaluated the effect of windows in both a foveal and peripheral relationship and found that performance on a foveal window deteriorates when there are peripheral windows, and the performance degradation is even *greater* if the information in the peripheral is dynamic or moving. Reeves and Nass (1996) measured brain waves with an EEG and found that attention increased every time motion appeared on a screen. Permanently moving animation on a screen makes it very hard for people to concentrate on reading text, if the brain wants to attend to the motion. Animation can also be very annoying.

Another current negative side effect of Web page animation is its close association with advertising. Animation, including scrolling text, is frequently being used by advertisers to try and gather the users' attention. Studies suggest that people have started equating animation with advertising, so animation as a screen element is being routinely ignored. Important animation may, therefore, be missed. Animated images also take longer to load.

Guidelines. Use animation sparingly. Only use it when it is an *integral part* of the textual content, or reinforces the content. Create *short segments*. There are many distractions people may encounter while watching animation, so long segments should be avoided. Animation, when used, should be capable of being *stopped* by the user so an image may be studied in detail. It should also be capable of being ended entirely so it is eliminated as a visual distraction. In conclusion, always avoid animation or special effects that detract from the screen's message.

Audition

- Uses:
  - As a supplement to text and graphics.
  - To establish atmosphere.
  - To create a sense of place.
  - To teach.
  - To sample.
- Advantages:
  - Does not obscure information on the screen.
  - Shorter downloading time than video.

- Disadvantages:
  — Is annoying to many people, including users and nonusers in the vicinity.
  — Can easily be overused, increasing the possibility that it will be ignored.
  — Is not reliable because:
    • Some people are hard of hearing.
    • If it is not heard, it may leave no permanent record of having occurred.
    • The user can turn it off.
    • Audio capability may not exist for the user.
- Guidelines:
  — When words are spoken:
    • The content should be simple.
    • The speed of narration should be about 160 words per minute.
  — When used to introduce new ideas or concepts the narration should be slowed.
  — Off-screen narration should be used rather than on-screen narration.
    • Unless the narrator is a recognized authority on the topic.
  — Create short segments.
  — Provide segments of high quality.
  — Provide audio controls.
  — Play background audio softly.

This discussion of audition focuses on sound as a communication medium for presenting meaningful information, words, music, and so on A discussion of sounds used to alert the user is found in Step 9.

Uses. Use audio as a *supplement* to text and graphics and only to reinforce visual content. Audio should never be used alone because of the disadvantages listed above. Audio can also be used to establish *atmosphere*. A particular type of music reflecting a Web site's content can be played to establish ambience and also to create orientation signposts fostering a *sense of place*. Audio can also be used to *teach* word pronunciation or to provide *samples* of music.

Advantages. An advantage of audio is its ability to offering commentary or help for a visual display. Audio does not obscure information on the screen, and it downloads faster than most other types of graphics.

Disadvantages. Audio's disadvantages are similar to those of sounds described in Step 9. Audio can be annoying to many people, including users and nonusers in the vicinity. It can easily be overused, increasing the possibility that it will be ignored. Audio is also not reliable because some people are hard of hearing, it may leave no permanent record of having occurred, it may not be available to the user, or it may be turned off. Loud audio can also be irritating, especially to those with sensitive hearing.

Guidelines. Williams (1998) in a multimedia literature review extracted most of the following guidelines. When words are spoken, the content should be simple, and the speed of narration should be about 160 words per minute. When the narration is used to introduce new ideas or new concepts the narration should be slowed. Off-screen (invisible) narration should be used rather than on-screen narration.

On-screen narration is acceptable, however if the narrator is a recognized authority on the topic being presented.

Other audition guidelines include these: Create *short segments*. There are many distractions people may encounter while listening to audio, so long segments should be avoided. Always provide audio segments of *high quality*. Research has found (Reeves and Nass, 1996) that while people will accept poor video, they are very affected by poor audio. Let users control the playing of audio. Provide the following *controls*: Play, Pause/Resume, Stop, Rewind, Fast Forward, and Volume. Any *background* audio should be subdued so it does not interfere with main information being presented on the screen.

Combining Mediums

- Combinations:
  - Use sensory combinations that work best together:
    - Auditory text with visual graphics.
    - Screen text with visual graphics.
- Integration:
  - Closely integrate screen text with graphics.
- Relevance:
  - Both the visual and auditory information should be totally relevant to the task being performed.
- Presentation:
  - Visual and auditory textual narrative should be presented simultaneously, or the visuals should precede the narrative by no more than 7 seconds.
  - To control attention, reveal information systematically.
    - Limit elements revealed to one item at a time and use sequential revelations for related elements.
  - Animation must show action initiation as well as the action's result.
  - Avoid animation that distracts from other more important information.
- Downloading times:
  - Consider downloading times when choosing a media.
- Testing:
  - Thoroughly test all graphics for:
    - Legibility.
    - Comprehensibility.
    - Acceptance.

Interface technology encourages inclusion of the various graphical media (images, photos, video, diagrams, drawings, and audio) along with text on a screen. The design issue is which mediums work best with other mediums, and which mediums should not be employed together. Before reviewing research on this topic, which does find performance advantages for certain combinations of multimedia, theories for why this may happen will be summarized.

The first theory is called the *dual code* theory. It proposes that people store information in two ways in memory: verbally and pictorially. This theory postulates that, because of this dual-storage capability, information communicated to a person in both a verbal and pictorial manner has a greater likelihood of being remembered than information arriving in only one format. Also postulated is that too much information arriving in one format can overtax that particular memory. Combining verbal audio with displayed text is one such overtaxing combination.

The second theory also proposes two independent working memories, but is slightly different in concept. The first type of memory is a visual-spatial sketchpad in which information accumulated visually is stored. This visual information may be graphical or textual in nature. The second type of working memory is a phonological loop for dealing with and storing auditory information. This theory postulates that performance may be improved for certain more complex tasks because working memory is expanded through the application of two senses. The general conclusion is that combining visual and verbal auditory information can lead to enhanced comprehension, when compared to relying on one sense alone.

The two theories diverge on the storage of audio. The former suggests that verbal audio and displayed text is stored together; the latter suggests that they are stored separately.

Combinations and integration. Williams (1998) in a literature review found that combining visual and verbal auditory information in multimedia design can lead to enhanced comprehension, when compared to use of these medias alone. Several recent studies have also explored the effects of various media, or combinations of media, on user performance. One such study is that of Lee and Bowers (1997). These researchers evaluated various mediums to see which yielded the best learning. The results, summarized in Table 11.2, compared a control group to groups learning material by the various methods described.

Another series of three studies were those of Tindall-Ford, Chandler, and Sweller (1997). They compared combinations of the following multimedia conditions for learning and performance:

Table 11.2   Learning Improvements for Various Media

MEDIUM	PERCENT MORE LEARNING
Hearing spoken text and viewing graphics	91%
Viewing graphics alone	63%
Viewing text and viewing graphics	56%
Hearing spoken text, viewing text, and viewing graphics	46%
Hearing spoken text and viewing text	32%
Viewing text alone	12%
Hearing spoken text alone	7%

From Lee and Bowers (1997).

- A visual diagram or table and separated visual text.
- A visual diagram and integrated visual text.
- A visual diagram or table and spoken instructions.

They found that the visual-audio combinations yielded reliably better performance for complex tasks, but no differences were found for easy tasks. They also found that visual text integrated into a diagram yielded better performance than separated visual text. They attributed the better results for the audiovisual combination and the integrated text and diagram alternative to reduced demands on working memory.

What can we conclude from these studies?

- **The proper multimedia combinations can improve learning and performance.** Hearing spoken text combined with a visual graphic is an especially useful combination, especially for complex tasks. All studies found this pairing useful.
- **Visual graphics do enhance learning and performance.** In the Bowers and Lee study, the various graphical combinations yielded the higher learning rates.
- **Single-dimensional textual media are not as successful when used alone.** In the Bowers and Lee study, viewing text or hearing spoken text alone yielded the lowest learning rates.
- **Hearing spoken text and viewing text at the same time may not be great, but it may not be terrible, either.** This combination yielded "middle-of-the-road" results in the Bowers and Lee study. The dual code theory would suggest, however, that its use be minimized. Exercise caution in this area.
- **Visual text should always be integrated with related visual graphics.** Tindall-Ford et al. found much better user performance when visual text was closely integrated with, or adjacent to, related visual graphics. It will be much easier for user to coordinate and integrate the visual materials. Presenting spatially separated text and related graphics places greater demands on working memory.

Relevance. Both the visual and auditory information should be totally relevant to the task being performed. All spoken text should reinforce presented graphics.

Presentation. Faraday and Sutcliffe (1997) also conducted a series of studies addressing multimedia design. Like the above-mentioned studies, they found displayed graphics (images and animation) improved user performance, specifically the recall of information. Based upon these studies, they developed the following guidelines. Provide sufficient *time* for reading screen graphic captions. Present simultaneously all visual and auditory *narrative information* to the user, or have the visual information precede the auditory narrative by no more than 7 seconds. To control the users' attention, *reveal* or expose information systematically on the screen, either from left to right or from top to bottom. Limit the information revealed to one item at a time, and sequentially reveal related elements. Finally, any *animation* must show an action being initiated as well as the action's result, and avoid any animation that distracts from other more important screen information.

Downloading times. Consider times in choosing a graphical medium. In general, downloading times range from the fastest, audio, to the slowest, video.

Testing. Thoroughly test all graphics for *legibility*. Make sure visual graphics are easy to see from a variety of viewing distances. Also test them for *comprehensibility*. Are visual graphics and related audio clear and understandable? Are the graphics *acceptable* to the using audience? This is especially critical if the users are multicultural. Always test graphics with all representative user groups. Testing methods are described more fully in Step 14 "Test, Test, and Retest."

Choose the Proper Colors

Color adds dimension, or realism, to screen usability. Color draws attention because it attracts a person's eye. If used properly, it can emphasize the logical organization of information, facilitate the discrimination of screen components, accentuate differences among elements, and make displays more interesting. If used improperly, color can be distracting and possibly visually fatiguing, impairing the system's usability. In this step we will:

- Come to understand color's characteristics.
  - What color is.
  - The uses of color.
  - Possible problems and cautions when working with color.
  - The results of color research.
  - Color and human vision.
- Come to understand how to use color.
- Choose the proper colors for textual graphic screens.
- Choose the proper colors for statistical graphics screens.
- Choose the proper color for Web screen text and images.

Effective use of color in screen design has taken great steps forward in the last four decades. Earlier text-based displays could only present a few colors, and many of the colors were not very legible. Color was often overused in combinations that reminded one more of a Christmas tree than of an effective source of communication. The evolution to graphical screens expanded the use of color, but did not immediately eliminate some of the color problems. Today, because technology has improved, as well as our understanding of what constitutes good design, colors in screens are being used much more effectively. Pastels have replaced bright reds and dark blues, and the number of colors presented at one time on a screen has been reduced, dramatically in some cases. This is not to say, however, that all the problems have been solved. A tour around the office will usually uncover some questionable, or awful, uses of color. Two of two most common problems are screen backgrounds being more attention-grabbing than the screen data (which is the most important element of a screen), and overuse of color as a graphic language or code (the color itself meaning something to the screen viewer). This latter kind of use forces the user to interpret a color's meaning *before* the message it is communicating can be reacted to.

In recent years, the development of the Web and the availability of monitors with significantly expanded color capability have initiated a replay of the early color-use problems that surfaced in both text-based and graphical systems. Infatuated with the almost unlimited supply of available colors, developers have eagerly raced to include a multitude of colors on Web pages, with too little thought given to the consequences for users. The "Christmas tree effect" has lived on as users struggled with illegible text and numerous visual distractions. Today, the use of color in Web pages has improved somewhat. Too many site designers still, however, associate good design with "splashy" color.

The discussion to follow begins by defining color. Next is a review of how color may be used in screen design and some critical cautions on its use. Then, the human visual system and its implications for color are discussed. Continuing, a series of general screen guidelines are presented for choosing and using colors. This is followed by a compilation of guidelines for specific kinds of screens: textual and graphical, statistical graphics, and Web screens and their associated graphical elements.

Color—What Is It?

Wavelengths of light themselves are not colored. What is perceived as actual color results from the stimulation of the proper receptor in the eye by a received light wave. The name that a color is given is a learned phenomenon, based on previous experiences and associations of specific visual sensations with color names. Therefore, a color can only be described in terms of a person's report of his or her perceptions. The visual spectrum of wavelengths to which the eye is sensitive ranges from about 400 to 700 millimicrons. Objects in the visual environment often emit or reflect light waves in a limited area of this visual spectrum, absorbing light waves in other areas of the spectrum. The dominant wavelength being "seen" is the one that we come to associate with a specific color name. The visible color spectrum and the names commonly associated with the various light wavelengths are shown in Table 12.1.

To describe a color, it is useful to refer to the three properties it possesses: hue, chroma or saturation, and value or intensity, as illustrated in Figure 12.1. *Hue* is the spectral wavelength composition of a color. It is to this we attach a meaning such as green or red. *Chroma* or *saturation* is the purity of a color in a scale from gray to the most vivid version of the color. The more saturated a hue is, the more visible it is at a distance. The less

Table 12.1 The Visible Spectrum

APPROXIMATE COLOR WAVELENGTHS IN MILLIMICRONS	
Red	700
Orange	600
Yellow	570
Yellow-green	535
Green	500
Blue-green	493
Blue	470
Violet	400

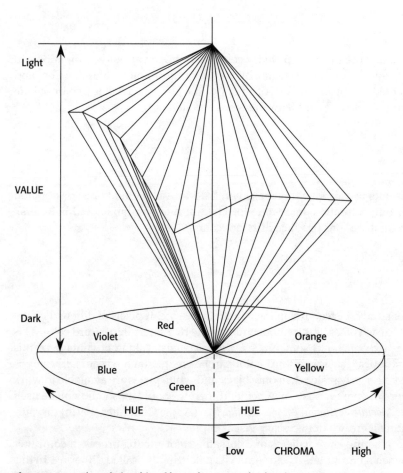

Figure 12.1 The relationship of hue, chroma, and value.

saturated, the less visible it is. *Value* or *intensity* is the relative lightness or darkness of a color in a range from black to white. Two-word descriptors, such as light red or dark blue, are usually used to describe lightness differences. Some hues are inherently lighter or darker than others, for example, yellow is very light and violet is very dark.

The primary colors of illuminated light are red, green, and blue, whose wavelengths additively combine in pairs to produce magenta, cyan, and yellow, and all the other visible colors in the spectrum. The three primary colors additively combine to produce white. The long-wavelength colors (red) are commonly referred to as warm, and short-wavelength colors (blue) as cool.

Color, then, is a combination of hue, chroma, and value. In any one instance what we call "blue" may actually be one of several hundred thousand "blues." This problem has confounded color research over the years. A "blue" may be unacceptable in one situation because it is highly saturated and dark, but perfectly acceptable in another, being less saturated and light. The exact measures of a color are rarely reported in the literature.

RGB

Many color monitors use the three primary colors of light, in various combinations, to create the many colors we see on screens. By adjusting the amounts of red, green, and blue light presented in a pixel, millions of colors can be generated. Hence, color palette editors exist with labels R, G, and B (or the words spelled out).

HSV

Some palette editors use a convention based on the Munsell method of color notation called HSV, for hue, saturation, and value (or HSL for hue, saturation, and lightness). Again, various combinations produce different colors.

Dithering

The eye is never steady, instead trembling slightly as we see. If pixels of different colors are placed next to each other, this tremor combines the two colors into a third color. This is referred to as *dithering*, and sometimes *texture mapping*. Taking advantage of this phenomena, an optical illusion, a third color can be created on a screen. Dithering is often used to create a gray scale when only black and white pixels are available to work with. A difference of opinion exists on whether dithering should, or should not, be used on a screen. *The Macintosh Human Interface Guidelines* (Apple Computer, 1992b) discourage its use, stating it creates unnecessary visual clutter.

In systems containing large palettes of colors, the color-mixing process a computer goes through when it encounters a color not in its palette is also called dithering. In this process palette colors are mixed to approximate the appearance of the desired color.

Color Uses

- Use color to assist in formatting a screen:
  — Relating or tying elements into groupings.
  — Breaking apart separate groupings of information.
  — Associating information that is widely separated on the screen.
  — Highlighting or calling attention to important information by setting it off from the other information.
- Use color as a visual code to identify:
  — Screen components.
  — The logical structure of ideas, processes, or sequences.
  — Sources of information.
  — Status of information.
- Use color to:
  — Realistically portray natural objects.
  — Increase screen appeal.

Color may be used as a formatting aid in structuring a screen, or it may be used as a visual code to categorize and identify information or data. It may also be used to portray objects naturally and make a screen more appealing to look at.

Color as a Formatting Aid

As a formatting aid, color can provide better structure and meaning to a screen. It is especially useful when large amounts of information must be included on a screen and spacing to differentiate components is problematic. For example, displaying groupings of information in different colors can enhance differentiation of the groupings. Spatially separated but related fields can also be tied together through a color scheme.

Color can also replace highlighting as a means of calling attention to information. Color is much more flexible than other techniques because of the number of colors that are available. Color, as an attention-getting mechanism must, however, be chosen in light of the psychological and physiological considerations to be described shortly.

Color as a Visual Code

A color code indicates what category the information being displayed falls into. It has meaning to the screen's user. A properly selected color-coding scheme permits a person to identify a relevant information category quickly, without having to read its contents first. This permits focusing on this category, while the remaining information is excluded from attention.

One common color-coding scheme used to differentiate screen components is to display screen captions and data in different colors. Another is to identify information from different sources—information added to a process from different locations, or text added to a message from different departments, may be colored differently. Using color-coding to convey status might involve displaying, in a different color, information that passed or failed system edits. Color can also be used as a prompt, guiding a person through a complex transaction.

To be effective, color as a visual code must be relevant and known. Relevance is achieved when the color enables a person to attend to only the information that is needed, and easily exclude that which is not needed. A relevant code, however, will be useless unless its meaning is also understood by the person who must use it. If a color's meaning is not known, one must first interpret its meaning. This can place burdens on a person's memory. It can also impede performance, requiring one to consult a manual or a legend in order to understand it.

Other Color Uses

Color can also be used to more realistically portray objects in the world around us that must be displayed on a screen. It is also thought that the addition of color increases a screen's appeal and makes working with a display more pleasant.

Possible Problems with Color

The simple addition of color to a screen will not guarantee improved performance. What may have been a poorly designed product will simply become a colorful poorly designed product. When used improperly, color may even impair performance by distracting the viewer and interfering with the handling of information. Possible problems may be caused by the perceptual system itself or the physiological characteristics of the human eye.

High Attention-Getting Capacity

Color has an extremely high attention-getting capacity. This quality causes the screen viewer to associate, or tie together, screen elements of the same color, whether or not such an association should be made. A person might search for relationships and differences that do not exist, or that are not valid. The result is often bewilderment, confusion, and slower reading. The effect achieved is often described as the Christmas tree mentioned earlier.

Interference with Use of Other Screens

Indiscriminate or poor use of color on some screens will diminish the effectiveness of color on other screens. The rationale for color will be difficult to understand and its attention-getting capacity severely restricted.

Varying Sensitivity of the Eye to Different Colors

All colors are not equal in the eye of the viewer. The eye is more sensitive to those in the middle of the visual spectrum (yellow and green), which appear brighter than those at the extremes (blue and red). Thus, text composed of colors at the extremes is thought to be more difficult to read. Research evidence on this topic is mixed. Several studies have found that acuity, contrast sensitivity, target recognition, legibility, and performance were not influenced by color. On the other hand, other studies have found advantages for central spectral colors in reaction times, resolution, and error rates.

Also, it is thought that some combinations of screen colors can strain the eye's accommodation mechanism. The wavelengths of light that produce blue are normally focused in front of the eye's retina, the red wavelengths behind it. Simultaneous or sequential viewing of red and blue causes the eye to continually refocus to bring the image directly onto the retina, thereby increasing the potential for eye fatigue. Again, the research evidence is mixed. Some studies have found this a problem while others have not.

What does one conclude after looking at the research addressing the above problems? The reasonable assumption is that they have neither been proved nor disproved. We have not properly defined all the terminal-based tasks being performed, and the exact qualities of the colors being studied. Also, the studies have used only a few of the many devices in existence. And, a firm definition of "visual fatigue" remains elusive. Finally, none of the studies have addressed extended terminal viewing. The prudent course is to be cautious and avoid using colors and combinations that color theory suggests can create problems.

The perceived appearance of a color is also affected by a variety of other factors, including the size of the area of color, the ambient illumination level, and other colors in the viewing area. Also, larger changes in wavelength are needed in some areas of the visual spectrum for a color change to be noticed by the eye. Small changes in extreme reds and purples are more difficult to detect than small changes in yellow and blue-green. Failure to consider the eye and how it handles color, then, can also lead to mistakes in color identification, misinterpretations, slower reading, and, perhaps, visual fatigue.

Color-Viewing Deficiencies

Another disadvantage of color is that about 8 percent of males and 0.4 percent of females have some form of color-perception deficiency—color blindness, as it is commonly called. In actuality, very few people are truly color-blind; most of those with problems simply have difficulties discriminating certain colors. A red viewing deficiency is called *protanopia*, a green deficiency is called *deuteranopia*, and a blue deficiency is called *tritanopia*. These common color deficiencies, their results, and the percentage of people who experience these problems, are summarized in Table 12.2. Total color blindness affects no more than 0.005 percent of both sexes. For an individual with color-perception deficiency, all the normal colors may not be discernible, but often differences in lightness or intensity can be seen. The important point: a person experiencing any form of color deficiency must not be prohibited from effectively using a screen.

Table 12.2   Results of Color-Defective Vision

ACTUAL COLOR	COLOR SEEN WITH:		
	RED-VIEWING DEFICIENCY (2.04%)	GREEN-VIEWING DEFICIENCY (6.39%)	BLUE-VIEWING DEFICIENCY (0.003%)
Red	Brown	—	—
Yellow	Greenish-Yellow	Orange	Deeper Yellow
Purple	Dark Blue	Red	Deep Red
Green	—	Light Brown	—
Brown	—	Reddish-Brown	—
Blue	—	—	Green

From Barnett (1993); Fowler and Stanwick (1995).

Cross-Disciplinary and Cross-Cultural Differences

Colors can have different meanings in different situations to different people. A color used in an unexpected way can cause confusion. An error signaled in green would contradict the expected association of red with stop or danger. The same color may also have a different connotation, depending upon its viewer. The color blue has the following quite different meanings:

- For financial managers—Corporate qualities or reliability.
- For health care professionals—Death.
- For nuclear reactor monitors—Coolness or water.
- For American movie audiences—Tenderness or pornography.

Differences in color connotations also exist between cultures. Red, for example, in the United States is associated with danger, in Egypt with death, and in India with life. Incorrect use in a different culture may cause severe problems. A listing of some common cultural associations with color was found in Table 10.2 in Step 10 "Provide Effective Internationalization and Accessibility."

Color appeal is also subjective. People have different tastes in color, what is pleasing to one person may be distasteful or unusable by someone else.

The proper use of color, then, requires an analysis of the expectations and experiences of the screen viewer. The use of color in design must always keep these possible problems clearly in focus. The designer must work to minimize their disruptive and destructive effects.

MAXIM   Poor use of color is worse than not using it at all.

Color—What the Research Shows

The effectiveness of color in improving the usability of a display has been studied for many years. The research results have been mixed. To illustrate, on a positive note, color has been shown to improve performance (Kopala, 1981; Nagy and Sanchez, 1992; Sidorsky, 1982), to improve visual search time (Christ, 1975; Carter, 1982), to be useful for organizing information (Engel, 1980), to aid memory (Marcus, 1986b), and to demarcate a portion of a screen (as opposed to lines or type font, Wopking, Pastoor, and Beldie 1985). Color has also created positive user reactions (Tullis, 1981), was preferred to monochromatic screens for being less monotonous and reducing eyestrain and fatigue (Christ, 1975), and is more enjoyable (Marcus, 1986b).

On the other hand, it has also been shown that color does not improve performance (Tullis, 1981), does not have much of an effect on reading text (Legge and Rubin, 1986), may impair performance (Christ and Teichner, 1973; Christ, 1975), and is less important than display spacing (Haubner and Benz, 1983). It has also been demonstrated that poor character-background color combinations lead to poorer performance (McTyre and Frommer, 1985). Finally, no evidence has been produced that color, as compared to black and white, can significantly improve aesthetics or legibility or reduce eyestrain (Pastoor, 1990).

Research has found, moreover, that as the number of colors on a display increases, the time to respond to a single color increases, and the probability of color confusion increases (Luria, Neri, and Jacobsen 1986). Many studies have found that the maximum number of colors that a person can handle is in the range of 4 to 10, with emphasis on the lower numbers (for example, Brooks, 1965; Halsey and Chapanis, 1951; Luria, Neri, and Jacobsen, 1986).

The conclusion to be derived from these studies is that for simple displays, color may have no dramatic impact. Indeed, a monochromatic display may serve the purpose just as well. As display complexity increases, however, so does the value of color. A second conclusion is that people like using color and think it has a positive influence on their productivity, even though it may not.

To be effective, color must be properly used. Poor use of color will actually impair performance, not help it. When using color, keep in mind its value will be dependent upon the task being performed, the colors selected, the number of colors used, and the viewing environment.

Color and Human Vision

To understand how color should be used on a screen, it is helpful to know something of the physiology of the human eye.

The Lens

Muscles control the lens of the eye. These muscles focus received wavelengths of light on the retina. The lens itself is not color corrected. The wavelengths of light that create different colors are focused at different distances behind the lens, the longer wavelengths (red) being focused farther back than the shorter wavelengths (blue). The result is that colors of a different wavelength from the color actually being focused by the lens will appear out of focus. To create a sharp image of the out-of-focus colors requires a refocusing of the eye. Excessive refocusing (such as between red and blue) can lead to eye fatigue.

The effect of this focusing for most people is that blues appear more distant and reds appear closer. This can give a three-dimensional appearance to what is being viewed. A critical problem is that the wavelength of light that creates blues can never be brought into focus on the retina but is always focused in front of it. A sharp blue image is impossible to obtain. Very pure or saturated colors require more refocusing than less pure or unsaturated colors. Therefore, a color with a large white component will require less refocusing.

The lens does not transmit all light wavelengths equally. It absorbs more wavelengths in the blue region of the spectrum than those in the other regions. Additionally, as the lens ages, it tends to yellow, filtering out the shorter blue wavelengths. Thus, as people get older, their sensitivity to blue decreases. The lens also refocuses for light waves of different brightness. Sharp contrasts in brightness in things being viewed can lead to visual fatigue as the eye continually makes muscular adjustments. Driving an automobile through a forest of trees on a bright sunny day illustrates this effect. The eye continually adjusts as the auto sequentially moves through areas of bright sunlight and patches of shadows.

The Retina

The retina is the light-sensitive surface of the eye. It comprises two kinds of receptors, rods and cones, which translate the incoming light into nervous impulses. Rods are sensitive to lower light levels and function primarily at night. Cones are stimulated by higher light levels and react to color. The sensitivity of cones to colors varies, different cones possessing maximum sensitivity to different wavelengths of light. About two-thirds (64 percent) of the cones are maximally sensitive to longer light wavelengths, showing a peak response at about 575 millimicrons. These cones have traditionally been referred to as "red" sensitive cones. In actuality, however, the peak sensitivity is in the yellow portion of the visual spectrum (see Table 12.1). About one-third (32 percent) of the cones achieve maximum sensitivity at about 535 millimicrons and are commonly referred to as "green" sensitive cones. The remainder (2 percent) primarily react to short light wavelengths, achieving maximum sensitivity at about 445 millimicrons. These are known as "blue" sensitive cones. Any light wave impinging on the retina evokes a response, to a greater or lesser degree, from most or all of these cones. A perceived "color" results from the proportion of stimulation of the various cone kinds.

Rods and cones vary in distribution across the retina. The center is tightly packed with cones and has no rods. Toward the periphery of the retina, rods increase and cones decrease. Thus, color sensitivity does not exist at the retina's outer edges, although yellows and blues can be detected further into the periphery than reds and greens. The very center of the retina is devoid of blue cones, creating a "blue-blindness" for small objects being looked at.

The receptors in the eye also adjust, or adapt, their level of sensitivity to the overall light level and the color being viewed. Adaptation to increases in brightness improves color sensitivity. Color adaptation "softens" colors.

The brightness sensitivity of the eye to different colors also varies. It is governed by output from the red and green cones. The greater the output, the higher the brightness, which results in the eye being most sensitive to colors in the middle of the visual spectrum and less sensitive to colors at the extremes. A blue or red must be of a much greater intensity than a green or yellow even to be perceived.

The ability of the eye to detect a form is accomplished by focusing the viewed image on the body of receptors to establish edges. Distinct edges yield distinct images. Edges formed by color differences alone cannot be accurately brought into focus and thus create fuzzy and indistinct images. A clear, sharp image requires a difference in brightness between adjacent objects, as well as differences in color.

The components of the eye—the lens and retina—govern the choices, and combinations, of colors to be displayed on a screen. The proper colors will enhance performance; improper colors will have the opposite effect, as well as increase the probability of visual fatigue.

MYTH If we can't do it right, do it big. If we can't do it big, do it in color.

Choosing Colors

When choosing colors for display, one must consider these factors: the human visual system, the possible problems that the colors' use may cause, the viewing environment in which the display is used, the task of the user, how the colors will be used, and the hardware on which the colors will be displayed. The primary objective in using color is communication, to aid the transfer of information from the screen to the user.

Choosing Colors for Categories of Information

- Choosing colors for categories of information requires a clear understanding of how the information will be used.
- Some examples:
  - If different parts of the screen are attended to separately, color-code the different parts to focus selective attention on each in turn.
  - If decisions are made based on the status of certain types of information on the screen, color-code the types of status that the information may possess.
  - If screen searching is performed to locate information of a particular kind or quality, color-code these kinds or qualities for contrast.
  - If the sequence of information use is constrained or ordered, use color to identify the sequence.
  - If the information displayed on a screen is packed or crowded, use color to provide visual groupings.
- Use color as a redundant screen code.

Categories. Color chosen to organize information or data on a screen must aid the transfer of information from the display to the user. This requires a clear understanding of how the information is selected and used. The examples above describe some common ways of classifying information for color-coding purposes.

Redundancy. Never rely on color as the only way of identifying a screen element or process. Users with a color-viewing deficiency may not be able identify a specific color when it is important. It is also important to remember that information on one screen may be used in more than one way. What is useful in one context may not be in another and may only cause interference. Therefore, when developing a color strategy, always consider how spatial formatting, highlighting, and messages may also be useful and employ these structural and coding methods as well.

Colors in Context

Colors are subject to contextual effects. The size of a colored image, the color of images adjacent to it, and the ambient illumination all exert an influence on what is actually perceived. At the normal viewing distance for a screen, maximal color sensitivity is not reached until the size of a colored area exceeds about a 3-inch square. Smaller images become desaturated (having a greater white component) and change slightly in color. Also, small differences in actual color may not be discernible. Blues and yellows are particularly susceptible to difficulties in detecting slight changes. Finally, small adjacent colored images may appear to the eye to merge or mix. Red and green, for example, might appear as yellow.

Adjacent images can influence the perceived color. A color on a dark background will look lighter and brighter than the same color on a light background, for example. A color can be *induced* into a neutral foreground area (gray) by the presence of a colored background. A red background can change a gray into a green. Induced colors are the complement of the inducing color. Looking at a saturated color for a period of time can also induce complementary afterimages. Colors also change as light levels change. Higher levels of ambient light tend to desaturate colors. Saturated colors will also appear larger than desaturated colors.

Usage

- Design for monochrome first.
- Use colors conservatively.
  - Do not use color where other identification techniques, such as location, are available.

Monochrome. Design for monochrome first, or in shades of black, white and gray. A screen should be as capable of being effectively used as if it were located in a monochrome environment. Spatial formatting, consistent locations, and display techniques such as highlighting and multiple font styles, should all be utilized to give information a structure independent of the color. Doing this will permit the screen to be effectively used:

- By people with a color-viewing deficiency.
- On monochrome displays.
- In conditions where ambient lighting distorts the perceived color.
- If the color ever fails.

Conservative Use. Use color sparingly since it has such a high attention-getting quality. Only enough colors to achieve the design objective should be used. More colors increase response times, increase the chance of errors due to color confusion, and increase the chance of the Christmas tree effect. If two colors serve the need, use two colors. If three colors are needed, by all means use three. A way to minimize the need for too many colors is not to use color in situations where other identification methods are available. A menu bar, for example, will always be located at the top of the screen. Its position and structure will identify it as a menu bar. To color-code it would be redundant.

Discrimination and Harmony

- For best absolute discrimination, select no more than four or five colors widely spaced on the color spectrum.
  — Good colors: red, yellow, green, blue, and brown.
- For best comparative discrimination, select no more than six or seven colors widely spaced on the color spectrum.
  — Other acceptable colors: orange, yellow-green, cyan, violet, and magenta.
- Choose harmonious colors.
  — One color plus two colors on either side of its complement.
  — Three colors at equidistant points around the color circle.
- For extended viewing or older viewers, use brighter colors.

Absolute discrimination. The population of measurable colors is about 7.5 million. From this vast number, the eye cannot effectively distinguish many more than a handful. If color memorization and absolute discrimination is necessary (a color must be correctly identified while no other color is in the field of vision), select no more than 4 to 5 colors widely spaced along the color spectrum. Selecting widely spaced colors will maximize the probability of their being correctly identified. Good choices are red, yellow, green, blue, and brown.

Two good color opponent pairs are red/green and yellow/blue. All of these colors except blue are easy to resolve visually. Again, be cautious in using blue for data, text, or small symbols on screens because it may not always be legible. If the meaning for each of more than five colors is absolutely necessary, a legend should be provided illustrating the colors and describing their associated meanings.

Comparative discrimination. If comparative discrimination will be performed (a color must be correctly identified while other colors are in the field of vision), select no more than six or seven colors widely spaced along the visual spectrum. In addition to those above, other colors could be chosen from orange, yellow-green, cyan, violet, and magenta. Again, be cautious of using blue for data, text, or small symbols. If the intent is to portray natural objects realistically, the use of more colors is acceptable.

Harmony. Choose harmonious colors. Harmonious colors are those that work well together or meet without sharp contrast. Harmony is most easily achieved with a monochromatic palette. For each background color, different lightness or values are established through mixing it with black and white. Marcus (1986a) suggests a minimum of three values should be obtained.

Harmonious combinations in a multicolor environment are more difficult to obtain. Marcus recommends avoiding complementary colors—those at opposite sides of the circle of hues in the Munsell color system, a standard commercial color system. He suggests using split complements, one color plus two colors on either side of its complement, or choosing three colors at equidistant points around the color circle.

Extended viewing. For older viewers or extended viewing, use bright colors. As eye capacity diminishes with age, data, text, and symbols in the less bright colors may be harder to read. Distinguishing colors may also become more difficult. For any viewer, long viewing periods result in the eye adapting to the brightness level. Brighter colors will be needed if either of these conditions exists.

Emphasis

- To draw attention or to emphasize elements, use bright or highlighted colors. To deemphasize elements, use less bright colors.
  — The perceived brightness of colors from most to least is white, yellow, green, blue, red.
- To emphasize separation, use contrasting colors.
  — Red and green, blue and yellow.
- To convey similarity, use similar colors.
  — Orange and yellow, blue and violet.

Drawing attention. To draw attention or emphasize, use bright colors. The eye is drawn to brighter or highlighted colors, so use them for the more important screen components. The data or text is the most important component on most screens, so it is a good candidate for highlighting or the brightest color. Danger signals should also be brighter or highlighted. The perceived brightness of colors, from most to least, is white, yellow, green, blue, and red.

Keep in mind, however, that under levels of high ambient illumination, colors frequently appear washed out or unsaturated. If some means of light attenuation is not possible, or if the colors chosen are not bright enough to counter the illumination, color should be used with caution.

Emphasizing separation. Use contrasting colors to emphasize separation. The greater the contrast, the better the visibility of adjacent elements. To emphasize the separation of screen components, use contrasting colors. Possible pairs would be red/green and blue/yellow.

Similarity. Use similar colors to convey similarity. Displaying elements in a similar color can bring related screen components together. Blue and green, for example, are more closely related than red and green.

Common Meanings

- To indicate that actions are necessary, use warm colors.
  — Red, orange, yellow.
- To provide status or background information, use cool colors.
  — Green, blue, violet, purple.
- Conform to human expectations.
  — In the job.
  — In the world at large.

Actions. The warm colors, red, yellow, and orange, imply active situations or that actions are necessary. Warm colors advance, forcing attention.

Status or background. The cool colors, green, blue, violet, and purple, imply background or status information. Cool colors recede or draw away.

Expectations. Conform to human expectations. Use color meanings that already exist in a person's job or the world at large. They are ingrained in behavior and difficult to unlearn. Some common color associations are the following:

- Red—Stop, fire, hot, danger.
- Yellow—Caution, slow, test.
- Green—Go, OK, clear, vegetation, safety.
- Blue—Cold, water, calm, sky, neutrality.
- Gray—Neutrality.
- White—Neutrality.
- Warm colors—Action, response required, spatial closeness.
- Cool colors—Status, background information, spatial remoteness.

Some typical implications of color with dramatic portrayal are:

- High illumination—Hot, active, comic situations.
- Low illumination—Emotional, tense, tragic, melodramatic, romantic situations.
- High saturation—Emotional, tense, hot, melodramatic, comic situations.
- Warm colors—Active, leisure, recreation, comic situations.
- Cool colors—Efficiency, work, tragic and romantic situations.

Proper use of color also requires consideration of the experiences and expectations of the screen viewers.

Location

- In the center of the visual field, use red and green.
- For peripheral viewing, use blue, yellow, black, and white.
- Use adjacent colors that differ by hue and value or lightness.

Central vision. The eye is most sensitive to red and green in the center of the visual field. The edges of the retina are not sensitive to these colors. If used in the viewing periphery, some other attention-getting method such as blinking must also be used.

Peripheral vision. For peripheral viewing, use blue, yellow, black, or white. The retina is most sensitive to these colors at its periphery.

Adjacent colors. Colors that appear adjacent to one another should differ in hue and lightness for a sharp edge and maximum differentiation. Also, adjacent colors that differ only in their blue component should not be used so that differentiation is possible. The eye is poorly suited for dealing with blue.

Ordering

- Order colors by their spectral position.
  — Red, orange, yellow, green, blue, indigo, violet.

If an ordering of colors is needed, such as from high to low, by levels of depth, and so on, arrange colors by their spectral position. There is evidence that people see the spectral order as a natural one. The spectral order is red, orange, yellow, green, blue, indigo, and violet, most easily remembered as "ROY G. BIV."

Foregrounds and Backgrounds

- Foregrounds:
  — Use colors that highly contrast with the background color.
  — For text or data, use:
    • Black.
    • Desaturated or spectrum center colors such as white, yellow, or green.
    • Warmer more active colors.
  — Use colors that possess the same saturation and lightness.
  — To emphasize an element, highlight it in a light value of the foreground color, pure white, or yellow.
  — To deemphasize an element, lowlight it in a dark value of the foreground color.

- Backgrounds:
  - Use a background color to organize a group of elements into a unified whole.
  - Use colors that do not compete with the foreground.
  - Use:
    - Light-colored backgrounds of low intensity: Off-white or light gray.
    - Desaturated colors.
    - Cool, dark colors such as blue or black.
    - Colors on the spectral extremes.

Foregrounds

Foreground colors should be as different as possible from background colors. A widely different foreground will maximize text legibility. With today's high-resolution monitors, the most recommended text color is black presented on a light-colored background of low intensity, either off-white or light gray. Bright white backgrounds should be avoided because of the harsh contrast between the dark text and the background.

Desaturated spectrum center colors, such white, yellow, or green, on dark backgrounds also work well. These colors do not excessively stimulate the eye and appear brighter to the eye. Saturated colors excessively stimulate the eye. Color theory also suggests using warmer, more active colors for foregrounds. Warmer colors advance, forcing attention. Exercise caution in using more fully saturated red and orange, however. They may be difficult to distinguish from one another.

Use foreground colors that possess the same saturation and lightness. Highlight elements in a light value of the foreground color. If off-white is the foreground color, highlight elements in pure white. Yellow can also be used to highlight elements. To deemphasize an element, lowlight it in a darker value of the foreground color. When lowlighting, a strong enough contrast with both the background and the non-lowlighted element must be maintained so that legibility and visual differentiation is possible.

The simultaneous use of highlighting and lowlighting should be avoided. Used together they may confuse the viewer. Also, as with other display techniques, be conservative in using highlighting and lowlighting, so that simplicity and clarity are maintained.

Backgrounds

A background color should organize a group of elements into a unified whole, isolating them from the remainder of the screen. Use colors that do not compete with the foreground. A background must be subtle and subservient to the data, text, or symbols on top of it.

As mentioned above, with today's high-resolution monitors, the most recommended background color is a low-intensity off-white or gray with black text. Pastoor (1990), in a study to be described shortly, also found that desaturated backgrounds in almost any color work well. Foreground colors must be chosen with consideration of the background color, however.

For dark backgrounds, use the cool, dark colors. Cool, dark colors visually recede, providing good contrast to the advancing lighter, foreground colors. Blue is especially good because of the eye's lack of sensitivity to it in the retina's central area and increased sensitivity to it in the periphery. Lalomia and Happ (1987), also in a study to be described shortly, found the best background colors to be black and blue. In a similar study, Pastoor (1990) found that cool colors, blue and bluish cyan, were preferred for dark background screens.

Also consider colors at the extreme end of the color spectrum. Marcus (1986a) recommends, in order of priority, the following background colors: blue, black, gray, brown, red, green, and purple.

Three-Dimensional Look

- Use at least five colors or color values to create a 3-D look on a screen.
    — Background: The control itself and the window on which it appears.
    — Foreground: Captions and lines for buttons, icons, and other objects.
      • Usually black or white.
    — Selected mode: The color used when the item is selected.
    — Top shadow: The bezel on the top and left of the control.
    — Bottom shadow: The bezel on the bottom and right of the control.

At least five colors or color values are needed to create a three-dimensional look on a screen (Fowler and Stanwick, 1995): the backgrounds of the control and the surface on which it is placed, the foreground (captions, lines, and so on), the selected mode, and the top and bottom shadows of the controls. These shadows assume an upper-left light source. Motif has created an algorithm to automatically calculate the top and bottom shadows, and the select color based upon the background (Kobara, 1991). Briefly, it recommends the following:

- **Background.** Midrange colors, 155–175 on the RGB scale.

- **Foreground.** Black or white, depending on the lightness or darkness of the background.

- **Selected mode.** About 15 percent darker than the background color, halfway between the background and bottom shadow. (Calculate this by multiplying the background color's RGB value by 0.85.)

- **Top shadow.** About 40 to 50 percent brighter than the background color. (Calculate this by multiplying the background color's RGB by 1.50.)

- **Bottom shadow.** About 45 to 60 percent darker than the background color. (Calculate this by multiplying the background's RGB values by 0.50.)

One reminder: A raised look should only be used on operable controls.

Color Palette, Defaults, and Customization

- Permit users to customize their colors.
- Provide a default set of colors for all screen components.
- Provide a palette of six or seven foreground colors.
  — Provide 2 to 5 values or lightness shades for each foreground color.
- Provide a palette of six or seven background colors.
- Never refer to a screen element by its color.

Customization. Because color preference is subjective, permit users to customize their displayed colors. While little research has been performed on color customization, Familant and Detweiler (1995) have measured the frequency of color changes by users. Compared were displayed color combinations that were judged to be "good" or "poor." They found that users with the poorer color combinations changed their screen colors more often than those with good combinations. Color satisfaction for those with "poor" color combinations must be fleeting. When color customization is permitted, whenever possible allow users to see the results of their color choices before they are applied. Include a sample screen in a preview function within the customization process.

Default set. While some users experiment with different color combinations, many others take what is provided them and never attempt to change it. Actually, many people do not know how to apply color to create a clear and appealing screen. Others may have the talent and skills but not the time to choose a proper combination. For these users, a preselected set of default colors should be developed for all screen elements.

Both the Macintosh and Microsoft Windows provide standard, well thought out color schemes. While thousands of colors may be available for display on a screen, most platforms recommend the use of restricted palettes. This is actually a good thing, reducing the probability of very poor color combinations and Christmas trees. Most Macintosh colors are subdued to avoid a "circus" effect on the screen (Apple, 1992b). Microsoft offers a number of predefined schemes such as "Arizona."

Do not provide the color spectrum; limit the number of choices available. A maximum of six or seven foreground and background colors will provide the necessary variety. It is also worthwhile to note that 2 to 5 values or lightnesses for each foreground color be developed.

With these palettes, however, some sort of guidance concerning maximum number of colors to use and what are good and poor combinations should be provided. Macintosh, for example, suggests that, if you create your own color schemes, colors compatible with the ones on the Color Control Panel be used. Guidelines will make the color selection process more efficient and reduce the likelihood of visually straining conditions developing.

Color reference. Finally, never refer to a screen element by its designed color. What was originally on the screen in yellow may not now be so on some users' screens.

Gray Scale

■ For fine discriminations use a black-gray-white scale.
— Recommended values are white, light gray, medium gray, dark gray, black.

The perception of fine detail is poor with color. The eye resolves fine detail much better on a black-white scale. Marcus (1986b) recommends five tonal values for black and white, higher-resolution screens: black, dark gray, medium gray, light gray, and white. He suggests the following general uses:

White:	Screen background.
	Text located in any black area.
Light Gray:	Pushbutton background area.
Medium Gray:	Icon background area.
	Menu drop shadow.
	Window drop shadow.
	Inside area of system icons.
	Filename bar.
Dark gray:	Window border.
Black:	Text.
	Window title bar.
	Icon border.
	Icon elements.
	Ruled lines.

Motif presents the following scheme for designing windows in a gray scale (Kobara, 1991).

Background:	A 30 percent light gray (RGB 79, 79, 79).
Foreground:	White (RGB 0, 0, 0).
Selected mode:	A 70 percent dark gray (RGB 181, 181, 181).
Top Shadow:	White.
Bottom Shadow:	Black (RGB 255, 255, 255).

Gray scale values must differ by at least 20 to 30 percent (White, 1990).

Text in Color

■ When switching text from black to color:
— Double the width of lines.
— Use bold or larger type:
— If originally 8 to 12 points, increase by 1 to 2 points.
— If originally 14 to 24 points, increase by 2 to 4 points.
■ Check legibility by squinting at text.
— Too-light type will recede or even disappear.

Text in color is not as visible as it is in black. Fowler and Stanwick (1995) report that the size of text has to be increased to maintain legibility when the text is switched from black to color. Lines should be doubled in width and type made larger or bolder. If the existing type ranges from 8 to 12 points, increase it one or two points. If the existing type ranges from 14 to 24 points, increase it by 2 to 4 points. They suggest that by squinting at it, you can check the legibility of type. A type that is too light will recede, or even disappear, from view.

Monochromatic Screens

- At the standard viewing distance, white, orange, or green are acceptable colors.
- At a far viewing distance, white is the best choice.
- Over all viewing distances, from near to far, white is the best choice.

Monochromatic, or one-color, screens are still found in graphical systems, most frequently on notebook PCs. In a study by Hewlett-Packard (Wichansky, 1986) white, orange, and green monochrome desktop display device screens were evaluated for performance and readability at various viewing distances. At the standard screen viewing distance (18 to 24 inches), no performance differences were found between white, orange, and green phosphor in either polarity (light characters on a dark background, or dark characters on a light background). Subjective ratings of ease of reading were highest for green and orange light background screens as compared to dark background screens, while no differences in ease of reading were found for either polarity with white phosphor at this distance. At a far viewing distance (4 to 5 feet), orange and green light background screens could be seen more clearly than dark background screens, while white screens were equally legible in either polarity. More errors were found with green than the other two colors.

A green screen yielded red or pink afterimages for 35 percent of the screen viewers; orange, blue afterimages for 20 percent; white yielded afterimages for 5 percent. A 35 percent pink afterimage rate for green screen viewing was also found by Galitz (1968).

Some conclusions:

- At standard viewing distances, no significant performance differences exist for white, orange, or green. All are acceptable. Subjective preferences may vary, however, so providing the viewer a choice of any of these colors is desirable.
- At far viewing distances, white is the more legible color and therefore the best choice.
- Over all viewing distances, white is the best choice.
- White has the lowest probability for creating visual afterimages.

Consistency

- Be consistent in color use.

Consistency in color usage should exist within a screen, a set of screens, and a system. A person can sense the relatedness of color in space and over time, thereby linking elements not seen immediately together. An identical background color in windows on different screens, for example, will be seen as related. Changing specific color meanings must be avoided. It will lead to difficulties in interpretation, confusion, and errors. In general, broadly defined meanings (such as red indicating a problem) permit more scope for variations without inconsistency.

Cultural, Disciplinary, and Accessibility Considerations

- Consider the impact of specific colors on:
  — Users of various cultures.
  — Users of various disciplines.
  — Users with color-viewing deficiencies.
  — Users relying on accessibility utilities.

As previously described, colors may possess different meanings and interpretations in different cultures and disciplines. Where applicable, color choices for screen elements should reflect these differences and not be offensive. See Table 10.2 in Step 10 for a summary of some cultural color differences. Also consider users with a color-viewing deficiency. If color is used as a code, it must be recognizable by all users. It is best to use color as a supplement to other coding methods such as location, size, or element orientation. See Table 12.2 for a summary of problem-creating colors for people with defective color vision. Colors chosen should also consider the impact of users relying on accessibility utilities. Some utilities, such as the Magnifier accessory included with Windows, alter the colors displayed on a screen.

Choosing Colors for Textual Graphic Screens

For displaying data, text, and symbols on a textual graphical screen (as opposed to statistical graphics screens to be described shortly) colors selected should have adequate visibility, meaning, contrast, and harmony.

- Use effective foreground/background combinations.
- Use effective foreground combinations.
- Choose the background color first.
- Display no more than four colors at one time.
- Use colors in toolbars sparingly.
- Test the chosen colors.

Effective Foreground/Background Combinations

Lalomia and Happ (1987) established effective foreground/background color combinations for the IBM 5153 Color Display. From a color set of 16 different foregrounds and 8 different backgrounds, 120 color combinations were evaluated for (1) response time to identify characters, and (2) subjective preferences of users. The results from each measure were ranked and combined to derive an overall measure of color combination effectiveness. The best and poorest color combinations are summarized in Table 12.3. In this table "Best" means the specified combination was in the top 20 percent for overall effectiveness; "Poor" means it was in the bottom 20 percent. Those combinations composing the "middle" 60 percent are not marked.

The results yield some interesting conclusions:

- The majority of good combinations possess a bright or high-intensity color as the foreground color.
- The majority of poor combinations are those with low contrast.
- The best overall color is black.

Table 12.3   Effective Foreground/Background Combinations

| FOREGROUND | BACKGROUND | | | | | | | |
	BLACK	BLUE	GREEN	CYAN	RED	MAGENTA	BROWN	WHITE
BLACK	x			Good		Good		Good
BLUE		x			Poor			Good
H.I. BLUE			Poor	Poor			Poor	Poor
CYAN	Good		Poor	x			Poor	
H.I. CYAN	Good	Good		Good	Good	Good		
GREEN	Good	Good	x	Poor	Good		Poor	Poor
H.I. GREEN		Good						
YELLOW	Good	Good		Good		Good		
RED			Poor		x	Poor	Poor	
H.I. RED			Poor					
MAGENTA			Poor		Poor	x	Poor	
H.I. MAGENTA	Good		Good			Poor		
BROWN			Poor			Poor	x	
GRAY		Poor			Poor		Poor	
WHITE		Good		Poor				x
H.I. WHITE	Good		Good	Good				

(H.I. = High Intensity)

From Lalomia and Happ (1987).

- The poorest overall color is brown.
- Maximum flexibility and variety in choosing a foreground color exists with black or blue backgrounds. (These backgrounds account for almost one-half of the good combinations.)
- Brown and green are the poorest background choices.

Bailey and Bailey (1989), in their screen creation utility Protoscreens, have a table summarizing research-derived good foreground/background combinations. This table, which uses the results of the Lalomia and Happ study plus some others, is shown in modified form in Table 12.4.

The studies referenced above did not control character-background luminance-contrast ratios. Because of the characteristics of the eye, some colors appear brighter to it than others. A conclusion of the Lalomia and Happ study was that good combinations usually possessed a bright or high-intensity foreground color.

Table 12.4 Preferred Foreground/Background Combinations from Protoscreens

BACKGROUNDS	ACCEPTABLE FOREGROUNDS	
Black	Dark Cyan Dark Yellow Dark White	Light Green Light Cyan Light Magenta Light Yellow Light White
Blue	Dark Green Dark Yellow Dark White	Light Green Light Cyan Light Yellow Light White
Green	Black Dark Blue	Light Yellow Light White
Cyan	Black Dark Blue	Light Yellow Light White
Red		Light Green Light Cyan Light Yellow Light White
Magenta	Black	Light Cyan Light Yellow Light White
Yellow	Black Dark Blue Dark Red	
White	Black Dark Blue	

Pastoor (1990) equalized luminance-contrast ratios at preoptimized levels for about 800 foreground/background color combinations. For light foregrounds and dark backgrounds, the ratio was 10:1; for light backgrounds and dark foregrounds, 1:6.5. He then had the combinations rated with the following results:

- For dark on light polarity:
  - Any foreground color is acceptable if the background color is chosen properly.
  - Increased saturation of the foreground only marginally affected ratings, implying that any dark, saturated, foreground color is satisfactory.
  - Saturated backgrounds yield unsatisfactory ratings.
  - Less saturated backgrounds generally receive high ratings with any foreground color.
- For light on dark polarity:
  - Combinations involving saturated colors tend to be unsatisfactory.
  - As foreground color saturation increases, the number of background colors yielding high ratings diminishes.
  - Generally, desaturated foreground/background color combinations yielded the best ratings.
  - Short wavelength, cool colors were preferred for backgrounds (blue, bluish cyan, cyan).

In general, Pastoor concluded that: (1) there was no evidence suggesting a differential effect of color on subjective ratings or performance (except that for light on dark polarity, blue, bluish cyan, or cyan were preferred as backgrounds), and (2) overall, desaturated color combinations yielded the best results.

Choose the Background First

When choosing colors to display, it is best to select the background color first. Then, choose acceptable foreground colors.

Maximum of Four Colors

While not experimentally verified, experience indicates that displaying more than four colors at one time on a textual screen gives rise to a feeling of "too much." Marcus (1986a) suggests an even more conservative approach, a maximum of three foreground colors and, even better, only two. An application of good use of color can often be viewed in one's living room. Note the use of color by the television networks when textual or tabular information is presented (for example, sport scores, news highlights, and so on). The use of only two, or sometimes three, colors is most commonly seen.

So, while more than four colors may be displayed over a period of time or on a series of screens, do not display more than four colors at one time on a single screen. For most cases, restrict the number of colors to two or three.

Use Colors in Toolbars Sparingly

Toolbar icons are usually small in size. Presenting them in color is rarely useful, most often disrupting legibility. Use color in toolbar icons simply and conservatively, and only if the color aids icon identification, makes it easier to distinguish icons, or adds meaning. A file folder in yellow or a "stop" icon in red are examples of good uses of color.

Test the Colors

Because color is such a complex phenomenon, because definitions of a color can vary, and because the hardware on which a color is used can affect its look, always test all chosen colors as part of the system testing process (see Step 14 "Test, Test, and Retest").

Choosing Colors for Statistical Graphics Screens

The visual, spatial, or physical representation of information—as opposed to numeric, alphanumeric, textual, or symbol representation—is known as *statistical* or data graphics. Common kinds of statistical graphics include bar graphs, line graphs, scatterplots, and pie charts. Color can also be used to render a statistical graphic screen more legible and meaningful.

Emphasis

- Emphasize the graphic's data.

The main emphasis of color in a statistical graphics screen should be in the data area. Brighter colors and highlighting should attract the eye to the presented data so that trends and conclusions can be quickly perceived. Supporting text, numbers, and legends should receive slightly less emphasis. Aids in data interpretation such as grids should receive the least emphasis.

Number of Colors

- Use no more than six colors at one time.
- Use one color of five values or lightness.

Experience indicates that displaying more than six colors at one time on statistical graphics screens is "too much." Even five or six colors, however, may be distracting or confusing if they are not properly chosen or are not harmonious. Marcus (1986a) suggests a more pleasing arrangement can often be achieved for graphics with five or less segments by using one color and displaying each segment in a different value or lightness.

Backgrounds

- Surround images:
  — In a neutral color.
  — In a color complementary to the main image.

A neutral background will help set off a full color. A background in the complementary color of the main image will minimize visual afterimages.

Size

- Provide images of an adequate size for the task.
- If the image changes in size, use colors that exhibit a minimum shift in hue or lightness.
  — White, yellow, and red on dark backgrounds.

As color areas decrease in size, they appear to change in lightness and saturation. Similar colors may look different, and different colors may look similar. Interactions with the background color also increase. Thin gray images (lines or borders, for example) appear as a desaturated color complement of their background.

Provide *adequately sized* images. Where color identification is important, an image should be large enough to eliminate these distortions. For images *changing in size*, use colors that exhibit minimal hue or lightness shifts. Marcus (1986b) recommends that white, yellow, and red be used for light text, thin lines, and small shapes on dark backgrounds (blue, green, red, light gray).

Status

- To indicate a status, use the following colors:
  — *Proper, normal, or OK:* Green, white, or blue.
  — *Caution:* Yellow or gold.
  — *Emergency or abnormal:* Red.

To indicate a status, use green, white, or blue to indicate OK; yellow or gold for caution; and red for emergency or abnormal. The use of red, yellow, and green are well-learned color conventions.

Measurements and Area-Fill Patterns

- Display measurements in the following colors:
  — Grids: Gray
  — Data points: Yellow

— Variance or error bars: Blue
— Out of specified range data: Red
— Captions and labels: Lavender, lime green, or cyan

■ Display area-fill patterns in the following colors:
— Widely spaced dots: Red
— Closely spaced dots: Green
— Wide dashed lines: Magenta
— Narrow dashed lines: Cyan
— Wide crosshatch: Blue
— Narrow crosshatch: Yellow

For *measurements*, Smith (1986) recommends the above. They balance emphasis considerations (gray for grids, yellow for data points, lavender, lime green, or cyan for labels) and human expectations (red for out-of-specified range). Marcus (1986a) recommends that all text and the horizontal and vertical axis lines of a statistical graphic should be off-white. This will aid in focusing users' main attention on the colored data. To ensure that fill-in area patterns are identifiable, discriminable, and free from unintended brightness effects, Smith (1988) recommends the above.

Physical Impressions

■ Size:
— To convey an impression of:
• Larger: Use bright or saturated colors.
• Smaller: Use dark or desaturated colors.
• Similar: Use colors of equal lightness.

■ Weight:
— To convey an impression of:
• Heavy: Use dark, saturated colors.
• Light: Use light, desaturated colors.

■ Distance:
— To convey an impression of:
• Close: Use saturated, bright, long-wavelength (red) colors.
• Far: Use saturated, dark, short-wavelength (blue) colors.

■ Height:
— To convey an impression of height, use desaturated, light colors.

■ Depth:
— To convey an impression of depth, use saturated, dark colors.

■ Concentration level:
— To convey an impression of concentration level, use:
• High: Saturated colors.
• Low: Desaturated colors.

- Magnitude of change:
  — To convey an impression of magnitude of change, use:
    • Lowest: Short-wavelength (blue) colors.
    • Highest: Long-wavelength (red) colors.

- Actions:
  — To convey an impression of action, use:
    • Required: Long-wavelength (red) colors.
    • Not required: Short-wavelength (blue) colors.

- Order:
  — To convey an impression of order with color, use:
    • Low end of a continuum: Short-wavelength (blue) colors.
    • High end of a continuum: Long-wavelength (red) colors.
  — When displaying an array of ordered colors, position:
    • Short-wavelength colors at the left side or at the bottom.
    • Long-wavelength colors at the right side or at the top.
  — To convey an impression of order with value or lightness, use the lightness order of a color (darkest to lightest or vice versa).

- Neutrality:
  — To convey an impression of neutrality, use black, gray, and white.

Colors yield different physical impressions. Bright, saturated colors convey a feeling of large and close. Dark, saturated colors mean heavy, far, and impression of depth. Desaturated, light colors indicate a light weight and height. Desaturated dark colors mean smaller. Long-wavelength (red) colors are associated with high rate of change, action required, and the high end of a continuum. Short-wavelength (blue) colors are associated with low rate of change, no actions required, and the low end of a continuum. Neutrality is best indicated by black, gray, or white.

Choosing Colors for Web Pages

- Purpose:
  — Color must always have a meaningful purpose.
- Palette:
  — Use the browser 216-color palette.
- Presentation:
  — Minimize the number of presented colors.
  — Always consider color in context.
  — Use similar or the same color schemes throughout.
    • For foregrounds: Use black or strong colors for text and headings.
  — For backgrounds: Use weaker contrasting colors such as off-white or light gray.
  — Use a uniform color in large areas.

— The smaller the element, the more contrast is required between it and its background.
— Larger images should use:
  • Flat, Web-safe colors.
  • Fewer colors than small images.
— Select colors that can be easily reproduced in black and white.

■ Links:
— Use default colors for links.
  • Make unselected/unvisited links blue.
  • Make selected/visited links purple.
— Do not display non-link text in link colors.

■ Testing:
— Test all colors.

Purpose. Color should always be used for a meaningful purpose. Acceptable uses include highlighting or calling attention to information, grouping related information, designating selected links, giving a site an identity, or communicating realism for images. Color without a purpose is gratuitous and visually distracting.

Palette. Use colors that succeed on a variety of platforms or browsers. There are 216 colors (out of the standard 256 colors) that will always look the same on any monitor at any resolution. This is called the *browser-safe* palette, and it is illustrated on several Web sites. A search on "color palette" or a similar term will lead to these Web sites.

Presentation. Colors should be carefully chosen to aid users in understanding content, to keep a page well balanced, and to keep it graphically simple. Always *minimize* the number of presented colors. Too much color makes it difficult for people to notice something that might be really important, and makes it difficult to comprehend how color is being used to aid in understanding the screen's content. Christmas trees should be reserved for December 25; the "Las Vegas effect" (as the gratuitous use of color is also sometimes called) should be confined to a region in southern Nevada. Minimizing the use of color will also have page download benefits. Fewer colors means faster downloads.

Always consider color in *context*, never in isolation. One background color interacts with other background colors. Foreground text colors and graphics interact with background colors. When choosing colors, consider these interactions and use colors that work well together. Use *similar* or the same color schemes throughout a Web site. This will give the site an identity and help the user maintain a sense of place.

Foreground colors should be as different as possible from *background* colors. A contrasting foreground will maximize text legibility. A background color should organize a group of elements into a unified whole, isolating them from the remainder of the screen. Use background colors that do not compete with the foreground. A background must be subtle and subservient to the data, text, or symbols on top of it. With today's high-resolution monitors, the most recommended foreground text color is black presented on a light-colored background of low intensity, either off-white or light gray. Most other pastel colors, especially spectrum center colors, have also been found to be acceptable as backgrounds

(Pastoor, 1990). Use dark backgrounds only when establishing contrast between an area of the screen and the main screen body. High intensity colors as backgrounds (such as red, magenta and bright green) must be avoided as they can be visually fatiguing when viewed for a period of time. Short wavelength, cool colors (blue and black) have been found to be preferred for dark backgrounds (Lalomia and Happ, 1987). Cool, dark colors visually recede, providing good contrast to the advancing lighter, foreground colors. Blue is especially good because of the eye's lack of sensitivity to it in the retina's central area and increased sensitivity to it in the periphery.

When choosing foreground and background colors, ensure that contrasting combinations are selected. See Tables 12-3 and 12-4 for color selection guidance. Also, always test all selected foreground and background colors. What may look good in theory may not always look as good in reality.

Use a *uniform* color in large screen areas. Large areas of the same color download faster. They compress well and are an efficient use of the GIF format. The *smaller* the element, the more contrast is required between it and its background. To reduce image file sizes for *larger* images, use flat Web-safe colors. Also use fewer colors with smaller images. Finally, select colors that can be easily *reproduced* in black and white on a screen or printer. This ensures that those who use a monochrome display or print in black and white will have a faithful reproduction of the intended screen.

MAXIM   *Content* **is always more important than color.**

Links. Unselected/unvisited links must be distinguishable from selected/visited links. Stick with the default colors of *blue* for links already followed and *purple* for links not yet ventured down. While the choice of blue as a text color was poor because of its degraded reading ability, it is well learned, its use is recommended because it is now very familiar. Using nonstandard link colors can lead to severe problems. It is difficult to remember what color means what, increasing link selection errors. It can also lead to confusion with normal underlined text in a document. Never display general screen text in the link colors of blue and purple. This will create confusion between linked and non-linked text. It is acceptable, however, to use these colors in text that is large and decorative in nature and acting as a graphic and not plain text.

Testing. The possibility always exists that identical colors may appear differently on different monitors and platforms. Color choices should be tested on a variety of displays.

Uses of Color to Avoid

- Relying exclusively on color.
- Too many colors at one time.
- Highly saturated, spectrally extreme colors together:
  — Red and blue, yellow and purple.
- Low-brightness colors for extended viewing or older viewers.

- Colors of equal brightness.
- Colors lacking contrast:
  — For example, yellow and white; black and brown; reds, blues, and browns against a light background.
- Fully saturated colors for text or other frequently read screen components.
- Pure blue for text, thin lines, and small shapes.
- Colors in small areas.
- Color for fine details.
- Non-opponent colors.
- Red and green in the periphery of large-scale displays.
- Adjacent colors that only differ in the amount of blue they possess.
- Single-color distinctions for color-deficient users.
- Using colors in unexpected ways.
- Using color to improve legibility of densely packed text.

The proper use of color in screen design also suggests some things to avoid.

Relying exclusively on color. Consider the needs of color-blind viewers and the effects of ambient lighting on color perception. Do not underestimate the value and role of other techniques such as spatial formatting and component locations in good screen design.

Too many colors at one time. Using too many colors at one time can eliminate the benefits of color. Response times are increased, erroneous associations made, the handling of information is interfered with, and confusion is created. The objective is a screen that communicates; a colorful screen is not the objective. Use just enough colors to create effective communication. Again, consider the value of other techniques such as spatial formatting and consistent component locations in good design.

Highly saturated, spectrally extreme colors together. Spectrally extreme combinations can create eye focus problems, vibrations, illusions of shadows, and afterimages. In addition to red/blue and yellow/purple, other combinations that might cause problems are yellow/blue, green/blue, and red/green.

Low-brightness colors for extended viewing or older viewers. The eye adapts to color during extended viewing. The eye's capability also diminishes with age as the amount of light passing through the lens decreases. All colors will look less bright, and colors that are dim to begin with may not be legible. Brighter colors are needed to prevent reading problems.

Colors of equal brightness. Colors of equal brightness cannot be easily distinguished. A brightness difference must exist between adjacent colors.

Colors lacking contrast. Colors lacking contrast also cannot be easily distinguished. Similar foreground and background colors often do not have sufficient contrast with each other.

Fully saturated colors for frequently read screen components. Fully saturated colors excessively stimulate the eye, possibly causing visual confusion and fatigue.

Pure blue for text, thin lines, and small shapes. Because of its physical make-up, the eye has difficulty creating a clear and legible image of small blue shapes. They will look fuzzy.

Colors in small areas. Distortions in color, lightness, and saturation may occur for small areas of color.

Colors for fine details. Black, gray, and white will provide much better resolution. Reserve other colors for large areas or attracting attention.

Non-opponent colors. Non-opponent colors, red/yellow or green/blue, produce poorer images. Opponent colors, red/green or yellow/blue are good combinations for simple displays.

Red and green in the periphery of large-scale displays. The edges of the retina are not particularly sensitive to red and green. Avoid these colors in the periphery, especially for small symbols and shapes. Yellow and blue are much better peripheral colors.

Adjacent colors only differing in the amount of blue they possess. Because of the eye's difficulty in dealing with blue, differences in color based upon varying amounts of blue in the color's mixture will not be noticed.

Single color distinctions for color-deficient users. For those people with color-viewing deficiencies, distinguishing certain colors may be difficult or impossible. Always provide a redundant coding scheme.

Using colors in unexpected ways. Colors have become associated with certain meanings. Red, for example, is always associated with stop or danger. To display a critical or error message in green would violate an ingrained association and cause confusion. Always use colors in the way people expect them to be used.

Using color to improve legibility of densely packed text. Space lines between paragraphs of text or after about every five lines of data will work much better.

Too many colors at one time (again). Never overuse color (again, this is important). Too many colors at one time may make a screen confusing or unpleasant to look at. Use only enough color to fulfill the system's objectives.

Organize and Layout Windows and Pages

During the design process to this point, the individual elements, or building blocks, of screens will have been identified, and each element's content and wording established. A logical flow of information will also have been determined. The next step is to organize and lay out individual windows and Web pages clearly and meaningfully. Proper screen presentation and structure will encourage quick and correct information comprehension, the fastest possible execution of tasks and functions, and enhanced user acceptance. In this step, we will address:

- Organizing and laying out graphical and Web screens to encourage quick and accurate information comprehension and control execution.
  - Organizing for meaningfulness and efficiency.
  - Creating groupings.
  - Providing alignment and balance.

In graphical user interfaces, components to be included on windows include a title, screen controls, headings, other screen content, and possibly instructional messages. On Web pages, components to be included consist of elements such as the page title, textual content, graphics, headings, screen controls, links, and other necessary components.

Organizing and Laying Out Screens

How a screen is organized and how its information is actually presented are crucial to achieving the design goals of fast and accurate comprehension and control execution.

Following is a summary of numerous design principles that can be applied toward these ends. They have all been fully addressed in earlier chapters but are restated here for quick referral and as a reminder of their importance.

General Guidelines

- Amount of information:
  — Present the proper amount of information on each screen.
    - Too little is inefficient.
    - Too much is confusing.
  — Present all information necessary for performing an action or making a decision on one screen, whenever possible.
- Organization:
  — Provide an ordering that:
    - Is logical and sequential.
    - Is rhythmic, guiding a person's eye through the display.
    - Encourages natural movement sequences.
    - Minimizes pointer and eye movement distances.
- Control placement:
  — Position the most important and frequently used controls at the top left.
  — Maintain a top-to-bottom, left-to-right flow.
  — If one control enables or affects another, the enabling control should be above or to the left of the enabled control.
  — Place the command buttons that affect the entire window horizontally, and centered, at the window's bottom.
- Navigation:
  — The flow of interaction should:
    - Require as little cursor and pointer travel as possible.
    - Minimize the number of times a person's hand has to travel between the keyboard and the mouse.
  — Assist users in navigating through a screen by:
    - Aligning elements.
    - Grouping elements.
    - Using line borders.
- Aesthetics:
  — Provide a visually pleasing composition through:
    - Adequate use of white space.
    - Balance.
    - Groupings.
    - Alignment of elements.
- Visual clutter:
  — Avoid visual clutter by:
    - Maintaining low screen density levels.
    - Maintaining distinctiveness of elements.

- Focus and emphasis:
  - — Provide visual emphasis to the most important screen elements, its data or information.
  - — Sequentially, direct attention to items that are:
    1. Critical.
    2. Important.
    3. Secondary.
    4. Peripheral.
- Consistency:
  - — Provide consistency.
    - With a person's experiences and cultural conventions.
    - Internally within a system.
    - Externally across systems.

These guidelines, along with many others, were fully addressed in Step 3 "Understand the Principles of Good Screen Design." In brief, present the proper amount of information in each window. Never cram information into it. Keep the proportion of the window devoted to information or "ink" to no more than 30 to 40 percent of the window's entire area. Always leave a sufficient margin around all screen elements and between elements and the screen border. The window will look much more appealing to the viewer. Provide an ordering that is logical, sequential, and rhythmic to guide a person's eye through the display. Other important factors include maintaining a top-to-bottom, left-to-right flow; efficiency in navigation; a visually pleasing composition, achieved by means of balance, groupings, and alignment; the proper emphasis of elements; and being consistent.

Organization Guidelines

Organizational guidelines to be addressed include those relating to groupings, borders, dependent controls, alignment, and balance.

Creating Groupings

- General:
  - — Provide groupings of associated elements.
    - Elements of a radio button or check box control.
    - Two or more related fields or controls.
  - — Create groupings as close as possible to 5 degrees of visual angle.
- White space:
  - — Provide adequate separation of groupings through the liberal use of white space.
  - — Leave adequate space:
    - Around groups of related controls.
    - Between groupings and window borders.
  - — The space between groupings should be greater than the space between fields within a grouping.

- Headings:
  - — Provide section headings and subsection headings for multiple control groupings.
  - — Provide headings that meaningfully and concisely describe the nature of the group of related fields.
- Borders:
  - — Enhance groupings through incorporation of borders around:
    - Elements of a single control.
    - Groups of related controls or fields.
  - — Individual control borders should be visually differentiable from borders delineating groupings of fields or controls.
    - Provide a border consisting of a thin line around *single* controls.
    - Provide a border consisting of a slightly thicker line around *groups* of fields or controls.
  - — Do not place individual field or control borders around:
    - Single entry fields.
    - Single list boxes.
    - Single combination boxes.
    - Single spin boxes.
    - Single sliders.
  - — Do not place borders around command buttons.

Individual controls with multiple parts, such as radio buttons or check boxes, should be identifiable as a single entity. A series of related controls should also be presented as related. Create groupings to do this as often as possible. Groupings aid learning and provide visual appeal. The optimum group size is five degrees of visual angle. At the normal viewing distance of a screen this is a circle 1.67 inches in diameter. On a text-based screen this is equivalent to about six to seven lines at a width of 12 to 14 characters. Examples of groupings are shown in Figure 13.1.

Groupings can be made visually obvious through liberal use of white space. Sufficient space should be left between all groupings of controls, and groupings and the window borders, as illustrated in Figure 13.2.

Headings should also be used to give groupings of controls or information an identity. This aids comprehension and learning of what is presented. See Figure 13.3.

Borders

Groupings can be further enhanced through the use of borders. Inscribe line borders around elements of a single control such as a radio button or check box and/or groups of related controls or fields. Individual control borders should be visually differentiable from borders delineating groupings of fields or controls. Provide a border consisting of a thin line around single controls and a slightly thicker line around groups of fields or controls.

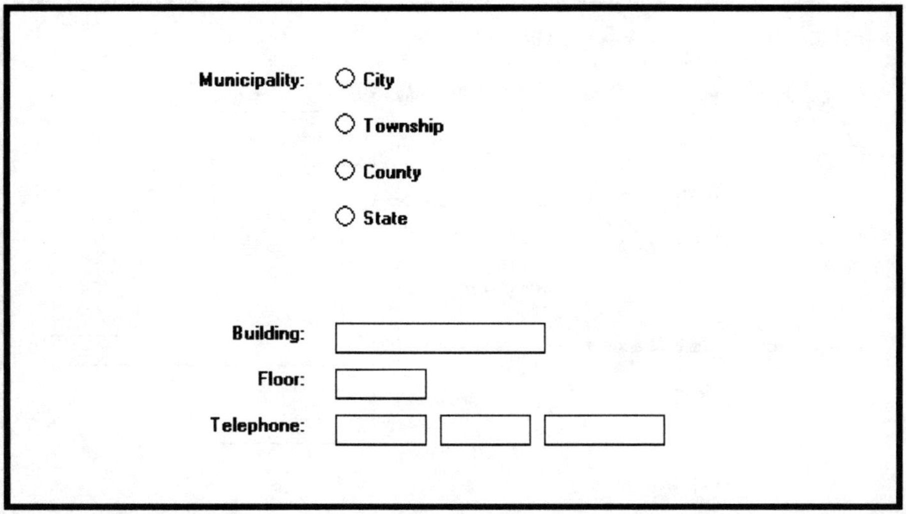

Figure 13.1   Groupings.

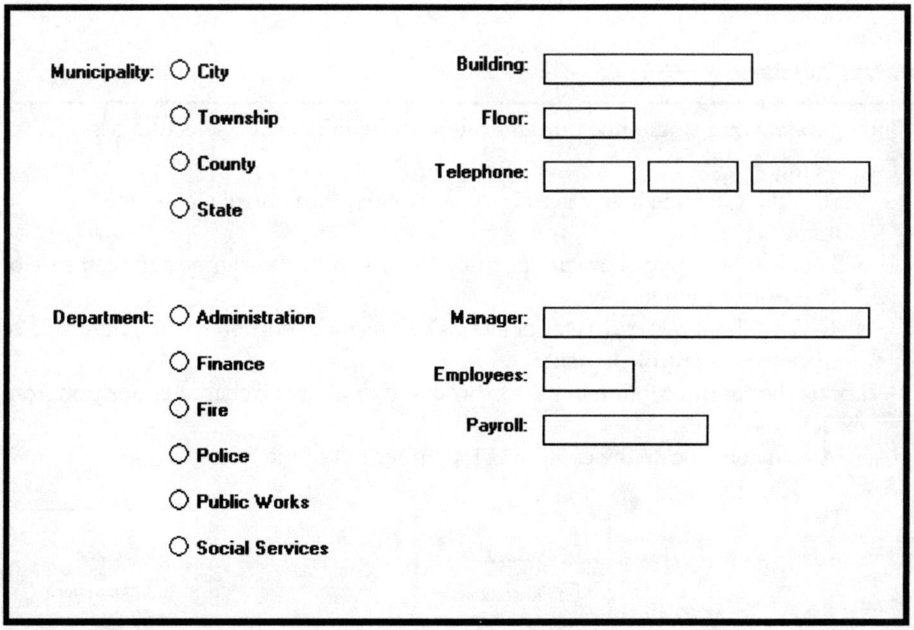

Figure 13.2   Groupings using white space.

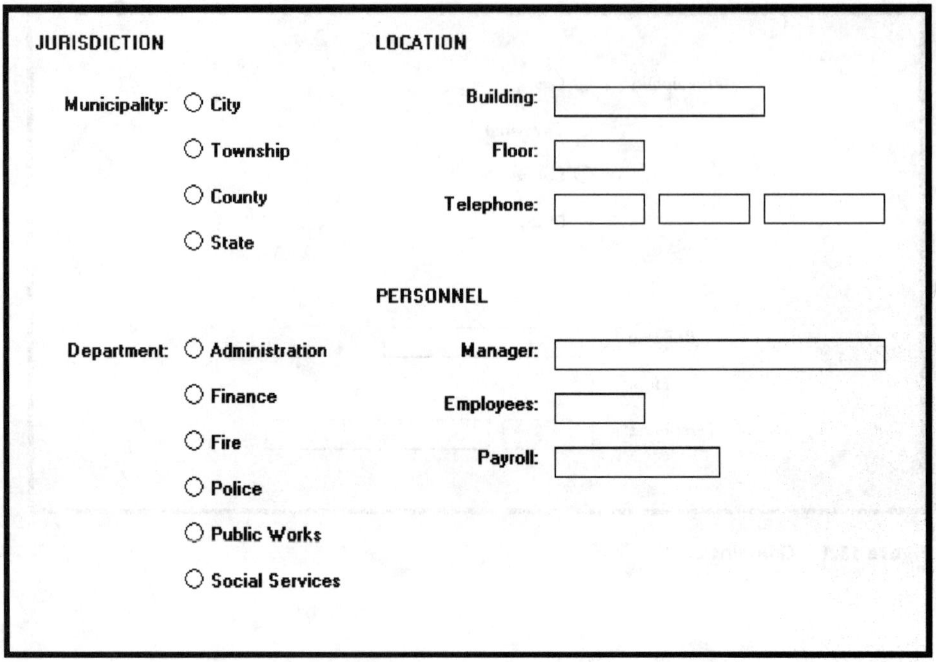

JURISDICTION   LOCATION

Municipality: ○ City   Building:

            ○ Township   Floor:

            ○ County   Telephone:

            ○ State

                    PERSONNEL

Department: ○ Administration   Manager:

            ○ Finance   Employees:

            ○ Fire   Payroll:

            ○ Police

            ○ Public Works

            ○ Social Services

Figure 13.3   Groupings with section headings.

Control Borders

■ Incorporate a thin single-line border around the elements of a selection control.

■ For spacing:
— Vertically, leave one line space above and below the control elements.
— Horizontally:
    • Leave at least two character positions between the border and the left side of the control elements.
    • Leave at least two character positions between the border and the right side of the longest control element.
— Locate the control caption in the top border, indented one character position from the left border.
    • Alternately, locate the caption at the upper left of the box.

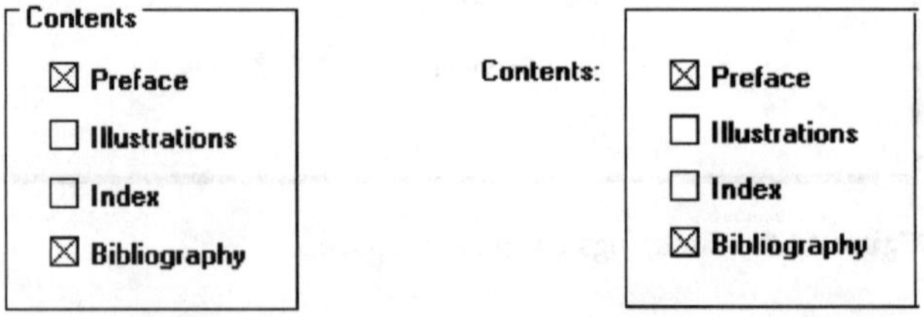

Contents
  ☒ Preface
  ☐ Illustrations
  ☐ Index
  ☒ Bibliography

Contents: ☒ Preface
           ☐ Illustrations
           ☐ Index
           ☒ Bibliography

Figure 13.4

— If the control caption exceeds the length of the choice descriptions, extend the border two character positions to the right of the caption.

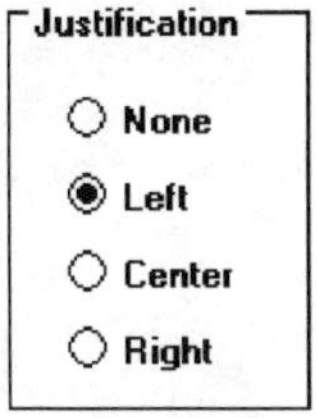

Figure 13.5

Thin line borders may be used to surround some boxed-in controls, particularly radio buttons and check boxes. Control captions should be located upper left within the border itself, or to the left of the box. The spacing guidelines are to prevent cramping the text within the border. Some examples of control borders are illustrated in Figures 13.6 and 13.7.

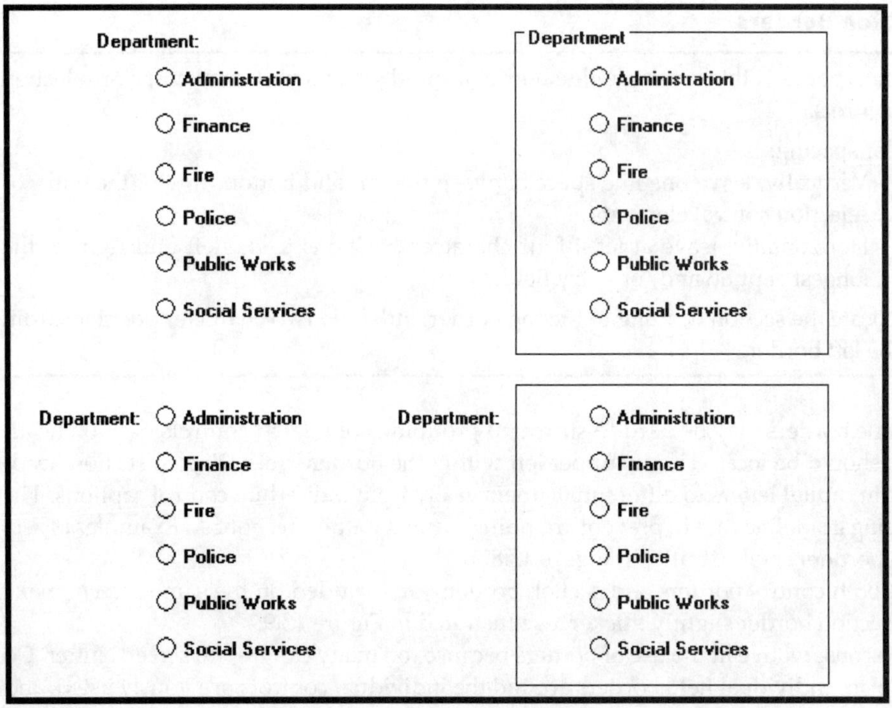

Figure 13.6   Examples of vertically arrayed controls without and with borders.

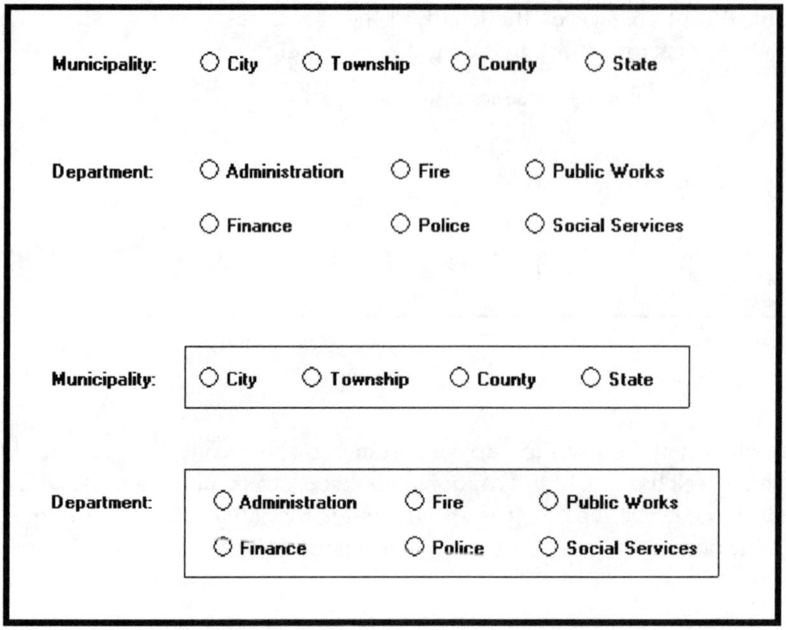

Figure 13.7   Examples of horizontally arrayed controls without and with borders.

Section Borders

- Incorporate a thicker single-line border around groups of related entry or selection controls.
- For spacing:
  - Vertically, leave one line space between the top and bottom row of the entry or selection control elements.
  - Horizontally, leave at least four character positions to the left and right of the longest caption and/or entry field.
- Locate the section heading in the top border, indented two character positions from the left border.

Line borders may be used to surround groupings of related controls. Section headings should be located at the upper left within the border itself. Display section headings in capital letters to differentiate them easily from individual control captions. The spacing guidelines are to prevent cramping the text within the border. Examples of section borders are illustrated in Figure 13.8.

If both control borders and section borders are included on the same screen, make the section border slightly thicker, as illustrated in Figure 13.9.

Be conservative in the use of borders because too many can lead to screen clutter. Do not place individual field borders around the individual controls previously listed, and illustrated in Figure 13.10. The nature of their design provides them with a border. Also, because of the potential for clutter, do not place a border around groups of pushbuttons.

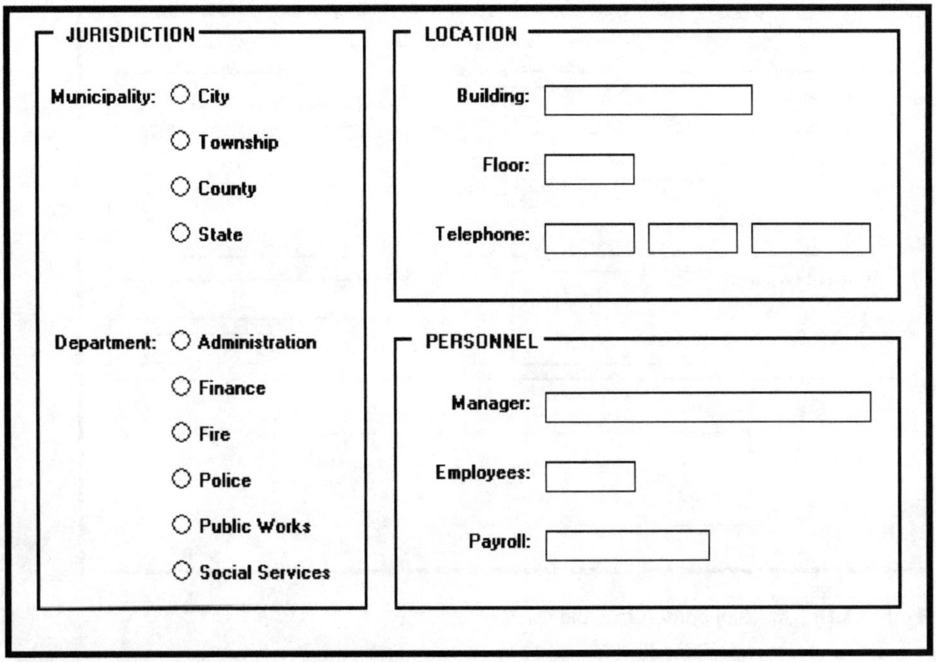

Figure 13.8 Grouping of sections using borders.

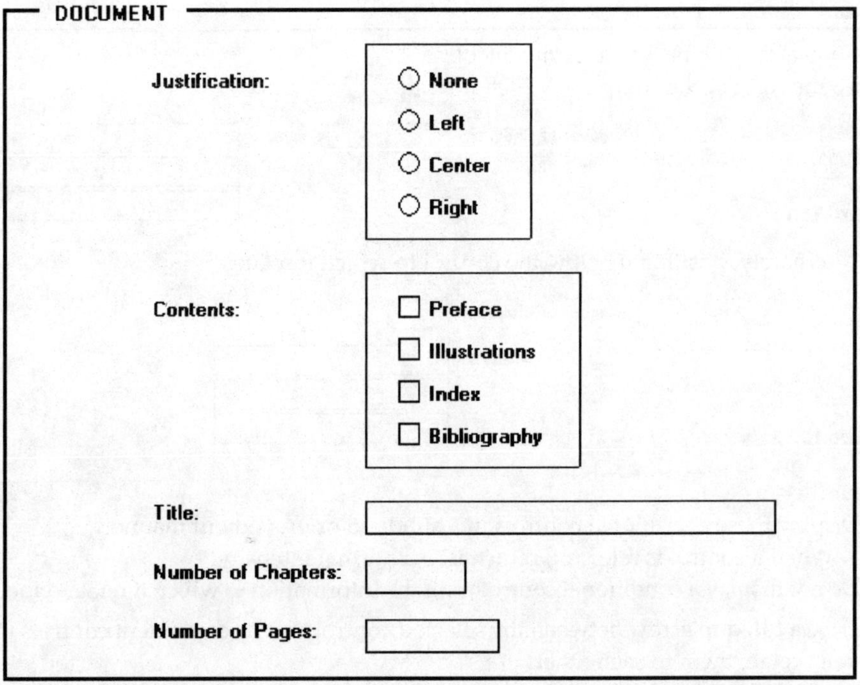

Figure 13.9 Differentiable control and section borders.

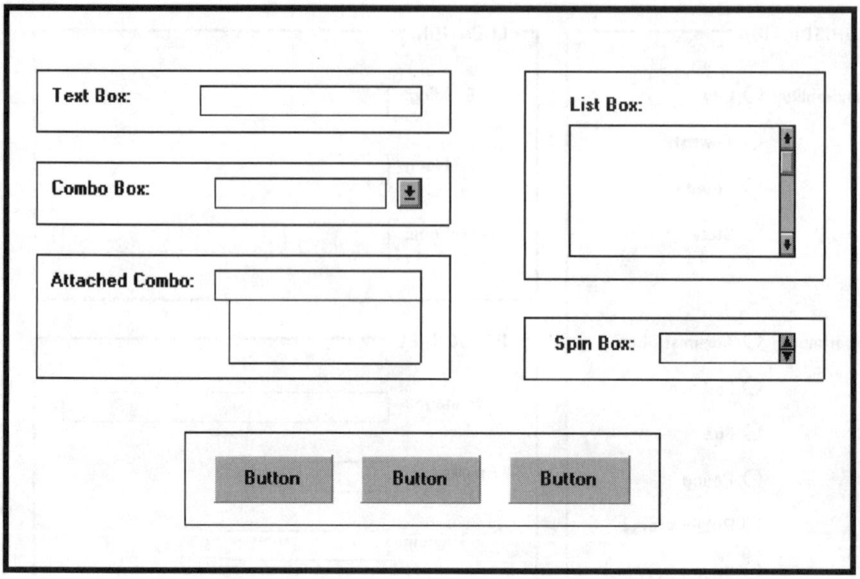

Figure 13.10 Kinds of borders to avoid using.

Dependent Controls

■ Position a conditional control, or controls:
— To the right of the control to which it relates.

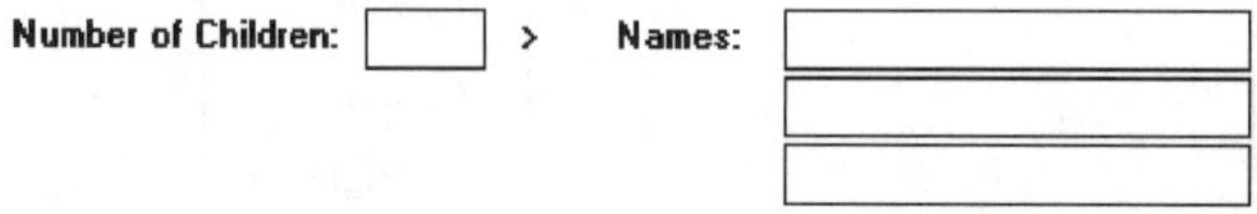

Figure 13.11

— Alternately, position it below the control to which it relates.

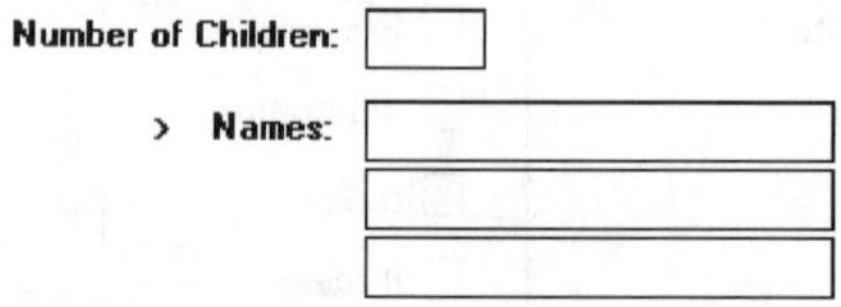

Figure 13.12

■ Either:
— Display these conditional controls in a subdued or grayed out manner.
  • When a control is relevant, return it to a normal intensity.
— Do not display a conditional control until the information to which it relates is set.
■ Inscribe a filled-in arrow between the selected control and its dependent controls to visually relate them to each other.

In some circumstances, a control may be active only under certain conditions. Only when a particular response is made is this additional information needed. For example, a question such as "Do you have any children?" might necessitate knowing their names. If this question is answered affirmatively, a field requesting their names can be displayed at that point on the screen. If a "No" response is given, the tab will cause the cursor to move to the next field, and the children's names field will not appear.

Locate a dependent or conditional control to the right of or below the field or choice that necessitates it. Exact positioning will depend upon the flow of eye movement through the screen and screen space constraints. The displayed arrow serves to tie the dependent control to the triggering control. The control field may either be shown in a grayed out or subdued manner, or not displayed at all until it is needed.

Displaying a control as grayed out or subdued allows the user to be aware of its existence but reduces the visual competition between it and other needed information on the screen. Not displaying dependent fields until they are triggered reduces screen clutter. Hiding their existence, however, does not give the screen user a full picture of all the possibly needed data and the relationships that may exist. Hiding them, then, may result in a slight learning price, depending upon the complexity of the needed data. The recommendation is to display them grayed out.

One caution: Place dependent controls within a window only when their frequency of use is moderate or high. Infrequently used dependent information is best located in a dialog box. The extra step needed to occasionally obtain the dialog box is more then compensated for by the additional screen space made available and the reduction in screen clutter.

Aligning Screen Elements

- Minimize alignment points on a window.
  - Vertically.
  - Horizontally.

Fewer screen alignment points reduce a screen's complexity and make it more visually appealing. Aligning elements will also make eye and pointer movement through the screen much more obvious and reduce the distance both must travel. Screen organization will also be more consistent and predictable. Alignment is achieved by creating vertical columns of screen fields and controls and also horizontally aligning the tops of screen elements.

> **MAXIM**   **Designers work hard so users don't have to.**

Fields or controls vertically columnized may be oriented in two directions, vertically or horizontally. Vertical orientation, a top-to-bottom flow through controls and control components, is the recommended structure.

Vertical Orientation and Vertical Alignment

- Radio buttons/check boxes:
  - Left-align choice descriptions, selection indicators, and borders.
  - Captions:
    - Those inscribed within borders must be left-aligned.

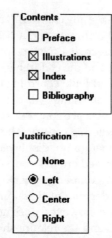

Figure 13.13

- Those located at the left may be left- or right-aligned.

■ Text boxes:
   — Left-align the boxes. If the screen will be used for inquiry or display purposes, numeric fields should be right-aligned.
   — Captions may be left- or right-aligned.

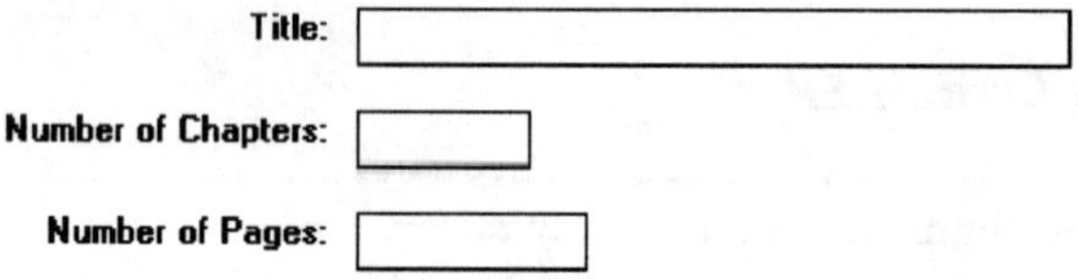

Title: [   ]

Number of Chapters: [   ]

Figure 13.14   Number of Pages: [   ]

■ List boxes:
   — Left-align fixed list boxes.
   — Captions:
      - Those located above the boxes must be left-aligned.

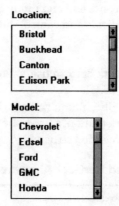

Figure 13.15

- Those located at the left may be left- or right-aligned.

- Drop-down/pop-up boxes, spin boxes, combo boxes:
  — Left-align control boxes.
  — Field captions may be left- or right-aligned.

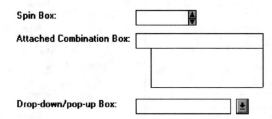

Figure 13.16

- Mixed controls
  — Left-align vertically arrayed:
    - Text boxes.
    - Radio buttons.
    - Check box boxes.
    - Drop-down/pop-up list boxes.
    - Spin boxes.
    - Combination control boxes.
    - List boxes.
  — Captions may be left- or right-aligned.

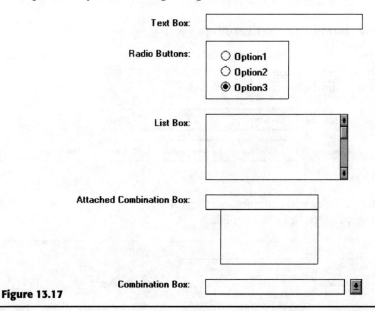

Figure 13.17

Elements and information should be organized vertically (top to bottom) as well. Two, and sometimes three, columns of controls and fields may occasionally be created. When multiple columns are presented and no section borders are used, column separation and downward flow may be emphasized through line borders, as illustrated in Figure 13.18.

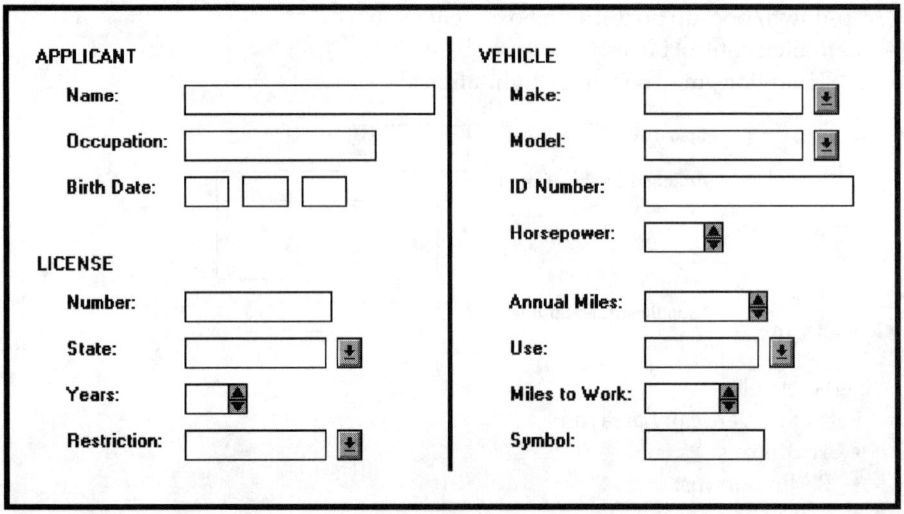

Figure 13.18   Multicolumn controls with a separation border.

In some cases, window space constraints may dictate a horizontal orientation of controls, most noticeably radio buttons and check boxes. Again the pattern created must be consistent, predictable, and distinct.

Horizontal Orientation and Vertical Alignment

■ Radio buttons/check boxes selection controls:
  — Align leftmost radio buttons and/or check boxes.
  — Field captions may be left- or right-aligned.

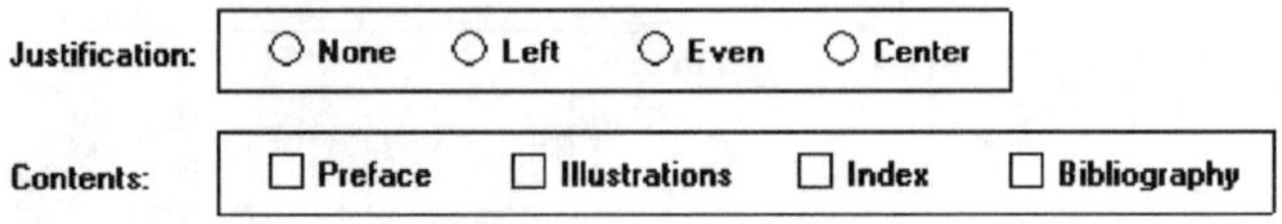

Figure 13.19

■ Text boxes:
  — Left-align text boxes into columns.
  — Captions may be left- or right-aligned.

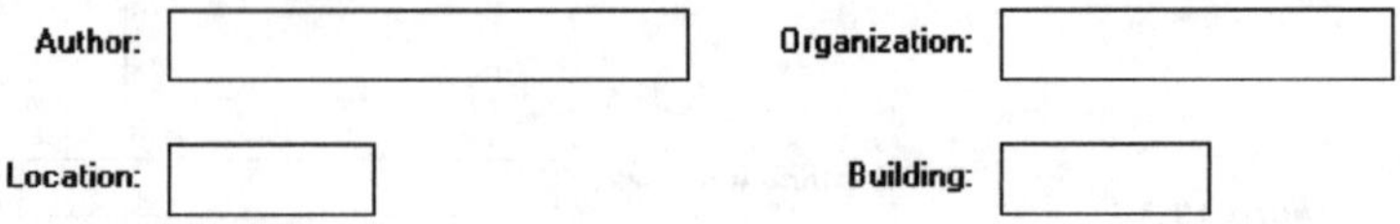

Figure 13.20

  • Numeric data should be right-aligned.

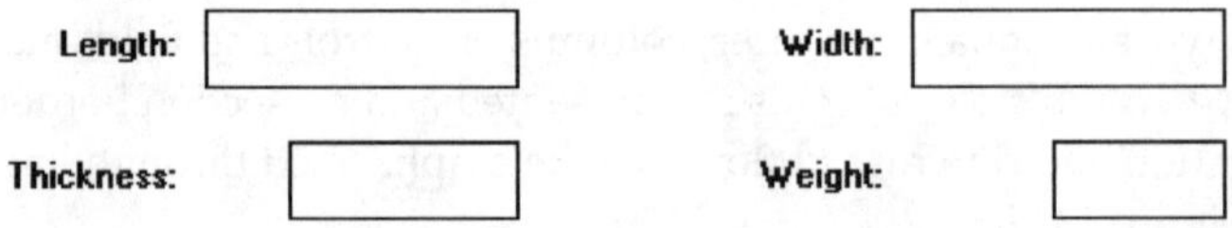

Figure 13.21

- Mixed text boxes and selection controls:
  — Align leftmost radio buttons and/or check boxes.
  — Align the leftmost text box under the leftmost choice description button or box.
  — Captions may be left- or right-aligned.

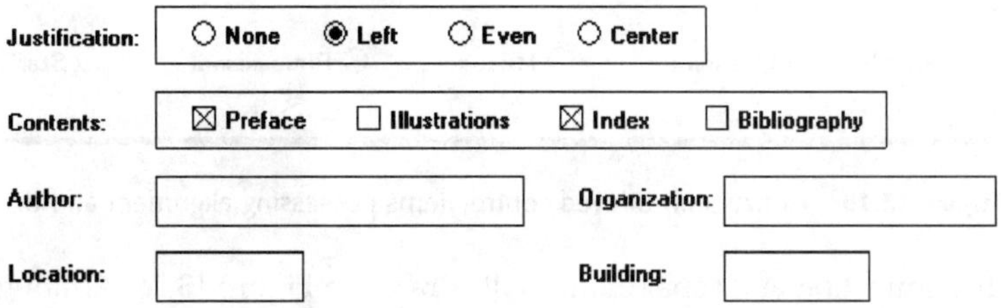

Figure 13.22

For horizontally oriented controls, indistinctiveness can be caused if the item descriptions are positioned as close to a following button or box as they are to the button or box they relate to, as illustrated in Figure 13.23. While the objective is to create as few vertical alignment points as possible, this is usually not practical. For check boxes and radio buttons, most often the result will be inconsistently spaced item descriptions, as illustrated in Figure 13.24. Vertical alignment of items in several adjacent controls can also create a false vertical orientation perception, which is also illustrated in Figure 13.24. Final positioning will be a compromise between alignment and providing clear item distinctiveness, as illustrated in Figure 13.25. With a vertical orientation of radio buttons and check boxes, all these problems are avoided. With a horizontal orientation, borders aid

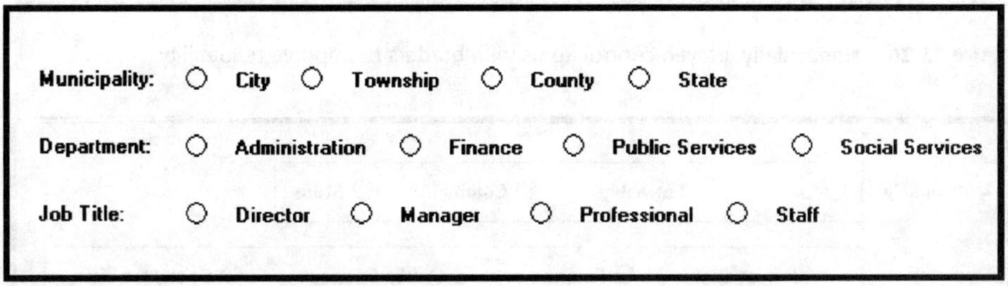

Figure 13.23 Horizontally arrayed radio buttons with poor item differentiation.

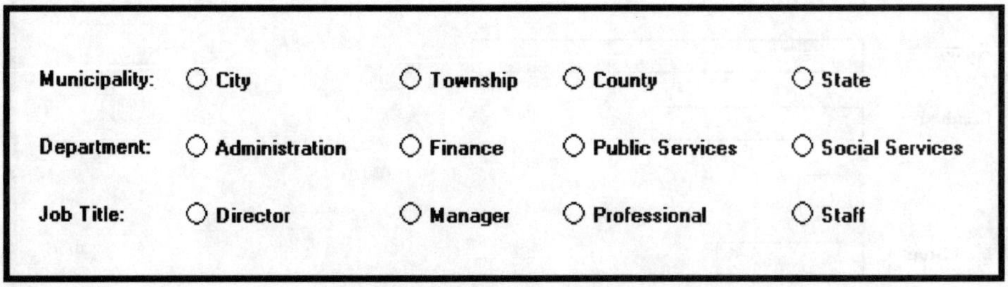

Figure 13.24 Horizontally arrayed control items with inconsistent spacing and a false vertical orientation.

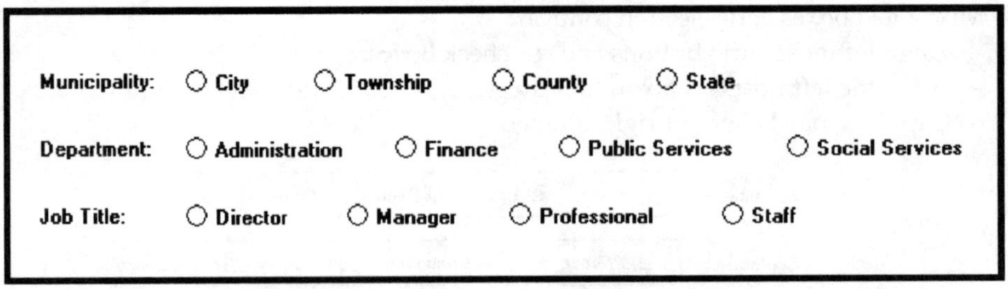

Figure 13.25 Horizontally arrayed control items possessing alignment and distinctiveness.

discrimination and separation, as illustrated in Figure 13.26. Although the examples in the previous guidelines illustrate text boxes structured left to right, every attempt should be made to maintain a top-to-bottom orientation of single entry and selection fields. The fields in the example will be more effectively structured as illustrated in Figure 13.27.

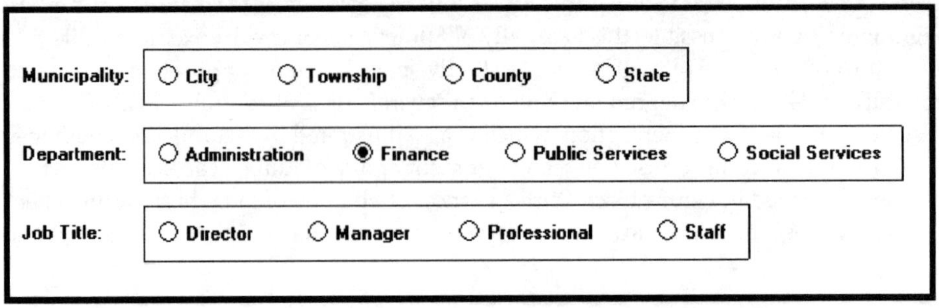

Figure 13.26 Horizontally arrayed control items with borders to improve readability.

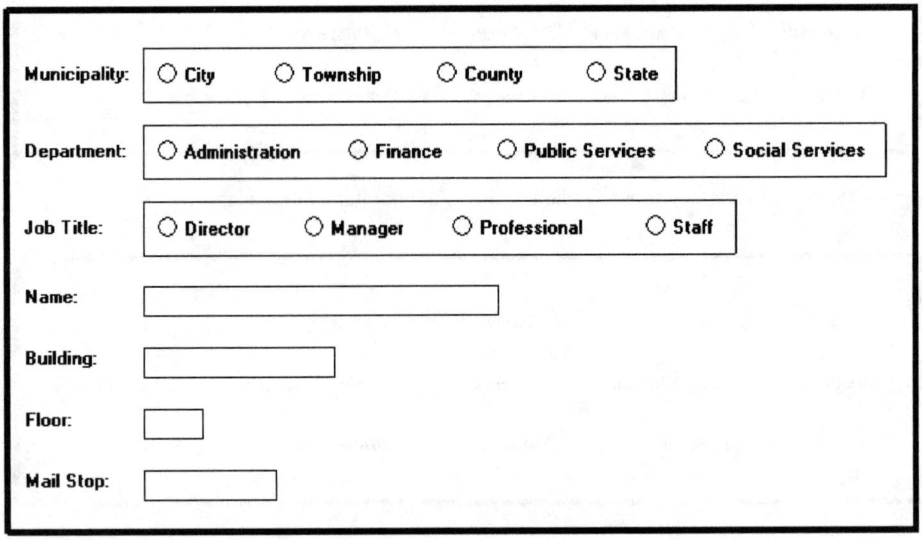

Figure 13.27 Vertical orientation of text boxes.

Horizontal Alignment

- Text boxes:
  — Align by their tops horizontally adjacent text boxes.

- Radio buttons/check boxes:
  — Align by their tops horizontally adjacent radio button and/or check box controls.

- Fixed list boxes:
  — Align by their tops horizontally adjacent fixed list boxes.

- Drop-down/pop-up list box, spin box, combo boxes:
  — Align by their tops horizontally adjacent entry/selection fields.

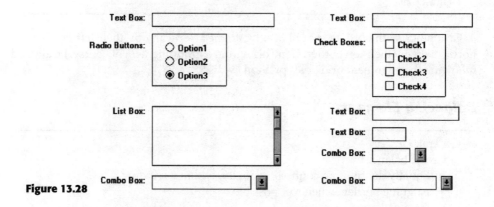

Figure 13.28

- Mixed text boxes and selection controls:
  — Align by their tops:
    - Text boxes.
    - Radio buttons.
      — If a control border exists, align by top border.
    - Check boxes.
      — If a control border exists, align by top border.
    - Drop-down/pop-up list boxes.
    - Spin boxes.
    - Combination boxes.
    - List boxes.

Arrangement of controls horizontally always consists of aligning them by their tops. Since controls may be of different heights, screen efficiency occasionally dictates that a control must be positioned in an area where it does not align horizontally with another control. When this occurs, attempt to align it horizontally with the bottom of an adjacent control, as illustrated by the list box and adjacent combo box in the above example. Do not cramp a control, however, to achieve bottom alignment.

Section Alignment

- Align by their left side vertically arrayed groupings containing section borders.
- Align by their top horizontally arrayed groupings containing section borders.

```
┌ Frame1 ──────────────┐   ┌ Frame3 ──────────────┐
│                      │   │                      │
│                      │   │                      │
│                      │   │                      │
└──────────────────────┘   │                      │
                           └──────────────────────┘
┌ Frame2 ──────────────┐   ┌ Frame4 ──────────────┐
│                      │   │                      │
│                      │   │                      │
└──────────────────────┘   └──────────────────────┘
```

Figure 13.29

Groupings with borders should also be aligned vertically by their left border and horizontally by their top border. Controls within a grouping will, of course, be aligned following the alignment principles previously discussed.

Balancing Elements

- General:
  — Create balance by:
    - Equally distributing controls, spatially, within a window.
    - Aligning borders whenever possible.
- Individual control borders:
  — If more than one control with a border is incorporated within a column on a screen:
    - Align the controls following the guidelines for multiple-control alignment.
    - Align the left and right borders of all groups.
    - Establish the left and right border positions according to the spacing required for the widest element within the groups.

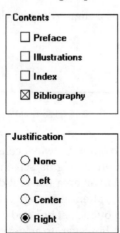

Figure 13.30

— With multiple groupings and multiple columns, create a balanced screen by:
   • Maintaining equal column widths as much as practical.
   • Maintaining equal column heights as much as practical.

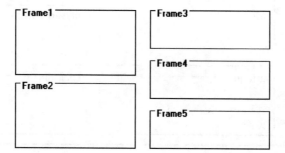

Figure 13.31

■ Section borders:
   — If more than one section with borders is incorporated within a column on a screen:
      • Align the left and right borders of all groups.
      • Establish the left and right border positions according to the spacing required by the widest element within the groups.

```
┌ DOCUMENT ─────────────────────────────┐
│                                        │
│   Justification:   ● None              │
│                    ○ Left              │
│                    ○ Center            │
│                    ○ Right             │
│                                        │
│   Contents:        ☒ Preface           │
│                    ☒ Illustrations     │
│                    ☒ Index             │
│                    ☒ Bibliography      │
│                                        │
├ AUTHOR ────────────────────────────────┤
│                                        │
│   Name:        ┌──────────────────┐    │
│                └──────────────────┘    │
│   Telephone:   ┌──────────┐            │
│                └──────────┘            │
└────────────────────────────────────────┘
```

Figure 13.32

— With multiple groupings and multiple columns, create a balanced screen by:
   • Maintaining equal column widths as much as practical.
   • Maintaining equal column heights as much as practical.

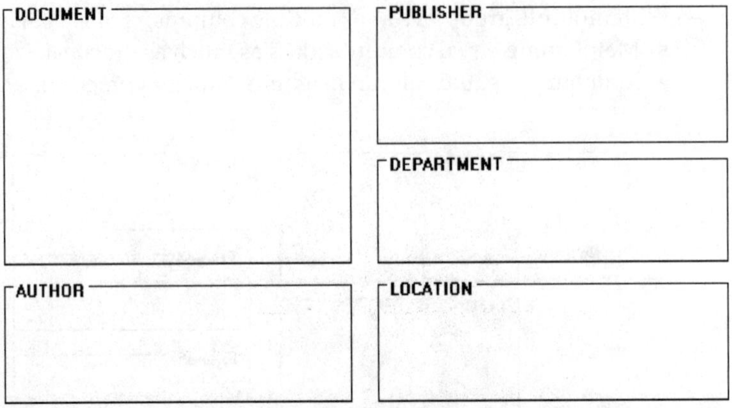

Figure 13.33

Screen balance should be attained as much as possible. Do not sacrifice screen functionality to achieve balance, however. Never rearrange controls to simply make the screen "look nice." A meaningful order of elements is most important. The "look" will be the best that can be achieved within the limits imposed by functionality.

One additional point about alignment. While these guidelines suggest aligning section, radio button, and check box borders on the right side as well as the left, a glance back at Figure 13.9 will reveal an instance where this was not done. The Justification and Contents borders were not right-aligned because the text boxes within that grouping created a ragged right edge. Aligning just these two controls would have served no purpose. So, all alignment and balancing must occur within the context of the *whole* screen.

Control Navigation

- Tab/arrow keys:
  - Use the tab key to move between operable window controls, in the logical order of the controls.
    - Do not tab to field captions/labels.
  - Radio buttons:
    - Use arrow keys to move through radio buttons within a single control.
  - Check boxes:
    - Use the Tab key to move between, when they are independent controls.
    - Within a border or group box, use arrow keys to move between the check boxes since they appear as a logical group.
  - List boxes:
    - Use arrow keys to navigate within list box choices.
- Command buttons
  - For exiting or expanding/feature dialog command buttons:
    - Tab to them at the end of the screen control tabbing sequence.
  - For a command button with a contingent relationship to a control in the window body:
    - Tab to it at the logical point in the tabbing sequence within the window.

- Keyboard equivalents:
  — Use keyboard equivalents (mnemonics) for direct access to each control, whenever possible.
    - Mnemonic designations must be unique within a window.

Use the tab key to move between operable window controls, in the logical order that the controls are organized. Do not tab to control captions but the control itself. For a grouping of radio buttons, use the arrow keys to move through an array of buttons. For check boxes, use the tab key to move between them when they are arrayed as independent controls. When check boxes are located within a border or group box, use the arrow keys to move between the boxes since they appear as a logical group. Always use arrow keys to navigate within a listing of choices.

Tab to exiting or expanding/feature dialog buttons at the end of the screen control tabbing sequence. If a button has a contingent relationship to a control in the window body, tab to it at the logical point in the tabbing sequence within the window.

Use keyboard equivalents (mnemonics) for direct access to each window control, whenever possible. Mnemonic designations must be unique within a window. The command buttons OK and Cancel are not typically assigned mnemonics, the Enter and Esc keys being used instead.

Window Guidelines

- Organization:
  — Organize windows to support user tasks.
  — Present related information in a single window whenever possible.
  — Support the most common tasks in the most efficient sequence of steps.
  — Use:
    - Primary windows to:
      — Begin an interaction and provide top-level context for dependent windows.
      — Perform a major interaction.
    - Secondary windows to:
      — Extend the interaction.
      — Obtain or display supplemental information related to the primary window.
    - Dialog boxes for:
      — Infrequently used or needed information.
      — "Nice-to-know" information.
- Number:
  — Minimize the number of windows needed to accomplish an objective.
- Size:
  — Provide large enough windows to:
    - Present all relevant and expected information for the task.
    - Not hide important information.
    - Not cause crowding or visual confusion.
    - Minimize the need for scrolling.
    - Less than the full size of the entire screen.

— If a window is too large, determine:
  - Is all the information needed?
  - Is all the information related?

These guidelines, and many others, were presented and fully discussed, in Step 5 "Select the Proper Kinds of Windows." In summary, always organize windows to support user tasks. Support the most common tasks in the most efficient sequence of steps. Minimize the number of windows needed to accomplish an objective. In general, present all related information in a single window whenever it is possible to do so. A window should be large enough to accommodate the amount of data a person would typically expect to see. The needed information can only be determined through thorough task analysis.

The necessity for window scrolling should also be avoided whenever possible. If all the relevant controls or data cannot be placed within the confines of a single window, place that which is less frequently needed on another window. Do not make the default size of a window the full screen. The option to maximize a window always exists.

Finally, use primary windows, secondary windows, and dialog boxes consistently and in the manner they are intended to be used.

Web Page Guidelines

The following specific Web page layout principles must also be considered in page design.

Page Layout

- General:
  - Provide a layout that is:
    - Efficient
    - Logical.
    - Consistent.
    - Self-explanatory.
    - Scannable.
  - Strike a proper balance between:
    - Textual information.
    - Graphics.
    - Links.
- Layout Grid:
  - Create and use a layout grid.
- Elements:
  - Include no more than seven distinct elements per page.
- Size:
  - Minimize page length.
    - Restrict it to two or three screens of information.

- — Anticipate page breaks.
- — Avoid horizontal scrolling.
- Organization:
  - — Place critical or important information at the very top so it is always viewable when the page is opened.
    - Locate it within the top 4 inches of page.
  - — Position remaining elements according to importance.
  - — Reduce graphic complexity and textual density toward the page bottom.
- Formatting:
  - — Provide sufficient white space.
    - A minimum of 30 percent.
  - — Keep the length of textual lines short.
    - A maximum of two alphabets.
  - — Keep text and related graphics close to each other.
  - — Provide adequate horizontal spacing.
  - — Use horizontal rules sparingly.
- Other:
  - — Use frames with caution.
    - Consider them for global elements.
  - — Change the organization and structure only when significant benefits exist.

Well-organized, thoughtfully laid out, and consistent Web pages will permit people to easily learn a site's structure, allow users to effectively and quickly scan its pages, and will foster interest in its content. A well-designed page will possess the following qualities.

General

Efficient. A page will be more powerful if more is said with less. Every element of the design must support the goal of the message being presented. Eliminate all superfluous elements. Avoid clutter that prevents people from finding what they want. Exercise extreme care in using decorative elements.

Logical and consistent. A logical and consistent layout of the site and its pages will enable people to quickly find what they are looking for. As said earlier in this book, people develop expectations for how to find different types of information and how to perform particular tasks. A layout that matches a person's expectations speeds learning and enables prediction of where to find things and how to do things. Illogical and inconsistent structures lead only to user frustration.

Self-explanatory. Each page should be self-explanatory, giving a clear indication of what Web site it belongs to and where it fits within the structure of the Web site's information space. Present the proper information, and arrange it, so users always know where they are. Remember, most pages can be accessed from outside the site.

Scannable. Allow people to easily scan a page and select relevant and useful information. To foster scannability, include headings that accurately reflect the content of text. Also create short paragraphs and use simple bulleted lists (complex bullets, such as diamonds and fingers, may create unnecessary visual noise). Avoid the use of too many links and use plenty of white space.

Proper balance. Always strike a proper balance between textual information, graphics and navigation links. A page's elements must balance, interact with, and support each other. As mentioned earlier, studies show people prefer textual content, so do not clutter up the page with too many graphics, particularly at the top. A large top graphic may push important textual content and navigation links off the bottom of the page where they cannot be seen. Always make sure text is visible first so people can start reading right away. Conversely, densely packed text will be difficult to read. Long and detailed textual information can usually be relegated to secondary pages.

MYTH **This way of doing it must be right because (_fill in the blank_) does it that way.**

Layout Grid

To provide both structure and consistency to a Web site, establish a standard layout grid, or grids, for each of the site's pages. Multiple, but similar, grids may be necessary for site pages with different purposes or varying complexity. These design grids will be composed of rectangular sections into which the page's navigation components (headings, text, and graphics) will be placed. To develop the grids:

- Gather representative samples of the contents of site pages. Include all types of pages: navigation pages, content pages, simple pages, and complex pages.
- Experiment with various arrangements for all kinds of pages, painting or sketching patterns of organization on sample pages.
- Follow all layout guidelines (alignment, balance, and so on) and evolving page organizational standards in the sketching process.
- Maintaining as much consistency between pages types as possible, establish a design grid (or grids) for the identified page types.
- Plug in content (navigational components, text, and graphics) for each page.

Ideally, one standard design grid may satisfy the needs of many Web sites. Larger sites with more content may require multiple grids. Keep in mind that fewer grids are better, and, if you use multiple grids, maintain as much consistency as possible between the grids' layouts.

The use of the grids on all pages will provide a unifying character within and between pages, a standard look and feel. Regular and repeating organizational patterns help readers to understand site's organization and aid them maintaining a sense of place. Grids allow pages to be laid out without the designer having to stop and rethink the basic design approach for every new page. Pressing needs of the moment will also have much less of an influence on design. Examples of page layout grids, both poor and good, are illustrated in Figure 13.34. The poor grid is haphazard in design, and there is little connection of the elements. The good grid reflects much greater alignment and better visual connection of elements. It is structured and more consistent. The good grid has a visual complexity measure, as described in Step 3, 47 percent lower than the poor grid.

Elements

To keep pages simple, restrict the number of distinct functional elements on a page to seven or fewer. Elements include such things as the title, the navigation bar, the textual link listing to major site areas, textual content, graphics, and the page footer. The more elements on a page, the greater the competition between the elements for a person's attention. To many elements will eventually overwhelm the user's information-processing system.

Size

Page length. The many issues associated with page length were thoroughly described in Step 3 (Vertical scrolling, user memory requirements, user tasks, and monitor sizes, for example.) so optimum page length must balance all these factors. In general, the best approach seems to be to minimize a page's length, restricting it to two or three screens of information.

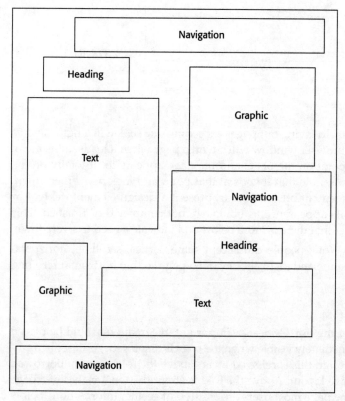

POOR GRID

Figure 13.34   Page layout grids.

(continues)

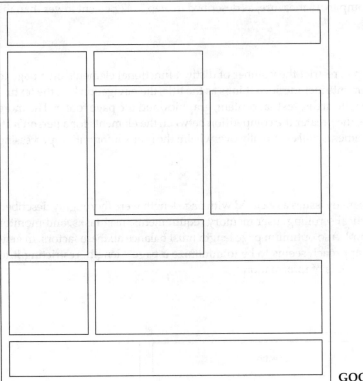

GOOD GRID

Figure 13.34 Continued

Anticipate page breaks. In laying out pages exceeding one screen in length, always consider where the browser window will cut off a page when it loads. If the break occurs at a logical point on the page, and the page appears to fit totally on the screen, people may assume that it ends at that point and look no further down. Where potential screen cut-offs can occur, present a design element (textual or graphical) that, by its appearance, is obviously not completed or finished. This will signal to the user that there is more below and indicate a need to scroll down.

Horizontal scrolling. While people can accept some vertical scrolling, horizontal scrolling is cumbersome and disliked. Lay out a page so that horizontal scrolling is never necessary.

Organization

Important elements at the top. Critical or important information should be placed where it will be immediately visible when the page is displayed. As described earlier, in Web page design this is referred to as "above the fold," a term borrowed from newspaper page layout. Above the fold is about the top 4 inches of a page and is the area of the page most users are assured of seeing. Information "below the fold" will usually require scrolling to access and may not always be seen.

Generally, the top of the page should be more dense and packed with more useful and interesting information than the area lower down. Include in this area the page title, links to other important content and pages, and summary information so the user can determine whether continued reading is desirable.

Positioning. The effect of presented information drops very quickly as one moves lower down the page. Visually prioritize the page information space by establishing an information hierarchy, using contrast, size, location pattern, and other concepts discussed in Step 3.

Reduced complexity. Reduce graphic complexity and textual density as one moves lower down a page or to interior site pages. Produce diminishing or thinning vertical gradients of complexity, providing quieter and less-distracting design elements. This will allow people to focus on the content, which must have some interest since they have navigated that far. To be distracted by irrelevant information or useless animation at that point can be very irritating.

Formatting

White space. To enhance readability and organization, and make the page more inviting, allow a sufficient amount of white space on each page. According to many experts, white space should consume at least 30 percent of a page. (Remember, white space is a design element, not something to always be consumed.) Of the remaining 70 percent of space, restrict text to no more than another 30 percent. The remaining 40 percent may be used for graphics. If the entire 40 percent is not used for graphics, use it for more white space, not additional text.

Textual line length. For easier reading, restrict textual lines to no more than the length of two alphabets, or 52 characters.

Text and related graphics. Keep text and any related graphics close to each other. The viewer will assume a connection between elements located in close proximity. Also, keep chunks of related text in closer proximity than unrelated text, to ensure a connection.

Horizontal spacing. Provide sufficient horizontal spacing so that groupings of information are obvious. A chunk of text, its heading, and any related graphic should be readily discernible as a grouping.

Horizontal rules. Use horizontal rules sparingly on pages. These rules can break up page flow and signal a page's end when it is not intended. Use horizontal rules only if the objective is break the flow. Uses might be, for example, to separate standard header and footer information from basic page content.

Other

Frames. Use frames with caution. As was discussed in Step 4 "Develop System Menus and Navigation Schemes," frames can be confusing for many users. They may cause problems with scrolling, bookmarking, and printing. They also reduce the content window size. Frames, however, may be useful for global page elements such as navigation links or corporate/organization information. If a person arrives at a framed page from a search facility, the page is seen without the accompanying frames. The site name and a link to the home page must always be provided on the content page so the user does not reach a dead-end.

Change. In an environment as volatile and changing as the Web, the urge to try the newest and latest concepts in design and layout always exists. Use restraint. A Web site's fashion should be evident in its content, not its design. Fashion changes all the time, and constant changes in design will continually antagonize users who have invested time and effort in understanding a site's structure and organization. Change the organization and structure only when significant benefits for the user and the Web site owner are perceived to exist.

Home Page

- Limit to one screen.
- Clearly identify the Web site's content and purpose.
- Elements to include:
  — Site overview or map.
  — Navigation links to most (if not all) of the site or major sections.
  — Some useful content.

A site's home page is a concrete and visual anchor point; a safe haven to return to when one is confused or decides to do something else. The home page also gives people a first impression of a site, and first impressions can create a positive or negative feeling, or a feeling somewhere in between. A negative first impression can lead to rejection, a positive first impression create an urge for further exploration. In many ways, the home page is a site's most important page.

One screen. Keep the home page to one screen. All important elements should be viewable without scrolling so they will not be missed. Elements of less importance and those not vital to site use (corporate or organizational identification information or e-mail links, for example) may be included below the visible area, however.

Content and purpose. The home page should clearly identify the Web site's content and purpose. Assume that potential users know nothing about the site and what is presented within it. Describe who the site is intended for or of interest to. Describe the kinds of information available. The home page must convince users to stay by telling them what they will find within the site.

Elements. Elements to include on the home page include a site overview or map, navigational links to most (if not all) of the site or its major sections, and a small amount of useful content. The home page may also be used to promote site areas that should be seen, and new or changed content.

Page Elements

A large number of items might be included within any Web site's pages. Table 13.1 provides a summary of possible components.

Table 13.1 Possible Web Page Components

COMPONENT	PURPOSE	PAGE FREQUENCY	LOCATION
Page title.	To clearly identify and describe page.	Every page.	Top
Navigation bar.	To allow global site navigation.	Every page.	Top
Table of contents.	To list page contents.	If longer than 2 to 3 screens.	Top
Site identifier (trademark, logo, or organizational identification).	To identify page's owner. A strong navigational and orientation cue.	Every page.	Top
Search facility.	To provide a means for locating content of interest.	Every page.	Top
Page's author or contact person.	To identify page's author, or to indicate page's contact person.	Every page.	Footer
Contact e-mail address.	To solicit queries or comments.	Every page.	Footer
Comment facility.	To solicit queries or comments.	As necessary.	Footer
Other contact details (telephone number, mailing address, etc.).	To identify other methods for soliciting queries or comments.	As necessary.	Footer
Copyright information.	To identify page's legal ownership. To caution against unauthorized use.	Every page.	Footer
Date of creation or update.	To indicate currency of information.	Every page.	Footer
Links to:			
Skip to main content.	An accessibility consideration.	Every page.	Top
Other major sections of site.	To provide easy access to all major site content.	Every page.	Top, footer also for long pages
Home page.	To return to home page.	Every page.	Top, footer also for long pages
Index page.	To return to index.	Every page.	Top, footer also for long pages

(continues)

Table 13.1 Continued

COMPONENT	PURPOSE	PAGE FREQUENCY	LOCATION
Site map or directory.	To return to site map or directory.	Every page.	Top, footer also for long pages
Next page.	To go to next page in a sequence.	Every page (if applicable).	Bottom
Previous page.	To return to previous page.	Every page (if applicable).	Bottom

Screen Examples

Following are more examples of good and poor design. Included are redesigns of the screens critiqued in Step 3.

Example 1

Here is a poorly designed screen and its redesigned version.

Screen 1.1

A very poor screen: Captions are not discernible from choice descriptions, and the initial choice descriptions are not left-aligned. The radio buttons and check boxes are not strongly associated with their respective descriptions, and they also *follow* their respec-

Screen 1.1

TEXT PROPERTIES

Family
- ○ Courier
- ○ Helvetica
- ○ Sans Serif
- ○ Times

Pitch
- ○ 10 CPI
- ○ 12 CPI
- ○ 15 CPI
- ○ Proportional

Border

Size
- ○ Small
- ○ Medium
- ○ Large

Style
- ☐ Bold
- ☐ Italic
- ☐ Underline

Color
- ○ Black
- ○ Blue
- ○ Green
- ○ Red

OK   Apply   Cancel   Help

Screen 1.2

tive descriptions, certainly causing selection confusion. The horizontal orientation of choices is not efficient for human scanning. No perception of groupings exists. The ordering scheme of Family, Style, and Color is questionable. Alphabetic ordering would seem to be more appropriate.

Screen 1.2

A much better screen. The title is capitalized to set it off from the remainder of the screen. The radio buttons and check boxes are arrayed vertically to facilitate scanning and comparison of alternatives. All controls are enclosed in borders to focus the viewer's attention to them. While the overall organization does not assist the viewer in establishing a scanning direction (horizontal or vertical), the kind of information presented does not make this critical. The screen can be effectively used from left to right or from top to bottom. Family, Style, and Color are alphabetized. Using the complexity measure discussed in Step 3, this redesigned screen is 42 percent less complex than the original.

Example 2

This is a representation of an actual screen from Microsoft Windows. Two alternate designs are presented.

```
┌─────────────────────────────────────────────────────────────┐
│  ·  PIF EDITOR                                               │
├─────────────────────────────────────────────────────────────┤
│                                                             │
│   Program Filename:    ┌──────────────────────────────────┐ │
│                        └──────────────────────────────────┘ │
│   Window Title:        ┌──────────────────────────────┐     │
│                        └──────────────────────────────┘     │
│   Optional Parameters: ┌──────────────────────────────────┐ │
│                        └──────────────────────────────────┘ │
│   Start-up Directory:  ┌──────────────────────────────────┐ │
│                        └──────────────────────────────────┘ │
│                                                             │
│   Video Memory:      ○ Text      ○ Low Graphics   ○ High Graphics │
│                                                             │
│   Memory Requirements:  KB Required  ┌──────┐  KB Desired  ┌──────┐ │
│                                                             │
│   EMS Memory:        KB Required  ┌──────┐   KB Limit   ┌──────┐ │
│                                                             │
│   XMS Memory:        KB Required  ┌──────┐   KB Limit   ┌──────┐ │
│                                                             │
│   Display Usage:  ○ Full Screen      Execution:  ○ Background │
│                   ○ Windowed                     ○ Exclusive │
│                                                             │
│   ☐ Close Window on Exit                                     │
│                                                             │
└─────────────────────────────────────────────────────────────┘
```

Screen 2.1

Screen 2.1

This is a screen with several faults. On a positive note, the captions on the left side are nicely aligned, as are the top four text boxes. The box alignment, however, breaks down in the middle of the screen. Also, what appear to be captions (because they possess an ending colon) are really headings, communicating a false message to the viewer (Memory Requirements, EMS Memory, and XMS Memory). The word "memory" repeated four times in succession seems redundant, indicating the potential for a heading. One radio button field (Video Memory) is arrayed horizontally, the others (Display Usage and Execution) are arrayed vertically. The control "Close Window on Exit" seems lost.

Screen 2.2

This is a much-improved alternative. Groupings of elements are provided. Section borders, with titles, are included in the upper part of the screen to strengthen the perception of groupings. Control borders in the lower part of the screen serve the same purpose. Proper alignment of data fields is achieved in the top two sections of the screen. The redundant word "memory" is incorporated as a section heading. Section headings are displayed capitalized to distinguish them from control captions. Subsection headings are created in the Memory section where the heading-caption confusion previously existed. Subsection headings are set off by capitalization and arrows.

Screen 2.2

The radio buttons/check boxes at the bottom of the screen are arrayed horizontally to provide screen balance. The "Close Window on Exit" control field is given an (admittedly redundant) caption to allow a control border consistent with its neighbors and to create screen balance. The Video (Memory) control remains, as a trade-off, arrayed horizontally. It would have been desirable to organize its choices vertically, but the best overall fit within the screen is achieved by horizontal orientation. This redesigned version of the screen is actually 4 percent *more* complex than the original. The addition of headings and subheadings added to its complexity measure. In spite of this, it is a better screen. Additional information added to a screen to aid understanding can sometimes increase its complexity. So, use the complexity measure as a guide, not as an absolute and final measure of a screen's effectiveness.

Screen 2.3

Here is another redesigned version of this screen. The Memory section has been restructured to maintain a top-to-bottom flow. The trade-off is that two columns are now required to present the information. This version is 8 percent more complex than the original, again because of the added information. Which version do you prefer, 2.2 or 2.3?

```
                           PIF EDITOR

  ┌APPLICATION──────────────────────────────────────────────┐
  │    Program Filename:  [                              ]   │
  │    Window Title:      [                            ]     │
  │    Optional Parameters: [                          ]     │
  │    Start-up Directory:  [                          ]     │
  └─────────────────────────────────────────────────────────┘
  ┌MEMORY───────────────────────────────────────────────────┐
  │  ┌Real──────────────────┐  ┌EMS────────────────────────┐ │
  │  │  Required: [      ] KB│  │  Required: [      ] KB    │ │
  │  │  Desired:  [      ] KB│  │  Limit:    [      ] KB    │ │
  │  └──────────────────────┘  └───────────────────────────┘ │
  │  ┌XMS───────────────────┐  ┌Video──────────────────────┐ │
  │  │  Required: [      ] KB│  │      ○ Text               │ │
  │  │  Limit:    [      ] KB│  │      ○ Low Graphics       │ │
  │  │                      │  │      ○ High Graphics      │ │
  │  └──────────────────────┘  └───────────────────────────┘ │
  └─────────────────────────────────────────────────────────┘
  ┌Display Usage──┐ ┌Execution──────┐ ┌Window───────────────┐
  │  ○ Full Screen│ │  ○ Background  │ │  ☐ Close on Exit    │
  │  ○ Windowed   │ │  ○ Exclusive   │ │                     │
  └───────────────┘ └───────────────┘ └─────────────────────┘
```

Screen 2.3

Example 3

These are redesigned versions of the banking screen presented in Step 3.

Screen 3.1

The original screen.

Screen 3.2

The Name field is given a caption and a single alignment point is established for both captions and data. Captions and data are now much more readable. Name format instructions (1st, 2nd, and so on) are established as prompts. This prompt designation is signaled by placing them in italics to subdue them visually. The prompt for Date of Birth is placed to the right of its text box, out of the way but still easily viewable. This also permits the alignment point for the text boxes to be moved closer to the captions. Date is also segmented into its component pieces. The command buttons are positioned at the bottom. No groupings are established, however. This screen is 9 percent less complex than the original.

Personal Details Customer

| 1st Given Name | 2nd Given Name (if any) | Surname | OK |

Courtesy Title:

Sex: ○ Male   ○ Female   ○ Unknown

Marital Status: ○ Married   ○ Single   ○ All Others

Date of Birth (dd/mm/yyyy):

Daytime Phone No:

Home Address:

City/Town/Suburb: Postcode:

Apply Cancel Help

Screen 3.1

PERSONAL DETAILS - CUSTOMER

(1st)   *(2nd - if any)*   *(Surname)*

Name:

Courtesy Title:

Sex: ○ Male   ○ Female   ○ Unknown

Marital Status: ○ Married   ○ Single   ○ All Others

Date of Birth: /   /   *(dd/mm/yyyy)*

Daytime Phone No:

Home Address:

City/Town/Suburb: Postcode:

OK   Apply   Cancel   Help

Screen 3.2

PERSONAL DETAILS - CUSTOMER

	(1st)	(2nd - if any)	(Surname)

Name:

Courtesy Title:

Sex:
- ○ Male
- ○ Female
- ○ Unknown

Marital Status:
- ○ Married
- ○ Single
- ○ All Others

Date of Birth: /   /   (dd/mm/yyyy)

Daytime Phone No:

Home Address:

City/Town/Suburb: Postcode:

[OK] [Apply] [Cancel] [Help]

Screen 3.3

Screen 3.3

This screen is identical to the above version except that Sex and Marital Status are arrayed vertically. This screen is 17 percent less complex than the original.

Screen 3.4

The elements are now grouped with group boxes and section headings. Name is segmented into its three components. Address details are moved closer to the customer's name. Sex and Marital Status must be arrayed horizontally because of space constraints caused by the groupings. This screen is 4 percent less complex than the original. Which of these do you prefer, 3.2, 3.3, or 3.4?

Example 4

These are redesigned versions of the drawing program screens presented in Step 3.

Screen 4.1

The original PRINT MERGE screen.

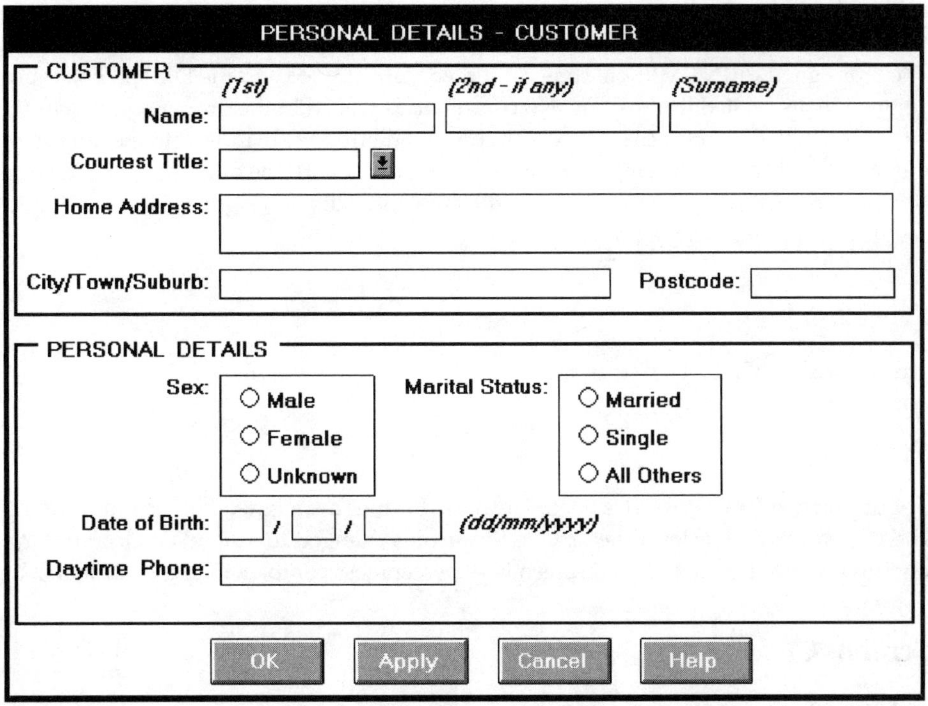

Screen 3.4

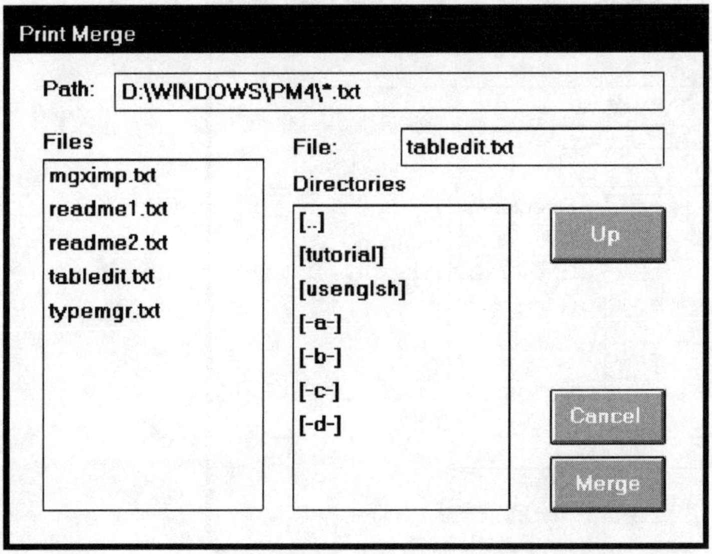

Screen 4.1

Screen 4.2

The redesigned PRINT MERGE screen. Elements are aligned and the File text box is positioned by its related list box. The Up command is placed in the proper contingent relationship to the Directories list box. The command buttons are moved to the bottom of the screen and Merge is changed to OK for consistency with the other screens. The title is capitalized for consistency with the other screens. This redesigned screen is 29 percent less complex than the original.

Screen 4.3

The original PAGE SETUP screen.

Screen 4.4

The redesigned PAGE SETUP screen. The radio buttons are aligned for vertical scanning and placed within borders. The "inches" control is changed to a standard drop-down/pop-up list box. This redesigned screen is 19 percent less complex than the original.

Screen 4.5

The original EXPORT screen.

PRINT MERGE

Path: D:\WINDOWS\PM4*.txt

File: tabledit.txt

mgximp.txt
readme1.txt
readme2.txt
tabledit.txt
typemgr.txt

Directories: [..]
[tutorial]
[usenglsh]
[-a-]
[-b-]
[-c-]
[-d-]

Up - >

OK   Cancel

Screen 4.2

PAGE SETUP

Orientation: ○ Portrait   ○ Landscape

Page Size: ○ Letter   ○ Legal   ○ Tabloid

○ A3   ○ A4   ○ A5   ○ B5

○ Custom   ○ Slide

Horizontal: 11.70   Inches

Vertical: 8.27   Inches

[Paper Color...]   [Add Page Frame]   [OK]   [Cancel]

Screen 4.3

PAGE SETUP

Orientation: ○ Portrait
               ○ Landscape

Page Size: ○ Letter   ○ A3   ○ Custom
               ○ Legal   ○ A4   ○ Slide
               ○ Tabloid   ○ A5
                           ○ B5

Horizontal: 11.70   inches

Vertical: 8.27   inches

[Paper Color...]   [Add Page Frame]   [OK]   [Cancel]

Screen 4.4

```
┌─────────────────────────────────────────────────────────────┐
│ ████████████████████████████████████████████████████████████│
│ EXPORT                                                        │
│                                                               │
│  ┌───────────────────────────┐                                │
│  │ CorelDRAW!         .CDR ▲ │                                │
│  │ CorelDRAW! 1.xx    .CDR ║ │                                │
│  │ Postcript[EPS]     .EPS ║ │                                │
│  │ Windows Metafile   .WMF ║ │                                │
│  │ PCX                .PCX   │                                │
│  │ TIFF               .TIF ▼ │                                │
│  └───────────────────────────┘                                │
│                                                               │
│  ☐ Selected Object(s) Only       ☐ Include All Artistic Attributes │
│  ☐ Include Image Header           ☐ All Fonts Resident         │
│                                                               │
│  Resolution:   ○ Course (40)   ○ Low(75)   ○ Medium(150)   ○ High(300) │
│                                                               │
│  Fixed Size:   ○ 128X128    ○ 256X256    ○ 512X512           │
│                                                               │
│                                      ┌────────┐  ┌────────┐    │
│                                      │   OK   │  │ Cancel │    │
│                                      └────────┘  └────────┘    │
└─────────────────────────────────────────────────────────────┘
```

Screen 4.5

Screen 4.6

The redesigned EXPORT screen. The radio buttons and check boxes are aligned for vertical scanning and placed within borders. The check boxes are given a caption, as is the list box. For balance purposes, the controls are arrayed in two columns. This redesigned screen is 5 percent less complex than the original.

Example 5

Here are redesigned versions of the word-processing screens presented in Step 3.

Screen 5.1

The original FOOTNOTE OPTIONS screen.

Screen 5.2

The redesigned FOOTNOTE OPTIONS screen. Elements are aligned, including the single check boxes. Headings are capitalized and left-justified within the borders. "Position" and "Separator" are combined into one grouping called "LOCATION." This redesigned screen is 13 percent less complex than the original.

EXPORT

Format:

CorelDRAW!	.CDR
CorelDRAW! 1.xx	.CDR
Postcript[EPS]	.EPS
Windows Metafile	.WMF
PCX	.PCX
TIFF	.TIF

Resolution
- ○ Course (40)
- ○ Low (75)
- ○ Medium (150)
- ○ High (300)

Include
- ☐ Selected Object(s) Only
- ☐ All Artistic Attributes
- ☐ Image Header
- ☐ All Fonts Resident

Fixed Size
- ○ 128x128
- ○ 256x256
- ○ 512x51

[OK]   [Cancel]

Screen 4.6

Footnote Options

Numbering

Numbering Method: [   ]⬍   Characters: [   ]

Style in Text: [   ]⬇

Style in Note: [   ]⬇

☐ Restart Numbering on Each Page

Spacing

Line Spacing in Notes: [   ]

Spacing Between Notes: [   ]

Continued Notes

☐ Print (Continued...) Message

Minimum Note Ht: [   ]

Position

[   ]⬍

Separator

[   ]⬍

[OK]   [Cancel]

Screen 5.1

Screen 5.2

Screen 5.3

The original LOCATION OF FILES screen.

Screen 5.4

The redesigned LOCATION OF FILES screen. The section headings are capitalized and left-justified in the borders. Visual competition with the text box information is now minimized. A grouping called FILES is created at the screen's top for consistency and balance. The single check box is aligned under the text boxes. This redesigned screen is 2 percent more complex than the original, again due to the added heading.

Example 6

Here is a redesigned version of the drawing program read-only/display screen presented in Step 3.

Screen 6.1

The original screen.

Location of Files

Backup Files:	
Documents:	c:\window\learn
Graphics Files:	c:\window\graphics
Printer Files:	c:\wpc
Spreadsheets:	

Macros/Keyboards/Button Bars

Files:	c:\window\macros

Styles

Directory:	c:\window
Filename:	c:\window\library.sty

Thesaurus/Speller/Hyphenation

Main:	c:\window
Supplementary:	c:\window

☐ Update Quick List with Changes

[OK]   [Cancel]

Screen 5.3

LOCATION OF FILES

FILES

Backup Files:	
Documents:	c:\window\learn
Graphics Files:	c:\window\graphics
Printer Files:	c:\wpc
Spreadsheets:	

MACROS/KEYBOARDS/BUTTON BARS

Files:	c:\window\macros

STYLES

Directory:	c:\window
Filename:	c:\window\library.sty

THESAURUS/SPELLER/HYPHENATION

Main:	c:\window
Supplementary:	c:\window

☐ Update Quick List with Changes

[OK]   [Cancel]

Screen 5.4

```
┌─────────────────────────────────────────────────────────────────┐
│                      walogo.tif Header Info.                      │
│  ┌─TIFF File format ──────────┐   ┌─Image size ─────────────────┐ │
│  │ Version #              42  │   │ Horizontal    1888    6.3   │ │
│  │ Byte order             II  │   │ Vertical      1656    5.5   │ │
│  │ NewSubFile Type         1  │   │ Units        Pixel   Inch   │ │
│  └────────────────────────────┘   └─────────────────────────────┘ │
│                                                                   │
│  ┌─Spatial Configuration ─────┐   ┌─Image resolution ───────────┐ │
│  │ Samples per pixel       1  │   │ Horizontal res.       300   │ │
│  │ Bits per sample         1  │   │ Vertical res.         300   │ │
│  │ Planar config.          1  │   │ Units                 dpi   │ │
│  └────────────────────────────┘   └─────────────────────────────┘ │
│                                     Palette: Red, Green, Blue     │
│  ┌─Photometric data ──────────┐   ┌─────────────────────────────┐ │
│  │ Photo Interpretation    1  │   │                             │ │
│  │ Resolution Unit      Inch  │   │                             │ │
│  │ Compression Type    PkBit  │   │                             │ │
│  └────────────────────────────┘   │                             │ │
│                                    │                             │ │
│   ┌────────┐  ┌────────────────┐   │                             │ │
│   │   OK   │  │ Display image  │   │                             │ │
│   └────────┘  └────────────────┘   └─────────────────────────────┘ │
└─────────────────────────────────────────────────────────────────┘
```

Screen 6.1

Screen 6.2

The redesigned screen. Headings are capitalized to set them off from the control captions. The headline style of presentation is consistently applied to all captions. The data fields are aligned and the Units in the IMAGE sections are moved to the top. This redesigned screen is 12 percent less complex than the original.

Example 7

Here are redesigned versions of the other read-only/display screen presented in Step 3.

Screen 7.1

The original STORY INFO screen.

Screen 7.2

The redesigned STORY INFO screen. Elements are aligned and incorporated within borders. Note that headings are not included within the borders. The command remains positioned in the upper-right corner, as is standard for this graphical system. This redesigned screen is 8 percent less complex than the original.

```
                     walogo.tif Header Info.

  ┌TIFF FILE FORMAT──────────┐   ┌IMAGE SIZE──────────────────┐
  │   Version #:          42 │   │   Units:         Pixel  Inch │
  │   Byte Order:         II │   │   Horizontal:    1888   6.3  │
  │   New Subfile Type:    1 │   │   Vertical:      1656   5.5  │
  └──────────────────────────┘   └──────────────────────────────┘

  ┌SPATIAL CONFIGURATION─────┐   ┌IMAGE RESOLUTION────────────┐
  │   Samples Per Pixel:    1 │   │   Units:              dpi    │
  │   Bits Per Sample:      1 │   │   Horizontal:         300    │
  │   Planar Configuration: 1 │   │   Vertical:           300    │
  └──────────────────────────┘   └──────────────────────────────┘

  ┌PHOTOMETRIC DATA──────────┐   Palette: Red, Green, Blue
  │   Photo Interpretation: 1 │   ┌──────────────────────────────┐
  │   Resolution Unit:   Inch │   │                              │
  │   Compression Type: PkBit │   │                              │
  └──────────────────────────┘   └──────────────────────────────┘

              [ OK ]      [ Cancel ]
```

Screen 6.2

Screen 7.3

Another version of the redesigned STORY INFO screen. Then only difference is that the command button is positioned at the bottom rather than at the side, creating a better balanced screen. On less complex screens this is another advantage of bottom positioning of command buttons.

```
  Story info                          [ OK ]
  ─────────────────────────────────

    File link:

    Textblocks:   1        First page:   4

    Char count:   1400     Last page:    4

    Overset chars:   0

    Total area:   23.413 sq inches

    Total depth:  7.400 inches
```

Screen 7.1

STORY INFORMATION

File Link:

OK

Textblocks:	1
Character Count:	1400
First Page:	4
Last Page:	4
Overset Characters:	0

| Area: | 23.413 sq inches |
| Depth: | 7.400 inches |

Screen 7.2

STORY INFORMATION

File Link:

Textblocks:	1
Character Count:	1400
First Page:	4
Last Pago:	4
Overset Characters:	0

| Area: | 23.413 sq inches |
| Depth: | 7.400 inches |

OK

Screen 7.3

Test, Test, and Retest

The design of graphical systems and Web pages, and their screens, is a complicated process. As has been shown, in both a host of factors must be considered. In graphical systems among the many design elements are the types of windows used, the way the windows are organized, what controls are selected to collect and present information, and the way the controls are organized within one window and between several windows. Web page design factors include the proper integration of text, graphics, navigation links, and controls, page size, writing for simplicity and clarity, the characteristics of browsers and monitors, and accessibility requirements. In both design processes numerous design trade-offs will be made. Also, some design decisions may be based on skimpy data and reflect the most educated guess possible at the moment. Finally, the implications for some design decisions may not be fully appreciated until the results can be seen.

To wait until after a system has been implemented to uncover and correct any system usability deficiencies can be aggravating, costly, and time-consuming for both users and developers. Indeed, after implementation many problems may never be corrected because of time constraints and costs. To minimize these kinds of problems, and ensure usability, interfaces must be continually tested and refined before they are implemented.

What follows is an overview of the testing process and the role it plays in design. Its purpose is to provide an awareness of the testing procedures and methods, and to summarize some basic testing guidelines. Testing steps to be reviewed are:

- Identifying the purpose and scope of testing.
- Understanding the importance of testing.
- Developing a prototype.

- Developing the right kind of test plan.
- Designing a test to yield relevant data.
- Soliciting, selecting, and scheduling users to participate.
- Providing the proper test facility.
- Conducting tests and collecting data.
- Analyzing the data and generating design recommendations.
- Modifying the prototype as necessary.
- Testing the system again.
- Evaluating the working system.

The Purpose of Usability Testing

Usability testing serves a twofold purpose. First, it establishes a communication bridge between developers and users. Through testing, the developer learns about the user's goals, perceptions, questions, and problems. Through testing, the user is exposed to the capabilities of the system early on, before design is solidified.

Second, testing is used to evaluate a product. It validates design decisions. It also can identify potential problems in design at a point in the development process where they can be more easily addressed. Testing also enables comparison of alternate versions of a design element, when a clear direction is not immediately evident. How well the interface and screens meet user needs and expectations can also be assessed.

Thorough testing also has one other benefit for the developer. It can prevent the massive embarrassment that often results from letting things "slip through the cracks."

The Importance of Usability Testing

A thorough usability testing process is important for many reasons, including all of the following.

Developers and users possess different models. As discussed earlier, developers and users have different expectations and levels of knowledge. Specialized knowledge possessed by the developers enables them to deal with complex or ambiguous situations on the basis of context cues not visible to the users. Developers also frequently use terminology that does not always match that of the users.

Developer's intuitions are not always correct. The intuition of designers, or anyone for that matter, no matter how good or bad they may be at what they do, is error prone. This is illustrated by the previously reported Tullis and Kodimer (1992) study evaluating several screen-based controls. They found that programmers' predictions of control usage speed correlated only .07 with actual measured speeds. They also found that programmers' predictions of user control preferences correlated only .31 with actuality. Intuition is too shallow a foundation on which to base design decisions.

There is no average user. We all differ—in looks, feelings, motor abilities, intellectual abilities, learning abilities and speeds, device-based control preferences, and so forth. In a keyboard data entry task, for example, the best operators will probably be twice as fast as the poorest and make 10 times fewer errors. The design must permit people with widely varying characteristics to satisfactorily and comfortably learn and perform the task or job.

It's impossible to predict usability from appearance. Just as it is impossible to judge a person's personality from his or her looks, it's impossible to predict a system's usability from its appearance.

Design standards and guidelines are not sufficient. Design standards and guidelines are an important component of good design, laying the foundation for consistency. But design standards and guidelines often fall victim to trade-offs. They also cannot address all the countless design element interactions that occur within a completed system.

Informal feedback is inadequate. Informal feedback is a hit-and-miss proposition. Parts of the system may be completely overlooked; significant problems in other parts may never be documented.

Products' built-in pieces almost always have system-level inconsistencies. This is a normal and expected result when different developers work on different aspects of a system. We might also say that developers differ—there is no average developer.

Problems found late are more difficult and expensive to fix. Unless they're really severe, they may never be fixed.

Problems fixed during development mean reduced support costs later. Support costs are directly proportional to the usability problems that remain after development. The more problems, the higher the support costs.

Advantages over a competitive product can be achieved. Many products can do something. The most successful products are those that permit doing something easily.

Scope of Testing

Testing should begin in the earliest stages of product development and continue throughout the development process. It should include as many of the user's tasks, and as many of the product's components, as reasonably possible. Always involve all members of the design team in the testing to ensure a common reference point for all. Involving all also permits multiple insights into the test results from the different perspectives of team members.

Prototypes

A prototype is primarily a vehicle for exploration, communication, and evaluation. Its purpose is to obtain user input in design, and to provide feedback to designers. Its major function is the communicative role it plays, not accuracy or thoroughness. A prototype enables a design to be better visualized and provides insights into how the software will look and work. It also aids in defining tasks, their flow, the interface itself, and its screens.

A prototype is a simulation of an actual system that can be quickly created. A prototype may be a rough approximation, such as a simple hand-drawn sketch, or it may be interactive, allowing the user to key or select data using controls, navigate through menus, retrieve displays of data, and perform basic system functions. A prototype need not be perfectly realistic, but it must be reasonably accurate and legible. A prototype also need not be functionally complete, possessing actual files or processing data. Today, many software support tools for prototyping are available that permit the prototype to be integrated directly into the application code.

A prototype may have great breadth, including as many features as possible to present concepts and overall organization, or it might have more depth, including more detail on a given feature or task to focus on individual design aspects. By nature, a prototype cannot be used to exercise all of a system's functions, just those that are notable in one manner or another.

Particularly useful early in design, a prototype should be capable of being rapidly changed as testing is performed. A prototype is characterized by its fidelity, the exactness and thoroughness of its replication of a system's screens and user interaction. Prototypes range in fidelity from low to high, from rough hand-drawn sketches to fully functioning software (Microsoft, 1995; Weinschenk, 1995; Winograd, 1995). Various kinds of prototypes, in general order of increased fidelity, are as follows.

Hand Sketches and Scenarios

- Description:
  - Screen sketches created by hand.
  - Focus is on the design, not the interface mechanics.
  - A low-fidelity prototype.

- Advantages:
  - Can be used very early in the development process.
  - Suited for use by entire design team.
  - No large investment of time and cost.
  - No programming skill needed.
  - Easily portable.
  - Fast to modify and iterate.
  - A rough approximation often yields more substantive critical comments.
  - Easier to comprehend than functional specifications.
  - Can be used to define requirements.

- Disadvantages:
  - Only a rough approximation.
  - Limited in providing an understanding of navigation and flow.
  - A demonstration, not an exercise.
  - Driven by a facilitator, not the user.

— Limited usefulness for a usability test.
— A poor detailed specification for writing the code.
— Usually restricted to most common tasks.

Description. The first, and simplest, prototype is a low-fidelity rough hand-drawn sketch, or mock-up, of the screens. These can start early in the design process and before any attempt is made to create a prototype using an available toolkit or interface builder. With sketches, the focus is on the design of individual screens, not the interface mechanics. The hand sketch should be an entity that has enough of a general look to suggest the functionality, interaction, and layout of screens. The goal is a rough vision, not a polished work of art. This sketch will be useful in defining and refining task organization, conceptual ideas, and the general layout of screens.

> **MYTH** **The design is finished.**

Advantages. Hand-drawn sketches of screens can be easily developed and used very early in the development process. Many usability problems can then be identified and corrected quickly. Sketches are also suitable for use by the entire development team, giving everyone a sense of what the real design issues are. Sketches require no large investment of time and money, and they are portable, placing few restrictions on where the testing may occur. Sketches can also be quickly modified and iterated, as many times as necessary. Because there has been no emotional investment in "code" and the status quo, there is no necessity for team members to defend something already created from hard work. Screen sketches are rough approximations, and rough approximations often yield more substantive suggestions or critical comments than actual screen-drawn versions. Their "draft" or "unpolished" look greatly softens the attitude that everything is cast in concrete. Sketches can also be used to define a system's requirements.

Disadvantages. Since hand-drawn sketches are rough approximations, they can only suggest the final layout of the interface. They are limited in helping understand system navigation and flow, and are a demonstration device driven by a facilitator, with the user assuming a more passive role. They are usually restricted to the most common user tasks. As a result, they possess limited usefulness for usability testing.

Sketch Creation Process*

- Sketch (storyboard) the screens while determining:
  — The source of the screen's information.
  — The content and structure of individual screens.
  — The overall order of screens and windows.

* Based on Weinschenk (1995).

- Use an erasable medium.
- Sketch the screens needed to complete each workflow task.
- Try out selected metaphors and change them as necessary.
- First, storyboard common/critical/frequent scenarios.
  — Follow them from beginning to end.
  — Then, go back and build in exceptions.
- Don't get too detailed; exact control positioning is not important, just overall order and flow.
- Storyboard as a team, including at least one user.
- Only develop online prototypes when everyone agrees that a complete set of screens has been satisfactorily sketched.

Sketch the screens while determining the source of the screen's information, the content and structure of the individual screens, and the overall flow of the screens. Use an erasable medium so that as ideas are explored and changed, the modifications will be easy to make. Sketch the screens needed to complete each task in the workflow. First, sketch the most common, critical, or frequent activities, following them from beginning to end. Then, go back and build in the exceptions. Try out all selected metaphors and modify them as necessary. Make sure the major user objects are very obvious. Avoid getting too detailed. Most important is the overall screen flow, order, and structure. Approximate the positioning of controls simply to verify fit. Exact positioning will come later. Sketch the screens as a team, including at least one user. To avoid solidifying the product too soon, develop online prototypes only when everyone agrees a complete set of screens have been satisfactorily sketched.

Interactive Paper Prototypes

- Description:
  — Interface components (menus, windows, and screens) constructed of common paper technologies (Post-It notes, transparencies, and so on).
  — The components are manually manipulated to reflect the dynamics of the software.
  — A low-fidelity prototype.
- Advantages:
  — More illustrative of program dynamics than sketches.
  — Can be used to demonstrate the interaction.
  — Otherwise, generally the same as for hand-drawn sketches and scenarios.
- Disadvantages:
  — Only a rough approximation.
  — A demonstration, not an exercise.
  — Driven by a facilitator, not the user.
  — Limited usefulness for usability testing.

Description. Another simple low-fidelity prototype involves use of common office supplies such as Post-It notes, transparencies, markers, and scissors. Menu bars, pull-down menus, pop-up windows, screen bodies, and so on reflecting system tasks are created using these media. Then, the components are manually manipulated to illustrate the dynamics of the software. The purpose of this kind of prototype is to provide a sense of the dynamics of a program without actually having to build a functional version of it. The objective, again, is to create a rough vision, not a polished piece of art, in order to elicit substantive suggestions and critical comments. The goal is not to show how the system or Web site will look, but to assess if people can easily use it.

Advantages. Interactive paper prototypes are more illustrative of program dynamics than simple screen sketches. System components can be manipulated to demonstrate the interactive nature of the system. The other paper prototype advantages are generally the same as those described for hand-drawn sketches and scenarios.

Disadvantages. The disadvantages are similar to those for hand-drawn sketches. They are only rough approximations, are demonstrations and not exercises, are driven by a facilitator not the user, and possess limited usefulness for usability testing.

Programmed Facades

- Description:
  - Examples of finished dialogs and screens for some important aspects of the system.
  - Created by prototyping tools.
  - Medium-fidelity to high-fidelity prototypes.
- Advantages:
  - Provide a good detailed specification for writing code.
  - A vehicle for data collection.
- Disadvantages:
  - May solidify the design too soon.
  - May create the false expectation that the "real thing" is only a short time away.
  - More expensive to develop.
  - More time-consuming to create.
  - Not effective for requirements gathering.
  - Not all of the functions demonstrated may be used because of cost, schedule limitations, or lack of user interest.
  - Not practical for investigating more than two or three approaches.

Description. To provide a realistic surface view of a real program and to illustrate some of the program's functioning, a programmed facade can be created. Using prototyping tools such as Hypercard, Supercard, and Toolbook, examples of finished dialogs and screens for some important aspects of the system are constructed and viewed. A facade is very shallow, duplicating only a small portion of what is ultimately intended in both depth and breadth. Because of this shallow nature, it is best described as a medium-fidelity to high-fidelity prototype.

Advantages. While much is missing underneath, what is visible can provide a good impression of finished design. Programmed facades also provide a good detailed specification for writing code, and can be a vehicle for the actual collection of data.

Disadvantages. First, a highly polished product can foster a sense of finality because of its appearance. Significant reorganization or restructuring suggestions may be inhibited, with the focus simply being on screen cosmetics. Second, the false expectation that the real thing is only a short time away may easily be created, even though much work still remains to be done. Programmed facades are also much more expensive to develop than paper-based prototypes, and they take much longer to create. Also not all of the functions demonstrated may eventually be used because of cost, schedule limitations, or lack of user interest, and they are not practical for investigating more than two or three alternate design approaches.

Prototype-Oriented Languages

■ Description:
— An example of finished dialogs and screens for some important aspects of the system.
— Created through programming languages that support the actual programming process.
— A high-fidelity prototype.

■ Advantages:
— May include the final code.
— Otherwise, generally the same as those of programmed facades.

■ Disadvantages:
— Generally the same as for programmed facades.

Description. To present an example of completed dialogs and screens for some parts of the system, prototypes can be constructed using programming languages that support the actual programming process. Examples include Power Builder, Visual Basic, and so on. Using these tools, a high-fidelity, real program can be created to illustrate some of the program's functioning and the mechanics of the interface. One consideration to be decided up front: Will the prototype software be a "throw-away," or the actual system software? This will have implications concerning the amount of programming effort expended on the prototype.

Advantages. The greatest advantage of this kind of prototype is that it may include the actual code needed for the system. Otherwise, advantages are generally the same as those of programmed facades.

Disadvantages. Like a programmed facade, a danger is that the highly polished product can foster a sense of finality because of its appearance, inhibiting reorganization or restructuring suggestions, the focus simply being on screen cosmetics. Other disadvantages are also similar to those of programmed facades.

Comparisons of Prototypes

The fidelity of the prototypes described above varies from low to high. Does fidelity affect a prototype's usefulness as a testing tool? Two recent studies have addressed this issue. The first study, by Catani and Biers (1998), examined prototypes created at three fidelity levels: low (paper), (medium) screen shots, and high (using a prototype-oriented language—Visual Basic). There were no significant differences in the number and severity of problems identified with each kind of prototype. There was also a high degree of commonality in the specific problems uncovered.

The second study, reported by Uceta, Dixon, and Resnick (1998), compared a paper-based prototype with a computer-based prototype. Both interfaces were identical except for the medium of presentation. Most of the usability problems were found using both approaches, the results being statistically comparable. Identifying problems using the paper prototype, however, took about 30 percent longer than using the computer-based prototypes.

The results of these studies indicate that prototype fidelity seems to have no impact on the identification of usability problems. Other prototyping issues (prototype creation time and cost, testing time, and so on) remain important issues in usability testing, however. It seems reasonable that any system development effort should use combinations of these prototyping techniques throughout the entire design cycle in order to visualize the design, solicit users' input, and obtain needed feedback for the developers. Successively increasing the complexity of the prototypes as development moves toward the final solution, allows users to continually get a better idea of how the system will actually look and work. This will give them greater and greater insights into how the system may be improved.

Kinds of Tests

A test is a tool that is used to measure something. The "something" may be:

- Conformance with a requirement.
- Conformance with guidelines for good design.
- Identification of design problems.
- Ease of system learning.
- Retention of learning over time.
- Speed of task completion.
- Speed of need fulfillment.
- Error rates.
- Subjective user satisfaction.

A test is usually formal; it is created and applied intentionally and with a purpose. It is usually based upon some kind of criteria, an understanding of what a good result would be. Several testing techniques, at varying levels of sophistication and cost, are available to exercise the system.

Guidelines Review

- Description:
  - A review of the interface in terms of an organization's standards and design guidelines.
- Advantages:
  - Can be performed by developers.
  - Low cost.
  - Can identify general and recurring problems
  - Particularly useful for identifying screen design and layout problems.
- Disadvantages:
  - May miss severe conceptual, navigation, and operational problems.

Description. A *guidelines review* is an inspection of an interface's navigation and screen design and layout in the context of an organization's standards and design guidelines. A checklist summarizing a system's standard or guideline document is prepared and is used as the basis for the comparison. Failure to comply with a guideline or standard indicates that a design modification may be necessary.

Advantages. Software developers can perform this kind of test. Its advantages include its low cost and its ability to identify recurring and general problems. It is particularly useful in identifying screen design and layout problems.

Disadvantage. Because this review tends to be static in nature, it may miss severe conceptual, navigation, and operational problems.

Heuristic Evaluation

- Description:
  - A detailed evaluation of a system by interface design specialists to identify problems.
- Advantages:
  - Easy to do.
  - Relatively low cost.
  - Does not waste user's time.
  - Can identify many problems.
- Disadvantages:
  - Evaluators must possess interface design expertise.
  - Evaluators may not possess an adequate understanding of the tasks and user communities.
  - Difficult to identify systemwide structural problems.
  - Difficult to uncover missing exits and interface elements.
  - Difficult to identify the most important problems among all problems uncovered.
  - Does not provide any systematic way to generate solutions to the problems uncovered.

- Guidelines:
  — Use 3 to 5 expert evaluators.
  — Choose knowledgeable people:
    • Familiar with the project situation.
    • Possessing a long-term relationship with the organization.

Description. In a *heuristic evaluation*, interface specialists study a system in depth and look for properties they know, from experience, will lead to problems. The interface is judged for its compliance with recognized usability principles, the heuristics.

Advantages. A heuristic evaluation is relatively easy to do and its cost is fairly low (See "Heuristic Evaluation Process" below). It does not waste the user's valuable time. It also can identify many usability problems (See the research studies below).

Disadvantages. The evaluators should possess user interface expertise; this greatly restricts the population from which evaluators can be are chosen. Because of the small size of this available group, evaluators may not possess an adequate understanding of the system tasks and the user communities. (Even expert reviewers have great difficulty knowing how typical users, especially first-time users, will really behave.)

With this method of evaluation, it is difficult to identify deeper design problems, including systemwide structural problems, missing exits, and missing interface elements or features. It is also difficult to identify the most important problems among those documented. Finally, this method does not provide any systematic way to generate solutions to the problems uncovered.

Guidelines. Based upon a study, Nielsen (1992) suggests that the optimum expert group size to satisfactorily perform a heuristic evaluation is 3 to 5 people. He found that different evaluators tend to find different problems, and one person will never be able to find the number of usability problems that several people will. Nielsen also found that including more than five evaluators does not gain enough additional usability information for the extra cost involved. Ideally, evaluators used should be familiar with the project situation and possess a long-term relationship with the developing organization. This suggestion is often difficult to achieve, however.

Heuristic Evaluation Process

- Preparing the session:
  — Select evaluators.
  — Prepare or assemble:
    • A project overview.
    • A checklist of heuristics.
  — Provide briefing to evaluators to:
    • Review the purpose of the evaluation session.
    • Preview the evaluation process.
    • Present the project overview and heuristics.
    • Answer any evaluator questions.
    • Provide any special evaluator training that may be necessary.

■ Conducting the session:
— Have each evaluator review the system alone.
— The evaluator should:
  • Establish own process or method of reviewing the system.
    — Provide usage scenarios, if necessary.
  • Compare his or her findings with the list of usability principles.
  • Identify any other relevant problems or issues.
  • Make at least two passes through the system.
— Detected problems should be related to the specific heuristics they violate.
— Comments are recorded either:
  • By the evaluator.
  • By an observer.
    — The observer may answer questions and provide hints.
— Restrict the length of the session to no more than 2 hours.

■ After the session:
— Hold a debriefing session including observers and design team members where:
  • Each evaluator presents problems detected and the heuristic it violated.
  • A composite problem listing is assembled.
  • Design suggestions for improving the problematic aspects of the system are discussed.
— After the debriefing session:
  • Generate a composite list of violations as a ratings form.
  • Request evaluators to assign severity ratings to each violation.
  • Analyze results and establish a program to correct violations and deficiencies.

Preparing the session. First, as described above, *select* 3 to 5 evaluators. Ideally, the evaluators used should be familiar with the project situation and possess a long-term relationship with the developing organization. Then, *prepare or assemble* a project overview and a checklist of heuristics. A useful checklist may be available from one or more of the evaluators. Examples of checklists are found in Tables 14.2 and 14.3. Finally, provide a *briefing* to the evaluators to review the purpose of the evaluation session, to preview the entire evaluation process that is being undertaken, to present the project overview and heuristics, and to answer any questions the evaluators may have. Any special evaluator training that may be necessary can also be provided at this time. This briefing session will normally consume 45 to 60 minutes.

Conducting the session. Each evaluator should inspect the system *alone*, not with or in the presence of other evaluators. This is to ensure independent and unbiased evaluations from each evaluator. Allow the evaluators to establish their *own process or method* of reviewing the system. Ideally, let the evaluator use the system without procedural assistance, browsing as is felt necessary. If, however, the evaluators are not familiar with the system's content and purpose, they may be provided with scenarios listing the steps a user would take to perform a sample set of realistic user tasks.

During the session, the evaluators will compare their findings with the list of usability principles. *Detected problems* should be related to the specific heuristics they violate. Multiple heuristics can be linked to any one identified problem. Other relevant problems or issues can also be noted. Two or more passes should be made through the system.

Evaluator *comments* can be recorded either by the evaluator or by an observer. Evaluator-written comments require additional effort by the evaluator during the review process and can break the continuity of the evaluation process. Having an observer record the evaluator's verbal comments adds to the overhead of the session, but reduces the evaluator's workload and allows greater focusing on the review process. If the same observer is used for all evaluation sessions, session results should be available faster since the observer only needs to understand and organize one set of personal notes, not multiple reports or reviews written by all session participants. The observer may answer questions and provide hints to the evaluator, as necessary. Evaluators not familiar with the system's content will occasionally need advice. Also precious time will not be wasted by the evaluator's struggling with the interface's mechanics. Observer comments should be restricted to situations where the evaluator is clearly confused or in trouble.

MAXIM   **Not even the most brilliantly conceived and ingenious computer system can do all that it was designed to do—or even a small part of what it was designed to do—unless the brilliance of its operation and purpose is matched by the cunning simplicity of its user interface. (Hicks and Essinger, 1991)**

Finally, to minimize evaluator fatigue, restrict the *length of a session* to about 2 hours. For large or complicated interfaces that require more time to evaluate, it is better to split the session into several sessions, each concentrating on a part of the interface.

After the session. When all evaluator and/or observer notes have been complied, hold a *debriefing session,* no more than 2 hours in length. Include all observers and design team members. Have each evaluator present the problems detected and the heuristic each violated. Assemble a composite list of usability problems (if one has not yet been compiled). Solicit and discuss design suggestions for improving the problematic aspects of the system.

After the debriefing session, form the composite list of violations into a ratings form. Request the evaluators to assign severity ratings to each violation on a scale ranging from "usability catastrophe" to "not a usability problem," as shown in Table 14.1. It is difficult to obtain these estimates during the evaluation process, where the focus is on finding problems. Then, analyze the results and establish a program to correct the necessary violations and deficiencies. The ratings will identify the most serious problems, the first in need of attention.

Heuristic Evaluation Effectiveness

One of the earliest papers addressing the effectiveness of heuristic evaluations was by Nielsen (1992). He reported that the probability of finding a *major* usability problem averaged 42 percent for single evaluators in six case studies. The corresponding probability for uncovering a *minor* problem was only 32 percent. He also found that the actual

Table 14.1   Severity Ratings in Heuristic Evaluation

0 = I don't agree that this is a usability problem at all.
1 = A cosmetic problem only. Need not be fixed unless extra time is available.
2 = A minor usability problem. Fixing should be given a low priority.
3 = A major usability problem. Important to fix and should be given a high priority.
4 = A usability catastrophe. Imperative to fix before the product can be released.

From useit.com

number of located minor problems exceeded the number of major problems uncovered by about a 3:1 ratio (152 minor problems versus 59 major problems). Minor design problems are normally more prevalent in design (for example, inconsistent use of typefaces) and, consequently, show up in greater numbers in this kind of evaluation. Minor problems, such as inconsistencies, are more susceptible to identification by inspection, and may not be noticed in testing with actual users, who are focusing on a task or procedure. Nielsen suggests that severity ratings are especially useful in prioritizing minor problems.

For a number of years, Bailey (2001) has questioned the effectiveness of heuristic evaluations, as now conducted. In a 1992 article (Bailey, Allan, and Raiello, 1992) he suggested that many of the "problems" identified by heuristic evaluations were really not problems at all. He recently bolstered his argument by reporting on three studies looking at their effectiveness (Catani and Biers, 1998; Rooden, Green, and Kanis, 1999; Stanton and Stevenage, 1998). In each study, he determined what the heuristic evaluators thought the problems were, and then he compared these determinations with the problems users actually had in performance testing. The results showed that about one-third (36 percent) of identified problems were actually usability problems, and almost one-half (43 percent) of the problems identified by evaluators *did not* turn out to be problems at all. The evaluators also missed about one-fifth (21 percent) of the problems users actually had. He concluded that when a heuristic evaluation is conducted, about one-half of the problems identified will be problems, and one-half will not be problems.

Bailey ends his article not by suggesting that heuristic evaluations are bad, but that the heuristics themselves must be greatly improved. (The messenger is all right—the problem is the message.) He recommends establishing more solidly research-based heuristics. The most used set of heuristics can be traced back to a paper by Molich and Nielsen in 1990, and revised by Nielsen in 1994 (Bailey, 1999b). The research foundation of these papers is somewhat suspect. Bailey suggests a better research-based set of heuristics will lead to improved evaluation results, for example, those proposed by Gerhardt-Powals (1996). This set of heuristics is summarized in Table 14.2.

Web heuristics are still an evolving entity and must also be validated through research. The set proposed by Levi and Conrad (1996), and summarized in Table 14.3, seem a good place to start.

In conclusion, heuristic evaluations are useful in identifying many usability problems and should be part of the testing arsenal. Performing this kind of evaluation before beginning actual testing with users will eliminate a number of design problems, and is but one step along the path toward a very usable system.

Table 14.2 Research-Based Set of Heuristics

1. Automate unwanted workload.
   - Free cognitive resources for high-level tasks.
   - Eliminate mental calculations, estimations, comparisons, and unnecessary thinking.

2. Reduce uncertainty.
   - Display data in a manner that is clear and obvious.

3. Fuse data.
   - Reduce cognitive load by bringing together lower-level data into a higher-level summation.

4. Present new information with meaningful aids to interpretation.
   - Use a familiar framework, making it easier to absorb.
   - Use everyday terms, metaphors, and so on.

5. Use names that are conceptually related to functions.
   - Context-dependent.
   - Attempt to improve recall and recognition.

6. Group data in consistently meaningful ways to decrease search time.

7. Limit data-driven tasks.
   - Reduce the time needed to assimilate raw data.
   - Make appropriate use of color and graphics.

8. Include in the displays only that information needed by a user at a given time.
   - Allow users to remain focused on critical data.
   - Exclude extraneous information that is not relevant to current tasks.

9. Provide multiple coding of data where appropriate.

10. Practice judicious redundancy.
    - To resolve the conflict between heuristics 6 and 8.

From Gerhardt-Powals (1996).

Table 14.3 Possible Web Page Heuristics

1. Speak the user's language.
   - Use familiar words, phrases, and concepts.
   - Present information in a logical and natural order.

2. Be consistent.
   - Indicate similar concepts through identical terminology and graphics.
   - Adhere to uniform conventions for layout, formatting, typefaces, labeling, and so on.

3. Minimize the user's memory load.
   - Take advantage of recognition rather than recall.
   - Do not force users to remember key information across documents.

4. Build flexible and efficient systems.
   - Accommodate a range of user sophistication and diverse user goals.
   - Provide instructions where useful.
   - Lay out screens so that frequently accessed information is easily found.

(continues)

Table 14.3   Continued

5. Design aesthetic and minimalist systems.
   • Create visually pleasing displays.
   • Eliminate information that is irrelevant or distracting.

6. Use chunking.
   • Write materials so that documents are short and contain only one topic.
   • Do not force the user to access multiple documents to complete a single thought.

7. Provide progressive levels of detail.
   • Organize information hierarchically, with more general information appearing before more specific detail.
   • Encourage the user to delve as deeply as needed, but to stop whenever sufficient information has been obtained.

8. Give navigational feedback.
   • Facilitate jumping between related topics.
   • Allow the user to determine his/her current position in the document structure.
   • Make it easy to return to an initial state.

9. Don't lie to the user.
   • Eliminate erroneous or misleading links.
   • Do not refer to missing information.

From Levi and Conrad (1996).

Cognitive Walkthroughs

- Description:
  — Reviews of the interface in the context of tasks users perform.
- Advantages:
  — Allow a clear evaluation of the task flow early in the design process.
  — Do not require a functioning prototype.
  — Low cost.
  — Can be used to evaluate alternate solutions.
  — Can be performed by developers.
  — More structured than a heuristic evaluation.
  — Useful for assessing "exploratory learning."
- Disadvantages:
  — Tedious to perform.
  — May miss inconsistencies and general and recurring problems.
- Guidelines:
  — Needed to conduct the walkthrough are:
    • A general description of proposed system users and what relevant knowledge they possess.
    • A specific description of one or more core or representative tasks to be performed.
    • A list of the correct actions required to complete each of the tasks.

— Review:
  • Several core or representative tasks across a range of functions.
  • Proposed tasks of particular concern.
— Developers must be assigned roles of:
  • Scribe to record results of the action.
  • Facilitator to keep the evaluation moving.
— Start with simple tasks.
— Don't get bogged down demanding solutions.
— Limit session to 60 to 90 minutes.

Description. In a *cognitive walkthrough*, developers walk through an interface in the context of representative user tasks. Individual task actions are examined and the evaluators try to establish a logical reason why the user would perform each examined action. Actions are compared to the user's goals and knowledge. Discrepancies and problems are noted and analyzed and the tasks modified as necessary. Walkthroughs require that the task definition methodology must have been properly accomplished in the system requirements stage. The user's goals and assumptions must also be clearly defined before the walkthrough is performed.

Advantages. Walkthroughs permit a clear evaluation of the task flow early in the design process, before empirical user testing is possible. The earlier a design flaw can be detected, the easier it is to fix it. They can also be used to evaluate alternate design solutions. Walkthroughs are of low cost and can be performed by developers. They are also more structured than a heuristic evaluation, being less likely to suffer from subjectivity because of the emphasis on user tasks. Walkthroughs are very useful for assessing "exploratory learning," first-time use of a system without formal training.

Disadvantages. A cognitive walkthrough is tedious to perform, and it may miss inconsistencies and general and recurring problems.

Guidelines. Needed to conduct the walkthrough are a general description of proposed system users and what relevant knowledge they possess, a specific description of one or more core or representative tasks to be performed, and a listing of the correct actions required to complete each of the tasks. The walkthrough should review several core or representative tasks across a range of functions, as well as proposed tasks of particular concern to the developers. Start with simple tasks to get the brain juices flowing. Don't get bogged down looking for solutions to problems. Avoid detailed screen designs; they often inhibit assessment of the big picture. Limit a session to 60 to 90 minutes.

Think-Aloud Evaluations

■ Description:
— Users perform specific tasks while thinking out load.
— Comments are recorded and analyzed.

- Advantages:
  — Utilizes actual representative tasks.
  — Provides insights into the user's reasoning.
- Disadvantages:
  — May be difficult to get users to think out loud.
- Guidelines:
  — Develop:
    • Several core or representative tasks.
    • Tasks of particular concern.
  — Limit session to 60 to 90 minutes.

Description. In a *think-aloud evaluation*, users perform specific tasks while thinking out load. The objective is to get the user to talk continuously. All comments are recorded so all thoughts are captured and subtle points are not missed when analysis occurs.

Advantages. This kind of evaluation utilizes actual representative tasks. Valuable insights into why the user does things are obtained.

Disadvantages. It may be difficult to get all people to think out loud.

Guidelines. Develop core or representative task scenarios, or scenarios of proposed tasks of particular concern. Limit a session to 60 to 90 minutes.

Usability Test

- Description:
  — An interface evaluation under real-world or controlled conditions.
  — Measures of performance are derived for specific tasks.
  — Problems are identified.
- Advantages:
  — Utilizes an actual work environment.
  — Identifies serious or recurring problems.
- Disadvantages:
  — High cost for establishing facility.
  — Requires a test conductor with user interface expertise.
  — Emphasizes first-time system usage.
  — Poorly suited for detecting inconsistency problems.

Description. A *usability test* evaluates an interface under real-world or controlled conditions. Specific tasks are performed by users, measures of performance taken, and the results compared with the previously defined performance goals. Evaluators also gather data on problems that arise. Errors, confusion, frustrations, and complaints can be noted and discussed with the user. It is also useful to have the user talk aloud about what he or she is doing. Failure to meet these usability design objectives will indicate that redesign is necessary.

Advantages. Usability tests incorporate a realistic work environment. Tasks are performed in an actual work setting, either a usability laboratory or another controlled setting. A usability test can identify serious or recurring problems, avoiding low-priority items

Disadvantages. Its most serious problem is the high cost associated with establishing a facility to perform the testing. To effectively perform usability test also requires a test conductor with user interface expertise. A usability test also emphasizes first-time or early system use, collecting little data concerning use of a system by experienced system users. These tests are also poorly suited to detecting problems with consistency.

Classic Experiments

- Description:
  — An objective comparison of two or more prototypes identical in all aspects except for one design issue.
- Advantages:
  — Objective measures of performance are obtained.
  — Subjective measures of user satisfaction may be obtained.
- Disadvantages:
  — Requires a rigorously controlled experiment to conduct the evaluation.
  — The experiment conductor must have expertise in setting up, running, and analyzing the data collected.
  — Requires creation of multiple prototypes.
- Guidelines:
  — State a clear and testable hypothesis.
  — Specify a small number of independent variables to be manipulated.
  — Carefully choose the measurements.
  — Judiciously select study participants and carefully or randomly assign them to groups.
  — Control for biasing factors.
  — Collect the data in a controlled environment.
  — Apply statistical methods to data analysis.
  — Resolve the problem that led to conducting the experiment.

Description. When two or more design alternatives exist, either of which may appear possible, a *classic experiment* may be developed to compare them directly. Two or more prototypes are constructed, identical in all aspects except for the design issue (type of control, wording of an instruction, and so forth). Speed and accuracy measures are collected and user preferences solicited.

Advantages. Objective measures of performance and subjective measures of user satisfaction are obtained, thereby permitting a better-informed selection of the best alternative.

Disadvantages. A rigorously controlled experiment, and experimental environment, is required to conduct the evaluation. The experiment conductor must have expertise in setting up, running, and analyzing the data collected. Multiple prototypes reflecting the design issues must also be created.

Guidelines. General steps to be followed in conducting an experiment are the following. First, state a clear and testable hypothesis (screen background color will affect screen readability). Specify a small number of independent variables to be manipulated (five screen background colors). Carefully choose the measurements (screen reading time and reading errors). Judiciously select study participants and carefully or randomly assign them to groups (ascertain reading speeds and equalize mean speeds for groups). Control for biasing factors (ensure that the same monitor is used for all experimental sessions). Collect the data in a controlled environment (within a usability laboratory). Apply statistical methods to data analysis, and resolve the problem that led to conducting the experiment (choose the best screen background color for the system).

Focus Groups

- Description:
  — A discussion with users about interface design prototypes or tasks.
- Advantages:
  — Useful for:
    • Obtaining initial user thoughts.
    • Trying out ideas.
  — Easy to set up and run.
  — Low cost.
- Disadvantages:
  — Requires experienced moderator.
  — Not useful for establishing:
    • How people really work.
    • What kinds of usability problems people have.
- Guidelines:
  — Restrict group size to 8 to 12.
  — Limit to 90 to 120 minutes in length.
  — Record session for later detailed analysis.

Description. In a *focus group*, a small group of knowledgeable users and a moderator are brought together to discuss an interface design prototype or proposed design tasks. The discussion is loosely structured but must be focused on a specific topic or topics.

Advantages. A focus group is a useful method for obtaining initial thoughts or trying out ideas. They are easy to set up and run and have a fairly low cost.

Disadvantages. Focus groups do require an experienced moderator. Also, they are not useful for establishing how people really work and what kinds of usability problems people have.

Guidelines. A focus group should be restricted in size to 8 to 12 people. An individual session should consume no more than 90 to 120 minutes. Recording of the session, either by video or audio, will permit later detailed analysis of participants comments. The recording can also be played for the entire design team again, providing insights into user needs for all developers.

Choosing a Testing Method

Unfortunately, there is little published detailed advice on which tests to use, when to use them, and which tests work best together. Beer, Anodenko, and Sears (1997) suggest a good pairing is cognitive walkthroughs followed by think-aloud evaluations. Using cognitive walkthroughs early in the development process permits the identification and correction of the most serious problems. Later, when a functioning prototype is available, the remaining problems can be identified using a think-aloud evaluation.

A substantial leap forward in the testing process would be the creation of a software tool simulating the behavior of people. This will allow usability tests to be performed without requiring real users to perform the necessary tasks. One such example is a system, described by Hornof and Kieras (1997), called Executive Process Interactive Control (EPIC). Formal evaluations by a tool such as this have the potential to greatly improve the quality of many user interfaces.

In conclusion, each testing method has strengths and weaknesses. A well-rounded testing program will use a combination of some, or all, of these methods to guarantee the usability of its created product. It is very important that testing start as early as possible in the design process and, continue through all developmental stages.

Developing and Conducting the Test

A usability test requires developing a test plan, selecting test participants, conducting the test, and analyzing the test results.

The Test Plan

- Define the scope of the test.
- Define the purpose of the test.
  - Performance goals.
  - What the test is intended to accomplish.

- Define the test methodology.
  - — Type of test to be performed.
  - — Test limitations.
  - — Developer participants.
- Identify and schedule the test facility or location.
- Develop scenarios to satisfy the test's purpose.

An inadequately planned test can waste time and money, and provide flawed or misleading information.

Scope. How extensive and detailed will the test be? A test's scope will be influenced by a variety of factors. Determinants include the following issues: (1) The *design stage:* early, middle, or late—the stage of design influences the kinds of prototypes that may exist for the test, (2) the *time available* for the test—this may range from just a few days to a year or more, (3) *finances allocated* for testing—money allocated may range from one percent of a project's cost to more than 10 percent, (4) the project's *novelty* (well defined or exploratory)—this will influence the kinds of tests feasible to conduct, (5) expected *user numbers* (few or many) and *interface criticality* (life-critical medical system or informational exhibit)—much more testing depth and length will be needed for systems with greater human impact, and (6) finally, the development team's *experience* and testing knowledge will also affect the kinds of tests that can be conducted.

Purpose. Define the purpose of the test in simple statements, including performance goals, what the test is expected to accomplish in system learning, use of screens, system navigation, and efficiency of operation. Learning issues will center on effectiveness in starting to use the system, recognizing system features, and exploring system features. Screen issues will be directed toward general screen layout, including efficiency and aesthetics, and recognition and understanding of screen-based controls, icons, and messages. Navigational issues involve use of system navigation methods, including menus, buttons, and icons. Operational issues include how many steps are needed to accomplish a task, system responsiveness, and forms of system feedback provided.

Methodology. Define the specific *type* of test to be carried out. Also identify any test *limitations.* Set reasonable expectations. If the test is measuring only a part of a system or its behavior, the results must be interpreted with this limitation in mind. Identify all *participants* from the development team.

Test Facility or Location. Select the location where the test will be conducted, in a usability lab, a conference room, or some other location. The location should be away from distractions and disturbances. If the test is being held in a usability laboratory, the test facility should resemble the location where the system will be used. It may be an actual office designated for the purpose of testing, or it may be a laboratory specially designed and fitted for conducting tests. The advantage of a laboratory from a data collection perspective is that it can be designed with one-way mirrors for observers and easily equipped with recording devices such as video cameras. The physical environment—lighting, temperature, and so on—can also be more precisely controlled.

MYTH **Testing would be nice, but it is costly and we don't have time for it.**

Scenarios. Task scenarios to adequately satisfy the test's purpose must be identified and constructed. Ideally, the entire system will be tested, but time and costs often limit what can actually be done. When time or cost constraints exist, good candidates for testing include the user's most important tasks or the most representative tasks. Always test the functions or features whose design foundation is not as solid as desired. These are features where the trade-off issues were not clear-cut, not strongly pointing to one design alternative over other possible alternatives.

After preparing task scenarios, try them out and refine them as necessary. Make sure they are clearly written and capable of being performed in the allocated testing time.

The testing of Web sites will follow the same methodology as that for graphical systems. Web sites, however, present some unique issues that must also be addressed. Many of these important issues are summarized in Table 14.4. This listing is not intended to be all-inclusive. It is simply presented as a reminder of "what not to forget to do."

Table 14.4 Some Things to Remember to Test in Web Site Design

TEST:	ENSURE THAT:
All the browsers, servers, and monitors used.	Different servers and browsers don't introduce adverse new behaviors. Different monitors don't negatively affect color appearance, legibility, and page size.
At different dial-up speeds.	Download times are satisfactory for all users.
The navigation design.	Users know how to find information. The navigation sequence through related information makes sense. Users know where they are in the Web site's structure. Users know how to return to visited points when they are browsing. All links are working properly. Unnecessary links are found and removed.
The visual design style.	The style reflects the site's purpose. The style creates a positive and proper impression of the organization owning the site. The style is compatible with user tasks and needs.
Content legibility and readability.	The design succeeds for all default fonts. All grammar and spelling is correct.

(continues)

Table 14.4 Continued

TEST:	ENSURE THAT:
Backgrounds and color.	Backgrounds are compatible with foregrounds. Backgrounds are not distracting. Monitor color rendering differences do not negatively affect site usability.
Graphics and icons.	Graphics are meaningful and efficient. Graphics are not distracting to the user.
Page breaks.	Actual page breaks are obvious. False signals for page breaks do not exist.
Page printing.	The page prints completely and does not bleed off the page.
Accessibility.	Compatibility with accessibility utilities. Compatibility with accessibility guidelines.

Test Participants

■ Assemble the proper people to participate in the test.

Assembling the proper people to participate in the test is critical to its success. Always recruit participants with the proper qualifications, those currently performing the job where the product will ultimately be used. While the "boss" may profess to be knowledgeable, he or she is too far removed from the grind of daily activities and seldom knows exactly what is going on. Also, recruit participants covering the spectrum of user characteristics, including age, gender, and experience, in order to allow general conclusions based on the test results. Recruit strangers, not friends. A stranger is less likely to withhold comments that might possibly hurt the tester's feelings. There will also be less embarrassment if problems are uncovered.

Nielsen (2000) recommends that the optimum number of users for a usability test is five. He states that research indicates about 85 percent of a system's usability problems will be identified with five participants, and the law of diminishing returns sets in at this point. It is much better, he reasons, to conduct more types of tests with fewer participants, than to conduct fewer tests with more participants. All in all, this is a very reasonable recommendation. One caveat—if a system like a Web site has several highly distinct groups of users (children, parents, and senior citizens, for example) then their interface behaviors may differ. In this case, each different group must be tested. He recommends using 3 to 4 users from each category if one is testing two groups of users, and three users from each category if one is testing three or more user groups. Also, do not forget to include users with disabilities.

Always advise selected test participants of what to expect in the test. They will approach the test with less apprehension. Finally, never refer to test participants as "subjects." While many of us, including myself, have been conditioned to use this term, and have used it for very many years, the correct term today is "evaluator" or "participant."

Test Conduct and Data Collection

To collect usable data, the test should begin only after the proper preparation. Then, the data must be properly and accurately recorded. Finally, the test must be concluded and followed up properly. Following are guidelines for conducting a usability test. Many are from Schrier (1992).

Usability Test Guidelines

- Before starting the test:
    - Explain that the objective is to test the software, not the participants.
    - Explain how the test materials and records will be used.
    - If a consent agreement is to be signed, explain all information on it.
    - If verbal protocols will be collected, let participants practice thinking aloud.
    - Ensure that all participants' questions are answered and that participants are comfortable with all procedures.
- During the test:
    - Minimize the number of people who will interact with the participants.
    - If observers will be in the room, limit them to two or three.
    - Provide a checklist for recording:
        - Times to perform tasks.
        - Errors made in performing tasks.
        - Unexpected user actions.
        - System features used/not used.
        - Difficult/easy-to-use features.
        - System bugs or failures.
    - Record techniques and search patterns that participants employ when attempting to work through a difficulty.
    - If participants are thinking aloud, record assumptions and inferences being made.
    - Record the session with a tape recorder or video camera.
    - Do not interrupt participants unless absolutely necessary.
    - If participants need help, provide some response.
        - Provide encouragement or hints.
        - Give general hints before specific hints.
        - Record the number of hints given.
    - Watch carefully for signs of stress in participants:
        - Sitting for long times doing nothing.
        - Blaming themselves for problems.
        - Flipping through documentation without really reading it.
    - Provide short breaks when needed.
    - Maintain a positive attitude, no matter what happens.

- After the test:
  — Hold a final interview with participants; tell participants what has been learned in the test.
  — Provide a follow-up questionnaire that asks participants to evaluate the product or tasks performed.
  — If videotaping, use tapes only in proper ways.
    • Respect participants' privacy.
    • Get written permission to use tapes.

Before Starting the Test

Most people participating in a test will approach it with some anxiety. Fears may exist that they themselves are being judged, or apprehension may be caused by a general fear of the unknown, a common human trait. These fears must be put to rest. Before the test begins, all participants must be told exactly what will happen in the test. Explain that the test objective is to evaluate the software, not the participants themselves. Also explain how the test materials and records will be used. If participants will be signing a consent agreement, review and explain all information on it before it is signed. If verbal protocols will be collected, that is, if the participants are going to be asked to think aloud, let participants practice this process. For most people this is not a common experience, and it may require getting used to. Finally, do not start the test session until all participants' questions are answered and people are comfortable with all of the test procedures. Providing this kind of information, and preparation, will enable participants to relax faster at the start of the test.

During the Test

Minimize the number of people who will interact with participants. Many and strange voices must be avoided because they can be very distracting and disturbing. If observers will be in the room during the test, limit their number to two or three. Observers must *never* talk during the test.

For data recording, provide observers with a checklist reminding them what to record and for use in actually recording data. Useful information to collect includes the time needed to perform each of the test tasks, errors made, any unexpected actions taken by the participants, how often system features are used, those features that are not used, difficulties in using features, features that are particularly easy to use, and system bugs or system failures. When participants encounter a difficulty, record the techniques and search patterns they employ when attempting to work through the difficulty. If participants are thinking aloud, record the assumptions and inferences they make as they proceed. If practical, record the test with a tape recorder or video camera. This will permit more leisurely review of the test session later. Details missed during the session will be uncovered, and comparisons can be made between the approaches and activities of the different participants. The entire design team will also be allowed to later review and evaluate the test results.

Never interrupt a test participant unless it is absolutely necessary. If, however, it is sensed that participants need help, provide a response of some kind, first through encouragement and then through hints. Provide general hints before specific hints, and record the number of hints given. Watch carefully for signs of stress. If it is detected, again give encouragement or provide hints, or provide a break. Signs of stress include a participant's sitting for a long time doing nothing, blaming him- or herself for problems, and flipping through documentation without really reading it. Provide short breaks when they are needed, and maintain a positive attitude no matter what happens (everything probably will). A tester with a negative attitude will influence the participants in the same way, and the data collected will be contaminated.

After the Test

At the test's conclusion, hold a closing interview with the participants. During this interview, questions that occurred to the tester during the actual test can be asked; the participants can also ask questions, and the tester can tell the participants some of what has been learned. This will make the participants feel that their effort was worthwhile. Also provide follow-up questionnaires that ask participants to evaluate the product or tasks performed. Finally, if videotaping is performed, respect the participant's privacy when the tape is later shown. If necessary, obtain the participant's written permission to later use the tape.

Analyze, Modify, and Retest

- Compile the data from all test participants.
- List the problems the participants had.
- Sort the problems by priority and frequency.
- Develop solutions for the problems.
- Modify the prototype as necessary.
- Test the system again, and again.

Data analysis. Compile all the data collected from all test participants by listing the problems the participants had, sorting the problems by priority and frequency. See Table 14.1 for a problem-rating scheme. Make the results available to the entire design team for analysis, again to provide multiple insights into problem solutions. Then, develop solutions for the problems. Get expert advice if the solutions are not obvious.

Prototype modification. Prototypes must, of course, be modified based on the design recommendations made during testing, and the solutions decided upon.

Test again. The testing process continues in an iterative manner until all problems are satisfactorily solved and all criteria are met. After the prototyping is complete and all code written, a final system test must be performed to assure no software bugs exist and performance meets all specifications. The screens and interface must also be again tested to assure all established usability criteria are being met. The design steps and methods are identical to those for prototype testing.

Evaluate the Working System

■ Collect information on actual system usage through:
— Interviews and focus group discussions.
— Surveys.
— Support line.
— Online suggestion box or trouble reporting.
— Online bulletin board.
— User newsletters and conferences.
— User performance data logging.
■ Respond to users who provide feedback.

Testing never stops with system implementation. The interface, like any part of a system, must be continually evaluated to ensure that it is achieving its design objectives. Problems detected can be corrected in system enhancements and new releases. This type of evaluation is necessary for a variety of reasons.

Problems will have slipped through the cracks. In spite of all the preimplementation testing performed, problems will still exist. It is impossible to exercise all aspects of a system in a testing environment as thoroughly as is done in actual system use. Also, actual use can capture the experiences of all users, not simply those used in the various testing phases.

Initially impressive features may later be regarded as frustrating or completely ignored. Initial impressions may change over time. Some parts of a system, which in the testing process were seen as neat or helpful, may, in everyday use, be found to have little or no value.

Experienced users are more sensitive to time delays. Response times that seemed adequate in the testing process may, as users become experienced, become a source of great irritation.

Customizable interfaces may change. Over a period of time customization may change the interface so much that original features are lost and tasks become more difficult to perform.

The external environment may have changed. The original system hardware used in the testing process may change over time. Added elements or features may affect the system's usability in a negative way, or allow enhancement of the interface.

Many of the techniques used in requirements determination and prototype evaluation can also be applied in this evaluation phase.

Interviews and focus group discussions. Individual user interviews can identify specific areas of concern. These can be pursued to the level of detail needed. Focus groups can then be conducted to determine the generality of the identified problems.

Surveys. A survey or questionnaire is administered to users to obtain feedback on usability problems. These surveys can use e-mail, the Web, or traditional mail.

Support line. Information collected by the unit that helps customers with day-to-day problems can be analyzed (Customer Support, Technical Support, Help Desk, and so on).

Online suggestion box or trouble reporting. An online suggestion box can be implemented to solicit comments or enhancement suggestions.

Online bulletin board. An electronic bulletin board can be implemented to solicit comments, questions, or enhancement suggestions.

User newsletters and conferences. Improvements can be solicited from customer groups who publish newsletters or convene periodically to discuss software usage.

User performance data logging. The system software can capture users' usage patterns and problems doing real tasks. When one uses log data, however, a user's goals and needs can only be surmised.

Respond to users who provide feedback. When feedback is received, respond in an appreciative manner to the person providing it. A positive relationship will be established, and the person will be more likely to provide additional feedback. A failure to respond will discourage future suggestions and indicate to the user that his or her needs are not important. Finally, if a system change is made based upon a suggestion, inform the user or users making the suggestion of the change.

Additional Reading

For the reader who needs much more detailed information on usability testing, the following are recommended. For a demonstration of the importance of usability testing to the success of a software development project, see Bias and Mayhew's *Cost-Justifying Usability* (1994). For a step-by step guide, including checklists and insights, see Dumas and Redish's *A Practical Guide to Usability Testing* (1993). For a practical handbook, see Nielsen's *Usability Engineering* (1993). For discussions of usability testing methods, see Nielsen and Mack's *Usability Inspection Methods* (1994). Extensive accessibility testing guidelines will be found in the Web sites of IBM and Microsoft. An accessibility validation tool is contained in the Web site of Cast Bobby www.cast.org/bobby/.

A Final Word

Enjoy your journey through the wonderful world of graphical interface and Web page development. Application of these many principles in design will aid greatly in creating a product that satisfies all your client's needs. A happy and satisfied client, of course, also means a happy and satisfied developer. Good luck!

References

Andre, A.D. and Wickeans, C.D. (1995). "When users want what's NOT best for them." *Ergonomics in Design*. October.

Apple Computer, Inc. (1992a). *Guide to Macintosh Software Localization*. Reading, MA: Addison-Wesley.

Apple Computer, Inc. (1992b). *Macintosh Human Interface Guidelines*. Reading, MA: Addison-Wesley.

Baca, B. and Cassidy, A. (1999). "Intranet development and design that works," *Proceedings of the Human Factors and Ergonomics Society—1999*, 777–790.

Baddeley, A. (1992). "Working memory." *Science*, 255, 556–559.

Baecker, R., and Small, I. (1990). "Animation at the interface." In *The Art of Human-Computer Interface Design*, B. Laurel (ed.). Reading, MA: Addison-Wesley.

Bailey and Bailey Software Corporation. (1989). *Protoscreens*. Ogden, UT: Bailey and Bailey Software Corporation.

Bailey, Bob. (1999a) *UI Design Update Newsletter*. http://www.humanfactors.com/library/feb992.htm. February.

Bailey, Bob. (1999b) *UI Design Update Newsletter*. http://www.humanfactors.com/library/may992.htm, May.

Bailey, Bob. (1999c) *UI Design Update Newsletter*. http://www.humanfactors.com/library/dec992.htm, December.

Bailey, Bob. (2000) *UI Design Update Newsletter*. http://www.humanfactors.com/library/aug002.htm, August.

Bailey, Bob. (2001) *UI Design Update Newsletter*. http://www.humanfactors.com/library/jan012.htm, January.

Bailey, R.W., Allan, R.W., and Raiello, P. (1992). "Usability testing vs. heuristic evaluation: A head-to-head comparison." *Proceedings of the Human Factors Society 36th Annual Meeting*, Santa Monica, CA: Human Factors Society.

Barmack, J.E. and Sinaiko, H.W. (1966). *Human Factors Problems in Computer-Generated Graphic Displays*. Institute for Defense Analysis (AD-636170).

Barnett, R. (1993). *Forms Analysis and Design*. Belconnen ACT, Australia: Robert Barnett and Associates Pty. Ltd.

Beasley, R. and Waugh, M. (1997). "Predominant Initial and Review Pattern Navigation in a Fully Constrained Hypermedia Hierarchy: An Empirical Study" (11 Aug. 1997) Retrieved via Netscape. http://aace.virginia.edu/aacr/pubs/jemh/v6n2.html# Predominant.

Beer, T., Anodenko, T., and Sears, A. (1997). "A Pair of Techniques for Effective Interface Evaluation: Cognitive Walkthroughs and Think-Aloud Evaluations," *Proceedings of the Human Factors and Ergonomics Society 41st Annual Meeting*, 380–384.

Bennett, J.L. (1979). "The commercial impact of usability in interactive systems." *Man-Computer Communication, Infotech State-of-the-Art*, Vol. 2. B. Schackel, ed. Maidenhead: Infotech International.

Bennett, J.L. (1984). "Managing to meet usability requirements." In *Visual Display Terminals: Usability Issues and Health Concerns*. J.L. Bennett, D. Case, J. Sandelin, and M. Smith, eds. Englewood Cliffs, NJ: Prentice Hall.

Berry, Dick. (2000) "The user experience #2 It's a matter of style—GUI versus the Web," User Experience Design, IBM Ease of Use Team, http://www-106.ibm.com/developerworks/library/w-berry2.html, October.

Bias, Randolph G. and Mayhew, Deborah J. (Eds.). (1994). *Cost-Justifying Usability*. Boston Academic Press.

Billingsley, P. (1988). "Taking panes: Issues in the design of windowing systems." In *Handbook of Human-Computer Interactions*, M. Helander, ed. Amsterdam: Elsevier Science Publishers.

Billingsley, P. (1996). "Standards: Simplifying conformance." *SIGCHI Bulletin*. 28: 36–38.

Bishu, Ram R. and Zhan, P. (1992). "Increasing or decreasing? The menu direction effect on user performance." *Proceedings of the Human Factors Society 36th Annual Meeting*, Santa Monica, CA: Human Factors Society.

Black, J.B., Carroll, J.M., and McGuigan, S.M. (1987). "What kind of minimal instruction manual is most effective?" *Proceedings of CHI+GI. 1987*. New York.

Blinn, B. and Biers, D.W. (1999). "Searching hard-copy (paper) vs. electronic (CRT) documents: Role of experience, amount of text displayed, and the book metaphor." *Proceedings of the Human Factors and Ergonomics Society*, 447-451.

Bonsiepe, G. (1968). "A method of quantifying order in typographic design." *Journal of Typographic Research*, 2, 203–220.

Bouch, A., Kuchinsky, A., and Bhatti, N. (2000). "Quality is in the eye of the beholder: Meeting users' requirements for Internet quality of service," *CHI 2000*, 297–304.

Bouma, H. (1970). "Interaction effects in parafoveal letter recognition." *Nature*. 226: 177–178.

Boyarski, D., Neuwirth, C., Forlizzi, J., and Regli, S.H. (1998). "A study of fonts designed for screen display." *CHI 98 Conference Proceedings*, 87–94.

Brewster, S.A., Wright, P.C., and Edwards, A.D.N. (1993). "An evaluation of earcons for use in auditory human-computer interfaces." *INTERCHI 93*. Amsterdam.

Brooks, R. (1965). "Search time and color coding." *Psychonomic Science*. 2: 281–282.

Brown, C.M. (1988). *Human-Computer Interface Design Guidelines*. Norwood, NJ: Ablex Publishing Co.

Bury, K.F., Boyle, M. , Evey, R.J., and Neal, A.S. (1982). "Windowing versus scrolling on a visual display terminal." *Human Factors* 24: 385–394.

Byrne, M.D. (1993). "Using icons to find documents: simplicity is critical." *INTERCHI 93.* Amsterdam, April 24–29.

Byrne, M.D., John, B.E., Wehrle, N.S., and Crow, D.C. (1999). "The tangled web we wove: A taskonomy of WWW use." *CHI 99 Conference Proceedings,* 544–551.

Card, S.K., Moran, T.P., and Newell, A. (1983). *The Psychology of Human-Computer Interaction.* Hillsdale, NJ: Lawrence Erlbaum.

Carroll, J.M., and Carrithers, C. (1984). "Blocking learner error states in a training-wheels system." *Human Factors* 26: (4)377–389.

Carroll, J.M., Smith-Kerker, P.L., Ford, J.R., and Mazur, S.A. (1986). *The Minimal Manual* (Research Report RC 11637). Yorktown Heights, NY: IBM T.J. Watson Research Center.

Carter, R.L. (1982). "Visual search with color." *Journal of Experimental Psychology: Human Perception and Performance.* 8: 127–136.

CAST.org. "Welcome to Bobby Worldwide (2001)," http://www.cast.org/bobby/.

Catani, M.B. and Biers, D.W. (1998). "Usability evaluation and prototype fidelity: Users and usability professionals," *Proceedings of the Human Factors and Ergonomics Society 42nd Annual Meeting,* 1331–1335.

Charness, N. and Dijkstra, K. (1999). "Age, luminance, and print legibility in homes, offices, and public places." *Human Factors,* 41 (2)173–193.

Christ, R.E., and Teichner, W.H. (1973). "Color research for visual displays." *JANAIR* (Report No. 730703), New Mexico: New Mexico State University.

Christ, R.E. (1975). "Review and analysis of color coding research for visual displays." *Human Factors* 17: (6)542–570.

CNN. (April 9, 1997). "Inventor of Computer 'Mouse' Finally Cashes a Big Check." www.cnn.com/TECH/9704/09/mouse.inventor/.

Cohen, S. (1994). "Most comfortable listening level as a function of age," *Ergonomics,* 37 (7)1269–1274.

Coll, R.A., Coll, J.H., and Thakur, G. (1994). "Graphs and tables: A four-factor experiment." *Communications of the ACM.* 177–85.

Cope, M.E. and Uliano, K.C. (1995). "Cost-justifying usability engineering: A real world example." *Proceedings of the Human Factors Society 39th Annual Meeting,* Santa Monica, CA: Human Factors Society.

Czaja, S.J. (1997) "Computer technology and older adults," In *Handbook of Human-Computer Interaction (2nd Edition),* M.E. Helander, T.K. Landauer and P. Prabhu (eds.) New York: Elsevier, 797–812.

Damodaran, L., Simpson, A., and P. Wilson. (1980). "Designing systems for people." *NCC.* Manchester and Loughborough University of Technology.

Danchak, M.M. (1976). "CRT displays for power plants." *Instrumentation Technology.* 23: (10)29–36.

del Galdo, E. (1990). "Internationalization and translation: Some guidelines for the design of human-computer interfaces." *Designing User Interfaces for International Use,* J. Nielsen, (ed.). Amsterdam: Elsevier Science Publishers.

Digital Equipment Corp. (1988). *XUI Style Guide* (Order No. AA-MG20A-TE). Maynard, MA.

Dillon, A. (1992). " Reading from paper versus screen: A critical review of the empirical litereature," *Ergonomics,* 35 (10)1297–1326.

DiPierro, C., Nachman, G., and Raderman, (2000) "Screen Size and Web Browsing."*UI Design Update Newsletter*, February.

Dumas, Joseph S. and Redish, Janice C. (1993) *A Practical Guide to Usability Testing.* Norwood, NJ: Ablex Publishing.

Dvorak, A., Merrick N.F., Dealey, W.L., and Ford, G.C. (1936) "Typewriting Behavior: Psychology Applied to Teaching and Learning Typewriting." New York: American Book Co.

Eberts, R. (1997). "Cognitive modeling." In *Handbook of Human Factors and Ergonomics,* Second Edition, G. Salvendy (ed.). New York: John Wiley and Sons.

Elkerton, J. (1988). "Online aiding for human-computer interfaces." In *Handbook of Human-Computer Interaction.* M. Helander, ed. Amsterdam: Elsevier Science Publishers.

Elkerton, J. and Palmiter, S.L. (1991). "Designing help using a GOMS model: An information retrieval evaluation." *Human Factors* 33: (2)185–204.

Ellis, R.D. and Kurniawan, S.H. (2000). "Increasing the usability of online information for older users: A case study in participatory design," *International Journal of Human-Computer Interaction,* 12 (2)263–276.

Engel, F.L. (1980). "Information selection from visual displays." In *Ergonomic Aspects of Visual Display Terminals*, E. Grandjean and E. Vigliani (eds.). London: Taylor and Francis Ltd.

Faraday, P. and Sutcliffe, A. (1997). "Designing Effective Multimedia Presentations," *Proceedings of CHI'97,* 272–278.

Fath, J.L. and Henneman, R. L. (1999). "On the development of user interface design guidelines for electronic commerce." *Proceedings of the Human Factors and Ergonomics Society—1999,* 192–198.

Familant, M.E., and M.C. Detweiler. (1995). "Do human factors color recommendations have any practical value?" *Proceedings of the Human Factors and Ergonomics Society 39th Annual Meeting*, Santa Monica, CA: Human Factors Society.

Festa, P. (1998). *Web design not what you pay for.* http://www.news.com/News/Item/0,4,21150,00.html.

Fitts, P.M. (1954). "The information capacity of the human motor system in controlling the amplitude of movement." *Journal of Experimental Psychology, 47,* 381–391.

Fowler, S.L., and Stanwick, V.R. (1995). *The GUI Style Guide,* Cambridge, MA: Academic Press.

Fuccella, Jeanette, Pizzolato, Jack, and Franks, Jack. (1999). "Finding out what users want from your Web site: Techniques for gathering requirements and tasks." June.

Galitz, W.O. (1968). "CRT viewing and visual aftereffects." *UNIVAC Internal Report.* Roseville, MN.

Galitz, W.O. (1980). *Human Factors in Office Automation.* Atlanta, GA: Life Office Management Association.

Galitz, W.O. (1981). *Handbook of Screen Format Design.* Wellesley, MA: QED Publishing Group.

Galitz, W.O. (1992). *User-Interface Screen Design.* Wellesley, MA: QED Publishing Group.

Galitz, W.O. and DiMatteo, A. (1974). "EIS forms and screens design manual." *International Report*. Philadelphia, PA: INA Corporation.

Garver, W.W. (1993). "Synthesizing auditory icons." *INTERCHI 93*. April 24–29, Amsterdam.

Gerhardt-Powals, J. (1996). "Cognitive engineering principles for enhancing human-computer performance," *International Journal of Human-Computer Interaction*, 8 (2), 189–211.

Gould, J.D. (1988). "How to design usable systems." *Handbook of Human-Computer Interaction*, M. Helander (ed.). Amsterdam: Elsevier Science Publishers.

Gould, J.D., Boies, S.J., Meluson, M., Rasamny, M., and Vosburgh, A.M. (1988). "Empirical evaluation of entry and selection methods for specifying dates." *Proceedings of the Human Factors Society 32nd Annual Meeting*, Santa Monica, CA: Human Factors Society.

Greene, S.L., Gould, J.D., Boies, S.JU., Meluson, A., and Rasamny, M. (1988). "Entry-based versus selection-based interaction methods." *Proceedings of the Human Factors Society 32nd Annual Meeting*, Santa Monica, CA: Human Factors Society.

Greene, S.L., Gould, J.D., Boies, M.R., Rasamny, M., and Meluson, A. (1992). "Entry and selection based methods of human-computer interaction." *Human Factors* 34: (1)97–113.

Grose, E., Parush, A., Nadir, R., and Shtub, A. (1998). "Evaluating the layout of graphical user interface screens: validation of a numerical computerized model." *International Journal of Human-Computer Interaction*, 10 (4)343–360.

Grok Dot Com, www.grokdot.com.com

Guastello, S.J., Traut, M., and Korienek, G. (1989). "Verbal versus pictorial representation of objects in a human-computer interface." *International Journal of Man-Machine Studies*. 31: 99–120.

Gugerty, L., Halgren, S., Gosbee, J., and Rudisill, M. (1991). "Using GOMS models and hypertext to create representations of medical procedures for online display." *Proceedings of the Human Factors Society 35th Annual Meeting*, Santa Monica, CA: Human Factors Society.

Gujar, A.U., Harrison, B.L., and Fishkin, K.P. (1998). "A comparative evaluation of display technologies for reading." *Proceedings of the Human Factors and Ergonomics Society 42nd Annual Meeting*, 527–531.

Halsey, R.M. and Chapanis, A. (1951). "On the number absolutely identifiable spectral hues." *Journal of Optical Society of America*. 41: 1057–1058.

Harrison, S.M. (1995). "A comparison of still, animated, or nonillustrated on-line help with written or spoken instructions in a graphical user interface." *Proceedings of CHI 95*. May 7–11, Denver, CO.

Hatfield, D. (1981). *Conference on Easier and More Productive Use of Computer Systems*. Ann Arbor, MI. (In Shneiderman, 1986).

Haubner, P., and Benz, C. (1983). "Information display on monochrome and colour screens." *Abstracts: International Scientific Conference on Ergonomic and Health Aspects in Modern Offices*. November 7–9, Turin, Italy.

Haubner, P. and Neumann, F. (1986). "Structuring alphanumerically coded information on visual display units." *Proceedings: International Scientific Conference: Work with Display Units*. May 12–15, Stockholm, Sweden.

Hicks, R. and Essinger, J. (1991). *Making Computers More Human: Designing for Human-Computer Interaction*. Oxford: Elsevier Advanced Technology.

Hollands, J.G. and Spence, I. (1992). "Judgments of Change and Proportion in Graphical Perception." *Human Factors*, 34: (3)313–334.

Hornof, A.J., and Kieras, D.E. (1997). "Cognitive Modeling Reveals Menu Search Is Both Random and Systematic," *Proceedings of CHI '97*, 107–114.

Hornof, A.J. and Kieras, D.E. (1999). "Cognitive modeling demonstrates how people use and anticipate location knowledge of menu items." *CHI 99 Conference Proceedings*, 410–417.

Horton, W. (1994). *The Icon Book*. New York: John Wiley and Sons.

Howe, Walt. (2001). "A Brief History of the Internet." http://www.walthowe.com/navnet/history.html.

Howlett, V. (1995). *Visual Interface Design for Windows*. John Wiley and Sons.

Hulteen, Eric, (1988) in Walker, 1989.

Hutchins, E.L., Hollan, J.D., and Norman, D.A. (1986). "Direct manipulation interfaces." In *User Centered System Design: New Perspectives on Human-Computer Interaction*. Hillsdale, NJ: Lawrence Erlbaum Associates.

International Business Machines Corporation (IBM). (1987). *Systems Application Architecture Common User Access, Panel Design and User Interaction* (SC26-4351-0). Boca Raton, FL: IBM.

International Business Machines Corporation (IBM). (1989a). *System Application Architecture Common User Access, Advanced Interface Design Guide* (SC26-4582). Cary, NC: IBM.

International Business Machines Corporation (IBM). (1989b). *Systems Application Architecture Common User Access, Basic Interface Design Guide* (SC26-4583). Cary, NC: IBM.

International Business Machines Corporation (IBM). (1991). *Systems Application Architecture Common User Access Advanced Interface Design Reference* (SC34-4289).

International Business Machines Corporation (IBM). (1992). *Object-Oriented Interface Design: IBM Common User Access Guidelines*. Carmel, IN: Que Corporation.

International Business Machines (IBM). (2001). "Cost Justifying Ease of Use." http://www-3.ibm.com/ibm/easy/eou_ext.nsf/Publish/23.

Intons-Peterson, M.J., Rocchi, P., West. T., McLellan, K., and Hackney, A. (1998). "Aging, optimal testing times, and negative priming." *Journal of Experimental Psychology: Learning, Memory, and Cognition*, 24 (2)362–376.

Intons-Peterson, M.J., Rocchi, P., West. T., McLellan, K., and Hackney, A. (1999). "Age, testing at preferred or nonpreferred times (testing optimality), and false memory." *Journal of Experimental Psychology: Learning, Memory, and Cognition*, 25 (1) 23-40.

Johnsgard, T.J., Page, S.R., Wilson, R.D., and Zeno, R.J. (1995). "A comparison of graphical user interface widgets for various tasks." *Proceedings of the Human Factors and Ergonomics Society 39th Annual Meeting*, Santa Monica, CA: Human Factors Society.

Karat, C. (1997). "Cost-justifying usability engineering in the software life cycle." In *Handbook of Human-Computer Interaction*, M. Helander, T. Landauer, and P. Prabhu (eds.). Elsevier Science, Amsterdam.

Karat, C.M., Halverson, C., Horn, D., and Karat, J. (1999). "Patterns of Entry and Correction in Large Vocabulary Continuous Speech Recognition Systems," *CHI 99 Conference Proceedings*, 568–575.

Karat, C.M., Halverson, C., Horn, D., and Karat, J. (1999). "Patterns of entry and correction in large vocabulary continuous speech recognition systems, *CHI99 Conference Proceedings*, 568–175.

Keil, M., and Carmel, E. (1995). "Customer-developer links." *Communications of the ACM*. 38: (5)33–34.

Kobara, S. (1991). *Visual Design with OSF/Motif*. Reading, MA: Hewlett-Packard/Addison-Wesley.

Koenemann, J. and Belkin, N. (1996). "A case for interaction: a study of interactive information retrieval behavior and effectiveness." *Proceedings CHI 96: Human Factors in Computing Systems*, ACM Press, New York, NY, 205–212.

Kohl, J.R., Barclay, R.O., Pinelli, T.E., Keene, M.L., and Kennedy, J.M. (1993). "The impact of language and culture on technical communication in Japan." *Technical Communication*.

Kopala, C.J. (1981). "The use of color coded symbols in a highly dense situation display." *Proceedings of the Human Factors Society 23rd Annual Meeting*, Santa Monica, CA: Human Factors Society.

KYE Systems Corp. (1995). *Genius EasyScan/Color PRO User's Guide*.

Lai, Y. and Waugh, M.L. (1995). "Effects of three different hypertextual menu designs on various information searching activities." *Journal of Multimedia and Hypermedia*, 4: (1)25–52.

Lalomia, M.J. and Happ, A.J. (1987). "The effective use of color for text on the IBM 5153 color display. *Proceedings of the Human Factors Society 31st Annual Meeting*, Santa Monica, CA: Human Factors Society.

Larson, K., and Czerwinski, M. (1998). "Web page design: Implications for memory, structure and scent for information retrieval." *CHI 98 Conference Proceedings*, 25–32.

Lee, A.Y. and Bowers, A.N. (1997). "The Effect of Multimedia Components on Learning," *Proceedings of the Human Factors and Ergonomics Society 41st Annual Meeting*, 340–344.

Legge, G.E. and Rubin, G.S. (1986). "Psychophysics of reading IV. Wavelengths effects in normal and low vision." *Journal of the Optical Society of America*. 3: 40–51.

Levi, Michael D. and Conrad, Frederick G. (1996). "Usability Testing of World Wide Web Sites," http://stats.bls.gov/ore/htm_papers/st960150.htm.

Levine, R. (1995) "*Guide to Web Style*." Sun Microsystems, Inc. http://www.sun.com/styleguide.

Lewis, J.R. (1999). "Effect of Error Correction Strategy on Speech Dictation Throughput." *Proceedings of the Human Factors and Ergonomics Society*, 457–461.

Lind, N.E., Johnson, M., and Sandblad, B. (1992). "The art of the obvious." *CHI 95*. May 3–7, Monterey, CA.

Luria, S.M., Neri, D.F., and Jacobsen, A.R. (1986). "The effects of set size on color matching using CRT displays." *Proceedings of the Human Factors Society 30th Annual Meeting*, Santa Monica, CA: Human Factors Society.

MacKenzie, J.S., Sellen, A., and Buxton, W. (1991). "A comparison of input devices in elemental pointing and dragging tasks." *CHI 91*.

Maguire, M.C. (1985). "A review of human factors guidelines and techniques for the design of graphical human-computer interfaces." *Comput and Graphics* 9: (3)25.

Mallory, K., et al. (1980). "Human engineering guide to control room evaluation. Essex Corporation." *Technical Report NUREG/CR-1580*. Alexandria, VA.

Mandel, T. (1994). *The GUI-OOUI War: Windows vs. OS/2, the Designer's Guide to Human-Computer Interfaces*. New York: Van Nostrand Reinhold.

Marcus, A. (1984). "Icon design requires clarity, consistency." *Computer Graphics Today*.

Marcus, A. (1986a). "Proper color, type use improve instruction." *Computer Graphics Today*.

Marcus, A. (1986b). "Ten commandments of color." *Computer Graphics Today*.

Marcus, A. (1992). *Graphic Design for Electronic Documents and User Interfaces*. New York: ACM Press.

Martin, J. (1973). *Design of Man-Computer Dialogues*. Englewood Cliffs, NJ: Prentice Hall.

Mayhew, D.J. (1992). *Principles and Guidelines in Software User Interface Design*. Englewood Cliffs, NJ: Prentice Hall.

McTyre, J.H. and Frommer, W.D. (1985). "Effects of character/background color combinations on CRT character legibility." *Proceedings of the Human Factors Society 29th Annual Meeting*, Santa Monica, CA: Human Factors Society.

Mead, S.E., Spaulding, R.A., Sit, B.M., and Walker, N. (1997). "Effects of age and training on World Wide Web navigation strategies." *Proceedings of the Human Factor and Ergonomics Society 41st Annual Meeting*, 152–156.

Microsoft Corporation. (1992). *The Windows Interface: An Application Design Guide*. Redmond, WA: Microsoft Press.

Microsoft Corporation. (1995). *The Windows Interface Guidelines for Software Design*. Redmond, WA: Microsoft Press.

Microsoft 2001, msdn.Microsoft.com.library, 2001.

Microswitch (A Honeywell Division). (1984). *Applying Manual Controls and Displays: A Practical Guide to Panel Design*. Freeport, IL: Microswitch.

Miller, G.A. (1956). "The magical number seven, plus or minus two: Some limits on our capability for processing information." *Psychological Science*. 63: 87–97.

Molich, R. and Nielsen, J. (1990). "Improving a human-computer dialogue," *Communications of the ACM*, 33 (3)338–348.

Mori, H. and Hayashi, Y. (1993). "Visual interference with user's tasks on multi-window system." *Proceedings of the Fifth International Conference on Human-Computer Interaction*. 80–85.

Morimoto, K., Kurokawa, T., and Nishimura, T. (1993). "Dynamic representation of icons in human-computer interaction." *Proceedings of the Fifth International Conference on Human-Computer Interaction*.

Morrison, J.B., Pirolli, P., and Card, S.K. (2001). "A Taxonomic Analysis of What World Wide Web Activities Significantly Impact People's Decisions and Actions." Interactive poster, presented at the Association for Computing Machinery's *Conference on Human Factors in Computing Systems*, Seattle, March 31–April 5, 2001.

Nagy, A.L. and Sanchez, R.R. (1992). "Chromaticity and luminance as coding dimensions in visual search." *Human Factors* 34: 601–614.

National Language Technical Center. (1991). *National Language Design Guide: Designing Enabled Products*. Vol. 1. Canada: National Language Technical Center.

Nelson, T. (1980). "Interactive systems and the design of virtuality." *Creative Computing*. l6 (11)56 ff., and 6 (12)94 ff.

Nielsen, J. (1990). "Usability testing of international interfaces." In *Designing User Interfaces for International Use*, J. Nielson (ed.). New York: Elsevier.

Nielsen, J. (1992). "Finding usability problems through heuristic evaluation." *Proceedings: CHI 95*. May 3–7, Monterey, CA.

Nielsen, J. (1994). "Enhancing the explanatory power of usability heuristics," *CHI'94 Conference Proceedings*.

Nielsen, Jakob (1993). "Usability Engineering." Boston, MA: Academic Press .

Nielsen, Jakob (1996). "Top Ten Mistakes in Web Design." *Jakob Nielsen's Alertbox for May 1996*. www.useit.com/alertbox/9605.html.

Nielsen, Jakob (1997a). "The Difference Between Web Design and GUI Design." *Jakob Nielsen's Alertbox for May 1, 1997*. www.useit.com/alertbox/9705a.html.

Nielsen, Jakob (1997b). "The Difference Between Intranet and Internet Design." *Jakob Nielsen's Alertbox for September 15, 1997. w*ww.useit.com/alertbox/9709b.html.

Nielsen, Jakob (1999a). "Intranet Portals: The Corporate Information Infrastructure," *Jakob Nielsen's Alertbox*. www.useit.com/alertbox/990404.html, April 4.

Nielsen, Jakob (1999b). "'Top Ten Mistakes' Revisited Three Years Later." *Jakob Nielsen's Alertbo*. www.useit.com/alertbox/990502.html, May 2.

Nielsen, Jakob (2000). "Is Navigation Useful?" *Jakob Nielsen's Alertbox*. www.useit.com/alertbox/20000109.html, January 9.

Nielsen, Jacob, and Mack, Robert L. (Eds.) (1994). *Usability Inspection Methods*. New York: John Wiley and Sons.

NIST, 2001, www.nist.gov/webmetrics.

Omanson, R. C., Cline, J.A., Kilpatrick. C.E., and Dunkerton, M.C. (1998). "Dimensions affecting Web site identity." *Proceedings of the Human Factors and Ergonomics Society 42nd Annual Meeting*, 429–433.

Omoigui, N., He, L., Gupta, A., Grudin, J. and Sanocki, E. (1999). "Time-compression: Systems, concerns, usage, and benefits, *CHI 99 Conference Proceedings*, 136–143.

Open Software Foundation. (1993). *OSF/Motif Style Guide*. Englewood Cliffs, NJ: Prentice Hall.

Ozok, A.A. and Salvendy, G. (2000). "Measuring consistency of Web page design and its effects on performance and satisfaction, *Ergonomics*, Vol. 43, No. 4, 443–460.

PBS Life on the Internet, http://www.pbs.org/internet/timeline/timeline-txt.html.

Pastoor, S. (1990). "Legibility and subjective preference for color combinations in text." *Human Factors* 32: (2)157–171.

Piolat, A., Roussey, J.Y., and Thunin, O. (1998). "Effects of screen presentation on text reading and revising." *International Journal of Human Computer Studies*, 47, 585–589.

Popowicz, A. (1995). "Collecting user information on a limited budget." *SIGCHI Bulletin*. 27: (4)23–28.

Pressman, R.S. (1992). "Software Engineering: A Practitioner's Approach." New York: McGraw Hill.

Ramsay, J., Barbesi, A., and Preece, J. (1998). "A psychological investigation of long retrieval times on the World Wide Web," *Interacting with Computers*, 10, 77–86.

Reeves, B., and Nass, C. (1996). "The media equation: How people treat computers, television, and new media like real people and places." New York: Cambridge University Press.

Rogers, Y. (1989). "Icons at the interface: Their usefulness." *Interacting with Computers: The Interdisciplinary Journal of Human-Computer Interaction.* 1: (1)105–117.

Rooden, M.J., Green, W.S., and Kanis, H. (1999). "Difficulties in usage of a coffeemaker predicted on the basis of design models," *Proceedings of the Human Factors and Ergonomics Society,* 476–480.

Russo, P., and S. Boor. (1993). "How fluent is your interface? Designing for international users." *INTER 93.* April 24–29, Amsterdam.

Rutkowski, C. (1982). "An introduction to the human applications standard computer interface, part 1: Theory and principles," *BYTE 7.* 11: 291–310.

Schrier, J.R. (1992). "Reducing stress associated with participating in a usability test." *Proceedings of the Human Factors Society 36th Annual Meeting,* Santa Monica, CA: Human Factors Society.

Selvidge, P.R., Chaparro, B., and Bender, G.T. (2000). "The world wide wait: Effects of delays on user performance," *Proceedings of the IEA 2000/HGES 2000 Congress,* 1-416 to 1-419.

Shackel, B. (1981). "The concept of usability." *Proceedings of IBM Software and Information Usability Symposium.* September 15–18, Poughkeepsie, NY.

Shackel, B. (1991). "Usability—context, framework, definition, design and evaluation." In *Human Factors for Informatics Usability,* B. Schackel and S.J. Richardson (eds.). Cambridge, U.K.: Cambridge University Press.

Shannon, C.E. and Weaver, W. (1949). *The Mathematical Theory of Communication.* Urbana, IL: The University of Illinois Press.

Sharit, J. and Czaja, S.J. (1994). "Ageing, computer-based task performance, and stress: Issues and challenges," *Ergonomics,* 37 (4)559–577.

Shneiderman, B. (1982). "The future of interactive systems and the emergence of direct manipulation." *Behaviour and Information Technology, I.* 237–256.

Shneiderman, B. (1987). *Designing the User Interface: Strategies for Effective Human-Computer Interaction.* Reading, MA: Addison-Wesley.

Shurtleff, M. (1993). "Say cheese! Guidelines for the use of photorealism in graphical user interfaces." *CSTG Bulletin.* 15–17.

Sidorsky, R.C. (1982). "Color coding in tactical displays: Help or hindrance." *Army Research Institute Research Report.*

Simkin, D. and Hastie, R. (1987). "An information-processing analysis of graph perception." *Journal of the American Statistical Association.* 82: 454–465.

Simmons, T. and Manahan, M. (1999). "The Effects of Monitor Size on User Performance and Preference," *Proceedings of the Human Factors and Ergonomics Society.*

Smith, D.C., Harslem, E.F., Irby, C.H., Kimball, R.B., and Verplank, W.L. (1982). "Designing the star user interface." *Byte.*

Smith, S.L., and J.N. Mosier. (1986). *Guidelines for Designing User-Interface Software* (Mitre ESD-TR-86-278 MTR 10090). Hanscom AFB, MA.

Smith, W. (1986). "Computer color: Psychophysics, task application, and aesthetics." *Proceedings: International Scientific Conference: Work with Display Units.* May 12–15, Stockholm, Sweden.

Smith, W. (1988). "Standardizing colors for computer screens." *Proceedings of the Human Factors Society 32nd Annual Meeting,* Santa Monica, CA: Human Factors Society.

Spool, J.M., Scanlon, T., Schroeder, W., Snyder, C., and DeAngelo, T. (1997). "Web Site Usability: A Designer's Guide." North Andover, MA: User Interface Engineering.

Stanton, N.A. and Stevenage, S.V. (1998). "Learning to predict human error: Issues of acceptability, reliability and validity," *Ergonomics*, 41 (11)1737–1747.

Streveler, D.J. and Wasserman, A.I. (1984). "Quantitative measures of the spatial properties of screen designs." *INTERACT '95. Human-Computer Interaction*. England.

Stromoski, R. (1993). "Fighting the futz factor." *Information Week*. February 15: 55.

Suhm, B., Myers, B., and Waibel, A. (1999). "Model-Based and Evaluation of Multimodal Interactive Error Correction." *CHI 99 Conference Proceedings*, 584–591.

Sukaviriya, P. and Moran, L. (1990). "User interfaces for Asia." In *Designing User Interfaces for International Use*, J. Nielsen (ed.). New York: Elsevier.

Sun Microsystems, Inc. (1990). *Open Look Graphical User Interface Application Style Guidelines*. Reading, MA: Addison-Wesley.

Sun Microsystems, Inc. (1998), www.sun.com/sunonnet/.

Taylor, D. (1992). *Global Software*. New York: Springer Verlag.

Thacker, P. (1987). "Tabular displays: A human factors study." *CSTG Bulletin*. 14: (1)13.

Thecounter.com. (2001) www.thecounter.com/stats/.

Thovtrup, H., and Nielsen, J. (1991). "Assessing the usability of a user interface standard." *Proceedings: CHI 91*. 335–342.

Tindall-Ford, S., Chandler, P., and Sweller, J. (1997). "When two sensory modes are better than one," *Journal of Experimental Psychology; Applied*, 3 (4)257–287.

Tinker, M.A. (1955). "Prolonged reading tasks in visual research." *Journal of Applied Psychology*, 39: 444–446.

Tripathi, P.D. (1992). "English: 'The Chosen Tongue,'" *English Today*. 8 (4)3–11.

Tufte, E.R. (1983). *The Visual Display of Quantitative Information*. Cheshire, CT: Graphics Press.

Tullis, T. (1981). "An evaluation of alphanumeric, graphic, and color information displays." *Human Factors* 23: 541–550.

Tullis, T. (1983). "Predicting the usability of alphanumeric displays." Ph.D. diss., Rice University.

Tullis, T. (1993). "Is user interface design just common sense?" *Proceedings of the Fifth International Conference on Human-Computer Interaction*. 9–14.

Tullis, T. and Kodimer, M.L. (1992). "A comparison of direct-manipulation, selection, and data-entry techniques for reordering fields in a table." *Proceedings of the Human Factors Society 36th Annual Meeting*, Santa Monica, CA: Human Factors Society.

Uceta, F.A., Dixon, M.A., and Resnick. M.L. (1998). "Adding Interactivity to Paper Prototypes," *Proceedings of the Human Factors and Ergonomics Society 42nd Annual Meeting*, 506–511.

Usability.gov/guidelines.

useit.com, "Severity Ratings for Usability Problems," http://www.useit.com/papers/heuristic/severityrating.html.

User Interface Engineering. (2001) http://world.std.com/~uieweb/tips.htm.

Verplank, B. (1988). "Designing graphical user interfaces." *Proceedings: CHI 88*. May 15.

Vitz, P.C. (1966). "Preference for different amounts of visual complexity." *Behavioral Science*, 2: 105–114.

Walker, M.A. (1989). "Natural language in a desktop environment." In *Designing and Using Human-Computer Interfaces and Knowledge Based Systems*, G. Salvendy and M.J. Smith (eds.). Amsterdam: Elsevier Science Publishers.

Weinschenk, S. (1995). "Storyboarding the information process." *Session Proceedings, BFMA The 26th International Symposium on Forms and Information Systems*. May 7–11, St. Louis, MO.

Weinschenk, S. (2001). "Page Design for Web Documents." http://www.wein schenk.com/guidelinesdemo/presweb.html.

White, J.V. (1990). *Color for the Electronic Age*. New York: Watson-Guptill Publications.

Whiteside, J., Jones, S., Levy, P.S., and Wixon, D. (1985). "User performance with command, menu, and iconic interfaces." *Proceedings CHI 85*.

Wichansky, A.M. (1986). "Legibility and user acceptance of monochrome display phospher colors." *Proceedings: International Scientific Conference: Work with Display Units*. May 12–15, Stockholm, Sweden.

Williams, J.R. (1998). "Guidelines for the Use of Multimedia in Instruction." *Proceedings of the Human Factors and Ergonomics Society 42nd Annual Meeting*, 1447–1451.

Winograd, T. (1995). "From programming environments to environments for designing." *Communications of the ACM*. 38: (10)65–74.

Wopking, M., Pastoor, S., and Beldie, I.O. (1985). "Design of user guidance in videotex systems." *Proceedings of the 11th International Symposium on Human Factors in Telecommunications*. Boston: Information Gatekeepers.

World Wide Web Consortium. (2001). www.w3.org.

Wright, P. (1991). "Designing and evaluating documentation for I.T. users." In *Human Factors for Informatics Usability*, B. Shackel and S.J. Richardson (eds.). Cambridge U.K.: Cambridge University Press.

Wright, P., Lickorish, A., and Milroy, R. (1994). "Remember while mousing: The cognitive cost of mouse clicks." *SIGCHI Bulletin*, 26: (1)41–45.

Zahn, C.T. (1971). "Graph-theoretical methods for detecting and describing gestalt clusters." *IEEE Transactions on Computers, X-20*. 68–86.

Zaphiris, P. and Mtei, L. (1998). "Depth versus breadth in the arrangement of Web links." www.otal.umd.edu/Shore/bs04/.

Zhan, P., Bishu, R.R., and Riley, M.W. (1993). "Screen layout and semantic structure in iconic menu design." *Proceedings of the Fifth International Conference on Human-Computer Interaction*.

Ziefle, M. (1998). "Effects of display resolution on visual performance." *Human Factors*, 40 (4)555–568.

Index

A

Abbreviations or acronyms usage, 518
Accessibility, 578–587
   cognitive disabilities, 583–584
   design, 579–587
   design considerations, 73, 83
   documentation, 586–587
   hearing disabilities, 582
   physical movement disabilities, 582–583
   seizure disorders, 584
   speech or language disabilities, 583
   types of disabilities, 578–579
   visual disabilities, 579–581
   Web page design, 584–586
Aesthetically pleasing design, 41
Animation
   icons, 601, 602
   multimedia, 609, 614–615
Application versus object or data
   orientation, 26
ARPANET, 9, 10
Assistance. *See* Guidance and assistance
Auditory
   icons, 601, 602–603
   multimedia, 615–617
Axes, 211

B

Balance, 120–121
Balloon tips, 492–494
Bar graphs, 219–221

Borders, 658, 660–664
   control borders, 660–662, 672–673
   section borders, 662–664, 673–674
Browsers, 230–232, 287
Browsing, 192, 193, 196
Business function. *See* Understand business
   function
Buttons, 405–420
   activation, 416–417, 420
   advantages, 405
   command, 406, 407–417, 674
   customization, 419
   defaults, 414–415
   description, 405
   disadvantages, 405
   expansion, 414
   help command, 559–560
   intent indicators, 413–414
   keyboard equivalents and accelerators,
     415–416, 420
   labels, 408–409
   location, 410–411, 419
   number of, 409–410
   organization, 412–413, 418–419
   purpose, 405
   radio, 427–435
   size, 409, 418
   structure, 417–418
   styles, 406
   toolbars, 406, 417–420
   usage, 405, 407, 417